KT-477-761

OPERATIONS STRATEGY

Visit the *Operations Strategy,* Second Edition, Companion Website at **www.pearsoned.co.uk/slack** to find valuable **student** learning material including:

- Study guides for each chapter to help test your understanding

OPERATIONS STRATEGY

Second Edition

Nigel Slack

Michael Lewis

FT Prentice Hall
FINANCIAL TIMES

An imprint of **Pearson Education**
Harlow, England • London • New York • Boston • San Francisco • Toronto • Sydney • Singapore • Hong Kong
Tokyo • Seoul • Taipei • New Delhi • Cape Town • Madrid • Mexico City • Amsterdam • Munich • Paris • Milan

Pearson Education Limited
Edinburgh Gate
Harlow
Essex CM20 2JE
England

and Associated Companies throughout the world

Visit us on the World Wide Web at:
www.pearsoned.co.uk

First published 2002
Second edition 2008

ISBN 978-0-273-69519-6

British Library Cataloguing-in-Publication Data
A catalogue record for this book is available from the British Library

10 9 8 7 6 5 4 3 2 1
11 10 09 08 07

Typeset in 9.5/12pt Stone Serif by 3
Printed and bound in Great Britain by Ashford Colour Press, Gosport

The publisher's policy is to use paper manufactured from sustainable forests.

Brief contents

Contents

Cases studies 333

Supporting resources

Visit **www.pearsoned.co.uk/slack** to find valuable online resources

Companion Website for students
- Study guides for each chapter to help test your understanding

For instructors
- Complete, downloadable Instructor's Manual
- PowerPoint slides that can be downloaded and used for presentations

For more information please contact your local Pearson Education sales representative or visit **www.pearsoned.co.uk/slack**

List of figures and tables, and exhibits from case studies

Figures

Tables

Exhibits from case studies

Bunge Limited

IKEA's global sourcing challenge: Indian rugs and child labour

McDonald's Corporation

Kuhn Flowers

Preface

Operations strategy can have a huge impact on the competitive success of any type of enterprise. Not just in the short term, but on an enduring basis. Just look at those companies that have transformed their prospects through the way they manage their operations resources strategically. Amazon, Google, IKEA, Tesco, Singapore Airlines, SAB Miller, Seven-Eleven Japan, Toyota, Zara and many more, all have developed their strategic operations capabilities to the point where they represent a formidable asset. (And all are amongst the many examples to be found in this book.) These firms have found that it is the way they manage their operations that sets them apart from, and above, their competitors.

The dilemma is that when we talk about 'operations', we must include the majority of the firm's resources, because contributing to creating the firm's services and products is such an all-consuming task. And when something is all around us, like operations resources are, it can be difficult to see them in their entirety. This is the paradox of operations strategy. It lies at the heart of how organisations manage their strategic intent in practice and is vitally important for long-term success. Yet, it is also so all-embracing that it becomes easy to underestimate the significance of the subject.

If you doubt the importance of the subject, the following are just some of the decisions with which operations strategy is concerned.

- How should the organisation satisfy the requirements of its customers?
- What intrinsic capabilities should the organisation try and develop as the foundation for its long-term success?
- How specialised should the organisation's activities become?
- Should the organisation sacrifice some of its objectives in order to excel at others?
- How big should the organisation be?
- Where should the organisation locate its resources?
- When should it expand or contract, and by how much?
- What should it do itself and what should it contract out to other businesses?
- How should it develop relationships with other organisations?
- What type of technology should it invest in?
- How should it organise the way it develops new products and services?
- How should it bind together its resources into an organisational structure?
- How should the organisation's resources and processes be improved and developed over time?
- What guiding principles should shape the way any organisation formulates its operations strategies?

All these questions are not merely important, they are fundamental. No organisation whether large or small, for-profit or not-for-profit, in the services or manufacturing sector, international or local, can ignore such questions. Operations strategy is central, ubiquitous, and vital to any organisation's sustained success.

New to this edition

The success of the previous edition was helped by the many suggestions we received from fellow teachers of operations strategy. They have been kind enough to provide further feedback that has informed the changes we have made for the second edition. These changes include the following:

- a more focused approach that highlights the very key issues, especially in treating capacity strategy, supply network strategy, technology strategy and operations strategy formulation;
- new and updated examples, which cover the topical issues in operations strategy;
- a more focused approach to the 'process' of operations strategy;
- a new chapter on the 'substitutes for strategy', that is the relatively new approaches to improving operations that are not strategies as such, but can be an important part of an operations strategy;
- a new chapter on the implementation of operations strategy;
- ten longer cases that can be used to form the basis of a whole course in operations strategy.

The aim of this book

The aim of this book is to provide a treatment of operations strategy which is clear, well structured, and interesting. It seeks to apply some of the ideas of operations strategy to a variety of businesses and organisations. The text provides a logical path through the key activities and decisions of operations strategy as well as covering the broad principles which underpin the subject and the way in which operations strategies are put together in practice.

More specifically, the text aims to be:

- *Balanced in its treatment of the subject*. In addition to taking the orthodox 'market-led' approach to operations strategy, the book also provides an alternative but complementary 'resource-based' perspective.
- *Conceptual in the way it treats the decisions, activities and processes which together form an organisation's operations strategy*. Although some examples are quantified, the overall treatment in the book is managerial and practical.
- *Comprehensive in its coverage of the more important ideas and issues which are relevant to most types of business*. In any book covering such a broad area as operations strategy, one cannot cover everything. However, we believe that the more important issues are all addressed.
- *Grounded in the various bodies of knowledge which underpin operations strategy*. Most chapters introduce concepts and principles, often from other academic disciplines, which illuminate the particular operations strategy issue being discussed.

- *International*. In the examples it uses, the book describes practical operations strategy issues.

Who should use this book?

This book is intended to provide a broad introduction to operations strategy for all students who wish to understand the strategic importance and scope of the operations function, for example:

- MBA students, who should find that it both links and integrates their experience and study of operations management with their core studies in business strategy;
- higher-level undergraduates studying business or technical subjects, although we assume a prior knowledge of the basics of operations management;
- postgraduate students on other specialised Master's degrees should find that it provides them with a well-grounded approach to the subject;
- executives will also be able to relate the practical and pragmatic structure of the book to the more conceptual and theoretical issues discussed within the structure.

Distinctive features

Clear structure

The book employs coherent models of the subject that run through each part of the text and explain how the chapters fit into the overall subject. Key questions set the scene at the beginning of each chapter, and provide a structure for the summary at the end of each chapter.

Illustration-based

The study of operations, even at a strategic level, is essentially a practical subject and cannot be taught in a purely theoretical manner. Because of this we have used both abstracted examples and 'boxed' examples which explain some issues faced by real operations.

Theory

Operations strategy is a practical subject which is driven by theoretical ideas. Most chapters contain one or more theories which explain the underpinning ideas which have contributed to our understanding of the issues being discussed.

Case studies

The book includes a number of case studies suitable for class discussion. The cases are long enough to provide depth and serve as illustrations, which can be used to supplement class sessions.

Selected further reading

Every chapter ends with a list of further reading which takes the topic covered in the chapter further, or treats some important related issues.

Companion Website

A website is available which helps students to develop a firm understanding of each issue covered in the book and provides lecturers with pedagogical assistance. There is also a teacher's manual available. Go to **www.pearsoned.co.uk/slack**.

Chapters

Chapter 1 defines operations strategy in terms of the reconciliation between market requirements and operations resources.

Chapter 2 looks at three interrelated issues which affect reconciliation – how operations change over time, how operations deal with trade-offs, and how trade-offs can be used to understand 'targeted', or focused, operations.

Chapter 3 examines those decisions which shape the overall capacity of the operations resources, particularly the level of capacity and where the capacity should be located and deals with the dynamics of the capacity decision by examining how capacity is changed over time.

Chapter 4 looks at supply networks, particularly the nature of the relationships which develop between the various operations in a network, the advantages of taking a total network perspective and how networks behave in a dynamic sense.

Chapter 5 characterises the various types of process technology which are at the heart of many operations, in particular, it looks at the effects of some newer types of technology on operations capabilities and proposes some ideas which help operations to choose between different technologies and implement them once chosen.

Chapter 6 examines the way operations resources can be developed and improved within the organisation, especially how capabilities can be directed, developed and deployed in a cycle of improvement.

Chapter 7 applies some of the issues covered in the previous chapters to the activities associated with product and service development and organisation.

Chapter 8 will look at what reconciling market requirements and operational resources actually means in practice, particularly the achievement of some kind of 'fit' between what the market wants and what the operation can deliver.

Chapter 9 examines some of the popular approaches to improving operations performance. These are Total Quality Management (TQM), Lean operations, Business Process Reengineering (BPR), Enterprise Resource Management (ERP) and Six Sigma. Although they are not strategies as such, implementing any of them is a strategic decision.

Chapter 10 looks at some of the issues concerning the implementation of operations strategy. In particular, it explores how implementation is shaped by strategic, organisational, methodological, delivery and operational contexts.

Acknowledgements

Again we have been fortunate enough to receive advice from a number of leading academics and industrialists. In particular Pär Åhlström of Chalmers University, David Barnes of the Open University, Alan Betts of ht2, Ruth Boaden of Manchester Business School, Mike Bourne of Cranfield University, Paul Coghlan of Trinity College Dublin, Henrique Correa of Rollins College, Roland van Dierdonck of the University of Ghent, Kasra Ferdows of Georgetown University, Keith Goffin of Cranfield University, Mike Gregory of Cambridge University, Christer Karlsson of Copenhagen Business School, Bart McCarthy of Nottingham University, John Mills of Cambridge University, Chris Morgan of Cranfield University, Andy Neely of Cranfield University, Ken Platts of Cambridge University, Martin Spring of Lancaster University and Ann Vereecke of the Univerity of Ghent.

Our academic colleagues at Warwick and Bath Universities also helped us, both by contributing ideas and by creating a lively and stimulating work environment. At Warwick, our thanks go to Hilary Bates, Stuart Chambers, Dr Simon Croom, Dr Mihalis Giannakis, Prof. Bob Johnston, Dr Zoe Radnor, Dr Mike Shulver, Dr Rhian Silvestro, Paul Wally and in particular, Dawei Lu of Warwick Manufacturing Group who provided both ideas and materials for examples. At Bath our thanks go to Dr Alistair Brandon-Jones, Professor Andrew Brown, Professor Chris McMahon, Professor Steve Culley, Dr Mickey Howard, Dr Thomas Johnsen. Also research students Catherine Phillips, Richard Johns, Lisa Brodie, Richard Battams and Jens Roehrich.

We are also grateful to many friends, colleagues, and company contacts. In particular, thanks to go Peter Norris of the Royal Bank of Scotland, David Garman of TDG plc, Rupert Gasser, Tyko Persson and Hans Mayer of Nestlé, Gillian McGrattan of Grant Thornton, Philip Godfrey and Cormack Campbell of OEE, and John Tyley of Lloyds TSB, Professor Kasra Ferdows of Georgetown University, Professor Glenn Schmidt, also of Georgetown University, Professor Jose Machuca, Dr Andrew Court of QinetiQ, Tony Solomons, Chris Spencer and Maurice Dunster of Waitrose, John Palmer of the Welsh Assembly, Nathan Travis of Gloucestershire Fire and Rescue, John Richardson of Elizabeth Shaw, Dr Hanno Kirner of Rolls Royce Motors and Dr Karin Breu of Said Business School, University of Oxford.

Mary Walton is the coordinator of the Warwick Business School Operations Management Group. She will claim that she did not contribute to this book. In fact her cheerful disposition and (largely forlorn) efforts to keep us organized have contributed more than she could imagine.

The team from Pearson Education provided their usual high professional support.

Every word of this book, together with many words which were discarded during the writing process, was word processed by Angela Slack. The task of typing and retyping the manuscript, providing PowerPoint versions of all the illustrations, organising the writing process, and generally making some kind of sense of eccentric word processing styles was a truly amazing effort. We owe Angela our thanks for her effort and her (almost) infinite patience.

Finally, and most importantly, we would like to thank our wives, Angela and Helen, for their forbearance and their unwavering support.

Nigel Slack
Michael Lewis

Publisher's acknowledgements

We also are grateful to the following for permission to reproduce copyright material:

Figures 3.12 and 4.9: Slack, N., Chambers, S. and Johnston, R (2007) *Operations Management*, Fifth Edition. Harlow: Financial Times Prentice Hall, Reproduced with permission from Pearson Education Ltd. Reproduced with permission; Figure 4.10: Harland, C.M. (1996) 'Supply chain management: relationships, chains and networks', *British Journal of Management*, 1(7). Reproduced with permission of Blackwell Publishing; Figure 4.12: Adapted from Fisher, M.C. (1997) 'What is the right supply chain for your product?', *Harvard Business Review*, March–April, 105–16. Copyright © Harvard Business School Publishing Corporation, all rights reserved. Reproduced with permission from Harvard Business School Publishing Corporation; Figure 8.13: Adapted from Christensen, C.M. (1997) *The Innovator's Dilemma: When New Technologies Cause Great Firms to Fail*. Boston, MA: Harvard Business School Press, Introduction, p. xvi. Copyright © Harvard Business School Publishing Corporation, all rights reserved. Reproduced with permission from Harvard Business School Publishing Corporation.

Table 4.3: Lee, H.L. et al (1997) 'The bullwhip effect in supply chains', *MIT Sloan Management Review*, Spring 1997, article no. 3837. Copyright © 1997 by Massachusetts Institute of Technology, all rights reserved. Distributed by Tribune Media Services. Reproduced by permission; Table 6.4: Bohn, R.E. (1994) 'Measuring and managing technical knowledge', *MIT Sloan Management Review*, Fall 1994, article no. 3615, Table 1. Copyright © 1994 by Massachusetts Institute of Technology, all rights reserved. Distributed by Tribune Media Services. Reproduced by permission; Case study 5, Exhibit 6: Society of American Florists. Reproduced with permission; Case study 5, Exhibit 7: Society of American Florists, American Floral Endowment Consumer Tracking study. Reproduced with permission.

Page 335: West, Jonathan (2001) 'Bunge Limited', *Harvard Business School Cases*. Copyright © 2001 President and Fellows of Harvard College; 364: Bartlett, Christopher A., Dessain, Vincent and Sjoman, Anders (2006) 'IKEA's global sourcing challenge: Indian rugs and child labour', *Harvard Business School Cases*. Copyright © 2006 President and Fellows of Harvard College; 378: Stonebraker, P.W. and Polbitsyn, S.N. 'From Russia with love', CIBER Case Collection, sponsored by the Indiana University Center International Business Education and Research and distributed by the European Case Clearing House (ECCH) at Babson. Copyright © 2004 by Peter William Stonebraker and Sergey Nicholaievich Polbitsyn; 390: Upton, David (2002) 'McDonald's Corporation (Abridged)', *Harvard Business School Cases*. Copyright © 2002 President and Fellows of Harvard College.

In some instances we have been unable to trace the owners of copyright material, and we would appreciate any information that would enable us to do so.

What is operations strategy?

Introduction

For many in business the very idea of an 'operations strategy' is a contradiction in terms. After all, to be involved in the strategy process is the complete opposite of those day-to-day tasks and activities associated with being an operations manager. Yet at the same time we know that operations can have a real strategic impact. For many *enduringly* remarkable enterprises, from Amazon to IKEA, and from Toyota to Zara – operations resources are central to long-term strategic success. Moreover, these firms have found that it is the way they manage their operations that sets them apart from, and above, their competitors. More generally, all operations need to prevent strategic decisions being frustrated by poor operational implementation. But the focus of this book, the notion of operations strategy itself, is to ensure that all operating capabilities provide competitive advantage. In this chapter we look at four perspectives on operations strategy that define the subject, and focus in particular on two perspectives – market requirements and operations resources (Figure 1.1).

KEY QUESTIONS

- *What is 'operations' and why is it so important?*
- *What is strategy?*
- *What is operations strategy?*
- *How should operations reflect overall strategy?*
- *How can operations strategy learn from operational experience?*
- *How do the requirements of the market influence operations strategy?*
- *How can the intrinsic capabilities of an operation's resources influence operations strategy?*
- *What is the difference between the 'content' and the 'process' of operations strategy?*
- *What are operations strategy performance objectives?*
- *What are operations strategy decision areas?*
- *How do performance objectives relate to decision areas?*

What is 'operations' and why is it so important?

'Operations' is the activity of managing the resources and processes that produce and deliver goods and services. Every organisation, no matter in what sector, has an operations function (even if it is not called by this name) because every organisation

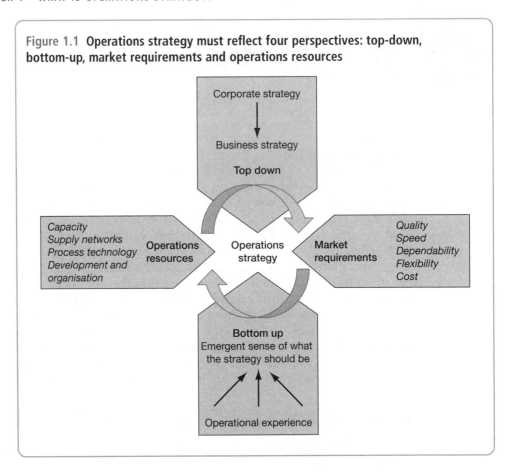

Figure 1.1 Operations strategy must reflect four perspectives: top-down, bottom-up, market requirements and operations resources

produces some mix of goods and services.[1] All operations transform resource inputs into outputs of products and services. This is called the 'input-transformation-output' model of operations. Some resource inputs are actually changed or 'transformed' (usually some combination of physical materials, information and customers). So, predominantly, a television factory processes materials, a firm of accountants processes information, while a theatre processes customers. Other resource inputs do the transforming. These are usually classified into the physical facilities (buildings, machines, equipment, computers, etc.) and the human resources (staff) who operate, support and manage the processes. Most operations produce both products *and* services. But some, such as an aluminium smelter, mainly produce products with only a peripheral service element. Others, such as a psychotherapy clinic, produce almost pure services.

Note that we are treating all types of operation here, both manufacturing and service. Hotels produce accommodation services, financial services invest, store, move, or sell us money and investment opportunities, and manufacturing businesses physically change the shape and the nature of materials to produce products. Although these businesses are from different sectors (banking, hospitality, manufacturing, etc.), they share a very similar set of issues and problems. In fact, there are often bigger differences *within* economic sectors than *between* them.

Three levels of input-transformation-output

Operations management uses the input-transformation-output model to analyse businesses at three levels. The most obvious level is that of the business itself, or more specifically, the operations function of the business. But any operation can also be viewed as part of a greater network of operations. It will have operations that supply it with the products and services it needs to make its own products and services. And unless it deals directly with the end consumer, it will supply customers who themselves may go on to supply their own customers. Moreover, any operation could have several suppliers, several customers and may be in competition with other operations producing similar services to those it products itself. This collection of operations is called the supply network. Also, inside the operation, there will be a network of processes. And within each process there will be a 'network' of individual resources (technology and people). At each level of analysis, operations managers must understand the capabilities of each element, and the relationship between them. This idea is called the hierarchy of operations (see Figure 1.2).[2]

Through the management of its resources and its networks at all levels operations management can contribute to the success of any organisation by providing what the business needs to survive and prosper (higher margins, innovate new products, unique competencies, etc.) and by satisfying its customers. It does this by achieving four broad objectives.

- It can reduce the **costs** of producing products and services by being efficient in the way it transforms inputs into outputs.

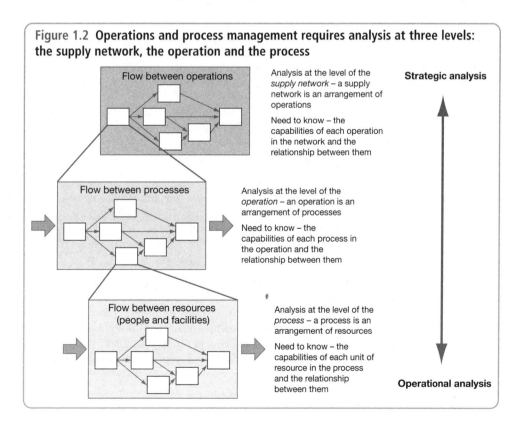

Figure 1.2 Operations and process management requires analysis at three levels: the supply network, the operation and the process

- It can increase **revenue** by promoting outstanding customer satisfaction through its ability to provide exceptional quality, responsiveness, reliability and flexibility.
- It can reduce the amount of **investment** (*capital employed*) that is necessary to produce the required type and quantity of products and services. It can do this by increasing the effective capacity of the operation and by being innovative in how it uses its physical resources.
- It can provide the basis for **future innovation** by building a solid base of operations-based capabilities, skills and knowledge within the business.

These four ways in which operations can contribute to any enterprise's success are undeniably strategic. Achieving them may come through a detailed and sustained focus on operations resources and processes, but their combined effect has real value at a strategic level.

Example **There's no such thing as manufacturing strategy – it's all service strategy**[3]

In all but the most commodity-like of products, the physical presence of the product is not what brings in the revenue, rather it is the knowledge and service embedded in or around the product. This is a simple message but one that is only reluctantly being accepted by some manufacturing companies. Yet, many successful 'manufacturers' derive more than half their revenues from services. Rolls Royce, which manufactures aero and other engines, GE, which manufactures many high-tech products, and many other companies are all forecasting a continued rise in service revenues.

Of course, much of these revenues would not be there if they didn't make the product in the first place. Earning money from maintaining aircraft engines, for example, is at least partly dependent on having the depth of knowledge of the engine and its technology that comes from actually having manufactured it. The idea of manufacturers moving towards service (which is known by the rather ugly word 'servitisation') is not a plea to manufacture less, but rather to think of manufacturing as just one component in delivering service value to customers.

Look at AES, a UK-based engineering company that manufactures engineering seals (mechanical devices that fit on rotating machines such as pumps and stop liquids from leaking out). Because its business also involves specifying the seals for its customers, it has become as much an engineering consultant as it is a manufacturer. Chris Rea, the Chairman and owner of AES, says:

'Service is a vital part of the company's strategy. Of the company's 920 employees, just under half are in service-related jobs – most concerned with specifying the nature of the seal that AES will make for individual customers from 20 million possible types. Our product is not a commodity. We believe our customers need an element of consultancy to make sure they get the best value from what we can provide.'

But consultancy is only one of many services available to 'manufacturers'. Design services, installation services, spare parts supply, maintenance, online remote diagnostics, training, regular updating of control systems, the list is virtually endless. Even companies who cannot exploit some of these revenue streams can still gain from thinking of themselves as service providers. Even when a product can be made cheaper in Asia or eastern Europe, advice, delivery and extended service can still go some way to overcome cost disadvantages.

What is strategy?

We have used the word 'strategy' several times. So what exactly is strategy? Surprisingly, it is not easy to answer what seems like a straightforward question. Linguistically the word derives from the Greek word *strategos*, meaning 'leading an army'. And although there is no direct historical link between Greek military practice and modern ideas of strategy, the military metaphor is powerful. Both military and business strategy can be described in similar ways, and include some of the following:

- setting broad objectives that direct an enterprise towards its overall goal;
- planning the path (in general rather than specific terms) that will achieve these goals;
- stressing long-term rather than short-term objectives;
- dealing with the total picture rather than stressing individual activities;
- being detached from, and above, the confusion and distractions of day-to-day activities.

Later views of strategy have introduced some of the practical realities of business based on observations of how organisations really do go about making (or not making) strategic decisions. These include the following considerations.

- Business objectives may not ever become 'clear'. In fact, most organisations will have multiple objectives that may themselves conflict. For example, an outsourcing decision may improve profitability but could involve a firm in long-term reputational risk.
- Markets are intrinsically unstable in the long-term so there must be some limit to the usefulness of regarding strategy as simply planning what to do in the future. It may be more important to keep close to what is actually happening in the market and adapt to whatever circumstances develop.
- Many decisions are far less formal than the simple planning model assumes. In fact, many strategic decisions 'emerge' over time rather than derive from any single formal senior management decision.
- Organisations do not always do in practice what they say they do, or even what they want to do. The only way to deduce the effect strategy of an organisation is to observe the pattern of decisions that it makes over time.

In this book we recognise the problematic nature of strategy. Nevertheless, we do offer some models and approaches that implicitly assume that managers can have some influence over the strategic direction of their organisation – even if this influence may, at times, be limited. So, notwithstanding the uncertainties and complexities of real strategy making, it is our belief that some kind of structure, model, or plan can help most managers to understand what they believe they should be doing.

Example **Sometimes any plan is better than no plan**

There is a famous story that illustrates the importance of having some kind of plan, even if hindsight proves it to be the wrong plan.[4] During manoeuvres in the Alps, a detachment of Hungarian soldiers got lost. The weather was severe and the snow was deep. In these freezing

▶

conditions, after two days of wandering, the soldiers gave up hope and became reconciled to a frozen death on the mountains. Then, to their delight, one of the soldiers discovered a map in his pocket. Much cheered by this discovery, the soldiers were able to escape from the mountains. When they were safe back at their headquarters, they discovered that the map was not of the Alps at all, but of the Pyrenees. The moral of the story? A plan (or a map) may not be perfect but it gives a sense of purpose and a sense of direction. If the soldiers had waited for the right map, they would have frozen to death. Yet, their renewed confidence motivated them to get up and create opportunities.

Operations strategy – operations is not always operational

One of the biggest mistakes a business can make is to confuse 'operations' with 'operational'. Operational is the opposite of strategic; it means detailed, localised, short-term, day-to-day. Earlier we defined operations management as 'the activity of managing the resources and processes that produce and deliver goods and services'. Operations strategy is concerned less with individual processes and more with the total transformation process that is the whole business. It is concerned with how the competitive environment is changing and what the operation has to do in order to meet current and future challenges. It is also concerned with the long-term development of its operations resources and processes so that they can provide the basis for a sustainable advantage. If a business does not fully appreciate the strategic impact that effective operations and process management can have, it is missing an opportunity. Perhaps more significantly, many of the businesses that seem to be especially competitively successful, and which appear to be sustaining their success into the longer-term, have a clear (and often innovative) operations strategy. Just look at some of the high-profile companies quoted in this book, or that feature in the business press. From Tesco to IKEA, from Ryanair to Singapore Airlines, it is not just that their operations strategy provides these companies with adequate support; it is their operations strategy that is the pivotal reason for their competitive superiority.

Yet, some businesses, like Coca Cola or Heinz, are more marketing and brand driven. But even these types of business need a strong operations strategy. Their brand position may be shaped in the consumer's mind by their promotional activities, but it would soon erode if they could not deliver products on time, or if their quality was sub-standard, or if they could not introduce new products in response to market trends. So, for example, a 'fast moving consumer goods' (FMCG) company that has operations that are capable of mastering new process technologies, or flexing their capacity, or running agile yet efficient supply chains, or continually cutting cost out of the business through its improvement programme, will have a huge advantage over less capable rivals.

Example   Singapore Airlines[5]

Singapore International Airlines (SIA), one of the most consistently profitable airlines in the world, the winner of numerous 'Best Airline' and service awards and an industry leader in service innovation. The Singapore Airlines Group became the world's largest carrier by market capitalisation in 2006/7, it ranks amongst the top 15 carriers worldwide in terms of dollar passenger kilometres and is the largest airline in Asia. It has consistently led the industry in its ability to introduce new in-flight communications and entertainment systems. In 2005, it was one of the earliest to introduce high-speed, in-flight internet service and became the first airline to offer live international television broadcasts, the first to offer free in-cabin language lessons, and the first to provide live news feeds on its KrisWorld entertainment system.

Nor is SIA's investment limited to in-cabin technology. It has a history of purchasing and operating long-range, state-of-the-art aircraft, while balancing the increase in its operational capacity with the opening up of new routes.

At the same time, the company sells aircraft on a regular basis, so that cash can be generated and the fleet constantly renewed. In 2005, the airline unveiled the slogan 'First to fly the A380 – experience the difference in 2006', to promote itself as the world's first airline to take delivery of the A380-800 double-decker super jumbo, although in the event technical difficulties at Airbus delayed the aircraft's introduction.

SIA's subsidiaries provide local and tourist flights, a cargo operation, and Singapore Air Terminal Services (SATS) which provides ground services such as baggage handling, check-in and ticketing. Its maintenance operation also provides services to other airlines and has joint venture agreements with Pratt and Whitney, the US engine manufacturer, and the Japanese Taiko Engineering with whom it operates a maintenance operation in Xiamen, China. In its passenger operations, alliances enhance geographical reach. The idea is to extend operational frontiers without incurring major capital costs, while winning customer support by offering seamless travel. Changi, one of the world's most efficient airports, is the company's home. It is also its cargo hub, whose handling infrastructure boasts a state-of-the-art system which can make an online booking from any one of the cities where the airline has cargo offices.

So how has SIA managed to sustain its success over the decades in an industry notorious for boom and bust? It has consistently focused on getting its operations management *and strategy* right. *'[We] offer our customers the very best services, cut our costs to the bone and generate a surplus to continue the unending process of renewal.'* In particular, SIA's Managing Director, Dr Cheon Choong Kong, emphasises the importance of the passengers. *'The only way to meet the customers' needs is to consider every detail about service. This means both getting the major decisions on structure and investment right, and never underestimating the importance of the attention to detail.'* Of course, Singapore Airlines has got its brand building right (using the 'Singapore Girl' tag line), and has managed its finances professionally. However, it could not have done any of these things without a strong and effective operations strategy. It is the decades of consistently good decision making in terms of building its capabilities, knowing what to outsource and what to keep in-house, being able to operationalise the concept of service excellence, having the capability to continually innovate, that have proved to be the foundations of its long-term success.

Four perspectives on operations strategy

Just as there is no overall agreement about what 'strategy' means, there is no universal agreement on how 'operations strategy' should be described. Different authors have slightly different views and definitions of the subject. Between them, four 'perspectives' emerge.

- Operation strategy is a **top-down** reflection of what the whole group or business wants to do.

- Operations strategy is a **bottom-up** activity where operations improvements cumulatively build strategy.
- Operations strategy involves translating **market requirements** into operations decisions.
- Operations strategy involves exploiting the capabilities of **operations resources** in chosen markets.

None of these four perspectives alone gives the full picture of what operations strategy is. But together they provide some idea of the pressures which go to form the content of operations strategy. We will treat each in turn (see Figure 1.3).

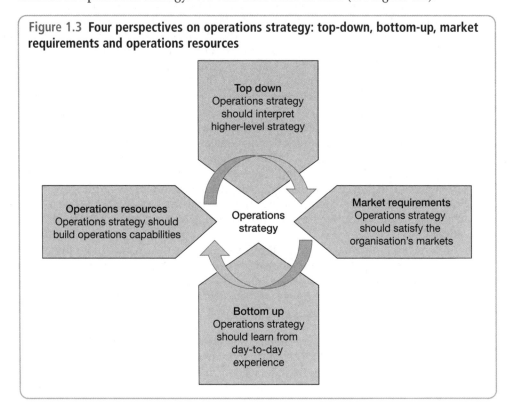

Figure 1.3 **Four perspectives on operations strategy: top-down, bottom-up, market requirements and operations resources**

The top-down perspective – operations strategy should interpret higher-level strategy

Arguably the traditional view of operations strategy is that it is one of several functional strategies which are governed by decisions taken at the top of the organisation and which set the overall strategic direction of the organisation. This is called a 'top-down' approach to the management of operations. So, if the organisation is a large, diversified corporation, its corporate strategy will consist of decisions about what types of business the group wants to be in, in what parts of the world it wants to operate, what businesses to acquire and what to divest, how to allocate its cash between its various businesses, and so on. Within the corporate group, each business unit will also need to put together its own business strategy which sets out its individual mission and objectives, as well as defining how it intends to compete in its markets.

Similarly, within the business each function will need to consider what part it should play in contributing to the strategic and/or competitive objectives of the business by developing a functional strategy which guides its actions within the business. So, in the 'top-down' view, these three levels of strategy – corporate, business and functional – form a hierarchy, with business strategy forming the context of functional strategies and corporate strategy forming the context of business strategies.

For example, a manufacturer of metrology instruments is part of a group which contains several high-tech companies. It has decided to compete by being the first in the market with every available new product innovation. Its operations function, therefore, needs to be capable of coping with the changes that constant innovation will bring. It must develop processes which are flexible enough to manufacture novel parts and products. It must organise and train its staff to understand the way products are developing so that they can put in place the necessary changes to the operation. It must develop relationships with its suppliers which will help them to respond quickly when supplying new parts. Everything about the operation, its technology, staff, and its systems and procedures, must, in the short term, do nothing to inhibit the company's competitive strategy.

The bottom-up perspective – operations strategy should learn from day-to-day experience

In reality, the relationship between the levels in the strategy hierarchy is more complex than the top-down perspective implies and certainly does not represent the way strategies are always formulated. Businesses, when reviewing their strategies, will (hopefully) consult the individual functions within the business. In doing so they may also incorporate the ideas that come from each function's day-to-day experience. Therefore, an alternative view to the top-down perspective is that many strategic ideas emerge over time from actual experiences. Sometimes companies move in a particular strategic direction because the ongoing experience of providing products and services to customers at an operational level convinces them that it is the right thing to do. There may be no high-level decisions examining alternative strategic options and choosing the one that provides the best way forward. Instead, a general consensus emerges, often from the operational level of the organisation. The 'high level' strategic decision making, if it occurs at all, may confirm the consensus and provide the resources to make it happen effectively. This idea of strategy being shaped by experience over time is sometimes called the concept of emergent strategies.[6] Strategy gradually becomes clearer over time and is based on real-life experience rather than theoretical positioning. Indeed, strategies are often formed in a relatively unstructured and fragmented manner to reflect the fact that the future is at least partially unknown and unpredictable. This may seem not to be a particularly useful guide for specific decision making. Yet, while emergent strategies are less easy to categorise, the principle governing a bottom-up perspective is clear: *'shape the operation's objectives and action, at least partly, by the knowledge it gains from its day-to-day activities'*. The key virtues required for doing this are an ability to learn from experience and a philosophy of continual and incremental improvement that is built into the strategy-making process.

For example, the manufacturer of metrology instruments, described earlier, discovers that continual product innovation both increases its costs and confuses its customers. The company's designers therefore work out a way of 'modularising' their product designs so that one part of the product can be updated without interfering with the design of the main body of the product. This approach becomes standard design practice within the company. Note that this strategy has emerged from the company's experience. No top-level board decision was probably ever taken to confirm this practice, but nevertheless it emerges as the way in which the company organises its designs. Figure 1.4 illustrates both the top-down and bottom-up for this example.

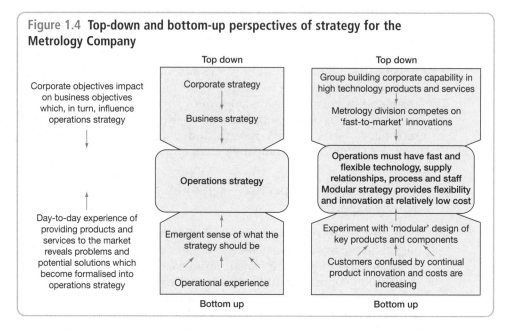

Figure 1.4 **Top-down and bottom-up perspectives of strategy for the Metrology Company**

The market requirements perspective – operations strategy should satisfy the organisation's markets

It may seem obvious that whatever the operations strategy of an organisation, it must in some way reflect the requirements of the organisation's markets. Indeed, a sensible starting point for any operations strategy is to look to its markets and ask the simple but important question, 'How can operations help the organisation to compete in its market place?' Remember though that the organisation itself usually has some influence over what its markets demand, if for no other reason than that it has chosen to be in some markets rather than others. Therefore, by choosing to inhabit a particular market position, the organisation is, to some extent, influencing how easy it is for the operations function to support the market position. This opens up the possibility that, in some circumstances, it may be sensible to shift the markets in which the organisation is trying to compete in order to reflect what its operation is good (or bad) at. We shall discuss this in more detail later, for now we return to the important point that operations strategy must reflect the organisation's market position. And the starting point for this is to develop an understanding of what is required from the operation in order to support the market position. One problem with this is that the concepts, language and, to some extent, philosophy used by the marketing function to help them understand markets are not always useful in guiding operations activities. So, descriptions of market needs developed by marketing professionals usually need 'translating' before they can be used in an operations strategy analysis.

Market positioning is influenced by (amongst other things) customers and competitors. Both, in turn, influence operations strategy. Market segmentation is a common approach to understanding markets by viewing heterogeneous markets as a collection of smaller, more homogeneous, markets. Usually this is done by assessing the needs of different groups of potential users in terms of the needs which will be satisfied by the product or service. Segmentation variables help to classify these needs. The marketing purpose of segmentation is to ensure that the product or service specification, its price, the way it is promoted and how it is channelled to customers are all appropriate to customer needs. However, market segmentation is also important in shaping operations strategy. The same needs that define markets will shape the objectives for operation's attempt to satisfy those needs. Similarly, how an organisation chooses to position itself in its market will depend on how it feels it can achieve some kind of advantage over its competitors. This, of course, will depend on how its competitors have positioned themselves. Although one particular segment of a market may look attractive, the number of other companies competing in it could deter any new entrants. However, if a company sees itself as having the operations capability of servicing that market better, even in the face of the competition from other firms, it may be worth entering the market. So, both customer and competitor analysis is a prerequisite to developing an effective operations strategy.

For example, the original business of a medium-sized theatre lighting company was devoted to designing the lighting arrangements and hiring the necessary equipment for theatrical and entertainment events, exhibitions and conferences. The company could supply any specialist lighting equipment, partly because it held a wide range, and partly because it had developed close relationships with other equipment hire firms. It also focused on the 'top end' of the lighting market, targeting customers who were less price-conscious. This was becoming a problem in the theatre lighting and exhibition markets because competition was forcing margins lower as competitors undercut prices. Soon they realised that the greatest potential for profitable growth lay in the conference market where competition was not yet as fierce, and where its high (but expensive) service levels, ability to give presentation advice and innovation were valued. Figure 1.5 illustrates how this analysis of the company's customers and competitors sets the performance objectives for its operations strategy.

In this case the 'translation' logic goes something like the following:

(a) There are several segments in the lighting design and supply market, but the fastest growing segment is the conference market.

(b) Competition is getting tougher in the theatre market because the large international lighting groups are able to provide lower-cost lighting solutions. Also exhibition venues are increasingly developing in-house operations and encouraging exhibitors to use the in-house service. Margins are being squeezed in both markets.

(c) Therefore, the company has chosen to target the broad conference market were margins and growth is higher.

(d) They believe they can differentiate themselves from competitors by their aesthetically innovative designs, ability to give good presentation advice, high customisation of lighting solutions, and fast and reliable supply.

(e) Operations therefore, needs to prioritise high-quality technical and aesthetic consultancy advice, customisation, fast response and dependability.

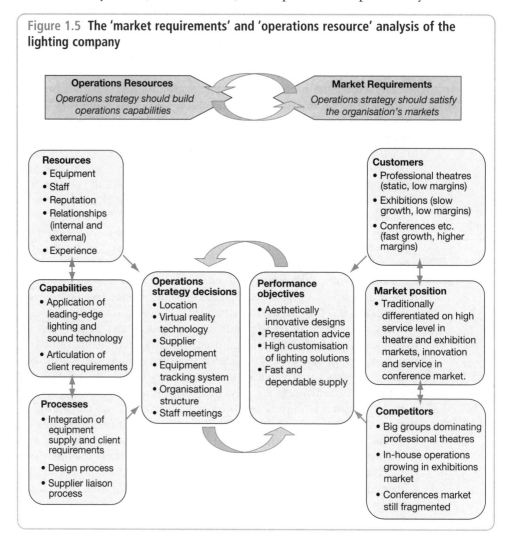

Figure 1.5 The 'market requirements' and 'operations resource' analysis of the lighting company

Although these are somewhat simplified statements, they demonstrate a path of increasing specificity, with increasing meaning to the operations function of the business. Not all businesses work through this logic in such a systematic way, nor is it intended to be a prescription as such, but it is an example, however, of how the market-operations *translation* process can work.

Performance objectives

The last stage of analysis in Figure 1.5 needs more explanation. This is the stage that identifies the *performance objectives* for the operation. That is, the aspects of operations performance that satisfy market requirements and therefore that the operation is expected to pursue. Many authors on operations strategy have their own set of performance objectives, and no overall agreement exists on terminology. They are referred to variously as 'performance criteria', operations 'strategic dimensions', 'performance dimensions', 'competitive priorities', 'strategic priorities'. Here, we will be using the term *performance objectives*. While there are differences between authors as to exactly what these performance dimensions are, there are some commonly used categories. Here, we will use a set of five performance objectives which have meaning for any type of operation (though obviously their relative priorities will differ). Within these five we will subsume the other dimensions. They are:

- quality
- speed
- dependability
- flexibility
- cost.

Each will be examined in more detail later in this chapter.

The operations resource perspectives – operations strategy should build operations capabilities

The majority of most organisations' resources are within its operations function. No surprise then, that long-term resource management is often regarded as the underlying rationale for operations strategy. The problem is again one of translation because the approach and terminology which are useful for understanding a firm's resources are not necessarily appropriate to clarify the nature of the decisions which shape those resources. A useful starting point is to understand, 'what we have' – that is, the totality of the resources owned by (or available to) the operation. Next one needs to link the broad understanding of resources and processes with the specific operations strategy decisions ('what actions we are going to take'). To achieve this linkage we need a concept to bridge the gap between the sometimes fuzzy understanding of 'what is there' and the necessarily more specific 'what should we do?' stages. In the operations resource perspective we use the concept of operations capabilities.

Operations resources, processes, routines and capabilities

Listing its resources provides a first step in understanding an operation, but this is rather like describing an automobile by listing its component parts. To understand how an operation works we need to examine the interaction between its resources. For example, how different resources, such as processing centres, are positioned relative to each other, how staff are organised into units and so on. These arrangements of resources constitute the processes of the operation that describe the way things happen in the operation. To return to the automobile analogy, processes are the mechanisms that power, steer and control its performance. Yet, even this technical explanation of an automobile's mechanisms does not convey either the full extent of how it performs on the road or its style, feel and 'personality'. Similarly, any view of an operation that limits itself to a description of its obvious tangible resources and processes fails to move our knowledge of the operation beyond the most basic level. Any audit of a company's resources and processes needs to include the organisation's intangible resources. These are the factors which may not be directly observable but are nonetheless significant in enabling any company to function. They include such things as:

- supplier relationships, contracts and mutual understanding of how suppliers are managed;
- knowledge of, and experience in, dealing with technology sources and labour markets;
- process knowledge relating to the day-to-day production of products and services;
- new product and service development skills and procedures;
- contacts and relationships in the market which enable an understanding of market trends and more specific customer needs.

Notice how many of the issues concerning intangible assets involve not so much what an operation has but what it does. All operations have documented procedures to formalise their regular activities, such as 'generating orders', 'fulfilling orders', 'developing new products and services', and so on. But they also have ways of getting things done which are less formally documented. The effectiveness of these informal practices depends on the relationships between individual staff, their shared values and understandings of overall objectives, the tacit (non-articulated) knowledge accumulated by individuals, an understanding of 'who knows what' and 'who can get things done', and so on. It is these informal arrangements of a company's resources that go a long way to explaining the effectiveness of its operations. Not that the formal processes are unimportant. It is the combination of formal and informal processes, explicit and tacit knowledge, the intrinsic attributes of the company's resources and the way in which these resources are deployed that describes an operation's abilities. The collective term for both formal and informal processes is the 'routines' of the firm. Accountants have considerable trouble when dealing with intangible resources (or invisible assets as they are sometimes called). Yet, intangible assets are often the reason for a firm's success. Bill Gates, of Microsoft, points out that '. . . *our primary assets, which are our software and software development skills, do not show up in the balance sheet at all'*.[7]

Example **Amazon, So what exactly is your core competence?[8]**

It started to become clear in October 2006. The founder and boss of Amazon was out speaking about the company's plans at a number of public events. Although Amazon was generally seen as an internet book retailer and then a more general internet retailer, Jeff Bezos was actually pushing three of Amazon's 'utility computing' services. These were a company that provides cheap access to online computer storage, a company that allows program developers to rent computing capacity on Amazon systems, and a service that connects firms with other firms which perform specialist tasks that are difficult to automate.

The problem with online retailing, said Bezos, is its seasonality. At peak times, such as Christmas, Amazon has far more computing capacity than it needs for the rest of the year. At low points it may be using as little as 10 per cent of its total capacity. Hiring out that spare capacity is an obvious way to bring in extra revenue. In addition, by 2006 Amazon had developed a search engine, a video download business, a service (Fulfilment By Amazon) that allowed other companies to use Amazon's logistics capability including the handling of returned items, and a service that provided access to Amazon's 'back-end' technology.

Amazon's apparent redefinition of its strategy was immediately criticised by some observers. '*Why not*', they said, '*stick to what you know, focus on your core competence of internet retailing?*' Bezos's response was clear. '*We are sticking to our core competence; this is what we've been doing for the last 11 years. The only thing that's changed is that we are exposing it for (the benefit of) others.*' At least for Jeff Bezos, Amazon is not so much an internet retailer as a provider of internet-based technology and logistics services.

The concepts of intangible (or invisible) resources and of routines are central to what is sometimes called the 'resource-based view' (or RBV) of strategic management. The resource-based view is centred on the notion that most companies consider themselves to be particularly good at some specific activities, but try to avoid head-to-head competition in others. The terms distinctive capabilities or distinctive competence are used to describe those unique aspects of operations through which the firm competes. While the concept of capability or competence remains somewhat ambiguous (and the words themselves are often used interchangeably), the central idea is very close to the resource-based view of the firm, namely that externally unobservable (within-firm) factors are at least as important as observable industry market (between-firm) factors in determining competitive advantage. However, resource-based capabilities are not a substitute for sensible market positioning (even though they may be a better predictor of sustainable competitive advantage). Rather the idea is that its operations capabilities can allow a company to take up an attractive market position and can protect it from competitive threat. Furthermore, the sustainability of any market advantage will depend upon the advantage not being 'competed away' too quickly. For example, a computer chip company, such as Intel, might, at any point in time, possess a significant capability-based performance advantage over its competitors. Yet, in such a hyper-competitive market its advantage may be 'competed away' relatively quickly, possibly in months rather than years. But even here a resource-based advantage is still exceptionally valuable, even if the advantage is relatively short-lived compared with other industries. RBV is explained further in the appendix to this chapter.

As an example, return to the lighting business described ealier. Its market requirements analysis had indicated a shift towards targeting commercial companies who needed lighting designs (and often specialised equipment) for sales promotion events, conferences, displays and exhibitions. An analysis of the firm's resources, processes and capabilities revealed that the company's history and experience of advising theatrical producers was a valuable asset, particularly in the conference market. It allowed them to excel at understanding how to translate someone else's vision into theatrical reality. Furthermore, their lighting and sound technicians were experienced at re-programming equipment and configuring equipment to fit almost any concept their clients wanted. These skills, combined with an intimate network of contracts with equipment and software suppliers, enabled the company to outperform competitors and eventually dominate this (for them) new market. In order to maintain its competitive advantage, it opened new sites in a number of locations where existing and potential customers were located, all of which had a resident lighting and sound design expert. The company also developed a virtual reality simulation which helped demonstrate to potential customers how a set might look. This simulation was developed in consultation with key equipment suppliers, to utilise their expertise. In order to make all equipment readily available at all sites it installed a computer-based equipment tracking and scheduling system which was integrated across all sites. The company also organised periodic 'state of play' conferences where all staff discussed their experiences of serving clients. Some suppliers and customers were invited to these meetings.

Consider this example and how its resources have helped it to compete so effectively. Figure 1.5 illustrates how the firm has 'translated' an understanding of its resources to a set of operations strategy decisions. The translation logic goes something like this.

(a) We have a set of equipment which is sophisticated and useful in the theatre lighting business. We also have some staff that have sound and lighting design expertise.

(b) As a company we have developed a reputation for being able to take a theatre director's 'vision' for a production, and use our knowledge to make it reality, even improving the original vision.

(c) What allows us to do this so well is the way we have 'grown up together' and are able to understand all the stages of satisfying customers, from an understanding of what equipment is available right through to managing the design, installation, operating and dismantling of the production.

(d) These capabilities are particularly attractive in the commercial conference market. This is now the firm's target market.

(e) In order to consolidate and sustain this competitive position, the company makes a number of resource decisions as to how its capabilities can be preserved, developed and deployed, for example concerning, location, virtual reality technology, supplier development, tracking systems, organizational structure, etc.

Example SAB Miller[9]

SAB Miller, originally South African Breweries, provides an example of a company whose overall strategy has been significantly dictated by its acquired capabilities. Founded in 1895 in Johannesburg, it has grown to be the world's second-largest brewer. As well as producing a massive 98 per cent of all the beer sold in its native South Africa, it has expanded globally, especially in the rest of sub-Saharan Africa, China, central and eastern Europe, South America and, most recently, in the USA.

During its main growth period immediately after South Africa's first democratic elections, it expanded, not by building new capacity, but either by buying existing local companies or through joint-venture partnerships, usually with the backing of the host government. Often it bought controlling stakes in newly privatised state breweries, a strategy it used in Tanzania, Zambia, Mozambique, Hungary and China. Globally, the beer industry may not be very heavily consolidated but at a national level there are rarely more than a handful of companies. Typically, the top two companies share 80 per cent of a national beer market. Thus, SAB can dominate a local market by acquiring underperforming, but high market share, companies and applying its highly professional operations expertise to their production, distribution and marketing operations.

SAB Miller's particular competence has been the ability to enter an underdeveloped but high-volume market, adapt to its specific operating conditions, and quickly develop world-class operations standards, low-cost facilities and efficient distribution networks. Most importantly, it can achieve these characteristics of developed-country brewing in developing-country conditions. In other words, it concentrated on doing what competitors found difficult – overcoming poor infrastructure, unreliable communications, sometimes less than helpful officialdom, natural disasters, labour unrest, even political revolutions. Although the specific problems in each country were different, the skills and procedures that the company had developed on the back of its experience helped it to move quickly down the learning curve at each new acquisition, adapting its operations to suit local economic and cultural conditions. Even before it entered a new market SAB sent in technical and marketing/distribution teams. Local managers were trained at SAB's training institute and considerable effort was put into capturing the learning its expatriate and local managers gained at each new acquisition. So, for example, Hungary acted as a hub of knowledge and expertise for developing the company's new Central European operations until they reached the SAB standards of quality and operating efficiency. Any difficulties (not unknown in such unpredictable markets) and the company used SWAT teams of technical specialists. Even so, the business was inevitably risky. The collapse of the Russian economy in 1998, and the resulting squeeze on profit margins, caused the company to write down its beer-making assets in Russia from $85 million to $15 million before they had even started production.

In 2002, however, the company broke with its previous strategy and bought Miller, a 'mainstream' US brewer with substantial US sales. Now it was doing what it had previously avoided, competing directly against established competitors (notably Anheuser-Busch) in developed markets where its operations-based capabilities counted for less. The company's hopes of introducing new (to the US) brands such as Peroni into the US market were not totally fulfilled because of American consumers' dislike of imported beers. This, according to one commentator, *'has left the company with no other option but to go head-to-head with Anheuser-Busch in a very public Miller-Budweiser duel'*. Yet, SAB Miller also continued to expand in non-Western markets. The company's $7.8 billion purchase of Colombia's Bavaria in 2005 was one of the biggest acquisitions in the industry's history. In the same year it acquired the Fuyang City Snowland Brewery Company bringing the number of SAB Miller breweries in China to 38.

So what is operations strategy?

The four perspectives on operations strategy which we have outlined need not necessarily conflict. Nor are they 'alternative' views of how operations strategy should be formulated. Operations managers can hold all four views simultaneously. They simply represent alternative starting points for understanding the nature, scope and rationale of operations strategy. Bringing all four views together can even expose the dilemmas inherent within an operations strategy. In fact, operations strategy can be seen as the attempt to reconcile all four perspectives; the top-down with the bottom-up view and the market requirements with the operations resource view.

In particular, the tension between the market requirements perspective and the operations resource perspective is central to all operations strategy decision making. Operations managers must obviously satisfy the requirements of the market if their enterprise is to survive in the long-term. Yet, simply following a market is unlikely to provide long-term competitive advantage. After all, competitors will themselves be attempting to do the same thing. To escape from being permanently 'jerked around' by the dynamics of the market, operations should also be attempting to develop the long-term capabilities that competitors will find difficult to imitate. This is why our definition of operations strategy, and the main theme throughout this book, encompasses the reconciliation of market requirements with operations resources.

This is actually a very complex interaction. Partly the complexity lies in the difficulty most organisations have in clarifying either the nature of market requirements or the characteristics of their operations resources. Sometimes this is simply because not enough effort is put into clarifying their intended markets. Some operations strategies are formulated without the context of a well-understood market and/or business strategy. But, even in better-managed companies, market requirements may be unclear. For example, a company may compete in many different markets which exhibit sometimes subtle, but nevertheless important, differences in their requirements. Furthermore, markets are dynamic. Neither customers nor competitors are totally predictable. Customer behaviour may change for reasons which become clear only after the event. Competitor reaction, likewise, can be unpredictable and sometimes irrational. Above all, it is important to understand that the links between customers, competitors and market positioning are not always obvious. Market positioning is not an exact science and the strategic reconciliation process of operations strategy may have to take place under conditions of both uncertainty and ambiguity. The operations resources side of the equation may be equally unclear. Businesses do not always know the value, abilities, or performance of their own resources and processes. Notwithstanding the popularity of the 'core competence' concept, organisations frequently find difficulty in identifying what are, could be, or should be, their core competences. More significantly, the resources and processes within the operation are not deterministically connected, like some machine where adjustments to levers of control lead inexorably to a predictable and precise change in the behaviour of the operation. The cause–effect mechanisms for most operations are, at best, only partially understood.

A company may find that its intended market position is matched exactly by the capabilities of its operations resources, the strategic decisions made by its operations managers having, over time, generated precisely the right balance of performance objectives to achieve a sustainable competitive advantage in its markets. Then again, it may not. In fact, even where it is understood, the capabilities of its operations resources are unlikely to be in perfect alignment with the requirements of its markets. The objective of operations strategy is to attempt this alignment over time without undue risk to the organisation. Operations managers must attempt to do this through the process of reconciliation, a process which is ongoing and iterative. We can include this concept of 'reconciliation' into our definition of operations strategy.

> Operations strategy is the total pattern of decisions which shape the long-term capabilities of any type of operation and their contribution to overall strategy, through the reconciliation of market requirements with operations resources.

The content and process of operations strategy

A conventional and (sometimes) useful distinction that is often used when discussing strategy is that between 'content' and 'process'. 'Content' means the collection of decisions which are made (deliberately or by default) within the operations strategy domain. Content is concerned with the strategic decisions which shape and develop the long-term direction of the operation and form the 'building blocks' of an operations strategy. 'Process' means the way in which operations strategies are (or can be) formulated. It is a reflection both of what operations managers should do and what they actually do in practice. It is the procedures which are, or can be, used to formulate operations strategy. The process of operations strategy determines how an operation pursues the reconciliation between its market requirements and operations resources in practice. However, there are significant overlaps between content and process. For example, part of the 'content' of operations strategy is concerned with the organisational structure and responsibility relationships within the operations function. Yet, these issues have a direct impact on the process of how the organisation formulates its own operations strategies. Nevertheless, despite the overlap, it is conventional to treat content and process separately. More importantly it allows us to examine the set of issues associated with each in a logical manner. Chapters 2 to 7 of this book are concerned with issues of the *content* of operations strategy, while Chapters 8, 9 and 10 are concerned with the operations strategy *process*.

The content of operations strategy – an overview

Operations strategy is concerned with the reconciliation of market requirements and operations resources. It attempts to influence the way it satisfies market requirements by setting appropriate performance objectives. It attempts to influence the capabilities of its operations resources through the decisions it takes in how those resources are deployed. So, the content of operations strategy is the interaction between the operation's performance objectives and the decisions that it takes concerning resource deployment. Figure 1.6 illustrates this idea. It particularly highlights the importance of,

● understanding the relative importance of the operation's performance objectives; and

● understanding the influence on them of the decision areas that determine resource deployment.

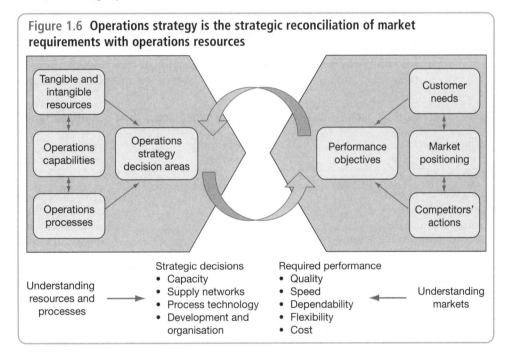

Figure 1.6 **Operations strategy is the strategic reconciliation of market requirements with operations resources**

Performance objectives

In Figure 1.6 the market requirements perspective on operations strategy was summarised in terms of five generic performance objectives: quality, speed, dependability, flexibility and cost. Their purpose is to articulate market requirements in a way that will be useful to operations. However, before we can pursue the idea of performance objectives further we must take a step back in order to consider market positioning and how competitive factors are used to describe positioning.

A company may try to articulate its position in the market in a number of ways. It might compare itself with a competitor, for example 'We wish to offer a wider range of products than Gap, but not be as expensive as Donna Karan'. Alternatively, they might associate themselves with the needs of a particular customer group. For example, 'We wish to provide a level of service and attention which discerning business people expect when they stay at our hotels'. Either way, they finish up defining market position in terms of a number of dimensions, for example, range, price, quality of service, etc. These dimensions on which a company wishes to compete are called competitive factors. Different words will be used for different types of operation and their relative importance will change depending on how the company wishes to compete. Nevertheless, their common characteristic is that they describe the things that a customer can see or experience. Table 1.1 illustrates this idea for two contrasting operations. This clusters the competitive factors for each operation into the five generic performance objectives which they represent.

Note that the two operations we have used as examples in Table 1.1 have a different view of each of the performance objectives. So, for example, the mortgage service sees quality as being at least as much about the manner in which their customers relate to their service as it does about the absence of technical errors. The steel plant, on the other hand, while not ignoring quality of service, primarily emphasises product-related technical issues. Different operations will see quality (or any other performance objective) in different ways, and emphasise different aspects. Broadly speaking though, they are selecting from the same pool of factors which together constitute the generic performance objective, in this case 'quality'. So, each of the performance objectives represents a cluster of competitive factors grouped together

Table 1.1 Competitive factors for two operations grouped under their generic performance objectives

Mortgage services Associated competitive factors include ...	Performance objectives	Steel plant Associated competitive factors include ...
Professionalism of staff Friendliness of staff Accuracy of information Ability to change details in future	Quality	Percentage of products conforming to their specification Absolute specification or products Usefulness of technical advice
Time for call centre to respond Prompt advice response Fast loan decisions Fast availability of funds	Speed	Lead-time from enquiry to quotation Lead-time from order to delivery Lead-time for technical advice
Reliability of original promise date Customers kept informed	Dependability	Percentage of deliveries 'on time, in full' Customers kept informed of delivery dates
Customisation of terms, such as duration/life of offer Cope with changes in circumstances, such as level of demand	Flexibility	Range of sizes, gauges, coatings, etc. possible Rate of new product introduction Ability to change quantity, composition and timing of an order
Interest rate charged Arrangement charges Insurance charges	Cost	Price of products Price of technical advice Discounts available Payment terms

for convenience. Sometimes operations may choose to re-bundle, using slightly different headings. For example, it is not uncommon in some service operations to refer to 'quality of service' as representing all the competitive factors we have listed under quality and speed and dependability. In practice, the issue is not so much one of universal definition but rather consistency within one, or a group of operations. At the very least it is important that individual companies have it clear in their own minds what list of generic performance objectives is appropriate to their business, what competitive factors each represents, and how each competitive factor is to be defined. However, not that cost is different from the other performance objectives. While most competitive factors are clear manifestations of their performance objectives, the competitive factors of 'price' are related to the cost performance objective. So, an improvement in cost performance does not necessarily mean a reduction in the price charged to customers. Firms that achieve lower costs may choose to take some, or all, of the improvement in higher margins rather than reduce prices.

Decision areas

Also in Figure 1.6 is a set of 'decision areas'. This is the set of decisions needed to manage the resources of the operation. Again, different writers on operations strategy use slightly different groupings and refer to them collectively in slightly different ways, such as operations policy areas, sub-strategies or operations tasks. We shall refer to them throughout this book as operations strategy decisions or decision areas, and the groupings of decision areas which we shall use are as follows.

Capacity strategy

This concerns how capacity and facilities in general should be configured. It includes questions such as: 'What should be the overall level of capacity?'; 'How many sites should the capacity be distributed across, and what size should they be?'; 'Should each site be engaged in a broad mixture of activities, or should they specialise in one or two?'; 'Exactly where should each site be located?'; 'When should changes be made to overall capacity levels?'; 'How big should each change in capacity be?'; 'How fast should capacity expansion or reduction be pursued?'; and so on. Chapter 3 will deal with the decisions concerning capacity strategy.

Supply network strategy, including purchasing and logistics

This concerns how operations relate to its interconnected network of other operations, including customers, customers' customers, suppliers, suppliers' suppliers, and so on. All operations need to consider their position in this network, both to understand how the dynamic forces within the network will affect them, and to decide what role they wish to play in the network. Decisions here include such things as: 'How much of the network do we wish to own?'; 'How can we gain an understanding of our competitive position by placing it in a network context?'; 'How do we predict and cope with dynamic disturbances and fluctuations within the network?'; 'Should we attempt to manage the network in different ways depending on the types of market we are serving?'; 'How many suppliers should we have?'; 'What should be the nature of our relationship with our suppliers, purely market-based or long-term partnerships?'; 'What are the appropriate ways of managing different types of supplier relationships?'; and so on. Chapter 4 deals with supply network strategy.

Process technology strategy

This concerns the choice and development of the systems, machines and processes which act directly or indirectly on transformed resources to convert them into finished products and services. Decisions here include such things as: 'How should we characterise alternative process technology?'; 'How should we assess the consequences of choosing a particular process technology?'; and so on. Chapter 5 will deal with process technology decisions.

Development and organisation

This concerns the set of broad- and long-term decisions governing how the operation is run on a continuing basis. Decisions here include such things as: 'How do we enhance and improve the processes within the operation over time?'; 'How should resources be clustered together within the business?'; 'How should reporting relationships be organised between these resources?'; How should new product and service development be organised?'. We devote two chapters to these areas. Chapter 6 will deal with the strategic improvement, and Chapter 7 with product and service development.

Why these decision areas?

All these decision areas will be familiar to managers in a wide variety of operations. However, it is possible to support this intuitive list of decision areas with a slightly more rigorous approach. To do this let us indulge in some simple ratio analysis.

Essentially, ratio analysis is an attempt to decompose a fundamental ratio of some element of performance into other ratios by inserting the same measure on the top and bottom of the resulting ratios. The idea is to split the fundamental ratio into other measures so that we can understand how it is built up. The best-known examples of this occur in financial accounting. Here we will do it in a slightly different way by inserting measures which have some meaning in an operations context. We are not proposing this ratio analysis as a practical analysis tool. Rather it is intended to provide some underpinning for each decision area. Figure 1.7 shows how we can do this for the fundamental ratio of profit divided by total assets, or return on assets (ROA).[10]

The simple ROA ratio, profit over total assets, is broken down into 'profit/output' and 'output/total assets'. This first ratio (in effect, average profit) can be further broken down into average revenue minus average cost. Operations affect the former through its ability to deliver superior levels of competitive performance (better quality, speed, dependability and flexibility). It affects the latter through the more productive use of its resources (lower costs). These are the two measures which have been seen as the great operations balancing act, keeping revenue high through standards of service and competitive pricing while keeping costs low. Both are a function of an organisation's success in achieving an effective and efficient operation through its development and organisation decisions. These attempt to ensure that improvement and learning continually reduce costs, while the performance of products and services and its level of service to customers are continually increased.

The other part of the decomposed ROA ratio – output/total assets – represents the output being produced for the investment being put into the operation. It is shown in Figure 1.7 broken down into three ratios: 'output/capacity', 'fixed assets/total assets' and 'capacity/fixed assets'.

Figure 1.7 Decomposing the ratio profit/total assets to derive the four strategic decision areas of operations strategy

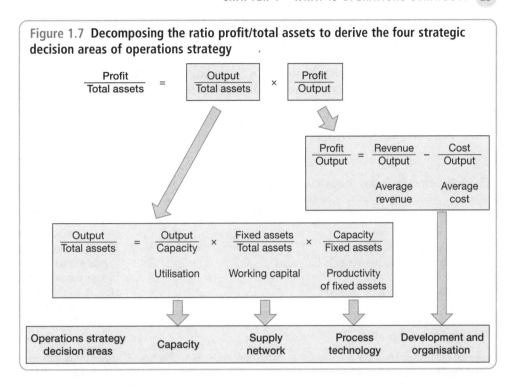

'Output/capacity', or the utilisation of the operation, is determined by the balance of demand on the operation and its long-term ability to meet that demand. To improve ROA, utilisation needs to be as close to 1 as possible. To do this, either demand must be generated to match capacity, or the operation must develop an ability to adjust its capacity to match demand. This ratio is largely a function of an organisation's capacity decisions. Has it managed to balance the provision of capacity with demand (output) and can it change its capacity to meet changing levels of demand?

'Fixed assets/total assets' is a ratio partially governed by the working capital requirements of the business. The smaller the working capital required by the operation, the closer fixed assets is to total assets. For the operations function, working capital minimisation is often a matter of reducing the inventories in its supply network, a function of an organisation's supply network decisions. Can the supply network maintain appropriate delivery of its products and services without carrying excessive levels of inventory?

'Capacity/fixed assets' is sometimes called the productivity of fixed assets. It is a measure of how much the operation has had to spend in order to acquire, or develop, its capacity. To some extent this is determined by the skill of the operation's designers and technologists. An operation that achieves the required capacity levels without needing large amounts of capital expenditure will have a better ratio than the operation that has 'thrown money at the problem'. This ratio is largely a function of an organisation's process technology decisions. Has it invested wisely in appropriate process technologies, which can create a sufficient volume of appropriate products and/or services, without excessive capital expenditure?

Obviously, this is not a totally clean categorisation. In some way all the decision areas will have some impact on all the ratios. For example, a company's development and organisation strategy includes such issues as how improvement is encouraged, how the organisation's structure works and how performance is measured. This will affect many of these ratios. Its main focus, however, is likely to be on improving average profit, by reducing costs through operations efficiency and increasing revenue through improved operations effectiveness at delivering its products and services.

Table 1.2 sets out some typical decisions which need to be taken in two very different types of operation, clustered under the four areas.

Table 1.2 **Some decisions in each decision area for a hotel chain and an automobile manufacturer**

Hotel chain	Decision area	Automobile manufacturer
How many rooms and other facilities should each hotel have? Should each hotel have the same set of facilities? Where should our hotels be located? How do we manage the long-term expansion or contraction of capacity in each region?	Capacity	How big should each plant be? Should we focus all production on one model on a single site? Where should each site be located? How do we manage the long-term expansion or contraction of overall capacity?
What activities should we be performing in-house and what should we buy in? Do we develop franchise opportunities on our sites? Should we form alliances with other vacation or travel companies?	Supply networks	What parts should we be making in-house and what should we buy in? How do we coordinate deliveries from our suppliers? Should we form long-term supply alliances? How many 'first tier' suppliers should we have?
To what extent should we be investing in multi-functional information systems? Should all information systems be linked to a central system?	Process technology	What processes should be receiving investment for automation? How can investment in technology increase our flexibility while keeping costs low? Should our process technologies be integrated?
How can we integrate new services features smoothly into our existing operation? What should be the reporting responsibility relationships within and between hotels? Should we promote company-wide improvement initiatives? How do we make sure sites learn from each other?	Development and organisation	How can we bring new products to market quickly? Should we develop products on common platforms? How do we manage product variety? What should be the reporting responsibility relationships within and between sites? Should we promote company-wide improvement initiatives? How do we make sure sites learn from each other?

Structural and infrastructural decisions

A distinction is often drawn in operations strategy between the strategic decisions that determine an operation's structure, and those that determine its infrastructure. Structural issues primarily influence the physical arrangement and configuration of the operation's resources. Infrastructural strategy areas influence the activities that take place within the operation's structure. This distinction in operations strategy has been compared to that between 'hardware' and 'software' in a computer system. The hardware of a computer sets limits to what it can do. Some computers, because of their technology and their architecture, are capable of higher performance than others, although those computers with high performance are often more expensive. In a similar way, investing in advanced process technology and building more or better facilities can raise the potential of any type of operation. But the most powerful computer can only work to its full potential if its software is capable of exploiting the potential embedded in its hardware. The same principle applies with operations. The best and most costly facilities and technology will only be effective if the operation also has an appropriate infrastructure which governs the way it will work on a day-to-day basis.

However, it is a mistake to categorise decision areas as being either entirely structural or entirely infrastructural. In reality, all the decision areas have both structural and infrastructural implications. Capacity strategy, since it is concerned with the physical size and location of operations, is mainly a structural issue, but can also affect the organisation's reporting relationships systems and procedures. Similarly, supply network decisions have much to do with whether the organisation chooses to perform in-house and what it chooses to buy in, but this needs infrastructural support for communications and the development of relationships. Process technology, likewise, has its structural aspects that will partly determine the physical form of the operation, but much of an operation's process technology will be devoted to driving the systems, procedures and monitoring systems that form its infrastructure. Even decisions within the development and organisation category, while primarily being concerned with infrastructure, can have structural elements. A set of reporting relationships embedded within an organisational structure may reflect different locations and different process technologies. It is usually best to consider a spectrum as illustrated in Figure 1.8.

Figure 1.8 Operations strategy decision areas are partly structural and partly infrastructural

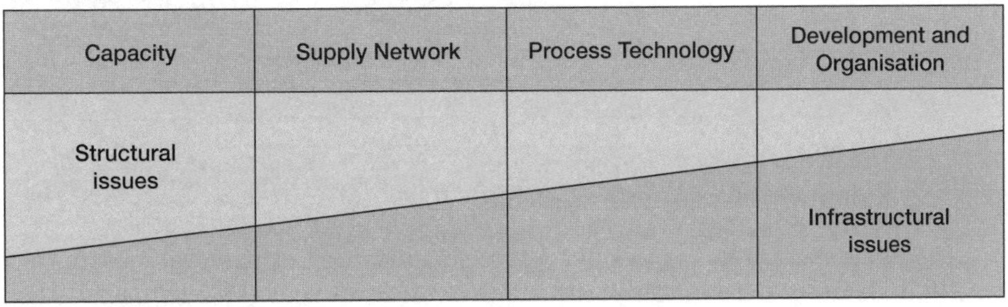

The operations strategy matrix

We can now bring together the two perspectives of market requirements and operations resources to form the dimensions of a matrix. This 'operations strategy matrix' describes operations strategy as the intersection of a company's performance objectives with its decision areas (see Figure 1.9). It emphasises the intersections between what is required from the operations function (the relative priority given to each performance objective), and how the operation tries to achieve this through the set of choices made (and the capabilities which have been developed) in each decision area, and although sometimes complex, the matrix can, at the very least, be considered a checklist of the issues which are required to be addressed. Any operation which claims to have an operations strategy will presumably be able to have some kind of story to tell for each of the intersections. It should be able to explain exactly how capacity strategy is going to affect quality, speed, dependability, flexibility or cost. It should be able to explain exactly how flexibility is influenced by capacity, supply network, process technology, and development and organisation decisions, and so on. In other words, the matrix helps operations strategies to be comprehensive. Also, it is unlikely that all the intersections on the matrix will necessarily be of equal importance. Some intersections will be more critical than others. Which intersections are critical will, of course, depend on the company, and the nature of its operations, but they are likely to reflect the relative priority of performance objectives and those decisions areas that affect, or are affected by, the company's strategic resources. The example of Seven-Eleven Japan illustrates how the matrix can be used to describe a company's operations strategy.

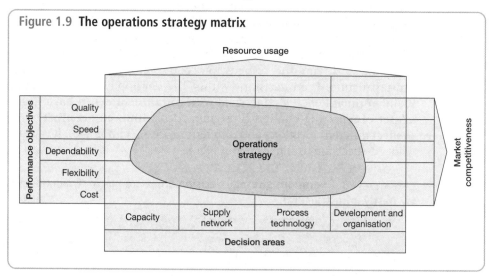

Figure 1.9 The operations strategy matrix

Example Seven-Eleven Japan[11]

Economic stagnation and lack of consumer confidence in Japan over most of the last decade hit its retail sector particularly hard. An exception was Seven-Eleven Japan (7-Eleven), a franchise convenience store chain, with over 11,500 outlets in Japan and established in 1973. The 7-Eleven organisation has maintained its position in the industry by growing profits to a level almost unequalled in the Japanese retail industry and is now the largest retailer in Japan. Its secret behind years of growth has been its advanced inventory management system supported by sophisticated information technology.

Company legend has it that Toshifumi Suzuki, the Chairman and CEO of 7-Eleven, was inspired to devise his item-by-item control when he tried to buy a shirt at a retail shop. He did not find a suitable size because the shop had sold out, even though he was himself average sized. On enquiry, the shop assistant told him that they always ordered the same amount of stock in all sizes irrespective of demand. 7-Eleven determined never to run needless risks of this type with its customer loyalty. The company's Total Information System (TIS) integrates all information from its stores, head office operations, district offices, suppliers, combined distribution centres and its field 'counsellors'. This system drives the company's inventory management and distribution/delivery systems. 7-Eleven has, over the years, encouraged its vendors to open common distribution centres where similar categories of goods, such as milk and dairy products, are combined for delivery to the stores on one truck. Thus, small deliveries are made on a regular basis which reduces the need for stock space in the stores but also guards against stock-outs. These common distribution centres also reduce the total number of deliveries a day to individual stores. In 1980 a typical store would receive over 30 deliveries per day; by 1999 this had shrunk to under 10. The company further refined this common distribution centre process by grouping items for each centre, not by type but rather by storage temperature, for example frozen foods, chilled foods, room temperature process foods, hot foods, etc. This grouping helps to maintain product quality. The Total Information System also allows the company to respond to changes in trends and customer demand. With an average floor space of just over 1000 square feet, 7-Eleven stores must make sure that every product sold is earning its shelf space. Networked cash registers and hand-held terminals allow sales staff to input details of the type of customer making each purchase. This is tracked, along with the time of day when the products are purchased, and analysed daily by product, customer type, and store. The aggregated results, as well as the data from individual stores, are used by 7-Eleven's field counsellors whose job it is to develop franchisees and 'help the stores to make more money'. By combining advanced information and distribution systems, 7-Eleven has been able to minimise the time between the receipt of orders from stores and the delivery of goods.

7-Eleven's expansion was carefully planned to ensure that it has a minimum presence of 50 stores in any area, thus reducing advertising and distribution costs. Franchisees were chosen partly by location and partly for their willingness to fit in with 7-Eleven procedures. To maintain the welfare of franchisees, the company tries to ensure that skills and learning are shared between stores to continually enhance operations best practice. It seems to be paying off. Average daily sales per 7-Eleven store are more than 30 per cent higher than its main rival. Presumably this is why 7-Eleven's franchisees are prepared to pay relatively high royalty fees compared with its rivals.

The operations strategy matrix analysis for Seven-Eleven Japan

For a company like Seven-Eleven Japan, it is possible to find some kind of relationship between each performance objective and every decision area. However, in Figure 1.10, we have confined ourselves to some of the critical issues described in the Example. This operations strategy matrix has been adapted slightly to combine speed and dependability under the single performance objective 'availability'. The relative degree of 'criticality' has also been indicated. Arguably, the pivotal intersection in this company's operations strategy matrix is that between its process technology, in the form of its Total Information System, and the flexibility which this gives it to understand and respond to both sales and suppliers' trends. Many of the other cells in the matrix derive from this particularly critical cell. Here process technology is enabling strategic action both in the development of the company's supply networks and in its general development and organisation strategy. Similarly, the enhanced flexibility, which the TIS gives, helps to reduce cost, increase availability and maintain quality.

As in most analyses of this type, it is the interrelationship between the intersections (cells) of the matrix which are as important to understand as the intersections themselves. It is also worth noting that one column of issues (those concerned with supply networks) has all its cells filled in. Again, this is not unusual. In this case the reason lies in the purpose of this company. It is essentially a supply organisation. Its only reason for existence is to supply its franchise holders. Not surprising then that it should be particularly concerned with supply network issues.

Figure 1.10 Operations strategy matrix for Seven-Eleven Japan

Resource development

Market competitiveness

	CAPACITY	SUPPLY NETWORK	PROCESS TECHNOLOGY	DEVELOPMENT AND ORGANISATION
QUALITY of products and services		Distribution centre grouping by temperature **		Information sharing and parenting system spread service ideas **
Speed and dependability combined to indicate AVAILABILITY		Distribution centres and inventory management systems give fast stock replenishment **		
FLEXIBILITY of response to sales and customers' trends		TIS allows trends to be forecast and supply adjustments made *	TIS gives sophisticated analysis of sales and supply patterns daily ***	
COST in terms of minimising: • operating cost • capital cost • working capital	Area dominance reduces distribution and advertising costs *	Common distribution centres give small, frequent deliveries from fewer sources **		Field counsellors with sales data help stores to minimise waste and increase sales **
	• Location of stores • Size of stores	• Number and type of distribution centres • Order and stock replenishment	• The total information system (TIS)	• Franchisee relationships • New product/ service development • Approach to operations improvement

*** Very critical
** Critical
* Secondary

SUMMARY ANSWERS TO KEY QUESTIONS

What is 'operations' and why is it so important?

'Operations', is the activity of managing the resources and processes that produce and deliver goods and services. All operations transform resource inputs into outputs of products and services and can be analysed at three levels: that of the business itself, as part of a greater network of operations, and at the level of individual processes within the operation. Operations management contributes to the success of any organisation by reducing costs, by increasing revenue by reducing capital employed, and by providing the basis for future innovation.

What is strategy?

Strategic decisions are those that, set broad objectives that direct an enterprise towards its overall goal, plan the path that will achieve these goals, stress long-term rather than short-term objectives, deal with total picture rather than with individual activities, and are often seen as above or detached from routine day-to-day activities. However, it is not easy to totally characterise strategy or strategic decisions. Some organisations make no explicit strategic decisions as such. Rather they develop over time, often with strategies that 'emerge' from their ongoing experience of doing business. Furthermore, the strategy as espoused by an organisation may not always be reflected in what it actually does. This is why strategy is often taken to be the 'pattern of decisions' that indicate the company's overall path.

What is operations strategy?

Operations strategy is the total pattern of decisions which shape the long-term capabilities of any kind of operation and their contribution to overall strategy, through the ongoing reconciliation of market requirements and operation resources. All businesses have markets, all businesses own or deploy resources; therefore all businesses are concerned with the reconciliation of markets and resources.

How should operations reflect overall strategy?

An operations strategy will be one of several functional strategies which are governed by the decisions which set the overall strategic direction of the organisation. This is called the 'top-down' approach. So, corporate strategy should be reflected in the strategies of each business unit, which should, in turn, inform the strategy of each business function.

How can operations strategy learn from operational experience?

An alternative view to the top-down perspective (one that is based on observing how strategy happens in practice) is the bottom-up perspective that stresses how strategic ideas emerge over time from actual experiences. Companies adopt strategies partly because of their ongoing experience, sometimes with no high-level decision making involved. The idea of strategy being shaped by experience over time is also called the concept of emergent strategies. Shaping strategy from the bottom up requires an ability to learn from experience and a philosophy of continual and incremental improvement.

How do the requirements of the market influence operations strategy?

Two important elements within markets are customers and competitors. The concept of market segmentation is used to identify target markets which have a clear set of requirements and where a company can differentiate itself from current, or potential, competitors. On the basis of this, the company takes up a market position. This market position can be characterised in terms of how the company wishes to compete for customers' business. By grouping competitive factors into clusters under the heading of generic performance objectives (quality, speed, dependability, flexibility and cost), market requirements are translated into a form useful for the development of the operation.

How can the intrinsic capabilities of an operation's resources influence operations strategy?

Over time, an operation may acquire distinctive capabilities, or competences, on the basis of the accumulation of its experiences. These capabilities may be embedded within a company's intangible resources and its operating 'routines'. So, they concern both what the operation has and what it does. Operations shapes these capabilities (consciously or unconsciously) through the way it makes a whole series of decisions over time. These decisions can be grouped under the headings of capacity, supply network, process technology, and development and organisation.

What is the difference between the 'content' and the 'process' of operations strategy?

The reconciliation process is not a straightforward task. Neither markets nor resources are always easy to understand. Markets are uncertain and volatile whereas resource competences can be diffuse and difficult to pin down. Two sets of issues help to untangle this complexity. The first concerns the 'content' of operations strategy, that is, the building blocks from which any operations strategy will be formed. This includes the definition attached to individual performance objectives, together with a prioritisation of those performance objectives. It also includes an understanding of the structure and options available in the four decision areas of capacity, supply networks, process technology, and development and organisation. The second set of issues concern the 'process' of operations strategy, that is, how the reconciliation process takes place.

What are operations strategy performance objectives?

Performance objectives are the general classifications under which we group competitive factors. Competitive factors are the dimensions of performance which define the company's intended market position. Here we use the five generic performance objectives of quality, speed, dependability, flexibility and cost. The exact definition of these five performance objectives will differ for individual operations. Nevertheless, the categories are broadly applicable in most circumstances. Each performance objective will have an effect both inside and outside the operation. The relative priorities of performance objectives will be influenced by customer importance and performance against competitors. The highest-priority objectives for operations are usually those that customers find important but where performance is relatively poor compared to competitors.

What are operations strategy decision areas?

Operations strategy decision areas are grouping of decisions which shape the operation's resources. Here we use the four broad groupings of capacity, supply networks, process technology, and development and organisation. These four groupings are used partly because they relate to common operations strategy practice and partly because they all have a clear influence on an organisation's return on investment. Furthermore, they apply to all types of operation. The individual decisions within each group may vary, depending on the type of operation, but the groupings themselves are generic.

How do performance objectives relate to decision areas?

Performance objectives and decisions areas interact in a way that can be described by the operations strategy matrix. When devising an operations strategy it is important to ensure that, in terms of the matrix, the strategy is comprehensive (all obvious aspects are at least considered) and has the critical intersections identified.

Further reading

Bettley A., Mayle, D. and Tantoush, T. (eds) (2005) *Operations Management: A Strategic Approach*. London: Sage Publications.

Hayes, R.H., Pisano, G.P., Upton, D.M. and Wheelwright, S.C. (2004) *Operations, Strategy, and Technology: Pursuing the Competitive Edge*. New York: John Wiley & Sons.

Hayes, R.H., Pisano, G.P. and Upton, D.M. (1996) *Strategic Operations: Competing Through Capabilities: Text and Cases*. New York: The Free Press.

Hill, T. (2000) *Manufacturing Strategy*, 2nd edn. Macmillan Press.

Mintzberg, H. and Quinn, J. (1990) *The Strategy Process: Concepts, Contexts, and Cases*. Upper Saddle River, NJ: Prentice Hall.

Peteraf, M. (1993) 'The cornerstones of competitive advantage: a resource-based view', *Strategic Management Journal*, Vol. 14.

Skinner, W. (1978) *Manufacturing in the Corporate Strategy*. John Wiley & Sons.

Slack, N., Chambers, S., Johnston, R. and Betts, A. (2006) *Operations and Process Management: Principles and Practice for Strategic Impact*. Harlow, UK: Financial Times Prentice Hall.

Stalk, G., Evans, P. and Shulman, L. (1992) 'Competing on capabilities: the new rules of corporate strategy', *Harvard Business Review*, March–April.

Wernerfelt, B. (1984) 'A resource-based theory of the firm', *Strategic Management Journal*, No. 5.

Whittington, R. (1993) *What Is Strategy – and Does It Matter?*, Routledge.

Swink, M. and Way, M.H. (1995) 'Manufacturing strategy: propositions, current research, renewed directions', *International Journal of Operations and Production Management*, 15(7).

Appendix: the resource-based view of the firm

The resource-based view (RBV) of the firm has its origins in early economic theory. Some of the initial works in strategic management also included consideration of the firm's internal resources.[12] The 'SWOT' (strengths/weaknesses, opportunities, threats) approach saw competitive advantage as exploiting the opportunities raised in the competitive environment using the firm's strengths, while neutralising external threats and avoiding being trapped by internal weaknesses. While one school of thought, the 'environmental' school, focused on a firm's opportunities and threats, the other, the 'resource based', focused on firm's strengths.[13] Each school is grounded on different economic theories. The environmental approach adopted neo-classical economics, and more specifically industrial organisations (IO) theory,[14] whereas the resource-based theory has many similarities to the 'Austrian school', which stresses the importance of entrepreneurship, and behavioural economics. The two schools of thought differ in the way they explain why some companies outperform others over time – what strategists call a 'sustainable competitive advantage' (SCA).

Through the 1970s and 1980s, the dominant school, the environmental school, saw a firm's performance as being closely related to the industrial structure of its markets. In this view, key strategic tasks centred on competitive positioning within industrial sectors. The firm itself is seen as an allocator of resources between different product-market opportunities. The implication of this is that a firm should analyse the forces present within the environment in order to assess the profit potential of the industry, and then design a strategy that aligns the firm to the environment.

The 'resource-based' explanation of why some companies manage to gain sustainable competitive advantage, by contrast, focuses on the role of the resources which are (largely) internal to the company's operations. Put simply, 'above average' performance is more likely to be the result of the core capabilities (or competences) inherent in a firm's resources than its competitive positioning in its industry.

The RBV also differs in its approach to how firms protect any competitive advantage they may have. The environmental view sees companies as seeking to protect their competitive advantage through their control of the market. For example, by creating barriers to entry through product differentiation, or making it difficult for customers to switch to competitors, or controlling the access to distribution channels (a major barrier to entry in petrol retailing, for example, where oil companies own their own retail stations), and so on. By contrast, the RBV sees firms being able to protect their competitive advantage by building up 'difficult-to-imitate' resources. Thus, the resources which a firm possesses are closely linked to its ability to outperform competitors. Certain of these resources are particularly important, and can be classified as 'strategic' if they exhibit the following properties.[15]

- They are scarce – unequal access to (or information about) resources can lead to their uneven distribution amongst competing firms. In this way, scarce resources such as specialised production facilities, experienced engineers, proprietary software, etc. can underpin competitive advantage.

- They are imperfectly mobile – some resources are difficult to move out of a firm. For example, resources that were developed in-house, or are based on the experience of the company's staff, cannot be traded easily. As a result, the advantages which they create are more likely to be retained over time.

- They are imperfectly imitable and imperfectly substitutable – these critical dimensions help define the overall sustainability of a resource-based advantage. It is not enough only to have resources which are unique and immobile. If a competitor can copy these resources or, less predictably, replace them with alternative resources, then their value will quickly deteriorate. Again, the more the resources are connected with tacit knowledge and routines embedded within the firm, the more difficult they are for competitors to understand and to copy.

Extended Resource-Based Theory (ERBT)[16]

Although 'classic' RBT has obvious appeal, research has emerged on resource-based advantage within a broader network context: the so-called 'extended' RBT. ERBT assumes that strategic resources lying beyond the boundaries of the firm can be used to generate 'relational' or 'collaboration specific quasi-rents', emphasising their reliance on inter-firm relationships. ERBT shares explicit links with the broader supply literature and, in particular, work focused on determining appropriate levels of *synergy* between firms, with specific reference to issues such as the development and evolution of buyer–seller relationships, strategic returns from collaboration (e.g. supplier development), economic value of market power, etc. ERBT is founded on the assumption that strategic resources lying beyond the boundaries of the firm can be accessed, especially given the existence of certain types of inter-firm relationships. It represents an extension of RBT because, the structure and function of these relationships relates to the specificity of the resources to be transferred. Research focused on inter-firm knowledge transfer has explored the performance implications of strong and weak ties between network nodes. It is argued that weak ties (i.e. those lacking history, reciprocity, emotional intensity, etc.) are best suited to transfer of codified technical-type information, but are less suited to richer knowledge transfer. For example, strong ties were central to the development of Toyota's hugely effective supply network.

Notes on the chapter

1 In some organisations the operations manager could be called by some other name. For example, he or she might be called the 'fleet manager' in a distribution company, or the 'administrative manager' in a hospital, or the 'store manager' in a supermarket.

2 Slack, N., Chambers, S. and Johnston, R. (2007) *Operations Management*, 5th edn., Harlow: Financial Times Prentice Hall.

3 Sources include: company websites (2007); Marsh, P. (2006) 'The masters of good service', *Financial Times*, 30 June.

4 Weick, K.E. (1990) 'Cartographic myths in organizations', in Huff, A. (ed.) *Managing Strategic Thought*. London: Wiley.

5 Singapore Airlines' website (2007).

6 Mintzberg, H. and Quinn, J. (1990) *The Strategy Process: Concepts, Context, and Cases*. Upper Saddle River, NJ: Prentice Hall.

7 Source: Microsoft website (2007).

8 Source: 'Lifting the bonnet', *The Economist*, 7 October 2006.

9 Sources: Company information (2007); Maitland, A. (2000) 'A troubled history is no small beer', *Financial Times*, 19 December.

10 An idea put forward by Eilan, S. and Gold, B. (1978) *Productivity Measurement*. Oxford: Pergamon Press.

11 Lee, H.L. and Whang, S. (2001) 'A tale of two retailers', *Supply Chain Management Review*, 3 January.

12 Learned, E.C., Christensen, C., Andrews, K. and Guth, W. (1969) *Business Policy: Text and Cases*. Homewood IL: Irwin.

13 Penrose, E. (1959) *The Theory of the Growth of the Firm*. Oxford: Blackwell.

14 Bain, J.S. (1968) *Industrial Organization*. New York: John Wiley & Sons.

15 Barney, J. (1991) 'The resource-based model of the firm: origins, implications and prospects; and firm resources and competitive advantage', *Journal of Management*, 17(1).

16 For example, see: Dyer, J.H. and Nobeoka, K. (2000) 'Creating and managing a high

performance knowledge-sharing network: The Toyota Case', *Strategic Management Journal*, Vol. 21, pp. 345–67; Granovetter, M.S. (1973) 'The strength of weak ties', *American Journal of Sociology* 78, pp. 1360–80; Ireland, R.D., Hitt, M.A. and Vaidyanath, D. (2002) 'Alliance management as a source of competitive advantage', *Journal of Management*, 8(3), pp. 413–66; Madhok, A. and Taliman, S.B. (1998) 'Resources, transactions and rents: managing value through interfirm collaborative relationships', *Organization Science*, 9, pp. 326–39; Matthews, J.A. (2003) 'Competititve Dynamics and economic learning: an extended resource-based view', *Industrial and Corporate Change*, 12(1), pp. 115–45; Matthews, J.A. (2003) 'Strategizing by firms in the presence of markets for resources', *Industrial and Corporate Change*, 12(6), pp. 1157–93; Szulanski, G. (2000) 'The process of knowledge transfer: a diachronic analysis of stickiness', *Organisational Behaviour and Human Decision Processes*, 82, pp. 9–27.

Operations performance

Introduction

In this chapter we look at how we judge the performance of operations, primarily in terms of the five performance objectives: quality, speed, dependability, flexibility and cost. We then look at three related aspects of performance which are fundamental to understanding operations strategy. First, we examine how the relative importance of different aspects of performance changes over time. This is because the relative importance of the market requirements and operations resource perspectives do not stay constant over time. Sometimes market requirements dominate and operations resources must be made to fit whatever the market dictates. At other times, the capabilities and constraints of operations resources will place restrictions on the organisation's choice of its market positioning. Second, we look at how performance objectives trade off against each other. Operations are often called on to enhance some specific aspects of their performance. The key issue is, do improvements in some aspects of performance necessarily mean a reduction in the performance of others? Third, we examine how exceptional performance levels can be reached by focusing on a limited set of objectives and exploiting the trade-offs between objectives (see Figure 2.1).

Figure 2.1 **This chapter examines how the relative importance of the market requirements and operations resource perspectives change over time, how performance objectives trade-offs between each other and how operations focus can lead to exceptional performance**

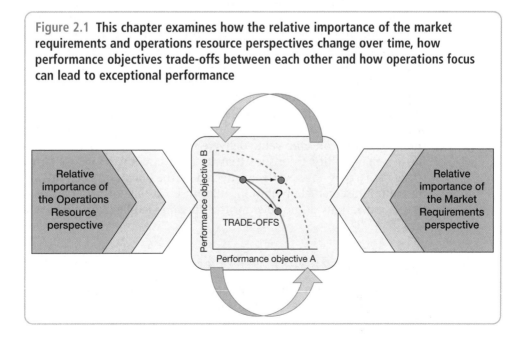

KEY QUESTIONS

- *What are operations performance objectives?*
- *Do the role and key performance objectives of operations stay constant or vary over time?*
- *Are trade-offs between operations performance objectives inevitable or can they be overcome?*
- *What are the advantages and disadvantages of focused operations?*

Operations performance objectives

Assessing the performance of anything at any time is hardly ever straightforward. Perceived performance is a function of, amongst other things, who you are (customer, employee, stockholder, etc.), your objectives (often disputed), timescale (what is judged as good now may not be appropriate next year), measurability (how do you measure trust, relationship, security, etc.?), and how comprehensive you want to be (do you really want to measure everything that every customer may find important?). Nevertheless, for operations strategy to be effective performance must be assessed in some way, and an obvious starting point is to consider the operation's range of stakeholders – the people and groups, who may be influenced by, or influence, the operation's strategy. Some are internal, for example the operation's employees; others are external, for example: customers, society or community groups, and a company's shareholders. External stakeholders may have a direct commercial relationship with the organisation, for example: suppliers and customers; others may not, such as, industry regulators. In not-for-profit operations, these stakeholder groups can overlap. So, voluntary workers in a charity may be employees, shareholders and customers all at once. However, in any kind of organisation, it is a responsibility of the operations function to understand the (sometimes conflicting) objectives of its stakeholders and set its objectives accordingly.

Figure 2.2 illustrates some main stakeholder groups together with some of the aspects of operations performance in which they will be interested for a global parcel delivery company. The company is clearly concerned to satisfy its customers' requirements for fast and dependable services at reasonable prices, as well as helping and improving its own suppliers (a whole range of organisations, from those who print packets to those who clean the offices). Similarly, it is concerned to ensure the long-term economic value delivered to its stockholders. But the company also has a responsibility to ensure that its own employees are well treated and that society at large is not negatively affected by the operation's activities – the company must minimise vehicle pollution, minimise wastage of materials or energy, ensure that its operations do not disrupt the life and well-being of those who live nearby, and so on.

The five generic performance objectives

Understanding broad stakeholder objectives is important, mainly because different or conflicting priorities between stakeholder groups often provide the backdrop to operations strategy decision-making. But, in practical terms, an operation requires a

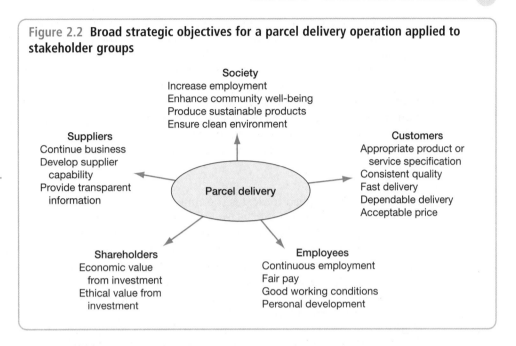

Figure 2.2 **Broad strategic objectives for a parcel delivery operation applied to stakeholder groups**

more tightly defined set of objectives. These are the five generic 'performance objectives' that were briefly introduced in the previous chapter and that apply to all types of operation. It is worth examining each of them in a little more detail. Not to present any precise definitions, but rather to illustrate how the terms, quality, speed, dependability, flexibility and cost, may be used to mean slightly different things depending on how they are interpreted in different operations. This is not to imply that broad stakeholder objectives are irrelevant to operations strategy, far from it. But the five generic performance objectives have meaning for all types of operation and relate specifically to operations' basic task of satisfying customer requirements.

Quality

Many definitions of quality refer to the 'specification' of a product or service, usually meaning high specification; as in 'the Mercedes-Benz S Class is at the quality end of the market'. Quality can also mean appropriate specification; meaning that the products and services are 'fit for purpose'; they do what they are supposed to do. 'Fit for purpose' quality includes two concepts which are far more usefully treated separately. One is the level of the product or services specification, the other is whether the operation achieves conformance to that specification.

Specification quality is also a multidimensional issue. We needed to use several aspects of specification in the automobile example above, even to reach a crude indication of what type of car is being produced. So any product or service needs to use several dimensions of specification to define its nature. These dimensions can be separated into 'hard' and 'soft' aspects of specification quality. Hard dimensions are those concerned with the evident and largely objective aspects of the product or service. Soft dimensions are associated with aspects of personal interaction between customers and the product (or more usually) service. Table 2.1 identifies some hard and soft dimensions of specification quality, though each list will change depending on the type of product or service being considered.[1]

Conformance quality is more a concern of the operation itself. It refers to the operation's ability to produce goods and services to their defined specification reliably and consistently. This is not always a simple matter of yes it can, or no it cannot. Rather the issue is often a matter of how closely the operation can achieve the product or service specification consistently. Here there is a difference between hard and soft dimensions of specification. Generally, the conformance to soft dimensions of quality is more difficult to measure and more difficult to achieve. This is largely because soft dimensions, being related to interpersonal interaction, depend on the response of individual customers relating with individual staff.

Speed

At its most basic, speed indicates the time between the beginning of an operations process and its end. It is an elapsed time. This may relate to externally obvious events; for example, from the time when the customer requests a product or service, to the time when the customer receives it. Or it may be used internally in the operation; for example, the time between when material enters an operation and when it leaves fully processed. As far as operations strategy is concerned, we are usually interested in the former. Part of this elapsed time may be the actual time to 'produce the product or service' (the 'core' processing time). It may also include the time to clarify a customer's exact needs (for example, designing a product or service), the 'queuing' times before operations resources become available, and after the core processing, the time to deliver, transport and/or install the product or service. Figure 2.3 illustrates some of the significant 'process' times which signify the steps in customer response for two operations – a hospital and a software producer. One issue for these organisations' operations is how to define the speed of delivery. Clearly, limiting it to the elapsed time taken by the core process (though this is the part they can most directly control) is inadequate. From the customers' view, the total process starts when they become aware that they may need the product or service and ends when they are completely satisfied with its 'installation'. Some may even argue that, given the need continually to engage the customer in other revenue-generating activities such as maintenance or improvement, the process never ends.

Dependability

The term dependability here is used to mean keeping delivery promises – honouring the delivery time given to the customer. It is the other half of total delivery performance along with delivery speed. The two performance objectives are often

Table 2.1 Examples of hard and soft dimensions of specification quality

'Hard' dimensions of specification quality	'Soft' dimensions of specification quality
E.g.	E.g.
Features	Helpfulness
Performance	Attentiveness
Reliability	Communication
Aesthetics	Friendliness
Security/safety	Courtesy
Integrity	
Etc.	Etc.

Figure 2.3 Significant times for the delivery of two products/services

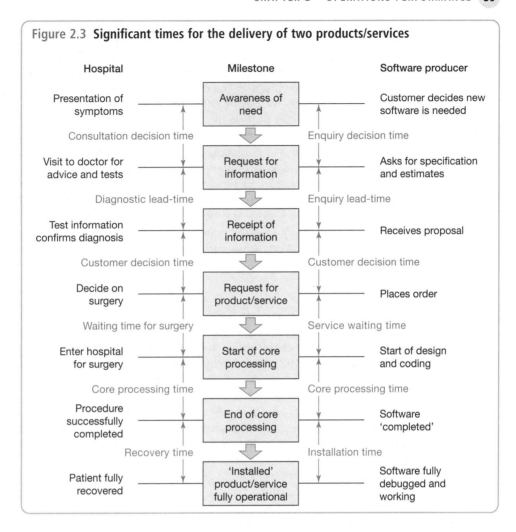

linked in some way. For example, theoretically, one could achieve high dependability merely by quoting long delivery times. In which case the difference between the expected delivery time and the time quoted to the customer is being used as an insurance against lack of dependability within the operation. However, companies that try to absorb poor dependability inside long lead-times can finish up being poor at both. There are two reasons for this. First, delivery times tend to expand to fill the time available. Attempting to discipline an operation to achieve delivery in two weeks when three are available is unambitious and allows the operation to relax its efforts to use all the available time. Second, long delivery times are often a result of slow internal response, high work-in-progress, and large amounts of non-value-added time. All of these can cause confusion, complexity and lack of control, which are the root causes of poor dependability. Good dependability can often be helped by fast throughput, rather than hindered by it. In principle, dependability is a straightforward concept:

Dependability = due delivery time − actual delivery time.

When delivery is on time, the equation should equal zero. Positive means it is early and negative means it is late. What, though, is the meaning of 'due time'? It could be the time originally requested by the customer or the time quoted by the operation. Also, there can be a difference between the delivery time scheduled by Operations and that promised to the customer. Delivery times can also be changed, sometimes by customers, but more often by the operation. If the customer wants a new delivery time, should that be used to calculate delivery performance? Or if the operation has to reschedule delivery, should the changed delivery time be used? It is not uncommon in some circumstances to find four or five arguable due times for each order. Nor is the actual delivery time without its complications. When, for example, should the product or service be considered to have been delivered? Here we are facing a similar issue to that posed when considering speed. Delivery could be when the product or service is produced, when the customer receives it, when it is working, or when they are fully comfortable with it. Then there is the problem of what is late. Should delivery to the promised minute, hour, day, week or even month be counted as on time?

Flexibility

The word 'flexibility' means two different things. One dictionary definition has flexibility meaning the 'ability to be bent'. It is a useful concept which translates into operational terms as the ability to adopt different states – take up different positions or do different things. So one operation is more flexible than another if it can do more things – exhibit a wide range of abilities. For example, it might be able to produce a greater variety of products or services, or operate at different output levels. Yet, the range of things an operation can do does not totally describe its flexibility. The same word is also used to mean the ease with which it can move between its possible states. An operation that moves quickly, smoothly and cheaply from doing one thing to doing another should be considered more flexible than one that can only achieve the same change at greater cost and/or organisational disruption. Both the cost and time of making a change are the 'friction' elements of flexibility. They define the response of the system – the condition of making the change. In fact, for most types of flexibility, time is a good indicator of cost and disruption, so response flexibility can usually be measured in terms of time. So the first distinction to make is between range flexibility – how much the operation can be changed; and response flexibility – how fast the operation can be changed.

The next distinction is between the way we describe the flexibility of a whole operation and the flexibility of the individual resources which, together, make up the system. Total operations flexibility is best visualised by treating the operation as a 'black box' and considering the types of flexibility which would contribute to its competitiveness. For example:

- *product or service flexibility* – the ability to introduce and produce novel products or services or to modify existing ones;
- *mix flexibility* – the ability to change the variety of products or services being produced by the operation within a given time period;
- *volume flexibility* – the ability to change the level of the operation's aggregated output;
- *delivery flexibility* – the ability to change planned or assumed delivery dates.

Each of these types of total operations flexibility has its range and response components, described in Table 2.2.

Cost

Cost is here treated last, not because it is the least important performance objective, but because it is the most important. To companies that compete directly on price, cost will be clearly their major performance objective. The lower the cost of producing their products and services, the lower can be the price to their customers. Yet, even companies that compete on things other than price will be interested in keeping their costs low. Other things being equal, every euro, dollar or yen removed from an operation's cost base is a further euro, dollar or yen added to its profits. Not surprisingly, low cost is a universally attractive objective.

Here we are taking a broad definition of 'cost' as it applies in operations strategy. In this broad definition, cost is any financial input to the operation that enables it to produce its products and services. Conventionally, these financial inputs can be divided into three categories.

Operating expenditure – the financial inputs to the operation needed to fund the ongoing production of products and services. It includes expenditure on labour, materials, rent, energy, etc. Usually the sum of all these expenditures is divided by the output from the operation (number of units produced, customers served, packages carried, etc.) to give the operation's 'unit cost'.

Capital expenditure – the financial inputs to the operation that fund the acquisition of the 'facilities' which produce its products and services. It includes the money invested in land, buildings, machinery, vehicles, etc. Usually the funding for facilities is in the form of a lump sum 'outflow' investment followed by a series of smaller inflows of finance, in the form of either additional revenue or cost savings. Most

Table 2.2 **The range and response dimensions of the four types of total operations flexibility**

Total operations flexibility	Range flexibility	Response flexibility
Product/service flexibility	The range of products and services which the company has the design, purchasing and operations capability to produce	The time necessary to develop or modify the products or services and processes which produce them to the point where regular production can start
Mix flexibility	The range of products and services which the company produces within a given time period	The time necessary to adjust the mix of products and services being produced
Volume flexibility	The absolute level of aggregated output which the company can achieve for a given product or service mix	The time taken to change the aggregated level of output
Delivery flexibility	The extent to which delivery dates can be brought forward	The time taken to reorganise the operation so as to replan for the new delivery date

methods of investment analysis are based on some form of comparison between the size, timing and risks associated with the outflow and its consequent inflows of cash.

Working capital – the financial inputs needed to fund the time difference between regular outflows and inflows of cash. In most operations, payments must be made on the various types of operating expenditure which are necessary to produce goods and services before payment can be obtained from customers. Thus, funds are needed to bridge the time difference between payment out and payment received. The length of this time difference, and therefore the extent of the money required to fund it, is largely influenced by two processes – the process that handles the day-to-day financial transactions of the business, and the operations process itself which produces the goods and services. The faster the financial process can get payment from customers and the more it can negotiate credit delays to its suppliers, the shorter the gap between money going out and money coming in, and the less working capital is required. Similarly, the faster the operations process can move materials through the operation, the shorter the gap between obtaining the materials and having products and services ready for sale. This argument may also apply to information processing or even customer processing operations if operating expenditure is associated with the information or customers entering and progressing through the operation process.

The internal and external effects of the performance objectives

The whole idea of generic performance objectives is that they can be clearly related to some aspects of external market positioning, and can be clearly connected to the internal decisions which are made concerning the operations resources. Because of this, it is worthwhile examining each of the performance objectives in terms of how they affect market position outside the operation and operations resources inside the operation. Table 2.3 identifies some of these effects. What is interesting is that whereas the consequences of excellent performance outside the operation are specific and direct, the consequences inside the operation are more interdependent. So, for example, a high performance in terms of speed of delivery outside the operation gives clear benefits to customers who value short delivery times for products or queuing times for services. If an operation competes on speed of delivery, then it will need to develop the speed objective inside its operations. Internally, fast throughput time will presumably help it to achieve short delivery times to its external customers. However, there are other benefits which may come through fast throughput times inside the operation. Materials, information or customers moving rapidly through an operation can mean less queuing, lower inventory levels, a lower need for materials, information or customers to be organised and tracked through the process. All this adds up to lower processing costs in general. This gives operations strategy one of its more intriguing paradoxes. Even if a performance objective has little value externally in terms of helping the company to achieve its desired market position, the operation may still value high performance in that objective because of the internal benefits it brings.

The relative priority of performance objectives differs between businesses

Not every operation will apply the same priorities to its performance objectives. Businesses that compete in different ways should want different things from their

Table 2.3 Internal and external benefits of excelling at each performance objective

Operations resources Potential internal benefits include . . .	Performance objective	Market requirements Potential external benefits include . . .
Error-free processes Less disruption and complexity More internal reliability Lower processing costs	Quality	High specification products and services Error-free products and services Reliable products and services
Faster throughput times Less queuing and/or inventory Lower overheads Lower processing costs	Speed	Short delivery/queuing times Fast response to requests
Higher confidence in the operation Fewer contingencies needed More internal stability Lower processing costs	Dependability	On-time delivery/arrival of products and services Knowledge of delivery times
Better response to unpredicted events Better response to variety of activities Lower processing costs	Flexibility	Frequent new products and services Wide range of products and services Volume adjustments Delivery adjustments
Productive processes Higher margins	Cost	Low prices

operations functions. So, a business that competes primarily on low prices and 'value for money' should be placing emphasis on operations objectives such as cost, productivity and efficiency, one that competes on a high degree of customisation of its services or products should be placing an emphasis on flexibility, and so on. Many successful companies understand the importance of making this connection between their message to customers and the operations performance objectives that they emphasise. For example:[2]

'Our management principle is the commitment to quality and reliability . . . to deliver safe and innovative products and service . . . and to improve the quality and reliability of our businesses.'

(Komatsu)

'The management team will . . . develop high quality, strongly differentiated consumer brands and service standards . . . use the benefits of the global nature and scale economies of the business to operate a highly efficient support infrastructure (with) . . . high quality and service standards which deliver an excellent guest experience . . .'

(InterContinental Hotels Group).

'A level of quality durability and value that's truly superior in the market place . . . the principle that what is best for the customer is also best for the company . . . (our) . . . customers have learnt to expect a high level of service at all times – from initiating the order, to receiving help and advice, to speedy shipping and further follow-up where necessary . . . (our) . . . employees "go that extra mile".'

(Lands' End)

The relative priority of performance objectives differs between different products and services within the same businesses

If, as is likely, an operation produces goods or services for more than one customer group, it will need to determine a separate set of competitive factors, and therefore, different priorities for the performance objectives for each group. For example, one of the most obvious differences to be found within an airline's activities is that between the operations supporting business and first-class travellers on one hand, and those supporting economy-class travellers on the other. This is shown in Figure 2.4.

Figure 2.4 Different product groups require different performance objectives

	First/Business Class	Economy class
Services	First/Business Class cabin, airport lounges, pick-up service	Economy cabin
Customers	Wealthy people, business people, VIPs	Travellers (friends and family), holiday makers, cost-sensitive business travellers
Service range	Wide range, may need to be customised	Standardised
Rate of service innovation	Relatively high	Relatively low
Volume of activity	Relatively low volume	Relatively high volume
Profit margins	Medium to high	Low to medium

Main competitive factors	Customisation, extra service, comfort features, convenience	Price, acceptable service

Performance objectives	Quality (specification and conformance), Flexibility, Speed	Cost, Quality (conformance)

The polar representation of performance objectives

A useful way of representing the relative importance of performance objectives is shown in Figure 2.5(a). This is called the polar representation because the scales which represent the importance of each performance objective have the same origin. A line describes the relative importance of each performance objective. The closer the line is to the common origin, the less important is the performance objective to the operation. Two services are shown, a newspaper collection recycling (NC) service and general recycling (GR) service. Each essentially provides a similar type of service, but for different markets, and therefore different objectives. Of course, the polar diagram can be adapted to accommodate any number of different performance objectives. For example, Figure 2.5(b) shows a proposal for using a polar diagram to assess the relative performance of different police forces in the UK. Note that this proposal uses three measures of quality (reassurance, crime reduction and crime detection), one measure of cost (economic efficiency), and one measure of how the police force develops its relationship with 'internal' customers (the criminal justice agencies). Note also that actual performance as well as required performance is also marked on the diagram.

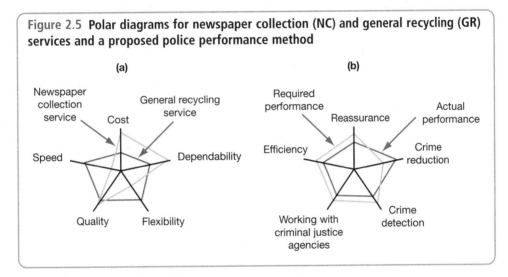

Figure 2.5 Polar diagrams for newspaper collection (NC) and general recycling (GR) services and a proposed police performance method

Order-winning and qualifying competitive factors

One way of determining the relative importance, or at least the different nature, of competitive factors is to distinguish between what are sometimes called 'order-winning' and 'qualifying' factors.[3] Although not a new idea, it is a particularly useful one. Different authors use different terms, so order-winners can also be called competitive edge factors, critical or primary factors, motivating factors, enhancing factors, and so on. Qualifiers sometimes go under the names hygiene factors or failure preventors.

Order-winning factors are things that directly and significantly contribute to winning business. They are regarded by customers as key reasons for purchasing the product or service. They are, therefore, the most important aspects of the way a company defines its competitive stance. Raising performance in an order-winning factor will either result in more business or improve the chances of gaining more business. Of course, some order-winning factors are more important than others. In Figure 2.6 the slope of the line indicates how sensitive competitive benefit is to an operation's achieved performance in the factor.

Qualifying factors may not be the major competitive determinants of success, but are important in another way. They are those aspects of competitiveness where the operation's performance has to be above a particular level just to be considered by the customer. Below this 'qualifying' level of performance the company probably won't even be considered by many customers. Above the 'qualifying' level, it will be considered, but mainly in terms of its performance in the order-winning factors. Any further improvement in qualifying factors above the qualifying level is unlikely to gain much competitive benefit.

Delights

In addition to order-winners and qualifiers, some authorities add a third category, generally known as 'delights'. Notwithstanding its rather off-putting name, delights are aspects of performance that customers have not yet been made aware of, or that are so novel that no one else is aware of. If an organisation presents customers with a 'delight', the implication is that, because the customers are unaware of it, no competitor has offered it to them. For example, healthcare companies that supply products and services to clinics and hospitals have always been aware that they need to supply their customers in a fast and efficient manner. Factors such as the range of products supplied and the dependability of supply would be regarded as qualifiers, with speed of supply and cost regarded as order-winners. Thus, the basis of competition was relatively clear. Then one or two companies started to offer a much more comprehensive service, which included, in effect, taking over the whole supply responsibility for individual customers. A hospital could not just buy products from a company, it could hand over total responsibility for forecasting demand, purchasing, delivery, and storage of its supplies. This was a 'delight' to the hospitals that were able to effectively outsource the supply of these items enabling them to concentrate on their core task of curing and caring for the sick.

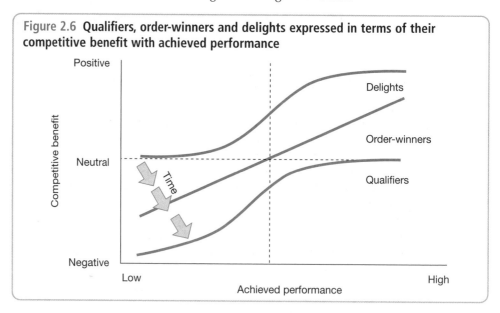

Figure 2.6 Qualifiers, order-winners and delights expressed in terms of their competitive benefit with achieved performance

The benefits from order-winners and qualifiers

The distinction between qualifiers, order-winners and delights does illustrate the important point that competitive factors differ, not only in their relative importance, but also in their nature. This is best thought of as how the competitive benefit, which is derived from a competitive factor, varies with how well an operation performs in delivering that competitive benefit. In other words, it is an indication of the benefits an operation gains by being good at different aspects of performance. Figure 2.6 shows the benefits from qualifiers, order-winners and delights as performance levels vary. No matter how well an organisation performs at its qualifiers, it is not going to achieve high levels of competitive benefits. The best that it can usually hope for is neutrality. After all, customers expect these things, and are not going to applaud too loudly when they receive them. They are the givens. However, if the organisation does not achieve satisfactory performance with its qualifiers, it is likely to result in considerable dissatisfaction amongst customers – what in Figure 2.6 is termed as negative competitive benefit. In effect, there is a discontinuity in the benefit function. This is different from an order-winner which can achieve negative or positive competitive benefit, depending on performance, and whose benefit function is far more linear. The advantage of order-winners (and why they are called order-winners) is that high levels of performance can provide positive competitive benefit, and hence more orders.

The benefits to be derived from 'delights' are also shown on Figure 2.6. The absence of delights (that is, very low achieved performance) will not upset customers because they didn't expect them anyway. However, as the operation starts to perform successfully in terms of its 'delights', the potential for customer satisfaction and therefore positive competitive benefit, could be very significant. Note that for something to be classed as a delight it is both novel (and therefore unexpected) and genuinely adds value for customers. The idea is that the combination of added value together with its unexpected nature will make delights, when delivered effectively, particularly attractive. But because they are unexpected, the competitive benefit will not become negative for the very reason that customers are not aware of the delights.

Two points should be made about 'delights'. The first is that the curves in Figure 2.6 are conceptual. They are there to illustrate an idea rather than to be drawn with any degree of precision. (Nevertheless, the theory of delights is closely associated with what some people know as the Kano model, which product designers can use in a more quantitative manner.[4]) The other point to make is that delights apply only at one point in time. By definition, because delights rely on their novelty, when offered in the market they will no longer be novel. This means that competitors can attempt to imitate them. So, in the example of the healthcare companies discussed previously, when they introduced their enhanced service it provided considerable competitive advantage for the few companies that could satisfactorily deliver the service. Since that time many more companies have introduced similar services. Therefore, what was once a delight became an order-winner, with customers choosing suppliers on the basis of the effectiveness of their supply chain management service. In time, it may even become a qualifier, where all companies who wish to compete in the market for healthcare supplies are expected to offer this service. So, what were once delights will over time erode as competitors achieve high levels of performance in the same competitive factors.

This prompts an interesting debate for any organisation. How sustainable are the order-winners and delights on which your business depends? Figure 2.7 illustrates a matrix that will allow for this kind of analysis. For any particular product or service it is important first to understand what competitive factors are order-winners, what are qualifiers, and what (if any) are delights. But because delights and order-winners can both erode over time, in the future what will happen is that some (if not all) delights will become order-winners and some (if not all) order-winners will become qualifiers. There is a general drift downwards (as shown by the arrows in the figure) as competitors catch up or exceed one's level of performance. Usually the cell in the matrix that is the most problematic is that marked as 'tomorrow's delights'. This prompts the intriguing question of 'What is the organisation doing today in order to develop the things that will delight its customers tomorrow?'

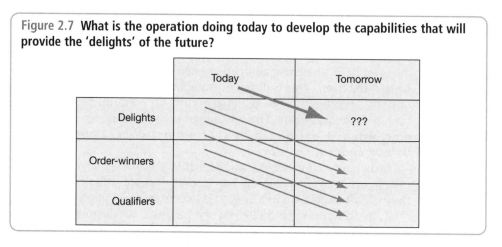

Figure 2.7 **What is the operation doing today to develop the capabilities that will provide the 'delights' of the future?**

Criticisms of the order-winning and qualifying concepts

Not everyone agrees with the idea of categorising competitive factors as order-winners or qualifiers. There are two major criticisms:[5] The first is that order-winners and qualifiers are based on how potential purchasers of services and products behave when considering a single transaction. Increasingly though, purchasers of both consumer and 'industrial' services and goods do not consider a single transaction but rather think in terms of longer-term relationships. Some purchasers may be willing to accept occasional lapses in performance in either order-winners or qualifiers because they wish to preserve the long-term relationship with their supplier. So the relationship itself both transcends the idea of order-winners and qualifiers and becomes the major order-winning competitive factor itself. Second, the original interpretation of the order-winner/qualifier concept is based on considering past sales data, including the reaction of individual customers for individual orders. A more traditional, market-based, approach would treat far larger groups of customers in its segmentation procedures.

The relative importance of performance objectives change over time

In addition to the 'erosion' effect mentioned previously, there are more generic changes caused by the way markets change over time and operations resource capabilities develop over time. Not surprising then that the nature of the reconciliation process, and therefore the role of operations strategy, changes over time, though the stimulus for change may vary. At some times markets change fast. Competitors may be particularly aggressive, or novel products or services may redefine customer expectations. If so, the competitive agenda for the business will be influenced largely by how the organisation positions itself in its markets.

Changes in the firm's markets – the product/service life cycle influence on performance

One way of generalising the market requirements that operations need to fulfil is to link it to the life cycle of the products or services that the operation is producing. The exact form of product/service life cycles will vary, but generally they are shown as the sales volume passing through four stages – introduction, growth, maturity and decline. The important implication of this for operations management is that products and services will require operations strategies in each stage of their life cycle (see Figure 2.8).

Figure 2.8 The effects of the product/service life cycle on operations performance objectives

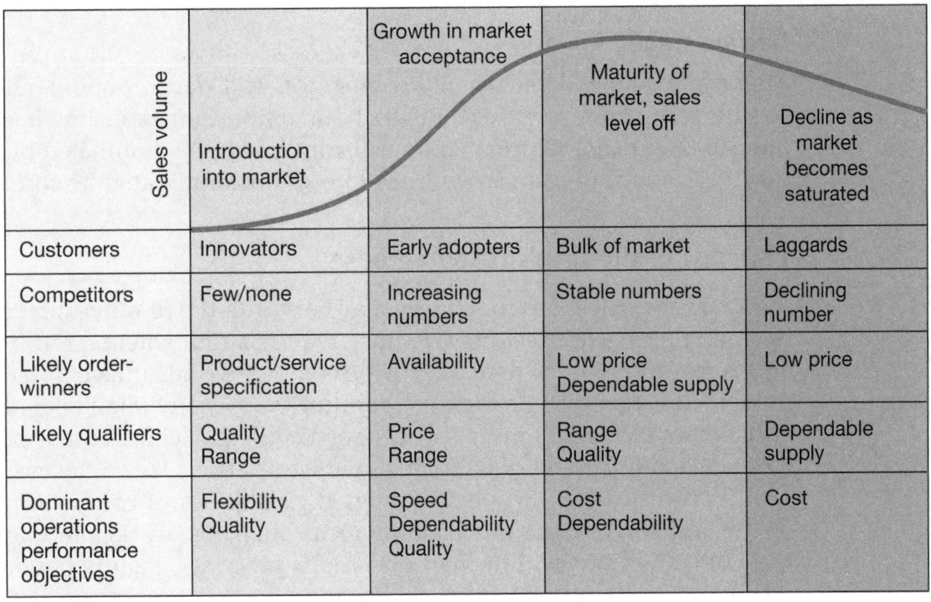

	Introduction into market	Growth in market acceptance	Maturity of market, sales level off	Decline as market becomes saturated
Customers	Innovators	Early adopters	Bulk of market	Laggards
Competitors	Few/none	Increasing numbers	Stable numbers	Declining number
Likely order-winners	Product/service specification	Availability	Low price Dependable supply	Low price
Likely qualifiers	Quality Range	Price Range	Range Quality	Dependable supply
Dominant operations performance objectives	Flexibility Quality	Speed Dependability Quality	Cost Dependability	Cost

(Vertical axis: Sales volume)

Introduction stage

When a product or service is first introduced, it is likely to be offering something new in terms of its design or performance. Few competitors will be offering the same product or service, and because the needs of customers are not perfectly understood, the design of the product or service could frequently change. Given the market uncertainty, the operations strategy of the company needs to develop the flexibility to cope with these changes and the quality to maintain product/service performance.

Growth stage

As the volume of products or services grows, competitors start to develop their own products and services. In the growing market, standardised designs emerge.

Standardisation is helpful in that it allows the operation to supply the rapidly growing market. Keeping up with demand could prove to be the main operations preoccupation. Rapid and dependable response to demand will help to keep demand buoyant while ensuring that the company keeps its share of the market as competition starts to increase. Also, increasing competition means that quality levels must be maintained.

Maturity stage

Eventually demand starts to level off. Some early competitors will have left the market and the industry will probably be dominated by a few larger companies. The designs of the products or services will be standardised and competition will probably emphasise price or value for money, although individual companies might try to prevent this by attempting to differentiate themselves in some way. So operations will be expected to get the costs down in order to maintain profits or to allow price cutting, or both. Because of this, cost and productivity issues, together with dependable supply, are likely to be the operation's main concerns.

Decline stage

After time, sales will decline and competitors will start dropping out of the market. To the companies left there might be a residual market, but if capacity in the industry lags demand, the market will continue to be dominated by price competition. Operations objectives will therefore still be dominated by cost.

Changes in the firm's resource base

At other times the focus for change may be within the resources and processes of the operation itself. New technologies may require a fundamental rethink of how operations resources can be used to provide competitive advantage. Internet-based technologies, for example, provided opportunities for many retail operations to shift, or enhance, market positioning. Other operations-based changes may be necessary, not to change, but merely to maintain a market position. They may even reflect opportunities revealed by the operations-based capabilities of competitors. For example, for the last two decades much of the focus of change in US and European automotive companies was within their operations processes, mainly because of the lower operations costs realised by their Japanese competitors. Again, this balance may change as niche markets become more distinctive. But this is the point. Although different industries may have a predisposition towards market or operations concerns, the relative balance is likely to experience some kind of change over time.

Mapping operations strategies

To understand how an organisation's operations strategy changes over time is to understand how it views its markets, how it sees the role of its operations resources, and most of all, how it has attempted to achieve reconciliation between the two. It also illustrates how an organisation understands its markets and how its resources evolve, often reacting to external pressures and internal possibilities. Of course, the minutiae of the thousands of decisions which constitute the mechanics of the reconciliation process over time are the key to understanding how the balance between markets and resources moves. Ideally we need to map the pattern and flow of each of these decisions, but this would be an immense task if our historical perspective is to be longer than a few years. Often, though, it is the nature of an organisation's products or services which one looks to see how the internal reconciliation process resolved itself. Products and services are after all the outward manifestation of the reconciliation process. Within their design they embody the characteristics which the company hopes will satisfy the market and at the same time exploit its resource capabilities. The example on 'VW: the first 70 years' illustrates this.

Example VW: The first 70 years[6]

For years Ferdinand Porsche had dreamt of designing a 'people's car'. Presenting his ideas to the Reich government in 1934, he found enthusiastic support for the idea. By 1939 the factory was completed, although the Second World War meant that it was almost immediately turned over to the production of war vehicles. By the end of the war, two-thirds of the factory had been destroyed; the local infrastructure was in ruins; and both material and labour were in desperately short supply. Although attempts were made to sell the plant, no one seemed to want a ruined plant.

In 1948, the occupying authorities put in Heinrich Nordhoff, to run the business. Nordhoff had faith in the basic concept of Porsche's design but added an emphasis on quality and engineering excellence. Throughout the 1950s the company overcame the difficulties of manufacturing in a recovering economy, and expanded both its manufacturing and its sales operations. The car itself, however, hardly changed at all. In fact, Nordhoff actively suppressed any change to the design. Nothing would be allowed to interfere with the core values of a simple, cheap, robust and standardised people's car. Yet, the world was changing. Local economies were recovering fast and customers were demanding more choice and touches of luxury in their motor vehicles. Eventually Volkswagen was forced to introduce a new model (the 1500). In all essentials, however, the company strategy was unchanged. During the early part of the 1960s, the 1500 model helped to take some of the pressure off the company. But consumer tastes were still moving faster than the company's response. Although sales held up, increased costs, together with stiff price competition, were having a severe effect on the company's profitability. By the end of the 1960s profits were declining and, in an attempt to find a new way forward, Volkswagen introduced several new products and acquired some smaller companies, most notably Auto Union GmbH from Daimler Benz, which later would form the nucleus Audi.

Out of this somewhat rudderless period (Nordhoff had died in 1968), the company eventually started to find a coherent strategy, with new models formed around the designs emerging from Audi. More in tune with modern tastes, they were front wheel drive, water cooled and more stylish than the old Beetle. Also the company started to rationalise its operations to ensure commonality between models and bring enhanced organisation to its global manufacturing operations and the company resumed profitable growth in 1975. During the remainder of the 1970s and through the 1980s, Volkswagen continued to produce its successful Polo, Golf and Passat models. Production facilities continued to expand around the world, but never again, Volkswagen vowed, would they be left behind consumer tastes. Design and product performance moved to the front of VW's strategy and all models were updated at regular intervals. The next big challenge for the company came, not from the inadequacy of its models, but from its manufacturing facilities.

In the early 1990s Volkswagen's models were still highly regarded and commercially successful, but costs were significantly above both its local European rivals and its Japanese

▶

competitors. And, although by now it was by far the largest auto-maker in Europe, the prospects for VW looked bleak. Management structures were bureaucratic, labour costs in Germany were significantly higher than other European and US levels. And one estimate had Volkswagen needing to operate at 95 per cent of capacity just to cover its costs. The break-even points of its rivals were significantly lower, at around 70 per cent. A fundamental cost-cutting exercise was seen by many commentators as the only thing that would save the company.

By the late 1990s, once more things were looking brighter. The company had negotiated pay and flexibility deals with its employees, successfully cut the costs of buying parts from its supply base (at one point hiring the controversial José Ignacio López from General Motors) and was continuing to introduce its new models. The most eye-catching of these was the New Beetle, a design based on the old Beetle but with thoroughly modern parts under its skin. Just as significantly, the company worked on the commonality of its designs. Within the VW group several models, although looking different on the surface, were based on the same basic platform. Yet, the company found that there were limits to how far one could sell essentially the same car as different brands at different prices, and it eventually devised a less obvious modular design strategy. The 2000s saw continued cost pressure from (mainly Japanese) competitors. In response VW's production shifted increasingly to lower-cost locations such as eastern Europe and China. At the same time, it started to seriously adopt lean principles in all its operations.

Understanding VW's operations strategy over time[7]

Like any company, VW's strategy has changed over time, and in turn, so has its operations strategy. The requirements of the market have changed, as world markets have grown, matured and become increasingly sophisticated over time, but also in response to how VW's competitors have behaved. Thus, VW markets which were small, local and disrupted at the beginning of the period became increasingly large, international and differentiated over time. Also competitive pressure counted for little at the beginning of the period, but by the 2000s automobile markets had become fiercely competitive. Likewise the nature of VW's operations resources has changed, starting with a desperate effort merely to satisfy even the most primitive of markets. Then, at various times through the next 50 years, VW's operations resources became more systematised, considerably larger, and far more complex, involving an interconnected network of internationally located operations.

Figure 2.9 shows the relative significance of market requirements and operations resources over time. This gives an indication of the relative degree of strategic activity within the firm's operations over time. It also gives us a clue as to the *role* of operations strategy over time. At some stages the role of operations strategy is relatively minor, often confined merely to implementing the company's market strategy. So, during the period 1959 to 1964 the firm's strategy was driven largely by a desire to change its market position slightly through the introduction of the 1500 model. The firm's operations strategy was limited to ensuring that the new model could be manufactured satisfactorily. Similarly, in the period 1976 to 1989, the firm's focus was mainly on how its markets could be segmented in order to achieve successful differentiation of its various products. At other times the strategy of the company not only relies on its operations capabilities but could be described as being driven by them. So, in the period 1946 to 1951 the company's strategy was dictated largely by the ability of its operations resources to produce the cars in suf-

Figure 2.9 Market requirements, operations resources and strategic reconciliation at VW over 70 years

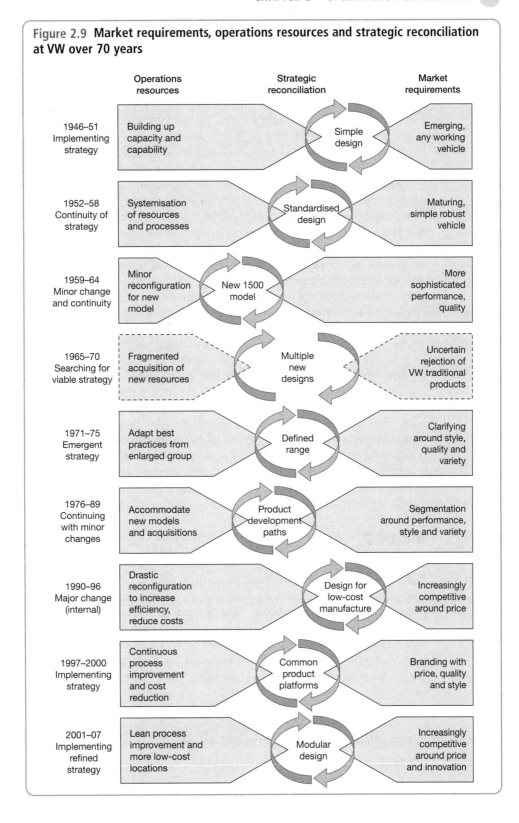

ficient quantity to satisfy its emerging market. Similarly, in the period 1990 to 1996, and again from 2001 to 2007, the firm's profitability, and even survival, depended on the ability of its operations resources to reduce its cost base significantly. In both these periods the company's market activity was, to some extent, driven by its operations capabilities (or lack of them). At other times the relative roles of market and operations strategy are more balanced. (Even if they are balanced, only in terms of their mutual confusion, as they were in the 1965 to 1970 period.)

The key point here is not so much that the firm's operations strategy is at times better or worse than at other times. Rather it is that, over the long term, any firm can expect the role of its operations strategy to change as its circumstances change. However, one should not infer that the role of operations is exclusively driven by environmental forces. Interwoven with environmental pressures are a whole set of significant choices VW has made. The company chose to suppress new designs in the 1950s, it chose to try out many designs in the late 1960s and it chose to develop its common products platform strategy in the late 1990s. The development of operations strategy over time is a combination of uncontrollable environmental forces and factors which can be more readily influenced. Above all, it is determined by choices about how operations resources are developed and the role we expect of the operations function within the firm. Notice how the two major crises for VW, in its loss of strategic direction in the late 1960s and its loss of cost control in the early 1990s, were preceded by a period where operations strategy had a relatively minor role within the company. Note also how VW's operations objectives changed as market circumstances changed. In its early history, the very basic objective of making products available (a combination of *speed* and *dependability*) was pre-eminent in an environment where basic resources were difficult to obtain. Latterly, the company, by now far larger and more complex, was struggling with the task of reducing its *costs* while maintaining its performance in other areas. The issue here is, because of changing market requirements, *not all performance objectives are equally important.* But also, from a resource perspective, *operations cannot be exceptionally good at every single aspect of performance at the same time.*

Trade-offs

Volkswagen emphasised different aspects of performance at different points in time. And, in order to excel in some particular aspects of performance, they would, to some extent, sacrifice performance in others. This idea is usually referred to as the *trade-off concept*. It is fundamental to our understanding of operations strategy. Perhaps most important, the idea of trade-offs is also at the heart of how operations seek to improve their performance over time. One of the many questions central to improvement efforts is, 'what do we want to be particularly good at?' Is there one particular aspect of performance which we wish to stress above everything else *('with us it is quality first, second and third')*?, or are we trying to achieve a balance between objectives *('we wish to offer the customer a wide range of services but not to the extent that costs get out of control')*? In order to answer these questions, we need to understand the way performance objectives relate to each other. This is where trade-offs come in.

What is a trade-off?

All of us are familiar with the simple idea that (much as we would like) we cannot have everything. Most of us want some combination of health, wealth and happiness. But we also know that sometimes we must sacrifice one to get the others. Driving ourselves too hard at work may give us wealth but can have negative effects on both health and happiness. Of course, we cannot let the wealth objective decrease too far or our poverty will undermine happiness and even health. We all instinctively understand that (a) the three objectives are related, (b) because some resource is finite (time, ability, etc.) we must, to some extent, trade off each objective against the others, (c) the trade-off relationship is not simple and linear (we do not decrease, or increase, our health by a fixed amount for every €1,000 earned), (d) the nature of the relationship will differ for each individual (some of us can derive great happiness *and* well-being from the process of making money) and perhaps most importantly, (e) none of us is always totally certain just how our own trade-offs operate (although some of us are better at knowing ourselves than others).

That these ideas also apply to operations was first articulated by Professor Wickham Skinner at Harvard University. As ever in those days, he was speaking of manufacturing operations, but broadly the same principles apply. He said:

> '[. . .] *Few executives realise the existence of trade-offs. Yet, most managers will readily admit that there are compromises or trade-offs to be made in designing an airplane or a truck. In the case of an airplane, trade-offs would involve matters such as cruising speed, take-off and landing distances, initial costs, maintenance, fuel consumption, passenger comfort, and cargo or passenger capacity. A given stage of technology defines limits of what can be accomplished in these respects. For instance, no one today can design a 500-passenger plane that can land on a carrier and also break the sonic barrier. Much the same thing is true of manufacturing. The variables of cost, time, quality, technological constraints, and customer satisfaction place limits on what management can do, force compromises, and demand an explicit recognition of a multitude of trade-offs and choices.'*[8]

Why are trade-offs important?

We judge the effectiveness of any operation by how well it performs. The call centre that can respond to our call and solve our problems within seconds, any time of the day or night, is superior to one that takes several minutes to answer our call and does not operate through the night. The plant that can deliver products in 24 hours is judged superior to one that takes three days. Plants turning over their stock 25 times a year are superior to ones which, operating under similar conditions, only manage to turn over stock seven times a year, and so on. Yet, in making our judgement we recognise two important characteristics of operations performance. The first is that all measures of performance will not have equal importance for an individual operation. Certain aspects of performance will outweigh others, their relative importance being determined by both the competitive characteristics of the market in which the operation is competing and, more importantly, the way in which the company chooses to position itself within that market. The second characteristic of performance which will shape our view of the operation is that we recognise that aspects of performance will, to some extent, trade off against each other. So for example, we are less impressed with the call centre that answers our calls quickly at all times of the day or night if its costs of running the operation make it necessary to charge us higher fees, or if the plant that delivers within 24 hours is achieving this only by investing in high levels of finished goods inventory. Though maybe we will be more indulgent towards the operation if we discover it has deliberately positioned itself in the market to compete primarily on instant response or fast delivery. Then the cost implications of high finished goods inventory may not matter so much. The operations have chosen to 'trade off' higher costs or high inventory to achieve fast response and fast delivery. However, we would be even more impressed with the call centre if it had 'overcome' the trade-off and was achieving both fast and 24-hour response *and* low cost levels. Similarly with the manufacturing plant, if it was achieving both fast delivery *and* low inventories. In both these examples we are using a broad understanding of the relationship between different performance objectives to judge the effectiveness of their operations management. But we are also implying that, in order to improve, these operations must overcome the trade-offs by changing the nature of the relationship between performance objectives.

Are trade-offs real or imagined?

Skinner's original idea of trade-offs was both straightforward and intuitively attractive. Essentially, it formalised the notion that there is no such thing as a free lunch. Any operation, like any machine, is 'technologically constrained'.[9] It, therefore, cannot provide all things to all people. The trade-off relationships between competitive objectives (cost, quality, delivery, variety, inventory, capital investment, etc.) mean that excellence in one objective usually means poor performance in some or all of the others. Operations that attempt to be good at everything finish up by being mediocre at everything. Therefore, the key issue of operations strategy is to *position* the competitive objectives of the operation to reflect the company's overall competitive strategy. Although Skinner has subsequently modified his original ideas, he maintains their essential validity: *'trade-offs . . . are as real as ever but they are alive and dynamic'*.[10]

The counter-view came from a new breed of more evangelical academics and consultants inspired by the perceived success of some (mainly Japanese) companies in overcoming, at least some, trade-offs, most notably that between cost and quality. They embraced the 'bottom up' improvement techniques of 'world class' operations. Both trade-offs and positioning, they claimed, are illusions. Trade-offs are not real, therefore positioning is not necessary. Citing the success of many companies that achieved improvements in several aspects of performance *simultaneously*, they dismiss trade-offs as distractions to what should be the real imperative of operations, namely improvement. Making choices between alternative aspects of performance leads to 'merely good', as opposed to 'outstanding' achievements. This is what some called 'the tyranny of either/or'. Rather than accepting the either/or approach, they recommend the more positive 'and/also' approach, which works towards 'having it all'. New forms of operations organisation and practice could overcome the 'technical constraints' of any operation, this being especially true if they are applied with a radical creativity hitherto unexpected in operations managers.

In spite of the appealing positive approach of this school, it could not fully explain away the intuitive appeal of the trade-off concept, and several attempts at an inclusive compromise which brings the two schools together were proposed. For example, it was suggested that some trade-offs did still, and would always, exist, while others had, for all practical purposes, been overcome by the new technologies and methodologies of manufacturing. Others suggested that while all trade-offs were real in the very short term, they could all be overcome in the long term. Most recent authors hold that 'trading-off' and 'overcoming trade-offs' are in fact distinct strategies, either of which may be adopted at different times by organisations. Neither are they mutually exclusive; operations may choose to trade off by repositioning the balance of their performance, both as a response to changes in competitive strategy and to provide a better starting point for improvement. And key to overcoming trade-off constraints is the building of appropriate operating capabilities. Thus, operations performance improvement is achieved by overcoming trade-offs, which, in turn, is achieved through enhanced operations capabilities.

The position taken in this book is close to the last school of thought. That is, that while there is a clear requirement for operations managers to position their operation such that they achieve the balance between performance objectives which are most appropriate for competitive advantage, there is also a longer-term imperative which involves finding ways of overcoming the intrinsic trade-offs caused by the constraints imposed by the operation's resources.

Example | **Faster, cheaper . . . splat[11]**

On 3 December 1999 the Mars Polar Lander approached the outer layers of the Martian atmosphere. Its mission was to release two Deep Space 2 microprobes that would penetrate the plant's surface, analyse its soil and broadcast the results back to NASA. On entering the atmosphere the vehicle broke off contact. This was entirely as planned. It was then supposed to resume contact after landing. It never did. No one knows why. The best guess is that problems with its braking rockets caused it to crash disastrously into the surface of the planet. More embarrassing, this was the second Mars disaster. Only a few weeks earlier the Mars Climate Orbiter had probably burnt up in the Martian atmosphere. Both failures were later blamed on NASA's policy which it called *Faster, Better, Cheaper* (FBC). Later this approach would be rechristened by critics as *Faster, Cheaper . . . Splat!*

FBC was a deliberate attempt to overcome what had always been seen in space exploration as a trade-off relationship. An old engineering proverb put it succinctly, 'Faster, better, cheaper – choose two of the above'. FBC challenged this and wanted all three. Critics of the FBC philosophy claimed that cutting budgets (cheaper) and going for ambitious project delivery dates (faster) had resulted in worse rather than better solutions. Certainly the panel set up to investigate the Mars programme failures concluded that the Mars projects were under-funded by as much as 30 per cent. Cost cutting had gone too far, especially in terms of getting rid of its more experienced engineers, who, being older and experienced, were expensive. In the previous five years more than 4,500 scientists and engineers had left NASA, of whom only 1,000 were younger than 40. The panel also pointed out that the Mars projects had been very tight on time. There is a relatively small launch window for missions to Mars which occurs only once every 26 months. The panel concluded that, with its budget cut and its launch date fixed, the only way for managers to operate when things started going wrong was to run an unacceptable degree of risk. Later NASA admitted that it had probably 'pushed the FBC philosophy too hard', and that it was 'time to rethink the approach'. Arguments still rage as to whether there is an absolute trade-off between speed, cost and quality in NASA projects, or whether the FBC philosophy is essentially the right approach that was just pushed too far.

Trade-offs and the efficient frontier

Figure 2.10(a) shows the relative performance of several companies in the same industry in terms of their cost efficiency and the variety of products or services that they offer to their customers. Presumably all the operations would ideally like to be able to offer very high variety while still having very high levels of cost efficiency. However, the increased complexity that a high variety of product or service offerings brings will generally reduce the operation's ability to operate efficiently. Conversely, one way of improving cost efficiency is to severely limit the variety on offer to customers. The spread of results in Figure 2.10(a) is typical of an exercise such as this. Operations A, B, C, D all have chosen a different balance between variety and cost efficiency. But none is dominated by any other operation in the sense that another operation necessarily has 'superior' performance. Operation X however, has an inferior performance because operation A is able to offer higher variety at the same level of cost efficiency and operation C offers the same variety but with better cost efficiency. The convex line on which operations A, B, C and D lie is known as the 'efficient frontier'. They may choose to position themselves differently (presumably because of different market strategies) but they cannot be criticised for being ineffective. Of course, any of these operations that lie on the efficient frontier may come to believe that the balance they have chosen between variety and cost efficiency is inappropriate. In these circumstances they may choose to reposition themselves at some other point along the efficient frontier. By contrast, operation X has also chosen to balance variety and cost efficiency in a particular way but is not doing so effectively. Operation B has the same ratio between the two performance objectives but is achieving them more effectively. Operation X will generally have a strategy that emphasises increasing its effectiveness before considering any repositioning.

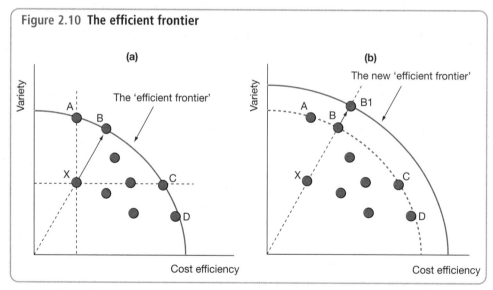

Figure 2.10 The efficient frontier

However, a strategy that emphasises increasing effectiveness is not confined to those operations that are dominated, such as operation X. Those with a position on the efficient frontier will generally also want to improve their operations effectiveness by overcoming the trade-off that is implicit in the efficient frontier curve. For example, suppose operation B in Figure 2.10(b) is the metrology systems company described earlier in this chapter. By adopting a modular product design strategy it improved both its variety and its cost efficiency simultaneously (and moved to position B1). What has happened is that operation B has adopted a particular operations practice (modular design) that has pushed out the efficient frontier. This distinction between positioning on the efficient frontier and increasing operations effectiveness to reach the frontier is an important one. Any operations strategy must make clear the extent to which it is expecting the operation to reposition itself in terms of its performance objectives and the extent to which it is expecting the operation to improve its effectiveness.

Improving operations effectiveness by using trade-offs

Improving the effectiveness of an operation by pushing out the efficient frontier requires different approaches depending on the original position of the operation on the frontier. For example, in Figure 2.11 operation P has an original position that offers a high level of variety at the expense of low-cost efficiency. It has probably reached this position by adopting a series of operations practices that enable it to offer the variety even if these practices are intrinsically expensive. For example, it may have invested in general purpose technology and recruited employees with a wide range of skills. Improving variety even further may mean adopting even more extreme operations practices that emphasise variety. For example, it may reorganise its processes so that each of its larger customers has a dedicated set of resources that understands the specific requirements of that customer and can organise itself to totally customise every product and service it produces. This will probably mean a further sacrifice of cost efficiency, but it allows an ever greater variety of products or services to produced (P1). Similarly, operation Q may increase the effectiveness of its cost efficiency, by becoming even less able to offer any kind of variety (Q1). For both operations P and Q effectiveness is being improved through increasing the focus of the operation on one (or a very narrow set of) performance objectives and accepting an even further reduction in other aspects of performance.

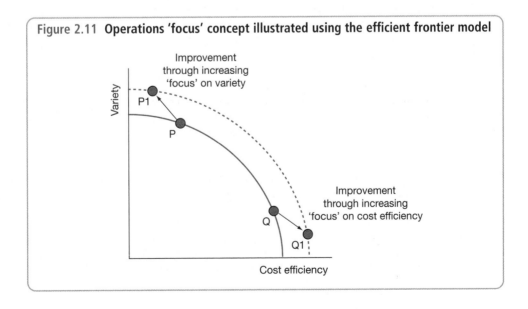

Figure 2.11 **Operations 'focus' concept illustrated using the efficient frontier model**

For example, if an audit firm designed an operation to carry out *only* simple standard audits on small to medium-sized engineering manufacturing companies, it could develop processes and procedures specifically to meet the needs of such clients. It could devise expert systems to automate much of its decision-making and it could train its staff with only the knowledge to carry out such audits. Focused and efficient, the operation could achieve exceptional productivity provided the demand could keep it fully employed. However, such an operation is something of a one-trick pony. Ask it to do anything else and it would have considerable difficulty. Increasing the variety placed on the operation outside its design specification would have an immediate and significant impact on its costs. In effect, designing the operation this way has made the relationship curve between variety and cost concave

Example | Flat beds trade off utilisation for comfort

At one time most airlines operated a 'twin class' system – First Class and Economy Class. Then came Business Class, with service standards placed between First and Economy. Ideally designed for the burgeoning business travel market, it attracted customers from both the First and Economy Classes. British Airways' strategy was typical. On most non-European sectors, BA offered all three levels of cabin service to their customers, with First and Business Classes particularly popular on long-haul flights, the transatlantic route being the single biggest market. By the mid-1990s, the first class market seemed to be in terminal decline, with many airlines pulling out of the First Class product entirely and, instead, concentrating on offering superior service in Business Class.

British Airways took a different view and believed that the whole concept of First Class travel needed to be redefined, and in early 1994 BA decided to refurbish their First Class cabins. Existing First Class cabins had 18 passenger seats, each with a 62 inch seat pitch, serviced by four cabin crew. BA's research using passenger focus groups showed that the most important factors associated with First Class travel were, in fact, space related. The main challenge was to create maximum passenger space within the existing area and simultaneously boost revenues from this segment. BA's answer was a new design for their First Class cabins, the 'Bed in the Sky' – a private first class seat encased in a shell that could transform itself into a completely horizontal bed. With the help of in-cabin technology, all control facilities were accessible within an arm's length of the passenger seat – audio/video, light switches, call buttons, etc. However, the more spacious seats meant that cabin size, in terms of seating, was reduced to 14 passenger seats. BA was also able to complement the new cabin designs with improved standards of cabin service and cuisine.

Refitting all their long-haul aircraft in this way succeeded in repositioning BA's First Class product so it had a unique First Class offering with no comparable competition. But it also had spent money to have fewer seats. Service quality was improved, but its costs per passenger were higher. This meant that BA had to increase its seat utilisation (the proportion of seats actually filled with paying passengers) in order to generate higher revenues from its improved service. In fact, BA were able to arrest the decline in first class travel, and increase its market share and revenues in the segment (revenues exceeded the business plan proposals by over 10 per cent). BA had traded off cost efficiency (it went down) for service quality (it went up). This paid off because of the extra revenue it brought. So successful was this exercise that BA repeated the strategy in its Business Class products. But now many other airlines have implemented a similar strategy, so the concept of 'erosion of delights' applies. Flat beds have become an 'order-winner', even in Business Class.

rather than convex. Asking the operation to move away from the performance objectives for which it was specifically designed brings an immediate penalty. Asking it to move even further away from its design specification also brings a cost, but not one to match that initial penalty.

Targeting and operations focus

The idea of repositioning the trade-off balance between conflicting performance objectives underpins one of the most effective 'types' of operations strategy – *focused* operations. This concept of focus is both powerful and proven because at its heart lies a very simple notion, that many operations are carrying out too many (often conflicting) tasks. The obvious result is that they are unable to perform them all with any real degree of success, whereas concentrating on one or two specific objectives, even at the expense of adopting a vulnerable 'concave' trade-off curve as discussed previously, can lead to substantially superior performance in those few objectives. It means redeploying operations resources to the needs of only a very specific part of the market.

The concept of focus

Most of the early work on what was then called the 'focused factory' concept was carried out by Wickham Skinner of Harvard Business School. Based on his ideas of how trade-offs dominated operations decision making, he argued that one way of achieving an effective operations strategy is through the concept of factory focus. This meant that first a business should establish a consistent set of policies for the various elements of its operations, which will support, not only each other, but also marketing requirements. Second, because of the inherent trade-offs, one operation cannot provide peak performance in all performance objectives at the same time. In his article, 'The Focused Factory',[12] Skinner based these arguments on his observations of a variety of US industries in the early 1970s. He found that most factories were trying to tackle too many tasks and therefore trying to achieve too many objectives. Because of this they were failing to perform well in any single objective. He concluded that a factory that was focused on a narrow range of products, and aimed at satisfying a particular section of the market, would outperform a plant that was attempting to satisfy a broader set of objectives. The equipment, systems and procedures that are necessary to achieve a more limited range of tasks for a smaller set of customers could also result in lower (especially overhead) costs. Focus, according to Skinner, can be expressed as dedicating each operation to a limited, concise, manageable set of products, technologies, volumes and markets, then structuring policies and support services so they focus on one *explicit* task, rather than on a variety of inconsistent, conflicting, *implicit* tasks.

Focus as operations segmentation

In Chapter 1 we briefly described how marketing managers attempt to understand their markets through the process of segmentation. Market segmentation breaks heterogeneous markets down into smaller, more homogeneous, markets. Within operations resources, what we have called 'focus' is very similar to the process of segmentation. In fact, it can be regarded as operations segmentation. Operations, like markets, are complex. A whole range of different skills, process technologies, flow sequences, knowledge applications, individual decisions, and so on, come together to create a range of different products and/or services. Operations managers spend much of their time attempting to split up the tasks of managing these resources in order to simplify them and thereby manage them more effectively. In effect, they are segmenting their operations resources. And, just as in marketing there are continual debates around the best way to segment markets, so in operations there are similar debates as to the most sensible way to segment resources. Ideally, operations segmentation and market segmentation should correspond. That is, separate clusters of resources clearly and distinctively serve individual market segments. The major problem with the whole idea of focus, however, is that what is a sensible basis for segmenting markets does not always map onto the ideal basis for segmenting operations resources. For example, an advertising agency may segment its market by the size of the promotional accounts of its clients. Ideally, it may wish to have different service offerings for large, medium and small accounts. Each of these offerings would have different mixes of services specialising in different types of communication, such as TV, posters, radio, press, etc. In this way they can position themselves as 'one-stop shops' that will produce entire marketing campaigns seamlessly for each market segment. However, from an operations viewpoint, the

Example   Ryanair[13]

It all started with Southwest Airlines in the USA, which began operating back in 1971 and proved that, by organising its airline operations ruthlessly around providing a low-cost 'no frills' service, it could both grow its customer base and do so profitably. Around the world, and especially in Europe, Southwest's example inspired a number of imitators, who likewise focused on focus. In Europe the European Airlines Deregulation Act prompted the emergence of several low-cost airlines (LCAs). The larger airlines had been drawn towards longer-haul routes where their interconnecting network of services and their extended levels of service were a major attraction. So, even in Europe, which has a viable and popular rail network, several companies saw the opportunity to offer low-cost, short-haul services. Companies such as Ryanair adopted similar strategies for keeping costs down. To some extent these strategies included trading off levels of service for reduced costs. So complimentary in-flight service was kept to a minimum, secondary and sometimes less convenient airports were used, and one standard class of travel was offered. In other ways these companies attempted to overcome trade-offs by focusing their operations. For example, they focused on a standardised fleet of aircraft, thus keeping maintenance costs down. They focused on their key processes such as passenger handling while outsourcing more peripheral processes. They focused on direct sales to their customers, often pioneering low-cost channels such as the internet. They also focused on those elements of the process which hinder the effective utilisation of their expensive resources, such as reducing aircraft turn-round time at the airports.

To keep focused, however, requires a clarity of vision. Ryanair's boss, Michael O'Leary's policy on customer service is also clear:

'Our customer service is about the most well defined in the world. We guarantee to give you the lowest air fare. You get a safe flight. You get a normally on-time flight. That's the package. We don't, and won't, give you anything more. Are we going to say sorry for our lack of customer service? Absolutely not. If a plane is cancelled, will we put you up in a hotel overnight? Absolutely not. If a plane is delayed, will we give you a voucher for a restaurant? Absolutely not.'

company's creative staff (its main resource) may retain their creativity more effectively if they work in teams focused on specific media. So, for example, one team specialising in TV advertising, another in press campaigns, and so on. So, what is ideal for the market (one-stop shops by size of promotional spend) does not match the ideal way of organising resources to maintain or improve their effectiveness (in this case, creativity).

The 'operation-within-an-operation' concept

Any decision to focus an operation might appear to carry with it the need to set up completely new operations if further products/services are added to the range, and it is true that in some cases a failure to do this has undermined successful operations. However, it is not always feasible, necessary or desirable to do this and the 'operation-within-an-operation' (or 'plant-within-a-plant', or 'shop-within-a-shop') concept is a practical response that allows an organisation to accrue the benefits of focus without the considerable expense of setting up independent operations. A portion of the operation is partitioned off and dedicated to the manufacture of a particular product/delivery of a particular service. The physical separation of products/services will allow the introduction of independent workforces, control systems, quality standards, etc. In addition, this approach allows for easier supervision, motivation and accounting.

Types of focus

Just as there are many ways of segmenting markets, so there are several approaches to focusing operations. The organisation of technologies, staff and processes can be based on several criteria. Table 2.4 illustrates some of the more common approaches to focus. These can be placed on a spectrum from those that take market-related factors as being an appropriate way to segment operations resources, through to those that allow the resource characteristics themselves to dictate how operations are split up.

- *Performance objective focus.* The operation is set up solely to satisfy the performance requirements of a particular market or market segment. So all products or services produced in an operation have very similar characteristics in terms of generic performance objectives.

- *Product/service specification focus.* The operation is set up for a clearly defined product or service, or range of products or services, the implication being that each defined range of products or services is targeted at a clearly defined market segment.

- *Geographic focus.* Sometimes operations can be segmented in terms of the geographic market they serve. This may be because the characteristics of a company's different market segments are largely defined by their geographic location. Alternatively, it may mean that the nature of the service offered by an operation is geographically limited. Most high-contact operations, such as fast-food restaurants, would fall into this category.

- *Variety focus.* A company may wish to segment its operations in terms of the number of different activities (usually dictated by the number of different products or services) it is engaged in. So, for example, one site may concentrate on relatively low variety or standardised products and services while another concentrates on high variety or customised products and services.

Table 2.4 **Firms can use various criteria to 'focus' their operations**

	Focus criteria	*Ideal operations resource conditions*	*Ideal market requirements conditions*
Operations segmentation based on market criteria	**Performance objectives** Cluster products/services by market requirements	Products and services with similar market requirements have similar processing requirements	Market segmentation is based clearly on customer requirements
	Product/service specification Limits number of products/services in each part of the operation	Similar products and services require similar technologies, skills and processes	Products and services are targeted on specific market segments
	Geography Clusters products/services by the geographic market they serve	The geographic area where products and services are created has a significant impact on operations performance	Market segmentation can be based on geographic regions
	Variety Separately clusters high-variety products/services and low-variety products/services together	The nature of technology, skills and processes is primarily determined by the variety with which products/services are created	Market segmentation can be based on the degree of product/service choice required by customers
	Volume Separately clusters high-volumeproducts/ services and low-volume products/services together	The nature of technology, skills and processes is primarily determined by the volume at which products/services are created	Market segmentation can be summarised as 'mass markets' versus more 'specialised markets'
Operations segmentation based on resource criteria	Process requirements Cluster products/services with similar process requirements together	The process requirements (types of technology, skills, knowledge, etc.) of products/services can be clearly distinguished	Products and services with similar processing requirements are targeted on specific market segments

- *Volume focus.* High-volume operations, with their emphasis on standardisation and repetition, are likely to need different process technologies, labour skills and planning and control systems from those with lower volume. Volume focus extends this thinking to the creation of separate operations for different volume requirements.

- *Process requirements focus.* Here, a particular technology is the point of focus for the operation. This allows the organisation to concentrate on extending its knowledge and expertise about the process. Over the life cycle of a production/service system, the likely advantage to be gained from a process focus will change. As an operation starts up and moves into the growth phase, building process capability will be critical; however, as volumes stabilise, the process itself will become more stable. A process focus can also become very significant as volumes decline and the organisation seeks to redirect its operations. However, many firms choose to close an operation rather than redirect it.

Benefits and risks in focus

Different kinds of focus criteria carry different kinds of benefits and risk. However, usually the benefits and risks of focus can be summarised as follows.

Benefits include:

- *Clarity of performance objectives*. Clearly targeted markets imply at least some degree of discrimination between market segments. This in turn makes easier the task of prioritising those few performance objectives which are important for that market. This allows operations managers to be set relatively unambiguous and non-conflicting objectives to pursue in their day-to-day management of resources.

- *Developing appropriate resources*. A narrow set of focused resources allows those resources to be developed specifically to meet the relatively narrow set of per-

---

Example | **Burning your bridges (or boats)[14]**

The nature of focus is that it is not ambiguous. Opting for excellence in a narrow set of objectives at the expense of the ability to be excellent at the others calls for a significant level of commitment to the objectives which have been chosen. The idea of commitment to a strategy has long been debated in business strategy and, before that, in military strategy.

A classic military illustration of commitment is shown in Figure 2.12. Two armies want to occupy an island, though neither is particularly keen to fight the other for it. Suppose Army 1 occupies the island pre-emptively and burns the bridge behind it. Army 2 then is likely to cede the island because it realises that Army 1 has no option other than to fight if Army 2 attacks. By restricting its own flexibility (to retreat) and ensuring its commitment, Army 1 has won the island without having to fight.

Figure 2.12 Burning bridges behind you increases commitment but reduces flexibility

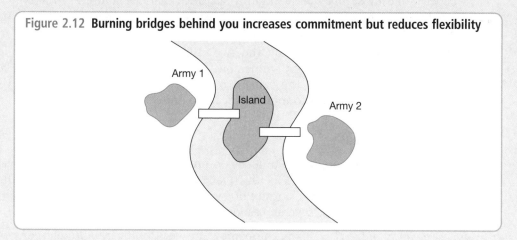

An example of this is the action taken by the Spanish conquistador, Hernán Cortés. In 1518 he landed his 12 ships on the coast of Mexico and soon determined to strike inland to the Aztec capital to defeat the Emperor Montezuma. However, Montezuma's troops had such a fearsome reputation that Cortés' men were somewhat reluctant to face the far larger Aztec army, especially since they knew that capture would mean a horrible death. Discontent reached such a pitch that one group of men planned to steal a ship and sail back to their homes. Cortés' solution to this was to execute the chief conspirators and beach nine of his 12 ships. In the face of such focused commitment, his men had little option but to follow him.

formance objectives required by the market. Process technologies, skills and infra-structural resources can all be organised so as to trade off unimportant aspects of performance for those valued by the target market.

● *Enhanced learning and improvement.* A combination of clear objectives, together with resources organised to meet those objectives, can enhance an operation's ability to manage its learning and improvement of its processes. Certainly the opposite holds true. Broad and/or confused objectives, together with complex resource structures, make it difficult to build process knowledge, learn how to extend the capabilities of processes or thereby improve their performance.

The risks involved in focus include:

● *Significant shifts in the marketplace.* Although less common than 'scare stories' often suggest, it is clear that a dramatic shift in the overall competitive environment can undermine the effectiveness of a focus strategy. For example, in turn-of-the-twentieth-century New England, one firm dominated the market for domestic and commercial ice throughout North America. It had established an immensely successful and highly focused production and distribution system but it was powerless when a technical innovation – the domestic refrigerator – effectively removed its market.

● *Few economies of scale.* Within an operation, focusing often involves separating out resources which were once bundled together. This allows these resources to be developed appropriately for the market they serve but, because they no longer form part of a larger whole, they may not be able to achieve the same economies of scale as before. For example, a corporate purchasing department, buying goods and services for a whole corporation, may achieve economies of scale in the use of its resources and in its purchasing power. Splitting up such a department between businesses may allow them to enhance their capabilities in the type of purchasing necessary for each individual business but this may be gained at the expense of buying power and efficiency.

● *Structural vulnerability.* Combine the two risks above and any focused set of resources may be structurally vulnerable. Relatively minor changes in market requirements may destroy the benefits of being close to a market while, at the same time, there are few economies of scale to protect their viability.

Drifting out of focus

Even when operations are set up to focus on one clearly specified set of objectives, they can, over time, drift out of focus. In fact some authorities would argue[15] that unfocused operations are often a result of a gradual, but insidious, drift away from a clear strategy. There can be several reasons for this.

● *New products and services.* Many companies, after developing new products or services, look to their existing operations to produce/deliver them. There is clearly a temptation to do this without examining the specific requirements of that particular product/service and evaluating the merits (and costs) of developing a new operation. Problematically, it is the firm's most successful operations that are perceived as being most able to cope with new products/services – even if their success is built upon focus.

● *Strategy drift.* In the absence of a clear competitive direction, managers often attempt to perform equally well against all of the many operations performance measures that exist. This (as discussed earlier) can lead to the dilution of the overall strategic impact of the firm.

- *Control by specialist.* Specialists in areas such as process technology, computer systems, inventory control, etc. will tend, in the absence of a more explicit operations strategy, to develop their own 'systems', which protect their own organisational position, or optimise their local objectives, at the expense of greater strategic objectives.

- *Company-wide solutions.* Looking for panaceas in the belief that one solution can cure all the problems of every operation, without sufficient regard for the need to tailor solutions to suit particular circumstances.

- *Business growth.* When operations have to stretch or be reconfigured to deal with larger volumes, this often leads to a loss of focus.

SUMMARY ANSWERS TO KEY QUESTIONS

What are operations performance objectives?

Operations strategy must include a relatively wide range of objectives that take into account the needs and aspirations of its stakeholders. However, because operations strategy is always concerned with addressing customers' needs, in this book we focus primarily on the five generic performance objectives of quality, speed, dependability, flexibility, and cost. Each of these performance objectives has both internal and external effects. Externally their relative importance will differ depending on the nature of the markets served by the operation and/or its products and services. Internally these objectives can be mutually dependent. One way of distinguishing between the relative importance of each performance objective is by classifying them as order-winners and qualifiers, and more recently, as 'delights'.

Do the role and key performance objectives of operations stay constant or vary over time?

Both. Markets change, and the capabilities of operations resources develop over time. Therefore, not only does operations strategy change, the relative importance of its performance objectives will change. In fact, over the long term, the operations strategies of most enterprises can be seen to vary, either in response to deliberate attempts to change overall strategic direction, or in a more emergent sense where a consensus of the most appropriate strategic direction forms through accumulated operational experience.

Are trade-offs between operations performance objectives inevitable, or can they be overcome?

Both. Yes, trade-offs are always, to some extent, inevitable in that pushing an operation to extremes in one aspect of performance will inevitably mean some sacrifice in other aspects of performance. Yet, trade-offs can, at the margin, be overcome. In fact, the whole concept of operations performance improvement is, in effect, an attempt to overcome trade-offs. It is, therefore, the responsibility of all operations managers to seek ways of overcoming trade-offs.

What are the advantages and disadvantages of focused operations?

The benefits of focus include achieving a *clarity* of performance objectives which aids day-to-day decision-making, developing resources in a manner *appropriate* to achieve a narrow set of objectives, and the enhanced *learning* and improvement that derives from concentrating on a narrow set of tasks. On the other hand, the problems with focus include the dangers inherent if there are significant *shifts in the marketplace* which may leave the operation 'stranded' with an inappropriate performance mix, the reduction in opportunities for *economies of scale* as operations are segmented internally, and some *structural vulnerability* because of the first two issues.

Further reading

Boyer, K.K. and Lewis, M.W. (2002) 'Competitive priorities: investigating the need for trade-offs in operations strategy', *Production and Operations Management*, 11(1).

Dale, B. (2003) *Managing Quality*. Blackwell.

Hayes, R. and Pisano, G.P. (1996) 'Manufacturing strategy: at the intersection of two paradigm shifts', *Production and Operations Management*, 5(1).

Hayes, R., Pisano, G.P., Upton, D. and Wheelwright, S. (2005) *Pursuing the Competitive Edge*. New York: John Wiley & Sons.

Liker, J.K. (2004) *The Toyota Way: 14 Management Principles from the World's Greatest Manufacturer*. McGraw-Hill.

Mintzberg, H. and Walters, J.A. (1985) 'Of strategies: deliberate and emergent', *Strategic Management Journal*, July–September.

Neely, A. (2005) *Measuring Business Performance*. London: Economist Books.

Parmenter, D. (2007) *Key Performance Indicators (KPI): Developing, Implementing and Using Winning KPIs*. John Wiley & Sons.

Notes on the chapter

1 Driver, C. and Johnston, R. (2000) 'Understanding service customers: the value of hard and soft attributes', Warwick University Working Paper.

2 All quotes taken from company websites.

3 Hill, T. (1993) *Manufacturing Strategy*. London: Macmillan.

4 Kano, S.T., Seraku, N. and Takahashi, F. (1984) 'Attractive quality and must-be quality', *Journal of the Society of Quality Control*, 14(2).

5 Spring, M. and Bowden, R. (1997) 'One more time: how do you win orders: a critical appraisal of the Hill manufacturing strategy framework', *International Journal of Operations and Production Management*, 17(8).

6 Based partly on information provided by Volkswagen Kommunikation (2007) and *The Economist* (2005) 'Dark days for Volkswagen', 16 July.

7 Mintzberg, in his classic paper, Mintzberg, H. (1978) 'Patterns of strategy formulation', *Management Science*, 24(9), carried out an analysis of VW on which the first part of this analysis is based.

8 Skinner, W. (1969) 'Manufacturing – missing link in corporate strategy', *Harvard Business Review*, May–June, p. 136.

9 Skinner, W. (1969) Ibid.

10 Skinner, W. (1992) 'Missing the links in manufacturing strategy', in Voss, C.A., *Manufacturing Strategy – Process and Content*. London: Chapman & Hall.

11 Oberg, J. (2000) 'Houston we have a problem', *New Scientist*, 15 April.

12 Skinner, W. (1974) 'The focused factory', *Harvard Business Review*, May–June, p. 113.

13 Keenan, S. (2002) 'How Ryanair puts its passengers in their place', *The Times*, 19 June.

14 For further discussion see Ghemawat, P. and del Sol, P. (1998) 'Commitment versus flexibility?', *California Management Review*, 40(4).

15 Hill, T. (1993) op. cit.

Capacity strategy

Introduction

Capacity is the first of the operations strategy decision areas to be treated, and, for operations managers, it is a fundamental decision. After all, the purpose of operations strategy is to provide and manage the capacity to supply demand. Also, capacity strategy decisions affect a large part of the business (indeed capacity decisions can create a large part of the business), and the consequences of getting them wrong are almost always serious and sometimes fatal to a firm's competitive abilities. Too much capacity under-utilises resources and drives costs up. Too little capacity limits the operation's ability to serve customers and therefore earn revenues. The risks inherent in getting capacity wrong lie both in having an inappropriately configured set of resources and in mismanaging the process of changing capacity over time. This chapter will look at the principles behind how operations configure, and reconfigure, their capacity (Figure 3.1).

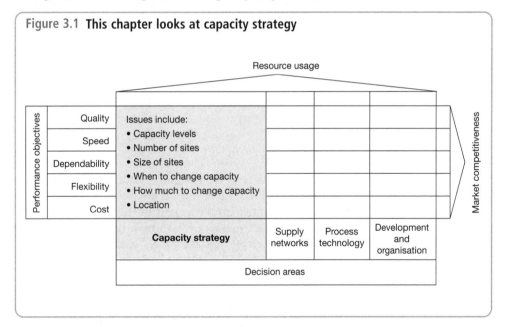

Figure 3.1 **This chapter looks at capacity strategy**

What is capacity strategy?

An operation's capacity dictates its potential level of productive activity. It is, the maximum level of value-added activity over a period of time that the operation can achieve under normal conditions. Operations strategy is the set of decisions concerned with how operations configure and change their overall capacity in order to

- *What is capacity strategy?*
- *How much capacity should an operation have?*
- *How many separate sites should an operation have?*
- *What issues are important when changing capacity levels?*
- *Where should capacity be located?*

achieve a particular level of output potential. Note that capacity is not the same as output. Demand may not be sufficient to warrant an operation producing at full capacity, and in many high customer contact operations, such as theatres, 'output' (i.e. the number of customers entertained) cannot normally exceed demand.

The capacity strategy of an operation defines its overall scale, the number and size of different sites between which its capacity is distributed, the specific activities allocated to each site and the location of each site. All these decisions are related. For example, an air conditioning servicing operation will have sites with relatively small individual capacity if it chooses to have many sites located no more than 30 minutes' travelling time from any customer. If it relaxed this 'response time' to 60 minutes, it could have fewer, larger sites. Together these decisions determine the configuration of an operation's capacity, its overall shape, size and deployment. An appropriate configuration of capacity for one set of products or services, and pattern of demand, will not necessarily be appropriate for another. So when the nature of competition shifts in some way, companies often need to reconfigure their capacity. This process of changing (or reconfiguring) capacity is also part of capacity strategy. It usually involves deciding when capacity levels should be changed (up or down), how big each change step should be and overall how fast capacity levels should change.

Capacity at three levels

The provision of capacity is not just a strategic issue. It takes place in all operations minute by minute, day by day and month on month. Every time an operations manager moves a staff member from one part of the operation to another, he or she is adjusting capacity within the operation. Similarly, when setting shift patterns to determine working hours, effective capacity is being set. Neither of these decisions is strategic – they do not necessarily impact directly on the long-term physical scale of the operation. But shift patterns will be set within the constraints of the physical limits of the operation, and the minute-by-minute deployment of staff will take place within the constraints of the number and skills of the people present within the operation at any time. Thus, although capacity decisions are taken for different time-scales and spanning different areas of the operation, each level of capacity decision is made with the constraints of a higher level.

Table 3.1 illustrates this idea. Note, though, that the three levels of capacity decision used here are, to some extent, arbitrary and there is, in practice, overlap between the levels. Also, the actual time-scales of the three levels will vary between industries.

Table 3.1 **Three levels of capacity decision**

Level	Time-scale	Decisions concern provision of ...	Span of decisions	Starting point of decision	Key questions
Strategic capacity decisions	Years–Months	Buildings and facilities Process technology	All parts of the process	Probable markets to be served in the future Current capacity configuration	How much capacity do we need in total? How should the capacity be distributed? Where should the capacity be located?
Medium-term capacity decisions	Months–Weeks	Aggregate number of people Degree of subcontracted resources	Business – site	Market forecasts Physical capacity constraints	To what extent do we keep capacity level or fluctuate capacity levels? Should we change staffing levels as demand changes? Should we subcontract or off-load demand?
Short-term capacity decisions	Weeks–Hours–Minutes	Individual staff within the operation Loading of individual facilities	Site Department	Current demand Current available capacity	Which resources are to be allocated to what tasks? When should activities be loaded on individual resources?

The overall level of operations capacity

The first capacity-related decision faced by any operation is 'How much capacity should we have?', or put simply, 'How big should we be?' It sounds a straightforward question, but is in fact influenced by several factors particular to each operation and its competitive position. Each of the main factors which will influence the overall level of capacity will be discussed in this section. Figure 3.2 illustrates them. As usual, some of the factors are primarily related to the requirements of the market, while others are largely concerned with the nature of the operation's resources.

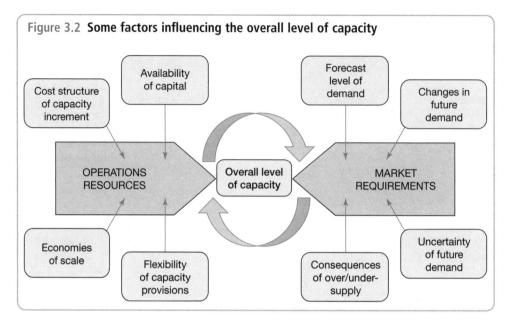

Figure 3.2 **Some factors influencing the overall level of capacity**

Forecast demand

Only rarely will a business decide to invest in a level of capacity which is exactly equal to its expectation of future demand. However, it is a starting point in trying to understand why operations finish up the size they are. So, for example, if a leisure business believes there is likely to be a demand for 500 rooms per night at a newly developed resort location, then it may build a 500-roomed hotel. If an insurance company's call centre is forecast to handle 500,000 calls per week and one operator can handle a call every three minutes, then it may build a 625-station call centre (operators have 40×60 minutes a week, so can receive 2400/3 = 800 calls a week, so 500,000/800 = 625 operators are needed). But capacity decisions are not always as simple as this. Although a 'single point' forecast of future demand for an operation's products and services will have a major influence on how big its operations will be, other considerations will affect the decision. It is these other factors, acting to modify a simple demand forecast, which reveal much about the strategic context of operations decisions.

Example   IKEA exploits the scale factor[1]

Sometimes capacity decisions can be made with the objective of influencing demand itself. The most obvious example of this is the 'category killer' in retailing. These are highly efficient operations which sell a specific category of goods at keen prices, often from large 'edge-of-town' superstores. One of the best-known category killers in retailing is IKEA, the furniture and homeware chain which started life in Sweden but has now spread all over the world. With over 210 giant stores operating in more than 30 countries, IKEA sells, *'a wide range of well designed, functional home furnishing products at prices so low that as many people as possible will be able to afford them'*. This IKEA concept *'guides the way IKEA products are designed, manufactured, transported, sold and assembled.'* The name IKEA comes from the initials of its founder, Ingvar Kamprad, I and K, plus the first letters of Elmtaryd and

Agunnaryd, which are the names of the farm and village where he grew up. In the 1950s Kamprad, who was successfully selling furniture through a catalogue operation, built a showroom in Stockholm. Not in the centre of the city where land was expensive, but on the outskirts of town. Instead of buying expensive display stands, he simply set the furniture out as it would be in a domestic setting. Instead of moving the furniture from the warehouse to the showroom area, customers pick the furniture up from the warehouse themselves. The furniture is usually designed to be stored and sold as a 'flat pack' which the customer assembles at home. The stores are all designed around the same self-service concept – that finding the store, parking, moving through the store itself, and ordering and picking up goods should be simple, smooth and problem-free. But it is the company's huge capacity at each site that allows it to offer customers the range of choice which attracts them in large numbers. The large numbers mean high throughput which, in turn, means not only that the company can build large capacity, low 'transaction cost' sites, but also that it can win substantial discounts from suppliers, reducing costs even further (and attracting even more customers).

Uncertainty of future demand

Even when the demand for an operation's products or services can be reasonably well forecast, the uncertainty inherent in all estimates of future demand may inhibit the operation from investing to meet the most likely level of demand. The economics of the operation may mean that, should the lower level of demand occur, the financial consequences would be unacceptable to the company. There are also other consequences of over- and under-supply. For example, the availability of excess capacity may give an operation the flexibility to respond to short-term surges in demand. This could be especially valuable when either demand needs to be satisfied in the short term, or when satisfying short-term demand can have long-term implications, so immediately after the introduction of a new product or service, especially when there are several competitors, is a bad time not to be able to satisfy demand. Market share lost at this point may never be regained. Paradoxically though, in some circumstances, under-supplying a market may increase the value (and, therefore, price) of an operation's goods or services. Such a scarcity-based strategy, however, does rely on an appropriate market positioning and a confidence in the lack of competitor activity.

Changes in demand – long-term or short-term demand?

In addition to any uncertainty surrounding future demand, there is also the question of the time-scale over which demand is being forecast. For example, short-term expected demand may be higher than expected long-term sustainable demand. In which case, does an organisation plan to provide capacity to meet the short-term peak, or alternatively, plan to satisfy only longer-term sustainable levels of demand? Conversely, short-term demand may be relatively low compared to longer-term demand. Again, there is the same dilemma. Should the operation build capacity for the short or long term? Like many capacity strategy decisions, this is related to the economies of scale of individual operations and the ease with which they can add or subtract increments of capacity. The dynamics of changing capacity levels will be discussed further in the next chapter. Here we are concerned with the decision of where initially to pitch capacity levels.

Long-term demand lower than short-term demand

Suppose a confectionery company is launching a new product aimed at the children's market. From previous experience it realises that it must make an initial impact in the market with many sales based on the novelty of the product, in order to reach a lower but sustainable level of demand. It estimates that initial demand for the product will be around 500 tons per month. However, longer-term demand is more likely to settle down to a reasonably steady level of 300 tons per month.

A key issue here is whether the higher level of demand will sustain for long enough to recoup the extra capital cost of providing capacity to meet that high level. Furthermore, even if this is the case, can an operation with a nominal capacity of 500 tons per month operate sufficiently profitably when it is only producing 300 tons per month? If the answer to either of these questions is 'No', then a capacity-based analysis would tend to discourage investment at the higher level of capacity. The main problem with this approach is that it may prove to be self-fulfilling. Under-supplying the market may depress demand which would otherwise have grown to justify the 500 tons per month capacity level. More likely, competitors will take advantage of the company's inability to supply to increase their own share of the market. Of course, the company may wish to counteract any under-supply by adopting pricing and promotion strategies that minimise the effects of, or even exploit, product shortage. The lesson here is that setting the initial capacity level cannot be done in isolation from the company's market positioning strategy.

Short-term demand lower than long-term demand

Again, the issues here are partly concerned with economies of scale versus the costs of operating at levels below the operation's capacity. If the economies of scale of providing capacity at the higher level of demand mean that the profits generated in the long term are worth the costs associated with under-utilisation of capacity in the short term, then building capacity at the higher level may be justified. Once more though, the relationship between capacity provision, costs, and market positioning needs to be explored. Initial over-capacity may be exploited by producing at higher volume, therefore lower costs, and pricing in order to take market share or even stimulate the total market. Indeed, over-capacity may be deliberately provided in order to allow such aggressive market strategies.

The availability of capital

One obvious constraint on whether operations choose to meet demand fully is their ability to afford the capacity with which to do it. So, for example, a company may have developed a new product or service which they are convinced will be highly attractive in the marketplace. Sales forecasts are extremely bullish, with potential revenues being two or three times higher than the company's present revenue. Competitors will take some time to catch up with the company's technological lead and so they have the market to themselves for at least the next two years. All of this sounds very positive for the company; its products and services are innovative, the market appears to want them, forecasts are as firm as forecasts can be, and the company is in a position to make very healthy profits for at least the next two years. But consider what the company will have to do to its resource base. Irrespective of how novel or technologically difficult the new processing requirements are, there will certainly be a lot more of them. The company will need to increase its operations resources by two or three hundred per cent. The question must arise of whether it can afford to do this, or more accurately, whether it is prepared to face the consequences of doing this. Borrowing enough cash to double or triple the worth of the company may not be possible from conventional sources of lending. The owners may not wish to float the company at this stage. Other sources of finance, such as venture capitalists, may demand an equity stake. Under these circumstances the company may forgo the opportunity to meet forecast demand fully. Even though in pure accounting terms the return on any investment in operating capacity may be perfectly acceptable, the consequence in terms of ownership or vulnerability of the company to being taken over may not be worth risking. An alternative for the company may be to increase capacity only as fast as their currently feasible borrowing capability will allow. The risk then is that competitor companies will have the time to enter the market and reduce its longer-term potential for company.

The cost structure of capacity increments – break-even points

One of the most basic, and yet most important, issues in capacity strategy is concerned with the relationship between the capacity of an operation, the volume of output which it is actually processing, and its profitability. Simple break-even analysis can illustrate the basics of this. Each additional unit of capacity results in a fixed-cost break. The fixed costs of a unit of capacity are those expenditures that have to be incurred irrespective of how much the capacity is actually being used. The variable costs of operating the capacity are those expenditures that rise proportionally to output. As volume increases for one operation, the additional capacity required can move an operation through its 'break-even' point from profitability to loss. Further additions to the capacity of the operation will be needed to cope with increased demand. Each addition brings a new set of fixed costs. Fixed-cost breaks may mean that there are levels of output within which a company might not wish to operate. This issue is particularly important when the fixed costs of operation are high compared with the variable costs.

Figure 3.3 shows how this might be in one operation. Each unit of capacity can process 4000 units of output per month. The fixed costs of operating this capacity are $2000 per month and the variable costs $0.25 per unit. The revenue from each unit processed to the operation is $0.9 per unit. Demand is forecast to be steady at around 9000 units per month. To meet this demand fully, three units of capacity would be needed, though the third unit would be much under-utilised. As Figure 3.3 shows, meeting demand fully, the company's total costs are higher than its total revenue. It would, therefore, be operating at a loss. Under these circumstances, the company might very well choose to process only 8000 units per month, not meeting demand but operating more profitably than if they were meeting demand.

Economies of scale

If the total cost of the output from an operation is its fixed costs plus its output multiplied by its variable costs per unit, then we can calculate the average cost per unit

Figure 3.3 **Cost, volume, profit illustration**

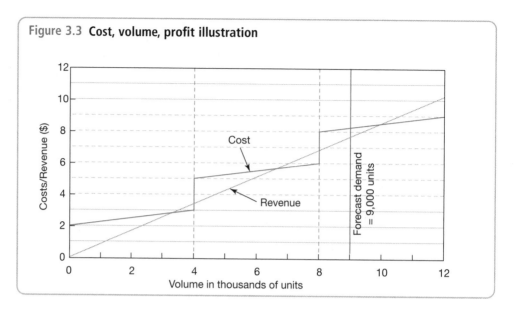

of output simply by dividing total costs by the output level. So, for example, Figure 3.4 (a) shows the unit cost for an increment of capacity of the operation described earlier. In reality though, the real average cost curve may be different from that shown in Figure 3.4 (a) for a number of reasons.

The real maximum capacity may be larger than the theoretical maximum capacity. For example, the theoretical capacity in Figure 3.4 (a) was based on an assumption that the operation would be working 112 hours a week (14 shifts a week out of a possible 21 shifts a week) whereas the operation is theoretically available 168 hours a week. Utilising some of this unused time for production will help to spread further the fixed costs of the operation but could also incur extra costs. For example, overtime payments and shift premiums together with incrementally higher energy bills may be incurred after a certain level of output.

There may also be less obvious costs of operating above nominal capacity levels. Long periods of overtime may reduce productivity levels, reduced or delayed maintenance time may increase the chances of breakdown, operating facilities and equipment at a higher rate or for longer periods may also expose problems which hitherto lay dormant. These 'diseconomies' of over-using capacity can have the effect of increasing unit costs above a certain level of output.

However, all the fixed costs are not usually incurred at one time at the start of operations. Rather they occur at many points as volume increases. Furthermore, operations managers often have some discretion as to where these fixed-cost breaks will occur. So, for example, the manager of a delivery operation may know that at the level of demand forecast for next month a new delivery vehicle should be purchased. This extra vehicle (together with the extra fixed cost it brings) could be purchased now in order to improve service delivery next month, when it is technically needed, or delayed beyond next month. This last option may involve taking the risk that any vehicle breakdown would leave the operation dangerously short of capacity but may yet be preferred if the operations manager has little faith in next month's level of demand being sustained.

All these points taken together mean that, as is illustrated in Figure 3.4 (b), in practice, unit cost curves:

- are capable of being extended beyond nominal capacity;
- often show increases in cost beyond a certain level of volume;
- are best represented by a band within which the true cost will lie, rather than a smooth, clean line.

Example **So why should Cemex want to be bigger?[2]**

Cemex is a growing global producer and distributor of ready-mix concrete, aggregates and building materials in more than 50 countries. It has grown from being a local player to one of the top global companies in the industry, with an annual production capacity of approximately 98 million metric tonnes of cement. So what advantages does Cemex see itself as gaining from its capacity growth? Cemex is well aware of the obvious advantages that come from conventional economies of scale. But, in addition, the company makes sure that it exploits its process knowledge across its capacity:

'We always look for ways to improve our productivity and operating efficiency. As a part of this process, we have implemented several standardised worldwide platforms designed to reduce our costs, streamline our processes, and extract synergies from our global operations. Through these platforms, we have developed and deployed centralised management-information systems throughout our operations – including administrative, accounting, purchasing, customer-management, budget-preparation, and control systems – to help us lower our costs.'

Or as the boss of Cemex, Lorenzo Zambrano, says:

'Scale gives us substantial economies, sure. It also lets us implement the Cemex way. Central control and the transfer of knowledge and best practice, that's what makes us efficient.'

As the company expands there is also an 'economy of growth' effect.

'With each international acquisition, we have refined the technological and managerial processes required to integrate acquisitions more rapidly and smoothly into our corporate structure. Consequently, we have been able to consolidate our acquisitions more quickly and efficiently.'

Or, put another way, the more the company expands its overall capacity, the better it becomes at doing it.

The factors that go together to reduce costs as volume increases are often called economies of scale. Those that work to increase unit costs for increased output beyond a certain volume are called diseconomies of scale. What we have described above are the economies and diseconomies of scale for a single increment of capacity within an operation. Yet, the same logic can be applied for the whole operation. As more units of capacity are added, the total fixed costs per unit of potential output tend to decrease. So, for example, the number of people staffing support services such as maintenance, supervision, warehousing, etc. is unlikely to double when the capacity of the whole operation doubles.

As the size of the operation increases it becomes possible eventually to replace the capacity which has been built up incrementally over time with new, larger and more integrated units. This may allow two further economies of scale. The first comes through the increases in operations efficiency which can be gained by integrating,

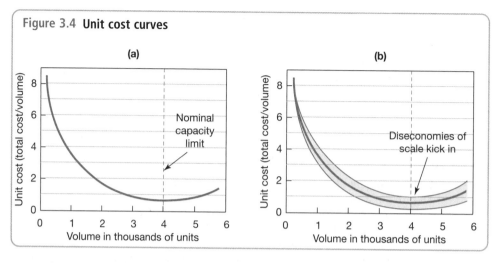

Figure 3.4 **Unit cost curves**

or combining, the processes established separately over time. So, for example, each increase of capacity may have included a particular kind of machine which could be replaced by a larger, more efficient machine once total capacity exceeds a certain level. Second, the capital costs of building operations do not increase proportionally to their capacity. The reason for this is that whereas the capacities of many types of facilities and equipment which go into an operation are related to their volume (a cubic function), the capital cost of the facilities and equipment are related to its surface area (a square function). Generally the cost (C_y) of providing capacity in one increment of size y is given as follows:[3]

$$C_y = Ky^k$$

where K is a constant scale factor and k is a factor which indicates the degree of economies of scale for the technology involved (usually between 0.5 and 1.0).

There may be, however, significant diseconomies of scale as the size of one site increases. The most significant of these are related to the complexity inherent in a large operation. As organisations grow larger they may become more unwieldy and need a greater degree of planning and coordination. More activities are needed just to keep the organisation operating and more staff are needed to manage the extra support processes. All this not only adds cost, it can make the whole operation incapable of responding to changes in customer demands. Very large operations find it difficult to be flexible because even if they can sense changes in the markets, they may not be able to respond to them. As operations grow communication also becomes more complex, which in turn provides more opportunities for miscommunication and errors.

Example **Can you get too big?[4]**

Founded in 1980 as one small store in Austin, Texas, Whole Foods Market® is now the world's leading retailer of natural and organic foods. Whole Foods Market is keen to point out that, as a company, it is:

'highly selective about what we sell [and is] ... dedicated to stringent quality standards, and committed to sustainable agriculture ... [believing] ... in a virtuous circle entwining the food chain,

human beings and Mother Earth: each is reliant upon the others through a beautiful and delicate symbiosis.'

The group tries to obtain its products locally where possible, often from small suppliers. Yet, although the company has been highly successful and has undoubtedly brought the benefits of organic food to millions of customers, in recent years it has started to receive criticism from the 'progressive' and 'liberal' groups who would normally be seen as its natural allies. And much of the criticism is associated with the company's scale.

Here are quotes from some websites critical of the company.

'Many people love the community at Whole Foods – this is what brought us to work here in the first place. But many of us have also seen that as the company has grown, the focus has shifted to profits and expansion at the expense of worker respect and fair compensation.'

'Like many "green lifestyle"-branded corporations, Whole Foods understands that marketing to educated, middle-class shoppers with disposable income is more effective when it is framed less as a sales pitch than as consumer education for a worthy cause (e.g. support for organic farmers; GE-free foods; your health). But the trouble is even the most informative marketing remains ultimately still, well ... a sales pitch. In other words, driven by profit. And sometimes, duplicity.'

'Whole Foods Market refuses to support better working conditions for strawberry workers.'

What is demonstrated here are two negative consequences of scale for a company like Whole Foods Market. First, the special interest groups that are attacking Whole Foods Market are doing so partly because it is so successful and, therefore, big. There is less publicity to be gained by attacking the little guy. Second, the very nature of what Whole Foods Market is selling conflicts in some people's minds with large-scale operation. Organic food is associated with small, local (and probably amateurish) operations. No matter how much it tries to promote its values, perhaps some of its customers will never be able to reconcile them with high-capacity, large-scale operations.

Flexibility of capacity provision

Committing to an investment in a particular level of capacity may be managed in such a way as to facilitate later expansion. Effective capacity requires all the required resources and processes to be in place in order to produce goods and services. This may not necessarily imply that all resources and processes are put in place at the same time. It may be possible, for example, to construct the physical outer shell of an operation without investing in the direct and indirect process technologies which will convert it into productive capacity. There may be capital expenditure efficiencies to be gained by constructing a larger building than is strictly necessary in the medium term, which can be fitted out with equipment when demand justifies it in the future. Clearly there is some risk involved in committing even part of the capital expenditure necessary before demand is certain. However, such a strategy is frequently employed in growing markets. Figure 3.5 shows alternative capacity strategies, and the resultant cash flow profiles, for an operation which is planning to expand its capacity to meet the forecast demand. One option involves building the whole physical facility (with a larger net cash outflow) but only equipping it to half its potential physical capacity. Only when demand justifies it would expenditure be made to fully exploit this capacity. The alternative is to build a fully equipped facility of half the capacity. A further identical capacity increment would then be added as required. Although this latter strategy requires a lower initial cash outflow, it shows a lower cumulative cash flow in the longer term.

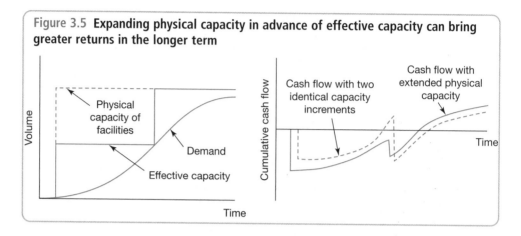

Figure 3.5 **Expanding physical capacity in advance of effective capacity can bring greater returns in the longer term**

The number and size of sites

The decision of how many separate operational sites to have is concerned with where a business wants to be on the spectrum between many small sites on one hand and few large sites on the other. Once again, we can think of this decision as the reconciliation of market factors and resource factors. This is illustrated in Figure 3.6. Separating capacity into several small units may be necessary if demand for a business's products or services is widely distributed. This will be especially true if customers demand high absolute levels, or immediate service. Of course, dividing capacity into small units may also increase costs because of the difficulty of exploiting the economies of scale possible in larger units. A small number of larger units may also be less costly to supply with their input resources. There again, in material transformation operations, a single large unit will bear extra transportation costs in supplying its distributed market.

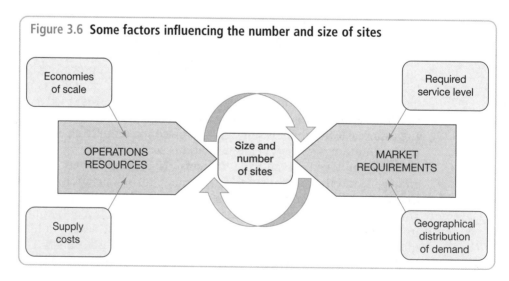

Figure 3.6 **Some factors influencing the number and size of sites**

Distribution operation

Suppose a company which stores and distributes books to book shops is considering its capacity strategy. Currently in its European market it has three distribution centres, one in the UK, one in France and one in Germany. The UK depot looks after the UK and Ireland, the French depot looks after France, Spain, Portugal and Belgium, and the German depot looks after the rest of Europe. The company is facing conflicting pressures. On one hand, it wants to minimise the total operations cost of its distribution services; on the other hand, it wishes to improve its level of service to its customers. In order to explore alternatives to its existing depots, it engages a firm of consultants to evaluate two alternative proposals which had been discussed within the company. Option 1 would require the company to concentrate its operations in one central depot which would serve the whole of Europe. It is likely that this would be in the Netherlands, probably in Rotterdam. Option 2 would require the company to move in the opposite direction, in the sense that it envisages a depot to be located in each of its six sales regions in western Europe. These regions are the Iberian peninsula, the UK, France and the Benelux countries, Italy, Germany, and Scandinavia. The consultants decide to simulate the alternative operations in order to estimate (a) the cost of running the depots (this includes fixed costs such as rent and local taxes, heating, wages, security, and working capital charges for the inventory, etc.), (b) transportation costs of delivering the books to customers, and (c) the average delivery time in working days between customers requesting books and them being delivered. Table 3.2 shows the results of this simulation.

From Table 3.2 one can see that concentrating on one large site gives substantial economies of scale in terms of the costs of running the depot but increases transportation costs, and (because there is further, on average, to travel) increases the average delivery time. Conversely, moving to several smaller sites increases depot costs but reduces transportation costs as well as improving the average delivery time. The company is here in a dilemma. By moving to one large site it can save €9.1 million per year (the savings on depot costs easily outweighing the increase in transportation costs). Yet, delivery times will increase on average by 1.4 days. Alternatively, moving to six smaller sites would increase costs by €9.3 million per year, yet gives what looks like a significant improvement in delivery time of 2.5 days. In theory the financial consequences of the different delivery times could be calculated, combined with the capital costs of each option, and a financial return derived for each option. In practice, however, the decision is probably more sensibly approached by presenting a number of questions to the company's managers.

- Is an increase in average delivery time from 6.3 to 7.7 days likely to result in losses of business greater than the €9.1 million savings in moving to a large site?

- Is the increase in business which may be gained from a reduction in delivery time from 6.3 days to 3.8 days likely to compensate for the €9.3 million extra cost of moving to six smaller sites?

- Are either of these alternative positions likely to be superior to its existing profitability?

One final point: in evaluating the sizes and number of sites in any operation, it is not just the increase in profitability which may result from a change in configuration that needs to be considered, it is whether that increase in profitability is worth

Table 3.2 Analysis of existing operation and two options

Capacity configuration	Depot costs (€ millions)	Transport costs (€ millions)	Average delivery time (working days)
Current three sites • Toulouse • Birmingham • Hamburg	55.3	15.6	6.3
One large site • Rotterdam	41.1	20.7	7.7
Six smaller sites • Madrid • Paris • Stockholm • Milan • Berlin • Birmingham	68.8	11.4	3.8

the costs of making the change. Presumably, either option will involve this company in not only capital expenditure, but also a great deal of management effort and disruption to its existing business. It may be that these costs and risks outweigh any increase in profitability.

Capacity change

Planning changes in capacity levels would be easy if it were not for two characteristics of capacity: lead-time and economies of scale. If capacity could be introduced (or deleted) with zero delay between the decision to expand (or contract) and the capacity coming on (or off) stream, an operation could wait until demand clearly warranted the change. The fact that changing capacity takes time means that decisions need to be made before demand levels are known for sure. So deciding to change capacity inevitably involves some degree of risk, but so does delaying the decision, because delay may still mean that capacity is not appropriate to demand. And all this is made even more problematic because of economies of scale (the tendency for both capital and operating costs to reduce as the increment of capacity increases). This means that, when changing capacity levels, there is pressure to make the change big enough to exploit scale economies. Again though, this carries risks that demand will not be sufficient for the capacity to be utilised sufficiently for the scale economies to be realised. Conversely, changing capacity by too little may mean opportunity risks of tying the operation in to small, non-economic units of capacity. Put both long lead-times and significant economies of scale together and capacity change decisions become particularly risky.

Timing of capacity change

The first decision in changing capacity levels is when to make the change. As with so many capacity decisions, the forecast level of future demand will be a major influence on the timing of capacity change. Capacity will be increased, or decreased, when forecasts indicate that extra capacity is needed, or current capacity not needed. Forecasting though, especially with the long-term planning horizons necessary for capacity planning, is a very uncertain process. Therefore, the degree of confidence an operation has in its forecasts will likewise influence the timing decision, as will the response of the market to under- or over-capacity. If competitive conditions dictate fast response times, then an operation might err on the side of timing capacity change to ensure over-capacity. Conversely, if customers are willing to wait, or if alternative supplies can be arranged, then there are fewer risks in under-capacity. Nor is the timing decision exclusively dictated by customers. Competitor activities and responses may also prompt capacity change. An operation may choose to invest in capacity even before demand warrants it just to pre-empt a competitor getting in first. The economics of the investment may even mean that whoever expands their capacity first renders capacity expansion by any other operation uneconomic. Figure 3.7 illustrates the factors that influence the timing decision.

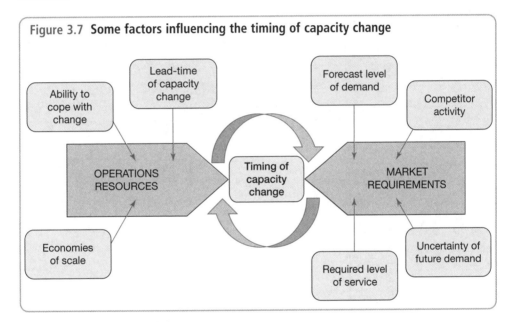

Figure 3.7 **Some factors influencing the timing of capacity change**

Generic timing strategies

There are three generic strategies for timing capacity change.

- Capacity leads demand – timing the introduction of capacity in such a way that there is always sufficient capacity to meet forecast demand.
- Capacity lags demand – timing the introduction of capacity so that demand is always equal to or greater than capacity.
- Smoothing with inventories – timing the introduction of capacity so that current capacity plus accumulated inventory can always supply demand.

For example, Figure 3.8 shows the forecast demand for an air conditioning company that has decided to build 400-unit/week capacity plants to meet the growth in demand. Figure 3.8(a) illustrates capacity leading and lagging strategies, while Figure 3.8(b) illustrates the 'smoothing with inventories' strategy. Each strategy has its own advantages and disadvantages. These are shown in Table 3.3. The actual approach taken by any company will depend on how it views these advantages and disadvantages. For example, if the company's access to funds for capital expenditure is limited, it is likely to find the delayed capital expenditure requirement of the capacity-lagging strategy relatively attractive.

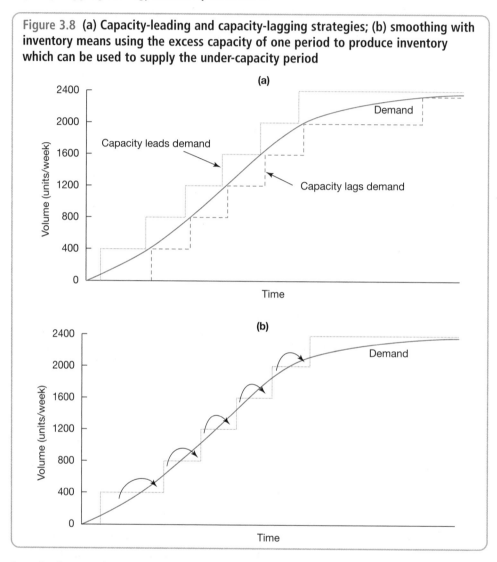

Figure 3.8 (a) Capacity-leading and capacity-lagging strategies; (b) smoothing with inventory means using the excess capacity of one period to produce inventory which can be used to supply the under-capacity period

Pure leading and pure lagging strategies can be implemented so that no inventories are accumulated. All demand in one period is satisfied (or not) by the activity of the operation in the same period. For a customer-processing operation there is no alternative to this. An hotel cannot satisfy demand in one year by using rooms which were vacant the previous year. For some materials- and information-processing operations, however, the output from the operation that is not required in one period can be stored for use in the next period. Inventories can be used to obtain the advantages of both capacity-leading and capacity-lagging. In Figure 3.8(b) plants have been introduced such that over-capacity in one period is used to make air con-

Table 3.3 **The advantages and disadvantages of pure leading, pure lagging and smoothing with inventories strategies of capacity timing**

	Advantages	*Disadvantages*
Capacity-leading strategy	Always sufficient capacity to meet demand, therefore revenue is maximised and customers satisfied. Most of the time there is a 'capacity cushion' which can absorb extra demand if forecasts are pessimistic. Any critical start-up problems with new plants are less likely to affect supply to customers.	Utilisation of the plants is always relatively high. Risks of even greater (or even permanent) over-capacity if demand does not reach forecast levels. Capital spending on plant early.
Capacity-lagging strategy	Always sufficient demand to keep the plants working at full capacity, therefore, unit costs are minimised. Over-capacity problems are minimised if forecasts are optimistic. Capital spending on the plants is delayed.	Insufficient capacity to meet demand fully, therefore, reduced revenue and dissatisfied customers. No ability to exploit short-term increases in demand. Under-supply position even worse if there are start-up problems with the new plants.
Smoothing-with-inventories strategy	All demand is satisfied, therefore, customers are satisfied and revenue maximised. Utilisation of capacity is high and therefore costs are low. Very short-term surges in demand can be met from inventories.	The cost of inventories in terms of working capital requirement can be high. This is especially serious at a time when the company requires funds for its capital expansion. Risks of product deterioration and obsolescence.

ditioning units for the following or subsequent periods. This may seem like an ideal state. Demand is always met and so revenue is maximised. Capacity is usually fully utilised and so costs are minimised. The profitability of the operation is therefore likely to be high. There is a price to pay, however, and that is the cost of carrying the inventories. Not only will these have to be funded, but the risks of obsolescence and deterioration of stock are introduced.

Leading, lagging or smoothing

Which of these strategies is used and at what time is partly a matter of the company's competitive objectives at any point in time? Just as significant, though, is the effect these strategies have on the financial performance of the organisation. Both the capacity-leading strategy and the smoothing-with-stocks strategy will tend to increase the cash requirements of the company through earlier capital expenditure and higher working capital respectively. Sometimes companies may wish to time capacity introduction in order to have a particular effect on the balance of cash requirement and profitability. It may be that some strategies of capacity change improve profitability at the expense of long-term cash requirements, while others minimise longer-term cash requirements but do not yield as high a level of short-term profitability. Thus, capacity strategy may be influenced by the required financial performance of the organisation, which in turn may be a function of where the company is raising its finance, on the equity markets or from long-term loans.

The magnitude of capacity change

Earlier we examined some of the advantages of large capacity increments (economies of scale, category killer effects, etc.). Large units of capacity also have some disadvantages when the capacity of the operation is being changed to match changing demand. If an operation where forecast demand is increasing seeks to satisfy all demand by increasing capacity using large capacity increments, it will have substantial amounts of over-capacity for much of the period when demand is increasing, which results in higher unit costs. However, if the company uses smaller increments, although there will still be some over-capacity it will be less than that using large capacity increments. This results in higher capacity utilisation and therefore lower costs. Remember, though, that the larger increments of capacity can be intrinsically more efficient (because of economies of scale) when they are well utilised. For example, suppose that the air conditioning unit manufacturer forecasts demand increase over the next three years, as shown in Figure 3.9(a), to level off at around 2,400 units a week. If the company seeks to satisfy all demand by building three plants, each of 800 units capacity, the company will have substantial amounts of over-capacity for much of the period when demand is increasing. Over-capacity means low capacity utilisation, which in turn means higher unit costs. If the company builds smaller plants, say 400-unit plants, there will still be over-capacity but to a lesser extent, which means higher capacity utilisation and possible lower costs.

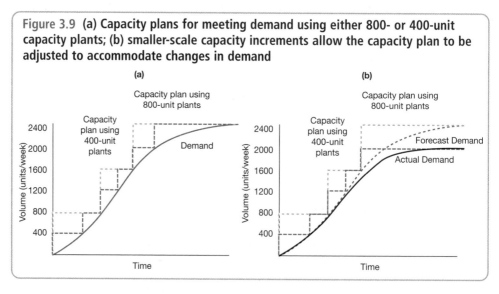

Figure 3.9 **(a) Capacity plans for meeting demand using either 800- or 400-unit capacity plants; (b) smaller-scale capacity increments allow the capacity plan to be adjusted to accommodate changes in demand**

Risks of over-capacity with large capacity increments

The inherent risks of changing capacity using large increments can also be high. For example, if the rate of change demand unexpectedly slows, the capacity will be only partly utilised. However, if smaller units of capacity are used the likelihood is that the forecast error would have been detected in time to delay or cancel the capacity adjustment, leaving demand and capacity in balance. For example, if demand does not reach 2,400 units a week but levels off at 2,000 units a week, the final 800-unit plant will only be 50 per cent utilised. However, if 400-unit plants are used the likelihood is that the over-optimistic forecast would have been detected in time. Figure 3.9(b) shows the consequences of adopting each of the two strategies in this case.

Example   Why industries have more capacity than they need[5]

There are few industries where the total demand for products and services matches the cumulative capacity of all the firms in the industry. In many industries capacity far exceeds demand. The automotive, computer chips, steel, chemicals, oil and hotel industries all have significant over-capacity because of over-investment and/or a collapse in demand. Take the automobile industry for example. One estimate claimed that the industry worldwide was wasting $70 billion a year because of over-capacity. By 2000, around 30 per cent of all car-making capacity was unused. The lost profit amounted to around $2,000 per car, which is more than the combined industry profits worldwide. This is partly bad news for those firms with the higher level of over-capacity because most car plants can only make significant profits when operating at over 80 per cent of capacity. However, over-capacity may not be viewed with too much alarm. Many of the well-known Western hotel chains in Asia, such as Westin and Sheraton, do not own the property itself, but confine themselves to managing it. The owner may be a local property developer or business person who invested for prestige or tax purposes. Many of the management contracts of this type, put together in the boom times, included fees based on a percentage of total revenue as well as a percentage of gross operating profits. So, even with no profit, the management company could make healthy returns. By contrast, other hotel chains, such as Shangri-La Asia, Mandarin-Oriental and Peninsular Hotels, both owned and managed their hotels. Because of this they were far more exposed to the consequences of over-capacity because it hit profits directly.

So why do companies invest, even when there is a high risk of industry over-capacity and thus under-utilised operations? One reason, of course, is optimistic forecasting. The risks of mis-forecasting are high, especially when there is a long gap between deciding to build extra capacity and the capacity coming on stream. A second reason is that all capacity is not the same. Newer operations are generally more efficient and may have other operations advantages compared to older operations using less state-of-the-art technologies. Thus, there is always the chance that a new operation coming on stream will attract business at the expense of older capacity. A third reason is that investment decisions are usually made by individual firms, whereas industry over-capacity is a result of all their decisions taken together. So a firm might be able to reduce its costs by investing in new capacity but the prices it receives for its products and services are partly determined by the cumulative decisions of its competitors. This also explains why it is not always easy to reduce over-capacity in an industry. Often it is in nobody's interest to be the first mover to shut down capacity. The costs of closing down capacity are paid by its owner. The benefits, however, in terms of higher prices and margins, are spread across the industry as a whole. So every firm wants capacity to be reduced as long as it is not its own capacity.

Balancing capacity change

During 2006 the price of oil (and therefore petrol) shot up to unprecedented levels (in dollar terms). Why was this? Well, there was uncertainty in the supply of crude oil and demand from developing economies was growing, but the reason that these elements of supply and market uncertainty had such a dramatic effect was because there was a shortage of refining capacity. The oil companies had failed to plan for sufficient refinery capacity and the bottleneck in the supply chain had increased the fear of shortages. So planning for capacity change must take into account that the capacity of a whole chain of operations will be limited by the lowest capacity or 'bottleneck' part of the chain. For example, if the 800-unit capacity air conditioning plant, introduced earlier, not only assembles products but also manufactures the parts from which they are made, then any change in the assembly plant must be matched by changes in the ability to supply it with parts. Similarly, further down the chain, operations such as warehousing and distribution may also have to change their capacity. For the chain to operate efficiently, all its stages must have more or less the same capacity. This is not too much of an issue if the economic increment of capacity is roughly the same for each stage in the chain. However, if the most cost-effective increment in each stage is very different, changing the capacity of one stage may have a significant effect on the economics of operation of the others. For example, Figure 3.10 illustrates the air conditioning plant example. Currently the capacity of each stage is not balanced. This could be the result of many different factors involving historical demand and capacity changes. The bottleneck stage is the warehouse, which has a weekly capacity of 900 units. If the company wants to increase output from its total operations to 1,800 units a week, all four stages will require extra capacity. The economy of scale graphs for each stage is illustrated. They indicate that for the parts manufacturing plant and the distribution operation, operating cost is relatively invariant to the size of capacity increment chosen. Presumably this is because individual trucks and/or machines can be added within the existing infrastructure. However, for both the assembly plant and the warehouse, operating costs will be dependent on the size of capacity increment chosen. In the case of the assembly plant the decision is relatively straightforward. A single addition to the operation of 800 units will both minimise its individual operating costs and achieve the required new capacity. The warehouse has more of a problem. It requires an additional capacity of 900 units. This would involve either building units of sub-optimum capacity or building two units of optimal capacity and under-utilising them with its own cost penalties.

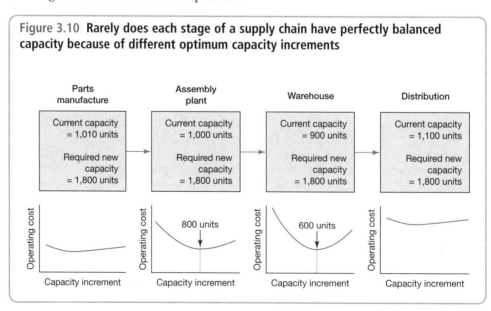

Figure 3.10 Rarely does each stage of a supply chain have perfectly balanced capacity because of different optimum capacity increments

The same issues apply on a wider scale when independent operations are affected by imbalance in the whole chain. Air travel is a classic example of this. Three of the most important elements in the chain of operations that provides air travel are the terminals which provide passenger facilities at airports, the runways from which aircraft take off and land, and the aircraft themselves operating on all the various sectors, which include the airport. Each of these stages, in planning their capacity, is subject to different pressures. Building new terminals is not only expensive in terms of the capital required, but also subject to environmental considerations and other issues of public concern. The individual aircraft that use these facilities are both far smaller units of capacity in themselves and form an element in the capacity chain which is subject to normal business commercial pressures. Different sizes of aircraft will be used for different routes depending on the 'density' (volume of demand) of the route. Because they represent relatively small units of capacity, the number of aircraft using an airport can change relatively smoothly over time. Runways and terminals, however, represent large increments of capacity and therefore change less frequently. Also, within each part of the chain the effective capacity may improve because of technical changes. Terminals are becoming more efficient in the way they can handle large amounts of baggage or even tag customers with micro-chipped tickets so that they can be traced and organised more effectively. All of which can, to some extent, increase the capacity of a terminal without making it any larger. Likewise, runways can accommodate more aircraft landing by providing more 'turn-offs' which allow aircraft to clear the main runway very soon after landing in order to let the next aircraft land. On high-density routes the aircraft themselves are getting larger. When the number of slots available to an airline is limited, and if route density warrants it, very large aircraft can increase the number of passengers carried per landing or take-off slot. However, these changes in effective capacity at each stage in the chain may affect the other stages. For example, very large aircraft have to be designed so as to keep the air turbulence they cause to a minimum so that it does not affect the time between landing slots. Also, very large aircraft may need different terminal equipment such as the air bridges which load and unload passengers.

Location of capacity

Often the reason why operations are where they are is not always obvious. Sometimes historical reasons dictated the location. Such operations are 'there because they're there'. Even more recent location decisions are not always logical. Entrepreneurial whim or lifestyle preference may overcome seeming locational disadvantages. In other cases the location decision is only reached after extensive thought and analysis.

The importance of location

The location decision is rarely unimportant but sometimes can be very important to the long-term health of an organisation. This is because the location decision can have a significant impact on both the investment in the operation's resources and in the market impact of the operation's resources. For example, locating a fire service station in the wrong place can both slow down the average time for the fire crew to respond to the call or increase the required investment to build the station, or both. Similarly, locating a manufacturing plant where it is difficult to attract labour with appropriate skills may affect the quality of its products (hence revenues), or the wages it has to pay to attract appropriate labour (hence costs).

| Example | Toyota moves to France[6] |

The last 20 years have been marked by the expansion of many Japanese manufacturing companies abroad. Consumer electronics and automobile manufacturers, especially, have set up plants around the world in their major markets of South East Asia, Europe and the United States. In the contest to attract Japanese inward investment in Europe, the UK was the clear winner. Some large early arrivals, such as Nissan, were attracted to the UK by generous government-funded financial support and tax concessions in regional development areas. Most of these were areas of high unemployment, yet with a tradition of industrial activity. Later arrivals had much fewer direct financial incentives, but saw the other advantages gained by the early arrivals. In some areas a critical mass of Japanese companies had developed, creating a flow of good publicity back to Japan and encouraging further interest. This success was reinforced by a growth in support infrastructure, such as Japanese schools, social activities, and even food retailing, to help expatriate families feel at home. Add to this that the English language is the most likely to be any Japanese manager's second language, the language commonality between the UK and the USA, climate similarity between the UK and Japan, and even factors such as the availability of golf courses, and the UK became the clear favourite for inward investment.

In December 1997, then, it came as a shock when Toyota, which already had a successful UK plant, decided to build its new European plant in the French city of Valenciennes. Located in the depressed north-eastern part of the country, the French government was able to offer attractive direct and indirect aid. There was also speculation that the British government's reluctance to join the initial group of countries participating in Europe's new single currency had also affected the decision. Yet, most industry commentators reckoned that the efficiency of Toyota's UK plant, together with the local infrastructure of suppliers it had built up, more than compensated for any currency risk. However, the really important factor was that the conservative French market much preferred cars made in France.

In the Toyota example it is clear that, in making its decision to move to France, it was acknowledging the importance of making its products in the same market where they were being sold. Toyota had been disappointed with its relatively poor performance in selling its products in continental Europe. The French motor market was notoriously chauvinistic but there were also genuine concerns that Toyota's models were out of touch with French, and indeed general continental European, preferences. In the end Toyota felt that the new small car, which was to be made at Valenciennes, stood a better chance of succeeding in France if it was made in France.

In addition to its effects on investment, costs and revenue there is often a considerable disruption cost whenever an organisation chooses to change its location. The costs of physically moving the operation's resources may be high but the risks involved may be even more important. Complex arrangements involving changes to many parts of the operation's resources invariably increase the risk of something going wrong with the move. Delays can mean inconvenience to customers, interruption of supply and increased costs. All this adds inertia to the location decision. Once made, a location decision is difficult to change, which is why few operations want to move frequently.

But organisations do move their location, and it is usually for one of two reasons. Either:

- there are changes in the demand for its goods and services; or
- there are changes in the supply of its input resources to the operation.

Where the stimulus for relocation is a change in demand it may be because of a change in the aggregated volume of demand. For example, if the demand for a clothing manufacturer's products is increasing beyond its capacity, the company could either expand at its existing site or, alternatively, if the site is not large enough, it could move to a larger site in another location. A third option would be to keep its existing site and find a second location for an additional plant. Two of these options involve a location decision. Similarly, a reduction in the aggregate volume of demand may mean the company under-utilising its site, selling or leasing part of the site, or moving to a smaller new site.

Some high customer contact operations do not have the choice of expanding on the same site to meet rising demand. For example, a fast-food restaurant chain competes, at least partially, by having locations close to its customers. As demand increases, it may well respond by investing in more locations. There will come a time, however, when locating a new restaurant in between the areas covered by two existing ones will, to some extent, cannibalise demand. The other reason for relocation is some kind of change in the cost or availability of its supply of inputs. An oil company, for example, will need to relocate as the oil it is extracting becomes depleted. A manufacturing company might choose to relocate its operations to a part of the world where labour costs are low. In other words, the labour costs differential, in the context of its competitive position, has changed. Similarly, the value of the land it has occupied compared with an alternative location may become too great to forgo the opportunity of releasing the value of the land.

Spatially variable factors

A prerequisite to effective location decisions is to understand the spatial characteristics of costs, revenues and investment. 'Spatially variable characteristics' are those whose value changes with geographical location. In not-for-profit organisations where revenue may not be a relevant objective, customer service may be used as a substitute. So, for example, the fire service may use average (or maximum) response time as its 'market phasing' objective. Figure 3.11 identifies some of the spatially variable factors which organisations may use in location decisions.

The suitability of the site itself

The intrinsic characteristic of a location may affect an operation's ability to serve its customers and generate revenue. For example, locating a luxury business hotel in a high-prestige site close to the business district may be appropriate for the hotel's customers. Move it one or two kilometres away where it is surrounded by warehouses and it rapidly loses its attraction.

The image of the location

Some locations are firmly associated in customers' minds with a particular image. Suits made and sold in Saville Row, which is the centre of the up-market bespoke tailoring district in London, may be little better than high-quality suits made else-

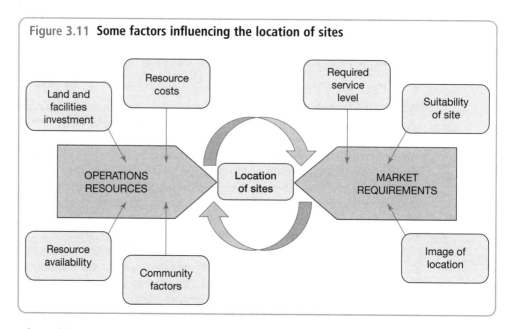

Figure 3.11 **Some factors influencing the location of sites**

where. However, a location there will establish a tailor's reputation and possibly its revenue. The availability of appropriate local skills can also have an impact on how customers see the nature of an operation's products or services. For example, science parks are located close to universities because they hope to attract companies interested in using the skills available there. An entertainment production company may locate in Hollywood, partly, at least, because of the pool of talent on which it can draw to produce high-quality (or at least high revenue earning) projects.

Service level

For many operations this is by far the most important demand-side factor. Locating a general hospital, for example, in the middle of the countryside may have many advantages for its staff and even maybe for its costs, but clearly would be very inconvenient for its customers. Not only would those visiting the hospital need to travel long distances, but those being attended to in an emergency would have to wait longer than necessary to be brought in for admission. Because of this, hospitals are located close to centres of demand. Similarly, with other public services, location has a significant effect on the ability of an operation to serve its customers effectively. Likewise, other high customer contact operations such as restaurants, stores, banks, etc. have revenues which are directly affected by how easily customers can access the service. Also, speed and dependability issues are becoming more important in many parts of manufacturing industry. Locating close to customers can be a competitive advantage or even a prerequisite for some customers. It is increasingly common for large manufacturers to demand that their suppliers build local plants, so as to ensure regular, fast and dependable supply. These may even be physically adjoining so that a supplier is able to deliver products through 'a hole in the wall' to its customer.

Land and facilities investment

If the operation is considering purchasing the land for its site this may be an important factor. If the operation is leasing the land then it is usually regarded as a supply-side cost factor. Certainly both land and rental costs vary between countries and cities. Companies sometimes locate where they already have available land, or even unused buildings, in order to avoid the investment costs.

In some location decisions, investment in the infrastructure needed to support the main operations facility can be as significant, if not more so, than the investment in the operation itself. At a simple level, infrastructural investment may include such things as building access roads, improving waste disposal, or building power generation support. At a more extensive level, a company locating in an under-developed part of the world may need to invest in road, or even rail, links. It may even be necessary to invest significantly in the local supply industry, either providing sites for suppliers or encouraging such things as producer cooperatives. Indeed, part of the deal which may be struck with the local government of the site may include a commitment to develop infrastructures.

Example | **Location clustering around the typewriter[7]**

In some ways Austin in Texas is an island of counter-culture surrounded by one of America's most conservative states. It is also home to a cluster of advanced technology industries. So why did Austin prove so attractive for companies like Samsung, Dell and IBM? Partly it goes back to a decision by IBM in 1967 to build a plant to make its (then revolutionary) Selectric typewriters. After that it expanded the plant to manufacture mainframe circuit boards and terminals, eventually also making its personal computers there. Because of IBM's dominance in the marketplace, other companies, including suppliers, such as Texas Instruments, also built plants there. A further boost came when Michael Dell, a drop-out student from the University of Texas at Austin, created his firm in the mid-1980s. Since then, literally thousands of other technology firms have followed. This is, in part, a further vindication for the idea that similar companies like to cluster together. Between them they soon create a critical mass of appropriate labour (computer geeks) and support industries. But it is also a testament to other, softer, factors. The 'quality of life' factor is important, particularly for computer-types who value the atmosphere, amenities (house prices are far lower than in Silicon Valley) and general atmosphere (Austin is the live-music capital of America). It is an area that revels in its quirkiness; its local slogan is 'Keep Austin Weird'. Along with this, Austin has one of the best universities in America and (quite important this) no local income tax.

Like many high-tech centres, it was severely hit by the technology crash of 2001 but it recovered. The latest industries to value Austin's attractions are those specialising in green technologies and online video gaming companies.

Resource costs – labour

Although wage and the other costs of employing people can vary between different areas in any country, it is more likely to be a significant factor when international comparisons are made. Here wage costs mean those costs to the organisation of paying wages directly to individual employees. Non-wage costs are the employment taxes, social security costs, holiday payments, and other welfare provisions which the organisation has to make in order to employ people. However, such labour costs should be treated with some caution. Two factors can influence them. The first is the productivity of labour. On an international level this is often inversely related to labour costs. This means that generally the average amount produced by each individual employed in a given unit of time is greater in countries with higher labour costs. This is at least partly because in countries with high labour costs there is more incentive to invest in productivity-enhancing technology. This effect goes some way in offsetting the large international variations in labour costs. The second factor is the rate of exchange of countries' currencies that may swing considerably over time. This in turn changes relative labour costs. Yet, in spite of these adjustments to the real value of relative labour costs, they may exert a major influence on the location decision, especially in industries such as clothing, where labour costs are a high proportion of total costs.

Resource costs – energy

Those operations which use large amounts of energy, for example aluminium smelting, may be influenced in their location decisions by the availability of relatively inexpensive energy. Low-cost energy sources may be direct, as in the availability of hydro-electric generation in an area, or indirect, for example a low-cost coal area which can be used to generate inexpensive electricity.

Resource costs – transportation

Transportation costs are clearly spatially variable because the operation's resources need to be transported (or transport themselves) from their point of origin to the operation itself. In many operations also, goods and services (or the people who perform the services) need to be transported from the operation to customers. Of course, not all goods and services are transported to customers. In operations such as hotels, retailers and hospitals, customers visit the operation to receive their services. In these cases we treat the ease with which customers access such services as a demand-side or revenue-influencing factor (or customer service factor in not-for-profit operations).

Proximity to sources of supply dominates location decisions where the cost of transporting input materials is high. So, for example, food processing or other agriculturally based activities are often located close to growing areas. Similarly, forestry and mining operations could only be located close to their sources of supply. Proximity to customers dominates location decisions where the transportation of products and services to customers is expensive or impossible. So, for example, many civil engineering projects are constructed where they are needed; similarly, accountancy audits take place at customers' own facilities because that is where the information resides.

Community factors

The general category of community factors are those influences on an operation's costs which derive from the social, political and economic environment of its location (see Figure 3.12). These include:

● government financial or planning assistance;
● local tax rates;
● capital movement restrictions;
● political stability;

- language;
- local amenities (schools, theatres, shops, etc.);
- history of labour relations, absenteeism, productivity, etc.;
- environmental restrictions and waste disposal.

Community factors can be particularly influential on the location decision. Some issues obviously affect the profitability of the operation. For example, local tax rates can clearly affect the viability of a new location. Others are less obvious. For example, the European country which has had the most inward investment from Japanese companies is the UK. Some investments, especially the early ones, were influenced by the UK government's generous financial support and tax concessions. Other factors included a relatively cheap but well-educated workforce. Yet, a less obvious but equally important factor was language. Many Japanese companies were accustomed to trading and producing in the USA. The English language is the first foreign language for most Japanese business people. Drawings of products and processes, for example, together with instruction sheets, computer programs, etc., were often immediately available for use without further translation for the UK. This means a lower risk of misunderstandings and mis-translation, smoothing communications between the new location and its Japanese head office.

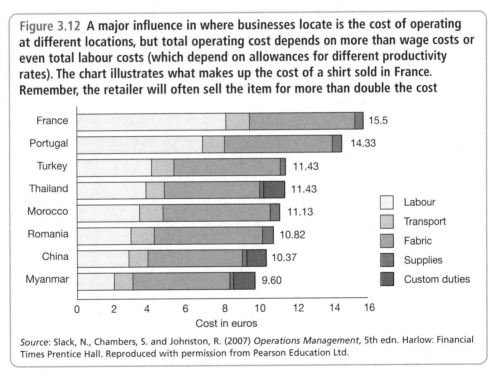

Figure 3.12 **A major influence in where businesses locate is the cost of operating at different locations, but total operating cost depends on more than wage costs or even total labour costs (which depend on allowances for different productivity rates). The chart illustrates what makes up the cost of a shirt sold in France. Remember, the retailer will often sell the item for more than double the cost**

Source: Slack, N., Chambers, S. and Johnston, R. (2007) *Operations Management*, 5th edn. Harlow: Financial Times Prentice Hall. Reproduced with permission from Pearson Education Ltd.

The nature of location decisions

Although all location decisions will involve some, or all, of the market requirement and operations resource factors outlined above, the nature of the decision itself can vary significantly. Locating new fast-food restaurant franchises is a very different type of decision from locating a new electronics factory, for example. The differences between these two location decisions (or indeed any other location decisions) can be characterised on two dimensions. These are the objectives of the location decision and the number of location options available. In many high contact operations, such as fast-food restaurants, retail shops and hotels, both costs and revenue are spatially variable. In other words, both the market and resource sides of the reconciliation process are significant. So, for example, locating a fast-food restaurant in an out-of-the-way location may allow it to operate with very low costs but its ability to attract customers (and therefore revenue) will be, likewise, very low. A more attractive location will undoubtedly be more expensive but would also attract higher custom. Most low-contact operations have revenues which are relatively invariant to location. Costs, however, will vary with location. Thus, location is largely one of cost minimisation, this being an approximation for profit maximisation.

The other major dimension of the location decision is concerned with the number of options between which a choice will be made. The electronics manufacturer may first decide on a relatively large geographic region, such as 'Hungary'. Once that broad decision is made, the number of possible sites is very large indeed, in fact, for all practical purposes, infinite. The decision process involves narrowing the number of options down to a smaller representative number which can be systematically evaluated against a common set of criteria. Many high-contact operations, however, are not located in this way. More likely, a company will first of all decide on a relatively limited area. For example, 'We wish to locate one of our franchises in Budapest'. Once this decision is made, the search begins for a suitable site. The choice then is between any site which may be immediately available or, alternatively, waiting until a more attractive site becomes available. Each decision is, in effect, a yes/no decision of accepting a site or, alternatively, deferring a decision in the hope that a better one will become available.

SUMMARY ANSWERS TO KEY QUESTIONS

What is capacity strategy?

Capacity-related decisions are conventionally divided into three time horizons – long-term strategic, medium-term, and short-term. Strategic decisions are those concerned with the provision of buildings, facilities and process technology, in all parts of the business, for at least months and probably years into the future. Capacity strategy includes a number of interrelated decisions, that include defining the overall scale of the operation, the number and size of the sites between which capacity is distributed, the specific activities allocated to each site, when capacity levels should be changed, how big each step change should be and the location of each site.

How much capacity should an operation have?

The starting point in determining overall capacity level will be the demand forecast. However, actual capacity may not be the same as forecast demand. It may be modified to account for the relative certainty, or uncertainty, of demand, long-term changes in expected demand level, the availability of capital needed, the ratio of fixed to variable costs, and general economies of scale. Also, a company may choose to provide more of one kind of resource (for example, the size of the physical building) before demand warrants it in order to save capital costs in the long run.

How many separate sites should an operation have?

The decision here concerns the choice between many small sites on one hand, or fewer larger sites on the other. The geographical distribution of demand, together with customers' required service level, will influence this decision, as will the economies of scale of the operation and the costs associated with supply. If demand is widely distributed between customers demanding high levels of service, and if there are no significant economies of scale or costs of supply, then the business is more likely to operate with many small sites.

What issues are important when changing capacity levels?

Capacity can be introduced to either lead or lag demand. Lead demand strategies involve early capital expenditure and under-utilisation of capacity but ensure that the operation is likely to be able to meet demand. Lagging capacity strategies involve later capital expenditure and full utilisation of the capacity but fail to fulfil forecast demand. If inventories are carried over so as to smooth the effects of introducing capacity increments, it may be possible to achieve both high sales and high utilisation of resources, therefore low costs. However, working capital requirements will be higher because the inventory needs to be funded. Changing capacity in large increments can minimise the costs of changing capacity (closure costs if demand is decreasing and capital expenditure if demand is increasing) but can also mean a significant mismatch between capacity and demand at many points in time. Conversely, changing by using small increments of capacity will match demand and capacity more exactly but require more frequent changes. Especially when increasing capacity, these changes can be expensive in capital cost and disruption terms. Often it is the risks of making too large a change in capacity that weigh heavily with operations, especially when forecasts of future demand are uncertain. Generally, the more uncertain is future demand, the more likely operations are to choose relatively small increments of capacity change. Notwithstanding this, there is a general pressure in many industries towards building new capacity even when over-capacity exists in the industry.

Where should capacity be located?

Required service levels from customers will influence this decision. Fast and regular supply implies location close to customer locations. Other market-related factors include the suitability of the site and the general image of its location. As far as operations resources are concerned, significant factors include the resource costs associated with the site, such as land and energy costs, the investment needed in land and facilities, the availability of any specialist resources required, and general community factors.

Further reading

DeToni, A., Filippini, R. and Forza, C. (1992) 'Manufacturing strategy in global market: an operations management model', *International Journal of Operations and Production Management*, 12(4).

DuBois, F.L., Toyne, B. and Oliff, M.D. (1993) 'International manufacturing strategies of US multinationals: a conceptual framework based on a four industry study', *Journal of International Business Studies*, 24(2).

Evans, P. and Wurster, W.S. (2000) *Blown to Bits: How the New Economics of Information Transforms Strategy*. Boston, MA: Harvard Business School Press.

Gunther, N.J. (2006) *Guerrilla Capacity Planning: A Tactical Approach to Planning for Highly Scalable Applications and Services*. Berlin and Heidelberg: Springer-Verlag.

Küpper, A. (2005) *Location-Based Services: Fundamentals and Operation: Fundamentals and Application*. Chichester: John Wiley & Sons.

Porter, M.E. (1989) 'Changing patterns of international competition', *California Management Review*, 28(2).

Tombak, M.M. (1995) 'Multinational plant location as a game of timing', *European Journal of Operational Research*, 86(4).

Wolfe, D. and Lucas, M. (eds) (2005) *Global Networks and Local Linkages: The Paradox of Cluster Development in an Open Economy*. School of Policy Studies, Queen's University.

Notes on the chapter

1 Source: company website (2007).
2 Source: company website (2007).
3 Hayes, R.H. and Wheelwright, S.C. (1984) *Restoring Our Competitive Edge*, New York: John Wiley & Sons.
4 Source: company website (2007).
5 Sources include: Liu, H.C.K. (2005) 'Scarcity economics and overcapacity', *Asia Times Online*, 28 July; *The Economist* (1999) 'Double parked', 9 January.
6 Sources: Toyota website (2007), *The Economist* (1997) 'Toyota learns French', 29 November.
7 Source: *The Economist* (2006) 'Blame it on the typewriter', 23 September.

Supply network strategy

Introduction

No operation, or part of an operation, can be seen as existing in isolation. All are part of an interconnected network of their own customers and suppliers and their customers' customers and suppliers' suppliers. Viewed one way, this network is the context in which an organisation's operations strategy is developed. Fundamental to the strategic design of any operation's resources are network-related questions such as: Should we do this activity ourselves or subcontract? Do we want to buy and incorporate any current suppliers into our current operation? How should we develop trading relationships with suppliers and customers? How do networks change or how are they changed over time? Figure 4.1 illustrates the coverage of this chapter.

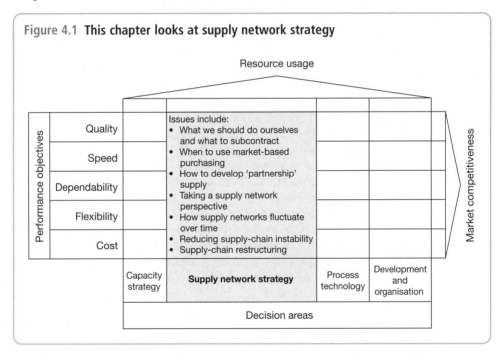

Figure 4.1 This chapter looks at supply network strategy

Resource usage

			Issues include:			
Performance objectives	Quality		• What we should do ourselves and what to subcontract			Market competitiveness
	Speed		• When to use market-based purchasing			
	Dependability		• How to develop 'partnership' supply			
	Flexibility		• Taking a supply network perspective			
			• How supply networks fluctuate over time			
	Cost		• Reducing supply-chain instability			
			• Supply-chain restructuring			

Capacity strategy	**Supply network strategy**	Process technology	Development and organisation

Decision areas

What is supply network strategy?

The broad subject of supply networks has been one of the most fashionable concepts within operations strategy over the past few years. Yet, many aspects of the concept are not new. After all, at the heart of the supply network concept is the idea of buyer–supplier relationships, something that has always been at the heart of all busi-

KEY QUESTIONS

- *What is supply network strategy?*
- *What are the arguments for and against outsourcing?*
- *What are the arguments for and against using traditional market relationships with suppliers?*
- *How do partnership relationships seek to gain the 'best of both worlds'?*
- *Are there 'natural' dynamic behaviours which supply networks exhibit?*
- *In what ways do companies try to change the nature of the supply network of which they are a part?*

ness. But in other ways, the idea of standing back and seeing each separate operation as part of an interconnected network of relationships is relatively new and has come to be seen as having important new implications. First a definition; a supply network is *'an interconnection of organisations which relate to each other through upstream and downstream linkages between the different processes and activities that produce value in the form of products and services to the ultimate consumer'*.[1] Figure 4.2 illustrates a supply network that we can use to make some general points.

The three main companies in this network (A, B and C) are at the centre of the network, because, in this case, the network has been drawn by Company A. Companies B and C could be its direct competitors or firms with which it cooperates. Company A is called the 'focal' company of the network and together with Companies B and C forms the 'focal level' of the network. In other words, the network is drawn from Company A's perspective. Company A's suppliers, together with its suppliers' suppliers and so on, form the upstream or supply side of the network, while its customers and customers' customers etc. form the downstream or demand side of the network. What is upstream and what is downstream is therefore defined only in terms of from whose perspective the network is being drawn.

Upstream and downstream here imply that the dominant flow in the network is from left to right. Note, however, that flow occurs in both directions, products and/or services one way and the information that triggers supply the other way. Of course, the products or services themselves may be defined in terms of information (being supplied with consultancy advice or market information, for example) but in Figure 4.2 the dotted lines are used to indicate the information that is the stimulus for supply. Much of modern supply network management is concerned as much with managing the flow of information upstream as it is with managing the flow of products and services downstream.

The various processes within Company A form the *internal* supply network. Outside its boundaries, Company A will have direct contact with a number of suppliers and a number of customers; this forms the *immediate* supply network. The linkages of suppliers to Company A's suppliers, and customers to Company A's customers, form its *total* supply network. The boundary between the internal network and the immediate network can change. Company A may cease to engage in one type of activity currently performed internally and instead buy in those services from a supplier. Conversely, it may choose to engage internally in an activity previously bought in from a supplier. Similarly, it may choose to expand or contract its

Figure 4.2 **Supply networks are the interconnections of relationships between operations**

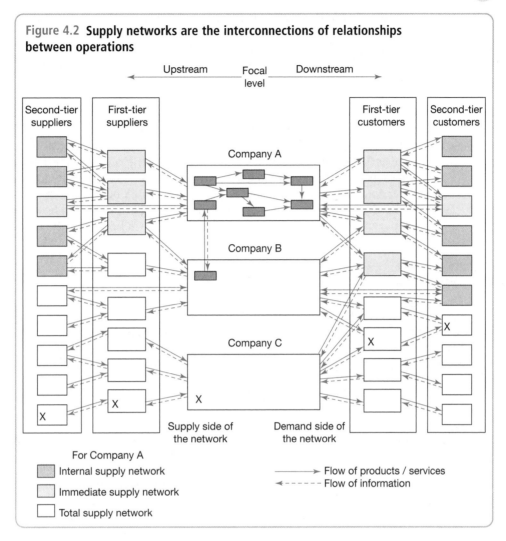

organisational boundaries downstream to its customers. This issue is conventionally referred to as the degree of vertical integration within Company A.

Companies that are predominantly part of the focal level's immediate supply network are called first-tier suppliers or first-tier customers. Those one level beyond this are called second-tier suppliers and customers, and so on. This does not mean that focal companies can trade only with first-tier customers and suppliers. In Figure 4.2 both Company A and Company B deal directly with a second-tier supplier and a second-tier customer. Competitors may trade, or even cooperate. It would appear that Company A occasionally subcontracts work to Company B. This may be because Company B has surplus capacity or because Company B can perform certain activities that Company A cannot.

The relationships between companies within the network are not always exclusive. Company A may purchase exactly the same products or services from a number of different suppliers, who in turn may 'multi-source' from several second-tier suppliers. Also the focal company's networks all involve several parallel relationships, each having several first-tier suppliers and several first-tier customers, which themselves may have more than one second-tier supplier or customer. But within these parallel relationships there are several supply chains. These are the sequential linkages of operations which intersect at the focal company. So, for example, the operations marked with an **X** form one of the supply chains passing through Company C.

Supply network strategy

Supply network strategy is the strategic direction of an organisation's relationships with suppliers, customers, suppliers' suppliers, customers' customers, etc. In particular, it includes such issues as ensuring that the organisation has an understanding of its supply networks, determining appropriate supply network relationships for its various activities, understanding supply network behaviour, in particular how the dynamics of a supply network will affect the organisation and how networks can be managed (or at least influenced) for the long-term benefit of the organisation.

Example **What's the nationality of your car?[2]**

On average, car companies source around three-quarters of their parts externally. This means that although an automobile company may be thought of as German or Italian or British, many (if not most) of its components may have been sourced abroad, and it may also have been assembled abroad. This can give some problems to cars whose brand is associated with a particular nationality, or whose core markets are particularly 'patriotic'. Italians may prefer to buy Fiat cars because Fiat is an Italian company, even though, in reality, many Fiats are now produced in Turkey and Poland. More than half of German buyers choose cars produced by German-owned companies. Yet, there is a good chance that the car has been made in Poland or Slovakia. Even the most nationally conservative French buyers will buy 'French' cars even though Citroën and Peugeot have plants in Slovakia. Buy an Audi TT in the UK and it was probably made in Hungary. Mercedes' ML-Class is built in the United States as is BMW's X5. Porsche builds the Boxter sports car in Finland. Even the Aston Martin, beloved by James Bond fans for its Britishness, has its front seats, automatic transmission, steering components, crank shafts, stability control, and its engine made in Germany. Even stranger, buy a Nissan Micra in Europe and you will find that it was designed in London, engineered in Bedfordshire and manufactured in Sunderland. It's more British than the Aston Martin.

Why take a supply-network perspective?

So, how does a 'perspective' help to give a general strategic advantage to an operation? A 'perspective' does not change anything in reality. No resources are reconfigured. No markets are changed. Taking a 'network perspective' is not a decision as such; it is merely a way of seeing operations in the context of the other operations with which they interact. Yet, the network perspective encourages some particularly significant aspects of operations strategy thinking which were previously underemphasised.

It enhances understanding of competitive and cooperative forces

When a business sees itself in the context of the whole network it may help it to understand why its customers and suppliers act as they do. Any operation has only two options if it wants to understand its ultimate customers at the end of the network. It can rely on all the intermediate customers and customers' customers, etc., which form the links in the network between the company and its end customers, to transmit the end customer needs efficiently back up the network, or it can take the responsibility on itself for understanding how customer–supplier relationships transmit competitive requirements through the network. Increasingly, organisations are taking the latter course. Relying exclusively on one's immediate network is seen as putting too much faith in someone else's judgement of things which are central to an organisation's own competitive health. There is also a further category of companies in the supply network – 'complementors'. Most businesses would find their lives more difficult if it were not for 'complementors' – other businesses providing complementary services and products (for example, internet retailers depend on 'order fulfilment' delivery companies). Figure 4.3 illustrates the 'value net' for a company. It sees any company as being surrounded by four types of players: suppliers, customers, competitors and complementors.[3]

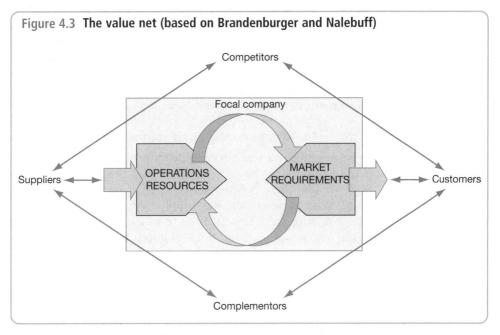

Figure 4.3 **The value net (based on Brandenburger and Nalebuff)**

Complementors enable customers to value your product or service more when they have their product and service as opposed to when they have yours alone. Competitors are the opposite; they make customers value your product or service less when they can have their product or service, rather than yours alone. Also competitors can be complementors and vice versa. For example, adjacent restaurants may see themselves as competitors for customers' business. A customer standing outside and wanting a meal will choose between the two of them. Yet, in another way they are complementors. Would that customer have come to this part of town unless there was more than one restaurant for him or her to choose between? Restaurants, theatres, art galleries, and tourist attractions generally, all cluster together in a form of cooperation to increase the total size of their joint market. It is important to distinguish between the way companies cooperate in increasing the total size of a market and the way in which they then compete for a share of that market. Historically, insufficient emphasis has been put on the role of the supplier. Harnessing the value of suppliers is just as important as listening to the needs of customers. Destroying value in a supplier in order to create it in a customer does not increase the value of the network as a whole. For example, pressurising suppliers because customers are pressurising you will not add long-term value. In the long term it creates value for the total network to find ways of increasing value for suppliers as well as customers. All the players in the network, whether they be customers, suppliers, competitors or complementors, can be both friends and enemies at different times. This is not 'unusual' or 'aberrant' behaviour. It is the way things are. The term used to capture this idea is 'co-opetition'.

It confronts the operation with its strategic resource options

A supply network perspective illustrates to any operation exactly where it is positioned in its network. It also, therefore, highlights where it is not. That is, it clearly delineates between the activities which are being performed by itself and those which are being performed by other operations in the network. This prompts the question of why the operations boundaries are exactly where they are. Should the operation extend its direct control over a greater part of the network through vertical integration? Alternatively, should it outsource some of its activities to specialist suppliers? Furthermore, should it encourage particular patterns of relationships in other parts of the network? Again, it is the network perspective that raises the questions: and sometimes helps to answer them.

It highlights the 'operation to operation' nature of business relationships

This may be the most far-reaching implication of a supply network perspective. It concerns the nature of the relationships between the various businesses in the network. Traditionally these relationships have been seen as 'customer–supplier' relationships. What is new in the way supply networks are now treated is that rather than conceptualising the relationship as 'doing business' with customers and suppliers, we are concerned with the 'flow of goods and services' between operations. Look at any supply network and the vast majority of businesses represented in it have other businesses as their customers rather than end customers. Not that the end customer is unimportant. But behind each business serving the end customer is a whole network of other businesses. To the end customer, it is the chain of operations lying behind the one they can see that is important. For that chain of operations the important questions are not 'How can I sell to my customer?' and 'How can I get supplies from my supplier?' Rather the questions should be 'How can my operation help my customer's operation to be more effective?' and 'How can my supplier's operation help my operation to be more effective?'

Global sourcing

Supply-network strategy is a global issue. Global sourcing means identifying, evaluating, negotiating and configuring supply across multiple geographies. Traditionally, even companies who exported their goods and services still sourced the majority of their supplies locally. Companies are now increasingly willing to look further afield for their supplies, and for very good reasons. Most companies report 10 per cent to 35 per cent cost savings by sourcing from low-cost-country suppliers.[4] Also there are other factors promoting global sourcing. The formation of trading blocs in different parts of the world (e.g. European Union, EU, the North American Free Trade Agreement, NAFTA, and the South American Trade Group, MERCOSUR) has lowered tariff barriers within those blocs. Transportation infrastructures are considerably more sophisticated and cheaper than they once were. Super-efficient port operations in Rotterdam and Singapore, for example, integrated road–rail systems, jointly developed auto route systems, and cheaper air freight have all reduced some of the cost barriers to international trade. But, most significantly, far tougher world competition has forced companies to look to reducing their total costs.

There are, of course, problems with global sourcing. The risks of increased complexity and increased distance need managing. The risks of delays and hold-ups can be far greater than when sourcing locally. Also negotiating with suppliers whose native language is different from one's own makes communication more difficult and can lead to misunderstandings over contract terms. Therefore, global sourcing decisions require businesses to balance cost, performance, service and risk, factors, not all of which are obvious. These factors are important in global sourcing because of non-price or 'hidden' cost factors such as cross-border freight and handling fees, complex inventory stocking and handling requirements, even more complex administrative, documentation and regulatory requirements, and issues of social responsibility.

This last point, that global sourcing requires extra attention to be placed on social responsibility has significant risk implications. Although the responsibility of operations to ensure that they only deal with ethical suppliers has always been important, the expansion of global sourcing has brought the issue into sharper focus. Local suppliers can (to some extent) be monitored relatively easily. However, when suppliers are located around the world, often in countries with different traditions and ethical standards, monitoring becomes more difficult. Not only that, but there may be genuinely different views of what is regarded as ethical practice. Social, cultural, and religious differences can easily make for mutual incomprehension regarding each others' ethical perspective. This is why many companies are putting significant effort into articulating and clarifying their supplier selection policies. The example on Levi Strauss' policy is typical of many organisations' approach to global sourcing. But it does not guarantee that all suppliers will conform.

> **Example** **Extracts from Levi Strauss' global sourcing policy[5]**
>
> Our Global Sourcing and Operating Guidelines help us to select business partners who follow workplace standards and business practices that are consistent with our company's values. These requirements are applied to every contractor who manufactures or finishes products for Levi Strauss & Co. Trained inspectors closely audit and monitor compliance among approximately 600 cutting, sewing, and finishing contractors in more than 60 countries. [. . .] The numerous countries where Levi Strauss & Co. has existing or future business interests present a variety of cultural, political, social and economic circumstances. [. . .] The Country Assessment Guidelines help us assess any issue that might present concern in light of the ethical principles we have set for ourselves. Specifically, we assess [. . .] the [. . .] Health and Safety Conditions Human Rights Environment, the Legal System and the Political, Economic and Social Environment would protect the company's commercial interests and brand/corporate image. The company's employment standards state that they will only do business with partners who adhere to the following guidelines:

▶

Child Labor: Use of child labor is not permissible. Workers can be no less than 15 years of age and not younger than the compulsory age to be in school. We will not utilize partners who use child labor in any of their facilities.

Prison Labor/Forced Labor: We will not utilize prison or forced labor in contracting relationships in the manufacture and finishing of our products. We will not utilize or purchase materials from a business partner utilizing prison or forced labor.

Disciplinary Practices: We will not utilize business partners who use corporal punishment or other forms of mental or physical coercion.

Working Hours: While permitting flexibility in scheduling, we will identify local legal limits on work hours and seek business partners who do not exceed them except for appropriately compensated overtime. Employees should be allowed at least one day off in seven.

Wages and Benefits: We will only do business with partners who provide wages and benefits that comply with any applicable law and match the prevailing local manufacturing or finishing industry practices.

Freedom of Association: We respect workers' rights to form and join organizations of their choice and to bargain collectively. We expect our suppliers to respect the right to free association and the right to organize and bargain collectively without unlawful interference.

Discrimination: While we recognize and respect cultural differences, we believe that workers should be employed on the basis of their ability to do the job, rather than on the basis of personal characteristics or beliefs. We will favor business partners who share this value.

Health & Safety: We will only utilize business partners who provide workers with a safe and healthy work environment. Business partners who provide residential facilities for their workers must provide safe and healthy facilities.

Inter-operations relationships in supply networks

To influence the nature of any operation's supply network we need to determine how the operation relates to other players in its network. Does it have a close and intimate knowledge of its immediate supply network? And does it make sure that its immediate supply network also has an intimate understanding of its own operations? Does it rely on other players only for trivial activities, or trust some important parts of the value-adding activities to other operations?

Types of relationship

Writers on supply network management have offered several ways of categorising the relationships between players in supply networks and again we distinguish between the market and resource perspectives of relationship.[6] In terms of the resources relationships with suppliers, what is the degree and importance of the activities that are performed in-house? – from doing everything in-house, through doing the most important things in-house, to totally outsourcing all activities. In terms of the market relationship, what are the number of separate supply relationships and how close are they? – from using many suppliers with little closeness in the relationships, through to a few close (or even one very close) supplier.

Figure 4.4 illustrates this. Different types of supply-network relationship can be positioned in terms of their implied resource scope and market relationships. At an extreme on both dimensions is the vertically integrated operation. This type of operation performs everything (or almost everything) within the organisation's boundaries. Unless the organisation has chosen to perform the same activity in many different parts of its operations there will be few (probably one) internal suppliers. This allows the potential for very close relationships. At the other extreme an operation may choose to do nothing in-house and buy in all its requirements – the so-called virtual company that retains relatively few physical resources. Its network is one of information and contacts with other players in the network who can supply all it requires to satisfy its own customers. (See the Example 'Virtually like the movies'.) When the nature of these supply relationships is temporary and market-based, it is called 'virtual spot trading'. Spot trading means that at any point in time an organisation looks at the spot price, or spot terms of supply, and makes a choice independently of what its previous or future choices might be. But not all virtual operations need be based on transactional market relationships. When almost all its activities are outsourced an organisation may seek to compensate for its lack of control by attempting to build long-term and close relationships with a relatively few suppliers. This is the long-term virtual operation.

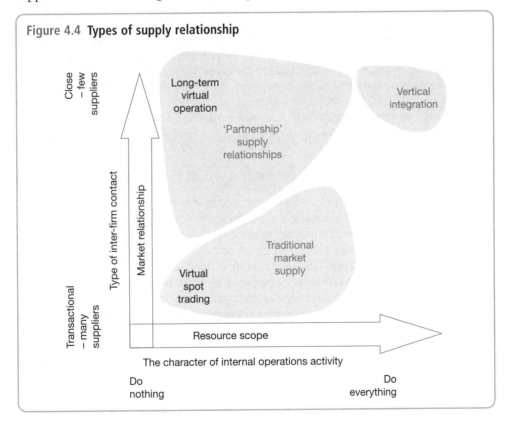

Figure 4.4 **Types of supply relationship**

Example **Virtually like the movies**[7]

As far as supply network management is concerned, could that most ephemeral of all industries, Hollywood's film-making business, hold messages for even the most sober of operations? It is an industry whose complexity most of us do not fully appreciate. The American writer Scott Fitzgerald said, 'You can take Hollywood for granted like I did, or you can dismiss it with the contempt we reserve for what we don't understand . . . not half a dozen men have ever been able to keep the whole equation of [making] pictures in their heads.' The 'equation' involves balancing the artistic creativity and fashion awareness, necessary to create a market for its products, with the efficiency and tight operations practices which get films made and distributed on time. But although the form of the equation remains the same, the way its elements relate to each other has changed profoundly. The typical Hollywood studio once did everything itself. It employed everyone from the carpenters, who made the stage, through to the film stars. Cary Grant was as much of an employee as the chauffeur who drove him to the studio, though his contract was probably more restrictive. The finished products were rolls of celluloid which had to be mass produced and physically distributed to the cinemas of the world.

No longer; studios now deal almost exclusively in ideas. They buy and sell concepts; they arrange finance; they cut marketing deals and, above all; they manage the virtual network of creative and not so creative talent that go into a film's production. A key skill is the ability to put together teams of self-employed film stars and the small, technical specialist operations that provide technical support. It is a world that is less easy for the studios to control.

The players in this virtual network, from film stars to electricians, have taken the opportunity to raise their fees to the point where, in spite of an increase in cinema attendance, returns are lower than at many times in the past. This opens opportunities for the smaller, independent studios. One way to keep costs low is by using inexpensive, new talent. Some of the most profitable films have been those that didn't cost a fortune to produce. Technology could also help this process. Digital processes allow easier customisation of the 'product' and mean that movies can be downloaded direct to cinemas (and direct to individual consumers' homes).

The outsourcing decision – vertical integration? Do or buy?

No single business does everything that is required to produce its products and services. Banks do not usually do their own credit checking, they retain the services of specialist credit checking agencies that have the resources to do it better. This is outsourcing; and has become an important issue for most businesses, because, although most companies have always outsourced some of their activities, a larger proportion of direct activities are now being bought from suppliers. Also many indirect processes, such as the more routine back-office processes are now being outsourced. This is often referred to as business process outsourcing (BPO). In a similar way many processes within the Human Resource function from simply payroll services through to more complex training and development processes, are being outsourced to specialist companies. Sometimes processes are still physically located where they were before, but the staff and technology are managed by the outsourcing service provider. The reason for outsourcing is usually to reduce cost. However, there can sometimes also be significant gains in the quality and flexibility of service offered. *'People talk a lot about looking beyond cost cutting when it comes to outsourcing companies' human resource functions',* says Jim Madden, CEO of Exult, the California-based specialist outsourcing company, *'I don't believe any company will sign up for this (outsourcing) without cost reduction being part of it, but for the clients whose human resource functions we manage, such as BP, and Bank of America, it is not just about saving money'.*

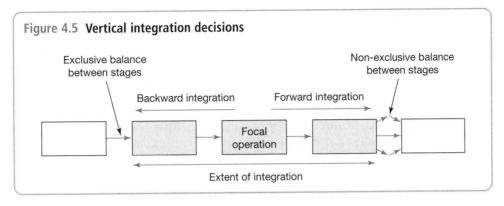

Figure 4.5 **Vertical integration decisions**

The outsourcing debate is just part of a far larger issue which will shape the fundamental nature of any business. Namely, what should the scope of the business be? In other words, what should it do itself and what should it buy in? This is often referred to as the 'do or buy decision' when individual components or activities are being considered, or 'vertical integration' when it is the ownership of whole operations that are being decided. Vertical integration is the extent to which an organisation owns the network of which it is a part. It usually involves an organisation assessing the wisdom of acquiring suppliers or customers. Vertical integration can be defined in terms of three factors (see Figure 4.5).[8]

The direction of vertical integration – should an operation expand by buying one of its suppliers or by buying one of its customers? The strategy of expanding on the supply side of the network is sometimes called backward or upstream vertical integration, and expanding on the demand side is sometimes called forward or downstream vertical integration.

The extent of vertical integration – how far should an operation take the extent of its vertical integration? Some organisations deliberately choose not to integrate far, if at all, from their original part of the network. Alternatively, some organisations choose to become very vertically integrated.

The balance among stages – is not strictly about the ownership of the network; but rather the exclusivity of the relationship between operations. A totally balanced network relationship is one where one operation produces only for the next stage in the network and totally satisfies its requirements. Less than full balance allows each operation to sell its output to other companies or to buy in some of its supplies from other companies. Fully balanced networks have the virtue of simplicity and also allow each operation to focus on the requirements of the next stage along in the network. Having to supply other organisations, perhaps with slightly different requirements, might serve to distract from what is needed by their (owned) primary customer. However, a totally self-sufficient network is sometimes not feasible, nor is it necessarily desirable.

Making the outsourcing/vertical integration decision

Whether it is referred to as do or buy, vertical integration or outsourcing, the choice facing operations is rarely simple. Organisations in different circumstances with different objectives are likely to take different decisions. Yet, the question itself is relatively simple, even if the decision itself is not: 'Does in-house or outsourced supply in a particular set of circumstances give the appropriate performance objectives that it requires to compete more effectively in its markets?' For example, if the main performance objectives for an operation are dependable delivery and meeting short-term changes in customers' delivery requirements, the key question should be: 'How does in-house or outsourcing give better dependability and delivery flexibility performance?' This means judging two sets of opposing factors – those which give the potential to improve performance, and those which work against this potential being realised. Table 4.1 summarises some arguments for in-house supply and outsourcing in terms of each performance objective.

Deciding whether to outsource

In addition to the effect on the operation's performance objectives, there are other issues when deciding if outsourcing is a sensible option. If an activity has long-term strategic importance to a company, it is unlikely to outsource it. For example, a retailer might choose to keep the design and development of its web site in-house even though specialists could perform the activity at less cost because it plans to move into web-based retailing at some point in the future. Nor would a company usually outsource an activity where it had specialised skills or knowledge. For example, a company making laser printers may have built up specialised knowledge in the production of sophisticated laser drives. This capability may allow it to introduce product or process innovations in the future. It would be foolish to 'give away' such capability. After these two more strategic factors have been considered the company's operations performance can be taken into account. Obviously, if its operation's performance is already too superior to any potential supplier, it would be unlikely to outsource the activity. But also even if its performance was currently below that of potential suppliers, it may not outsource the activity if it feels that it could significantly improve its performance. Figure 4.6 illustrates this decision logic.

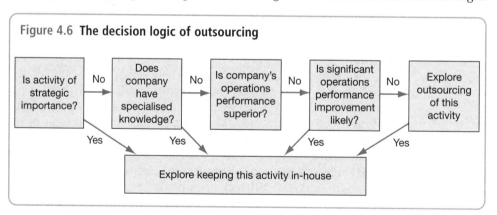

Figure 4.6 **The decision logic of outsourcing**

Some advantages and disadvantages of outsourcing

Although extensive vertical integration is no longer popular, there are still companies that avoid outsourcing. Indeed, very few companies are anywhere close to 'virtual'. Most justifications for doing things in-house fall under four categories.

Table 4.1 **How in-house and outsourced supply may affect an operation's performance objectives**

Performance objective	'Do it yourself' in-house supply	'Buy it in' outsourced supply
Quality	The origins of any quality problems are usually easier to trace in-house and improvement can be more immediate but can be some risk of complacency	Supplier may have specialised knowledge and more experience, also may be motivated through market pressures, but communication of quality problems more difficult
Speed	Can mean closer synchronisation of schedules which speeds up the throughput of materials and information, but if the operation also has external customers, internal customers may receive low priority	Speed of response can be built into the supply contract where commercial pressures will encourage good performance, but there may be significant transport/delivery delays
Dependability	Easier communications internally can help dependable delivery which also may help when internal customers need to be informed of potential delays, but as with speed, if the operation also has external customers, internal customers may receive low priority	Late delivery penalties in the supply contract can encourage good delivery performance, but distance and organisational barriers may inhibit in communication
Flexibility	Closeness to the real needs of a business can alert the in-house operation that some kind of change is required in its operations, but the ability to respond may be limited by the scale and scope of internal operations	Outsource suppliers are likely to be larger and have wider capabilities than in-house suppliers, this gives them more ability to respond to changes, but they can only respond when asked to do so by the customer and they may have to balance the conflicting needs of different customers
Cost	In-house operations give the potential for sharing some costs such as research and development, or logistics, more significantly in-house operations do not have to make the margin required by outside suppliers so the business can capture the profits which would otherwise be given to the supplier, but relatively low volumes may mean that it is difficult to gain economies of scale or the benefits of process innovation	Probably the main reason why outsourcing is so popular; outsourced companies can achieve economies of scale and they are motivated to reduce their own costs because it directly impacts on their profits, but extra costs of communication and coordination with an external supplier need to be taken into account

- It secures dependable delivery of input goods and services – supply may be unstable and subject to long-term gluts or shortages. One reason why the oil companies, which sell petrol, are also engaged in extracting it, is to ensure long-term supply.

- It may reduce costs – the most common argument here is that 'We can do it cheaper than our supplier's price'. Such statements are often made by comparing the marginal direct cost incurred by a company in doing something itself against the price it is paying to buy the product or service from a supplier.

- It may help to improve product or service quality – sometimes vertical integration can be used to secure specialist or technological advantage by preventing product and service knowledge getting into the hands of competitors.

- It helps in understanding other activities in the supply network – some companies, even those famous for their rejection of traditional vertical integration, do choose to own some parts of the supply network other than what they regard as core.

The arguments against doing things in-house tend to cluster around a number of observed disadvantages of those companies that have practised vertical integration extensively. These are:

- It creates an internal monopoly – the assumption is that external market mechanisms are more efficient at keeping operations close to market requirements than are any internally devised planning mechanisms. Operations, it is argued, will only keep sharp when they see a commercial need to do so.

- You can't exploit economies of scale – activities within an organisation are probably also carried out elsewhere in the industry so unless an operation has a unique process or, alternatively, is the overwhelmingly dominant player in the industry, specialist suppliers that can serve more than one customer are likely to have large volumes allowing specialists to get economies of scale.

- It results in loss of flexibility – vertically integrated companies by definition do most things themselves which means that a high proportion of their costs will be fixed relative to their variable costs which, in turn, means that any reduction in the total volume of activity can easily move the economics of the operation close to, or below, its break-even point.

- It cuts you off from innovation – suppliers (and customers) are a major source of innovation[9] because the ongoing information exchange between organisations is an ideal breeding ground for innovation, but isolate a process from the rest of the market by integrating it within the total organisation and it is cut off from its potentially richest sources of ideas.

- It distracts you from core activities – all organisations need to be good at certain things otherwise their customers would do them themselves. So, if you are earning profits by being good at something that others find difficult, then do not jeopardise it by doing other, less important things.

Traditional market-based supply

At the very opposite extreme from vertical integration is the idea that relationships are defined by 'pure' market forces. The justifications for market-based supply relationships are the mirror image of those used to justify vertical integration. There is little point in rehearsing these arguments again but it is worth noting that the case in favour of market-based relationships is usually based on the idea that a free market, with suppliers vying against each other for a customers' business, is the best long-term guarantee of low costs. No prospective supplier will survive under conditions of competitive markets, it is argued, unless the supplier is providing something very close to what the customers want. The dynamics of the market relationship can be exploited to minimise the cost of outsourced goods and services. Since outsourced goods and services are at least 50 per cent of most organisations' total costs this is important. Relatively small reductions in the price paid for outsourced goods and services can have a major effect on profits. For example, consider the following simple example.

Total sales	=	£10,000,000
Purchased goods and services	=	£7,000,000
Other costs	=	£2,500,000
Therefore, profit	=	£500,000

Profits can be doubled to £1,000,000 by any of the following:

- increasing sales revenue by 100 per cent;
- decreasing 'other costs', such as salaries, by 20 per cent;
- decreasing the cost of purchased goods and services by 7.1 per cent.

A doubling of sales revenue can occur in some fast-growing markets, but is by any standard an ambitious target for any marketing manager. Decreasing other costs by 20 per cent, especially if the majority of these are salaries, is again possible but difficult. However, reducing the cost of purchased goods and services by 7.1 per cent, although a challenging objective does seem the most realistic option. Because outsourcing costs are such a large proportion of total costs, relatively small changes in the price paid for outsourced goods and services will have a large impact on profits, and the higher the proportion of total costs devoted to outsourced goods and services, the more pronounced this effect is.

Problems with relying on market mechanisms

There are in practice some considerable problems in relying exclusively on market mechanisms, in particular, how to cope with buyer–supplier uncertainties, the cost of making purchase decisions and avoiding strategic risks.

Coping with buyer–supplier uncertainties

Relatively few purchasing decisions are made around a single unambiguous factor. Theoretically, if all companies in the market are offering exactly the same product with exactly the same conditions of delivery and quality, the purchasing company could make the decision of which company to use exclusively on the basis of price. Yet, there still may be issues of payment terms, long-term security of supply, ability to buy other goods and services in a one-stop-shop transaction, and so on. Purchasing on one factor only is unusual. It is found most frequently at the extreme upstream ends of supply networks where commodity-like products (and sometimes services) are being traded. For most purchase decisions several dimensions will need to be considered, and sometimes traded off. In order to make these trade-offs between cost, quality, delivery, product performance, flexibility and so on, the purchasing company needs to understand and evaluate all the options it faces. This is no mean task. There may be a large number of suppliers with subtly different product and service offerings which may themselves change in the near future. Thus there is 'market uncertainty' caused by a lack of perfect information. Managers are forced to decide under conditions of what is sometimes called 'bounded rationality'.

Even if it were possible to identify and evaluate all the real and potential offerings which the market could provide, it is sometimes difficult to get the required clarity of information internally. There may be some difficulty within a purchasing organisation of knowing exactly what is needed. Especially when technologies are newly emerging or complex, it is difficult to set down a precisely defined specification on which to evaluate purchasing opportunities. This is sometimes called 'need uncertainty'. There is also uncertainty concerning the degree of confidence the purchasing organisation has in its potential suppliers. Although a supplying company may be clear in saying what it will do, unless there is a history of proven reliable supply, how does the purchasing company know it can trust its supplier? This is called 'transaction uncertainty'.

Buyers will seek to minimise these uncertainties. Some industry associations provide data on their members to prospective purchasers of their members' services. In a similar way with consumer products, many of us buy automobile or hi-fi magazines which list these available products together with their performance and price details. At other times companies seek to limit the effort that goes into reducing uncertainty. Some companies have a list of preferred suppliers which contains details of companies supplying particular services from which alternative providers will be chosen on a transaction-by-transaction basis. Other methods of coping with uncertainty include working with internal designers to reduce any ambiguity around how products and services are specified internally. Likewise, transaction uncertainty can be reduced by seeking 'references' from other customers of potential suppliers.

The cost of making purchase decisions – transaction costs

The second problem with relying on market mechanisms is that they can be expensive to manage. Finding out information from suppliers, looking into the history and track record of potential suppliers, working with internal staff to understand exactly what is required, and so on, all need resourcing in some way. Decisions need to be made by sifting through the potential suppliers and periodically reviewing the decisions to check whether there are now better suppliers in the market. This is the traditional role of the purchasing function within businesses, which has always been faced with the 'perfect decision dilemma'. Put simply, in a free market, in order to reach the very best decisions as to which are the best set of suppliers to choose, you need a very large purchasing resource. In practice, companies will accept something less than a perfect decision in order to limit the resources needed to make the choice. It will do this by a number of common-sense mechanisms such as identifying the most important suppliers in terms of value of purchases, or in terms of long-term strategic impact, and concentrating on them. Nevertheless, the transaction cost which goes into the purchase decision when using free-market mechanisms is an important issue for companies adopting this approach.

Strategic risks

This final problem, with using market mechanisms is simply that if companies choose to outsource some of their activities to the 'best' suppliers, the market mechanisms that made those suppliers the 'best' could result in the suppliers becoming more powerful than the purchasing company. The purchasing company then is 'hollowed out'. It is left with few activities of long-term value or importance. So, if an operation is going to outsource some of its activities to the market, it should be very careful that it does not choose the wrong things to outsource. For example, when IBM started manufacturing personal computers, the industry was in a state of flux. Although clearly a significant development, few visionaries could see exactly how the market might develop. Because PCs were different from its current mainframe-type products, IBM set up a separate business to design, produce and sell these new products. Unable to perform every single activity necessary to the development of such products, IBM made (with hindsight) two important outsourcing decisions. It outsourced the design of its micro processor Intel and it outsourced the development of its operating system to a small but dynamic supplier called Microsoft.

Example | ## How Samsung made its breakthrough[10]

One of the best-known cautionary tales which illustrates the inherent dangers involved in subcontracting is that of General Electric's microwave oven experiences. Although the microwave industry at the beginning of the 1980s was dominated by Japanese domestic appliance manufacturers, such as Matsushita and Sanyo, General Electric was enjoying reasonable success in the US market with its purpose-designed microwave oven plant in Maryland. However, it soon came under price pressures from its Japanese competitors. What seemed an obvious solution was to subcontract the manufacture of some of its more basic models, where margins were relatively small. GE explored the idea of subcontracting these models to one of its main rivals, Matsushita, even though giving one of its main competitors such an advantage was considered risky. GE also found a small, but go-getting, Korean company that was already selling very simple (and very cheap) models in the USA. After much consideration, GE decided to continue making the top of the range models itself, subcontract its cheaper models to Matsushita, but also place a small order of 15,000 units of its cheaper models with the Korean company, partly to see whether they could cope with the order. Of course, it also made sense for GE to send its own engineers to help the Korean company transfer knowledge and ensure that quality standards would be maintained. The GE engineers found that, although the Korean company had little knowledge, they were very willing to learn. Eventually the Korean's production line started producing reasonable quality products, still at very low prices. Over time, the Korean company was given more and more orders by GE, which found that it was making more margin on the Korean sourced products than those coming out of its Maryland plant. This became particularly important as the market continued to mature and costs came under increased pressure. The Maryland plant attempted to cut its own costs but this proved especially difficult with so much of its volume now subcontracted to the Korean company. In the end, the Maryland plant was closed and GE withdrew entirely from the microwave-oven (indeed, the whole domestic-appliance) market. And the Korean company? It was called Samsung, and within 10 years of starting to make them, it became the world's largest manufacturer of microwave ovens.

The internet and e-procurement

By making it easier to search for alternative suppliers, the internet has changed the economics of the search process and offers the potential for wider searches. It also changed the economics of scale in purchasing. Purchasers requiring relatively low volumes find it easier to group together in order to create orders of sufficient size to warrant lower prices. E-procurement is the generic term used to describe the use of electronic methods in every stage of the purchasing process from identification of requirement through to payment, and potentially to contract management. Many of the large automotive, engineering and petrochemical companies, for example, have adopted such an approach. Typical of these companies' motives are those put forward by Shell Services International, part of the petrochemical giant:

> 'Procurement is an obvious first step in e-commerce. First, buying through the web is so slick and cheap compared to doing it almost any other way. Second, it allows you to aggregate, spend and ask: Why am I spending this money, or shouldn't I be getting a bigger discount? Third, it encourages new services like credit, insurance and accreditation to be built around it.'

Generally the benefits of e-procurement are taken to include the following:

- It promotes efficiency improvements (the way people work) in purchasing processes.
- It improves commercial relationships with suppliers.
- It reduces the transaction costs of doing business for suppliers.
- It opens up the marketplace to increased competition and therefore keeps prices competitive.
- It improves a business' ability to manage their supply chain more efficiently.

The cost savings from purchased goods may be the most visible advantages of e-procurement, but some managers say that it is just the tip of the iceberg. It can also be far more efficient because purchasing staff are no longer chasing purchase orders and performing routine administrative tasks. Much of the advantage and time savings come from more effective transactions. Purchasing staff can negotiate with vendors faster and more effectively. Online auctions can compress negotiations from months to one or two hours, or even minutes. Lucent's Vice-President of Purchasing sees e-procurement as being hugely important:

> 'When I think about the strides we have made in speed, efficiency and employee productivity it is incredible. With e-procurement, you get a standard interface [for purchasing] and eliminate redundancies. It is tremendously efficient – particularly from a time standpoint – because you eliminate paper approvals and procedures. There is a substantial reduction in transaction processing costs. Thanks to e-procurement, Lucent will achieve – or surpass – the 60% to 70% reduction in transaction processing time it set forth in its business plan. Everyone is trying to come up with a more effective cost structure to control spending. But if you don't have an efficient e-procurement platform, it is hard to understand where you are and hard to control costs. You can't take action unless you know where you are bleeding. When all the data are in one place, you can see problems quicker and easier and take the right action.'

Electronic marketplaces

E-procurement has grown largely because of the development over the last 10 years of electronic marketplaces offering services to both buyers and sellers. They are information systems that allow buyers and sellers to exchange information about prices and product and service offerings, and the firm operating the electronic marketplace acts as in intermediary. They can be categorised as consortium, private, or third party.

- A private e-marketplace is where buyers or sellers conduct business in the market only with its partners and suppliers by previous arrangement.
- The consortium e-marketplace is where several large businesses combine to create an e-marketplace controlled by the consortium.
- A third-party e-marketplace is where an independent party creates an unbiased, market-driven e-marketplace for buyers and sellers in an industry.

The internet is also an important source of purchasing information, even if the purchase is actually made by using more traditional methods. Also, even because many businesses have gained advantages by using e-procurement, it does not mean that everything should be bought electronically. When businesses purchase very large amounts of strategically important products or services, it will negotiate multimillion-euro deals, which involve months of discussion, arranging for deliveries up to a year ahead. In such environments, e-procurement adds little value. Deciding whether to invest in e-procurement applications (which can be expensive) say some authorities depends on what is being bought. For example, simple office supplies such as pens, paper clips and copier paper may be appropriate for e-procurement, but complex, made-to-order engineered components are not. Four questions seem to influence whether e-procurement will be appropriate.

Is the value of the spend high or low? High spending on purchased products and services give more potential for savings from e-procurement.

Is the product or commodity highly substitutable or not? When products and services are 'substitutable' (there are alternatives), e-procurement can identify and find lower cost alternatives.

Is there a lot of competition or a little? When several suppliers are competing, e-procurement can manage the process of choosing a preferred supplier more effectively and with more transparency.

How efficient are your internal processes? When purchasing processes are relatively inefficient, e-procurement's potential to reduce processing costs can be realised.

Partnership supply

The development of partnership relationships between customers and suppliers in supply networks is sometimes seen as a compromise between the 'extremes' of vertical integration and market trading. It attempts to achieve some of the closeness and coordination efficiencies of vertical integration without the necessity to own the assets and it attempts to achieve the sharpness of service and the incentive to continually improve, which is often seen as the benefit of traditional market trading. Yet, partnership is more than a mixture of vertical integration and market trading. It is an approach to how relationships in supply networks can be formed with a degree of trust that effectively substitutes for the ownership of assets. Partnership relationships can be viewed as strategic alliances that have been defined as: *'relatively enduring inter-firm cooperative arrangements, involving flows and linkages that use resources and/or governance structures from autonomous organisations, for the joint accomplishment of individual goals linked to the corporate mission of each sponsoring firm'.*[11] In such an alliance, partners are expected to cooperate, even to the extent of sharing skills and resources, to achieve joint benefits beyond those they could achieve by acting alone. Figure 4.7 identifies some of the major elements which contribute to the closeness necessary for partnership and divides them into those which are primarily related to the attitude with which the customer and supplier approach the relationship, and those which relate to the actions undertaken by both parties.

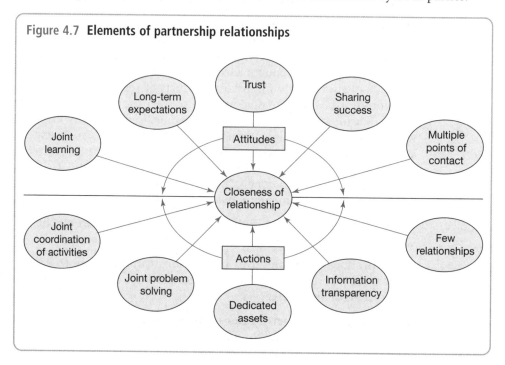

Figure 4.7 **Elements of partnership relationships**

Closeness

Closeness is the degree of intimacy, understanding and mutual support which exists between partners and reflects the degree of interdependence of the partners. An analogy is often drawn between the concept of closeness in business relations and how the word is used in personal relations. Interpersonal intimacy relies on the attitude with which individuals approach the relationship with their partner/friend, and is also affected by an accumulation of individual actions. Both are important. Intimacy relies on each partner's belief in the other's attitude and motivation in maintaining the relationship. It is that belief that helps dispel any doubt that we can rely on supportive actions from our partner. But it is also those actions which, over time, deepen and enhance the positive beliefs and attitudes concerning the relationship itself. In this way, closeness can be seen as both the result of, and the objective of, the interplay between attitudes towards the relationship and the ongoing activities which are the day-to-day manifestations of the relationship.

Trust

In this context trust means: *'the willingness of one party to relate with another in the belief that the other's actions will be beneficial rather than detrimental to the first party, even though this cannot be guaranteed.'*[12] The greater the degree of trust, the greater is the willingness to make oneself vulnerable to the actions of the other, even though this vulnerability is not as keenly felt because of the existence of trust. If there were no risk involved in a relationship there would be no need for trust, and without some degree of trust there is little justification for taking risks with a partner. Although most organisations are aware of different degrees of trust in their relationships with suppliers or customers, they do not always see trust as an issue to be managed explicitly. Sometimes this is the result of a broad philosophical view of the issue ('in the end suppliers will always look after their interests, it's foolish to believe otherwise'). At other times it may be that managers do not believe such a nebulous concept can be either analysed or indeed managed ('trust is one of those things which is either there or it isn't, you can't account for it like profit and loss'). However, almost all research in the area of supplier–customer relationships highlights the role of trust in determining the scope and limits to the relationship. Furthermore, it is at the heart of any understanding of partnership relationships. It is useful to think of trust in three stages.[13] Progression through these states of trust is often associated with time and the accumulation of positive, relationship-building experiences.

● Calculative trust is the most basic level of trust that arises because one of the parties calculates that trusting the partner is likely to lead to a better outcome than not trusting them. Underlying this is often the belief that the benefits from maintaining trust are greater than those from breaking it.

● Cognitive trust is based on a sharing of each partner's cognitions or understandings of aspects concerned with the relationship. By knowing how each other see the world, each partner is able to predict how the other will react. In other words, the other partner's behaviour can be anticipated, hence, it comes as no surprise and, therefore, will not threaten the relationship.

● Bonding trust is deeper. It is based on partners holding common values, moral codes and a sense of what obligations are due to each other. The partners identify with each other at an emotional level beyond the mere mechanics of the day-to-day transactions which occur. Trust is based on the belief that each party feels as well as thinks the same.

Sharing success

An attitude of shared success means that both partners recognise that they have more to gain through the success of the other partner than they have individually, or by exploiting the other partner. Both customers and suppliers are less interested in manoeuvring in order to get a bigger slice of the pie and are more interested in increasing the size of the pie. It is this belief that helps to prevent individual partners from acting against the interests of the other in order to gain immediate advantage, what economists call opportunistic behaviour. However, it must be clear that the size of pie will indeed be larger if both partners are to cooperate. It also is important to have an agreement as to how the larger pie will be divided up

Long-term expectations

Partnership relationships imply relatively long-term relationships between suppliers and customers. The deeper levels of trust require time to develop. Furthermore, there is no need to incur the transaction costs of frequent changes of partner, always assuming that the partner behaves in the best interests of the other. All of which points to long-term relationships – but not necessarily permanent ones. At the heart of the partnership concept is that either party could end the partnership. That is (partly) what keeps each motivated to do the best for the other. Maintaining the relationship is an affirmation that each partner has more to gain from the relationship than from ending it.

Multiple points of contact

Multiple points of contact means that communication between partners involves many links between many individuals in both organisations. Although this sounds like an action rather than an attitude, it is best thought of as an attitude which allows, and indeed encourages, multiple person-to-person relationships. It implies that both partners are sufficiently relaxed in their mutual dealings not to feel they have to control every discussion and development. Over time, this may lead to a complex web of agreements and understandings being formed, perhaps not in the legal contractual sense of a single 'all embracing' agreement, but as a multi-stranded, intertwined 'velcro-connected' binding of the two partners.

Joint learning

Again, this sounds like an action but in reality, though is more of an attitude that encourages approaching the relationship in a sense of mutual learning. Presumably, a partner has been selected on the basis that the partner has something to contribute beyond what the customer can do for themselves. While the customer would not necessarily wish to gain technical knowledge of these core processes (they have, after all, decided not to do these things themselves), it may be able to learn much about the application of whatever is supplied.

Few relationships

Partnership relationships do not necessarily imply single sourcing by customers, nor does it imply exclusivity by suppliers. However, even if the relationships are not monogamous, they are not promiscuous. Partnerships inevitably involve a limit on the number of other partnerships, if for no other reason than a single organisation cannot maintain intimacy in a large number of relationships. Furthermore, it also implies that the other partner has some say in the other's relationships. Generally, partners agree the extent to which they might form other relationships which may involve some longer-term threat to their partner.

Joint coordination of activities

Partly because there are fewer individual partners with whom to coordinate, the quantity, type and timing of product and service deliveries are usually subject to a greater degree of mutual agreement in a partnership relationship. However, notwithstanding the mutuality of interest, it is usually the customer side of a partnership which has a far greater say in the coordination of activities than the supplier. Customers, after all, are closer to the demand-driven end of a supply chain and thus subject to a greater degree of demand pull. A customer's increased involvement in a supplier's day-to-day planning and control (combined with a degree of trust) allows inventory to be reduced.

Information transparency

Open and efficient information exchange is a key element in partnership as well as the natural consequence of the various attitudinal factors discussed earlier. It means that each partner is open, honest and timely in the way they communicate with each other. As a way of encouraging appropriate decisions to be made by each party, and as a way of preventing misunderstanding between the parties, efficient information exchange and dissemination is vital. But, the nature of the information exchanged by the partners may become increasingly sensitive; meaning that it would be embarrassing to one party if the other leaked it. And, if the information is commercially valuable, leakage could mean one partner being placed at a commercial and/or strategic disadvantage.

Joint problem solving

Partnerships do not always run smoothly. In fact, the degree of closeness between partners would be severely limited if they did. When problems arise, either minor problems concerned with the day-to-day flow of products and services, or more fundamental issues concerned with the nature of the relationship itself, they will need to be addressed, by one or both partners. The way in which such problems are addressed is widely seen as being central to how the partnership itself develops. In fact, it can be argued that it is only when problems arise that the opportunity exists to explore fully many of the issues we have been discussing regarding trust, shared success, long-term expectations, and so on.

Dedicated assets

One of the more evident ways of demonstrating a commitment to partnership, and one of the most risky, is by one partner (usually the supplier) investing in resources which will be dedicated to a single customer. A company will only do this if it is convinced that the partnership will be long-term, that advantages can be gained by both parties and that the customer will not exploit the investment in order to bargain the price down below what was originally agreed.

Which type of relationship?

There is no simple formula for choosing what form of relationship to develop, but one can identify some of the more important factors which can sway the decision. Before doing so, however, it is worthwhile reminding ourselves that firms do not make an overall policy decision to adopt one of the three forms of relationship we have described here. Most have a portfolio of widely differing relationships where a whole set of factors have been influential. Figure 4.8 describes some of these in terms of market and resource factors.

From a market perspective, the most obvious issue will be how the firm intends to differentiate itself through its market positioning. If a firm is competing primarily on price then the relationship could be dictated by minimising transaction costs. If it is competing primarily on product or service innovation, then it may well wish to form a collaborative alliance with a partner with whom it can work closely. Unless, that is, the market from which innovations derive is turbulent and fast growing (as with many software and internet-based industries), in which case it might wish to retain the freedom to change partners quickly through the market mechanism. However, in such turbulent markets, a firm might wish to develop relationships that reduce its risks. One way to do this is to form relationships with many different potential long-term customers and suppliers, until the nature of the market stabilises. Opportunities to develop relationships, however, may be limited by the structure of the market itself. If the number of potential suppliers, or customers, is small, then it may be sensible to attempt to develop a close relationship with at least one customer or supplier. Opportunities to play off customers and suppliers against each other may be limited. Firms will also be influenced by likely competitor behaviour. For example, close partnership, or even vertical integration, may be seen as a defensive move against a competitor acquiring a major supplier or customer. From an operations resource perspective, economies of scale are important if the total requirement for a given product or service falls below the optimum level of efficiency. Low volume is one of the main factors that prevent firms doing things inhouse. The level of transaction costs also is important. Low transaction costs favour market-based relationships, while the possibility of jointly reducing transaction costs makes partnership an attractive option. Partnership is also attractive when there is the potential for learning from a partner. An absence of any potential learning suggests a more market-based relationship. Finally, although obvious, it is worthwhile pointing out that any sort of outsourcing, whether partnership or market-based, may be as a response to some sort of resource deficiency. That is, a firm will go outside for products and services if it does not have the resources to create them itself.

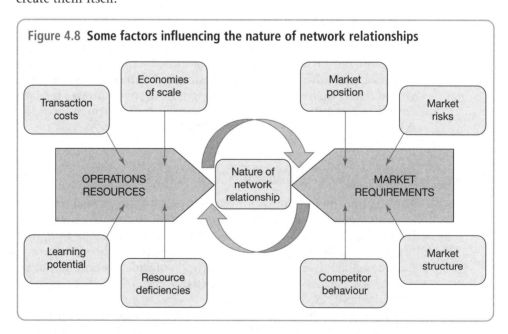

Figure 4.8 Some factors influencing the nature of network relationships

Network behaviour

Supply chains have their own dynamic behaviour patterns which tend to distort the smooth flow of information up the chain and product moving down the chain. Flow in supply chains can be turbulent, with the activity levels in each part of the chain differing significantly, even when demand at the end of the chain is relatively stable. Small changes in one part of the chain can cause seemingly erratic behaviour in other parts. This phenomenon is known as 'supply chain amplification', 'supply chain distortion', 'the Forrester effect'[14] (after the person who first modelled it), or most descriptively 'the bull whip effect'.[15]

For convenience we shall examine the underlying causes of supply chain behaviour in terms of their

- quantitative dynamics; and
- qualitative dynamics.

Quantitative supply chain dynamics

Inventory in supply chains has an 'uncoupling' effect on the operations they connect, which has advantages for each operation's efficiency, but it also introduces 'elasticity' into the chain which limits its effectiveness. This is because of the errors and distortions which are introduced to decision making in the chain. Not that the managers of each individual operation are acting irrationally. On the contrary, it is a rational desire by the operations in the supply chain to manage their production rates and inventory levels sensibly. To demonstrate this, examine the production rate and stock levels for the supply chain shown in Figure 4.9. This is a four-stage supply chain where an original equipment manufacturer (OEM) is served by three tiers of suppliers. The demand from the OEM's market has been running at a rate of 100 items per period, but in period 2 demand reduces to 95 items per period. All stages in the supply chain work on the principle that they will keep in stock one period's demand. This is a simplification but not a gross one. Many operations gear their inventory levels to their demand rate. The column headed 'stock' for each level of supply shows the starting stock at the beginning of the period and the finished stock at the end of the period. At the beginning of period 2 the OEM has 100 units in stock (that being the rate of demand up to period 2). Demand in period 2 is 95 and so the OEM knows that it would need to produce sufficient items to finish up at the end of the period with 95 in stock (this being the new demand rate). To do this it only need manufacture 90 items; this, together with five items taken out of the starting stock, will supply demand and leave a finished stock of 95 items. The beginning of period 3 finds the OEM with 95 items in stock. Demand is also 95 items and therefore its production rate to maintain a stock level of 95 will be 95 items per period. The OEM now operates at a steady rate of producing 95 items per period. Note, however, that a change in demand of only five items has produced a fluctuation of 10 items in the OEM's production rate.

Now carry the same logic through to the first-tier supplier. At the beginning of period 2 the second-tier supplier has 100 items in stock. The demand which it has to supply in period 2 is derived from the production rate of the OEM. This has dropped down to 90 in period 2. The first-tier supplier, therefore, has to produce sufficient to supply the demand of 90 items (or the equivalent) and leave one month's demand (now 90 items)

Figure 4.9 **Fluctuations of production levels along supply chain in response to small change in end-customer demand**

Period	Third-tier supplier		Second-tier supplier		First-tier supplier		Original equipment mfg.		Demand
	Prodn.	Stock	Prodn.	Stock	Prodn.	Stock	Prodn.	Stock	
1	100	100 100	100	100 100	100	100 100	100	100 100	100
2	20	100 60	60	100 80	80	100 90	90	100 95	95
3	180	60 120	120	80 100	100	90 95	95	95 95	95
4	60	120 90	90	100 95	95	95 95	95	95 95	95
5	100	90 95	95	95 95	95	95 95	95	95 95	95
6	95	95 95	95	95 95	95	95 95	95	95 95	95

Orders   Orders   Orders   Orders

[3]   [2]   [1]   OEM   Market

Items   Items   Items   Items

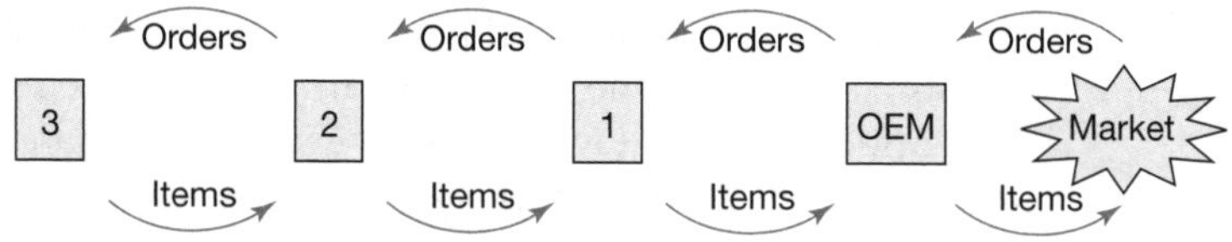

(Note – all operations keep one period's inventory)

Source: Slack, N., Chambers, S. and Johnston, R. (2007) *Operations Management*, 5th edn. Harlow: Financial Times Prentice Hall. Reproduced with permission from Pearson Education Ltd.

as its finished stock. A production rate of 80 items per month will achieve this. It will therefore start period 3 with an opening stock of 90 items but the demand from the OEM has now risen to 95 items. It therefore has to produce sufficient to fulfil this demand of 95 items and leave 95 items in stock. To do this it must produce 100 items in period 3, and so on. Note again, however, that the fluctuation has been even higher than that in the OEM's production rate, decreasing to 80 items per period, increasing to 100 items per period, and then achieving a steady rate of 95 items per period.

This logic can be extended right back to the third-tier supplier. If you do this you will notice that the further back up the supply chain an operation is placed the more drastic are the fluctuations caused by the relatively small change in demand from the final customer. In this simple case the decision of how much to produce each month was governed by the following relationship:

Total available for sale in any period = Total required in the same period
Starting stock + production rate = Demand + closing stock
Starting stock + production rate = 2 × demand (because closing stock must be equal to demand)

Production rate = 2 × demand − starting stock

Qualitative supply chain dynamics

Supply fluctuation is also caused because at each link in the chain, there is the potential for misunderstandings and misinterpretation both of what each operation wants and how each is seen to be performing. It may not be able to make the logical association between how it should be serving its customers and, therefore, what demands it should be placing on its own suppliers. There are three logical links which have to be correctly executed:

● understanding customer's needs correctly;

● understanding the association between what an operation's customers need and therefore what its suppliers should be providing;

● ensuring that suppliers really do understand what is required.

These three links represent the information specifying market requirements flowing back up the supply chain. For the chain to be working effectively it is also necessary to ensure that the performance of each part of the chain is monitored. Again, any operation in the chain can identify three logical links which must be in place for effective supply chain performance monitoring.

● Suppliers understand how they are performing.

● The operation itself understands the association between its supplier's performance and its ability to serve its own customers.

● The operation is correctly interpreting its customer's view of its own performance.

A model that identifies four types of mismatch that occur between and within each stage in a supply chain is shown in Figure 4.10 and Table 4.2; it pursues the analysis from the viewpoint of operation B – the focal operation. It highlights some obvious questions with which an operation can assess its own supply chain performance. Here it is enough to point out that, even in the simple three-stage supply chain shown in Figure 4.10, there are ample opportunities for gaps to exist between market requirements and operations performance within the chain.

Supply chain instability

Put together both qualitative and quantitative dynamics and it is easy to understand why supply chains are rarely stable. Figure 4.11 (see page 128) shows the fluctuations in orders over time in a typical consumer goods chain. One can see that fluctuations in order levels (the demand at the preceding operation) increase in scale and unpredictability the further back an operation is in the chain, with relatively small changes in consumer demand causing wild and disruptive activity swings at the first-tier, and subsequent suppliers. Four major causes of this type of supply chain behaviour can be identified.[16]

● **Demand forecast updating** – this was the cause of the dynamics which were illustrated in Figure 4.9. The order sent to the previous operation in the chain is a function of the demand it receives from its own customers, plus the amount needed to replenish its inventory levels. In effect, the view an operation holds about future demand is being changed every decision period.

● **Order batching** – every time a supermarket sells a box of breakfast cereal it does not order a replacement from its suppliers. Rather it waits until it needs to order

Figure 4.10 Potential perception mismatches in supply chains

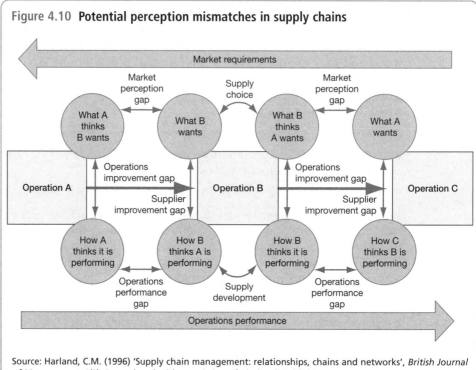

Source: Harland, C.M. (1996) 'Supply chain management: relationships, chains and networks', *British Journal of Management*, 1(7). Reproduced with permission of Blackwell Publishing.

a sufficient quantity to make the order administration, transport, etc. economic. This batching effect may be exaggerated further when many customers batch their orders simultaneously.

● **Price fluctuation** – businesses often use the price mechanism in the short term to increase sales. The result of price promotions is that customers place orders for quantities of goods that do not correspond to their immediate needs, inducing distortions into the supply chain. Promotions have been called the 'dumbest marketing ploy ever' in a now famous Fortune magazine article.[17]

● **Rationing and shortage gaming** – this cause of supply chain distortion occurs when a supplier rations supplies to its customers. If the customers are aware this is happening, it is in their interests to place a larger order in the hope that they will still get what they need, even after the order has been rationed down.

Network management

Operations spend most of their supply chain effort in trying to overcome the worst effects of supply chain dynamics. While the first step in doing this is clearly to understand the nature of these dynamics, there are several, more proactive, actions which operations take. These include: coordination activities, differentiation activities and reconfiguration activities.

Table 4.2 **Understanding the qualitative dynamics of supply chains**

Gaps	Definition	What it indicates	Questions to ask
Supply choice	The association between what an operation believes its customer wants and what it believes it needs from it supplier	The significance of a supply relationship for competitive success	What are the key competitive factors for our customers? Which of these rely on our supplier's performance?
Supply development	The association between how an operation views its own performance and how it views the performance of its suppliers	The effectiveness of a supplier relationship on competitive success	What have been our competitive successes and failures? To what extent were our competitive successes and failures the result of supplier performance?
The supplier improvement gap	The gap between our view of our own requirements and our view of our supplier's performance	Prioritisation for supplier development	What do we need from our suppliers? What are we getting from our suppliers? What are the main gaps?
The market perception gap	The gap between what we believe we need from our suppliers and what they think we need	The perceived differences in requirements between customers and suppliers	Can we be sure that our assumptions concerning our customer's needs and priorities are correct? Can we be sure that our suppliers have the correct assumptions regarding our needs and priorities?
The operations performance gap	The gap between how we see our suppliers' performance and how they see their own performance	The differences in perception of operations performance between customers and suppliers (objective performance could be different from both)	Can we be sure that our customers see our performance in the same way that we do? Can we be sure that our suppliers judge their own performance in the same way that we do?
The operations improvement gap	The gap between our perception of what our customers want and our perception of our own performance	The differences between an internal perception of performance and an internal perception of customers' requirements	Even assuming our perception of customers' needs and their view of our performance are correct, are we meeting our customers' requirements?

Coordination

Efforts to coordinate supply chain activity have been described as falling into three categories, as illustrated in Table 4.3.[18]

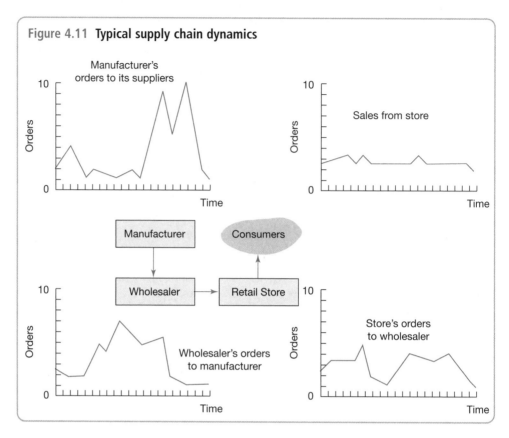

Figure 4.11 **Typical supply chain dynamics**

- *Information sharing* – demand information, not just from immediate customers, is transmitted up the chain so that all the operations can monitor true demand, free of the normal distortions. Information regarding supply problems, or shortages, may also be transmitted down the line so that downstream customers can modify their schedules and sales plans accordingly.

- *Channel alignment* – this is the adjustment of scheduling, material movements, pricing and other sales strategies, and stock levels to bring them into line with each other.

- *Operational efficiency* – each operation in the chain can reduce the complexity of its operations, reduce costs and increase throughput time. The cumulative effect of these individual activities is to simplify throughput in the whole chain.

Differentiation – matching supply network strategy to market requirements

Supply networks should differentiate between different market requirements. Supply chains, just like operations, need to ask, 'How do we compete?'. If the answer turns out to be, 'We compete in different ways in different parts of the market', then the supply chains serving those markets need to be organised in different ways. If a supply chain is organised in a standardised manner, notwithstanding the different market needs it is serving, it results in the supply distortions described previously. Here we will take an approach articulated by Marshall Fisher of Wharton Business School,[19] who makes a connection between different types of market requirements and different objectives for operations resources.

Table 4.3 **Coordinating mechanisms for reducing supply chain dynamic instability**

Causes of supply chain instability	Supply chain coordination activities		
	Information sharing	Channel alignment	Operational efficiency
Demand forecast update	Understanding system dynamics Use of point-of-sale (POS) data Electronic data interchange (EDI) Internet Computer-assisted ordering (CAO)	Vendor-managed inventory (VMI) Discount for information sharing Consumer direct	Lead-time reduction Echelon-based inventory control
Order batching	EDI Internet ordering	Discount for truck-load assortment Delivery appointments Consolidation Logistics outsourcing	Reduction in fixed cost of ordering by EDI or electronic commerce CAO
Price fluctuations		Continuous replenishment programme (CPR) Everyday low cost (EDLC)	Everyday low price (EDLP) Activity-based costing (ABC)
Shortage gaming	Sharing sales, capacity and inventory data	Allocation based on past sales	

Source: Adapted from Lee, H.L. *et al.* (1997) 'The bullwhip effect in supply chains', *MIT Sloan Management Review,* Spring. Copyright © 1997 by Massachusetts Institute of Technology, all rights reserved. Reproduced by permission.

Different market requirements

Operations producing one set of products and services may still be serving markets with different needs. For example, Volvo Heavy Truck Corporation selling spare parts, found itself with a combination of poor service levels at the same time as its inventory levels were growing at an unacceptable rate. Market analysis revealed that spare parts were being used in two very different situations. Scheduled maintenance was predictable, with spare parts ordered well ahead of time. Emergency repairs, however, needed instant availability and were far more difficult to predict. The fact that the parts are identical is irrelevant, they are serving two different markets with different characteristics. It is a simple idea and it applies in many industries. Chocolate manufacturers have their stable lines but also produce 'media related' specials which may last only a matter of months. Garment manufacturers produce classics, which change little over the years, as well as fashions that last only one season.

Different resource objectives

The design and management of supply chains involves attempting to satisfy two broad objectives – speed and cost. Speed means being responsive to customer demand within the chain. Its virtue lies in the ability it gives the chain to keep customer service high even under conditions of fluctuating or unpredictable demand. Speed can also keep costs down. Fast throughput in the supply chain means that products do not hang around in stock and, therefore, the chain consumes little working capital. Other contributors to keeping costs down include keeping the processes, especially manufacturing processes, well utilised.

Achieving fit between market requirements and supply chain resource policies

Professor Marshall Fisher's advice to companies reviewing their own supply chain policies is, first, to determine whether their products are functional or innovative, second, to decide whether their supply chain is efficient or responsive, and third, to plot the position of the nature of their demand and their supply chain priorities on a matrix similar to that shown in Figure 4.12.

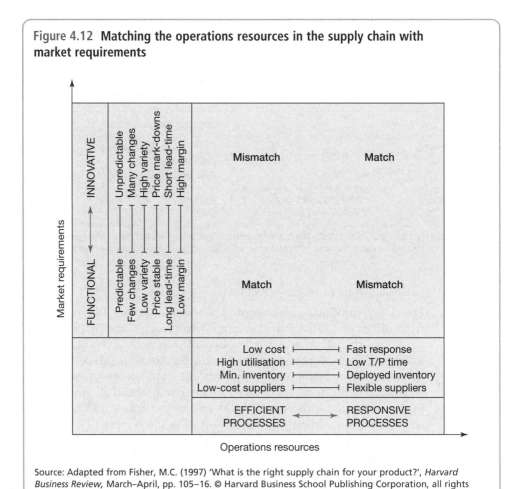

Figure 4.12 Matching the operations resources in the supply chain with market requirements

Reconfiguration

The most fundamental approach to managing network behaviour is to reconfigure the network so as to change the scope of the activities performed in each operation and the nature of the relationships between them. This could mean changing the trading relationships between operations in the network, or merging the activities currently performed in two or more separate operations into a single operation, or bypassing a stage in a current supply network. When one or more operations are bypassed in a supply chain the rather clumsy term 'disintermediation' is used. This need not mean that those bypassed operations become totally redundant; it just means that for some final customers they are not used. So, for example, when internet retailers started selling goods to consumers through their web sites, it 'disintermediated' retail stores. Yet, retail stores still exist, indeed the internet has become an alternative channel for providing service to customers.

Disintermediation is becoming a particularly significant issue because of the potential of technology to bypass traditional elements in supply chains. For example, originally corporate banks serving large business clients borrowed money on the capital markets at one rate of interest and lent it to their corporate clients at a higher rate of interest. This 'spread' between the two interest rates was how they earned their revenue. Other services which may have been provided to clients were used to justify, or even increase, this spread. Now large corporations have direct access to those same capital markets, partly because information technology makes it easy for them to do so. Corporate banking now makes its revenue by guiding and facilitating this process, advising clients on the best way to exploit capital markets. Corporate banks charge fees for these services. Disintermediation has caused the whole business model of corporate banking to change.

Supply chain vulnerability

One of the consequences of more efficient supply networks has been that companies need to take seriously the possibility of supply chain disruption. Supply networks have to cope with disruptions such as late deliveries, quality problems, incorrect information and so on. Yet, far more dramatic events can also cause disruption. For example, Land Rover (a division of the Ford Motor Company) had subcontracted the manufacture of its Discovery chassis to a single supplier that had become insolvent and was now in the hands of the receivers. The receivers were demanding an up-front payment of around £60 million to continue supply, arguing that they were legally obliged to recover as much money as possible on behalf of creditors. The outsourcing has made the supply networks more vulnerable, but there are also other factors which have increased vulnerability. Global sourcing means that parts are shipped around the world on their journey through the supply chain. Micro chips manufactured in Taiwan could be assembled to printed circuit boards in Shanghai which are then finally assembled into a computer in Ireland. Perhaps most significantly there tends to be far less inventory in supply chains that could buffer interruptions to supply.

> 'Potentially the risk of disruption has increased dramatically as the result of a too-narrow focus on supply chain efficiency at the expense of effectiveness. Unless management recognizes the challenge and acts upon it, the implications for us all could be chilling.'[20]

These 'chilling' effects can arise as a result of disruptions such as natural disasters, terrorist incidents, industrial or direct action such as strikes and protests, accidents such as fire in a vital component supplier's plant, and so on. Of course, many of these disruptions have always been present in business. It is the increased vulnerability of supply networks that has made many companies place more emphasis on understanding supply risks.

SUMMARY ANSWERS TO KEY QUESTIONS

What is supply network strategy?

A supply network is an interconnection of organisations which relate to each other through upstream and downstream linkages between the different processes and activities that produce value in the form of products and services to the ultimate consumer. Supply network strategy is the strategic direction of an organisation's relationships with suppliers, customers, suppliers' suppliers, customers' customers, etc. It includes understanding the supply network context, determining supply network relationships, understanding the dynamics of the supply network.

What are the arguments for and against outsourcing?

Deciding on the extent of vertical integration means that an operation draws the boundaries of its organisation in terms of the direction of integration, the extent, or span, of integration, and the balance between its vertically integrated stages. In doing so, an organisation is primarily trying to leverage the advantages of coordination, and cost reduction, as well as trying to secure product and process learning. However, the disadvantages of vertical integration can be significant. The internal monopoly effect is often held to inhibit improvement. In addition, vertical integration is said to limit economies of scale, reduce flexibility, insulate a firm from innovation, and be distracting from what should be the core activities of the firm.

What are the arguments for and against using traditional market relationships with suppliers?

At the opposite extreme from vertical integration is the use of market trading to buy in products and services. Because in most organisations a substantial part of costs are expended on bought-in products and services, this is an important issue. The advantages are largely concerned with overcoming the disadvantages of vertical integration. Primarily, that it gives an operation the flexibility to seek out the best deal in terms of cost innovation etc. However, the uncertainties, risks and, above all, transaction costs associated with pure market trading may also be significant.

How do partnership relationships seek to gain the 'best of both worlds'?

Long-term partnerships with a relatively small number of strategic partners have been put forward as a way of maintaining the coordination and low transaction cost effects of vertical integration, while at the same time avoiding the internal monopoly effect on operations improvement. The major problem with partnerships, however, is the difficulty of maintaining the attitudes and activities which bolster the high degree of trust which is necessary for them to work effectively.

Are there 'natural' dynamic behaviours which supply networks exhibit?

Yes. Because supply networks are interrelationships of independent operations, the way in which each operation relates to the others in the network provides an opportunity for supply network distortions. These distortions can be considered in both a quantitative and a qualitative sense. Quantitative distortions are caused by the necessity to manage the inventories between operations in the supply network. This can lead to short-term imbalance between supply and demand, the overall effect of which is to amplify the level of activity fluctuations back up the supply chain. So, relatively small changes in ultimate demand can cause very large changes in the output levels of operations upstream in the supply chain. Qualitative distortions can occur through misperceptions in the way market requirements are transmitted up a supply chain and the way in which operations performance is viewed down the supply chain. It can also be caused by mismatches between what is perceived as required by customers and suppliers and the performance which is perceived as being given to customers.

In what ways do companies try to change the nature of the supply network of which they are a part?

Operations attempt to overcome the worst effects of distortions in the supply chain, usually by one of three methods, coordination, differentiation and reconfiguration. Coordination attempts to line up the activities of operations in a supply chain through information sharing, channel alignment and changes in operational efficiency. Differentiation involves adopting different supply chain management strategies for different types of market. Reconfiguration involves changing the scope and shape of a supply chain. This may mean attempting to merge or reorder the activities in a supply chain, so as to reduce complexity or response times in the network. Increasingly, technology is having the effect of disintermediating operations in supply chains.

Further reading

Barney, J.B. (1999) 'How a firm's capabilities affect its boundary decisions', *Sloan Management Review*, Spring.

Brandenburger, A.M. and Nalebuff, B.J. (1996) *Co-opetition*. New York: Doubleday.

Caplan, S. and Sawhney, M. (2000) 'E-hubs: the new B2B market places', *Harvard Business Review*, May–June.

Child, J. and Faulkner, D. (1998) *Strategies of Co-operation: Managing Alliances, Networks and Joint Ventures*. Oxford: Oxford University Press.

Cohen, S. and Roussel, J. (2004) *Strategic Supply Chain: The Five Disciplines for Top Performance*. McGraw-Hill.

Evans, P. and Wurster, T.S. (2000) *Blown to Bits: How the New Economics of Information Transforms Strategy*. Boston, MA: Harvard Business School Press.

Farrington, B. and Lysons, K. (2005) *Purchasing and Supply Chain Management*, 7th edn. Harlow, UK: Financial Times Prentice Hall.

Harvard Business School (2006) *Harvard Business Review on Supply Chain Management*. Boston, MA: Harvard Business School Press.

Jarillo, J.C. (1993) *Strategic Networks: Creating the Borderless Organisation*. Oxford: Butterworth Heinemann.

Lorange, P. (1996) 'Interactive strategies – alliances and partnerships', *Long Range Planning*, 2(4).

Sinha, I. (2000) 'Cost transparency: the net's real threat to prices and brands', *Harvard Business Review*, March–April.

Notes on the chapter

1 Christopher, M. (2005) *Logistics and Supply Chain Management*, 3rd edn. Harlow, UK: Financial Times Prentice Hall.

2 Source: *Sunday Times* (2006) 'How British is that car?', 21 May.

3 Brandenburger, A.M. and Nalebuff, B.J. (1996) *Co-opetition*. New York: Doubleday.

4 Minahan, T. (2003) 'Global sourcing: what you need to know to make it work', CIO.com, 11 August.

5 Source: company website, www.levistrauss.com/responsibility/conduct/guide-lines

6 For example, see Ford, D.L. (1998) *Managing Business Relationships*. New York: John Wiley & Sons.

7 Sources: Mamet, D. (2007) *Bambi vs. Godzilla: On the Nature, Purpose, and Practice of the Movie Business*. New York: Pantheon Books. *The Entertainment Economy* (1998). London: Penguin Books.

8 Hayes, R. and Wheelwright, S.C. (1984) *Restoring our Competitive Edge: Competing Through Manufacturing*. New York: John Wiley & Sons.

9 von Hippel, E. (1988) *The Sources of Innovation*. New York: Oxford University Press.

10 Magaziner, I.C. and Patinkin, M. (1989) 'Fast heat: how Korea won the microwave war', *Harvard Business Review*, January–February.

11 Parkhe, A. (1993) 'Strategic alliance structuring: a game theoretic and transaction cost examination of interfirm co-operation', *Academy of Management Journal*, Vol. 36, pp. 794–829.

12 Child, J. and Faulkner, D. (1998) *Strategies of Co-operation: Managing Alliances, Networks and Joint Ventures*. Oxford: Oxford University Press.

13 Lane, C. and Backmann, R. (eds) (1998) *Trust Within and Between Organisations*. Oxford: Oxford University Press.

14 Forrester, J.W. (1961) *Industrial Dynamics*. Boston, MA: MIT Press.

15 Lee, H.L., Padmanabhan, V. and Wang, S. (1997) 'The bullwhip effect in supply chains', *Sloan Management Review*, Spring.

16 Ibid.

17 Sellers, P. (1992) 'The dumbest marketing ploy', *Fortune*, 126(5), pp. 88–93.

18 Lee, H.L. *et al.* (1977) op. cit.

19 Fisher, M.L. (1997) 'What is the right supply chain for your product?', *Harvard Business Review*, March–April, pp. 105–16.

20 Christopher, M. (2002) 'Business is failing to manage supply chain vulnerability', *Odyssey*, Issue 16.

Process technology strategy

Introduction

Technology has a profound impact on all operations. Yet, despite a widespread acceptance of its significance, strategic analysis too often treats it as a 'black box' fit only for technical experts. However, all operations need to understand the analytical dimensions for identifying the technical, managerial and 'operations strategy' characteristics of technology (Figure 5.1). This is an essential prerequisite for deciding 'what' technological options to explore. They need to clarify exactly 'why' the investments in process technology investments can give strategic advantage, and explore 'how' managers can make such investments work in practice; that is, how can they ensure that their investments are implemented so as not to waste the potential of the process technology? The risks associated with implementation are particularly important given the number of high-profile failures and claims of waste that seem to go hand-in-hand with such investments.

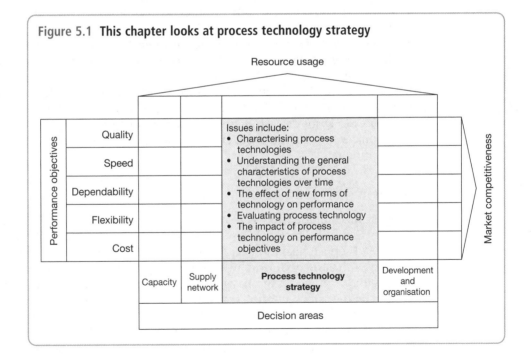

Figure 5.1 **This chapter looks at process technology strategy**

KEY QUESTIONS

- *What is 'process' technology strategy?*
- *What are suitable dimensions for characterising process technology?*
- *How do market volume and variety influence process technology?*
- *How can process technology be evaluated strategically?*

What is process technology strategy?

Although the word 'technology' is frequently used in managerial conversation, what does this term actually mean? We employ a generic definition for technology similar to that used as a corporate slogan by white goods manufacturer, Zanussi. In its advertisements Zanussi talks about its products being the result of *the appliance of science*. In this chapter we shall be examining how process technologies add value in the creation of products and services. Therefore, combining the Zanussi slogan with our transformation process view of operations, we can say that, *process technology is the 'appliance of science to any operations process'*. Note the 'process' in this definition. In this chapter we shall focus upon *process* technology as distinct from *product or service* technology. In manufacturing operations, it is a relatively simple matter to separate the two. For example, the product technology of a computer is embodied in its hardware and software. But the process technology that manufactured the computer is the technology that assembled all the different components. In service operations it can be far more difficult to distinguish process from product/service technology. For example, theme parks like Disney World use flight simulator technologies in some of their rides. These are large rooms mounted on a moveable hydraulic platform that, when combined with wide-screen projection, gives a realistic experience of, say, space flight. But is it product/service or process technology? It clearly processes Disney's customers, yet, the technology is also part of the product – the customers' experience. Product/service and process technologies are, in effect, the same thing.

Direct or indirect process technology

A common misapprehension is that the term 'process technology' describes only technology that acts directly on resource inputs to their operations. Yet, both manufacturing and service operations are increasingly reliant upon less 'direct' forms of technology. Infrastructural and information technologies that help control and coordinate direct processes are having a major impact on operations. In mass services like retailing, stock control systems link specific customer requirements into complex supply chains. Intelligent yield planning and pricing systems provide airlines with the cornerstone of their competitive strategies. Many professional service firms (consultants, accountants, engineers, etc.) utilise information databases in order to retain knowledge and experience. But the distinction between direct and indirect process technology is not always clear. For example, the 'direct' functional capabilities of an insurance company's IT system will define the types of product that the firm can offer. Yet, the same IT system's 'indirect' capability to forecast demand, schedule call centre staff to meet demand and issue billing details will be of equal importance.

Material, information and customer processing

In Chapter 1 we distinguished between operations that predominantly processed materials, information or customers. Process technologies can be similarly classified Table 5.1 shows some common process technologies of each type. Note that some of these technologies may have secondary, though important, elements in other categories. For example, many material processing technologies used in manufacturing, may also be processing information relating to the physical dimensions, or some other property, of what is being processed. A machine, while processing materials, may also be deciding whether tooling needs changing, whether to slow the rate of processing because of rising temperature, noting small variations in physical dimensions to plot on process control charts, and so on. In effect an important aspect of the technology's capability is to integrate materials and information processing. Similarly, internet-based technologies used by online retailers may be handling specific order information but are also integrating this information with characteristics of your previous orders, in order to suggest further purchases. Sometimes technologies integrate across all three types of technology. The systems used at the check-in gate of airports is integrating the processing of airline passengers (customers), details of their flight, destination and seating preference (information) and the number and nature of their items of luggage (materials).

Table 5.1 Some process technologies classified by their primary inputs

Material processing technologies	Information processing technologies	Customer processing technologies
Flexible manufacturing systems (FMS)	Optical character recognition machines	Surgical equipment
Weaving machines	Management information systems	Milking machines
Baking ovens	Global positioning systems	Medical diagnostic equipment
Automatic vending machines	Search engines on the internet	Body scanners
Container handling equipment	Online financial information systems	Aircraft
Trucks	Telecommunication technologies	Mass rapid transport (MRT) systems
Automated guided vehicles (AGVs)	Archive storage systems	Renal dialysis systems
Automatic warehouse facilities		Cinema digital projection
Low-temperature warehouses		Computer games
		Theme park rides

Process technology strategy

We define process technology strategy as *'the set of decisions that define the strategic role that direct and indirect process technology can play in the overall operations strategy of the organisation and sets out the general characteristics that help to evaluate alternative technologies'*.

Operations managers cannot avoid involvement with process technologies. They work with them on a day-by-day basis and should also be able to articulate how technology can improve operational effectiveness. Other functional areas will, of course, also be involved; Engineering/technical, Accountancy and Human Resources. Yet, it is operations that must act as 'impresario' for other functional areas' contributions, and who is likely to take responsibility for implementation.

And to carry out their 'impresario role', operations should have a grasp of the technical nature of process technologies. This does not necessarily mean that operations managers need to be experts in engineering, computing, biology, electronics, or whatever is the core science behind the technology, but they need to know enough about the technology to be comfortable in evaluating technical information, and be able to ask relevant questions of the technical experts. These questions include the following:

- What does the technology do which is different from other similar technologies?
- How does it do it?
- What constraint does using the technology place on the operation?
- What skills will be required from the operations staff in order to install, operate and maintain the technology?
- What capacity does each unit of technology have?
- What is the expected useful lifetime of the technology?

Process technology should reflect volume and variety

Although process technologies vary between different types of operation, there are some underlying characteristics that can be used to distinguish between them. These characteristics are strongly related to volume and variety, with different process technologies appropriate for different parts of the volume–variety continuum. High variety–low volume processes generally require process technology that is *general purpose,* because it can perform the wide range of processing activities that high variety demands. High volume–low variety processes can use technology that is more *dedicated* to its narrower range of processing requirements. Within the spectrum from general purpose to dedicated process technologies three characteristics in particular tend to vary with volume and variety. The first is the extent to which the process technology carries out activities or makes decisions for itself, that is, its degree of 'automation'. The second is the capacity of the technology to process work, that is, its 'scale' or 'scaleability'. The third is the extent to which it is integrated with other technologies; that is, its degree of 'coupling' or 'connectivity'. We shall look at each of these characteristics.

Scale/scalability – the capacity of each unit of technology

Scale is an important issue in almost all process technologies and is closely related to the discussion in Chapter 3 dealing with capacity strategy. Here we delve inside 'capacity' to explore how individual units of process technology go to make up the overall capacity of an operation. For example, consider a small regional airline serving just one main route between two cities. It has an overall capacity of 2,000 seats per day in either direction on its route. This capacity is 'defined' by its two 200-seater aircraft making five return journeys each day between the two cities. An alternative plan would be to replace its two identical 200-seat aircraft with one 250-seater and one 150-seater. This gives the company more flexibility in how it can meet varying demand levels throughout the day. It also may give more options in how its aircraft are deployed should it take on another route and buy additional aircraft. Of course, costs will be affected by the company's mix of aircraft. Generally, at full utilisation larger aircraft offer superior cost performance per passenger mile than smaller aircraft. The important point here is that by adopting units of process technology (aircraft) with different scale characteristics, the airline could significantly affect its operation's performance. Figure 5.2 notes some of the factors that influence the scale of process technology, including the following considerations.

What is the capital cost of the technology? Broadly speaking, the larger the unit of technology the more is its capital cost but the less its capital cost per unit of capacity. Similarly, the costs of installing and supporting the technology are likely to be lower per unit of output. Likewise, operating (as opposed to capital) costs per unit are often lower on larger machines, the fixed costs of operating the plant being spread over a higher volume.

Can the process technology match demand over time? As discussed in Chapter 3, there is a traditional trade-off between large increments of capacity exploiting economies of scale but potentially resulting in a mismatch between capacity and demand, and smaller increments of capacity with a closer match between capacity and demand but fewer economies of scale. The same argument clearly applies to the units of process technology that make up that capacity. Also, larger increments of capacity (and therefore large units of process technology) are difficult to stream on and off if demand is uncertain or dynamic. Small units of process technology with the same or similar processing costs as larger pieces of equipment would reduce the potential risks of investing in the process technology. This is why efficient but smaller-scale technologies are being developed in many industries. Even in industries where received wisdom has always been that large scale is economic (i.e. steel and electricity generation), smaller, more flexible operations are increasingly amongst the most profitable.

How vulnerable is the operation? Building an operation around a single large machine introduces greater exposure to the risk of failure. Suppose that the choice is between setting up a mail sorting operation with ten smaller or one very large machine. If there is a single machine failure, then the operation with ten machines is more robust, as 90 per cent of the mail can still be sorted. In the large-scale machine operation – no mail can be sorted.

What scope exists for exploiting new technological developments? Many forms of process technology are advancing at a rapid rate. This poses a threat to the useful life of large units of technology. If an operation commits substantial investment to a few large pieces of equipment, it changes them only infrequently and the opportunities for trying out new ideas are somewhat limited. Having a broader range of different technological options (albeit each of a smaller scale) makes it easier to take advantage of new developments – providing the operation can cope with potential inconsistencies.

From 'scale' to 'scalability'

Information processing technologies are an important exception to some of the issues discussed above. Information is transmitted far more easily between units of technology than either materials or customers. Information technology also has the capability of overcoming traditional links between volume and variety. Both of these factors mean that information technology processes can be linked relatively easily to combine their total processing capacity. Because of this, in many new technologies, the dynamic capacity challenges relate less to absolute scale and more to scalability. By scalability we mean the ability to shift to a different level of useful capacity quickly, cost-effectively and flexibly. Yet, one of the key challenges for information processing technology is still to judge how much computing capacity is required. This is especially true if the process technology is customer facing and in a dynamic marketplace (such as e-commerce) where demand uncertainty and variability are common. As many business-to-consumer internet-based businesses have discovered, too little capacity means that the technology (web-site server, etc.) can quickly become swamped and lead to extreme customer dissatisfaction. (It is worth reflecting at this point on your own experience of trying to connect to and use a very busy web site.) Conversely, too much technology means excess invested capital to service too few customers. There are a number of critical drivers underpinning scalability; these are also included in Figure 5.2.

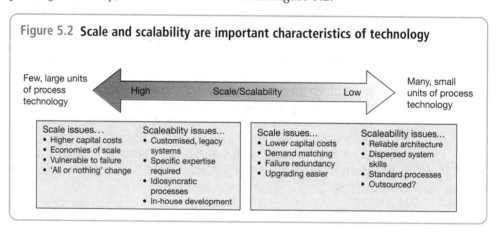

Figure 5.2 Scale and scalability are important characteristics of technology

The system architecture. Upgrading the functionality (what it can do) of an IT system is usually a matter of evolution rather than revolution. Because such technology changes quickly it is frequently being upgraded. Sometimes totally separate and only partially connected systems are installed alongside existing ones. So, because of upgrading, some systems finish up with patched and inconsistent system architectures. This does not mean that they are in themselves inefficient. However, it does make them difficult to scale up because they do not fit conveniently with other units of technology. Thus the underlying consistency and stability of an IT platform's architecture is an important determinant of its scalability. Also, a more stable platform often will have support staff who have developed a greater depth of expertise.

Underlying process standardisation. Often linked to stable system architectures are standardised processes. If the IT is stable, one of the possible reasons for changing a process is removed. On the other hand, processes which have been adapted to match system changes over time can become hugely idiosyncratic. So, a combination of processes which have developed independently of each other and 'legacy' IT systems (outdated but expensive to replace) can make scaling such operations difficult. It is partly because of these issues that many organisations have adopted 'off-the-shelf' internal business process management systems such as enterprise resource planning (ERP). Indeed, many adopters of ERP systems have chosen to change their business processes to match the IT rather than the other way around.

Degree of automation/'analytical content' – what can each unit of technology do?

No technology (as yet) operates continually, totally and completely in isolation, without ever needing some degree of human intervention. The degree of human intervention varies from almost continual (the driver's control over a bus) to the very occasional (an engineer's control in an automated pharmaceutical plant). This relative balance between human and technological effort is usually referred to as its capital intensity or degree of automation of the technology. Early applications of automation to material transformation processes revolved around relatively simple and regularly repeated tasks because technology is 'dumber' than humans; it cannot match people in many delicate tasks or those requiring complex (and especially intuitive) thought processes. But low automation often means higher direct costs, a requirement for control skills and human creativity. Whereas automated technology can repeat tasks endlessly and is capable of repeating these tasks with precision, speed and power. Figure 5.3 includes some of these factors

What degree of support is required? In many cases there have not been overall savings associated with automation, especially if a complex system requires regular and expensive maintenance. It is common for a shift towards greater capital intensity to necessitate the employment (either directly or contractually) of more engineers, programmers, etc. who normally come with a much higher price tag than the direct labour that was replaced.

How flexible is the process? If customer requirements change, how easy will it be to modify the technology? Can it cope with either new product possibilities or major volume shifts? Labour-intensive technologies can usually be changed more readily by controlling them in a different way. Capital-intensive technologies may have designed rigidities.

How dependable is the process? Although highly automated technology might require fewer people and have greater capability, it can be less robust than a combination of basic technology and less fragile than humans. Making changes to the technology can become longer and more difficult, subtle changes to input resources can have a huge impact, and so on. Tried and tested technology may appear to offer fewer differentiated benefits but it is often more robust.

From 'automation' to 'analytical content'

Again, information processing technologies are, to some extent, an exception. Even when considering automation of the most sophisticated forms of material and customer processing technology there is usually an underlying strategic choice to be made about the balance between people and technology. The choice is often between emphasising the power, speed and general physical abilities of automation against the flexible, intuitive and analytical abilities of human beings. However, an increasing number of purely information transformation processes are entirely automated (including most processing technology in the financial services sector, for instance). We need a different metric to differentiate between different information processing technologies which are 100 per cent 'automated', or very close to it.

Consider the range of new information-based technologies. Sophisticated data management and decision-making systems are being used to enhance existing processes.

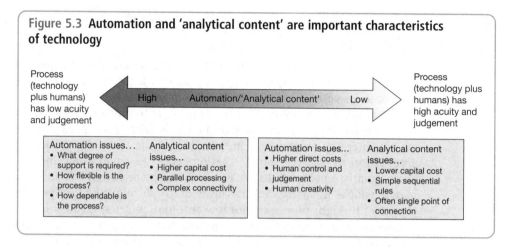

Figure 5.3 Automation and 'analytical content' are important characteristics of technology

These might include adding automatic measurement and process control to manufacturing technology or the use of expert systems to help authorise financial transactions. For example, American Express has its 'Authorizer's Assistant' system to help authorise transactions. This form of automation is very different from, say, that used to read bar-codes in a retail outlet. Both of them process information, but the former tackles far greater underlying task complexity. The characterising dimension for technology that can cope with the increasingly complex tasks is the degree of analytical resource or analytical content that the system can bring to bear on a task. Once again there are a number of different drivers that influence the analytical content of the technology (see Figure 5.3). These include the amount of parallel processing required and the level of customer interaction.

The amount of parallel processing required. One of the real operational attractions of IT is that it can transform sequential tasks into ones that can be carried out in parallel. This parallel processing could be in a complex multinational design process, such as that used by Ford for its global product development platform or more simply in IT 'work-flow' applications for compiling an insurance policy. In order to do this, and regardless of the precise tasks, the IT requires internal scheduling and data management protocols that are inherently more analytical than those employed in a straightforward sequential process.

The level of customer interaction. The greater the degree of customer interaction, often the greater the information 'richness' that must be input, processed and output. This can be directly related to the underlying task complexity with which the technology has to cope. Although using the keypad on your telephone to order cinema seats with a credit card is a valuable automated and interactive service, such a system is really only a virtual vending machine. The system has a finite (and relatively small) number of options (just like the limited range of snack foods in a vending machine). The analytical content of the system, such as checking seat availability and verifying the credit card, is relatively low (using the vending machine analogy again, it is like checking if a particular candy bar has run out and then verifying that coins are correct).

Degree of coupling/connectivity – how much is joined together?

Process technologies are increasingly coupled together. Many newer advanced manufacturing technologies derive their competitive cost and quality advantages from the 'coupling' or integration of activities that were previously separated. Coupling could consist of physical links between pieces of equipment, for example a robot removing a piece of plastic from an injection moulder and locating it in a machine tool for finishing, or it could mean merging the formerly managerial tasks of scheduling and controlling these machines with their physical activities to form a synchronised whole. Many of the direct benefits associated with increased coupling echo those described with respect to automation and scale (see Figure 5.4). For example, the integration of separate processes often involves high capital costs; increasing coupling removes much of the fragmentation caused by physical or organisational separation (what is called 'straight through processing' in financial services); closer coupling can lead to a greater degree of synchronisation thereby reducing work-in-process and costs; and closer integration can increase exposure (with positive and negative effects) if there is a failure at any stage.

From 'coupling' to 'connectivity'

Coupling in information processing technology once meant physically 'hard wiring' together disparate process elements and, as a result, was economically viable only at higher volumes and lacked the flexibility to cope with very high variety. However, more recently information processing has moved towards platform independence, allowing communication between computing devices regardless of their specification, and increasingly organisational boundaries. For example, supermarkets have dramatically altered the way they manage their buying process. Connected IT systems allow many suppliers access to a common data portal that gives real-time information about how products are selling in all stores. Such systems enable the supply companies to modify their production schedules in order to meet demand more precisely and ensure fewer stock-outs. Here the defining technological characteristic associated with platform independence is not coupling in the classic sense of integration, but rather a greater degree of connectivity. Two key drivers have allowed 'connectivity' to develop at such a phenomenal rate (see Figure 5.4).

Hardware development. Client/server systems have, for the past decade, been seen as the future of computing. These systems were initially promoted as a less costly replacement for mainframe technology. Yet, their real advantage has been their ability to permit the separation of the user interface, the processing application and data sources. This has encouraged the development of interconnection technology, including software protocols and connection technology (such as bandwidth enhancement).

Software development. Arguably, the distinguishing feature of the development of the World Wide Web has been the adoption of a universal browser interface, which has considerably expanded the potential for connectivity. The protocol known as HTML (HyperText Mark-up Language) tells any web browser the layout and functionality of any web page. Other developments, such as the equally platform-independent Java programming language (an object-oriented language developed by Sun Microsystems), can enhance content interaction and give more attractive web pages, but also allow for greater functional interconnectivity.

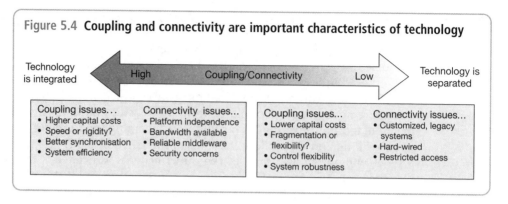

Figure 5.4 **Coupling and connectivity are important characteristics of technology**

The issues connected with connectivity are similar to those concerned with scalability and analytical content. Low connectivity is often associated with idiosyncratically designed, bespoke and 'legacy' IT systems. Often such systems come with restricted opportunities for the access which is a prerequisite to connectivity. High-connectivity technologies, on the other hand, are usually based on the platform independence discussed above and have the bandwidth capacity to enable rich communications. Sometimes, however, their very openness and easy access can give security concerns. Much new technology, although offering wonderful levels of connectivity creates new opportunities for fraud, 'denial of service' attacks, and so on.

Example **Will computers eventually do everything?[1]**

When the IBM computer 'Deep Blue' beat the world chess champion, Gary Kasparov, it reinforced an image that had been around in popular culture for years – that computers will eventually take over from human beings, either benignly in order to make our lives easier, or more worryingly, in some Terminator-type struggle for dominance. Even within the more mundane world of business, there is an underlying assumption that the limits to advances in process technology are governed by the limits to computing power, and the limits to computing power will take only a combination of time, money and effort to overcome. And a combination of sheer computing power and clever algorithms has now mastered most games enough to beat mere humans. But computers cannot, and probably will never be able to, perform certain tasks. Some problems are inherently non-computable. It can be mathematically proven that some tasks cannot be solved by computer, such as figuring out whether it is possible to cover an infinitely large plane with a given set of different tiles. This is not because computers are not powerful enough as such, it is just that a computer's logic cannot tackle such problems. Another class of problems which are puzzling to computers are those known as 'intractable' problems. For example, working out whether there is a guaranteed winning strategy for an arbitrary chess position cannot be solved, even with parallel processing, in less than many trillions of years. Another category of tasks which puzzles computers are known as 'NP-complete' problems. Working out the shortest route around several cities or putting together a typical school timetable are examples of this kind of problem. Perhaps the most problematic types of task are those that require creativity and/or intuition. Although computers can bring much needed discipline to such problems, they still need the human touch. Just as significant, computers cannot hold a decent conversation, and as customers we still feel more secure dealing with human beings, at least some of the time.

The product–process matrix

All three of these technology dimensions are strongly related. For example, the larger the unit of capacity, the more likely it is to be capital rather than labour intensive; this gives more opportunity for high coupling between its various parts. Conversely, small-scale technologies, combined with highly skilled staff, tend to be more flexible than large-scale, capital-intensive, closely coupled systems. As a result, these systems can cope with a high degree of product variety or service customisation ('boutique' strategy consulting firms are an example of this). Conversely, where flexibility is of little importance (with standardised, low-cost products such as industrial fastenings, or a mass transaction service such as letter sorting) but achieving dependable high volumes and low unit costs is critical, these inflexible systems come into their own. In IT-rich technologies, scalability generally depends upon connectivity (hence the emphasis upon standardisation in systems architecture and underlying operating processes). The analytical functionality that is so central to complex task automation normally requires different applications and data sources, so the greater the connectivity, the greater the analytical power, and so on. Remember though, although the three dimensions of process technology do often go together in this way, they do not always match perfectly.

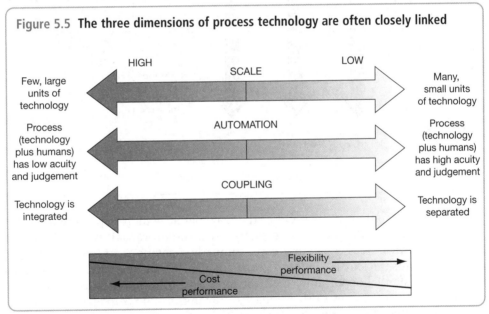

Figure 5.5 The three dimensions of process technology are often closely linked

Generally the characteristics of process technology affect cost and flexibility as shown in Figure 5.5. Several authors have also made a further link to the volume and variety requirements of the market. The logic goes something like this. Companies serving high-volume, and therefore usually low-variety, markets usually have a competitive position which values low prices, therefore low-cost operations are important, therefore process technologies need to be large, automated and integrated. Conversely, low-volume, high-variety operations need the flexibility that comes with small-scale, loosely coupled technologies with significant human intervention. This idea is incorporated in the product–process matrix, which was first described by Professors Robert Hayes and Stephen Wheelwright (both of Harvard Business

School). Although they used it to link the volume and variety requirements of the market with process design in general, here we use it to draw a link between volume and variety on the one hand and the three dimensions of process technology on the other. This is shown in Figure 5.6. The relationship between the volume/variety and process technology dimensions suggests that there is a 'natural' diagonal fit and that deviating from the 'diagonal' will, therefore, have predictable consequences for the operation.

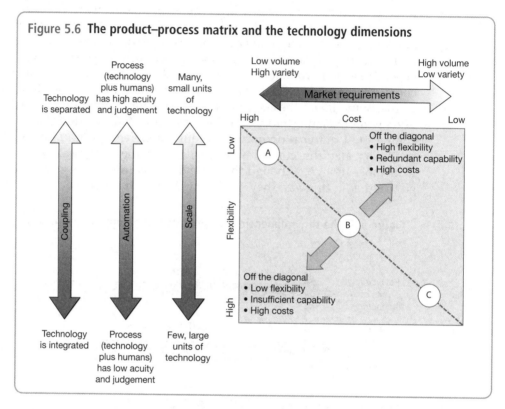

Figure 5.6 **The product–process matrix and the technology dimensions**

Operations to the right of the diagonal have more capability to deal with their requisite variety than is necessary. Such surplus capability will normally be associated with excess operating costs. Similarly, operations to the left of the diagonal have insufficient flexibility to cope with their requisite variety. This may result in substantial opportunity costs (being unable to fulfil orders economically), not to mention the competitive impact of having insufficient capability. Remember, though, that the matrix cannot prescribe the 'correct' process technology. It can, however, give a general idea of how an operation's process technology profile will need to be adapted as its market context changes.

Moving down the diagonal

Operations will change their position in the matrix. For example, a 'home-made' luxury ice-cream product, selling a few litres in a farm shop, might begin life by being manufactured in a farmer's own kitchen using domestic equipment (position A in Figure 5.6). Growth in sales (and health and safety legislation) would necessitate investment in a small production facility, although, because of the different varieties, the production unit will still need some flexibility (position B in Figure 5.6). Ultimately, if projected demand for some flavours and sizes reaches mass-market levels, major continuous-flow process investment will be necessary (position C in Figure 5.6). Equally, at this stage the product might become attractive to a large established manufacturer because the volume and variety of demand would match its existing integrated production facilities.

The natural trajectory of movement 'down' the product/process matrix can be observed in many different operational contexts. Many financial service firms, for instance, have been able to make major reductions in their back-office operations by reducing clerical and administrative staffing and cost levels through investment in large-scale, integrated, automated process technology. The example 'Voucher processing in retail banking' illustrates this.

Example | **Voucher processing in retail banking**

Although, throughout the financial services sector, volumes of paper-based transactions employing vouchers, such as cheques, are declining in absolute terms, the total volumes remain substantial. As a result, there remain substantial costs associated with the 'clearing' process (receiving paper transactions, checking data, updating accounts, transporting paper to other financial institutions). During most of the last 30 or 40 years banks in most developed countries have been merging and therefore getting larger. Simultaneously, they have attempted to standardise products and procedures within their own operations. Generally this has led to a lower variety of distinct activities being carried out in higher volume across a bank's network of operations. This is illustrated by the move from position 1 to 2 in Figure 5.7. At one time every branch had its own 'desktop' voucher processing technology, and customer service staff would have to spend a proportion of every day operating this system. Performing identical activities in a fragmented manner across hundreds or thousands of separate operations resulted in each individual back-office operation at each branch operating well below economic capacity levels. In the past 10 years, most banking businesses have reconfigured their technology to use a small number of large, automated voucher processing centres with high-volume, integrated processing lines, where optical character recognition technology reads thousands of cheques per minute and processes all the requisite data. This is shown as the move from 2 to 3 in Figure 5.7.

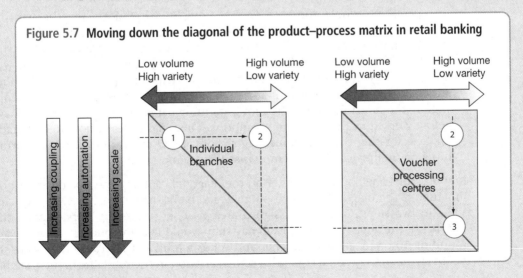

Figure 5.7 **Moving down the diagonal of the product–process matrix in retail banking**

Moving on the diagonal has its challenges

We can use the above example on how retail banking process technology has developed in retail banking to illustrate some general points about how operations change their position on the product/process matrix:

● A traditional branch dealt with nearly all the variety (services, products, etc.) that the bank offered, but equally dealt with relatively small volumes. While the branch network operated as a series of autonomous units, therefore, the small-scale, labour-intensive and stand-alone process technology appeared to be completely appropriate.

● When one begins to consider the entirety of the branch network, the absolute level of variety does not change, however, the total volume is far greater. This suggests that there was perhaps too much flexibility in the network as a whole and that there was substantial scope for simplification and redesign that might exploit larger-scale (lower unit cost) technology. Interestingly, one of the most significant challenges associated with the transition to stage 3 in Figure 5.7 was developing the (now critical) integrating systems that allowed relatively small volumes of vouchers to be moved from branch to centre and back again.

● After establishing their Voucher Processing Centres (VPC) networks (often overcoming a number of innovative technology implementation difficulties), many banks have substantially reduced the transaction unit costs associated with voucher processing. There is recognition that such systems are less flexible than before and more vulnerable to failure (as discussed earlier in this chapter). However, the risk was felt to be more than justified by the cost savings.

● Moving to a position on the diagonal towards the bottom of the matrix often requires a greater degree of standardisation and control in associated operations. In banking, for example, while voucher processing was performed at branches, small variation in procedure could be tolerated and even small errors rectified relatively easily. When vouchers were shipped to regional VPCs, branch procedures had to be totally standardised and any errors made by the branch could cause major disruption in the high-volume environment of the VPCs.

● An operation's whole approach to managing its technology, together with its organisational culture, will usually have to change as an operation's position on the diagonal changes. Many banks encountered unexpected problems when they moved over to large VPCs. Some of these were the result of having to cope with unfamiliar new technology. Most banks had anticipated that. What they had not anticipated was the change in managerial approach that was required. The people staffing the new VPCs were often long-standing bank employees. They had never before worked in high-volume operations. They had to learn how to be 'factory managers' rather than 'bank managers'. Some retail banks called their operations function 'manufacturing' to emphasise this point.

Moving from one point to another on the diagonal cannot always be done without moving off the diagonal at some point. Some banks made the move to very large VPCs in two steps. First, they assigned area voucher processing responsibility to a number of the larger branches. Each day they would take in vouchers from the surrounding 10 or 15 smaller branches and act as a mini VPC. Because they were still relatively small they could cope with some variation in their satellite branches' operating procedures. Unfortunately, when the move to full regional VPCs was made this tolerance of variety in branch operating procedures proved problematic for the (now inflexible) technology until all branches could be brought into using standardised procedures.

Market pressures on the flexibility/cost trade-off?

The traditional flexibility/cost trade-off inherent in the scale, automation and integration dimensions of process technology (and the product–process matrix for that matter) is coming under increasing pressure from more challenging and demanding markets. In many sectors, increased market fragmentation and the demand for more customisation is reducing absolute volumes of any one type of product or service. Simultaneously, shortening product/service life cycles can mean periodic step changes in the requirements placed on an operation and its process technology. This can severely reduce the potential for applying large-scale and relatively inflexible, though traditionally low-cost, technologies. Yet, at the same time, there is increasing pressure to compete on cost which is driving ongoing reductions in direct labour and placing increased emphasis on automation. In fact, for many traditionally labour-intensive sectors such as the banking industry referred to earlier, absence of sufficient technological investment (and the corresponding presence of 'too many staff') has a significant impact on analyst and shareholder confidence and therefore share price. Both these pressures are placing conventional process technology solutions under strain (see Figure 5.8). Of course, this competitive challenge has proved to be simply too much for many operations but, interestingly, many of those that have survived and prospered have not abandoned technology in their operations strategies. Rather, many operations have more fully embraced process technology, albeit in new IT-rich forms. Indeed, it is increasingly difficult to overstate the impact that information technology is having upon organisational life. There is almost no sphere of operations where computing technology in one form or another has not had a substantial impact

Process technology trends

So, markets seem to be demanding both greater flexibility and lower costs simultaneously from process technology. To the traditional mindset, which we illustrated in Figure 5.6, this seems to be difficult, bordering on impossible. Yet, remember our discussions on trade-offs between performance objectives back in Chapter 2. There we saw the development and improvement of operations (including process technology) as being a process of overcoming trade-offs. Now we must include developments in information technology, especially their effect of shifting traditional balances and trade-offs. In effect we have argued that emerging scalability, analytical content and connectivity characteristics have enabled process technologies to enhance their flexibility while still retaining reasonable efficiency and vice versa. In other words, these trends in process technology are having the net effect of overcoming some of the traditional trade-offs inherent within the dimensions of process technology. This has, for some industries, changed the nature of the product–process matrix, which we discussed earlier. Figure 5.9 shows how three separate but connected ideas have come together.

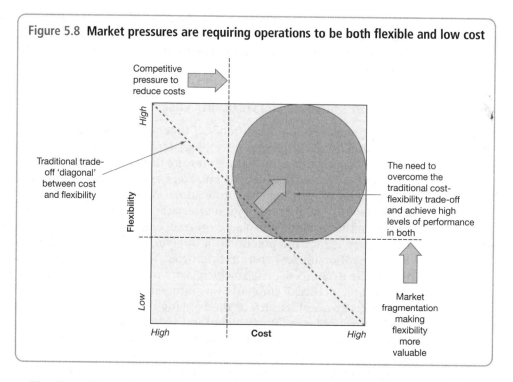

Figure 5.8 **Market pressures are requiring operations to be both flexible and low cost**

- The three dimensions of process technology – scale, automation and coupling – are related to the volume/variety characteristics of the market. In traditional process technologies, especially those with relatively little IT element, large, automated and tightly coupled technologies were capable of processing at low cost but had relatively little flexibility. This made them suitable for high-volume, low-variety processes. If process requirements were for high variety but low volume, process technology is likely to consist of smaller separated units with relatively little automation.

- Trends in the development of each dimension of process technology, especially those related to their increasing richness in information processing, are overcoming some of the traditional trade-offs within each dimension. In particular, technology with high levels of scaleability can give the advantages of flexible, small-scale technology and yet be quickly expanded if demand warranted it. Similarly, even high-volume information processing technology can still display the relatively high analytical content at one time reserved for more manual processes. Finally, technology with high connectivity can integrate processes without the rigidity once associated with high coupling.

- Market trends are themselves calling for simultaneously high performance in both cost and flexibility. No longer is it acceptable to suffer high costs if flexibility is demanded by the market, nor operations rigidity if costs need to be kept low. As far as market requirements are concerned, the ideal area in the traditional product–process matrix is one that delivers both low cost and high flexibility.

This is why information processing technology has had such an impact in so many industries. In effect, it has partially overcome some of the traditional trade-offs in choosing process technology. But note the words 'partially' and 'some'. There are

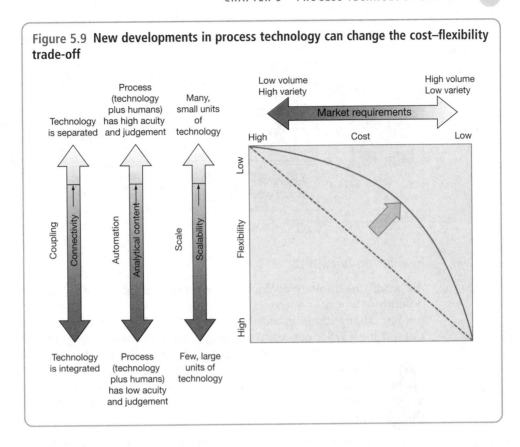

Figure 5.9 **New developments in process technology can change the cost–flexibility trade-off**

still trade-offs within technology choice even if they are not as obvious as they were once. Moreover, information processing and computing power has undoubtedly had a major impact on almost all technologies but there are still limits to what computers can do.

Evaluating process technology

Evaluating process technology quite literally means determining its value or worth. It involves exploring, understanding and describing the strategic consequences of adopting alternatives. Although there can be no 'all-purpose' list of attributes to be evaluated, indeed the precise nature of the attributes to be included in any evaluation should depend on the nature of the technology itself, it is useful to consider three generic classes of evaluation criteria:

- the feasibility of the process technology; that is the degree of difficulty in adopting it, and the investment of time, effort and money that will be needed;
- the acceptability of the process technology; that is how much it takes a firm towards its strategic objectives, or the return the firm gets for choosing it;
- the vulnerability associated with the process technology; that is the extent to which the firm is exposed if things go wrong, the risk that is run by choosing the technology (see Figure 5.10).

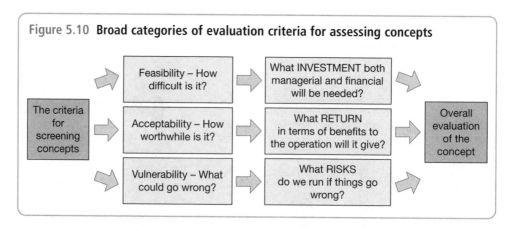

Figure 5.10 **Broad categories of evaluation criteria for assessing concepts**

Evaluating feasibility

All process technology decisions have resource implications – even the decision to do nothing liberates resources that would otherwise be used. In this context we are not just talking about financial resources which, although critical, are no help if, say, the technical skills necessary to design and implement a technology are not available. Therefore, if the resources required to implement technology are greater than those that are either available or can be obtained, the technology is not feasible. So evaluating the feasibility of an option means finding out how the various types of resource that the option might need match up to what is available. Four broad questions are applicable.

What technical or human skills are required to implement the technology? Every process technology will need a set of skills to be present within the organisation, so that it can be successfully implemented. If new technology is very similar to that existing in the organisation, it is likely that the necessary skills will already be present. If, however, the technology is completely novel, it is necessary to identify the required skills and to match these against those existing in the organisation.

What 'quantity' or 'amount' of resources is required to implement the technology? Determining the quantity of resources (people, facilities, space, time, etc.) required for the implementation of a technology is an important stage in assessing feasibility because it is time dependent. Rarely will a lack of sufficient, say, process engineers, rule out a particular process technology, but it could restrict when it is adopted. So, a firm may deliberately choose to delay some of its process technology decisions because it knows that its current commitments will not allow it. In order to assess this type of feasibility a company may compare the aggregate workload associated with its implementation over time with its existing capacity.

What are the funding or cash requirements? The previous two questions can be difficult to answer in a meaningful way but this does not diminish their significance. However, in any real investment evaluation one 'feasibility' factor will inevitably come to dominate all other considerations – do we have enough money? Because of this significance we will spend a little more time reviewing some of the many approaches that have been developed to aid managers in their analysis of cash flow and funding requirements over the lifetime of an investment project.

Can the operation cope with the degree of change in resource requirements? Even if all these resource requirements can quite feasibly be obtained individually by the organisation, the degree of change in the total resource position of the company might itself be regarded as infeasible. Consider, for instance, a bespoke manufacturer of road-racing bicycles being encouraged to leverage its reputation for high quality into the 'top end' of the mass cycle market (i.e. much higher volumes). This would require the firm to make substantial investment in automated tube welding equipment. The firm is confident that it will be able to obtain all the different categories of resource required for the project. It believes that it can recruit the appropriate expertise in sufficient quantity from the labour market. Furthermore, it believes that it could fund the project until it broke even. Yet, in the final analysis, the company regards the investment as unfeasible. It decides that absorbing such a radical new process technology in a relatively short time frame would put too great a strain on its own capacity for self-organisation. Thus, sometimes it is not the absolute level but rather the rate of change in resource requirements that renders a project unfeasible.

Assessing financial requirements

In most process technology decisions the most important feasibility question is, 'How much financial investment will the technology require, and can we afford it?' At its simplest, this could mean simply examining the one-off cost of the purchase price of the technology. Usually, though, an examination of the effect of the cash requirements on the whole organisation is necessary. If so, it is often necessary to simulate the organisation's cash flow over a period of time. Computing the total inflow of cash over time as it occurs, and subtracting from it the total outflow of cash as it occurs, leaves the net funding requirement for the option. For example, Figure 5.11 shows the net cash inflows likely to be earned if a proposed technology is adopted and the cash outflows associated with its purchase and implementation. The resulting cash requirements show that a maximum funding requirement of €1,050,000 occurs within the first eight months of the project, and diminishes only slowly for two years. After that, the project enjoys a large net inflow of cash. Of course, this analysis does not include the effects of interest payments on cash borrowed. When it is decided how the cash is to be raised (i.e. borrowed from a bank or private investor, raised from the equity markets) this can be included.

Evaluating acceptability

Evaluating acceptability can be done from many technical and managerial perspectives. Here we limit our discussion to cover the financial perspective on evaluation and the 'market requirements' and 'operations resource' perspectives. Figure 5.12 summarises the different elements of our analysis.

Acceptability in financial terms

Financial evaluation involves predicting and analysing the financial costs to which an option would commit the organisation, and the financial benefits that might accrue from acquiring the process technology. However, 'cost' is not always a straightforward concept. An accountant has a different view of 'cost' to that of an economist. The accountant's view is that the cost of something is whatever you had

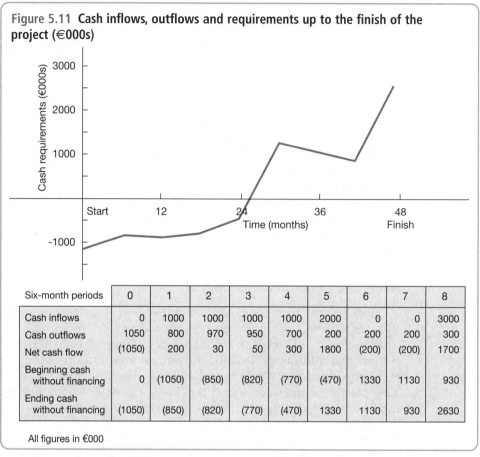

Figure 5.11 Cash inflows, outflows and requirements up to the finish of the project (€000s)

Six-month periods	0	1	2	3	4	5	6	7	8
Cash inflows	0	1000	1000	1000	1000	2000	0	0	3000
Cash outflows	1050	800	970	950	700	200	200	200	300
Net cash flow	(1050)	200	30	50	300	1800	(200)	(200)	1700
Beginning cash without financing	0	(1050)	(850)	(820)	(770)	(470)	1330	1130	930
Ending cash without financing	(1050)	(850)	(820)	(770)	(470)	1330	1130	930	2630

All figures in €000

to pay to acquire it originally. The economist, on the other hand, is more likely to define costs in terms of the benefits forgone by not investing elsewhere: that is, the opportunity cost of the technology. Thus, to the economist, the cost of investing in a process technology is whatever could be gained by investing an equivalent sum in the best feasible alternative investment. While opportunity costing has obvious intuitive attractions, and is particularly useful in process technology investments where alternative technologies may bring very different benefits, it does depend on what we define as the best feasible alternative use of our resources. The accountant's model of acquisition cost is at least stable – if we paid €1,000 for something, then its value is €1,000, irrespective of whatever alternative use we might dream up for the money.

The life-cycle cost

The concept of life-cycle costing is useful in process technology evaluation. It involves accounting for all costs over the life of the investment which are influenced directly by the decision. For example, suppose a company is evaluating alternative integrated warehousing systems. One system is significantly less expensive and seems at first sight to be the least costly. But what other costs should the company consider apart from the acquisition cost? Each system would require some initial development to remedy outstanding technical problems before installation. The sys-

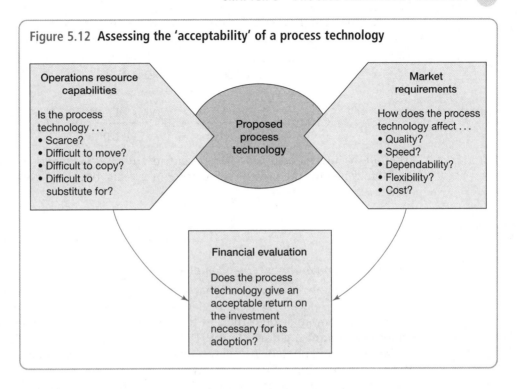

Figure 5.12 Assessing the 'acceptability' of a process technology

Operations resource capabilities

Is the process technology . . .
• Scarce?
• Difficult to move?
• Difficult to copy?
• Difficult to substitute for?

Proposed process technology

Market requirements

How does the process technology affect . . .
• Quality?
• Speed?
• Dependability?
• Flexibility?
• Cost?

Financial evaluation

Does the process technology give an acceptable return on the investment necessary for its adoption?

tems would also have to be 'debugged' before operation, but, more importantly, during its years of life the plant will incur operation and maintenance costs which will in part be determined by the original choice of system. Finally, if the company wants to look so far ahead, the disposal value of the plant could also be significant. In fact, total life-cycle costing is impossible in any absolute sense. The effects of any significant investment ripple out like waves in a pond, impinging on and influencing many other decisions. Yet, it is sensible to include more than the immediate and obvious costs involved in a decision, and a life-cycle approach proves a useful reminder of this.

The time value of money: net present value (NPV)

One of the most important questions to be answered in establishing the 'real' value of either costs or benefits is determining when they are incurred or realised. This dynamic is important because money in your hand today is worth more to you than the same money would be worth in a year's time. Conversely, paying out a sum in one year's time is preferable to paying it out now. The reason for this has to do with the opportunity cost of money. If we receive money now and invest it (in a bank account or in another project giving a positive return), then in one year's time we will have our original investment plus whatever interest has been paid for the year. Thus, to compare the alternative merits of receiving €100 now and receiving €100 in one year's time, we should compare €100 with €100 plus one year's interest. Alternatively, we can reverse the process and ask ourselves how much would have to be invested now, in order for that investment to pay €100 in one year's time. This amount (lower than €100) is called the present value of receiving €100 in one year's time.

For example, suppose current interest rates are 10 per cent per annum. The amount we would have to invest to receive €100 in one years' time is:

$$€100 \times \frac{1}{1.10} = €90.91$$

$$€100 \times \frac{1}{(1.10)} \frac{1}{(1.10)} = €100 \times \frac{1}{(1.10)^2} = €82/65$$

The rate of interest assumed (10 per cent in our case) is known as the discount rate. More generally, the present value of €x in n years' time, at a discount rate of r per cent is:

$$\frac{x}{(1 + r/100)^n}$$

Limitations of conventional financial evaluation

Conventional financial evaluation has come under criticism for its inability to include enough relevant factors to give a true picture of complex investments. Nowhere is this more evident than in the case of justifying investment in process technologies comprising a significant IT element. Here costs and benefits are uncertain, intangible and often dispersed throughout an organisation. Indeed, with all the talk about there being a 'new economy', the myriad discussions about computers removing cost (labour) from operational processes, or the impact of the creation of knowledge and information-based markets, you could be forgiven for thinking that the computer age was an unambiguously positive thing for business. Until recently, however, there has been little actual evidence that for all the IT investment that firms have made, there has been any real impact upon overall productivity.

Acceptability in terms of impact on market requirements

Extending the idea of considering all competitive benefits from an investment, we have argued elsewhere in this chapter that process technology can impact all of the generic operational performance objectives: quality, speed, dependability, flexibility and cost. The questions listed in Table 5.2 can help provide a framework for assessing the impact of any proposed investment on each of them. In order to illustrate this we have applied them to a generic analysis of the effect of process technology on the airline industry.

Although the examples in Table 5.2 were set in the airline industry, we could have done the same for any industry. The most important point to emerge from any similar analysis in any sector is that the market opportunities associated with process technology are far greater than the traditional narrow focus on cost reduction. Any sensible evaluation of process technology must include all the effects impacting on quality, speed, dependability, flexibility and cost. As we stressed in Chapter 2, the generic performance objectives are very rarely equally important for all types of operation. Their relative importance will reflect the actual and intended market position of the organisation. The implication of this for evaluating process technology is straightforward. Any evaluation must reflect the impact of process technology on each performance objective relative to their importance to achieving a particular market position. Often there will be trade-offs involved in adopting a new process technology. Reverting to our airline examples earlier, one advantage of having a fleet of mixed aircraft is the flexibility it provides to match aircraft to routes as the demand on different routes changes. Yet, different types of aircraft require different spare parts, different maintenance procedures, and different interfaces with ground technology and so on. This may add more cost and complexity to the total airline operations than is gained through the benefits of flexibility. For example, Airbus, the European airline consortium and great rival to the US aerospace giant Boeing, claims that its strategy of common cockpit and flight control systems across its range of planes saves considerable cost. Commonality in such systems allows pilots and ground crews to deal with similar systems with 120-seater to 400-seater aircraft.

Table 5.2 Evaluating the acceptability of process technology investment on market criteria

	Generic questions	*Example*
Quality	Does the process technology improve the specification of the product or service? That is, does it provide something better or different which customers value? Does the process technology reduce unwanted variability within the operation? Even if absolute specification quality is unaffected by process technology, it may contribute to conformance quality by reducing variability.	An airline investing in in-flight entertainment technology to enhance the specification of its flight services. An airline investing in maintenance equipment which keeps the performance of its aircraft and ancillary systems within very tight tolerances. This reduces the risk of failure in equipment as well as increasing the internal predictability of the airline's processes.
Speed	Does the process technology enable a faster response to customers? Does it shorten the time between a customer making a request and having it confirmed (or a product delivered etc.)? Does the process technology speed the throughput of internal processes? Even if customers do not benefit directly from faster process throughput within an operation, technology increasing 'clock speed' can benefit the operation by, for instance, reducing costs.	The check-in technology used by airlines at airport gates and lounges, in effect, allows customers' requests for seating or dietary requirements to be explored quickly and, if possible, confirmed. The technology which allows the fast loading of customers' bags and in-flight catering supplies, allows fuel to be loaded and engines to be checked, etc., all reducing the time the aircraft spends on the ground. This allows the aircraft to be used more intensively.
Dependability	Does the process technology enable products and/or services to be delivered more dependably? Although many of the causes of poor dependability may appear to be outside the control of an operation, technology may help to bring some of the factors within its control. Does the process technology enhance the dependability of processes within the operation? Again, even when customers see no direct result of more dependable technology, it can provide benefits for the operation itself.	Specialist navigation equipment installed in aircraft can allow them to land in conditions of poor visibility, thus reducing the possibility of delays due to bad weather. Customers benefit directly from such an increase in dependability. Airlines invest in advanced aircraft communications technology. Efficient communication between aircraft and control centres reduces the possibility of miscommunication, which, even when presenting no danger, can waste time and cause confusion. Indeed, an oft-cited concern of many airlines is that airports around the world do not always match their investment in communications technology – preventing maximum productivity gains from their equipment.

Table 5.2 **continued**

Flexibility	Does the process technology allow the operation to change in response to changes in customer demand? Such changes may be in either the level or nature of demand. Does the process technology allow for adjustments to the internal workings of the operations processes?	When an airline considers the mix of aircraft types to include in its fleet, it does so partly to retain sufficient flexibility to respond to such things as timetable change or unexpected demand. Some aircraft (notably the Boeing 777) permit the precise configuration of cabins and seating to be changed. While this may not happen very frequently, it offers airlines the flexibility to provide a different mix of services without having different types of aircraft.
Cost	Does the process technology process materials, information or customers more efficiently? As we mentioned previously, this is by far the most common basis for justifying new process technology, even if it is not always the most important. It is never unimportant, however. Does the process technology enable a greater effectiveness of the operations processes? Even if straightforward efficiency is unaffected, process technology can aid the deployment of the operations capabilities to increase profitability or general effectiveness.	A major driver for airlines to invest in new aircraft is the greater efficiency (€/passenger mile flown) of each new generation of aircraft that derives from the overall design of the aircraft and, most especially, the engines powering them. The 'yield management' decision support systems used by airlines enable them to maximise the revenue from flights by adjusting capacity and pricing strategies to match demand patterns.

Acceptability in terms of impact on operational resources

Using the generic performance objectives can help us to characterise the potential contribution that process technology can make to market requirements. At the same time, however, it is important to build up a picture of the contribution that process technology can make to the longer-term capability 'endowment' of the operation. We can use the dimensions described in Chapter 1 as being 'strategic' according to the resource-based view of the firm. As a reminder, these four dimensions are:

- the scarcity of resources;
- how difficult the resources are to move;
- how difficult the resources are to copy;
- how difficult the resources are to substitute for.

These four dimensions provide us with a 'first cut' mechanism for assessing the impact that a specific technological resource will have upon sustainable competitive advantage. Table 5.3 develops these four dimensions with examples.

Tangible and intangible resources

It is important to recall that in our discussion in Chapter 1 on the importance of operations resources and process we were careful to distinguish between tangible and intangible resources. Tangible resources are the actual physical assets which the company possesses. In process technology terms these will be the machines, computers, materials handling equipment, and so on, used within the operation. Intangible resources are not necessarily directly observable but nevertheless have value for the company. Things such as relationship and brand strength, supplier

Table 5.3 **The four dimensions of 'strategic' operations resources**

	Generic questions	*Example*
Scarcity	Does the technology represent any kind of first-mover advantage? In other words, how much of the developed technology (or perhaps its underlying R&D) is not possessed by competitors? Does the technology help create or exploit proprietary product/service knowledge, perhaps in the tangible form of a database?	Such resources might include bespoke production facilities in industries like petrochemicals and pharmaceuticals, where first-mover advantage often generates superior returns. Capturing customer data over time and then exploiting this information has long been a core element of airline competitive strategies – such information is extremely scarce.
Difficult to move	How much of the process technology was developed in-house? If a process technology is unique and, moreover, it was developed 'in-house', then such resources cannot easily be accessed without purchasing the firm. How many of the critical technological resources 'don't walk on legs'? In other words, highlight those resources that are more than contractually tied into the operation.	The value of resource immobility helps to explain the increased emphasis being placed upon infrastructure development in the management consulting sector – to facilitate the retention of skills, knowledge and experience. Mobility concerns in, say, the IT sector explain the emergence of more complicated contracts (constraining subsequent employment, etc.) and wage inflation for certain key staff.
Difficult to copy	How far down the 'learning curve' is the process technology? How strong is your legal protection? Patents offer some protection, even though the process is long, often expensive and may attract greater competitive risk than simply having better site security.	Experiences such as those documented in high-volume processes, like Intel and semiconductors, can create competitive performance barriers. In the competitive confectionery market, for instance, there is almost pathological secrecy associated with proprietary production processes but very little recourse to the filing of patents.
Difficult to create a substitute	What, if any, market mechanisms exist to prevent process technology simply becoming irrelevant through the introduction of a substitute?	Traditional EDI-type connections integrate supply chains but can also help to establish *de facto* standards and introduce switching costs. They can therefore prevent rivals offering substitute services.

relationships, process knowledge, and so on are all real but not always directly tangible. This concept of intangible resources is important when considering process technology. A unit of technology may not be any different physically from the technology used by competitors. However, its use may add to the company's reputation, skills, knowledge and experience. Thus, depending on how the process technology is used, the value of the intangible aspect of a process technology may be greater than its physical worth. If the usefulness of process technology also depends on the software it employs, then this also must be evaluated. Again, although software may be bought off the shelf and is therefore available to competitors, if it is deployed in imaginative and creative ways its real value can be enhanced.

Evaluating market and resource acceptability

Consider, for instance, a Windows-based data management system for a police force to help manage their crime laboratory. The lab is where samples from a range of crime scenes are tested in a large variety of different processes (DNA testing, finger-print analysis, etc.) that vary widely in their sophistication and complexity. Although speed is often of the essence in the lab, accuracy and dependability are equally critical, as is their legal requirement to store and access information over extended periods of time (for legal appeals, long-term investigations, etc.). While this operation does not have a market position as such, it still has a set of social and legal priorities which are its direct equivalent. Figure 5.13 illustrates this by adding a further line to the profile which indicates what the laboratory's performance targets are. Although the new process technology does not improve operations performance in all aspects of the crime lab's 'market' requirements, it does improve some specific areas of performance and does not appear to have any negative effects. However, it is when we turn our attention to the resource profile of the technology that the relevance for 'not for profit' operations of dimensions derived from a competitive marketplace needs to be more closely examined. Although we might see the usefulness of a unique and difficult-to-copy crime database in the 'war against crime', the positive advantage of having resources which rank highly on the RBV dimensions is not clear for an accountable public sector operation.

In other words, if a resource (like knowledge or experience) is difficult to move or copy this can contribute to sustainable advantage in a competitive marketplace. However, such characteristics can act against critical public sector objectives such as effective information transfer or even accountability over performance. In this type of application, therefore, it is necessary to see the resource characteristics as useful in a different way. So, for instance, imagine that the staff experience associated with analysing particular types of DNA evidence is crucial for the crime lab but very difficult to copy and therefore shared both within and between labs. The operations strategy response might therefore be to diminish (rather than embrace) this 'imitability' characteristic by developing systems and procedures that seek to codify (i.e. papers, technical diaries, open databases) and encourage regular sharing of experience (i.e. seminars, staff exchanges, apprenticeships).

Evaluating vulnerability

There have been some spectacular and very public failures associated with the introduction of new process technology (see the example 'Gardermoen Airport happy to come second'). Yet, presumably all of these process technology 'failures' were at one time determined to be both feasible and acceptable to the operation. Their subsequent failure highlights one further important issue to explore – vulnerability. That is, what exposure is the firm accepting if something goes wrong with the technology once the decision to invest is made?

Vulnerability because of changed resource dependencies

All process technologies depend for their effective operation on support services. Specific skills are needed if the technology is to be installed, maintained, upgraded and controlled effectively. In other words, the technology has a set of 'resource dependencies'. Changing to a different process technology often means changing

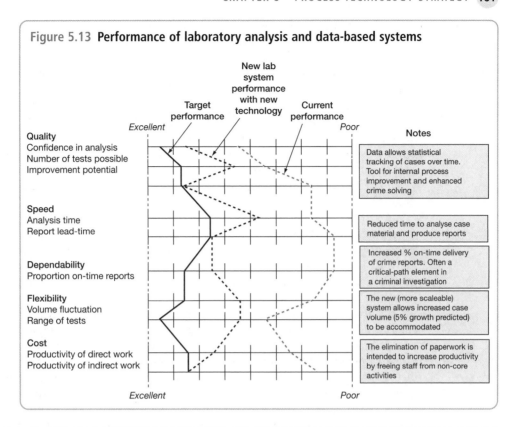

Figure 5.13 **Performance of laboratory analysis and data-based systems**

Gardermoen Airport happy to come second

In 2005 Denver International Airport (DIA) was voted 'Best Airport in North America' by the *Business Traveler Magazine*. But 10 years earlier its main claim to fame was its unpredictable baggage-handling system.

DIA had decided to be the pioneer in a new type of system where all bags would be individually handled on automatic carts or 'destination-coded vehicles'. So proud was the city, that its Mayor invited the press to witness the first run of the new automated baggage system. But it all went wrong: passengers' clothing was showered over the tracks and luggage was periodically thrown right off the belt. The baggage system continued to be a problem. Instead of the original $185 million, the eventual cost was over $300 million for only a partially operating system. The airport's opening was delayed three times and eventually a further $70 million had to be spent installing a conventional conveyor belt, and the system was finally scrapped completely in 2005.

This highly publicised failure caused Oslo's Gardermoen Airport to think twice before adopting its own new baggage-handling technology. However, Oslo learned from Denver's mistakes. Oslo's own system, the Dutch-manufactured Bagtrax system, was up to four times quicker than the conventional belt system, required less maintenance and was cheaper to operate. But unlike the, now defunct, Denver system, it was less complicated and less prone to breakdown. In effect, it allows the airport to tailor baggage delivery to requirements. A single bag could be sent to a single destination without having to start up a whole conventional belt system.

this set of resource dependencies. This may have a positive aspect. The skills, knowledge and experience necessary to implement and operate the technology can be scarce and difficult to copy and hence provide a platform for sustainable advantage. But there can also be a downside to a changed set of resources dependencies. For example, the specific skills needed to implement or operate a new process technology, because they are scarce, could become particularly valuable in the labour market. The company is vulnerable to the risk of the staff who have these skills leaving in order to leverage their value. This was a particular problem when many organisations were implementing enterprise resource planning (ERP) systems. The extensive training programmes necessary to give staff the skills to implement ERP systems shifted the 'knowledge power' to staff to the extent that it made staff retention difficult.

Issues of trust and power also influence the vulnerability created by dependence upon external organisations such as suppliers and customers. If there is a high degree of trust between a firm and its technology supplier, it can be entirely appropriate to become dependent for the installation, maintenance and upgrading of process technology upon a particular external provider. Dependence can also work the other way. Customers may ask for a particular piece of technology to be dedicated to their business. Again, this can be entirely legitimate if the operation trusts its customer to continue generating work for them over a suitable period. However, such exclusive relationships inevitably introduce vulnerabilities. For example, suppose an operation is choosing between alternative suppliers of software. One supplier seems to be particularly price competitive, very service-oriented and has developed a particularly effective leading-edge application. Unfortunately, this supplier is also smaller than the alternative suppliers. Although its products and service may be superior, it is itself more vulnerable to business pressures. If it went out of business the company would be left with unsupported infrastructure. Under these circumstances the company may decide that choosing this supplier would expose it to unacceptable levels of vulnerability.

SUMMARY ANSWERS TO KEY QUESTIONS

What is 'process' technology strategy?

Getting beyond a view of technology as a 'black box' is critical for any operations strategy. To help structure our review of technology we defined it in generic terms as the practical 'appliance of science'. Process technology is technology as applied to operational processes and is traditionally treated as separate from product/service technology. This distinction is inevitably less clear in many service operations where the product is the process. We can further classify two types of process technology. The first is that contributing 'directly' to the production of goods and services. The second type is the 'indirect' or 'infrastructure' technology that acts to support core transformation processes. Process technology strategy is the set of decisions that define the strategic role that direct and indirect process technology can play in the overall operations strategy of the organisation and sets out the general characteristics that help to evaluate alternative technologies.

What are suitable dimensions for characterising process technology?

Although generic dimensions will always fail to capture completely the rich detail of any individual piece of process technology, it is normally useful to describe scale (capacity of each technology unit), automation (what the machine can do) and coupling (how much is or can be joined together) characteristics. Although these three dimensions are unlikely to be equally relevant for all types of technology, they do offer a useful categorisation for comparing a range of process technology options.

We can modify our original dimensions (scale, automation and integration) to more accurately reflect the characteristics of IT-rich process technology. More suitable characteristics, therefore, are: scaleability, analytical content and connectivity. We argued that these new characteristics were overcoming the traditional flexibility/cost trade-off and that new process technologies were able to enhance operational flexibility while still retaining reasonable underlying efficiency and vice versa.

How do market volume and variety influence process technology?

There is often a 'natural' diagonal fit relationship between the volume/variety and process technology dimensions. For example, the larger the unit of capacity, the more likely that it is capital rather than labour intensive, which gives more opportunity for high coupling between its various parts. Where flexibility is unimportant but achieving dependable high volumes and low unit costs is critical, such inflexible systems come into their own. Conversely, small-scale technologies, combined with skilled staff, tend to be more flexible than large-scale, capital-intensive, closely coupled systems. As a result, these systems can cope with a high degree of variety.

How can process technology be evaluated strategically?

Evaluating process technology quite literally means determining its value or worth. It involves exploring, understanding and describing the strategic consequences of adopting alternatives. We outlined three possible dimensions:

1 The 'feasibility' of technology indicates the degree of difficulty in adopting it, and should assess the investment of time, effort and money that will be needed.

2 The 'acceptability' of technology is how much it takes a firm towards its strategic objectives. This includes contribution in terms of cost, quality, speed, etc. as well as the development of strategic resources. In general terms it is about establishing the return (defined in a very broad manner) the operation gets for choosing a process technology.

3 The 'vulnerability' of technology indicates the extent to which the firm is exposed if things go wrong. It is the risk that is run by choosing that specific technology.

Further reading

Bensaou, M. and Earl, M. (1998) 'The right mind-set for managing information technology', *Harvard Business Review*, September–October, pp. 119–28.

Davenport, T.H. (1993) *Process Innovation*. Boston, MA: Harvard Business School Press.

Edgerton, D. (2006) *The Shock of the Old: Technology in Global History Since 1900*. London: Profile Books

Hayes, R.H., Pisano, G.P., Upton, D.M. and Wheelwright, S.C. (2004) *Operations, Strategy, and Technology: Pursuing the Competitive Edge*. John Wiley & Sons.

McKeen, J.D. (2003) *Making IT Happen: Critical Issues in Managing Information Technology*. John Wiley & Sons Series in Information Systems.

Mills, P.K. and Moberg, D.J. (1990) 'Strategic implications of service technologies', Chapter 5 in Bowen, D.E., *et al.* (eds) *Service Management Effectiveness*. San Francisco: Jossey Bass, pp. 97–125.

Taninecz, G. (1996) 'What's the ROI?', *IW Electronics and Technology*, October, pp. 45–8.

Hayes, R.H. and Wheelwright, S.C. (1984) *Restoring our Competitive Edge*. New York: John Wiley & Sons, pp. 212–27.

Note on the chapter

1 Sources: *The Economist* (2007) 'Winning ways', 27 January; and Harel, D. (2000) *Computers Ltd: What They Really Can't Do*. Oxford: Oxford University Press.

Improvement strategy

Introduction

A large body of work has grown around how operations can be developed, enhanced and generally improved. Some of this focuses on specific techniques and prescriptions while some looks at the underlying philosophy of improvement. Of course, all of operations strategy is concerned with improving operations. Our treatment of the other 'content' decision areas in operations strategy, such as capacity, supply networks and technology, is all based on the implicit assumption that we take decisions in these areas in order to improve the operation. However, most organisations review their overall operations strategy relatively infrequently, and the final three chapters will look at the operations strategy formulation process, which presumably is done to improve overall performance. Between these times they do not expect the operation to 'freeze itself' between each major strategic review. Rather, organisations aspire to develop and improve their operations on a more routine basis. This chapter deals with the more ongoing improvement activity. We are concerned, not with strategy formulation on the grand scale, but with the more general issues of how companies can shape the routines which encourage the ongoing development of their operations (Figure 6.1).

KEY QUESTIONS

- *What are the differences between managing large 'breakthrough' improvement and managing continuous improvement?*
- *How do the needs of the market direct the ongoing development of operations processes?*
- *How can the ongoing management and control of operations be harnessed to develop their capabilities?*
- *What can operations do to deploy their capabilities into the market?*

Development and improvement

In this chapter we examine the development of operations resources and processes, that is, the way in which operations build their capabilities and by doing so improve their performance. Many authorities stress the importance of how organisations manage their development and improvement efforts. For example, '*The companies that are able to turn their . . . organisations into sources of competitive advantage are those that can harness various improvement programs . . . in the service of a broader [operations] strategy that emphasises the selection and growth of unique operating [capabilities].*'[1] But as with the previous chapter, we must accept some ambiguity as to the role of the

Figure 6.1 This chapter looks at development and organisation (operations development and improvement)

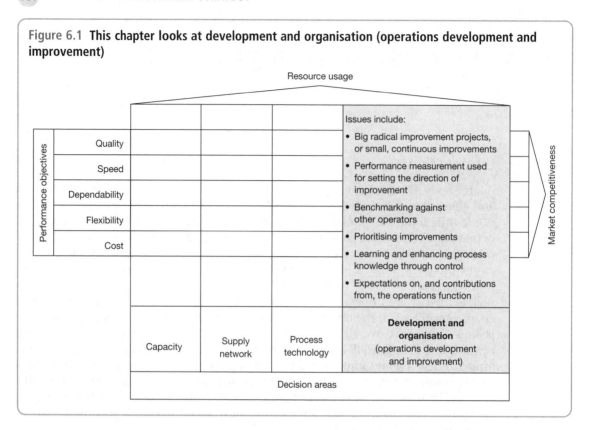

development and improvement activity within operations strategy. On one hand, it is a content decision area in the sense that there are decisions to be taken about how the operation thinks about and organises its own development. On the other hand, because we are dealing with the way in which improvement decisions are made, the topics covered in this chapter could also be considered part of the process of operations strategy formulation.

Process improvement

Most operations improvements are relatively minor ongoing changes to the operations processes. Every time a machine is adapted to facilitate faster changeover and any time a software failsafe routine is installed to prevent the mis-keyng of customer information, the operation is being improved. Sometimes, though, improvements are grander, involving major changes in capacity, supply networks, process technology and organisation. It is important therefore to apply some calibration to the degree of process improvement so that we can distinguish between different ways of treating different types of improvement. We will start by examining two particular strategies which represent different, and to some extent opposing, philosophies. These two strategies are breakthrough improvement and continuous improvement.

Breakthrough improvement

Breakthrough, or 'innovation'-based, improvement assumes that the main vehicle of improvement is major and dramatic change in the way the operation works, the total redesign of a computer-based hotel reservation system, for example. The impact of these improvements is relatively sudden, abrupt and represents a step change in practice (and hopefully performance). Such improvements are rarely inexpensive, usually calling for high investment, often disrupting the ongoing workings of the operation, and frequently involving changes in the product/service or process technology. Moreover, a frequent criticism of the breakthrough approach to improvement is that such major improvements are, in practice, difficult to realise quickly.

Continuous improvement

Continuous improvement, as the name implies, adopts an approach to improving performance which assumes more and smaller incremental improvement steps, for example simplifying the question sequence when taking a hotel reservation. This is also known as *kaizen*. While there is no guarantee that such a small step towards better performance will be followed by other steps, the whole philosophy of continuous improvement attempts to ensure that they will be. Continuous improvement is not concerned with promoting small improvements per se but it does see small improvements as having one significant advantage over large ones – they can be followed relatively painlessly by other small improvements. Thus, continuous improvement becomes embedded as the 'natural' way of working within the operation. So, in continuous improvement it is not the rate of improvement that is important, it is the momentum of improvement. It does not matter if successive improvements are small; what does matter is that every month (or week, or quarter, or whatever period is appropriate) some kind of improvement has actually taken place.

The differences between breakthrough and continuous improvement

One analogy which helps to understand the difference between breakthrough and continuous improvement is that of the sprint and the marathon. Breakthrough improvement is a series of explosive and impressive sprints. Continuous improvement, like marathon running, does not require the expertise and prowess required for sprinting; but it does require that the runner (or operations manager) keeps on going. Table 6.1 lists some of the differences between the two approaches. But, notwithstanding the fundamental differences between the two approaches, it is possible to combine the two, albeit at different times. Large and dramatic improvements can be implemented as and when they seem to promise significant improvement steps, but between such occasions the operation can continue making its quiet and less spectacular kaizen improvements.

The degree of process change

While continuous improvement implies relatively small changes to operations processes (but carried out frequently, in fact continually), breakthrough improvement implies substantially greater changes to processes. However, this dichotomy is a simplification used to highlight differences in improvement philosophy. The scale of improvement is a continuum. The scale shown in Table 6.2 characterises process change as being, in order of increasing degree of change, concerned with 'modification', 'extension', 'development' and 'pioneer' levels of change. Table 6.2 also illustrates what these degrees of process change could mean in two types of process.

Table 6.1 **Some features of breakthrough and continuous improvement (based on Imai)**[2]

	Breakthrough improvement	*Continuous improvement*
Effect	Short-term but dramatic	Long-term and long-lasting but undramatic
Pace	Big steps	Small steps
Time-frame	Intermittent and non-incremental	Continuous and incremental
Change	Abrupt and volatile	Gradual and constant
Involvement	Select a few 'champions'	Everybody
Approach	Individualism, individual ideas and efforts	Collectivism, group efforts, systems approach
Stimulus	Technological breakthroughs, new inventions, new theories	Conventional know-how and state of the art
Risks	Concentrated – 'all eggs in one basket'	Spread – many projects simultaneously
Practical requirements	Requires large investment but little effort to maintain it	Requires little investment but great effort to maintain it
Effort orientation	Technology	People
Evaluation criteria	Results for profit	Process and efforts for better results

Modifications to existing processes are relatively small changes where the nature of the activities within a process remain largely the same even if there are some minor rearrangements in the details of the sequence or arrangement of the activities within the process. At the other extreme, 'pioneer' change implies adopting radically different, or at least novel to the operation, types of change both to what is done in the process and how it is done. What we have termed extension and development lie in between these extremes. Continuous improvement is usually taken to mean degrees of process change limited to 'modification' or 'extension' changes to the process. Breakthrough improvement is usually assumed to mean what we have termed 'development' or 'pioneer' process change. For example, illustrations of business process reengineering (BPR) described in the press tend to be at this end of the scale, although some examples of BPR are relatively minor, what we have called 'extension' change. The most important issues here are, first, that the greater the degree of process change the more difficult that change is to manage successfully, and second, that many small changes need managing in a different way from few, relatively large changes.

Improvement cycles

A recurring theme in operations process development is the idea that continuous improvement is cyclical in nature – a literally never ending cycle of repeatedly questioning and adjusting the detailed workings of processes. There are many improvement cycles which attempt to provide a prescription for continuous improvement, some of them proposed by academics, others devised by consultancy firms. And although most of these cycles are not 'strategic', the concept of improvement as a cycle can be translated to mean an ongoing readjustment of strategic understandings, objectives and performance. In fact, the model of operations strategy and reconciliation between market requirements and operations resources itself implies ongoing cyclical readjustment. Market potential responds to the capabilities which the operations function is capable of deploying. Conversely, the operation adjusts its

Table 6.2 **The degree of process change can be characterised by changes in the arrangement and nature of process activities**

	Degree of process change			
	Modification	*Extension*	*Development*	*Pioneer*
Arrangement of activities (what is done)	Minor rearrangement of activities	Redesign of sequence or routing between activities	Redefinition of purpose or role activities	Novel/radical change
Nature of activities (how it is done)	No or little change to nature of activities	Minor change in nature of activities	Some change in core methodology/ technology process	Novel/radical change
Example: thin film precision coating process	New reel-change unit, allows faster changeovers	Clean-room filtering technology introduced which reduces contamination	High-energy drying allowing shorter drying path and energy savings	High-capacity machine with 'fluid electron' vacuum coating gives exceptional quality and low costs
Example: health monitoring/ diagnostics process	Patient completes pre-check-up questionnaire and brings it to regular check-up	Nurse performs initial checks at clinic, including new combined heart and respiration testing	Internet-based pre-visit routine allows test programme to be customised for each patient plus after-visit monitoring of patient health routine	Total remote testing/monitoring service using 'body shirts' which download via internet

resources and processes in response to the direction set by the company's intended market position. Also, within the operations function, operations capabilities are continually developed or evolved by learning how to use operations resources and processes more effectively. Similarly, within the marketing function, the company's intended market position may be refined and adjusted at least partly by the potential market positioning made possible because of operations capabilities.

Direct, develop and deploy

Figure 6.2 illustrates the strategic improvement cycle we shall use to structure this chapter. It employs the three 'operations strategy' elements of direct, develop and deploy described above, plus a market strategy element.

Direct. A company's intended market position is a major influence on how the operations function builds up its resources and processes. Some authorities argue that the most important feature of any improvement path is that of selecting a direction. In other words, even micro-level, employee-driven improvement efforts must reflect the intended strategic direction of the firm.

Develop. Within the operations function those resources and processes are increasingly understood and developed over time so as to establish the capabilities of the operation. Essentially this is a process of learning.

Deploy. Operations capabilities need to be leveraged into the company's markets. These capabilities, in effect, define the range of potential market positions which the company may wish to adopt. But this will depend on how effectively operations capabilities are articulated and promoted within the organisation.

Market strategy. The potential market positions which are made possible by an operation's capabilities are not always adopted. An important element in any company's market strategy is to decide which of many alternative market positions it wishes to adopt. Strictly, this lies outside the concerns of operations strategy. In this chapter we shall restrict ourselves to examining the direct, develop and deploy elements.

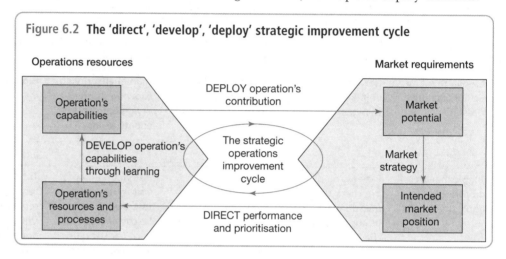

Figure 6.2 **The 'direct', 'develop', 'deploy' strategic improvement cycle**

In reality, the improvement process is never so straightforward, sequential or simple. This cyclical model is not prescriptive. Rather, it merely identifies the types of activity which together contribute to operations improvement at a strategic level. Moreover, no organisation would execute each link in the cycle in a rigorous sequential manner. The activities of directing the overall shape of the operation's resources and processes, developing their capabilities through learning, deploying the operation's contribution and deciding on market strategy, all should occur continually and simultaneously.

Setting the direction

An important element in the improvement process is the influence a company's intended market position has on the way it manages its resources and processes. In the view of many, it is the only important element. According to this view, operations improvement is a constant search for better ways of supporting the company's markets. And although the model of operations development used here (and our view of operations strategy generally) also takes into account the influence of operations capabilities on market position, the 'direction' to improvement provided by market requirements is clearly an important element. At its simplest, it involves translating the intended market position of the organisation into performance goals or targets for the operation. In fact, just as the whole improvement task can be seen as a cycle, so can each stage. In this case the cycle involves the ongoing refinement of these targets. For example, a company may decide that its customers place reasonable importance on its products being delivered on time. It, therefore, sets a target on-time delivery performance of 99.5 per cent. However, it finds that some customer requirements are so complex that manufacturing time is difficult to forecast and therefore delivery dates cannot be met. Because of this, its overall delivery performance is only 97 per cent. However, it emerges during discussions with those customers that they understand the inherent difficulty in forecasting delivery times. What is important to them is not that the original delivery date is met, but that they are given at least two weeks' notice of what the delivery date will actually be. Thus the failure of the operation's performance to match its target prompts the targets to be changed to reflect customers' real requirements more exactly. It is the cycle of setting targets and attempting to meet them that can lead to a more accurate interpretation of the real requirements of the market. In this section of the chapter we will briefly examine three approaches to managing this cycle: performance measurement systems, benchmarking, and 'importance–performance' comparisons (see Figure 6.3).

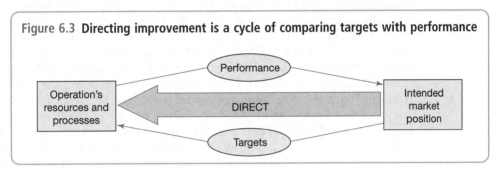

Figure 6.3 Directing improvement is a cycle of comparing targets with performance

Performance measurement

At a day-to-day level the direction of improvement will be determined partly by whether the current performance of an operation is judged to be good, bad or indifferent, so some kind of performance measurement is a prerequisite for directing improvement. Traditionally, performance measurement has been seen as a means of quantifying the efficiency and effectiveness of action.[3]

Performance measurement, as we are treating it in this chapter, concerns four generic issues:

- What factors to include as performance targets?
- Which are the most important?
- How to measure them?
- On what basis to compare actual against target performance?

What factors to include as performance targets?

In operations performance measurement there has been a steady broadening in the scope of what is measured. First, it was a matter of persuading the business that because the operations function was responsible for more than cost and productivity, it should therefore measure more than cost and productivity. For example,

'A ... major cause of companies getting into trouble with manufacturing is the tendency for many managements to accept simplistic notions in evaluating performance of their manufacturing facilities ... the general tendency in many companies is to evaluate

manufacturing primarily on the basis of cost and efficiency. There are many more criteria to judge performance'.[4]

After this, it was a matter of broadening out the scope of measurement to include external as well as internal, long-term as well as short-term, and 'soft' as well as 'hard' measures. The best-known manifestation of this trend is the 'Balanced Scorecard' approach taken by Kaplan and Norton.

The degree of aggregation of performance targets

From an operations perspective, an obvious starting point for deciding which performance targets to adopt is to use the five generic performance objectives, quality, speed, dependability, flexibility and cost. Of course, these can be broken down further into more detailed performance targets since each performance objective, as we have mentioned before, is in reality a cluster of separate aspects of performance. Conversely, they can be aggregated with composite performance targets. Broad aspects of performance such as 'customer satisfaction', 'operations agility' or 'productivity' can give a higher-level picture of both what is required by the market and what performance the operation is achieving. These broad targets may be further aggregated into even broader aims such as 'achieve market objectives' or 'achieve financial objectives', or even 'achieve overall strategic objectives'. This idea is illustrated in Figure 6.4. The more aggregated performance targets have greater strategic relevance in so much as they help to draw a picture of the overall performance of the business, although by doing so they necessarily include many influences outside those that operations strategy would normally address. The more detailed performance targets are usually monitored more closely and more often, and although they provide only a very limited view of an operation's performance, they provide in many ways a more descriptive and complete picture of what should be and what is happening within the operation. In practice, most organisations will choose to use performance targets from throughout the range.

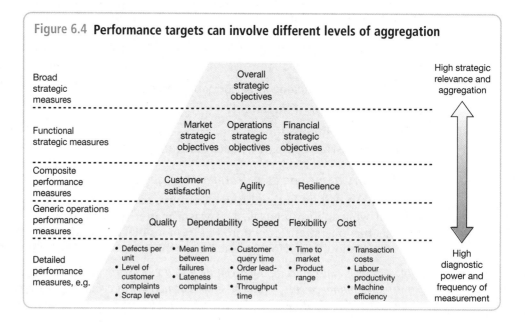

Figure 6.4 Performance targets can involve different levels of aggregation

The balanced scorecard approach

'The balanced scorecard retains traditional financial measures. But financial measures tell the story of past events, an adequate story for industrial age companies for which investments in long-term capabilities and customer relationships were not critical for success. These financial measures are inadequate, however, for guiding and evaluating the journey that information age companies must make to create future value through investment in customers, suppliers, employees, processes, technology, and innovation.'[5]

Generally operations performance measures have been broadening in their scope. It is now generally accepted that the scope of measurement should, at some level, include external as well as internal, long-term as well as short-term, and 'soft' as well as 'hard' measures. The best-known manifestation of this trend is the 'Balanced Scorecard' approach taken by Kaplan and Norton. As well as including financial measures of performance, in the same way as traditional performance measurement systems, the balanced scorecard approach, also attempts to provide the important information that is required to allow the overall strategy of an organisation to be reflected adequately in specific performance measures. In addition to financial measures of performance, it also includes more operational measures of customer satisfaction, internal processes, innovation and other improvement activities. In doing so it measures the factors behind financial performance which are seen as the key drivers of future financial success. In particular, it is argued, that a balanced range of measures enables managers to address the following questions (see Figure 6.5).

- How do we look to our shareholders (financial perspective)?
- What must we excel at (internal process perspective)?
- How do our customers see us (the customer perspective)?
- How can we continue to improve and build capabilities (the learning and growth perspective)?

The balanced scorecard attempts to bring together the elements that reflect a business' strategic position, including product or service quality measures, product and service development times, customer complaints, labour productivity, and so on. At the same time it attempts to avoid performance reporting becoming unwieldy by restricting the number of measures and focusing especially on those seen to be essential. The advantages of the approach are that it presents an overall picture of the organisation's performance in a single report, and by being comprehensive in the measures of performance it uses, encourages companies to take decisions in the interests of the whole organisation rather than suboptimising around narrow measures. Developing a balanced scorecard is a complex process and is now the subject of considerable debate. One of the key questions that have to be considered is how specific measures of performance should be designed? Inadequately designed performance measures can result in dysfunctional behaviour, so teams of managers are often used to develop a scorecard which reflects their organisation's specific needs.

Which are the most important performance targets?

One of the problems of devising a useful performance measurement system is trying to achieve some balance between having a few key measures on the one hand

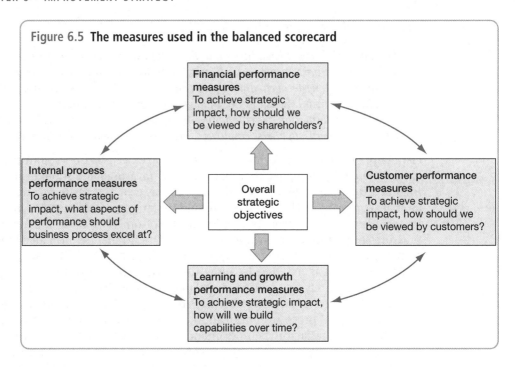

Figure 6.5 **The measures used in the balanced scorecard**

(straightforward and simple, but may not reflect the full range of organisational objectives), and, on the other, having many detailed measures (complex and difficult to manage, but capable of conveying many nuances of performance). Broadly, a compromise is reached by making sure that there is a clear link between competitive strategy, the key performance indicators (KPIs) which reflect the main performance objectives, and the bundle of detailed measures which are used to 'flesh out' each key performance indicator. Obviously, unless competitive strategy is well defined (not only in terms of what the organisation intends to do but also in terms of what the organisation will not attempt to do), it is difficult to focus on a narrow range of key performance indicators. So, for example, an international company which responds to oil exploration companies' problems during drilling by offering technical expertise and advice might interpret the five operations performance objectives as follows:

● *Quality*. Operations quality is usually measured in terms of the environmental impact during the period when advice is being given (oil spillage etc.) and the long-term stability of any solution implemented.

● *Speed*. The speed of response is measured from the time the oil exploration company decide that they need help to the time when the drilling starts safely again.

● *Dependability*. Largely a matter of keeping promises on delivering after-the-event checks and reports.

● *Flexibility*. A matter of being able to resource (sometimes several) jobs around the world simultaneously, i.e. volume flexibility.

● *Cost*. The total cost of keeping and using the resources (specialist labour and specialist equipment) to perform the emergency consultations.

The company's competitive strategy is clear. It intends to be the most responsive company at getting installations safely back to normal working, while also providing long-term effectiveness of technical solutions offered with minimum environmental impact. It is not competing on cost. The company therefore decides that speed and quality are the two performance objectives key to competitive success. This it translates into three key performance indicators (KPIs):

- the time from drilling stopping to it starting safely again;
- the long-term stability of the technical solution offered;
- the environmental impact of the technical solution offered.

From these KPIs several detailed performance measures were derived. For example, some of those which related to the first KPI (the time from drilling stopping to it starting again) were as follows:

- the time from drilling stopping to the company being formally notified that its services were needed;
- the time from formal notification to getting a team on site;
- on-site time to drilling commence time;
- time between first arrival on customer's site to getting full technical resources on site;
- etc.

How to measure performance targets?

The five performance objectives – quality, speed, dependability, flexibility and cost – are really composites of many smaller measures. For example, an operation's cost is derived from many factors which could include the purchasing efficiency of the operation, the efficiency with which it converts materials, the productivity of its staff, the ratio of direct to indirect staff, and so on. All of these factors individually give a partial view of the operation's cost performance, and many of them overlap in terms of the information they include. Each of them does give a perspective on the cost performance of an operation, however, which could be useful either to identify areas for improvement or to monitor the extent of improvement. If an organisation regards its 'cost' performance as unsatisfactory, therefore, disaggregating it into 'purchasing efficiency', 'operations efficiency', 'staff productivity', etc. might explain the root cause of the poor performance.

Table 6.3 shows some of the partial measures which can be used to judge an operation's performance.

On what basis to compare actual against target performance?

Whatever the individual measures of performance which we extract from an operation, the meaning we derive from them will depend on how we compare them against some kind of standard. So, for example, in Figure 6.6, one of the company's performance measures is delivery performance (in this case defined as the proportion of orders delivered on time, where 'on time' means on the promised day). The actual figure this month has been measured at 83 per cent. However, by itself it does not mean much. Yet, as Figure 6.6 shows, any judgement regarding performance is very dependent on the basis of comparing performance against targets.

Table 6.3 **Some typical partial measures of performance**

Performance objective	Some typical measures
Quality	Number of defects per unit
	Level of customer complaints
	Scrap level
	Warranty claims
	Mean time between failures
	Customer satisfaction score
Speed	Customer query time
	Order lead-time
	Frequency of delivery
	Actual versus theoretical throughput time
	Cycle time
Dependability	Percentage of orders delivered late
	Average lateness of orders
	Proportion of products in stock
	Mean deviation from promised arrival
	Schedule adherence
Flexibility	Time needed to develop new products/services
	Range of products/services
	Machine change – over time
	Average batch size
	Time to increase activity rate
	Average capacity/maximum capacity
	Time to change schedules
Cost	Minimum delivery time/average delivery time
	Variance against budget
	Utilisation of resources
	Labour productivity
	Added value
	Efficiency
	Cost per operation hour

An obvious basis for comparison involves using an historical standard. The graph in Figure 6.6 shows that, when compared to last year's performance of 60 per cent, this month's performance of 83 per cent is good. But there again, with an average performance last year of 60 per cent, the company is likely to have some kind of improvement goal in mind which represents what is regarded as a reasonable level of improvement. So, if the improvement goal was 95 per cent, the actual performance of 83 per cent looks decidedly poor. The company may also be concerned with how they perform against competitors' performance. If competitors are currently averaging delivery performances of around 75 per cent, the company's performance looks rather good. Finally, the more ambitious managers within the company may wish at least to try to seek perfection. Why not, they argue, use an absolute performance standard of 100 per cent delivery on time? Against this standard the company's actual 83 per cent again looks disappointing.

Benchmarking

Another very popular, although less 'day-to-day' method for senior managers to drive organisational improvement is to establish operational benchmarks. By high-

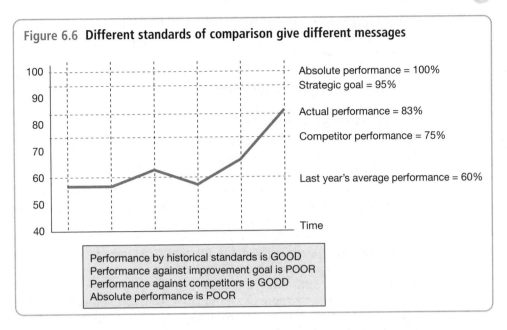

Figure 6.6 Different standards of comparison give different messages

Absolute performance = 100%
Strategic goal = 95%

Actual performance = 83%

Competitor performance = 75%

Last year's average performance = 60%

Time

Performance by historical standards is GOOD
Performance against improvement goal is POOR
Performance against competitors is GOOD
Absolute performance is POOR

lighting how key operational elements 'shape up' against 'best in class' competitors, key areas for focused improvement can be identified. Originally, the term 'benchmark' derives from land surveying where a mark, cut in the rock, would act as a reference point. In 1979 the Xerox Corporation, the document and copying company, used the term 'competitive benchmarking' to describe a process 'used by the manufacturing function to revitalise itself by comparing the features, assemblies and components of its products with those of competitors'.[6]

Since that time, the term benchmarking has widened its meaning in a number of ways.[7]

- It is no longer confined only to manufacturing organisations but is commonly used in services such as hospitals and banks.
- It is no longer practised only by experts and consultants but can involve all staff in the organisation.
- The term 'competitive' has been widened to mean more than just the direct comparison with competitors. It is now taken to mean benchmarking to gain competitive advantage (perhaps by comparison with, and learning from, non-competitive organisations).

Types of benchmarking

There are many different types of benchmarking (which are not necessarily mutually exclusive), some of which are listed below.

- Non-competitive benchmarking is benchmarking against external organisations which do not compete directly in the same markets.
- Competitive benchmarking is a comparison directly between competitors in the same, or similar, markets.
- Performance benchmarking is a comparison between the levels of achieved performance in different operations. For example, an operation might compare its

own performance in terms of some or all of our performance objectives – quality, speed, dependability, flexibility and cost – against other organisations' performance in the same dimensions.

- Practice benchmarking is a comparison between an organisation's operations practices, or way of doing things, and those adopted by another operation.

The objectives of benchmarking

Benchmarking is partly concerned with being able to judge how well an operation is doing. It can be seen, therefore, as one approach to setting realistic performance standards. It is also concerned with searching out new ideas and practices which might be able to be copied or adapted. For example, a bank might learn some things from a supermarket about how it could cope with demand fluctuations during the day. The success of benchmarking, however, is largely due to more than its ability to set performance standards and enable organisations to copy one another. Benchmarking is essentially about stimulating creativity and providing a stimulus which enables operations better to understand how they should be serving their customers. Many organisations find that it is the process itself of looking at different parts of their own company, or looking at external companies, that allows them to understand the connection between the external market needs which an operation is trying to satisfy and the internal operations practices it is using to try to satisfy them. In other words, benchmarking can help to reinforce the idea of the direct contribution which an operation has to the competitiveness of its organisation.

Importance–performance mapping[8]

Importance–performance mapping is a particularly useful approach to directing operations improvement because it explicitly includes both of the major influences on the generic performance objectives which define market requirements:

- the needs and importance preferences of customers; and
- the performance and activities of competitors.

Both importance and performance have to be brought together before any judgement can be made as to the relative priorities for improvement. Because something is particularly important to its customers does not mean that an operation should give it immediate priority for improvement. The operation may already be considerably better than its competitors in this respect. Similarly, because an operation is not very good at something when compared with its competitors' performance does not necessarily mean that it should be immediately improved. Customers may not particularly value this aspect of performance. Both importance and performance need to be viewed together to judge improvement priority.

Yet, although we have associated importance with the view of customers and performance with the activities of competitors, the approach may be adapted to deviate from this. For example, a company may choose to give importance to some aspect of operations activity even when customers do not find it important. If a company is working towards providing customised products or services in the near future, it may regard flexibility as being more important than do its customers who are, as yet, unaware of the change in the company's market stance. Neither is per-

formance always judged against competitors. Although it may be an obvious benchmark, it does presuppose the existence of competitors. Many not-for-profit organisations may not see themselves as having competitors as such. They could, however,
assess their performance against other similar organisations. Alternatively, they
could measure performance against customer perception or customer expectations.

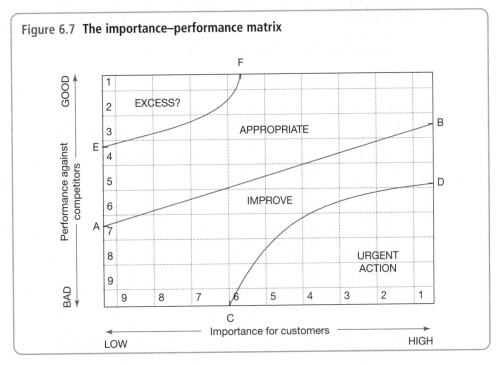

Figure 6.7 The importance–performance matrix

The importance–performance matrix

The priority for improvement which each competitive factor should be given can be
assessed from a comparison of their importance and performance. This can be
shown on an importance–performance matrix which, as its name implies, positions
each competitive factor according to its score or ratings on these criteria. Figure 6.7
shows an importance–performance matrix where both importance and performance
are judged using (in this case) a simple nine-point scale and where the matrix is divided into zones of improvement priority.

The first zone boundary is the 'lower boundary of acceptability' shown as line AB
in Figure 6.7. This is the boundary between acceptable and unacceptable performance. When a competitive factor is rated as relatively unimportant (8 or 9 on the
importance scale) this boundary will in practice be low. Most operations are prepared to tolerate performance levels which are 'in the same ballpark' as their competitors (even at the bottom end of the rating) for unimportant competitive factors.
They only become concerned when performance levels are clearly below those of
their competitors. Conversely, when judging competitive factors which are rated
highly (1 or 2 on the importance scale) they will be markedly less sanguine at poor
or mediocre levels of performance. Minimum levels of acceptability for these competitive factors will usually be at the lower end of the 'better than competitors' class.
Below this minimum bound of acceptability (AB) there is clearly a need for improve-

ment, above this line there is no immediate urgency for any improvement. However, not all competitive factors falling below the minimum line will be seen as having the same degree of improvement priority. A boundary approximately represented by line CD represents a distinction between an urgent priority zone and a less urgent improvement zone. Similarly, above the line AB, not all competitive factors were regarded as having the same priority. The line EF can be seen as the approximate boundary between performance levels which were regarded as 'good' or 'appropriate' on one hand and those regarded as 'too good' or 'excess' on the other. Segregating the matrix in this way results in four zones which imply very different priorities.

- *The 'appropriate' zone.* This zone is bounded on its lower edge by the 'lower bound of acceptability', that is, the level of performance below which the company, in the medium term, would not wish the operation to fall. Moving performance up to, or above, this boundary is likely to be the first-stage objective for any improvement programme. Competitive factors which fall in this area should be considered satisfactory, at least in the short to medium term. In the long term, however, most organisations will wish to edge performance towards the upper boundary of the zone.

- *The 'improve' zone.* Any competitive factor which lies below the lower bound of the 'appropriate' zone will be a candidate for improvement. Those lying either just below the bound or in the bottom left-hand corner of the matrix (where performance is poor but it matters less) are likely to be viewed as non-urgent cases. Certainly they need improving, but probably not as a first priority.

- *The 'urgent-action' zone.* More critical will be any competitive factor which lies in the 'urgent-action' zone. These are aspects of operations performance where achievement is so far below what it ought to be, given its importance to the customer, that business is probably being lost directly as a result. Short-term objectives must be, therefore, to raise the performance of any competitive factors lying in this zone at least up to the 'improve' zone. In the medium term they would need to be improved beyond the lower bound of the 'appropriate' zone.

- *The 'excess?' zone.* The question mark is important. If any competitive factors lie in this area their achieved performance is far better than would seem to be warranted. This does not necessarily mean that too many resources are being used to achieve such a level, but it may do. It is only sensible therefore to check if any resources which have been used to achieve such a performance could be diverted to a more needy factor – anything which falls in the 'urgent-action' area, for example.

Example TAG Transport

TAG Transport is a successful logistics company which is reviewing one of its fastest-growing services – an overnight, temperature-controlled, delivery service for chilled food. It is particularly keen to improve the level of service which it gives to its customers. As a first stage in the improvement process it has devised a list of the various aspects of its operations performance:

- Price/cost – the price (including discounts, etc.) which it can realise from its customers and the real internal cost of providing the service.

- Distribution quality – the ability to deliver goods in an undamaged state and its customers' perceptions of the appearance of its vehicles and drivers.
- Order/dispatch quality – the courtesy and effectiveness of its customer-facing call centre staff.
- Enquiry lead-time – the elapsed time between an enquiry from a new customer and providing a fully specified proposal.
- Drop time – the earliest time each morning when delivery can be made.
- 'Window' quote – the guaranteed time window around the drop time within which delivery should be made.
- Delivery performance – the proportion of actual deliveries made within the quoted 'window'.
- Delivery flexibility – the ability to change delivery destination.
- Volume flexibility – the ability to provide extra capacity at short notice.
- Documentation service – the reliability of documents such as temperature control charts supplied with each delivery.

Based on its discussions with customers, the laboratory manages to assign a score to each of these factors on the 1 to 9 scale. A score of 1 for 'importance' means that the factor is extremely important to customers and 9 means that it has no importance. For performance a score of 1 means that TAG is considerably and consistently better than any of its competitors; a score of 9 means that it is very much worse than any competitor. TAG plotted the importance and performance rating they had given to each aspect of performance on an importance–performance matrix. This is shown in Figure 6.8. It shows that the most important issue, delivery performance, is also where the company performs well against its competitors. Several issues need improving, however, three urgently. Enquiry lead-time, order/dispatch quality and delivery flexibility are all relatively important, yet, the company scores poorly against its competitors.

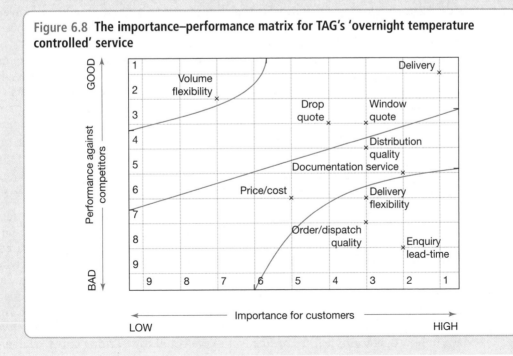

Figure 6.8 **The importance–performance matrix for TAG's 'overnight temperature controlled' service**

The sandcone theory

Techniques such as the importance–performance matrix assume that the improvement priority given to various aspects of operations performance is contingent upon the specific circumstances of an organisation's market position. But some authorities believe that there is also a generic 'best' sequence in which operations performance should be improved. The best-known theory of this type is sometimes called the sandcone theory. Although there are slightly different versions of this, the best known is that originally proposed by Arnoud de Meyer and Kasra Ferdows.[9] In fact, the sandcone model incorporates two ideas. The first is that there is a best sequence in which to improve operations performance, the second is that effort expended in improving each aspect of performance must be cumulative. In other words, moving on to the second priority for improvement does not mean dropping the first, and so on.

According to the sandcone theory; the first priority should be quality, since this is a precondition to all lasting improvement. Only when the operation has reached a minimally acceptable level in quality should it then tackle the next issue, that of internal dependability. Importantly though, moving on to include dependability in the improvement process should not stop the operation making further improvements in quality. Indeed improvement in dependability will actually require further improvement in quality. Once a critical level of dependability is reached, enough to provide some stability to the operation, the next stage is to turn attention to the speed of internal throughput, but again only while continuing to improve quality and dependability further. Soon it will become evident that the most effective way to improve speed is through improvements in response flexibility, that is, changing things within the operation faster; for example, reacting to new customer requirements quickly, changing production volumes rapidly and introducing new products faster. Again, including flexibility in the improvement process should not divert attention from continuing to work further on quality, dependability and speed. Only now, according to the sandcone theory, should cost be tackled head on.

The 'sandcone model' is so called because the sand is analogous to management effort and resources. To build a stable sandcone a stable foundation of quality improvement must be created. Upon such a foundation one can build layers of dependability, speed, flexibility and cost – but only by widening up the lower parts of the sandcone as it is built up (see Figure 6.9). Building up improvement is thus a cumulative process, not a sequential one.

Developing operations capabilities

Underlying the whole concept of continuous improvement is a simple yet far-reaching idea – small changes, continuously applied, bring big benefits. Small changes are relatively minor adjustments to resources and processes and the way they are used. In other words, it is the interaction between resources, processes and the staff who manage and operate them wherein lies the potential inherent in continuous improvement. It is the way in which humans learn to use and work with their operations resources and processes that is the basis of capability development. Learning, therefore, is a fundamental part of operations improvement. Here we examine two views of how operations learn. The first is the concept of the learning curve, a largely

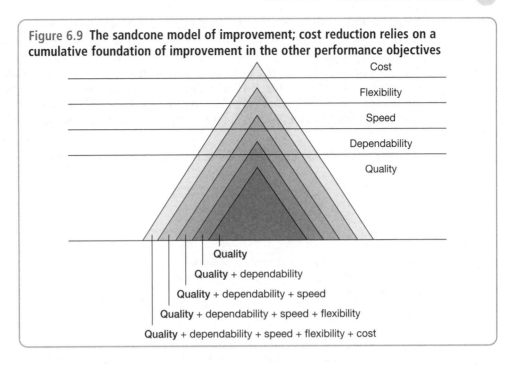

Figure 6.9 **The sandcone model of improvement; cost reduction relies on a cumulative foundation of improvement in the other performance objectives**

descriptive device which attempts to quantify the rate of operational improvement over time. Then we look at how operations' learning is driven by the cyclical relationship between process control and process knowledge.

The learning/experience curve

The relationship between the time taken to perform a task and the accumulated learning or experience was first formulated in the aircraft production industry in the 1930s. The learning curve argues that the reduction in unit labour hours will be proportional to the cumulative number of units produced and that every time the cumulative output doubles, the hours reduce by a fixed percentage. For example, in much labour-intensive manufacturing (e.g. clothing manufacture) a reduction in hours per unit of 20 per cent is found every time cumulative production has doubled. This is called an 80 per cent learning curve. When plotted on log-log paper, such a curve will appear as a straight line – making extrapolations (and strategic planning) more straightforward. Such 'learning' curves are still used in the aerospace, electronics and defence industries.

The patterns that exist in labour hours have also been found when costs are examined. They have been found not only in individual product costs but also in operation and industry-wide costs. When used to describe cost behaviour, the term 'experience curve' rather than learning curve is used. Where costs are not available, price has often been found to be a suitable proxy. An example of an experience curve is shown in Figure 6.10. It charts the progress of a 'voucher processing operation' in a bank. Voucher processing operations sort, read (using optical character recognition) and process the information from the paper documents generated by the branch operations of the bank. This figure shows how the average cost of processing a voucher reduced over time. To begin with, the operation had not used the type of large machines used in these processes, nor had it organised itself to receive the hundreds of thousands of vouchers from the branches it serviced. Over time it learned how to organise itself and to use the machines effectively. Although the data in Figure 6.10 stops at a point in time, future learning can be extrapolated from the operation's 'learning history'. This enabled the bank to establish its capacity requirements for the future, work out the cost savings from using such large processing operations and provide improvement targets for this and other similar operations.

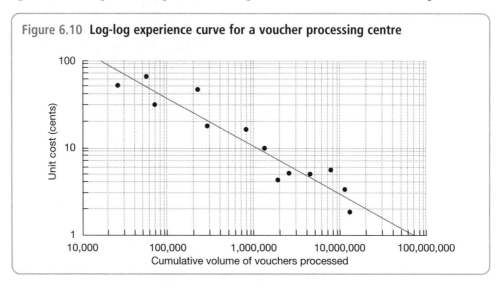

Figure 6.10 **Log-log experience curve for a voucher processing centre**

Limits to experience-curve-based strategies

There are clearly risks associated with any strategy that is based exclusively on one form of analysis. In this instance, basing the long-term competitive viability of a firm solely on the potential for ongoing cost reduction is open to a number of serious criticisms:

- Attributing specific costs is notoriously difficult and overhead costs are often arbitrarily allocated. In addition, units may perform poorly because they have the oldest capital equipment and their volume–variety mix may be inappropriate, factors which the experience may not capture.

- The product or service may be superseded. Innovation from within or (even less predictably) from outside of an industry can shift the competitive 'rules of the game'.

- Relentless pursuit of cost reduction (to the detriment of all the other key performance measures) can lead to operational inflexibility. Although traditional trade-off models are questioned in the 'world-class operations' paradigm, there remains an inevitable link between cost and flexibility.

- The control of cost is not the only way that an operation can contribute to the competitive position of the firm. Competing on quality, service, speed, etc. are all equally viable strategic options.

Process knowledge

Central to developing operations capabilities is the concept of process knowledge. The more we understand the relationship between how we design and run processes and how they perform, the easier it is to improve them. No process will ever reach the point of absolutely perfect knowledge – but most processes can benefit from attempting to move towards it. Moreover, few if any processes operate under conditions of total ignorance. Most operations have at least some idea as to why the processes behave in a particular way. Between these two extremes lies the path of process improvement along which operations managers attempt to journey. It is useful to identify some of the points along this path. One approach to this has been put forward by Roger Bohn.[10] He described an eight-stage scale ranging from 'total ignorance' to 'complete knowledge' of the process (see Table 6.4).

- *Stage 1, Complete ignorance.* There is no knowledge of what is significant in processes. Outputs appear to be totally random and unconnected with any phenomena that can be recognised.

- *Stage 2, Awareness.* There is an awareness that certain phenomena exist and that they are probably relevant to the process, but there is no formal measurement or understanding of how they affect the process. Managing the process is far more of an art than a science, and control relies on tacit knowledge (that is, unarticulated knowledge within the individuals managing the system).

- *Stage 3, Measurement.* There is an awareness of significant variables that seem to affect the process with some measurement, but the variables cannot be controlled as such. The best that managers could do would be to alter the process in response to changes in the variables.

- *Stage 4, Control of the mean.* There is some idea of how to control the significant variables which affect the process, even if the control is not precise. Managers can control the average level of variables in the process even if they cannot control the variation around the average. Once processes have reached this level of knowledge, managers can start to carry out experiments and quantify the impact of the variables on the process.

- *Stage 5, Process capability.* The knowledge exists to control both the average and the variation in significant process variables. This enables the way in which processes can be managed and controlled to be written down in some detail. This in turn means that managers do not have to 'reinvent the wheel' when repeating activities.

- *Stage 6, Know how.* By now the degree of control has enabled managers to know how the variables affect the output of the process. They can begin to fine-tune and optimise the process.

- *Stage 7, Know why.* The level of knowledge about the processes is now at the 'scientific' level with a full model of the process predicting behaviour over a wide range of conditions. At this stage of knowledge, control can be performed automatically, probably by microprocessors. The model of the process allows the automatic control mechanisms to optimise processing across all previously experienced products and conditions.

- *Stage 8, Complete knowledge.* In practice, this stage is never reached because it means that the effects of every conceivable variable and condition are known and

Table 6.4 Characteristics of Bohn's eight stages of process knowledge

Stage term	Indication	Operations activity	Process learning	Process knowledge	To maintain	To move up
1 Complete ignorance	Pure chance	Expertise-based	Artistic	In people's heads		Tinkering
2 Awareness	Art				Pro-fessionalism	Develop standards and systematic measures
3 Measure-ment	Measure good output				Preserve standards	Eliminate causes of large disturbance to process
4 Control of mean	Mean made stable				Observe and correct deviations from limits	Eliminate causes of important variance, identify new sources of variability
5 Process capability	Process variation kept smaller than tolerance band		Natural experiments	Written and oral	Eliminate new causes of variability	Stabilise process transitions and differences in process conditions for different parts
6 Know how	Transitions between products and processes are known				Monitor process parameters and transitions and eliminate causes of new variability	Scientific experiment-ation and theory building on important variables for new product introduction
7 Know why	Science about all key variables	Procedure-based	Controlled experiments and simulations	Databases and software	Science enquiry and debate	Scientific experiment-ation and theory building on all variables
8 Complete knowledge	Know all variable and relationships for products now and in the future					

Source: from Bohn, R.E. (1994) 'Measuring and managing technical knowledge', *MIT Sloan Management Review*, Fall 1994, article no 3615. Copyright © 1994 Massachusetts Institute of Technology, all rights reserved. Reproduced with permission.

understood, even when those variables and conditions have not even been considered before. Stage 8, therefore, might be best considered as moving towards this hypothetically complete knowledge.

The strategic importance of operational knowledge

One of the most important sources of process knowledge are the routines of process control. Process control and especially statistically based process control, is one of the foundations of the Six Sigma improvement approach and is explained in Chapter 9. And while process control and process knowledge may seem surprisingly operational for a book about the more strategic aspects of managing operations, it is vital to establishing an operations-based strategic advantage. In reality, the strategic management of any operation cannot be separated from how resources and processes are managed at a detailed and day-to-day level. The process knowledge, process control cycle of capability development is one of the best illustrations of this. As an operation increases its process knowledge it has a better understanding of what its processes can do at the limits of their capability even though those limits are continually expanding. This allows them to develop better products and services not only because of the enhanced process capability but also because of the operation's confidence in that capability. Similarly, as process knowledge increases, some of the more obvious operations trade-offs can be overcome. Often processes become more flexible in terms of widening their range of capabilities, without excessive additional cost. This in turn allows the operation to produce a wider range of products and services. At the same time, fewer process errors mean better conformance quality and (usually) happier customers. Most staff too will prefer to work in a process that is under control. Certainly, process uncertainty can undermine staff morale. Retaining good staff within chaotic processes is not easy in the long term. Well-controlled processes will also have fewer errors and waste, therefore, high efficiency and, therefore, low cost. It can even affect relationships with suppliers. High levels of process knowledge imply an understanding of how input will affect the process. Armed with this knowledge, relationships with suppliers can develop on a more professional basis. The important point here is that whereas grappling with the details of process control may seem operational, its benefits are not. The increased revenue opportunities of better products and services, a wide product range and customer loyalty, together with better supply relationships, good staff and lower costs, are unquestionably strategic (see Figure 6.11).

Deploying capabilities in the market

Operations capabilities are of little benefit if not used. Indeed, it could be argued that operations capabilities do not really exist unless they are used. They remain nothing more than unrealised potential. A vital element in strategic operations improvement, therefore, is the ability to leverage developed operations capabilities into the market. Not that operations capability will necessarily exclusively define a company's market position. We are not suggesting that because a company's operations have a particular capability it should always attempt to exploit it in the market. But the deployment of capability does create potential in the market. How this potential is realised (or not) and how organisations target market segments is beyond the scope of this book. However, what is very much important to operations

---

Example | **Dell (part 1) – Learning how to turn difficulties into advantages[11]**

Michael Dell, a student at the University of Texas at Austin, had a side-line in buying up unused stock of PCs from local dealers, adding components, and re-selling the now higher-specification machines to local businesses. When the side-line grew to over $50,000 per month he quit university and founded a computer company which was to revolutionise the industry's supply network management. But he faced some real difficulties. First, the Dell organisation was just too small to develop and make its own components. Better, he figured, to learn how best to manage a network of committed specialist component manufacturers and take the best of what was available in the market. Dell says that his commitment to out-sourcing was always done for the most positive of reasons. *'Outsourcing, at least in the IT world, is almost always a way to get rid of a problem a company hasn't been able to solve itself . . . that's not what we're doing at all. We focus on how we can coordinate our activities to create the most value for customers.'* This meant devising new methods of working, a point emphasised by Michael Dell: *'When we launch a new product, their engineers are stationed right in our plants. If a customer calls up with a problem, we'll stop shipping product while they fix design flaws in real time.'* Dell has also enhanced the economic incentive to collaborate with suppliers. *'We can share design and performance databases with suppliers, enabling them to shorten product development times.'*

But the Dell company still faced a cost disadvantage against its far bigger competitors. Seeking ways to undercut its rivals, Dell decided to sell its computers direct to customers, bypassing retailers. This allowed the company to cut out the retailers' (often considerable) margin, which in turn allowed Dell to offer lower prices, but the move was controversial. Computers are complex purchases, it was argued, and customers need to have their hands held while they are making up their minds; they won't buy a product they can't see and touch. Yet, Dell realised that cutting out the link in the supply network between Dell and the customer also provided the company with significant learning opportunities. First, it offered an opportunity to get to know customers' needs far more intimately. At the simplest level, this allows the company to forecast based on the thousands of customer contact calls it receives every hour. In a longer-term sense, it allows the company to talk to customers about what they really want from their machines. In this way, design decisions are made in an environment of realistic customer awareness. Second, it allowed Dell to learn how to run its supply chain in a different way. The time taken for products to move from suppliers through the supply chain to the end customer could be cut, reducing Dell's level of inventory to under 10 days' worth, as opposed to over 80 days for some competitors. This gave Dell a significant cost advantage. So much so that it went on to become the largest personal computer company in the world. But no business model lasts for ever. See the Example, 'Dell (part 2) Things change OK?', in Chapter 8.

---

strategy is how the operation can deploy its capabilities to provide the potential for the organisation to inhabit profitable market segments.

Again, we use the idea of a cycle within the overall strategic improvement cycle. This is illustrated in Figure 6.12. Operations capabilities must provide a contribution to what the organisation regards as being its range of potential market positions, but how the operation can contribute to this potential is influenced strongly by the expectations which the rest of the organisation has for its operations.

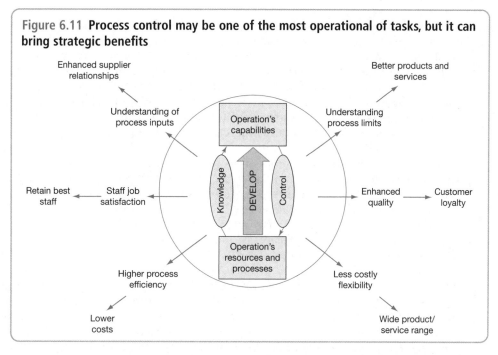

Figure 6.11 **Process control may be one of the most operational of tasks, but it can bring strategic benefits**

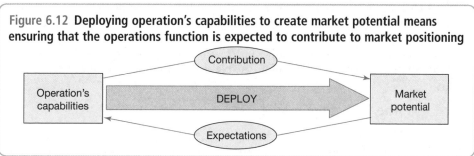

Figure 6.12 **Deploying operation's capabilities to create market potential means ensuring that the operations function is expected to contribute to market positioning**

Example | **Siemens leverages its global capabilities[12]**

Siemens, the leading European electrical engineering firm's story began in 1850 in a small workshop in Berlin. Now the company employs 430,000 people in 190 countries. Long before globalisation became fashionable, Siemens looked beyond national boundaries. It built lines from Finland to the Crimea for the Russian Empire, from London to Calcutta for the English Crown, as well as the Transatlantic cable linking Europe to the Americas, and it was doing business with China as early as 100 years ago. But now Siemens' commitment to China is much deeper. It has responded to the rise of low-cost manufacturing and the opening of the Chinese market by moving mass production to Asia.

Siemens' global network of operations exploits different capabilities in different parts of the world. In China and many of its other Asian plants, it has developed a low-cost base capability that helps it to export its more price-sensitive products to developing countries.It uses low-cost countries for making components for products that are assembled in Europe or America. But it also owns whole businesses, factories, service centres and distribution net-

▶

works around the world, as well as doing much of its product development abroad. *'We have to examine each stage of the value chain in each business area, from development to production, service and, of course, sales, and decide where to put it, based on customer proximity, skills and costs'*, says Dr Ulrich Stock, head of the company's 'Global Competitiveness' programme, For example, a lower-cost version of one of its medical body scanners, aimed at the Chinese market, was initially developed jointly between its Munich headquarters and in China, where it is also being manufactured. Now its Chinese operations have grown their capabilities to the point where the product is developed entirely in China and sold in developing countries worldwide.

The challenges in Siemens' European operations is different. Germany, in particular, is a high-wage economy where attempting to produce low cost products and services would be impossible. But it does have an extremely technically capable and increasingly flexible workforce. This means exploiting a different set of capabilities, so in its German home it now concentrates on the design and manufacture of high-added-value products. *'Of course Germany can't avoid this (low-cost) competition'*, says outgoing CEO Heinrich v. Pierer. *'But we shouldn't just look at the negative consequences of companies creating jobs abroad. These jobs also create jobs in Germany. Studies have shown that for every four jobs created abroad, one is created in Germany.'* Nevertheless, in high-wage countries like Germany, the relocation of operations to low-cost regions often creates anxiety. Klaus-Peter Gittler, head of the Global Manufacturing Concept initiative, says there has to be a change in attitudes. *'Highly industrialized countries like Germany need to have more courage and confidence in their own strengths. They have to be highly innovative and assume the role of trendsetter to justify their higher costs.'* In fact Siemens' electronics plant in Erlangen, which manufactures drives and controls for machine tools and production equipment and has 1,100 employees, was awarded the title of 'Best Factory in Europe' in 2007. Manufacturing lead-times at the plant were cut to just two to three days in order to implement state-of-the-art, just-in-time production. The concept is also driven by new, flexible working time models that allow the plant to absorb fluctuations in order volumes.

The four-stage model

The ability of any operation to contribute to opening up market potential for the organisation and the organisational aims, expectations and aspirations of the operations function has been captured in a model developed by Professors Hayes and Wheelwright of Harvard University.[13] With later contributions from Professor Chase of the University of Southern California,[14] they developed what they call the 'Four-Stage Model' which is ideal for evaluating the effectiveness of the contribution/expectation cycle. The model traces the progression of the operations function from what is the largely negative role of Stage 1 operations to it becoming the central element of competitive strategy in excellent Stage 4 operations (see Figure 6.13).

Stage 1 – internal neutrality

This is the very poorest level of contribution by the operations function. In a Stage 1 organisation, the operation is considered a 'necessary evil'. The other functions in the organisation regard it as holding them back from competing effectively. The operations function, they would say, is inward-looking and at best reactive. It certainly has very little positive to contribute towards competitive success. The best that can be expected from the operations function is to cure the most obvious problems. Certainly the rest of the organisation would not look to operations as the source of any originality, flair or competitive drive. The expectations on it are to be

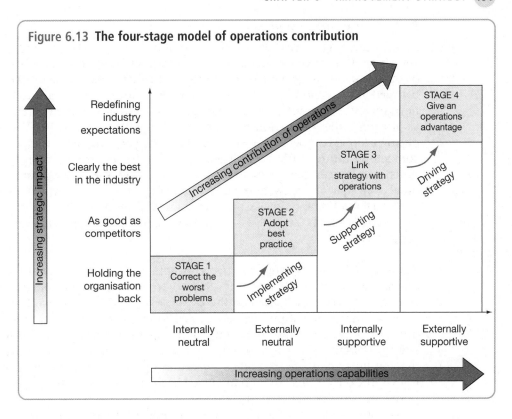

Figure 6.13 **The four-stage model of operations contribution**

'internally neutral', a position it attempts to achieve not by anything positive but by avoiding the bigger mistakes.

Stage 2 – external neutrality

The first step of breaking out of Stage 1 is for the operations function to begin comparing itself with similar companies or organisations in the outside market. A Stage 2 operation has achieved a sufficient level of capability to cease holding the company back, even if it may not yet be particularly creative in its contribution to competitiveness. It is expected, at least, to adopt 'best practice' and the best ideas and norms of performance from the rest of its industry. It is expected to be 'externally neutral' with operations capabilities similar to its competitors. This may not give the organisation any competitive advantage but neither is operations the source of competitive disadvantage.

Stage 3 – internally supportive

Stage 3 operations may not be better than their competitors on every aspect of operations performance but they are broadly up with the best. Nevertheless, good as they may be, Stage 3 operations aspire to be clearly and unambiguously the very best in the market. They try to achieve this level of contribution by a clear understanding of the company's competitive or strategic goals. Then they organise and develop their operations resources to excel in the things in which the company needs to compete effectively. The expectation on the operations function is to be 'internally supportive' by providing credible support to operations strategy.

Stage 4 – externally supportive

At one time, Stage 3 was taken as the limit of the operations function's contribution. Yet, Hayes and Wheelwright capture the emerging sense of the growing importance of operations management by suggesting a further stage – Stage 4. The difference between Stage 3 and Stage 4 is admitted by Hayes and Wheelwright to be subtle, but nevertheless important. A Stage 4 company is one that sees the operations function as providing the foundation for its future competitive success because it is able to deploy unique competencies which provide the company with the performance to compete in future market conditions. In effect, the contribution of the operations function becomes central to strategy making. Stage 4 operations are creative and proactive. They are likely to organise their resources in ways which are innovative and capable of adaptation as markets change. Essentially they are expected to be 'one step ahead' of competitors – what Hayes and Wheelwright call being 'externally supportive'.

Figure 6.13 brings together the two concepts of role and the contribution of the operations function. Moving from Stage 1 to Stage 2 requires operations to overcome its problems of implementing existing strategies. The move from Stage 2 to Stage 3 requires operations actively to develop its resources so that they are appropriate for long-term strategy. Moving up to Stage 4 requires operations to be driving strategy through its contribution to competitive superiority. Notice also how moving up from Stage 1 to Stage 4 requires operations progressively to adapt the roles of the operations function discussed in the previous chapter, implementer, supporter and driver, as shown in Figure 6.13.

Two points are important in understanding the power of the four-stage 1 to 4 model. First, it is linked to the company's aspirations (at least their operations management aspirations). In other words, there is an active desire (some might say even an evangelical desire) to improve the operation. Second, it is the endpoint of progression which emphasises the increasing importance and centrality of operations strategy to overall competitive advantage. The idea of a proactive and inventive 'Stage 4' operations function, described by Hayes and Wheelwright, foreshadows the somewhat later concept of 'world-class operations'. That is, the idea that companies should aspire not only to have performance levels equal to, or better than, any other similar business in the world, but should achieve this superiority because of their operations ability.

SUMMARY ANSWERS TO KEY QUESTIONS

What are the differences between managing large 'breakthrough' improvement and managing continuous improvement?

Although it is common to distinguish between major 'leaps forward' in terms of operations improvement on the one hand, and more continuous incremental improvement on the other, these are really two points on a spectrum describing the degree of operations change. Major improvement initiatives (such as most business process reengineering) are dramatic and radical changes in the way operations resources and processes are organised. They, therefore, need to be managed as projects with 'champions' and project managers being given responsibility to coordinate the individual ideas and efforts of the staff involved in the change. Continuous improvement, on the other hand, is less dramatic and longer term, involving small incremental steps. Change is gradual and constant and involves most or all staff. Here it is the collective motivation and culture which is important in maintaining the momentum of the improvement. Coordination becomes important because there will probably be many different small projects happening simultaneously. Continuous improvement is often described as a 'never-ending cycle'. In fact the concept of the cycle can also be used to put in place the routines and procedures which help to embed continuous improvement at a more strategic level. One such cycle uses the stages 'direct', 'develop', and 'deploy' to link market position to market potential.

How do the needs of the market direct the ongoing development of operations processes?

Usually market needs make their impact on how operations improve themselves through formal mechanisms such as performance measurement systems and benchmarking efforts, although these formal mechanisms are themselves cycles, in so much as they involve continually seeking gaps between the formal targets for the operation set by what the market requires and the actual performance of the operation. Designing performance measurement systems includes four generic issues. First, what factors to include as performance targets? It is likely that performance measures at different levels of aggregation will be needed. Approaches such as the 'balanced scorecard' approach have tried to encourage a broader view of performance measurement. The second question is, what are the most important performance targets? These are the aspects of performance which reflect the particular market strategy adopted by an organisation. Often these are contained in a small number of key performance indicators (KPIs). The third question is, how to measure the performance targets? Usually a number of measures are needed to describe broader or more aggregated performance measures adequately. The final question concerns the basis on which to compare actual against target performance. Different bases of performance can affect how we judge performance. Typically, bases for comparison are against historical standards, against improvement goals, against competitors or against some idea of absolute perfection. Benchmarking is also used to direct improvement within operations. One particular type of benchmarking is importance–performance mapping. This involves formally assessing the relative importance and performance of different aspects of the operation and plotting them on a matrix.

How can the ongoing management and control of operations be harnessed to develop their capabilities?

As operations gain experience they improve. In some ways this improvement is predictable and can be plotted over time using learning or experience curves. Of more immediate concern in operations strategy, however, is how operations can improve by building their capabilities over time. An important mechanism of capability building is the way in which operations increase their knowledge of their processes through attempting to control them. Process control (especially using approaches such as statistical process control) attempts to reduce the variation within a process. This will usually involve examining deviations from expected performance and 'problem solving' out the root causes of such variation. This in itself improves the process and makes it more predictable. Because it is more predictable it becomes easier to control, and so on. And although such control may be very operational in nature, the results of the improvement it brings can result in important strategic benefits.

What can operations do to deploy their capabilities into the market?

The extent to which an operation deploys its capabilities to create the potential for the organisation to operate in profitable parts of the market is shaped partly by the expectations placed on the operations function. The greater the expectations on the operations function, the more it will attempt to make a significant strategic contribution. The greater the contribution it makes, the higher the expectations of the rest of the organisation will be, and so on. One, relatively well known, model for assessing contribution is the Hayes and Wheelwright four-stage model. This model traces the progression of the operations function from the largely negative role of Stage 1, to becoming the central element in competitive strategy in so-called four-stage operations.

Further reading

Bessant, J. and Caffyn, S. (1997) 'High involvement innovation', *International Journal of Technology Management*, 14(1).

Davenport, T. and Prusak, L. (1998) *Working Knowledge: How Organisations Manage What They Know*. Boston, MA: Harvard Business School Press.

Dirgo, R. (2006) *Look Forward Beyond Lean and Six Sigma: A Self-perpetuating Enterprise Improvement Method*. Conyers, GA: J. Ross Publishing (hardcover).

Goldratt, E.M., Cox, J. and Whitford, J.C.D. (2004) *The Goal: A Process of Ongoing Improvement*, 3rd edn. Great Barrington, MA: North River Press.

Hammer, M. and Champy, J. (1993) *Reengineering the Corporation*. London: Nicholas Brearley Publishing.

Kaplan, R. and Norton, D. (1996) 'Using the balanced scorecard as a strategic management system', *Harvard Business Review*, January–February.

Leonard-Bart, D. (1995) *Wellsprings of Knowledge: Building and Sustaining the Sources of Innovation*. Boston, MA: Harvard Business School Press.

Neely, A.D. (1998) *Measuring Business Performance*. London: Economist Books.

Pisano, G.P. (1994) 'Knowledge, integration and the locus of learning: an empirical analysis of process development', *Strategic Management Journal*, Vol. 15, pp. 85–100.

Upton, D. (1996) 'Mechanisms for building and sustaining operations improvement', *European Management Journal*, 14(3).

Notes on the chapter

1 Hayes, R.H. and Pisano, G.P. (1996) 'Manufacturing strategy: at the intersection of two paradigm shifts', *Production and Operations Management*, 5(1).

2 Imai, M. (1986) *Kaizen – The Key to Japan's Competitive Success*. McGraw-Hill.

3 Neely, A.D. (1998) *Measuring Business Performance*. London: Economist Books.

4 Skinner, W. (1974) 'The focused factory', *Harvard Business Review*, May–June.

5 See Kaplan, R.S. and Norton, D.P. (1996) *The Balanced Scorecard*. Boston, MA: Harvard Business School Press.

6 Camp, C. (1989) 'Benchmarking: the search for best practices which lead to superior performance', *Quality Progress*, January–May.

7 Pickering, I.M. and Chambers, S. (1991) 'Competitive benchmarking: progress and future development', *Computer Integrated Manufacturing Systems*, 4(2).

8 This section is based on Slack, N. *et al.* (2007) *Operations Management*, 5th edn. Harlow, UK: Financial Times Prentice Hall.

9 Ferdows, K. and de Meyer, A. (1990) 'Lasting improvement in manufacturing', *Journal of Operations Management*, 9(2).

10 Bohn, R.E. (1994) 'Measuring and managing technical knowledge', *Sloan Management Review*, Fall.

11 Sources: Dell corporate website (2007); Dell, M. (1998) *Direct from Dell: Strategies That Revolutionised an Industry*. New York: Harper Business; *The Economist* (1996) 'Selling PCs like bananas', October; Magretta, J. (1998) 'The power of virtual integration: an interview with Dell Computer's Michael Dell', *Harvard Business Review*, March–April.

12 Sources: *Siemens Journal* (2007) 'The road to success', 15 February; *Siemens Journal* (2007) 'Global added value', 15 February; *The Economist* (2007) 'Home and abroad', 10 February.

13 Hayes, R.J. and Wheelwright, S.C. (1984) *Restoring Our Competitive Edge*. New York: John Wiley & Sons.

14 Chase, R.B. and Hayes, R.J. (1991) 'Beefing up operations in service firms', *Sloan Management Review*.

Product and service development and organisation

Introduction

The products and services produced by an operation are its 'public face' in so much as they are what markets judge a company on: good products and services equals good company. Because of this, it has always made sense to devote time and effort to how new products and services are developed. Moreover, it has long been accepted that there is a connection between how companies go about developing products and services and how successful those products and services are in the marketplace. Now two things have changed; both the speed and scale of market and technology changes has increased; second there is a greater understanding of how closely connected are the processes by which products and services are developed and the outcomes from those processes. Given that product and service development is a core issue for operations strategy, it is appropriate that it is treated here (Figure 7.1). And, even though it is a subject in its own right, it can still benefit from an operations strategy analysis.

Figure 7.1 This chapter looks at development and organisation strategy (product and service development and organisation)

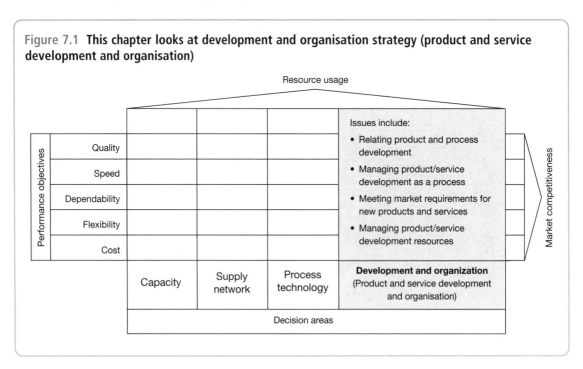

KEY QUESTIONS

● *Why is the way in which companies develop their products and services so important?*

● *What processes do companies use to develop products and services?*

● *How should the effectiveness of the product and service development process be judged in terms of fulfilling market requirements?*

● *What operations resource-based decisions define a company's product and service development strategy?*

The strategic importance of product and service development

Figure 7.2 illustrates some of the more important reasons why product and service development is seen as increasingly strategically important. From a market perspective, international competition has become increasingly intense. In many markets there are a number of competitors bunched together in terms of their product and service performance. Even small advantages in product and service specifications can have a significant impact on competitiveness. This has made customers both more sophisticated in exercising their choice and often more demanding in terms of wanting products and services that fit their specific needs. Also, markets are becoming more fragmented. Unless companies choose to follow relatively narrow niche markets, they are faced with developing products and services capable of being adapted in different ways to different markets. If this were not enough, product and service life cycles have become shorter. An obvious way to try to gain advantage over competitors is to introduce updated products and services. Competitors respond by doing the same and the situation escalates. While not every industry has such short life cycles as, say, the entertainment or fashion garment industry, the trend, even in industrial markets, is towards more frequent new product and service introductions.

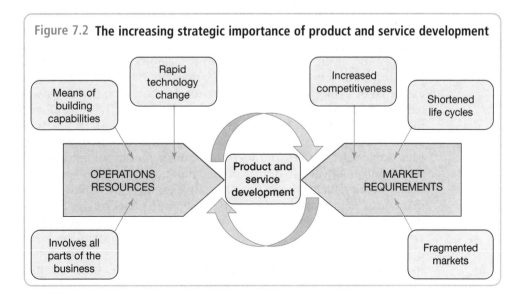

Figure 7.2 **The increasing strategic importance of product and service development**

A different, but equally important, set of pressures affect the operations resources which have to develop and deliver new products and services. Perhaps most importantly, rapid technology changes have affected most industries. For example, internet-based technologies have introduced startlingly new possibilities (and uncertainties) for almost all products and services in all industries. Partly because of the scale and pace of such technological developments, it has become increasingly obvious that effective product and service development places responsibilities on every part of the business. Marketing, purchasing, accounting, operations, are all, like it or not, an integral part of any organisation's ability to develop products and services effectively and efficiently. Every part of the business is now faced with the question, 'How can we deploy our competencies and skills towards developing better or different products and services?' New product and service development is now seen as the mechanism by which all parts of the business, but especially operations, leverages their capabilities into the marketplace.

Developing products and services and developing processes

For convenience and for ease of explanation we often treat the design of products and services on the one hand, and the design of the processes which produce them on the other, as though they were totally separate activities. In many organisations the two developments are organised separately. But this does not imply that they necessarily should be treated or organised separately, and they are clearly interrelated. It would be foolish to develop any product or service without taking into consideration the constraints and capabilities of the processes that will produce it. Similarly, developing processes to take advantage of new technologies or process methods will have implications for the development of products and services in the future. Successful developments often have a history of both product/service and process development.

The degree of product change is important

Just as it was important in the previous chapter to understand the degree of process change expected of the development process, so here it is important to understand the degree of product or service change. Again, we can construct a conceptual scale which helps to give some degree of discrimination between different levels of change. Also again, we can calibrate this scale from relatively minor modifications to a product or service at one extreme, through to the novel and/or radical changes exhibited by a 'pioneer' product or service. In the previous chapter we distinguished between what is done in a process and how it is done. The equivalent here is the distinction between what is seen externally to have changed in the product or service and how the product or service performs its function through its internal mechanisms. Table 7.1 describes four levels of change, 'modification', 'extension', 'development' and 'pioneer', in terms of the product or services' external and internal characteristics. It also shows two illustrative examples, one based on a company that manufactures exercise machines, the other a financial service company that runs a bank card service. Remember, though, that the level of change implied by these categories of development to products and services is approximate. What is important is to recognise that the nature of the product and service development process is likely to be different depending on the degree of product/service change.

Table 7.1 The degree of product/service change can affect both its external appearance and its internal methodology/technology

| | Degree of product/service change | | | |
	Modification	Extension	Development	Pioneer
External customer awareness (what is seen)	Little/none	More functionality	'Next generation' progression	Novel/radical change
Internal methodology/ technology (how it is done)	Minor/isolated	Some changes to original methodology/ technology	Extensive redesign of original method/ technology	Novel/radical change
Example: exercise machines	Minor engineering change to component parts	Extra options on control/display of computer	Aesthetic redesign and changes to internal resistance mechanism	'Total health monitoring' concept with intelligent machines' response to body monitoring and full automatic analysis
Example: bank card services	Minor changes to back-office procedures	Improvement of monthly statement with analysis of expenditure	Incorporation of smart-card technology	Ultimately flexible 'one card' concept with advanced smart-card capability and links with other financial services.

Relatively small 'modification' changes, such as those described in the two examples in Table 7.1, are likely to be relatively frequent and will probably be made using routine procedures. Most companies have standard procedures such as 'engineering change orders' (ECOs), where small changes are proposed in one part of the organisation and approved by other relevant departments. But although these small modifications may be incorporated into standard procedures, they may still require organisation-wide exposure, especially if the part of the product or service being modified has high 'connectivity'. Connectivity is the degree to which changes in one part of a product or service impacts on other parts. It is a concept which can also apply at an organisational level and is important in understanding why, as the degree of product or service change moves thorough 'extension' and 'development' to 'pioneer', the changes become more difficult and more risky. Fundamental changes to products and service almost always involve the whole organisation. So, in addition to the obvious difficulties of market acceptability and resource capability inherent in high degrees of product and service change, the coordination between functional strategies must be well managed.

Product and process change should be considered together

We can put together the degree of process change scale from the previous chapter with the scale indicating the degree of product/service change described in Table 7.1.

Example   Spangler, Hoover and Dyson[1]

In 1907 a janitor called Murray Spangler put together a pillowcase, a fan, an old biscuit tin, and a broom handle. It was the world's first vacuum cleaner. One year later he sold his patented idea to William Hoover whose company went on to dominate the vacuum cleaner market for decades, especially in its United States homeland. Yet, between 2002 and 2005 Hoover's market share dropped from 36 per cent to 13.5 per cent. Why? Because a futuristic looking and comparatively expensive rival product, the Dyson vacuum cleaner, had jumped from nothing to over 20 per cent of the market. In fact, the Dyson product dates back to 1978 when James Dyson noticed how the air filter in the spray-finishing room of a company where he had been working was constantly clogging with powder particles (just like a vacuum cleaner bag clogs with dust). So he designed and built an industrial cyclone tower, which removed the powder particles by exerting centrifugal forces. The question intriguing him was, *'Could the same principle work in a domestic vacuum cleaner?'* Five years and *five thousand* prototypes later he had a working design, since praised for its 'uniqueness and functionality'. However, existing vacuum cleaner manufacturers were not as impressed – two rejected the design outright. So Dyson started making his new design himself. Within a few years Dyson cleaners were, in the UK, outselling the rivals who had once rejected them. The aesthetics and functionality of the design help to keep sales growing in spite of a higher retail price. To Dyson good *'is about looking at everyday things with new eyes and working out how they can be made better. It's about challenging existing technology'.*

Dyson scientists were determined to challenge even their own technology and create vacuum cleaners with even higher suction. So they set to work developing an entirely new type of cyclone system. They discovered that a smaller diameter cyclone gives greater centrifugal force. So they developed a way of getting 45 per cent more suction than a dual cyclone and removing more dust, by dividing the air into eight smaller cyclones. This advanced technology was then incorporated into Dyson's new products.

This is done in Figure 7.3. Advanced or 'blue sky' research and development lies beyond both of these scales, but it is from this direction that most radical innovation emerges. The dotted lines indicate the degree of difficulty encountered in the development process. Put simply, product/service change is easier when the underlying processes which produce them are not being changed at the same time, and vice versa.

Figure 7.3 also shows three service/process developments at a bank. Making changes to the services offered in a bank branch involves relatively minor 'product' and process changes compared with the redesign of both product and process involved in a major new call centre. This, in turn, is less than the development of a totally new Internet banking service.

Managing the overlap between product and process development

Because it is often difficult to untangle a service 'product' from the process that produces it, operations developing new services know they have to develop new processes concurrently. But manufacturing operations are different. It is often both possible to develop products independently of the processes that make them and also common practice for many companies. Yet, because product development and process development are not the same thing, it does not mean that they should not overlap. In fact one of the more important trends in product design has been the considerable effort which recently has been put into managing the overlap. There are probably two reasons for this. First, there is a growing recognition that the design of products has a major effect on the cost of making them. Many decisions taken during the development of products such as the choice of material, or the way components are fastened together, will all define much of the cost of making the product. It clearly makes sense, therefore, to build into the development process the need to evaluate product design choices in terms of their effect on manufacturing processes as well as the functionality of the product itself. Second, the way overlap is managed between product and process development has a significant effect on the effectiveness and efficiency of the development process itself. This is particularly true for the time between the initial product or service concept and its eventual delivery into the market, and the overall cost of the total development effort. We shall deal with this issue later in the chapter.

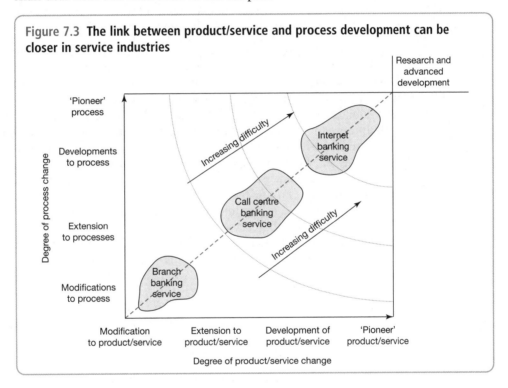

Figure 7.3 The link between product/service and process development can be closer in service industries

Modular design and mass customisation

Two separate, but related ideas – modularity in product and service design and mass customisation – have made an impact on product and service development. We will consider them separately and then bring the two ideas together.

Modularity – is a strategy for organising complex products (and services) and processes efficiently. A modular system is composed of units (or modules) that are designed independently but still function as an integrated whole.[2] So, rather than designing a product and service as a totally integrated and indivisible whole the design is divided into modules which can be put together in various ways. Putting different modules together will result in products or services with different functionality. Yet, because the modules themselves are standardised, they can be produced in a standardised low-cost manner. The most obvious examples of modular design are in the computer industry where relatively complex products can be built up using smaller subsystems. Customers who have different requirements can simply choose which modules they require within the overall product. Provided the overall architecture of the design (the way modules fit together and the functions they perform) and the interfaces between the modules allow for easy connection and communication, then modularity can offer considerable advantages. For example, innovative ideas can be tried out in one module without it necessarily interfering with the design of the product or service as a whole. So, suppose a medical centre offers a range of different health check-up services. If it designs its processes and systems to separate its different clinical procedures, it could introduce new tests in one area while leaving the others undisturbed. Of course, it would have to ensure that the interfaces between the improved test area and the other parts of its services processes (records, diagnostics, follow-up appointments, and so on) could handle any new information generated.

Mass customisation – is the ability to provide customers with high levels of variety and customisation through flexible and responsive processes and flexible product and service designs.[3] The vision of mass customisation is to reduce radically the effect of the assumed trade-off between variety and cost. Some authorities see it as an inevitable successor to mass production, while others argue that there is little essentially new in the idea, rather it pushes existing ideas such as flexibility and agility to their logical conclusion.[4] The mass customisation concept includes the ideas that, as far as market requirements are concerned, markets are becoming increasingly fragmented, while as far as operations resources are concerned, new forms of organisation and technology are allowing greater degrees of flexibility and responsiveness. Thus, it is possible to 'mass produce' a basic family of products or services which can still be customised to the needs of individual customers. The major management task, therefore, is to understand the implications of market and operations developments and harness them by embracing an attitude which stresses sensitivity to customers' individual needs and a willingness to supply them with customised offerings. This means changes in the way the operation produces its products and services and the way it markets them. But, of particular relevance here, it also implies a different approach to designing products and services. Predominantly this involves the standardisation and modularisation of components (see above) to increase variety while reducing production costs.

One much-quoted example of how modular design contributed to mass customisation is the way Black and Decker, the hand tool manufacturer, produced a wide range of well over one hundred basic hand tools, each with their own variants, from a relatively small set of modular and standardised components. The first consequence of this modular approach was more effective and efficient design.

> 'Much of the work in design and tooling was eliminated because of the standardisation of motors, bearings, switches, ... etc. New designs could be developed using components already standardised for manufacturing ability. The product did not have to start with a blank sheet of paper and be designed from scratch'.[5]

The second was drastically reduced production costs because standardised parts enabled standardised production processes.

Products and services from the long tail[6]

One of the most fashionable ideas of the last few years has been the 'theory of the Long Tail'. This idea is based around the ability of modern (often internet-based) technologies to earn profits from the 'Long Tail' of items that form the last 80 per cent of the traditional Pareto curve or 80:20 rule. Now that the internet allows access to these more obscure items, they are more accessible to consumers and therefore capable of being made profitable. Some organisations believe that the many thousands of items that make up the Long Tail can between them be as profitable as the one or two major selling 'hits'. The implication for new product and service development is that obscure items, if they are sufficiently attractive to consumers, will be discovered and eventually turn into hits. Increasingly, therefore, the hits, or big sellers, of tomorrow could be the niche products of today that have not yet been discovered by consumers in sufficiently large quantities.

Product and service development as a process

There are two views of how to characterise product and service development. One sees it as essentially a creative process where a technical understanding of the mechanisms involved in the service or product is brought together with ingenuity and flair. The emphasis should be on creativity, novelty and innovation. For all this to happen, the people involved must be given the space and time to be creative. Of course, the activity has to be managed but not to the point where it interferes with originality. Typically this view of product and service development sees the activity as a collection of, sometimes interdependent, projects. And although some aspects of project management may be relevant in guiding the activity, it cannot be regarded as a 'process'. Processes are what create products and services on a routine basis, whereas product and service development is the creation of original one-offs. Furthermore, the raw material of this knowledge is a substance which is difficult to define and even more difficult to identify. Product and service development, therefore, must focus on its outcome and not worry too much about how that outcome is achieved.

The counter-argument contends that, as with everything, output depends on process. Great ideas for products and services emerge from a process that makes them great. Therefore, of course, one should examine the process of product and service development. While no two development projects are exactly alike, there is sufficient commonality in all such projects to be able to model the process and work on improving its overall performance. The normal generic performance objectives which apply to any operations process, quality, speed, dependability, flexibility and cost, all have relevance to product and service development. Most companies would willingly adopt an approach which gave them higher-quality designs for new products and services, delivered faster and more dependably while maintaining sufficient flexibility to incorporate new ideas which are produced at lower cost. It makes sense, therefore, to apply similar approaches to improving product and service development processes as one would to any other process. Define the steps in the process, examine the characteristics of how prospective product and service designs flow through the resources which act upon them, look for bottlenecks and attempt to smooth them out, identify critical points in the flow and guard against quality failures at these points, and so on. This is the approach we shall take. Product and service development is a process, and needs to be managed strategically.

Product/service development – an operations strategy analysis

Product and service development can be treated as a coherent operation in its own right. We include it here as a part of the development and organisation decision area because developing products and services is clearly vital to any organisation's strategic development. However, the topic could be treated as an entirely separate function (which it is in many organisations). Indeed for professional design consultancies, for example, it is their whole reason for existing. We include the topic within operations strategy not because we believe product and service development should be always an integral part of the operations function organisationally. Rather, it is because of the difficulty in untangling the process of producing and delivering products and services and that of developing those products and services in the first place. Also, because we treat the topic as an integral part of operations strategy does not mean that no benefit can be derived from analysing product and service development as a distinct operations strategy in its own right.

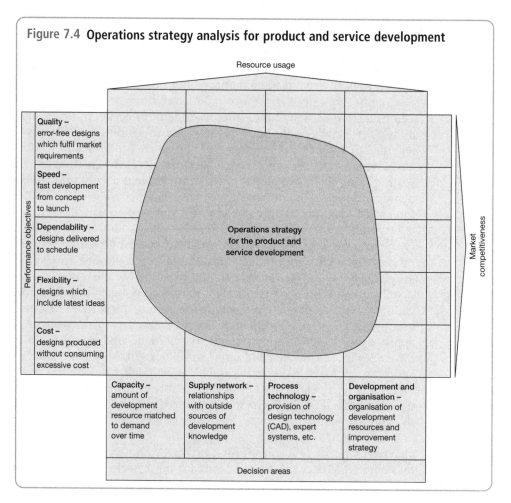

Figure 7.4 **Operations strategy analysis for product and service development**

For example, Figure 7.4 illustrates how an operations strategy matrix (discussed in Chapter 1) can be constructed for product and service development operations. The generic performance objectives of quality, speed, dependability, flexibility and cost can be used to describe the impact of new or modified products and services in the marketplace. In order to achieve competitive 'production' of product and service designs, the resources and processes which are used to develop them will themselves need organising along the lines of any other operation. The company's design capacity will have to be matched to the demand placed on it over time, relationships with an external supply network for design and development knowledge will have to be established, process technologies such as computer aided design (CAD) systems, expert systems, simulations, and so on may be needed, also the resources technology and processes used to develop products and services will need organising and themselves developing over time. All decision areas are of some relevance to most companies' development efforts.

The remainder of this chapter will first examine the nature of the product and service development process and then use the operations strategy approach to illustrate the requirements of the market and the capabilities of development resources.

Stages of development

Describing the way in which organisations develop products and services is problematic because different organisations will adopt different processes. Furthermore, what companies specify as a formal product or service development procedure, and what happens in reality, can be very different things. Yet, three ideas do seem to have found wide acceptance:

- The development process moves through a series of stages, some of which may be missed out and sometimes the process recycles back through stages. Somewhere towards the beginning of the process, there are stages concerned with collecting ideas and generating product and service concepts, and towards the end of the process, there are stages concerned with specifying the detail of the product or service.

- As the development process moves through these stages, the number of alternative design options reduces until one final design remains. The process often includes decision points which screen out options deemed to be unsatisfactory.

- As these possible design options are reduced there is a move from a state of uncertainty regarding the final design to a state of increasing certainty. One consequence of this is that the ability to change the design gets increasingly limited. Making changes at the end of the process can be considerably more expensive than making them at the beginning.

Different authors present different stage models which attempt to describe product and service development. These vary in the number and type of stages they include but are broadly similar. Figure 7.5 illustrates a typical stage model. Remember, though, that even if we assume that these stages are not sequential, it is a somewhat simplistic approach to describing what really happens in product and service development. The reality of bringing products and services from concept to market introduction is in reality both complex and messy.

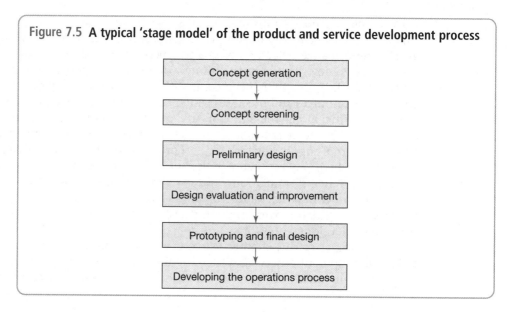

Figure 7.5 **A typical 'stage model' of the product and service development process**

Concept generation

Ideas for new product or service concepts may be generated from sources outside the organisation, such as expressed customers' needs or competitor activity, or from sources within the organisation such as sales staff and front-of-house operations staff, or, more formally, from the R&D department. There are many market research tools for gathering data in a formal and structured way from customers, including questionnaires and interviews. These techniques, however, usually tend to be structured in such a way as only to test out ideas or check products or services against predetermined criteria.

Concept screening

Not all concepts, or variants within a concept, have the potential to be developed through to market launch. The purpose of the concept-screening stage is to take the flow of concepts emerging from the development process and evaluate them. Concepts may have to pass through many different screens, and several functions might be involved, each using different criteria to screen the proposals. Screening may be divided into three sets of criteria related to market positioning, operations/technical implications and financial evaluation:

● Does the proposed product or service occupy a market position which is both attractive in its own right and consistent with the organisation's overall marketing strategy?

● Does the proposed product or service exploit existing operations resource capabilities or help the operation to develop attractive new capabilities?

● Is the investment in the proposed product or service feasible, and is the return from this investment acceptable?

Preliminary design

This stage represents the beginning of detailed work on the product or service design. It includes defining what will go into the product or service. This will require the collection of information about such things as the constituent component parts which make up the product or service package, the product/service structure, that is, the order in which the component parts of the package have to be put together, and the bill of materials (BOM), that is, the quantities of each component part required to make up the total package. This stage also may include specifying how the various components are put together to create the final product or service.

Design evaluation and improvement

This stage takes the preliminary design and attempts to improve it before the prototype product or services are tested in the market. There are a number of techniques that can be employed at this stage to evaluate and improve the preliminary design. Some of these techniques are concerned with costing the proposed product or service and identifying areas for cost improvement. Some are concerned with fully exploring the technical characteristics of the product or service in an effort to improve its overall value. Most are based on an approach which emphasises systematic questioning of exactly what each part of the product or service is intended to contribute to its overall value, why it is being done in a particular way and how it might be done differently. It is not the purpose of this book to explore any of these techniques in detail.

| Example | **Will airline passengers learn to love stealth technology?**[7] |

Predicting consumer reaction is an important part of all product and service design. Air travel is no different. Also it is getting a bad press. It is crowded, it is the target of terrorists, it swamps the areas around airports with noise pollution, and above all, it is destroying the planet with its carbon emissions. But there may be a technical solution – a design that could have a significant impact on at least the last two problems, noise pollution and fuel efficiency.

A joint research project from the University of Cambridge and the Massachusetts Institute of Technology in collaboration with aerospace companies such as Boeing and Rolls Royce, have come up with a design that smoothes the airflow around an aircraft making it quieter and more fuel efficient. The researchers are proposing a mid-range aircraft that is slightly slower than current models. But the slower speed brings a dramatic reduction in noise levels. Furthermore, the aircraft could also glide into land at a low approach speed, and when it takes off it could climb steeply enough to make it almost inaudible outside the airport. There are several pieces of clever technology embedded in this design including smaller, quieter engines that have variable nozzles, constructing the aircraft from composites and eliminating the flaps on its wings. But there is also another element to the design which is its biggest snag. It would resemble current stealth bombers that are, in effect, a flying wing with the body of the aircraft blended in to the wing design. Passengers would have to sit in a wide cabin with little or no sight of the exterior conditions and surrounded by fuel and cargo carried in the wings. Even with views of the outside projected around the cabin; tests have indicated that passenger reaction is extremely negative.

So which will win? Fuel efficiency (yes votes from the green lobby and the airlines) and reduced noise pollution (again, yes votes from the green lobby together with anyone who lives near an airport), or will it be the reluctance of us all to purchase a service that reinforces the lack of control we have over our own destinies whilst flying?

Prototyping and final design

Often 'close to final' designs are 'prototyped'. Partly the next stage in the design activity is to turn the improved design into a prototype so that it can be tested. This may be to learn more about the nature of the proposed product or service but often it is also to reduce the risk inherent in going straight to market. Product prototypes may include clay models of car designs and computer simulations, for example. Computer simulations can be used as service prototypes but also can include the actual implementation of the service on a pilot basis. Many retailing organisations pilot new products and services in a small number of stores in order to test customers' reaction to them.

Developing the operations process

Most models of product and service development assume that the final stage will involve developing the operations processes which will eventually produce the designed product or service. Although we dealt with process development in the previous chapter, it is important to stress again that, in practice, product/service development on the one hand and process development on the other are inexorably linked. Placing this stage at the end of the development process, however, does reinforce the idea that, generally speaking, if the development process is intended to design products and services which will fulfil a market need, then process decisions can only take place after some product or service characteristics have been decided.

Product and service development as a funnel

Although stage models such as we illustrated in Figure 7.5 are useful in identifying the activities which must at some time take place within the overall development activity, they do not form a strict set of stages to which the development process must conform. In reality, stages may merge, the sequence of stages may vary and, almost always, the development process recycles back and forth between the stages. But the underlying ideas behind such stage models are widespread. For example, a common method of describing the product or service development process is to liken it to a funnel. The mouth of the funnel, being wide, can accommodate many alternative designs for the product or service. Indeed, theoretically, there will always be an infinite number of ways in which the benefits required from a product or service design can be delivered, even if some are only minor variants on each other. As the development process progresses, some design operations are discarded. There may be formal 'filters' at various points in the funnel whose sole purpose is to exclude some of the options. These filters often represent 'screens' which evaluate alternative designs against criteria of market acceptability, technical capability, financial return, and so on. Eventually, only one design option remains, which is then developed into its final form. The whole process moves from a broad concept capable of infinite interpretation at one end of the funnel to a fully formed and specified design at the other.

Just as the stage model in Figure 7.5 was a simplification, so is the concept of the development funnel. Do not expect that all product and service development will conform to the obvious and regular funnel shape as shown in Figure 7.6 (a). Most developments do not look like this, and more to the point, nor necessarily should they. Rather than see the funnel as a prescription for how development should be, it is better to see it as a metaphor for the design process which can be reshaped to reflect how the development process itself can be designed. The implication of this is that, even if an organisation does not want to progressively reduce its new product and service ideas using a perfectly smooth funnel, it certainly needs to understand what shape of funnel it really does want.

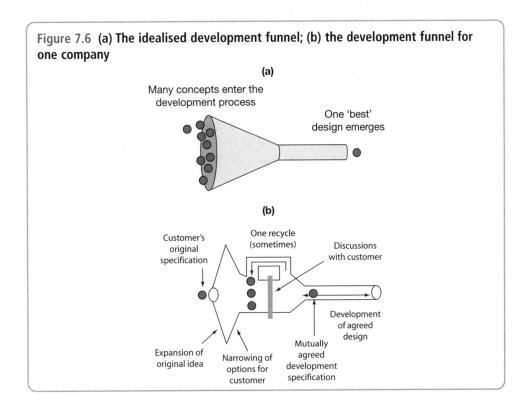

Figure 7.6 (a) The idealised development funnel; (b) the development funnel for one company

Consider the following quote from the vice-president in charge of product development in a company which makes advanced and customised electronic devices:

'Our customers put business our way mainly because we are experts in taking their problems and solving them. They usually give us an initial specification, to which we design, then at some time in the future they approve the design and we start to manufacture for them. What we have learnt to do right at the start of the development process is deliberately expand the number and scope of ideas beyond that which the customer first gives us. This can often result in a more creative solution than the customer had originally envisaged. After all, they are not the experts in this technology, we are. The trick is to not let this period last too long before we start narrowing down to two or three options which we can present to the customer. It is important to get to this stage before the customer's own internal deadline. That gives us time to refine ideas after we have presented them. Some designs will be recycled at this point if the customer wants a further development, but we have a rule that we only ever recycle once. From experience, if the customer wants further substantial changes then they are not even sure in their own mind what they really want. After this stage we go into the final development of a single design tied to a very tight specification agreed between ourselves and the customer.'

Figure 7.6 (b) illustrates how this particular executive saw the development funnel in her company. It may not be the perfect funnel of the textbooks, but it is well defined, well understood in the company, and can be easily communicated to the customer.

Simultaneous development

Earlier we described the development process as a set of individual, predetermined stages. Sometimes one stage is completed before the next one commences. This step-by-step, or sequential, approach was traditionally the typical form of product/service development. It has some advantages. It is easy to manage and control development projects organised in this way because each stage is clearly defined. In addition, each stage is completed before the next stage is begun, so each stage can focus its skills and expertise on a limited set of tasks. The main problem of the sequential approach is that it is both time consuming and costly. Any difficulties encountered during one stage might necessitate the design being halted while responsibility moves back to the previous stage. Yet often there is really little need to wait until the absolute finalisation of one stage before starting the next. Perhaps while generating the concept, the evaluation activity of screening and selection could be started. It would have to be a crude evaluation maybe, but nevertheless it is likely that some concepts could be judged as 'non-starters' relatively early on in the process of idea generation. Similarly, during the screening stage, it is likely that some aspects of the developing product or service will become obvious before the phase is finally complete. The preliminary work on these parts of the design could be commenced before the end of the final screening and selection process. In other words, one stage commences before the previous one has finished, so there is simultaneous or concurrent work at the stages (see Figure 7.7).

We can link this idea with the idea of uncertainty reduction discussed earlier. We made the point that uncertainty reduces as the design progresses. This also applies to each stage of the design, so uncertainty regarding the concept reduces through the concept generation stage, uncertainty about the preliminary design reduces through that phase, and so on. If this is so, then there must be some degree of certainty which the next stage can take as its starting point prior to the end of the previous stage. In other words, designers can be continually reacting to a preceding stage. However, this can only work if there is effective communication between each part of the stages.

A market requirements perspective on product and service development

Products and services are developed to satisfy market needs. It follows then that an important way of judging the effectiveness of the product and service development process is to judge how it performs in terms of quality, speed, dependability, flexibility and cost. These performance objectives have just as much relevance for the production of new product and service ideas or designs as they do for their ongoing production once they are introduced to the market. There is, however, a difference in judging how development processes satisfy market needs. When customers are both familiar and relatively satisfied with existing products and services they find it

Figure 7.7 **(a) Sequential arrangement of the stages in the development activity; (b) simultaneous arrangement of the stages in the development activity**

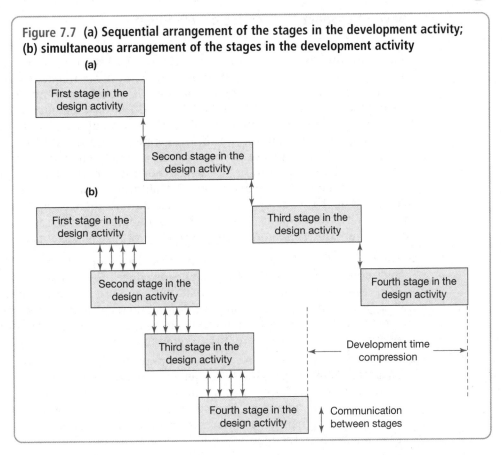

difficult to articulate their needs for novel products or services.[8] Customers often develop an enhanced understanding of their own needs only when they come into direct contact with the product or service and start to use it. Many software companies talk about the 'I don't know what I want but I'll know when I see it' syndrome, meaning that only when customers use the software are they in a position to articulate what they do or don't require.

Quality of product and service development

In Chapter 1, when we were discussing generic performance objectives, quality was not easy to define precisely. It is no easier when we are looking at the quality of product and service development. However, it is possible to distinguish high-quality product and service development from low-quality product and service development (although this is easier to do in hindsight). A useful approach if we wish to judge ongoing product and service development is to use the distinction between market requirements quality and operations resource quality. By market requirements quality we mean the ability of the output from the product or service development process (its final design) to meet the requirements of the company's intended market position. Operations resource quality indicates the extent to which the final design of the product or service allows the exploitation of the capabilities of the company's processes.

Speed of product and service development

Fast product and service development has become the norm in many industries. Sometimes this is because the pressures of market competition have forced companies to capture the markets' imagination with the frequent introduction of new offerings. Consumer electronics, for example, significantly increased the rate of new product introduction during the 1980s and 1990s. Sometimes it is the result of fast-changing consumer fashion. Getting to market quickly in order to capture a trend is important in many sectors of the garment and toy industries, for example. Sometimes fast development is the result of a rapidly changing technology base. Personal computers need to be updated frequently because their underlying technology is constantly improving. Sometimes all of these pressures are evident, as in many Internet-based services, for example. But no matter what pressures have motivated organisations to speed up their development processes, many have discovered that fast development brings a number of specific advantages.

- *Early market launch.* The most obvious advantage of an ability to develop products and services speedily is that they can be introduced to the market earlier and thus earn revenue for longer. Not only that, but if the product or service is the first of its type into the market, initially it has a hundred per cent market share, and customers may subsequently be reluctant to move to a competitor. Moreover, new offerings often can command price premiums.

- *Starting development late.* An alternative way of deploying a fast development advantage is by starting the development process late rather than introducing a product or service early. In some markets this has advantages, especially those where either the nature of customer demand or the availability of technology is uncertain and dynamic. In both cases fast development allows design decisions to be made closer to the point at which they are introduced to the market.

- *Frequent market stimulation.* Short development times allow the introduction of new or updated products or services more frequently. With a given set of development resourcing, if it takes 12 months to develop a new product and service, a company can only introduce a new or updated offering every 12 months. A six-month development process doubles their potential for making an impact in the market.

- *More opportunities for innovation.* In markets where the underlying 'technology' base is moving fast, it may be important to have frequent opportunities to introduce these new technologies as often as possible. Short development time with frequent updates produces more windows of opportunity for this type of innovation.

Dependability of product service development

Fast product and service development processes which cannot be relied on to deliver innovations dependably are, in reality, not fast at all. Development schedule slippage can extend development times, but worse, a lack of dependability adds to the uncertainty surrounding the development process. Conversely, processes that are dependable give stability and minimise development uncertainty. Yet, this poses a problem for most development processes. Unexpected technical difficulties, innovations that do not work or have to be modified, suppliers who themselves do not deliver solutions on time, customers or markets that change during the development process itself, and so on, all contribute to an uncertain and sometimes ambiguous environment. Certainly professional project management of the development process can help to reduce uncertainty. At least it should minimise the risk of internal disturbance to the development process if effective project management can prevent (or give early warning of) missed deadlines, detect bottlenecks and spot resource shortages. External disturbances to the process, however, will remain. Again, these may be minimised through close liaison with suppliers and effective market or environmental monitoring. Nevertheless, unexpected disruptions will always occur and the more innovative the development, the more likely they are to occur. This is why flexibility within the development process is one of the most important ways in which dependable delivery of new products and services can be ensured.

Flexibility of product and service development

Flexibility in new product and service development is usually taken to mean the ability of the development process to cope with external or internal change. The most common reason for external change is because the market in general, or specific customers, change their requirements. This may be prompted by their own customers and markets changing, or because developments in competitors' products or services dictate a matching or leapfrogging move in specification. Internal changes could include the emergence of superior materials or technical solutions. One suggestion for measuring development flexibility is to compare the cost of modifying a product or service design in response to such changes against the consequences to profitability if no changes are made. The higher the cost of modifying a product or service in response to a given change, the lower is the development flexibility.[9]

Two trends in many markets make development flexibility particularly important. The first is the pace and magnitude of environmental change. Although flexibility may not be needed in relatively predictable environments, it is clearly valuable in more fast-moving and volatile environments. The second factor, however, which amplifies environmental volatility is increasing complexity and interconnectedness of products and services. A bank, for example, may bundle together a number of separate services for one particular segment of its market. Privileged account holders may obtain special deposit rates, premium credit cards, insurance offers, travel facilities, and so on together in the same 'product'. Changing one aspect of this bundle may require changes to be made in other elements. So extending the credit card benefits to include extra travel insurance may also mean the redesign of the separate insurance element of the package.

One of the biggest benefits from development flexibility is that it can reduce development risk. Much development risk derives from the changes that occur during the development period. At the beginning of the development time, managers will presumably form a view concerning customer requirements, available technologies, and specification of competitor products and services. During the development period any, or all, of these might change. Customers may change their mind, either because their needs have changed or because they did not understand their own needs in the first place. The boundary of what was technologically possible may change as new technologies come onto the market, and competitors introduce rival products and services with superior or different performance. Development flexibility can help to minimise the impact of such occurrences.

The newspaper metaphor

Not all aspects of a development programme need to be flexible. Some aspects of a product or service may be judged unlikely to change over the development period, whereas others may be particularly difficult to forecast. It would seem sensible, therefore, to delay decisions regarding the uncertain elements until as late as possible in the process and build in sufficient flexibility in these elements rather than 'waste' it on the more stable elements. This is exactly how a daily newspaper designs its content. Special feature sections may be planned several weeks in advance and may even be printed well before their publication. Similarly, regular sections such as television times and advertisements are prepared several days before the newspaper is due to come out. On the day of publication, several stories may be vying for the front page. This is where flexibility is needed. The more flexible is the news desk in taking in new news and deciding the layout and priority of stories, the later the decision can be made and the more current the newspaper will be. Thus, in the development of any product or service, the more stable elements can be designed (in terms of making decisions around their form) well in advance, with their specification fixed early in the process. Other elements of the design can remain fluid so as to incorporate the latest thinking and then fixed only at the last moment.[10]

Incremental commitment

One method of retaining some flexibility in development processes is to avoid yes/no decisions. Alternative and parallel options can be progressed in stages. So, for example, an idea might be given approval to move to the next stage with no implied commitment to develop that idea through to the end of the project. One often quoted example concerns the development of the Boeing 777. Unusually for this type of product, the drawing which defined some parts had six or seven 'release levels'. This means that rather than confirming the final design of a part, it would be done in stages. So the design may be given approval for purposes of purchasing test materials but not for purposes of confirming tool design. This provided a more flexible way of delaying decisions until the last minute without holding up the whole development process.

Cost of product and service development

The cost of developing products and services is conventionally analysed in a similar way to the ongoing cost of producing the goods and services. In other words, cost factors are split up into three categories: the cost of buying the inputs to the process, the cost of providing the labour in the process, and the other general overhead costs of running the process. In most in-house development processes the latter two costs outweigh the former. As with day-to-day production of products and services, however, it is perhaps more revealing to consider how the other performance objectives drive cost:

- Quality – 'error-free' processes reduce reworking concepts and designs.
- Speed – fast development can use resources for shorter periods.

- Dependability – on-time development provides process stability, allows efficient resource planning and prevents expensive launch date slippage.

- Flexibility – the ability to delay design decisions can ensure the most appropriate options being chosen, preventing the costs of changing direction in the development.

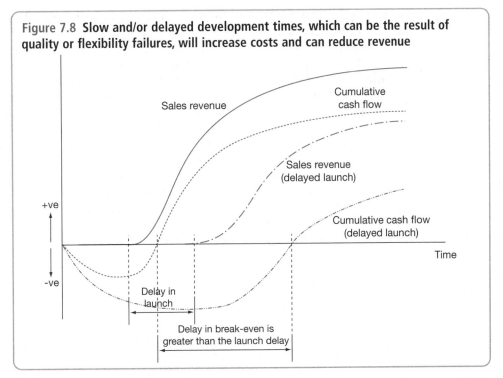

Figure 7.8 Slow and/or delayed development times, which can be the result of quality or flexibility failures, will increase costs and can reduce revenue

One way of thinking about the effect of the other development performance objectives on cost is shown in Figure 7.8. Whether through quality errors, intrinsically slow development processes, a lack of project dependability, or delays caused through inflexible development processes, the end result is that the development is late. Delayed completion of the development results in both more expenditure on the development and delayed (and probably reduced) revenue. The combination of both these effects usually means that the financial break-even point for a new product or service is delayed far more than the original delay in the product or service launch.

An operations resources perspective on product and service development

An operations resource perspective on product and service development involves examining the decision areas which we would normally use but applying them specifically to the development process. This is not difficult since all the categories can be applied directly. The capacity of the organisation's development processes needs managing over the long term, choices need to be made about whether some activities are performed in-house or subcontracted, investments in process technology are becoming an increasingly important element in managing new product and service development, and the organisation of the development process has become an important factor in managing the development process. Furthermore, behind each of these decisions lies the general objective of nurturing and exploiting the organisation's capabilities.

Product and service development capacity

As in any other process, the management of capacity involves deciding on the overall level of activity which an operation can support and also deciding how that level of support can be changed in order to respond to likely changes in demand. Essentially all the issues discussed in Chapters 4 and 5, in the context of the whole operation, also apply to the product and service development process. However, remember that the development process is a service in that it creates and works with knowledge for the benefit of its (usually internal) customers. This means that such options as building up an 'inventory' of designs is not usually feasible as such. Storing knowledge in a relatively developed form, however, may be possible. Indeed, in many ways, the whole development process can be characterised as building up and then deploying 'inventories' of design-based knowledge. Similarly, a 'capacity lagging' strategy (see Chapter 3) is not usually practical. The whole ethos of product and service development is one of broadly anticipating market requirements and attempting to bring ideas to market as early as possible. Deliberately planning to have a level of design capacity lower than the likely demand for such development rather implies extended time-to-market performance.

Uneven demand for development

The central issue for managing product and service development in many organisations is that the internal 'demand' for such development is uneven. Even in very large companies the rate of new service or product introduction is not constant. The need for product/service innovation is likely to be dictated by several complex and interrelated market factors. This may lead to several new offerings being introduced to the market close together, while at other times little development is needed, thus posing a resourcing problem. The capacity of a firm's development capability is often difficult to flex. The expertise necessary for development is embedded within designers, technologists, market analysts, and so on. Some expertise may be able to be hired in as and when it is needed, but much development resource is, in effect, fixed. Such a combination of varying demand and relatively fixed development capacity leads some organisations to be reluctant to invest in development capacity because they see it as an under-utilised resource. This may lead to a vicious cycle in which, although there is a short-term need for development resources, companies fail to invest in those resources because many of them (such as skilled development staff) cannot be hired in the short term, which leads to development projects being under-resourced with an increased chance of project overrun or failure to deliver appropriate technical solutions. This in turn may lead to the company losing business or otherwise suffering in the marketplace, which makes the company even less willing to invest in development resources (see Figure 7.9).

Product and service development networks

Most interest in supply networks has focused on the flow of parts, products (and occasionally services). Recently interest has also started to focus around the

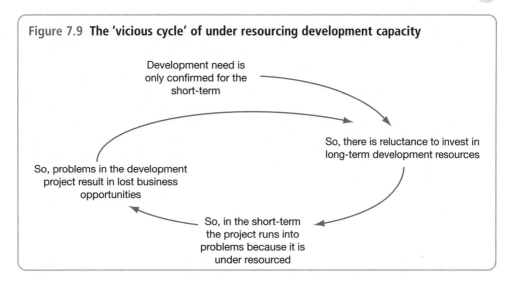

Figure 7.9 **The 'vicious cycle' of under resourcing development capacity**

exchange of product and service development knowledge, and the integrating of suppliers into the innovation process. This network of knowledge exchange is sometimes called the 'design (or development) network' or 'design chain' and in many ways the operations strategy decisions concerning conventional supply networks are also reflected in development networks. Two decisions in particular do much to determine the effectiveness of development networks. The first is the extent of vertical integration – the decisions of how much development to do in-house and how much to subcontract. The second is how to manage the relationship between the 'players' (most notably, customers and suppliers) in the network.

Example IBM develops its research base in China[11]

In the early years of the twenty-first century the idea of outsourcing manufacturing capability to China became well established. But perhaps of more long-term significance was the way in which global corporations started to outsource much of their research and development into the area. Yet, the first large company to establish a Chinese research and development presence was IBM, back in 1995. Now, there are hundreds of multinational research and development labs, but in 1995 it was seen as very much of a gamble. In fact, IBM has built research labs around the world, largely because the company is keen to attract the best talent. This was why IBM established its China Research Lab (CRL). And not only did China have technical talent in abundance, it was also clear that it would be the most important emerging market in the world. Having a research presence in the local market that understood its culture and language helped IBM establish close ties with customers who could become very important to its future growth. *'In the early days'*, says Dr. Katherine Shen who was the first employee of CRL, *'the problem was how to establish CRL in terms of capability and reputation. People had no way to foretell the future of the lab, and students on the hunt for jobs had never had the opportunity to work for this kind of organization before. People didn't know how many years the lab could survive.'*

▶

Now, with CRL firmly established with a reputation for the development of its own products, it has one particularly important tip for any other multinational establishing a remote development location. 'Make sure that you work closely with headquarters and business units in locations other than China'. This close collaboration with other labs allowed CRL to develop quickly. IBM sent its executives to visit CRL frequently, bringing new ideas and new understandings of how markets around the world were moving. Similarly, ERL established a programme of sending its own scientists around the world, not only to other IBM locations but to universities and independent research organisations. *'It's our experience'*, says CRL, *'that face-to-face communication plus conference calls works better than only knowing voices over the phone. Face-to-face communication is necessary for building trust and relationship between team members who are located across oceans.'*

In-house and subcontracted development

Companies position themselves on a continuum of varying degrees of design engagement with suppliers. At one extreme, a firm may retain all the necessary design capabilities in-house, while at the other end, it outsources all its development work, acting only as a focal point for the coordination of the design process. Between these extremes there exist options with varying degrees of internal and external design capability. In general, though, few companies are at the extremes of this continuum since process development necessitates some kind of interaction.

Design resources will be easy to control if they are kept in-house because they are closely aligned with the company's normal organisational structures, but control should be relatively loose because of the extra trust present in working with familiar colleagues. Outsourced design requires greater control and, because it has to be applied at a distance, contracts, often with penalty clauses for delay, may be needed. However, penalty clauses and contracts do not help to build long-term partnership relationships. In-house design has an advantage here because of its strong familiarity with the rest of the company's product or service range, operations processes, materials and market requirements. In contrast, outsourcing design can mean a weaker understanding in the short term, though if long-term relationships do develop, product and service familiarity will become stronger. The underlying capabilities built up through the development activity are generally assumed to be highly accessible when the development is done in-house. It is more difficult to provide access to tacit knowledge when it is housed outside the organisation. One motive behind companies investing heavily in common computer-aided design systems with their design suppliers is to ensure better accessibility. The overall cost of in-house versus outsourced development will vary, depending on the firm and the development project. An important difference, however, is that external developments tend to be regarded as a variable cost. The more external resources are used, the more the cost will be. In-house development is more of a fixed cost. Indeed a shift to outsourcing may occur because fixed development costs are viewed as too great. Paradoxically though, as external sourcing of development becomes an integral part of a company's strategy and relationships become stable, costs tend to be more or less fixed. Finally, a major driver of this decision can be the risk of knowledge leakage. Firms become concerned that experience gained through collaboration with a supplier of development expertise may be transferred to competitors. Again there is a paradox here. Companies usually outsource development primarily because of the supplier's capabilities which are themselves an accumulation of specialist knowledge from working with a variety of customers. Without such knowledge 'leakage' the benefits of the supplier's accumulated development capabilities would not even exist.[12]

Involving suppliers in development

The nature of the relationship with suppliers of product or service design services is not the same as when a supplier (even the same supplier) is providing product or services on an ongoing basis. For example, a component manufacturer, asked by a customer to design a new part, is providing a service rather than making a physical product. Even a supplier of services, in designing a new service for a customer, is engaged in a one-off (or at least relatively infrequent) exchange with its customer, in which its own knowledge is embedded in the design. In fact, a development relationship between customer and supplier is very similar to that between professional service firms, such as lawyers or consultants, and their clients. When choosing suppliers of design and development knowledge, companies often use criteria such as experience, trust, technical knowledge and 'relationship': a very similar list to that used to select their accountancy firm and their legal representatives.[13]

Characterising development relationships as professional services has practical implications, especially for suppliers. First, it emphasises the importance of customer perception of the 'process' of development as well as the final design which emerges from the process. Frequently demonstrating expertise during the development process allows suppliers to build their 'technical' reputation. Second, just as professional services, such as accountants, keep 'client files' which detail all contacts with individual clients, so design suppliers can use similar client knowledge management to manage the development of the relationship with customers. Third, it broadens the nature of contact with customers to include a more general responsibility for the development of relationships among other sources of expertise in the network. This has implications for the way suppliers might organise their design activity, for example in the way they attempt to respond to change in client needs during the creation of the design service, or in the use of implicit 'service guarantees'.

Involving customers in development

Few people know the merits and limitations of products and services better than the customers who use them. An obvious source, then, of feedback on product or service performance will be those who regularly use (or have ceased using) them. Different types of customer have the potential to provide different types of information. New users can pinpoint more attractive product and service features; those who have switched to a competitor offering can reveal its problems. A particularly interesting group of customers are the so-called 'lead users'.[14] Lead users have requirements of a product or service which will become more general in a market, but they are aware of these needs well ahead of the rest of the market. They also are users who will benefit significantly by finding a solution to their requirements. This may prompt them to develop or modify products or services themselves rather than wait for them to become commercially available. One reported example of lead-user research[15] concerns a new product development manager at Bose, the high-quality hi-fi and speaker company. On visiting his local music store, his professional ear noted the high quality of the background music being played. Investigating, he found that the store manager was using Bose speakers designed for home use but had attached metal strips around the speaker boxes so that they could be suspended close to the ceiling of the store. Inspired by this, Bose built prototypes of speakers which would satisfy the need for quality in-store speakers. These were taken back to the music store for further testing and eventually led to the company successfully entering the market for high-fidelity background music speakers.

Product and service development technology

One of the more significant changes in product and service development has been the growing importance of 'process' technology within the development process. Until relatively recently, although product/service technology knowledge was an important input into the development activity, technology used to process this knowledge was relatively unusual. It was limited to testing and evaluation technologies such as the mechanical devices which would simulate the stresses of everyday use on products such as automobiles or sports shoes, often testing them to destruction. Now process technologies are much more common, especially those based on computing power. For example, simulation software is now common in the design of everything from transportation services through to chemical factories. These allow developers to make design decisions in advance of the actual product or service being created. They allow designers to work through the experience of using the service or product and learn more about how it might operate in practice. They can explore possibilities, gain insights and, most important, they can explore the consequences of their decision decisions. In that sense, simulation is often a predictive rather than an optimising technology.

Knowledge management technologies

In many professional service firms, such as management consultancies, service development involves the evaluation of concepts and frameworks which can be used in client organisations to diagnose problems, analyse performance and construct possible solutions. They may include ideas of industry best practice, benchmarks of performance within an industry, and ideas which can be transported across industry boundaries. However, the characteristics of management consulting firms are that they are geographically dispersed and rarely are staff at their offices. The consultants spend most of their time in client organisations acquiring knowledge day by day. Yet, at the same time it is vital for such companies to avoid 'reinventing the wheel' continually. Any means of collectivising the cumulative knowledge and experience within the organisation must greatly assist the development of new concepts and frameworks. Most consultancy companies attempt to tackle this problem using knowledge management routines based on their intranet capabilities. This allows consultants to put their experience into a common pool, contact other staff within the company who have skills relevant to a current assignment, and identify previous similar assignments. In this way information is integrated into the ongoing knowledge development process within the company and can be tapped by those charged with developing new products.[16]

The significance of most of these development technologies is that they help to reduce the impact both of uncertainty and complexity. Simulation technologies allow developers to reduce their own uncertainty of how products and services will work in practice. Similarly, knowledge management systems consolidate and juxtapose information on what is happening within the organisation, thus presenting a more comprehensive vision and reducing uncertainty. CAD systems also help to deal with complexity by storing data on component details as they develop through various interactions. The absolute size and interrelatedness of some large products required sophisticated CAD systems if they are to be developed effectively. One of the most reported examples was the development of Boeing's 777 aircraft. The powerful CAD system used on this project was credited with Boeing's success in being able to involve its customers in the design process, allow more product configuration flexibility (such as the proportion of seats in each class, etc.), and still bring the huge project successfully to completion.

The organisation of product and service development

Amongst the criteria which are used to assess the effectiveness of different organisational forms, two in particular are important to product and service development – specialisation and integration. Specialisation is important because it encourages the depth of knowledge and technical understanding which is required in a concentrated form during the development process. Because of the (normally) finite time allowed for product and service development, technical knowledge needs to be deployed in a concentrated manner during limited windows of opportunity. Clustering resources around technical specialisms encourages the development of such concentrated knowledge. Integration is important because both product and services are composed of smaller components or subsystems. Coordinating the efforts of developers in different parts of a project and integrating their technical solutions in such a way as to reflect the market priorities within the development project is clearly an important aspect of any organisational structure. Both these criteria need to be incorporated in the organisational structure which is built to support a development project.

Project-based organisation structures

The total process of developing concepts through to market will almost certainly involve personnel from several different areas of the organisation. Most functions will have some part to play in making the decisions which will shape a final design. Yet, any development project will also have an existence of its own. It will have a project name, an individual manager or group of staff who are championing the project, a budget and, hopefully, a clear strategic purpose in the organisation. The organisational question is which of these two ideas – the various organisational functions which contribute to development, or the development project itself – should dominate the way in which the development activity is managed? The matrix form of organisation is a compromise between two (or more) approaches to clustering resources. It is an ideal model to examine the debates over an appropriate organisational form for development projects. Here the two conflicting approaches are the functional (specialist) dominated structure, and the project (or programme) dominated structure.

In a pure functional organisation all staff associated with the design project are based unambiguously in their functional groups. There is no project-based group at all. They may be working full-time on the project but all communication and liaison is carried out through their functional manager. The project exists only because of agreement between these functional managers. At the other extreme, all the individual members of staff from each function who are involved in the project could be moved out of their functions and perhaps even physically relocated to a 'task force' dedicated solely to the project. The task force could be led by a project manager who probably holds all the budget allocated to the design project. Not all members of the task force necessarily have to stay in the team throughout the development period, but a substantial core might see the project through from start to finish. Some members of a design team may even be from other companies. In between these two extremes there are various types of 'matrix' organisation with varying emphasis on these two aspects of the organisation (see Figure 7.10). And, although there are, in practice, an infinite number of structures, five stereotypical positions on the continuum are often discussed:

- *Functional organisation* – the project is divided into segments and assigned to relevant functional areas and/or groups within functional areas. The project is coordinated by functional and senior management.

- *Functional matrix* (or lightweight project manager) – a person is formally designated to oversee the project across different functional areas. This person has limited authority over functional people involved and serves primarily to plan and coordinate the project. The functional managers retain primary responsibility for their specific segments of the project.

- *Balanced matrix* – a person is assigned to oversee the project and interacts on an equal basis with functional managers. This person and the functional managers jointly direct work flow segments and approve technical and operational decisions.

- *Project matrix* (or heavyweight project manager) – a manager is assigned to oversee the project and is responsible for the completion of the project. Functional managers' involvement is limited to assigning personnel as needed and providing advisory expertise.

- *Project team* (or tiger team) – a manager is given responsibility for a project team composed of a core group of personnel from several functional areas and/or groups, assigned in a full-time basis. The functional managers have no formal involvement.

Effectiveness of the alternative structures

Although there is no clear 'winner' amongst the alternative organisational structures, there is wide support for structures towards the project rather than the functional end of the continuum. In one widely respected study, Professors Clark and Fujimoto argued that heavyweight project manager structures and dedicated project teams are the most efficient forms of organisation for product competitiveness, shorter lead-times and technical efficiency.[17] Other studies, although sometimes more equivocal, have shown that, in terms of the best total outcome from the development process, structures from balanced matrix through to project teams can all give high success rates. Perhaps of more interest is the suitability of the alternative structures for different types of product or service development project. Matrix structures are generally deemed to be appropriate for both simple and highly complex projects. Dedicated project teams, on the other hand, are seen as coming into their own especially in highly complex projects.

Yet again, there are advantages in functionally based development structures. In Chapter 10 we discuss how clustering resources around a functional specialism

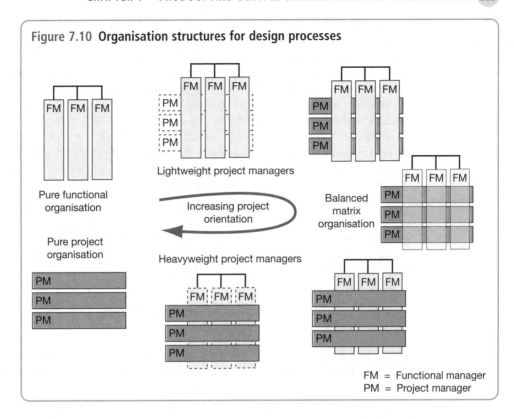

Figure 7.10 **Organisation structures for design processes**

FM = Functional manager
PM = Project manager

Pure functional organisation

Lightweight project managers

Balanced matrix organisation

Increasing project orientation

Pure project organisation

Heavyweight project managers

Example | **Changing development rules at Motorola[18]**

When the hugely popular RAZR (pronounced 'razor') phone was launched in late 2004, it was hailed as an iconic design. Yet, many industry commentators declared the product was a one-off from a once great company that would never regain its former status as a technology leader. It had already lost the position of market leader to Nokia some time earlier. But then followed the SLVR ('sliver'), a slim 'candy bar' design that offered an alternative to the RAZR's clamshell design, and the KRZR ('crazer'), a narrower version of the RAZR.

Much of the credit for the firm's return to successful new product development is credited to the way in which Motorola reorganised its development activities. *'One of the biggest changes at Motorola'*, says Jim Wicks, who heads the firm's 'consumer experience design' group, *'has been in the way that different teams, from design and engineering to marketing and finance, have got together to sort out the enormous complexities involved in developing new handsets. Co-operation improved because each group became willing to try something difficult that might help the others – without worrying too much about who would get blamed if they failed.'*

Now all the company's developers know that the rules of product development have changed. Even the company's hiring policy has changed, with more emphasis given to people and communication skills, as well as technical ability. *'After all'*, said one review of the company's success, *'when innovation involves complex interactions between many internal teams and outside partners – as it does at Motorola – the ability to communicate is prized'*.

helps the development of technical knowledge. Some organisations do manage to capture the deep technological and skills development advantages of functional structures, while at the same time coordinating between the functions so as to ensure satisfactory delivery of new product and service ideas. Perhaps the best known of these organisations is Toyota, the Japanese car giant. They have a strong functionally based organisation to develop their products. It adopts highly formalised development procedures to communicate between functions and places strict limits on the use of cross-functional teams. But what is really different is their approach to devising an organisational structure for product development which is appropriate for them. The argument which most companies have adopted to justify cross-functional project teams goes something like this:

> Problems with communication between traditional functions have been the main reasons for, in the past, failing to deliver new product and service ideas to specification, on time and to budget. Therefore, let us break down the walls between the functions and organise resources around the individual development projects. This will ensure good communication and a market-oriented culture.

Toyota and similar companies, on the other hand, have taken a different approach. Their argument goes something like this:

> The problem with cross-functional teams is that they can dissipate the carefully nurtured knowledge that exists within specialist functions. The real problem is how to retain this knowledge on which our future product development depends, while overcoming some of the traditional functional barriers which have inhibited communication between the functions. The solution is not to destroy the function but to devise the organisational mechanisms to ensure close control and integrative leadership which will make the functional organisation work.[19]

SUMMARY ANSWERS TO KEY QUESTIONS

Why is the way in which companies develop their products and services so important?

Competitive markets and demanding customers require updated and 'refreshed' products and services. Even small changes to products and services can have an impact on competitiveness. Markets are also becoming more fragmented, requiring product and service variants developed specifically for their needs. At the same time, technologies are offering increased opportunities for their exploitation within new products and services. Nor can one always separate the development of products and services on the one hand from the development of the processes that produce them on the other. Thus, product and service development influences and is influenced by almost all other decisions and activities within the operations function.

What processes do companies use to develop products and services?

There is no single product and service development process as such. However, there are many stage models which attempt to define and describe the various stages which a process should include. Typical of these stages are such activities as concept generation, concept screening, preliminary design, design evaluation and improvement, prototyping and final design, and developing the operations process. It is important to remember, though, that although these stages are often included (either formally or informally) within an organisation's product or service development process, they do not always follow each other sequentially. In reality the process may recycle through stages and even miss some out altogether. A common metaphor to illustrate the process is that of the 'funnel of development'. Again, though, the idea of many ideas passing through a funnel, being periodically screened and a single product or service design emerging from the end, is itself a simplification.

How should the effectiveness of the product and service development process be judged in terms of fulfilling market requirements?

The market effectiveness of any product or service development process can be judged in the same way as the day-to-day operations processes which produce the products and services themselves. That is, the development process can be judged in terms of its quality, speed, availability, flexibility and cost. Development projects must be error free, fast to market, deliver on time, retain sufficient flexibility to change as late as possible in the process, and not consume excessive development resources.

What operations resource-based decisions define a company's product and service development strategy?

Again, we can classify the decisions around the product or service development process in the same way as we can classify the decisions that specify the resources for day-to-day operations process. The overall development capacity of an organisation needs to be managed to reflect fluctuating demand for development activities, decisions must be made regarding the outsourcing of some, or all, of the development activity as well as the nature of the relationships with development 'suppliers', technologies such as computer aided design and simulation may be required to aid the development process, and the resources used for development need to be clustered into some form of organisational structure.

Further reading

Baldwin, C.Y. and Clark, K.B. (1997) 'Managing in an age of modularity', *Harvard Business Review*, September–October.

Cross, R. and Baird, L. (2000) 'Technology is not enough: improving performance by building organisational memory', *Sloan Management Review*, Spring.

Cooper, R.G. (2001) *Winning at New Products: Accelerating the Process from Idea to Launch*, 3rd edn. New York: Perseus Books.

Iansiti, M. and West, J. (1997) 'Technology integration: turning great research into great products', *Harvard Business Review*, May–June.

Trott, P. (2004) *Innovation Management and New Product Development*, 3rd edn. Harlow, UK: Financial Times Prentice Hall

Pisano, G.P. (1997) *The Development Factory*. Boston, MA: Harvard Business School Press.

Walker, S. (2006) *Sustainable by Design: Explorations in Theory and Practice*. London: Earthscan Publications.

Wheelwright, S.C. and Clark, K.B. (1995) *Leading Product Development*. New York: The Free Press.

Notes on the chapter

1 Sources include: Doran, J. (2006) 'Hoover heading for sell off as Dyson sweeps up in America', *The Times*, 4 February.

2 Baldwin, C.Y. and Clark, K.B. (1997) 'Managing in an age of modularity', *Harvard Business Review*, September–October.

3 Mass customisation was first fully articulated in Pine, B.J. (1993) *Mass Customisation: The New Frontier in Business Competition*. Boston, MA: Harvard Business School Press; See also Hart, C.W.L. (1995) 'Mass customisation: conceptual underpinnings, opportunities and threats', *International Journal of Service Industry Management*, 6(2).

4 Ahlström, P. and Westbrook, R. (1999) 'Implications of mass customisation for operations management', *International Journal of Operations and Production Management*, 19(3).

5 Lehnerd, A.P. quoted in Pine, B.J. (1993) op.cit.

6 Source: Anderson, Chris (2006) *The Long Tail: Why the Future of Business is Selling Less to More*. New York: Hyperion, pp. 11–30.

7 Source: *The Economist* (2006) 'Silent skies', 11 November.

8 von Hippel, E. (1988) *The Sources of Innovation*. New York: Oxford University Press.

9 Thomke, S. and Reinertsen, D. (1998) 'Agile product development', *California Management Review*, 41(1).

10 Ibid.

11 Source: Zhao, Chen (2006) 'IBM research in China', *Interactions,* March–April.

12 The above discussion is based on Twigg, D. (1997) 'A typology of supplier involvement in automotive product development', Warwick Business School Research Paper No. 271.

13 Haywood-Farmer, J. and Nollet, J. (1991) *Services Plus: Effective Service Management*. Boucherville, Quebec: Morin.

14 von Hippel, E., Churchill, J. and Sonnack, M. (1998) *Breakthrough Products and Services with Lead User Research*. New York: Oxford University Press.

15 Ibid.

16 Iansiti, M. and MacCormack, A. (1997) 'Developing products on internet time', *Harvard Business Review*, September–October.

17 Clark, K.B. and Fujimoto, T. (1991) *Product Development Performance*. Boston, MA: Harvard Business School Press.

18 Sources: Motorola website (2007); *The Economist* (2006) 'Motorola's boss, is combining slim mobile phones with big bets', 5 October.

19 Sobek, D.K. II, Licker, J.K. and Ward, A.C. (1998) 'Another look at how Toyota integrates product development', *Harvard Business Review*, July–August.

The process of operations strategy – sustainable alignment

Introduction

The process of strategy formulation is concerned with 'how' operations strategies are put together. It is important because, although strategies will vary from organisation to organisation, they should attempt to reconcile market requirements with operations resources. This is the first of three chapters that will focus explicitly on the process of operations strategy. It will look at the objective of formulation, namely, the achievement of some kind of alignment, or 'fit', between what the market wants, and what the operation can deliver, and how that 'alignment' can be sustained over time (Figure 8.1). The objective of the reconciliation process is both to satisfy market requirements through appropriate operations resources, *and* to develop those resources in the long term so that they can provide competitive capabilities in the longer term that are sufficiently powerful to achieve sustainable competitive advantage.

Figure 8.1 This chapter concerns the process of achieving sustainable alignment of market requirements with operations resources

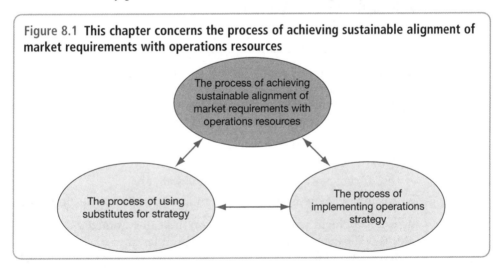

KEY QUESTIONS

- *What is 'sustainable alignment'?*
- *Why is sustainability of alignment so important?*
- *What is the formulation process trying to achieve?*
- *What are the practical challenges of formulating operations strategies?*

What is sustainable alignment?

The concept of 'sustainable alignment' in operations strategy is the active process of continually reconciling operational resources with market requirements so that there is an approximate degree of 'fit' or alignment between them. This is, in practice, more difficult that it sounds. The uncertain, and sometimes fickle, nature of many markets makes it difficult to interpret their behaviour in such a way as to provide operations with clear and unambiguous objectives. Similarly, the capabilities and constraints of the operation's resources and processes may themselves be less than predictable, especially when they are being introduced into an existing operation. The process of achieving alignment, therefore, is difficult even with internally coordinated communication between those parts of the firm responsible for market-facing activities and those responsible for internal resource-management activities. (Though in practice many of the problems of a lack of alignment between market requirements and operations resources are the result of different parts of the firm pursuing different objectives, or pursuing the same objective in different ways.) Figure 8.2 illustrates a conceptual model of what is meant by alignment.

The vertical dimension represents the nature and level of market requirements either because they reflect the intrinsic needs of customers or because their expectations have been shaped by the firm's marketing activity. This includes such factors as:

- strength of brand/reputation;
- degree of differentiation;
- extent of plausible market promises.

Movement along the dimension indicates a broadly enhanced level of market performance or market capabilities.

The horizontal scale represents the level and nature of the firm's operations resource and processes capabilities. This includes such things as:

- the performance of the operation in terms of its ability to achieve competitive objectives;
- the efficiency with which it uses its resources;
- the ability of the firm's resources to underpin its business processes.

Again, movement along the dimension indicates a broadly enhanced level of 'operations performance' and operations capabilities.

Achieving 'alignment' means achieving an approximate balance between 'required market performance' and 'actual operations performance'. So when alignment is achieved firms' customers do not need, or expect, levels of operations performance which it is unable to supply. Nor does the firm have operations strengths which are either inappropriate for market needs or remain unexploited in the market. The diagonal line in Figure 8.2, therefore, represents a 'line of fit with market and operations in balance. Be careful, however, in using this diagrammatic representation. It is a conceptual model rather than a practical tool. We have deliberately been vague in calibrating or even defining precisely the two axes in the figure. The model is intended merely to illustrate some ideas around the concept of alignment.

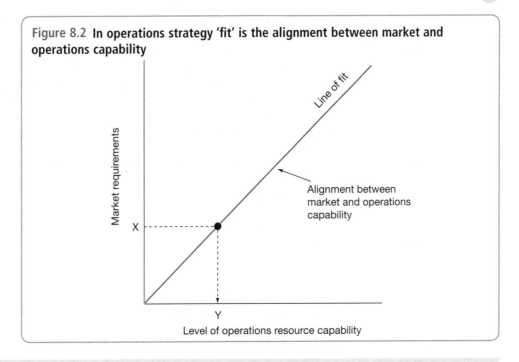

Figure 8.2 In operations strategy 'fit' is the alignment between market and operations capability

(Graph with y-axis labelled "Market requirements" and x-axis labelled "Level of operations resource capability". A diagonal "Line of fit" runs from bottom-left to top-right. A point on the line is marked, with dashed lines to X on the y-axis and Y on the x-axis. An arrow points to the line labelled "Alignment between market and operations capability".)

Example | **Is it 'Googley'?[1]**

To achieve its market objectives, a firm must be able to gain access to appropriate resources. If its most important resource is the people it employs, a firm may try and make sure that its people reflect the vision and culture.

For example, drivers on Highway 101 that passes through Silicon Valley, if they were paying attention, would have noticed a billboard that read: '[first10-digit prime found in consecutive digits of e].com'. Those drivers with both the intellectual curiosity and the mathematical knowledge would have realised that the number in question is 7427466391, and is a sequence that starts at the 101st digit of the constant e (the base of the natural logarithm). Those that looked up the web site then found a mathematically more difficult riddle to solve. Solving that led to another web page where they were invited to submit their CVs to Google. It was one of Google's ideas for attracting the type of clever but inventive staff that it needs, and a way of further establishing Google as the type of company that has the quirky vision to make it attractive to such people.

The tone of the billboard was, as it employees like to say, 'Googley' – something that evokes a 'humble, cosmopolitan, different, toned down, classiness'. At a recent conference, instead of the rock music and flashing lights used by most firms to introduce their speakers, Google played Bach's Brandenburg Concerto No. 3 and had a 'thought puzzle' placed on every seat. What ever else it is, Google is an organisation that thinks hard about what it is, what it wants to be, and how its people can sustain its position.

Should operations resources align with the market, or vice versa?

The task of achieving alignment can be approached in two ways. Firstly, and most commonly, an operation can seek to identify existing market requirements and then align its resources to match them. This approach has a number of intrinsic advantages, not least of which is the sheer availability of practical tools and techniques for classifying and identifying market requirements. This model also falls neatly into the traditional top-down hierarchy of strategies (discussed in Chapter 1) whereby operations' role is to support predetermined market decisions. The alternative approach is for the operation to analyse its resources and then seek market opportunities that align well with it (see Figure 8.3). In practice, however, this is difficult to do, so it is not surprising that the majority of models for operations strategy development start with market requirements and work through to the implications for operations resources. After all, all businesses have markets. They may not always be well understood and the business may not be good at identifying which part of a market it is trying to serve. However, all businesses have some idea of the requirements of their market. But, not every business understands its operations capabilities and many may not even have any 'distinctive' capabilities. And while we have continually stressed the importance of leveraging operations capabilities into the marketplace, this does presuppose that a business has some operations capabilities worth leveraging.

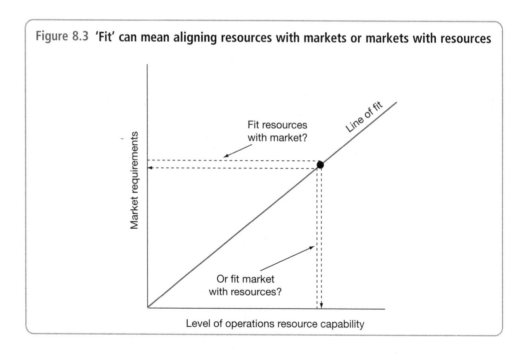

Figure 8.3 'Fit' can mean aligning resources with markets or markets with resources

The implication of this is that at relatively low levels of alignment between market requirements and operations resource capabilities, the concept of alignment may have to be largely market driven, that is, resources are shaped in order to align with market requirements. Such an approach would start with a formal statement of market positioning as derived from an organisation's understanding of the market segments it wishes to address and the activities of its competitors. Following on from this, generic operations performance objectives would be used as a device to translate market positioning into a statement of market requirements which was understandable and useful to the operations function. These objectives would influence the various operations strategy 'content' decisions which in turn, over time, shape the operations capabilities. As we shall see later, the practical frameworks designed to help formulate operations strategy are based on this approach which is summarised in Figure 8.4 (see page 232). At higher levels of alignment where demanding levels of market requirements are being matched with unique and strategic operations resources capabilities, it is those capabilities themselves that may dictate the search for markets which can fully appreciate them. Figure 8.4 also illustrates this operations resource perspective approach. Here the operations capabilities embedded within its tangible and intangible resources and its operations processes are articulated. The operations strategy 'content' decisions are made with the objective of enhancing the strategic capabilities of the organisation. These result in a particular set of operations performance objectives which define a potential set of market positions. The final market positioning strategy which is selected under a 'pure' version of this approach is the one that best exploits the organisation's core capabilities.

'Alignment' is both a static and a dynamic concept

Although the advantages of alignment might seem obvious, and are widely accepted managerial common sense, the underlying concept is not necessarily as straightforward as it sounds. This is because 'alignment' is both a static attribute and a dynamic process. It is not enough to achieve some degree of alignment to a single point in time, it also has to be sustained over time. For example, an online share trading operation may question its operations strategy by asking, 'How good are our back-office operations at delivering the response time which our share trading market requires?' Answering this question involves assessing how the share trading back-office operations are organised and their market performance. But, equally legitimate question are, 'How could the market change and make current performance inadequate?', or 'How long will it be before our investment in state-of-the-art processing technology has an impact?' These questions have more to do with the dynamic process of achieving alignment.

Achieving alignment at different levels

Look at our representation of alignment as the fit between market requirements and operations resources, and it becomes obvious that one can achieve this state of alignment at different levels. If the requirements placed upon the organisation by its markets are relatively undemanding, then the corresponding level of resource capability will not need to be particularly high. Or to put it another way, if you make relatively modest promises to your market, you do not need particularly well developed levels of operations capability to fulfil those promises. By extension, the more demanding the level of market requirements, or the more ambitious the promises made to the market, then the greater will have to be the level of operations resource capability. So, achieving alignment is a necessary but not sufficient condition for a successful operations strategy. Most firms would see their overall strategic objectives as achieving alignment at a level that implies some degree of long-term competitive success. In Figure 8.5 (see page 233) point A represents alignment at a low level, while point B represents alignment at a higher level. The assumption in most firms' operations strategies is that point B is a more desirable position than point A because it is more likely to represent a financially successful position. High levels of market performance, achieved as a result of high levels of operations resource capability being generally more difficult for competitors to match.

Figure 8.4 Align operations resources with market requirements, or align market positioning with operations resources capabilities

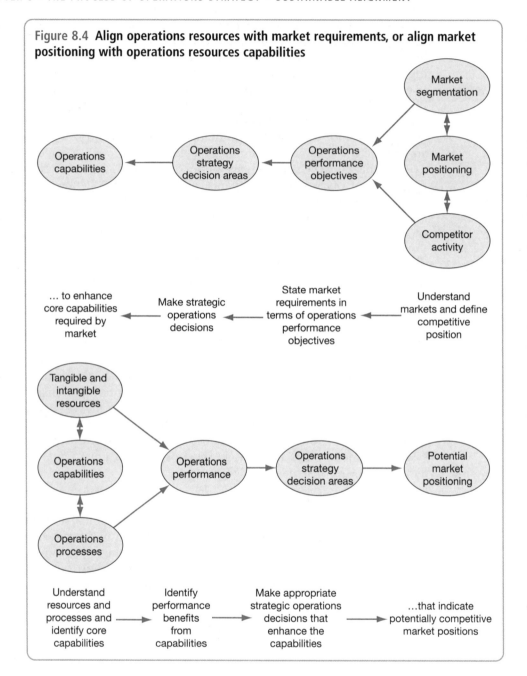

Tight alignment and loose alignment

So far in our diagrammatic representation of alignment we have represented alignment as being a single point of alignment between market requirements and operations resource capability. The implication of this is that there is a single 'tight' and well defined statement of market requirements together with a relatively narrow set of operations capabilities that correspond exactly with market requirements. Remember though that both market requirements and operations resource capabil-

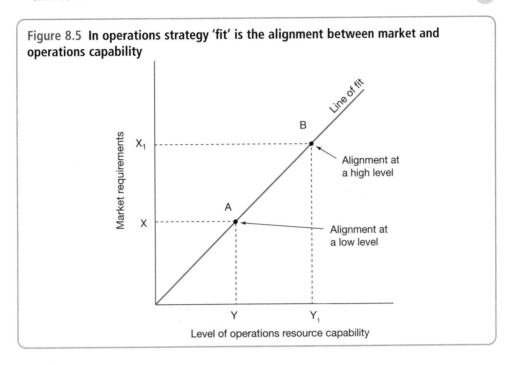

Figure 8.5 **In operations strategy 'fit' is the alignment between market and operations capability**

ities can change over time. Markets are dynamic and exhibit, sometimes unexpected, changes. Operations resource capabilities may change at a slower pace but are still subject to, sometimes unexpected, movements. Therefore, on our diagrammatic representation, the origin of the requirements and resources diagram can shift over time. So, if the alignment between operations capabilities and market requirements is too 'tight' or 'narrow' this could mean that, what was previously alignment between the two, can (relatively) move off the line of it. A looser or broader set of capabilities and market relationships however can provide some insurance against these unexpected shifts. This difference between tight and loose alignment is illustrated in Figure 8.6 (see page 234).

Sustaining alignment over time

Most organisations are as mortal as the people who create and run them. So why are those firms that last for many years the exception rather than the rule? Most new business ventures fail to make it past their first year. The obvious explanation is that firms fail to reconcile market requirements and operations resources because it is all too easy either to misinterpret customer requirements or fail to develop the requisite operational capabilities. At the same time, history is littered with companies that had their moment of competitive glory but then faded or disappeared for ever. They may have effectively reconciled operational resources and market requirements to achieve alignment at one point in time. Yet, subsequently they failed to sustain this position. And while many other factors, such as macroeconomic shifts and exchange rate fluctuations, have a huge influence on the success of organisations, the ongoing battle to reconcile resources and requirements to achieve sustainable alignment is clearly of great importance. This emphasises the idea that operations

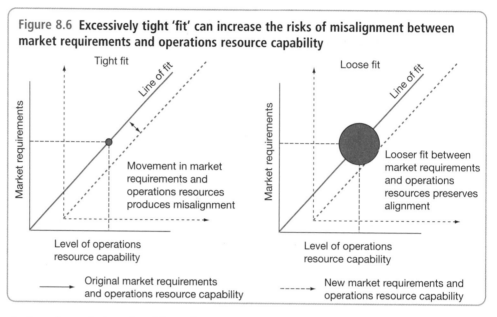

Figure 8.6 Excessively tight 'fit' can increase the risks of misalignment between market requirements and operations resource capability

strategy formulation should not be a one-off event. Strategies will be formed repeatedly over time in order to take into account changes in both operations resources and market requirements. At each of these 'formulation episodes' (which may be both frequent and informal), a key objective is likely to be the retention of 'alignment'. Sometimes this will mean maintaining alignment during an increase in both operations resource capabilities and market requirements. More realistically, even the most successful long-run firms will experience differing degrees of alignment between market requirements and their operational resources.

Example   Clean and Green (CAG) Recycling Services

With the widespread adoption of copying and printing technologies, paper usage for most firms exploded, leaving them with vast quantities of paper to dispose of. Recognising this requirement as a potential opportunity for a new business, 'Clean and Green' began operating in late 1990 as a venture in and around the town of Maastricht – initially targeting medium-sized businesses with a confidential paper removal and recycling service. Figure 8.7 illustrates their initial operations strategy matrix with critical intersections. The idea was to allow businesses to dispose of their paper without worrying about negative environmental impact (in effect CAG were also offering intangible enhancement to their clients' reputation for citizenship) while also preventing confidential information leaks. As a support to their relatively focused operations, their marketing effort emphasised the quality and dependability of the service. Initially, the operation consisted of dedicated collection receptacles and a number of vehicles (capacity and process technology decisions). Additionally, the firm made special contractual arrangements with paper producers (a supply network decision).

The firm entered the next phase of its development when 'green' politics were increasingly influential at the national and local level and many publicly provided recycling services were developed. Having built up a reputation with local businesses, the firm was invited by a consortium of local authorities to tender for a domestic paper collection con-

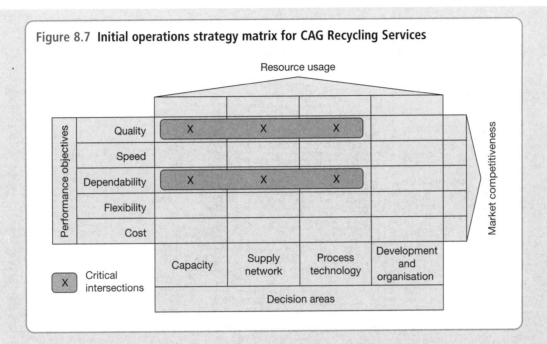

Figure 8.7 Initial operations strategy matrix for CAG Recycling Services

tract. This was not just an increase in requirements but also a very different kind of market. It required the collection and recycling of a wider range of paper from more sites and without any value being placed upon the confidentiality of their service. CAG needed to add capacity and enhance its process technology in order to both increase flexibility and reduce costs. After negotiating with the consortium (which was keen to assist in the development of a range of potential contractors), it was awarded a contract with an understanding that it would take almost 12 months to acquire and develop the requisite operational capability. Figure 8.8 illustrates how CAG's operations strategy evolved to cope with these new requirements.

After the award of this first very large contract, CAG won more public and private work and over time both added extra capacity and introduced other types (different materials, etc.) of recycling process. This was an essentially incremental process over a period of about four years, leveraging and developing existing capability while introducing new relationships with other physical recycling plants.

The firm's next significant strategic decision was to gamble on future recycling legislation in the Netherlands and the rest of Europe. Over an 18-month period CAG invested heavily in a 'complete recycling' capability which allowed it to collect a large percentage of all recyclable household waste. This meant extra collection capacity (vehicles and staff), different collection and sorting systems and new external relationships (including political lobbying). In particular, growth of the firm and the nature of the work meant that significantly more temporary staff were employed. This necessitated the introduction of new control and training systems (see Figure 8.9).

Future legislation was likely to 'require' much higher levels of domestic waste to be recycled which would introduce a step change in market requirements. Unlike CAG's previous experience, in trying to achieve a sustainable advantage for this new market, it deliberately developed capability before the market required it.

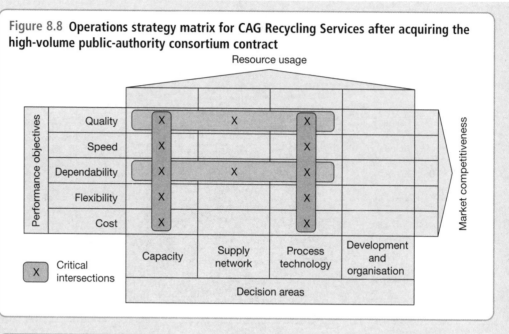

Figure 8.8 Operations strategy matrix for CAG Recycling Services after acquiring the high-volume public-authority consortium contract

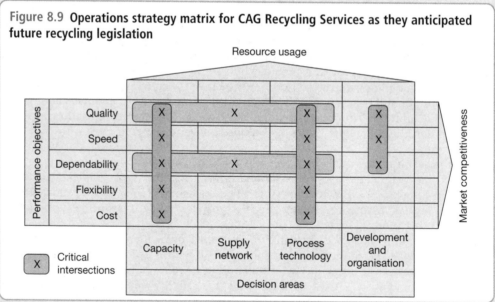

Figure 8.9 Operations strategy matrix for CAG Recycling Services as they anticipated future recycling legislation

CAG over time

The operations strategy matrix to describe CAG's changing issues over time allows us to see how different resource and requirement issues become more or less important as the company develops and allows us to discuss the complexity, coherence and comprehensiveness of the overall strategy. However, it does not fully capture the balancing act of reconciliation over time. Figure 8.10 represents this dynamic process.

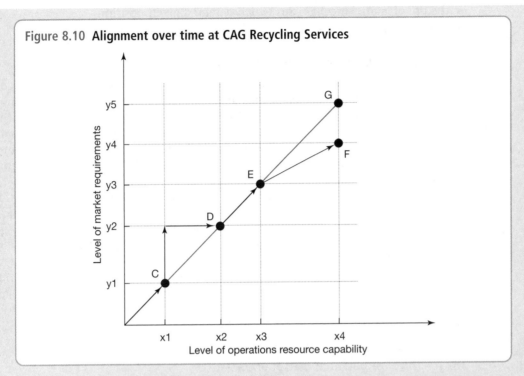

Figure 8.10 **Alignment over time at CAG Recycling Services**

CAG was the first in their area to offer a confidential and environmentally friendly paper disposal service and, therefore, the initial level of market requirement (shown as level y1 on Figure 8.10) exactly matched the operation's capability to deliver (x1). This 'start-up' phase is represented on the above figure by the transition to position C. Having built up a reputation with local businesses over a three-year period, the firm was invited by a consortium of local authorities to tender for a much larger single contract (market requirement, y2). It was awarded a contract with an understanding that it would take CAG a number of months to acquire and develop the requisite operational capability (x2). This transition from points C to D on the diagram is shown as a shift to the left of the 'line of alignment' – indicating that initially they had insufficient capability for the market requirements. After the award of this first large contract, the firm won more and more similar public and private work and over time (requirements shifting from y2 to y3) added gradually to its underlying capabilities. This incremental growth phase is represented by the transition from point D to E. The strategic decision to invest heavily in a 'complete recycling' capability (x3) allowed it to present a more extensive market offering (y3). It was then CAG's strategic strategy to anticipate the introduction of new legislation introducing a step change in market requirements (y5). On the diagram, position F is to the right of the 'line of alignment' (this indicates that they only currently need to meet y4 requirements) but they anticipate rapidly leveraging (i.e. moving to position G) these capabilities once the new market requirements are introduced.

'Static' and 'dynamic' sustainability

The CAG example reinforces the point that even the most successful and apparently problem-free development paths include times of mismatch between resources and requirements. More specifically, it illustrates the two basic models for assuring sustainability:

- the use of 'static' mechanisms which defend a given position;
- the use of 'dynamic' mechanisms which encourage innovation and change.

'Static' or defensive approaches to sustainability

'Static' mechanisms for achieving sustainability are concerned with preventing competitors from attacking existing market and resource positions, rather than trying to move to an entirely new position. So to some extent, it is a defensive rather than offensive approach. An operation can seek to identify the market isolating (barriers to entry) and resource isolating (barriers to imitation) mechanisms that minimise change and act to keep a lock on a specific resource/requirement position. It can do this using internal and external approaches.

Internal approaches exploit the idea that we have used before; that operations resources can be considered particularly valuable if they are scarce, difficult to move, difficult to copy or difficult to find substitutes for. Because they are difficult to replicate, such resources act to sustain competitive advantage by preventing competitors replicating their advantage. External mechanisms are based on the idea that the overall performance of a firm will depend on how well its strategy and its actions take into account the specific structure of the industry in which it is competing. In particular, the work of Michael Porter has been hugely influential in understanding this view. The forces Porter refers to can be summarised as:

(a) the bargaining power of suppliers and buyers;

(b) the threat of potential market entrants;

(c) the threat of substitute products/services; and

(d) the challenge from existing competitive rivals.

Table 8.1 offers some illustrations of how operations strategy can exploit both internal and external strategic attributes of sustainability.

'Dynamic' or offensive approaches to sustainability

Ultimately, even in the most isolated of market niches, customer requirements evolve and, as a result, operational capabilities also need to evolve. So, in addition to exploiting existing barriers to entry and imitation, operations can raise their game through innovation and change in order to achieve sustainability. Doing this involves the operation actively moving up the line of alignment and achieving a balance between market requirements and operations resources at a higher level. For instance, prior to the launch of the Federal Express 'next day' delivery service ('for when it absolutely, positively has to be there overnight') market analyses suggested that few organisations needed such a fast and dependable service.[2] Once launched, however, early adopters of the service, such as global industrial firms and professional and financial services, obtained competitive advantage from the speed and dependability benefits of overnight mail. As a result, increasing numbers of firms began to use the service. Although rivals eventually began to imitate the services, for a number of years this radical operating innovation proved to be hugely profitable for Federal Express, which, in effect, had gone to market with an entirely new set of capabilities delivering significantly improved speed and dependability performance.

Table 8.1 Internal and external 'defensive' static mechanisms of sustainability

'Defensive' static mechanisms of sustainability			
Internal	*Notes*	*External*	*Notes*
Scarcity	Scarce operational resources might include customised production facilities, or experienced operational staff embodying tacit knowledge developed over time, etc.	Bargaining power of buyers and suppliers	If an operation can control access to the market then other firms are effectively compelled to supply. Suppliers are able to exploit similar strategies if their products/services are seen as vital. The 'Intel Inside' marketing campaign was an example of such a strategy.
Difficult to move	Any operational resource (i.e. process technology) developed in-house cannot be accessed without purchasing the entire company. Because of greater labour mobility, critical skills and experiences can move to rivals quite easily. The resources that are the most difficult to move are therefore those that 'don't walk on legs' and are tied somehow into the operation.	The threat of potential market entrants	The threat posed by new entrants can be dramatically reduced if firms have an effective 'barrier to entry' (e.g. economies of scale in steel production, installed networks in telecommunications).
Difficult to copy	Although similar to the idea of mobility, the relative imitability of a resource is an important defensive characteristic. Any 'learning curve' effects that might exist in operations can make capabilities difficult to copy.	The threat of substitute products and/or services	Reducing the threat from substitute products/ services is an extension of the mechanisms associated with barriers to entry (see above), but specifically related to products and services, however. If the operation has established a dominant technological standard (e.g. Microsoft operating systems), this can be a major barrier to entry.
Difficult to create a substitute	No operation wants its operational resources to become irrelevant through the introduction of a substitute (or alternative) Yet, it can happen; the open protocols of the internet make switching and, hence, substitution far easier.	The challenge from existing competitive rivals	The challenge from existing rivals is strongly influenced by all of the categories discussed above. Additionally, because operations guard their process secrets, most firms 'reverse engineer' rival products/services to try to establish the nature of the process.

Example **Dell (part 2) – Things change OK?**[3]

What is right at one time may become a liability later on. For 20 years Dell had exhibited remarkable growth in the PC market. (See the Example, 'Dell (Part 1) – Learning how to turn difficulties into advantages' in Chapter 6.) Yet, by the mid 2000s, although still the largest seller of PCs in the world, growth had started to slow down and the company's stock market value had been downgraded. The irony of this is that, what had been one of the company's main advantages, its direct sales model using the internet and its market power to squeeze price reductions from suppliers, were starting to be seen as disadvantages.

Some commentators claimed that, although the market had changed, Dell's operating model had not. Over the 20 years Dell had developed a radically different and very successful set of operations based on an extremely efficient supply chain, low inventories, modular product designs that allowed it to customise to its individual customer requirements, and a direct link to customers. All of this allowed it to sell robust computers at low prices. Some of the questions raised by commentators focused on Dell's size. Perhaps it had grown so big that its lean supply model was no longer appropriate? How could a $56 billion company remain lean, sharp and alert? Other commentators pointed out that Dell's rivals had also now learnt to run efficient supply chains. ('Getting a 20 year competitive advantage from your knowledge of how to run supply chains isn't too bad.') However, one of the main factors was seen as the shift in the nature of the market itself. Sales of PCs to business users had become largely a commodity business with wafer-thin margins, and this part of the market was growing slowly compared with the sale of computers to individuals. Selling computers to individuals provided slightly better margins than the corporate market, but they increasingly wanted up-to-date computers with a high design value, and most significantly, they wanted to see, touch, and feel the products before buying them. This was clearly a problem for a company like Dell who had spent 20 years investing in its telephone and later, internet-based sales channels. Also, Dell's early attempts to move into products other than PCs, such as televisions, were also hindered by its lack of physical stores. What all commentators agreed on was that in the fast moving and cut-throat computer business, where market requirements could change overnight, operations resources must constantly develop appropriate new capabilities.

The Red Queen effect

In 1973, Leigh Van Valen was searching for a way to describe the discovery that he had made while studying marine fossils. He had established that no matter how long a family of animals had already existed, the probability that the family will become extinct is unaffected. In other words, the struggle for survival never gets easier. However well a species fits with its environment it can never relax. The analogy that Van Valen drew has a strong resonance with business realities. He recalled from Alice's adventures through the looking glass that she had encountered living chess pieces and, in particular, the Red Queen.

> 'Well, in our country', said Alice, still panting a little, 'you'd generally get to somewhere else – if you ran very fast for a long time, as we've been doing'. 'A slow sort of country!' said the Queen. 'Now, here, you see, it takes all the running you can do, to keep in the same place. If you want to get somewhere else, you must run at least twice as fast as that!'

(Lewis Carroll (1871), Alice Through the Looking Glass)

In many respects this is like business. The strategy that proves the most effective is the one that people will try to block or imitate. Innovations are soon countered in response by others that are stronger. The quality revolution in manufacturing industry, for example, is widely accepted, but most firms that have survived the past 15 years (in the automotive sector, for example) now achieve much higher levels of quality performance, reflecting greater depth of operational capability. Yet, their relative position has in many cases not changed. Their competitors who have survived have only done so by achieving similar levels of quality themselves.

Learning, appropriation and path dependency

For any operation to achieve 'dynamic' sustainability, its operations strategy needs to address three important issues:

- How can an operations strategy encourage the learning necessary to make sure that operations knowledge is carried forward over time?
- How can an operations strategy ensure that the organisation appropriates (captures the value of) the competitive benefits which are derived from any innovations?
- How can an operations strategy take into account the fact that innovations have a momentum of their own and are strongly path dependent (they are influenced by what has happened before)?

Organisational learning

In uncertain environments any organisation's ability to pre-plan or make decisions in advance is limited. So, rather than adhering dogmatically to a predetermined plan, it may be better to adapt as circumstances change. And, the more uncertain the environment, the more an operation needs to emphasise this form of strategic flexibility and develop its ability to learn from events. Generally, this strategic flexibility depends on a learning process which concerns the development of insights and knowledge, and establishes the connections between past actions, the results of those actions, and future intentions. The crucial issue here is an essentially pragmatic and practical one, 'How does an operations strategy encourage, facilitate and exploit learning, in order to develop strategic sustainability?' Initially this requires us to recognise that there is a distinction between single- and double-loop learning.[4]

Single- and double-loop learning

Single-loop learning is a phenomenon which is widely understood in operations management. It occurs when there is repetitive association between input and output factors. Statistical process control, for instance, measures output characteristics from a process, such as product weight, telephone response time, etc. These can then be used to alter input conditions, such as supplier quality, manufacturing consistency, staff training, with the intention of 'improving' the output. In Chapter 6 we indicated how such forms of control provide the learning which can form the basis for strategic improvement. Every time an operational error or problem is detected, it is corrected or solved, and more is learned about the process, but without questioning or altering the underlying values and objectives of the process.

Single-loop learning is of great importance to the ongoing management of operations. The underlying operational resources can become proficient at examining their processes and monitoring general performance against generic performance objectives (cost, quality, speed, etc.), thereby providing essential process knowledge and stability. Unfortunately, the kind of 'deep' system-specific process knowledge that is so crucial to effective single-loop learning can, over time, help to create the kind of inertia that proves so difficult to overcome when an operation has to adapt to a changing environment. All effective operations are better at doing what they have done before and this is a crucial source of advantage. But while an operation develops its distinctive capability only on the basis of single-loop learning, it is exposing itself to risks associated with the things that it does not do well (see Figure 8.11).

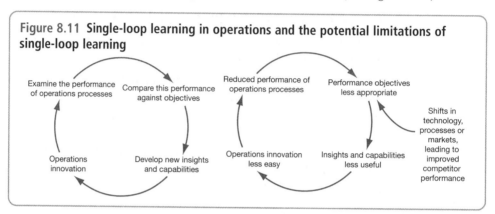

Figure 8.11 Single-loop learning in operations and the potential limitations of single-loop learning

Sustainable operations strategies therefore also need to emphasise learning mechanisms that prevent the operation becoming too conservative and thereby effectively introduce delays and inappropriate responses to major change decisions. Double-loop learning, by contrast, questions fundamental objectives, service or market positions or even the underlying culture of the operation. This kind of learning implies an ability to challenge existing operating assumptions in a fundamental way, seeking to re-frame competitive questions and remain open to any changes in the competitive environment. But being receptive to new opportunities sometimes requires the abandonment of existing operating routines at certain points in time – sometimes without any specific replacement in mind. This is difficult to achieve in practice, especially as most operations tend to reward experience and past achievement (rather than potential) at both an individual and group level. Figure 8.12 illustrates double-loop learning.

An operation needs both the limited single-loop learning, so it can develop specific capabilities, and the more expanded experience of double-loop learning. Single-loop learning is needed to create consistency and stability. At the same time, operations need double-loop learning for continual reflection upon their internal and external objectives and context. There has to be a continual balancing act if a sustainable position is to be developed. An operation may even have distinct phases or locations where it emphasises single- or double-loop learning, where companies will periodically engage in double-loop learning, searching to challenge accepted values and objectives while at the same time maintaining some (single-loop) operational routines. Inevitably perhaps, this means a degree of tension between preservation and change. For an operations strategy this tension is particularly keenly felt. The need for managers to question and challenge what is currently practised is clearly important but at the same time, operations are largely responsible for delivering the already established organisational mission.

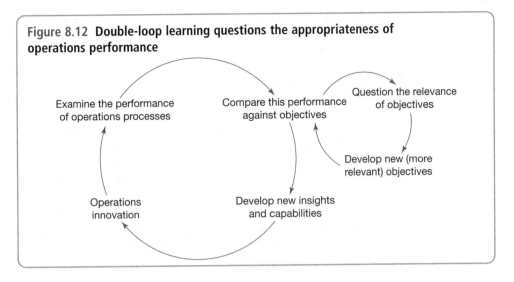

Figure 8.12 **Double-loop learning questions the appropriateness of operations performance**

Appropriating competitive benefits

One of the most surprising aspects of innovation is that, even if change works, and even if a market is created for a new product or service, there is no guarantee that the innovating operation will benefit commercially from the results. A critical question to ask in all strategic decisions is, 'who actually captures the profits?' Powerfully innovative firms like Xerox in the US (who invented many of the core personal computer and interface application concepts) and EMI in the UK (who developed one of the most widespread medical revolutions – magnetic resonance imaging) both failed to gain full competitive benefit from their efforts. The issues of appropriation (i.e. getting the benefit from innovation) are particularly significant for operations strategy because, as we discussed in Chapter 4, 'partnership' relationships have become more important. Products and services are often developed jointly with customers,[5] and companies are increasingly actively sharing knowledge with suppliers. For example, firms such as Bose have adopted particularly close relationships with suppliers, often involving exchanges of key staff. It is argued that the benefit for the customer is instant access to 'rich' supplier expertise on a range of current and future product issues. The main benefit for the supplier is the 'opportunity' to learn of 'potential' new contracts.[6] Issues of long-term intellectual property rights can become very difficult to manage in such circumstances.

Path dependencies and development trajectories

History matters when it comes to operations strategy. Very few operations have a completely blank sheet (or 'greenfield' scenario) when it comes to options and choices. Current resource and requirement positions act to constrain the future development paths, or trajectories, of the operation. In other words, operations capabilities are path dependent. For example, when chemical giant Monsanto first embarked upon their strategy to develop a biotechnology business, they had great difficulties in hiring new staff because they had no pre-existing capabilities for new staff to join, hence no visible career path, no guarantee of appropriate facilities, rewards and recognition and so on.

The influence of path dependency on sustainability is best summed up by the idea of capability and market trajectories. An operation may have been pursuing a particular strategy in each of its decision areas over a period of time. The pattern of these decisions will have become well established within the decision-making culture of the operation to the extent that the pattern of decisions may have established its own momentum. The organisation may have developed particular skills at making decisions to support its strategies and may be building upon the learning which it acquired from previous similar decisions. The decision area has developed its own trajectory. This may have both positive and negative effects. For example, a clothing retailer may have an operations strategy which includes aggressive capacity expansion. The result is that the company succeeds in capturing significant and profitable market share. For one or two years its skills at identifying, acquiring and commissioning new stores is a major factor in its ongoing success. However, its competitors soon start to adopt a similar expansion strategy and the company finds it increasingly difficult to maintain its market share. Yet, the policy of capacity expansion is so entrenched within the company's decision making that it continues to increase its floor space beyond the time when it should have been consolidating, or even reducing, its overall capacity. The trajectory of its capacity strategy, which was once a significant advantage, is now in danger of undermining the whole company's financial viability. What was once a core capability of the company has become a core rigidity.[7]

The same idea applies to the performance objectives which reflect market requirements. If an operation is used to thinking about quality, or speed, etc. in a particular way it will find it difficult to reconsider how it thinks about them internally and how it communicates them to its customers. Again, there is a momentum based on the trajectory of previous decisions. And again, this can have both positive and negative effects. Strong market-based trajectories can both lead to market success and expose companies to market vulnerability when challenged by radically new products and services. For example, Digital Equipment Corporation once dominated the minicomputer market. It was renowned for understanding its customers' requirements, translating these into products which matched its customers' requirements, and developing operations to support its product/market strategy. But eventually it was its very expertise at following its existing customers' requirements that caused it to ignore the threat from smaller and cheaper personal computers. Clayton Christensen, of Harvard Business School, has studied companies which found themselves in this position precisely because these firms listened to their customers, invested aggressively in new technologies that would provide their customers with more and better products of the sort they wanted, and because they carefully studied market trends they lost their positions of leadership; there are times at which it is right not to listen to customers . . .[8]

The innovator's dilemma[9]

Both market and capability trajectories are brought together in what Christensen calls the innovator's dilemma, the dilemma being that, especially when faced by radical shifts in the technological or operating model of a product or service, meeting long established customer needs can become an obstacle, rather than an enabler, of change. Christensen divides technologies into sustaining and disruptive technologies. Sustaining technologies are those that improve the performance of established products and services along the same trajectory of performance which the majority of customers have historically valued. Disruptive technologies are those that, in the short term, cannot match the performance that customers expect from products and services. They are typically simpler, cheaper, smaller and sometimes more convenient, but they do not often provide conventionally enhanced product or service characteristics. However, all technologies, sustaining or disruptive, will improve over time. Christensen's main point is that, because technology can progress faster than the requirements of the market, disruptive technologies will eventually enter the zone of performance which is acceptable to the markets (see Figure 8.13).

One example Christensen uses is that of the electric car. At the moment, no electric car can come close to the performance characteristics of internal combustion engines. In that sense, this technology is not an immediate threat to existing car or engine manufacturers. However, the electric car is a disruptive technology in so much as its performance will eventually improve to the extent that it enters the lower end of the acceptable zone of performance. Perhaps initially, only customers with relatively undemanding requirements will adopt motor vehicles using this technology. Eventually, however, it could prove to be the dominant technology for all types of vehicle. The dilemma facing all organisations is how to simultaneously improve product or service performance based on sustaining technologies, while deciding whether and how to incorporate disruptive technologies.

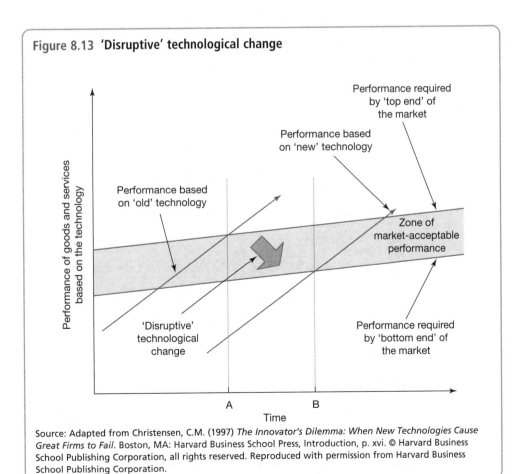

Figure 8.13 'Disruptive' technological change

What should the formulation process be trying to achieve?

Back in Chapter 1 we introduced the idea of the operations strategy matrix. We suggested that, because it emphasised the intersections between what is required from operations (in terms of the relative priority which should be given to each performance objective) and how the operation tries to achieve this through the choices made in each decision area, it was a useful device to describe any organisation's operations strategy. At least it could act as a checklist to ensure that the organisation had been reasonably comprehensive in considering different aspects of its operations strategy. In fact we can use the matrix to go further than merely describe an operations strategy. We can use it to question, develop and even formulate strategies. Indeed, using the matrix to check for comprehensiveness could be considered the first step in a formulation process. Here we will use the matrix to explore some of the most basic aspects of operations strategy formulation (see Figure 8.14):

- exploring what it means for an operations strategy to be comprehensive;

- ensuring there is internal coherence between the different decision areas;

- ensuring that decisions taken as part of the operations strategy process correspond to the appropriate priority for each performance objective;

- highlighting which resource/requirement intersections are the most critical with respect to the broader financial and competitive priorities of the organisation.

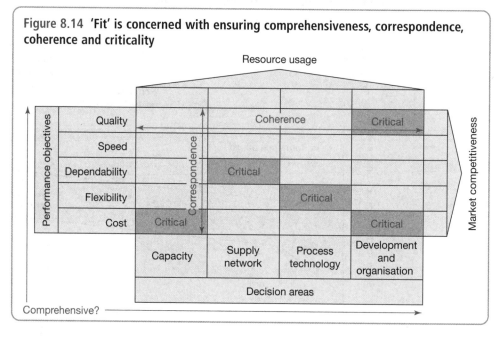

Figure 8.14 'Fit' is concerned with ensuring comprehensiveness, correspondence, coherence and criticality

Comprehensive

The notion of 'comprehensiveness' is a critical first step in seeking to achieve operations alignment. Business history is littered with world-class companies that simply failed to notice the potential impact of, for instance, new process technology, or emerging changes in their supply network. Also, many attempts to achieve alignment have failed because operations have paid undue attention to only one of the key decision areas.

Coherence

As a comprehensive strategy evolves over time, different tensions will emerge that threaten to pull the overall strategy in different directions. This can result in a loss of coherence. Coherence is when the choices made in each decision area do not pull the operation in different directions. For example, if new flexible technology is introduced which allows products or services to be customised to individual clients' needs, it would be 'incoherent' to devise an organisation structure which did not enable the relevant staff to exploit the technology because it would limit the effective flexibility of the operation. For the investment in flexible technology to be effective, it must be accompanied by an organisational structure which deploys the organisation's skills appropriately, a performance measurement system which acknowledges that flexibility must be promoted, a new product/service development policy which stresses appropriate types of customisation, a supply network strategy which develops suppliers and customers to understand the needs of high-variety customisation, a capacity strategy which deploys capacity where the customisation is needed, and so on. In other words, all the decision areas complement and reinforce each other in the promotion of that particular performance objective. The main problem with achieving coherence is that so many decisions are made which have a strategic impact; it is relatively easy to make decisions which inadvertently cause a loss of coherence.

Correspondence

Equally, an operation has to achieve a correspondence between the choices made against each of the decision areas and the relative priority attached to each of the performance objectives. In other words, the strategies pursued in each decision area should reflect the true priority of each performance objective. So, for example, if cost reduction is the main organisational objective for an operation then its process technology investment decisions might err towards the purchase of 'off-the-shelf' equipment from a third-party supplier. This would reduce the capital cost of the technology and may also imply lower maintenance and running costs. Remember, however, that making such a decision will also have an impact on other performance objectives. An off-the-shelf piece of equipment may not, for example, have the flexibility that more 'made-to-order' equipment has. Also, the other decision areas must correspond with the same prioritisation of objectives. If low cost is really important then one would expect to see capacity strategies which exploit natural economies of scale, supply network strategies which reduce purchasing costs, performance measurement systems which stress efficiency and productivity, continuous improvement strategies which emphasise continual cost reduction, and so on.

Criticality

In addition to the difficulties of ensuring coherence between decision areas, there is also a need to include financial and competitive priorities. Although all decisions are important and a comprehensive perspective should be maintained, in practical terms some resource/requirement intersections will be more critical than others. The judgement over exactly which intersections are particularly critical is very much a pragmatic one which must be based on the particular circumstances of an individual firm's operations strategy. It is, therefore, difficult to generalise as to the likelihood of any particular intersections being critical. However, in practice, one can ask revealing questions such as, 'If flexibility is important, of all the decisions we make in terms of our capacity, supply networks, process technology, or development and organisation, which will have the most impact on flexibility?' This can be done for all performance objectives, with more emphasis being placed on those having the highest priority. Generally, when presented with a framework such as the operations strategy matrix, executives can identify those intersections which are particularly significant in achieving alignment.

Analysis for formulation

Before we examine two specific operations strategy formulation models, it is worth noting that, however formulation is approached, it is likely to require some significant analysis. As one would expect in a process that reconciles market requirements with operations resource capabilities, the two chief areas of analysis concern markets and resources. The practical reason for emphasising the problems with this analysis is to help reinforce the balanced nature of the reconciliation between resources and requirements. Although analysis of the marketplace is generally characterised by better tools and techniques, in reality both are characterised by ambiguity and uncertainty.

Analysing market requirements

It is beyond the scope of an operations strategy book to explore the many practical models that exist to help practitioners assess the requirements of the marketplace. There is a rich and sophisticated literature on marketing stretching back over the history of modern business. However, simply because there are many highly structured, rational models for analysing the external environment, this does not imply that these analyses are foolproof. No matter how complex and detailed the model, regardless of how much time and effort is invested in the data collection, it is still an ambiguous and unreliable process.

Analysing operational resource capabilities

It can be difficult to analyse the external environment despite the widespread availability of practical tools and techniques designed to help in this process. But it can be even more difficult to analyse the 'inside' of the organisation. This aspect of strategy formulation is not supported by many practical frameworks. In fact Birger Wernerfelt, one of the first academics to advocate a resource-based view of the firm, argued that conceptually we tend to treat organisational resources as an 'amorphous heap'.[10] In fact, that widely applied strategy management tool, SWOT analysis is a good starting point for the analysis of operations resources. This mechanism explicitly links internal (strengths and weaknesses) and external (opportunities and threats) factors. And although SWOT analysis is extremely difficult to incorporate into an effective planning process, the 'strengths and weaknesses' part of SWOT is particularly useful. Table 8.2 lists some possible operations factors which might be included in such an analysis.

Although only a selection of general strengths and weaknesses, many weaknesses (in Table 8.2) are simply a lack of a particular strength, for example having 'in-house operations expertise' is a strength, while not having it is a weakness. But other strengths may conflict with each other. So achieving good 'economies of scale' can leave the operation open to 'under-utilisation of capacity' if demand drops. Similarly, 'resource capability' is only a strength if there are greater benefits of capturing extra demand than there are costs of providing the excess capacity. What are strengths in one set of circumstances could be weaknesses in another. It is important, therefore, to clarify the assumptions under which such lists are derived.

Although every SWOT analysis will be unique to the operation for which it is being devised, some general hints have been suggested that will enhance the quality of the analysis.[11]

- Keep it brief: pages of analysis are usually not required.
- Relate strengths and weaknesses, wherever possible, to key factors for success.
- Strengths and weaknesses should also be stated in competitive terms, if possible. It is reassuring to be 'good' at something, but it is more relevant to be 'better than the competition'.
- Statements should be specific and avoid blandness: there is little point in stating ideas that everyone believes in.
- Analysis should distinguish between where the company wishes to be and where it is now. The gap should be realistic.
- It is important to be realistic about the strengths and weaknesses of one's own and competitive organisations.

Table 8.2 **Some possible operations-related factors in a SWOT analysis**

Strengths	Weaknesses
Economies of scale	Uneconomic volume
Ability to adjust capacity	Under-utilisation of capacity
Reserve capacity	Insufficient capacity
Appropriate locations	Inappropriate locations
Long-term supplier relationships	Lack of power in supply market
Supply market knowledge	No long-term supply relationships
Supply chain control	Old process technology with poor performance
Advanced process technology knowledge	No capability to improve 'off the shelf' process technology
In-house process technology development capability	Rigid organisation or decision-making structure
Flexible organisational structure	No in-house operations expertise
In-house operations expertise	Static levels of operations performance
Continuous improvement culture	Poor product and service development skills
Effective product and service development processes	

Capabilities

Analysing strengths and weaknesses is the starting point for understanding resources, the next challenge is to understand the capabilities that they (may) represent. The idea of core capabilities is central to understanding how operations strategy can be sustained over time. But the idea of operations capabilities is not a straightforward one. Capabilities derive from strategically important assets – those which are scarce, difficult to move, difficult to copy and difficult to substitute for. But these types of assets are, by definition, more difficult to manage than those assets which are well understood, widely available and easy to copy. Practical analysis and implementation that is based upon a concept that is so ambiguous is therefore not always easy. However, it is possible to highlight a number of critical issues.

- Definitions (such as, what is capability?) can be important. As one confused engineer once exclaimed to one of the authors, *'this is very difficult you know, you don't walk around the factory and bang your head on the core capabilities of the firm!'* Yet, they do exist, and identifying them is an obvious first step in nurturing them. While complex definitions of different types of capability can be used, the more abstract the definition, the less likely it is that managers will find it useful. This drastically reduces the legitimacy of any decisions based upon the analysis and makes it harder for the dynamics of capability development to be incorporated on an ongoing basis. Therefore, if possible, keep definitions of capability as simple as is practical.

- The level of aggregation in how capabilities are defined is also critical. For instance, while one might reasonably assert that Sony's core capability is 'miniaturisation', this may be too generic for Sony's managers to act upon. Collis and Montgomery[12] illustrate this challenge with the example of a manufacturer of medical diagnostics test equipment that had defined its core capability as 'instrumentation'. Such an intuitively obvious definition was too broad for managers to act upon. Analysing to greater levels of disaggregation, however, revealed that their strength was mainly the result of competitive advantage in designing the human/machine interface. In order to exploit and deepen this competence, the firm hired ergonomists and set out to design a product for the fast-growing general practitioner market where the equipment would not be operated by skilled technicians.

- Articulating capabilities in very abstract terms may capture their essence but can make them difficult to use. Some degree of operationalisation is usually necessary. Collis and Montgomery[13] argue that *'evaluating whether Kraft General Foods or Unilever has better consumer marketing skills may be impossible, but analysing which is more successful at launching product-line extensions is feasible'*. In many ways such analyses are essentially forms of internal benchmarking and, as with that process, the greater the level of detail, the greater the cost and time necessary to perform the analysis.

- Much of the competence and capability literature regularly use the words 'core' or 'distinctive' to add extra emphasis to those capabilities that are most important to the business. Indeed the most celebrated of these authors, Prahalad and Hamel,[14] only use the phrase 'core competence'. Their implicit warning is to focus on the very few capabilities which really are 'core' to the sustainability of the operation.

- The practical consequences of identifying the 'core' capabilities within an operation are usually that additional resources will be acquired and deployed. This is clearly a political issue within the organisation. It can alter power balances, bolstering one set of managers, perhaps at the expense of others. It is important, therefore, to understand that asking managers to judge core capabilities is inevitably a political process. In one workshop, for example, a senior information technology (IT) manager was asked to rate the importance of 'managerial IT skills, knowledge and experience'. The answer was an unsurprising 'absolutely critical!'

Formulation models for alignment

At some time, most organisations will want to formulate their own operations strategy to cope with what they see as their individual competitive circumstances. There are many alternative procedures which have been suggested as providing the outline framework for developing an operations strategy, mostly in the form of simple stage models. Most consultancy companies have developed their own frameworks, as have several academics. It would be too lengthy a process to describe many of these frameworks. Many of them share some common elements, amongst them the following.

- A process which formally links the total organisation strategic objectives (usually a business strategy) to resource-level objectives.
- The formal listing of performance objectives as a translation device between market positioning objectives and operations strategy.
- A step which involves judging the relative importance of operations performance objectives in terms of customer preference.
- A step which includes assessing current achieved performance, usually as compared against competitor performance levels.
- An emphasis on operations strategy formulation as an iterative process.
- The concept of an 'ideal' or 'greenfield' operation against which to compare current operations. Very often the question asked is, 'If you were starting from scratch on a greenfield site how, ideally, would you design your operation to meet the needs of the market?' This can then be used to identify the differences between current operations and this 'ideal' state.
- A 'gap-based' approach. This is a well-tried approach in all strategy formulation which involves comparing what is required of the operation by the marketplace against the levels of performance which the operation is currently achieving.

Here we will confine ourselves to describing a couple of contributions from academics in the area. Two well-known procedures are briefly described here to give the flavour of how operations strategies are formulated in practice. These are the Hill framework and the Platts–Gregory procedure.

The Hill framework

One of the first, and certainly most influential, approaches to operations strategy formulation (although once again its development is largely connected with manufacturing operations) is that devised by Professor Terry Hill. The 'Hill framework' is illustrated in Figure 8.15. Hill's model, which is here adapted to the terminology used in this book, follows the well-tried approach of providing a connection between different levels of strategy making. It is essentially a five-step procedure. Step 1 involves understanding the long-term corporate objectives of the organisation so that the eventual operations strategy can be seen in terms of its contribution to these corporate objectives. Step 2 involves understanding how the marketing strategy of the organisation has been developed to achieve corporate objectives. This step, in effect, identifies the products/service markets which the operations strategy must satisfy, as well as identifying the product or service characteristics such as range, mix and volume, which the operation will be required to provide. Step 3 translates marketing strategy into what we have called performance objectives. These are the things which are important to the operation in terms of winning business or satisfying customers. Hill goes on to divide the factors that win business into order-winners and qualifiers (we explained this distinction in Chapter 2). Step 4 is what Hill calls 'process choice'. This is similar, but not identical, to the decision areas of capacity, supply networks and process technology. The purpose is to define a set of structural characteristics of the operations which are coherent with each other and correspond to the way the company wishes to compete. Step 5 involves a similar process but this time with the infrastructural features of the operation (broadly what we have called 'development and organisation' decisions).

Figure 8.15 The Hill methodology of operations strategy formulation

Step 1	Step 2	Step 3	Step 4	Step 5
Corporate objectives	Marketing strategy	How do products or services win orders?	Operations strategy	
			Process choice	Infrastructure
• Growth • Profit • ROI • Other 'financial' measures	• Product/service markets and segments • Range • Mix • Volumes • Standardisation or customisation • Innovation • Leader or follower	• Price • Quality • Delivery speed • Delivery dependability • Product/service range • Product/service design • Brand image • Technical service	• Process technology • Trade-offs embodied in process • Role of inventory • Capacity, size, timing, location	• Functional support • Operations planning and control systems • Work structuring • Payment systems • Organisational structure

Hill's framework is not intended to imply a simple sequential movement from step 1 to step 5, although during the formulation process the emphasis does move in this direction. Rather, Hill sees the process as an iterative one, whereby operations managers cycle between an understanding of the long-term strategic requirements of the operation and the specific resource developments which are required to support strategy. In this iterative process the identification of competitive factors in step three is seen as critical. It is at this stage that any mismatches between what the organisation's strategy requires and what its operation can provide become evident.

The steps in the Hill framework are closely related to classic corporate planning methodologies (with clear separations of responsibility, strong functional tasks, etc.), but Hill argues that whereas the first three elements are treated as interactive and iterative, the final two are commonly presented as straightforward, linear, logical implementation issues. This echoes the early works of Wickham Skinner who argued that operations was too often 'missing' from the corporate strategy debate.[15]

By stressing the iterative nature of his framework, Hill emphasises the need to improve the critical relationship between operations and marketing (too often a 'fault-line' in businesses) and facilitates this process by providing a framework that helps to simplify the complexity of manufacturing operations. This is essentially a mechanism for ensuring the coherence and correspondence of the overall strategy. Furthermore, he stresses that these reviews should not be static in so far as they should consider both existing products and plans for future products. This allows considerations of product (and process) life cycle to be included. With finite resources available, the framework can highlight some of the trade-offs that exist in any operations strategy.

The Platts–Gregory procedure

Although superficially similar to the Hill framework, the work of Ken Platts and Mike Gregory of Cambridge University adds at least one crucial element missing from Hill – namely a form of prioritisation based upon an assessment of relative, competitive performance. The overall framework comprises three distinct stages (see Figure 8.16, page 254).

- Stage 1 involves developing an understanding of the market position of the organisation. Specifically it seeks to identify the factors that are 'required' by the market and then compares these to a level of achieved performance.

- Stage 2 seeks to identify the capabilities of the operation. Decision categories (similar to those developed by Hayes and Wheelwright) are provided to help managers classify current operations practice and then link these practices to the priorities identified in stage 1.

- Stage 3 is the least structured of the elements, encouraging managers to review the different options they have for improvement and developing a new operations strategy – against the backdrop of market criteria.

Like many of the practical quality methodologies, the Platts–Gregory procedure develops a 'gap-based' model for driving improvement. Here the gap is between customers' view of what is important and the way in which the operation actually performs. In this way it is similar to the importance–performance matrix described in Chapter 6. But instead of a matrix the procedure uses profiles of market requirements and achieved performance to show up the gaps which the operations strategy must address. Figure 8.17 (see page 255) illustrates the use of these profiles.

The challenges to operations strategy formulation

Strategy is broad, abstract, concerned with generalities rather than details – almost theoretical in nature. By contrast, 'operations' is about 'doing the things'. Strategy is cerebral, operations is practical. Discussing the *process* of operations strategy

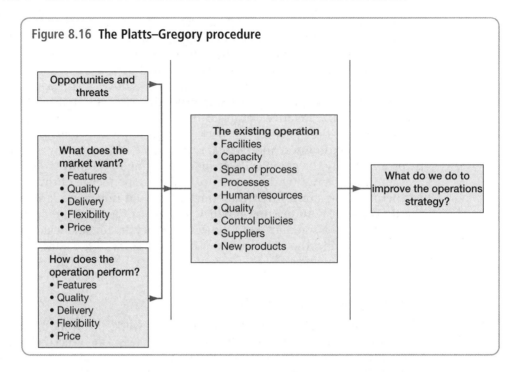

Figure 8.16 The Platts–Gregory procedure

highlights this tension between the strategic and operational aspects of operations management. We now deal with some practical aspects of formulating operations strategy. Because, although it is very easy to argue why alignment is a good thing, the practical challenges associated with achieving and maintaining alignment are immense.

What scope and unit of analysis?

One organisation's sub-strategy for operations will be another organisation's entire business strategy. For example, a medium-sized hotel chain can quite clearly consider its operations strategy as being concerned with the way it manages all its resources which produce its services. The scope of any operations strategy analysis would cover all the resources owned or controlled by the company. Each of the decision areas which we dealt with in this book would have some relevance for the analysis. But what of the far larger hotel and leisure group? One that has several types of hotel, branded in different ways and offering different types of service? It may also have theme parks, sports centres and other related businesses. Furthermore, it might both own and manage some of its resources while, in other parts of the group, it runs businesses which are owned by other people (a practice common in the hotel industry). How does this business start to consider its operations strategy? Including all the resources owned or managed by the group under one operations strategy is obviously out of the question. Different parts of the group will have different markets, different visions, serve different sets of customers and operate in different parts of the world. On the other hand, formulating an operations strategy for a single hotel within one part of the group might make no sense if the overall strategic objectives of that part of the group also apply to other hotels.

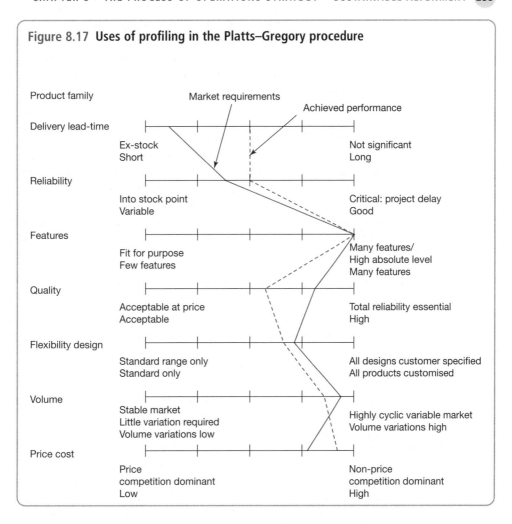

Figure 8.17 Uses of profiling in the Platts–Gregory procedure

Drawing a sensible boundary for an operations strategy analysis is therefore an important issue. Ideally, whatever resources lie within the boundary of analysis should have common, overall strategic objectives. This obviously makes the task of establishing a coherent operations strategy more straightforward. However, in practice, this is not always easy. Often the answer is defined in terms of the process of doing the analysis itself. Put simply, if putting an operations strategy together is difficult, then maybe you've got the boundary wrong. If it is not possible to devise a strategy which both corresponds to strategic objectives and is internally coherent, one possible reason is that the operations strategy is attempting to span too great a range of strategic objectives.

What is 'operations'?

The objectives, tasks and activities we have defined as 'operations' do not always match a coherent organisational function. Although many service organisations do have an explicit operations function, the notion of separating out the service 'product' from its production and delivery 'processes' is sometimes conceptually difficult. This can lead to a blurring between the boundaries of operations strategy, other functional strategies and the entire business strategy. Even in manufacturing businesses, where the idea and title 'operations' is more common, there are considerable overlaps between, say, Human Resource strategy, Engineering strategy and what we have included in Operations strategy. We would contend that including all the resources that produce the organisation's services and products within an operations strategy is usually the best starting point.

How explicit should a strategy be?

An operations strategy only exists formally in the documented decisions and actions agreed by whatever decision-making body drives the formulation process. But not every detail of an operations strategy is completely explicit. The degree to which it is made explicit is itself a formulation decision. Making an operations strategy analysis complex does not necessarily make it a better analysis. Indeed, many operations deliberately leave the overall direction of strategy quite 'light' in order to encourage creativity and dynamic problem solving.

What should be the role and position of operations?

In Chapter 6 we discussed the organisational role of the operations function, and the way in which the expectations which the rest of the organisation had for it influenced its contribution to overall strategic success. Clearly operations' role and expected contribution will shape the way in which it devises strategy. For example, if, historically, the contribution of operations has been poor and the expectations which the rest of the organisation have of it are consequently low (what, in Chapter 6, we noted as Hayes and Wheelwright's Stage 1), strategy will be mainly concerned with stopping holding the organisation back. This will include examining the root causes of the (probably numerous) operations failures, establishing 'base level' operations processes, bringing process technology investment up to a minimum level, and so on. Conversely, where the operations function is looked to as the main driver of the organisation's strategic direction (Hayes and Wheelwright's Stage 4), operations strategy formulation will be very different. Here the operations function will be looking for creative ways in which to leverage its superiority: redefining its customers' and suppliers' understanding of their relationships, timing each new innovation to maximise strategic advantage, and so on.

How should emergent strategies be treated?

Defining the content of an operations strategy is a necessary first step, but it is only the first step. The process of operations strategy puts those content decisions together. However, content decisions are not always clear. The exact timing of capacity change, the precise set of suppliers to partner with, the details of organisational structure, and so on might only be decided in vague terms. This is because the future is uncertain and the response of operations resources sometimes unclear. The details of content decisions may emerge only over time. Similarly, day-to-day operational experience in dealing both with markets and resources can lead to such a degree of 'refinement' of content decisions that the decision is in effect changed completely. This emergent aspect of the strategy process cannot be ignored in practice. This is why our definition of operations strategy does not view resources and requirements as naturally congruent but rather emphasises an ongoing process of reconciliation between them. Such an approach is more practical because at its heart lies the recognition that many environmental and operational variables are unknown in advance (and, in some cases, unknowable). This means that many strategic operations decisions will be made over time regardless of the formal formulation process.

Barriers to the formulation process

There are limits to the ability of any organisation to align itself to changing environmental requirements. This is because in any complex system there are certain resources and processes that tend to prevent adaptation/innovation rather than enable it, or, in other words, organisations are subject to a wide range of inertial forces. The dictionaries tend to define inertia as: 'the tendency to continue in the same state [or] to resist change', and as we discuss the practical challenges of achieving operational alignment, it is important to explore the sources of inertia. One of the most infamous examples of an operation that was unable to overcome inertia and adapt itself to a new set of market requirements is IBM between 1980 and the mid-1990s when it struggled to adapt to the world of the PC. (See the Example, 'IBM falls victim to a reluctance to change'.)

Example | **IBM falls victim to a reluctance to change**

In 1980 the US corporation, International Business Machines (IBM) posted profit figures of $3.6 billion. *Time* magazine described IBM as the 'colossus that works', echoing a widely held belief that this massive company was probably the best-managed organisation in the world. At that time it had over 300,000 staff, assets of $27 billion, sales of $26 billion. At this time IBM was often cited as an example of the benefits to be gained from 'alignment'. Although IBM was not really known for any specific radical innovations, it was widely viewed as simply being good at everything it did. Its operations strategy provided a strong degree of alignment with the dominant market requirements of cost and quality. Combining IBM's extensive sales, marketing and support network with an operations strategy that ensured well-designed products widely available at competitive prices offered IBM a 'tight alignment' with its core market.

The firm entered the 1990s, a decade widely predicted to see a global explosion in computer applications, as the largest computer firm in the world and in 1990 it made $6 billion profits. Incredibly, just two years later in 1992, the firm posted the largest loss in American corporate history – a staggering $4.97 billion! The share price collapsed from over $100 dollars to less than $50 and that same year the firm was forced to make nearly 50,000 people redundant. But of course, such a dramatic reversal of fortune does not truly happen overnight and in IBM's case its fall from a position of business 'super-stardom' reflected a series of poor corporate decisions over the previous decade. As discussed earlier, IBM's operational 'alignment' was primarily with the mainframe market and, although still a valuable and profitable business, the global computer industry was rapidly shifting towards smaller, personal computers. IBM launched its first PC in 1981 and it proved to be a great success, yet, as IBM attempted to further exploit this market opportunity, it made two fundamental errors of judgement relating to software (the Microsoft DOS and Windows operating systems) and hardware (the Intel 80386 microprocessor).

At the beginning of the 1980s, IBM passed up its option to acquire the operating system that evolved into DOS (Disk Operating System), leaving Bill Gates to buy it for only $75,000. This has now entered folklore as one of the greatest business mistakes, but in a similar vein,

▶

IBM signed a joint development agreement with Microsoft in 1985 that did not include its new project, Windows.

Intel's 80386 chip promised to be the fastest, most powerful processor on the market but IBM prevaricated over the decision to purchase this chip, diminishing its influence over the company that would eventually dominate PC hardware standards. In addition to these specific managerial blunders, changes in IBM's approach to its 'core' mainframe market also impeded the development of its PC business. IBM had traditionally leased many of its mainframes but in the early 1980s, the decision was taken to encourage customers to buy their machines outright. Although initially this gave a great boost to the firm's revenues, its longer-term impact was largely negative. IBM's renowned sales force no longer achieved commission through keeping established customers happy, rather they emphasised finding new buyers. At the same time, the sales commission on a mainframe was so much greater than that on a PC that there was little incentive to exploit existing relationships to promote PC sales.

It is easy to forget that in 1980 Microsoft was a start-up with fewer than 50 staff (IBM had 300,000 employees) and that despite phenomenal growth, by 1982 the combined market capitalisation of both Intel and Microsoft was only about one-tenth of IBM's. But many successful organisations contain the seeds of its own downfall – a phenomenon that has been explored by a number of authors, including Dorothy Leonard.[16] When discussing the relationship between what she calls core capabilities and core rigidities, Leonard offers the following quote from John F. McDonnell of the McDonnell Douglas Corporation to illustrate the phenomenon of success-enabled inertia:

> *'While it is difficult to change a company that is struggling, it is next to impossible to change a company that is showing all the outward signs of success. Without the spur of a crisis or a period of great stress, most organisations – like most people – are incapable of changing the habits and attitudes of a lifetime.'*

But why should this be so? Surely success generates revenue and profits that in turn can be invested in the future of the firm? Inertial forces need to be understood if their negative impact is to be overcome. If we explore the impact of high levels of success we can discern a number of specific structural issues that can increase the potential level of inertia. For instance:

- *Operations' resource profile.* Once an investment has been made in either tangible or intangible assets, this inevitably influences subsequent decision making. It is fairly obvious how certain assets are dedicated to specific tasks and not readily transferable, but more broadly the whole profile of an organisation's operations strategy can create inertial forces. For instance, IBM's vertically integrated production system made it the largest chip manufacturer in the world. This technological independence had an inevitable influence upon its delayed decision to purchase Intel's market-leading 80386 chip. Similarly, the agreement with Microsoft that overlooked Windows was internally justifiable because at that time the software was just a prototype and IBM had its own system in development.

- *Investment bias.* Operations will tend to invest further in those resource/requirement intersections that have proved successful. Regardless of whether this takes the form of extra capacity, additional R&D expenditure or staff recruitment, etc., investment here appears to offer a more reliable return. Given a finite resource base to draw upon, other aspects of the operation can easily suffer comparative neglect.

- *History*. Organisations become constrained by their own history. Once systems and procedure and 'ways of working' are established, it becomes difficult and expensive to change them. So, for example, even though IBM invented both floppy disk and hard drive technology, the firm saw itself as 'a supplier of integrated systems' and therefore it did not sell these components – effectively leaving other firms to make a fortune from IBM's invention.

- *Organisational structures/political forces*. Often overlooked in rational discussions of operations management, political forces have an enormous influence. In all operations there are individual managers and influential groups who compete for resources with their different priorities, opinions and values. In an organisation the size of IBM (in the mid-1980s) the combination of a cumbersome organisational structure (a single hierarchy for the whole business) and political machinations effectively killed off its entry into the PC market. Its first model, in 1981, had been very successful but the supposedly mass-market PC Jr model (intended for launch in July 1983) was delayed by senior management interference. It introduced an inferior keyboard, scrapped plans to sell it in department stores, missed the crucial Christmas sales period and priced it too high. A year later, it dropped the price, sold through different outlets and realised that it was too late – its competitors had developed new, more appealing models.

The influence of time and timing

Firms like Intel and Dell in the computer industry might, at any point in time, possess a significant design and manufacturing performance advantage over their competitors. Unfortunately, in their hyper-competitive markets the danger is that their advantage will be quickly 'competed away', with sustainability sometimes measured in months rather than years. Jeffrey Williams published a study of sustainability patterns in a range of industries.[17] He proposed a model classifying capability-based advantages according to how fast they can be duplicated. Nothing lasts for ever, and competitive success inevitably attracts imitators who offer superior product features or lower prices. Yet, it is also clear that some organisations are able to sustain the advantages of their products and services for much longer than others. For instance, throughout the 1990s in the PC industry, why was it that certain products like Microsoft's Office Suite of programs were highly stable, with functionality and prices essentially unchanged during more than 10 years, whereas physical products sold by Hewlett-Packard, Toshiba, Apple, etc. could last less than one year? In attempting to explain these and other differing patterns of sustainability, the following typology of resource life cycles offers some interesting insights.[18]

Slow cycle. Products and services in this class (Microsoft Word, British Airways flights through Heathrow) reflect resource positions that are strongly shielded from competitive pressures by mechanisms that are durable and enduring. In economic terms, such resources exploit scarcity characteristics that are derived from factors that are impossible (or at least extremely difficult) to imitate, such as unique geographical locations, long-standing brand reputations, personal client relationships, etc. Although being the first mover into a resource/market position is not a guarantee of advantage, in certain markets it can lead to incredibly sustainable positions.

Standard cycle. Products and services in this class (Toyota's cars, McDonald's fast food, Visa credit card services) exploit less specialised resources and, therefore, face higher levels of resource imitation pressure. Firms in this position often face direct competition over extended periods of time and this encourages a kind of trench warfare between established rivals (automobiles, banking, branded food, soft drinks, etc.). As a result, successful companies tend to emphasise discipline (control and coordination) in operations and products tend to be standardised for production at high volumes (product/service line rationalisations are common in this type of firm) and are strongly market share oriented. The huge financial and organisational commitments that derive from such strategies mean that firms tend to tread very carefully over their competitive territory. Indeed, efforts to streamline these operations and make them more lean can, if duplicated by rivals (and this is what normally happens!), bring on even more intense resource-imitation pressures – creating fast-cycle markets that they are poorly equipped to deal with.

Fast cycle. Products and services in this class (iPods, Intel microprocessors, Nokia mobile phones, corporate financial instruments) face the highest levels of resource imitation pressure. Such products/services are often idea driven and their economic half-life (the rate of product profit margin reduction minus reinvestment expenditure) is typically less than two years. Once established, these products do not require complex operations to support them and are increasingly outsourced to low-cost, focused producers. To maintain sustainable alignment, these firms must master competitive routines associated with innovation and time to market. In his article, Williams asks, 'How is a 1 Mbyte DRAM chip like a Cabbage Patch doll?'. Both products derive their value from the idea and information content is (unless protected by patents) inherently unsustainable.

The implications for management could seem counter-intuitive for operations managers used to emphasising speed and efficiency as key strategic goals. They include:

- *Determining the correct speed for innovation.* Too much innovation can become distracting for both the operation and its customers. The correct speed of innovation should depend upon the sustainability of the firm's resources. Williams cites the example of the Campbell Soup Company, which during the 1980s launched 300 products in a five-year period. Only a few were successful and the firm had to, according to CEO David Johnson, 'fight the motherhood of innovation'.

- *Resource cycles should influence diversification.* Business history is littered with examples of firms such as many defence contractors, who attempt to shift from their own 'slow cycle' markets into seemingly attractive 'medium cycle' or even 'fast cycle' markets. Their lack of understanding and capabilities in dealing with faster resource/requirement dynamics leaves them with over-engineered products, missed development lead-times, exorbitant production costs, etc. The key lesson becomes, 'beware of hidden barriers to entry'.

- *Look out for cycle time shifts.* Not all changes necessarily drive markets towards higher rates of imitation. For instance, the advent of hub and spoke control in airports gave less dominant regional airlines an invaluable source of competitive advantage over the major carriers. However, regardless of the direction of change, such shifts can be difficult to adjust to and therefore need to be actively sought out and analysed. At the same time, as in the airline example, they also represent major opportunities.

SUMMARY ANSWERS TO KEY QUESTIONS

What is 'sustainable alignment'?

Alignment is the state where an operation's capabilities match the requirements of its market. Its operations resources therefore are aligned with its external environment. It is important because it is the operationalisation of our definition of operations strategy – the reconciliation of market requirements and operations resources. In practical terms, most organisations will attempt to make their operations resources fit the requirements of their market. That is, they will start from a market perspective and work through to defining required operations capabilities. However, at higher 'levels of alignment' an organisation may start from the perspective of the unique capabilities of its operations and then attempt to leverage these into appropriate market positioning. Sustainability is the achievement of alignment over time. Maintaining an existing market requirements and operations capability balance is a 'static' approach to sustainability. Attempting to raise both operations capabilities and market requirements through a process of innovation is called a 'dynamic' approach to sustainability.

The extent of alignment within an organisation's operations strategy can be assessed by analysing it using the operations strategy matrix. Perfect alignment (in a static sense) is when all intersections on the operations strategy matrix are understood, so the strategy is comprehensive, there is internal coherence between the different decision areas in that the decisions taken in every area influence performance objectives in the same way, within each decision area the strategies correspond to the relative priorities of the company's performance objectives, and the critical intersections on the matrix are understood and identified.

Why is sustainability of alignment so important?

There is really no alternative to considering sustainability if an organisation wishes to survive. Even if an operation's ambitions are not to raise its level of alignment to higher levels of market requirements and operations capabilities, it needs to ensure that its position is not eroded.

What is the formulation process trying to achieve?

In terms of the operations strategy matrix, the formulation process is trying to make sure that the operations strategy:

- is comprehensive, covering all the important aspects of strategy;
- has internal coherence between the different decision areas;
- ensures that decisions correspond to the appropriate priority for each performance objective;
- highlights which resource/requirement intersections are the most critical with respect to the broader financial and competitive priorities of the organisation.

There are many and various frameworks put together by consultancy companies and academics. Two typical ones are the Hill framework and the Platts–Gregory procedure. Both are market driven in the sense that they start from a market perspective and work inwards towards the operations resources.

What are the practical challenges of formulating operations strategies?

Although most frameworks start with the requirement to understand markets, this is not always straightforward. Markets are, by their nature, dynamic and companies frequently mistake market reaction. Similarly, understanding operations resources is not straightforward. In particular, understanding the nature and value of intangible assets can be problematic. Also, the sheer inertia of organisations makes implementing strategic decisions difficult. In large companies especially, radical new changes in markets or internal technologies can often be underestimated.

Further reading

Christensen, C.M. (1997) *The Innovator's Dilemma: When New Technologies Cause Great Firms to Fail*. Boston, MA: Harvard Business School Press.

Cole, R.E. (1998) 'Learning from the quality movement: what did and didn't happen and why', *California Management Review*, 41(1), Fall, pp. 43–73.

Bettley A., Mayle, D. and Tantoush, T. (eds) (2005) *Operations Management: A Strategic Approach*. London: Sage.

Grant, R. (2004) *Contemporary Strategy Analysis*, 5th edn. Oxford: Blackwell Publishing.

Hayes, R.H., Pisano, G.P. and Upton, D.M. (1996) *Strategic Operations: Competing Through Capabilities: Text and Cases*. New York: The Free Press.

Hayes, R.H., Pisano, G.P., Upton, D.M. and Wheelwright, S.C. (2004) *Operations, Strategy, and Technology: Pursuing the Competitive Edge*. John Wiley & Sons.

Hayes, R.H., Wheelwright, S.C. and Clark, K. (1998) *Dynamic Manufacturing*. New York: The Free Press.

Hill, T. (1993) *Manufacturing Strategy: The Strategic Management of the Manufacturing Function*. Basingstoke, UK: Macmillan.

Leonard-Barton, D. (1995) *Wellsprings of Knowledge: Building and Sustaining the Sources of Innovation*. Boston, MA: Harvard Business School Press.

Tidd, J., Bessant, J. and Pavitt, K. (1997) *Managing Innovation: Integrating Technological, Market and Organizational Change*. Chichester, UK: John Wiley & Sons.

Utterback, J. (1994) *Mastering the Dynamics of Innovation*. Boston, MA: Harvard Business School Press.

Notes on the chapter

1 Source: *The Economist* (2006) 'Fuzzy maths', 13 May.
2 See James Gleick's fascinating book, *Faster* (Little Brown, 1999) for an exploration of the societal issues raised by the speed revolution.
3 Source: *The Economist* (2006) 'For whom the Dell tolls', 13 May.
4 Argyris, C. and Schon, D. (1978) *Organizational Learning*. Reading, MA: Addison-Wesley.
5 Lewis, M. (2000) 'Lean production and sustainable competitive advantage', *International Journal of Operations and Production Management*, 20(8).
6 Dixon, L. and Porter, A.M. (1994) *JITII: A Revolution in Buying and Selling*. Newton, MA: Cahners Publishing.
7 This idea is pursued in the context of product development by Dorothy Leonard in Leonard-Barton, D. (1992) 'Core capabilities and core rigidities: a paradox in managing new product development', *Strategic Management Journal*, Vol. 13, pp. 111–25.
8 Christensen, C.M. (1997) *The Innovator's Dilemma: When New Technologies Cause Great Firms to Fail*. Boston, MA: Harvard Business School Press.

9 This discussion is based on Slack, N., Chambers, S. and Johnston, R. (2007) *Operations Management*, 5th edn. Harlow, UK: Financial Times Prentice Hall.

10 Wernerfelt, B. (1984) 'A resource-based theory of the firm', *Strategic Management Journal*, Vol. 13, pp. 111–25.

11 Lynch, R. (1997) *Corporate Strategy*. Harlow, UK: Financial Times Prentice Hall.

12 Collis, D.J. and Montgomery, C.A. (1998) *Corporate Strategy: Resources and Scope of the Firm*. Boston, MA: Irwin.

13 Ibid.

14 Prahalad, C.K. and Hamel, G. (1990) 'The core competencies of the corporation', *Harvard Business Review*, May–June.

15 Skinner, W. (1969) 'Manufacturing – missing link in corporate strategy', *Harvard Business Review*, May–June.

16 Leonard-Barton, D. (1992) 'Core capabilities and core rigidities: a paradox in managing new product development', *Strategic Management Journal*, Vol. 13, pp. 111–25.

17 Williams, J. (1992) 'How sustainable is your competitive advantage?', *California Management Review*, 34(3).

18 Ibid.

The process of operations strategy – substitutes for strategy?

Introduction

Ask any organisation what is its operations strategy and you can expect a wide range of answers. Some will not even know what is meant by 'operations strategy', some will have a clearly worked out and thought through articulation of how they reconcile market requirements with operations resource capabilities. But many are likely to mention one of the 'new approaches' to operations that they have picked up, or been sold by consultants, or have judged to be particularly appropriate in improving their operations performance. Such responses might include, 'We are trying to make our operations as lean as possible', 'We are reengineering our operations to avoid organisational silos', 'We're investing in a total information system that will coordinate all our operations efforts (at least we hope it will coordinate them because it's really expensive!)', and so on. But are these approaches to operations strategy as such, or are they merely substitutes for strategy? In this chapter we will examine some of these approaches and the extent to which they can be seen as 'strategic' as well as discussing how they fit into operations strategy implementation (Figure 9.1).

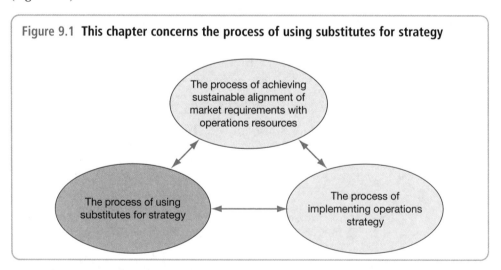

Figure 9.1 **This chapter concerns the process of using substitutes for strategy**

The process of achieving sustainable alignment of market requirements with operations resources

The process of using substitutes for strategy

The process of implementing operations strategy

'New' approaches to operations

One of the defining characteristics of business over the last two or three decades has been the number of 'new approaches' to the management of operations. Many of these new approaches have captured popular management imagination, at least for a short while. This is why many managers will say that their operations strategy is to implement Lean Operations principles, or Total Quality Management, or Business

KEY QUESTIONS

● *How does Total Quality Management fit into operations strategy?*

● *How do Lean Operations fit into operations strategy?*

● *How does Business Process Reengineering fit into operations strategy?*

● *How does Enterprise Resource Planning fit into operations strategy?*

● *How does Six Sigma fit into operations strategy?*

● *What place do these new approaches have in operations strategy?*

Process Reengineering, or Enterprise Resource Planning, or Six Sigma. What such responses indicate is that the company has opted to use a pre-packaged approach to improve its operations performance. And it is an increasingly common response. This is because either:

(a) they are an easily understood and a relatively simply way to tackle the complexities of modern operations; or

(b) they seem to have worked in other organisations; or

(c) they sound as if they are new and by implication, therefore, must be better than what went before; or

(d) they have been sold the idea by a consultant (or read about it in a book) and it's worth trying something new because many other things have failed to bring improvements.

So, are these approaches really strategic? Or are they simply a way of avoiding the difficult process of reconciling market requirements and operations resource capabilities?

The answer is probably that they are a bit of both. Why one adopts a particular approach and how it is implemented, is at least as important as which approach is adopted. Certainly some organisations have gained significant operations-based advantages from adopting Six Sigma or Lean Operations or Business Process Reengineering, or any of the other 'packaged' approaches to operations. None of these ideas is entirely without merit, and there have been many well reported triumphs. Particularly in the popular business press, these new approaches were hailed as almost a prerequisite to any kind of competitive success. However, it is evident that many organisations have failed to derive much, if any, benefit from their adoption, and partly as a result there has come a backlash. This is a natural phenomenon. No sooner is something set up as being the answer to sorting out operations' many problems, than someone wishes to knock it down again. There is always mileage for journalists and academics in 'smashing the myth', 'exposing the truth', etc. Yet, amidst these predictable reactions there were several studies that called into serious question the universal applicability and universal success of the new approaches. Although these studies do vary, many indicate that (at the most) only around one third of all initiatives involving these new approaches are deemed successful. Some companies that were the loudest in proclaiming their adherence to a new approach, with hindsight, seemed to have gained little benefit. So there began to develop a sense of real frustration at the inability of the new approaches to guarantee improvements.

Before anyone can judge whether any of these packaged solutions is right for them, they must understand what they are, their underlying philosophy, and how they differ from each other. In this chapter we look at five of the most commonly adopted of these solutions. They are as follows:

- Total Quality Management
- Lean Operations
- Business Process Reengineering
- Enterprise Resource Planning
- Six Sigma.

Total Quality Management (TQM)

Total quality management was one of the earliest management 'fashions'. Its peak of popularity was in the late 1980s and early 1990s. As such it has suffered from something of a backlash in recent years. Yet, TQM, or more properly the general precepts and principles that constitute TQM, is still hugely influential in organising operations improvement. Few, if any, managers have not heard of TQM and its impact on improvement. Indeed, TQM has come to mean more than simply 'avoiding errors'. It is also seen as an approach to the way operations and processes should be managed and, more significantly, improved, generally.

What is TQM?

A.V. Feigenbaum, generally held to be the originator of the term, defines TQM as, *'an effective system for integrating the quality development, quality maintenance and quality improvement efforts of the various groups in an organization so as to enable production and service at the most economical levels which allow for full customer satisfaction'.*[1] However, it was the Japanese who first made the concept work on a wide scale and subsequently popularised the approach and the term 'TQM'. It was then developed further by several, so called, 'quality gurus'. Each 'guru' stressed a different set of issues, from which emerged the TQM approach to operations improvement (although they rarely used the term 'TQM'). For example, W.E. Deming considered in Japan to be the father of quality control, asserted that quality starts with top management and is a strategic activity.[2] Deming's basic philosophy is that quality and productivity increase as 'process variability' (the unpredictability of the process) decreases. He emphasises the need for statistical control methods, participation, education, openness and purposeful improvement.

The elements of TQM

TQM is best thought of as a philosophy of how to approach the organisation of quality improvement. This philosophy, above everything, stresses the 'total' of TQM. It is an approach that puts quality (and indeed improvement generally) at the heart of everything that is done by an operation. This totality can be summarised by the way TQM lays particular stress on the following elements.

Meeting the needs and expectations of customers

There is little point in improvement unless it meets the requirements of the customers. However, in the TQM approach, meeting the expectations of customers means more than this. It involves the whole organisation in understanding the central importance of customers to its success and even to its survival. Customers are seen not as being external to the organisation but as the most important part of it.

Covering all parts of the organisation

One of the most significant elements of TQM is the concept of the internal customer and internal supplier. This means that everyone is a customer within the organisation and consumes goods or services provided by other internal suppliers, and everyone is also an internal supplier of goods and services for other internal customers. The assumption is that errors in the service provided within an organisation will eventually affect the external customer. TQM utilises this concept by stressing that each process in an operation has a responsibility to manage these internal customer–supplier relationships.

Including every person in the organisation

TQM uses the phrase 'quality at source', stressing the impact that each individual has on quality. In TQM the contribution of all individuals in the organisation is expected to go beyond understanding their contribution to 'not make mistakes'. Individuals are expected to bring something positive to improving the way they perform their jobs. The principles of 'empowerment' are frequently cited as supporting this aspect of TQM. When TQM practices first began to migrate from Japan in the late 1970s, the ideas seemed even more radical. Some Japanese industrialists even thought (mistakenly) that companies in Western economies would never manage to change. Take, for example, a statement by Konosuke Matsushito which, at the time, attracted considerable publicity.

> 'We are going to win and the industrial West is going to lose out – there is nothing much you can do about it, because the reasons for your failure are within yourselves. For you, the essence of management is getting the ideas out of the heads of bosses into the hands of labour. For us, the core of management is precisely the art of mobilizing and pulling together the intellectual resources of all employees in the service of the firm. Only by drawing on the combined brainpower of all its employees can a firm face up to the turbulence and constraints of today's environment. That is why our large companies give their employees three to four times more training than yours. This is why they foster within the firm such intensive exchange and communication. This is why they seek constantly everybody's suggestions and why they demand from the educational system increasing numbers of graduates as well as bright and well-educated generalists, because these people are the lifeblood of industry.'[3]

Examining all costs which are related to quality, especially failure costs

The costs of controlling quality can be large, so it is necessary to examine all the costs and benefits associated with quality. These costs of quality are usually categorised as prevention costs (identifying and preventing potential problems, improving the design of products and services and processes to reduce quality problems, training and development, process control, etc.), appraisal costs (the costs of controlling quality to check to see if problems or errors have occurred during and after production), internal failure costs (costs associated with errors which are dealt with inside the operation, scrap, rework, lost production time, failure-related disruption, etc.) and external failure costs (the loss of customer goodwill, litigation, guarantee and warranty costs, etc.).

Getting things 'right first time', i.e. designing-in quality rather than inspecting it in

TQM shifts the emphasis from reactive (waiting for something to happen) to proactive (doing something before anything happens). This change in the view of quality costs has come about with a movement from an inspect-in (appraisal-driven) approach to a design-in (getting it right first time) approach.

Developing the systems and procedures which support improvement

Typical of these is the ISO 9000 series which is a set of worldwide standards that establishes requirements for companies' quality management systems. It is different from, but closely associated with, TQM. ISO 9000 registration requires a third-party assessment of a company's quality standards and procedures and regular audits are made to ensure that the systems do not deteriorate.

Criticisms of TQM

Many of the criticisms of TQM tend to fall into two slightly conflicting categories. The first is that historically many TQM initiatives fail, or at least are not entirely successful. The second is that, even if TQM is not the label given to improvement initiatives, many of the elements of TQM such as continuous improvement, have now become routine.

As far as the first criticism is concerned, not all TQM initiatives which are launched, often with high expectations, will go on to have a major impact on performance. Companies who were in the vanguard of the TQM movement, such as Hewlett-Packard, admit that at one time they pushed quality for its own sake, and have shifted too much responsibility down to the shop floor. Similarly, *The Economist* magazine, reporting on some companies' disillusionment with their experiences, quoted from several surveys.[4] For example:

- *'Of 500 US manufacturing and service companies, only a third felt their Total Quality programmes had significant impact on their competitiveness.'*
- *'Only a fifth of the 100 British firms surveyed believed their quality programmes had achieved tangible results.'*
- *'Of those quality programmes that have been in place for more than two years, two thirds simply grind to a halt because of their failure to produce hoped-for results.'*

Also the excessive 'quality bureaucracy' associated with TQM, in particular, the continued use of standards and procedures, encourages 'management by manual' and over-systematised decision making, is expensive and time consuming. Furthermore, it is too formulaic, encouraging operations to substitute a 'recipe' for a more customised and creative approach to managing operations improvement.

As far as the second criticism ('We have incorporated much of TQM anyway') is concerned, it is undoubtedly true that some of the fundamentals of TQM have entered the vernacular of operations improvement. The idea of continuous improvement is perhaps the most obvious example. However, other elements such as the internal customer concept including service level agreements (SLAs), the idea of internal and external failure related costs, and many aspects of individual staff empowerment, have all become widespread. Yet, this is not really a criticism of TQM as such. Rather it is a criticism of the practice of 'packaging' individual improvement elements under a single improvement 'brand'. It is an issue that we shall return to later in this chapter.

Lessons from TQM

The core concept of a 'total, or holistic, view' of any issue is both powerful and attractive. At its simplest, it provides on outline 'checklist' of how to go about operations improvement. But it is also capable of being developed into a more sophisticated form. The best example of this is the EFQM Excellence Model, developed by the European Foundation for Quality Management (EFQM). Originally, the European Quality Award (EQA), awarded to the most successful exponent of total quality management in Europe each year, the model on which the award was based was modified and renamed The EFQM Excellence Model or Business Excellence Model. The EFQM Excellence Model is shown in Figure 9.2. The five 'enablers' are concerned with how results are being achieved, while the four 'results' are concerned with what the company has achieved and is achieving. The main advantage of using such models for self-assessment seems to be that companies find it easier to understand some of the more philosophical concepts of TQM when they are translated into specific areas, questions and percentages. Self-assessment also allows organisations to measure their progress in changing their organisation and in achieving the benefits of TQM. An important aspect of self-assessment is an organisation's ability to judge the relative importance of the assessment categories to its own circumstances.

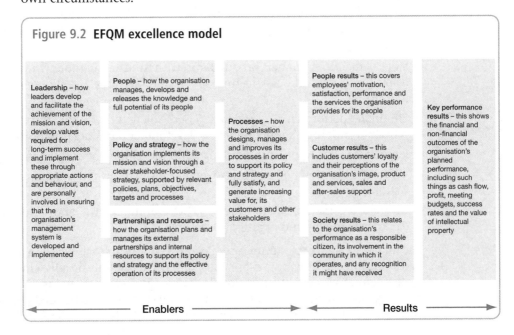

Figure 9.2 **EFQM excellence model**

Where does TQM fit into operations strategy?

Various authors have put forward prescriptions on how to integrate TQM into a business strategy. Many of these prescriptions stress that operations quality programmes should be both strategic and comprehensive. In other words, if one applied the operations strategy matrix to such an initiative, we would expect to see a spread of activities (albeit of differing priority) at the intersections with each of the decision areas. To test this assertion out, look at Deming's (one of the quality 'gurus') 14 points.[5] These are, in many ways, both a crystallisation of his lifetime of work in the improvement area and (because it was published relatively late in the quality boom) a summary of some other authorities' ideas on quality improvement. In order to translate these different elements onto the operations strategy matrix, we have listed each of Deming's 14 points followed by the operations strategy decision areas to which they relate.

- Plan for a long-term commitment to quality (development and organisation).
- Quality must be built into the processes at every stage (process technology, supply network, development and organisation).
- Cease mass inspection (process technology, supply network, development and organisation).
- Do not make purchase decisions on price alone (supply network, development and organisation).
- Identify problems and work continuously to improve the system (supply network, development and organisation).
- Implement SPC and quality training (process technology, development and organisation).
- Institute leadership and a human-centred approach to supervision (development and organisation).
- Eliminate fear (supply network, development and organisation).
- Break down barriers between departments (supply network, development and organisation).
- Stop demanding higher productivity without the methods to achieve them (capacity strategy, process technology, supply network, development and organisation).
- Eliminate performance standards based solely on output (capacity strategy, process technology, supply network, development and organisation).
- Remove barriers to pride in workmanship (development and organisation).
- Institute education and self-improvement programmes (development and organisation).
- Create a top management structure that emphasises the above 13 points every day (development and organisation).

The matrix in Figure 9.3 summarises Deming's points in each decision area and illustrates that the Deming points are comprehensive, though heavily emphasising the infrastructural aspects of operational change. However, changing behaviours and beliefs is not easy and requires constant emphasis over an extended period of time. The individual operations strategy matrix is essentially a 'snapshot' in time but for

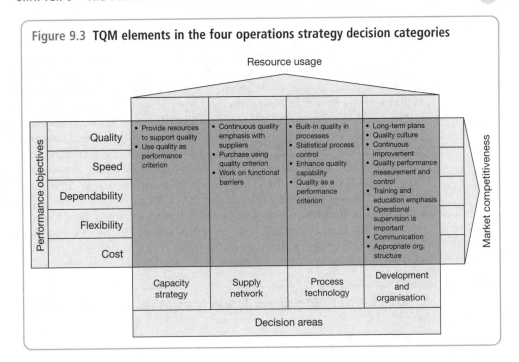

Figure 9.3 **TQM elements in the four operations strategy decision categories**

a strategy to be truly comprehensive, the different elements must not only be in place, but be in place over time.

Lean Operations

The idea of Lean Operations (also known as just-in-time, lean synchronisation, continuous flow operations, and so on) spread beyond its Japanese roots and became fashionable in the West at about the same time as TQM. And although its popularity has not declined to the same extent as TQM, over 25 years of experience (at least in manufacturing) have diminished the excitement once associated with the approach. But, unlike TQM, it was seen initially as an approach to be used exclusively in manufacturing. Because of this, lean has become newly fashionable as an approach that can be applied in service operations.

What is 'lean'?

The lean approach aims to meet demand instantaneously, with perfect quality and no waste. Put another way, it means that the flow of products and services always delivers exactly what customers want (perfect quality), in exact quantities (neither too much nor too little), exactly when needed (not too early or too late), exactly where required (not to the wrong location), and at the lowest possible cost. It results in items flowing rapidly and smoothly through processes, operations and supply networks. It is best illustrated with an example. Figure 9.4(a) shows a simple three-stage process. The traditional approach assumes that each stage in a process or supply network will be 'buffered' from the next stage downstream. These buffers 'insulate' each stage from its neighbours making each stage relatively independent so that if one stage stops operating for some reason, the next stage can continue, at least for a time. The larger the buffer inventory, the greater the degree of insulation between the stages, but throughput times will be slow because items will spend time waiting in the inventories. The main argument against this traditional approach lies in the very conditions it seeks to promote, namely the insulation of the stages from one another. When a problem occurs at one stage, the problem will not immediately be apparent elsewhere in the system, so the responsibility for solving the problem will be centred largely on the people within that stage. However, with a pure lean process, as shown in Figure 9.4(b), items will only flow from one stage of the process to another when the subsequent stage requests them. And that subsequent stage will request them only when it needs them. This means that problems at any stage are quickly exposed. The responsibility for solving the problem is now shared and is more likely to be solved. By preventing items accumulating between stages, the operation has increased the chances of the intrinsic efficiency of the process being improved. The lean approach exposes the process (although not suddenly) to problems, both to make them more evident and change the motivation towards solving the problems.

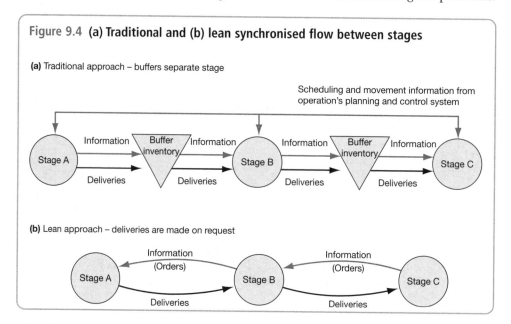

Figure 9.4 (a) Traditional and (b) lean synchronised flow between stages

(a) Traditional approach – buffers separate stage

Scheduling and movement information from operation's planning and control system

Stage A — Information — Buffer inventory — Information — Stage B — Information — Buffer inventory — Information — Stage C

Deliveries — Deliveries — Deliveries — Deliveries

(b) Lean approach – deliveries are made on request

Stage A — Information (Orders) — Stage B — Information (Orders) — Stage C

Deliveries — Deliveries

The elements of lean

To understand the elements of the lean approach, return to our simple example illustrated in Figure 9.4. Note how the trigger for any activity is the direct request of the internal customer. This reflects the emphasis that lean places on meeting the needs of customers exactly. Second, note how in the absence of inventories, items flow in a smooth and synchronous manner. In fact the term 'lean synchronisation' is perhaps a more accurate name for what we are here calling the lean approach. Third, note how the synchronisation leads to fewer inventories in the process, which in turn leads to a change in people's behaviour, involvement in, and motiv-ation for, improvement. Finally, note how this motivation to improve reinforces the quest for seeking out and eliminating waste within processes. It is these four elements of customer-based demand triggers, synchronised flow, enhanced improvement behaviour, and waste elimination that mesh together to form the lean approach (see Figure 9.5). We will briefly examine each in turn.

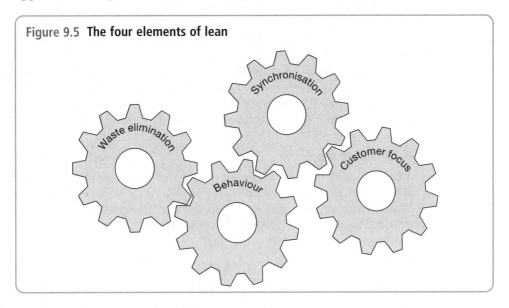

Figure 9.5 **The four elements of lean**

Customer-based demand triggers

In the lean approach, demand is to be met exactly when it is needed, no more no less, not early not late, and always to exact levels of quality. This is obviously easier when demand is predictable and, preferably, relatively steady. The implication of this is that the ability to implement lean principles are much enhanced when an organisation understands (and maybe to some extent controls) the nature and level of the demands on its resources. The most common approach to achieving customer-based triggering is by utilising 'pull' control as opposed to push control. Push control was illustrated in Figure 9.4(a) when any items that are processed by a stage are immediately pushed forward to the next stage irrespective of whether that customer stage actually requires them at that time. Pull control is implicit in Figure 9.4(b) where items are sent forward only in response a specific customer request.

Synchronised flow

Synchronised flow means that items in a process, operation or supply network flow smoothly and with even velocity from start to finish. This is a function of how inventory accumulates within the operation. Whether inventory is accumulated in order to smooth differences between demand and supply, or as a contingency against unexpected delays, or simply to batch for purposes of processing or movement, it all means that flow becomes asynchronous. It waits as inventory rather than progressing smoothly on. Of course, once this state of perfect synchronisation of flow has been achieved, it becomes easier to expose any irregularities of flow which may be the symptoms of more deep rooted underlying problems.

Involvement behaviour

Like TQM, the lean approach has always stressed the importance of staff involvement. However, often the way in which this was expressed using terms such as 'respect for humans' and 'enlightened vision', did not always resonate with Western perspectives on organisational behaviour. Indeed, the lean approach often seemed naïve, patronising, or worse to liberal Western eyes. Yet, return to the fundamental idea as illustrated in our simple example and we have something that is not fundamentally countercultural. Namely, that smooth flow and the absence of inventory motivates individuals to help their colleagues improve the whole process rather than focusing exclusively on their own area of direct responsibility. So behaviour is partly a function of synchronous flow which is itself a function of customer-based triggering of demand. Furthermore, it is these changes in motivation and behaviour which in turn lead on to the fourth element of waste elimination.

Waste elimination

This is arguably the most significant part of the lean philosophy; the elimination of all forms of waste, where waste is any activity that does not add value.

Identifying waste is the first step towards eliminating it. Toyota has described seven types. Here we consolidate these into four broad categories of waste that apply in many different types of operation.

Waste from irregular flow. Perfect synchronisation means smooth and even flow through processes, operations, and supply networks.

Waste from inexact supply. Perfect synchronisation also means supplying exactly what is wanted, exactly when it is needed. Any under or over supply and any early or late delivery will result in waste.

Waste from inflexible response. Customer needs can vary, in terms of what they want, how much they want, and when they want it. But unless an operation is flexible, it can make change only infrequently. This mismatch is the cause of much inventory, for example because machines make a large batch of similar products together.

Waste from variability. Synchronisation implies exact levels of quality. If there is variability in quality levels then customers will not consider themselves as being adequately supplied. Variability therefore is an important barrier to achieving synchronised supply. Symptoms of poor variability include the following.

Some organisations, especially now that lean is being applied more widely in service operations, view waste elimination as the most important of all the elements of the lean approach. In fact, they sometimes see the lean approach as consisting almost exclusively of waste elimination. What they sometimes fail to realise is that effective waste elimination is best achieved through changes in staff behaviour. It is the behavioural change brought about through synchronised flow and customer triggering that provides the window onto exposing and eliminating waste.

Capacity utilisation may be sacrificed in the short-term

A paradox in the lean concept is that it may mean some sacrifice of capacity utilisation. In organisations that place a high value on the utilisation of capacity this can prove particularly difficult to accept. It occurs because, when stoppages occur in the traditional system, the buffers allow each stage to continue working and thus achieve high capacity utilisation. The high utilisation does not necessarily make the system as a whole produce more because the extra production goes into the large buffer inventories. In a lean process, stoppages will affect the rest of the operation. This will lead to lower capacity utilisation, at least in the short term. However, there is no point in producing output just for it to increase inventory. In fact, producing just to keep utilisation high is not only pointless, it is counter-productive, because the extra inventory produced merely serves to make improvements less likely.

Criticisms of lean

The lean approach to people management can be viewed as, at best, patronising. It may be less autocratic than some earlier Japanese management practice, but it is not always in line with 'Western' job-design philosophies. Even in Japan the JIT approach is not without its critics. Kamata wrote an autobiographical description of life as an employee at a Toyota plant called *Japan in the Passing Lane*.[6] His account speaks of *'the inhumanity and the unquestioning adherence'* of working under such a system. Similar criticisms have been supported in some studies that point out some of the negative effects of the flexibility principles within the lean approach.[7]

Lean principles can also be taken to an extreme. When just-in-time ideas first started to have an impact on operations practice in the West, some authorities advocated the reduction of between-process inventories to zero. While in the long term this provides the ultimate in motivation for operations managers to ensure the efficiency and reliability of each process stage, it does not admit the possibility of some processes always being intrinsically less than totally reliable. An alternative view is to allow inventories around process stages with higher than average uncertainty. This at least allows some protection for the rest of the system. The same ideas apply to just-in-time delivery between factories. The Toyota Motor Corporation, often seen as the epitome of modern JIT, has suffered from its low inter-plant inventory policies. Both the Kobe earthquake and fires in supplier plants have caused production at Toyota's main factories to close down for several days because of a shortage of key parts. Even in the best regulated manufacturing networks, one cannot always account for such events.

The major weakness of lean principles is that they can break down when fluctuations in supply or demand become extreme, especially when they are also unpredictable. The pull control of hamburgers in a fast-food restaurant works perfectly well when demand stays within predictable limits. However, when subjected to an unexpected large influx of customers, it leaves most of those customers waiting for their meal. Similarly, in very complex and interrelated processes, lean principles are sometimes difficult to apply.

Example Toyota[8]

Seen as the leading practitioner and the main originator of the lean approach, the Toyota Motor Company has progressively synchronised all its processes simultaneously to give high quality, fast throughput and exceptional productivity. It has done this by developing a set of practices that has largely shaped what we now call 'lean' or 'just-in-time' but which Toyota calls the Toyota Production System (TPS). The TPS has two themes: 'just-in-time' and 'jidoka'.

Just-in-time is defined as the rapid and coordinated movement of parts throughout the production system and supply network to meet customer demand. It is operationalised by

▶

means of *heijunka* (levelling and smoothing the flow of items), *kanban* (signalling to the preceding process that more parts are needed) and *nagare* (laying out processes to achieve smoother flow of parts throughout the production process).

Jidoka is described as 'humanising the interface between operator and machine'. Toyota's philosophy is that the machine is there to serve the operator's purpose. The operator should be left free to exercise his/her judgement. Jidoka is operationalised by means of fail-safeing (or machine jidoka), line-stop authority (or human jidoka), and visual control (at-a-glance status of production processes and visibility of process standards).

Toyota believes that both just-in-time and jidoka should be applied ruthlessly to the elimination of waste, where waste is defined as 'anything other than the minimum amount of equipment, items, part and workers that are absolutely essential to production'. Fujio Cho of Toyota identified seven types of waste that must be eliminated from all operations processes. They are: waste from over production, waste from waiting time, transportation waste, inventory waste, processing waste, waste of motion and waste from product defects. Beyond this, authorities on Toyota claim that its strength lies in understanding the differences between the tools and practices used with Toyota operations and the overall philosophy of its approach to lean synchronisation. This is what some have called the apparent paradox of the Toyota production system, '*namely, that activities, connections and production flows in a Toyota factory are rigidly scripted, yet at the same time Toyota's operations are enormously flexible and adaptable. Activities and processes are constantly being challenged and pushed to a higher level of performance, enabling the company to continually innovate and improve.*'

One influential study of Toyota identified four rules that guide the design, delivery and development activities within the company.

- Rule one – all work shall be highly specified as to content, sequence, timing and outcome.

- Rule two – every customer–supplier connection must be direct and there must be an unambiguous yes or no method of sending requests and receiving responses.

- Rule three – the route for every product and service must be simple and direct.

- Rule four – any improvement must be made in accordance with the scientific method, under the guidance of a teacher, and at the lowest possible level in the organisation.

Lessons from lean

Looking back to when the lean approach was first introduced into Western manufacturing, it is easy to forget just how radical, and more importantly, counterintuitive it seemed. Although ideas of continuous improvement were starting to be accepted, the idea that inventories (especially in order to batch items) were generally a bad thing and that throughput time was more important than capacity utilisation seemed to border on the insane to more traditionally minded operations managers. So, as lean ideas have been gradually accepted, we have likewise come to be far more tolerant of ideas that are radical and/or counterintuitive. This is no mean legacy because it opened up the debate on operations and significantly broadened the scope of what are regarded as acceptable approaches.

Similarly, the idea that protecting parts of the operation (by buffering them with inventory) is not sensible in the long-term has also had profound effects. Opening up an operation's resources to its external customers is now seen as promoting the same behavioural change as reducing inventory between the stages of a process. It exposes the operation to the realities of the market and forces it to adapt to what the market really wants, often by increasing the flexibility of its resources.

A further legacy that the absorption of lean ideas has brought operations in general concerns the interdependence of a number of important ideas. Before the lean approach there was relatively little understanding of how inventory, throughput time, value-added and waste elimination, utilisation and flexibility all related to each other. Although the way in which lean philosophy integrated these ideas was novel, it was at least coherent. In fact, it legitimised the whole idea of a philosophy of operations. Prior to lean, operations was a relatively loose collection of ideas from the scientific management era of the early twentieth century, some elegant but relatively naïve mathematical modelling, and simple practical ideas based on pragmatic operations practice.

Lean principles were strongly influenced by Toyota and the work of Taiichi Ohno in particular. When this celebrated engineer wrote his book (after retiring from the firm in 1978) he was able to portray Toyota's manufacturing plants as embodying a coherent production approach. However, this encouraged observers to focus on the specific techniques of lean production and de-emphasised the importance of 30 years of 'trial and error'. The success of Toyota has much to do with the process of fit (see Chapter 8). Staff at Toyota worked over decades to ensure alignment between their intended market position and their operations resources. Maybe the real achievement of Toyota was not so much what they did but how long they stuck at it.

Example Volvo falls to the power of lean[9]

For almost 30 years, Volvo had acquired a reputation for experimenting with new models of work practice in its auto plants. In the 1970s Kalmar marked the first of Volvo's moves away from the traditional plant, breaking up the 'big factory' long assembly line into small 'mini factory' workshops. Most spectacularly, the assembly line itself was scrapped and cars were moved about the factory on independently moving trolleys.

Volvo moved to this design of process for one overriding reason – to attract workers into the factories. At the time, car assembly work was so unattractive that there were no indigenous Swedish workers in some parts of its more traditional Gothenberg plant. Low unemployment combined with a social reluctance to work on repetitive tasks made recruitment difficult. Later the Uddevalla plant was designed with teams of operators (called 'car builders', not 'assembly workers') working in parallel to build the whole car. The fully integrated teams were completely responsible, not only for building the car, but for many other indirect tasks such as quality, planning and, most radically of all, liaising with the customer sales end of the business. At the time, business was booming but the company was having some quality problems. It wanted highly skilled workers with personal dedication who would ensure the manufacture of high-quality products. However, in parallel with the Kalmar and Uddevalla experiments, Volvo's plant at Ghent in Belgium had been slowly adopting the principles of lean production which would eventually kill off the two more radical plants. It was the first plant outside Japan to be awarded the Total Productive Maintenance (TPM) award. It had also developed a form of teamwork, while still retaining the traditional line process design. By the late 1980s the cost and quality performance levels of Japanese-owned factories were making for intense competition in the automobile market. And while Volvo's more experimental plants were struggling to compete, the Ghent plant with its lean working principles was achieving levels of quality, cost and throughput time significantly superior to the company's other plants.

Where does lean fit into operations strategy?

Figure 9.6 summarises some of the elements of the lean approach, again using the four decision categories in the operations strategy matrix. This shows that the core principles of the lean approach are contained largely within the supply network and development and organisation decision areas. This is not surprising given the emphasis on flow (which is what supply network strategy is partly about) and improvement through waste elimination (an important part of development and organisation strategy). The role of process technology strategy is largely to ensure that technology choices support the core elements of lean through flexibility, reliability and reduced variability. Although there is only one entry under the category of capacity strategy, it is none the less important. If lean principles are to be adopted through the supply chain, then to maintain synchronous flow it will be necessary to tolerate reduced capacity utilisation. Or putting it the other way round, one cannot allow capacity bottlenecks to disturb smooth and synchronous flow through the chain. The implication is that under a lean approach more capacity may have to be provided than under a more traditional approach to managing supply chain throughput.

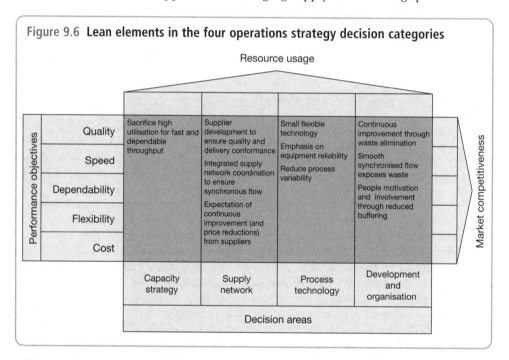

Figure 9.6 **Lean elements in the four operations strategy decision categories**

Business process reengineering (BPR)

The idea of business process reengineering originated in the early 1990s when Michael Hammer proposed that rather than using technology to automate work, it would be better applied to doing away with the need for the work in the first place ('don't automate, obliterate'). In doing this he was warning against establishing non-value added work within an information technology system where it would be even more difficult to identify and eliminate. All work, he said, should be examined for whether it adds value for the customer and if not processes should be redesigned to eliminate it. In doing this BPR was echoing similar objectives in both scientific management and more recently lean approaches. But BPR, unlike those two earlier approaches, advocated radical changes rather than incremental changes to processes. Shortly after Hammer's article, other authors developed the ideas, again the majority of them stressing the importance of a radical approach to elimination of non-value added work. This radicalism was summarised by Davenport[10] who, when discussing the difference between BPR and continuous improvement, held that, *'Today's firms must seek not fractional, but multiplicative levels of improvement – ten times rather than ten per cent'.*

What is BPR?

BPR has been defined as:[11]

'. . . the fundamental rethinking and radical redesign of business processes to achieve dramatic improvements in critical, contemporary measures of performance, such as cost, quality, service and speed.'

But there is far more to it than that. In fact, BPR was a blend of a number of ideas which had been current in operations management for some time. Lean concepts, process flow charting, critical examination in method study, operations network management and customer-focused operations all contribute to the BPR concept. It was the potential of information technologies to enable the fundamental redesign of processes, however, which acted as the catalyst in bringing these ideas together. It was the information technology that allowed radical process redesign even if many of the methods used to achieve the redesign had been explored before. For example,

'Business Process Reengineering, although a close relative, seeks radical rather than merely continuous improvement. It escalates the effort of . . . (lean) . . . and TQM to make process orientation a strategic tool and a core competence of the organization. BPR concentrates on core business processes, and uses the specific techniques within the . . . (lean) . . . and TQM tool boxes as enablers, while broadening the process vision.'[12]

The elements of BPR

The main principles of BPR can be summarised in the following points.

Rethink business processes

Rethink these processes in a cross-functional manner which organises work around the natural flow of information (or materials or customers). This means organising around outcomes of a process rather than the tasks which go into it. Underlying the BPR approach is the belief that operations should be organised around the total process which adds value for customers, rather than the functions or activities which perform the various stages of the value-adding activity. The core of BPR is a redefinition of the processes within an operation, to reflect the business processes which satisfy customer needs. Figure 9.7 illustrates this idea.

Strive for dramatic improvements

Strive for dramatic improvements in performance by radically rethinking and redesigning the process. It was this radical approach that generated much of the

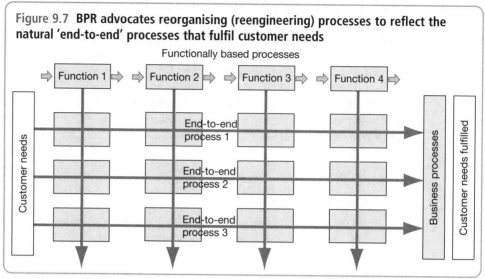

Figure 9.7 **BPR advocates reorganising (reengineering) processes to reflect the natural 'end-to-end' processes that fulfil customer needs**

publicity surrounding BPR when it was first proposed. But many would argue that it is inevitable that a BPR 'solution' will be radical when it seeks to redesign processes on an end-to-end basis as described above. Traditional organisational and functional boundaries will have to be reconfigured and individuals' jobs and responsibilities redefined. Furthermore, the use of new information technologies is likely to promote previously unexplored process designs. In fact, Hammer and Champy[13] discussed the role of what they termed 'disruptive technologies' that would directly challenge the orthodoxy of process design.

Have those who use the output from a process, perform the process

Check to see if all internal customers can be their own supplier rather than depending on another function in the business to supply them (which takes longer and separates out the stages in the process). In process design this idea is sometimes referred to as a 'short fat' process, as opposed to the more conventional multi-stage 'long thin' process.

Put decision points where the work is performed

Do not separate those who do the work from those who control and manage the work. Control and action are just one more type of supplier–customer relationship which can be merged.

Criticisms of BPR

BPR has aroused considerable controversy, mainly because BPR sometimes looks only at work activities rather than at the people who perform the work. Because of this, people become 'cogs in a machine'. Many of these critics equate BPR with the much earlier principles of scientific management, pejoratively known as 'Taylorism'. Generally, these critics mean that, like some forms of early scientific management, BPR is overly harsh in the way it views human resources. Certainly there is evidence that BPR is often accompanied by a significant reduction in staff. Studies at the time when BPR was at its peak often revealed that the majority of BPR projects could reduce staff levels by over 20 per cent.[14] Often BPR was viewed as merely an excuse for getting rid of staff. Companies that wished to 'downsize' were using BPR as the pretext, putting the short-term interests of the shareholders of the company above either their longer-term interests or the interests of the company's employees.

A combination of radical redesign together with downsizing could mean that the essential core of experience was lost from the operation. This leaves it vulnerable to any marked turbulence since it no longer possessed the knowledge and experience of how to cope with unexpected changes. This is a similar criticism to what we described in Chapter 8 as overly 'tight fit' between resources and market require-ments. When the operation's resources are designed to focus exclusively on one nar-rowly defined set of market requirements, it is vulnerable to any changes either in market requirements or its own resource capabilities. In this sense the outcome of a BPR project, even when implemented effectively, could be seen as carrying the same combination of advantages and disadvantages as the focus strategy described in Chapter 2. Namely, exceptional performance under a defined set of circumstances but excess risk when these circumstances no longer apply

Lessons from BPR

Although one of the later of the new approaches to operations, BPR is already suf-fering from a backlash. Perhaps this is not surprising given its radical nature. The greater the deviation from orthodoxy, the greater the level of criticism. Nevertheless, even with a relatively short experience of using BPR principles, certain lessons emerge.

- Don't dismiss radical approaches to reconfiguring operations resources. A radical reconfiguration may carry a higher risk but it is a legitimate alternative to incre-mental development. Although, like many of these new approaches, there are examples were expectations have not been met, there are also examples where radical redesign has brought significant benefits. General Motors, South West Airlines, Hewlett-Packard, and many other high-profile companies all claim to have experienced some significant success with BPR.

- New process technology, especially information technology, needs to be fully incor-porated into process redesign. These new technologies often have much more potential than simply speeding up, or doing better, what was done before. They both have capabilities (often associated with flexibility) that could be exploited in a new way and they may need new infrastructural support to develop their potential.

- Beware of the publicity that comes when a new approach is branded in a particu-lar way. Very soon after its introduction BPR had polarised expectations. Labour representatives assumed that it would always be used as a heartless exercise for 'employment bloodshed'. Business leaders, looking forward to often over inflated estimates of the saving that could be achieved, became disenchanted when these expectations were not met immediately.

- Many of the ideas generated by BPR and the debate it provoked were already com-monplace in manufacturing processes. BPR succeeded in moving the arena of this debate from manufacturing to direct service processes and even to non-operations processes. In that sense BPR helped to establish the idea that processes are ubiqui-tous in business and the same ideas and principles that shape process design within the operations function can also be used outside it.

- Beware of any approach that dismisses the contribution played by people in operations or processes. Even the originators of BPR later admitted that they had paid insufficient attention to human resources within process. Because of this the initial impression (that BPR inevitably meant trampling over human aspirations and potential) became difficult to reverse.

Where does BPR fit into operations strategy?

Figure 9.8 places some of the elements of BPR into our strategic decision areas. Again note how most of the elements lie within the infrastructural area of development and organisation. Organisationally BPR's recommendations regarding where decisions should be made and how processes should be conceptualised do much to shape the underlying philosophy of an operation's organisational design. Similarly, the idea that dramatic reductions in cost can be gained from eliminating unnecessary process steps is as much a state of mind as it is any change in the business' structural resources. Where structural resources are affected it is to emphasise the potential of process technology in facilitating cost reduction, recommend merging stages in the internal supply chain in order to simplify processes and implying that capacity should be balanced along end-to-end process lines rather than between functions as such.

Enterprise Resource Planning (ERP)

As information technology established itself within most businesses, the various functions within the business developed appropriate systems and databases to meet their own needs. Arguably, within operations the most significant of these systems was based around Materials Requirements Planning (MRP). Enterprise Resource Planning (ERP) systems attempt to integrate all these various systems. This allows changes made in one part of the business to be reflected immediately in information held for the benefit of other parts of the business, thereby improving both the communication and the effectiveness of the systems as a whole. However, this obvious and seemingly straightforward idea is, in practice, hugely complex and expensive to put into practice. And that is what ERP has become known for: its high cost and difficult implementation. Some large corporations are reported as having spent hundreds of millions of euros on their ERP systems. Even medium-sized companies can easily spend hundreds of thousands of euros. And although some authorities claim that even successfully implemented ERP systems will never offer any significant return on their investment, others argue that ERP was simply one of those things that any large company had to invest in simply to keep pace with its customers, suppliers, and competitors.[15] Certainly ERP has spawned a huge industry devoted to developing the computer systems needed to drive it. The (now) large companies which have grown almost exclusively on the basis of providing ERP systems include SAP, Oracle and Baan.

What is ERP?

One of the most important issues in resource planning and control is managing the sometimes vast amounts of information generated, not just from the operations function, but from almost every other function of the business. So, unless all rel-

Figure 9.8 **BPR elements in the four operations strategy decision categories**

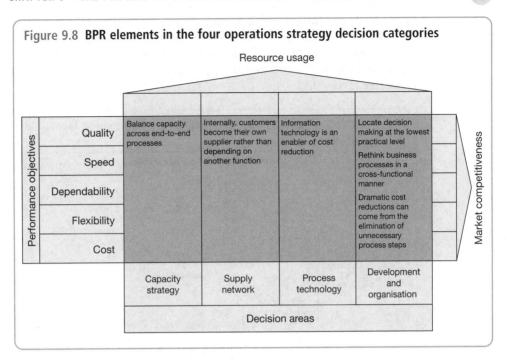

evant information is brought together and integrated it is difficult to make informed planning and control decisions. This is what Enterprise Resource Planning (ERP) is about. It is often described as a complete enterprise-wide business solution that integrates the planning, resource allocation and control activities of all parts of the business. The intent is that all transaction information is entered into the system at its source and done only once. Consider, for instance, a manufacturing firm receiving an order for a product. The transaction is entered (manually or through electronic data interchange (EDI)) into the system and the data is then sent to the master database, which accesses and updates the other business processes. For example, the finance process is instructed to raise an invoice, the sales and marketing processes are advised of sales and customer information, the production process triggers the manufacturing etc. If the system does not have its own scheduling software, it can (to varying degrees) be integrated with pre-existing packages.

From an operations perspective, ERP is part of a development that started with Materials Requirements Planning (MRP), an approach that became popular during the 1970s, although the planning and control logic that underlies it had been known for some time. It is a method (simple in principle but complex in execution) of translating a statement of required output into a plan for all the activities that must take place to achieve the required output. What popularised MRP was the availability of computer power to drive the basic planning and control mathematics in a fast, efficient, and most importantly, flexible manner. Manufacturing Resource Planning (MRP II) expanded out of MRP during the 1980s. This extended concept has been described as a game plan for planning and monitoring all the resources of a manufacturing company: manufacturing, marketing, finance and engineering. The strength of MRP and MRP II lay always in the fact that it could explore the consequences of any changes to what an operation was required to do. So, if demand changed, the MRP system would calculate all the 'knock-on' effects and issue instructions accordingly. The same principle applies to ERP, but on a much wider basis. ERP systems allow decisions and databases from all parts of the organisation to be integrated so that the consequences of decisions in one part of the organisation are reflected in the planning and control systems of the rest of the organisation (see Figure 9.9).

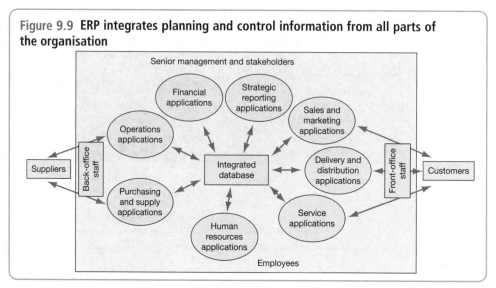

Figure 9.9 ERP integrates planning and control information from all parts of the organisation

The elements of ERP

The ERP system consists of software support modules such as: marketing and sales, field service, product design and development, production and inventory control, procurement, distribution, industrial facilities management, process design and development, manufacturing, quality, human resources, finance and accounting, and information services. Integration between the modules is stressed without the duplication of information. In addition to the integration of systems, ERP usually includes other features which make it a powerful planning and control tool:

● It is based on a client/server architecture; that is, access to the information systems is open to anyone whose computer is linked to central computers.

● It can include decision support facilities that enable operations decision makers to include the latest company information.

● It is often linked to external extranet systems, such as the electronic data interchange (EDI) systems, which are linked to the company's supply chain partners.

● It can be interfaced with standard applications programs which are in common use by most managers, such as spreadsheets, etc.

● Often, ERP systems are able to operate on most common platforms such as Windows NT, UNIX or Linux.

Arguably the most significant issue in many company's decision to buy an off-the-shelf ERP system is that of its compatibility with the company's current business processes and practices. Experience of ERP installation suggests that it is extremely important to make sure that one's current way of doing business will fit (or can be changed to fit) with a standard ERP package. If a business' current processes do not fit, it can either change its processes to fit the ERP package, or modify the software within the ERP package to fit its processes. Both of these options involve costs and risks. Changing business practices that are working well will involve reorganisation costs as well as introducing the potential for errors to creep into the processes. Adapting the software will both slow down the project and introduce potentially dangerous software 'bugs' into the system. It would also make it difficult to upgrade the software later on.

Supply network ERP

The step beyond integrating internal ERP systems with immediate customers and suppliers is to integrate it with the systems of other businesses throughout the supply network. This is often exceptionally complicated. Not only do different ERP systems have to communicate together, they have to integrate with other types of system. For example, sales and marketing functions often use systems such as Customer Relationship Management (CRM) systems that manage the complexities of customer requirements, promises and transactions. Getting ERP and CRM systems to work together is itself often difficult. Nevertheless, such web-integrated ERP applications are emerging. Although a formidable task, the benefits are potentially great. Transaction costs between supply network partners could be dramatically reduced and the potential for avoiding errors is significant. Yet, such transparency also brings risks. If the ERP system of one operation within a supply chain fails for some reason, it may block the effective operation of the whole integrated information system throughout the network.

Criticisms of ERP

ERP installation can be particularly expensive. Attempting to get new systems and databases to talk to old legacy systems can be very problematic. Not surprisingly, many companies choose to replace most, if not all, their existing systems simultaneously. New common systems and relational databases help to ensure the smooth transfer of data between different parts of the organisation.

There are also considerable 'adjustment costs' associated with many of the implementations. ERP implementations have developed a reputation for exceeding their budgets, with 200–300 per cent cost and time overruns being commonly cited for reasonably sized installations. Given that such systems are predicated on both substantial IT development and process redesign work, it should not be surprising that costs and timeframes proved to be larger and longer than predicted.

In addition to the obvious investment of time and effort, there is also the cost of providing training in new ways of working. Given that old systems, procedures and routines are being replaced in an ERP implementation, this retraining cost can be very significant. During the retraining period there may also be an increased chance of staff error which, combined with the novelty of the system, could cause further failures.

By definition ERP systems are 'enterprise wide'. This means that all parts of the enterprise must agree on a shared way of working (that coincides with the ERP system's underlying structure) and uniformly implement the system in the same way. There are two important implications of this. First, getting all parts of the enterprise to agree on a common business model is rarely straightforward, even supposing that the ERP system's business model is appropriate for the way the enterprise prefers to operate. Second, because all parts of the enterprise are linked together the whole business could be held back by the 'weakest link'. That is, inefficiency or incompetence in one part of the enterprise may hold back the whole business.

Note that these disadvantages of ERP are not so much concerned with the fundamental logic of integrating enterprise-wide information systems. Rather they are concerned with the sheer difficulty of making it happen. This leads some authorities to argue that the disadvantages of ERP systems are not really disadvantages. The question is really whether any individual firm has the money, time and talent to exploit the advantages of ERP.

Lessons from ERP

When ERP is implemented successfully it has the potential to significantly improve performance. This is partly because of the very much enhanced visibility that information integration gives, but it is also a function of the discipline that ERP demands. Yet, this discipline is itself a 'double-edged' sword. On one hand, it 'sharpens up' the management of every process within an organisation, allowing best practice (or at least common practice) to be implemented uniformly through the business. No longer will individual idiosyncratic behaviour by one part of a company's operations cause disruption to all other processes. On the other hand, it is the rigidity of this discipline that is both difficult to achieve and (arguably) inappropriate for all parts of the business. Nevertheless, the generally accepted benefits of ERP are as follows:

- greater visibility of what is happening in all parts of the business;
- forcing the business process-based changes that potentially make all parts of the business more efficient;
- improved control of operations that encourages continuous improvement (albeit within the confines of the common process structures);
- more sophisticated communication with customers, suppliers and other business partners, often giving more accurate and timely information;
- integrating whole supply chains including suppliers' suppliers and customers' customers.

An important justification for embarking on ERP is the potential it gives to link up with the outside world. For example, it is much easier for an operation to move into internet-based trading if it can integrate its external internet systems into its internal ERP systems. However, as has been pointed out by some critics of the ERP software companies, ERP vendors were not prepared for the impact of e-commerce and had not made sufficient allowance in their products for the need to interface with internet-based communication channels. The result of this has been that whereas the internal complexity of ERP systems was designed only to be intelligible to systems experts, the internet has meant that customers and suppliers (who are non-experts) are demanding access to the same information.

Where does ERP fit into operations strategy?

Figure 9.10 (see page 288) shows some of the key elements of ERP classified according to our operations strategy decision areas. In some ways it may seem that ERP is primarily a process technology decision. After all, it is an investment in 'indirect' process technology in so much as it supports the way the operation is managed.

Also, as we have stressed, it is a very significant investment. However, the investment has a very significant effect on the company's infrastructure, most notably the way in which the business is organised, the way processes relate to each other, the way data is treated, and the degree of training and development required to achieve commonality in working practice. Certainly, seeing ERP as simply a technology investment (although there are very significant technical issues to be overcome) is clearly a mistake. At its simplest level it still has a profound effect on the operation's development and organisation. In its more advanced forms when ERP extends to the supply network, it also will shape supply network strategy. Suppliers, customers and perhaps even competitors, may be required to adopt similar IT systems' protocols in order to communicate effectively. This in turn may also affect their own development and organisation decisions. Capacity strategy is probably the decision area least affected by ERP implementation. One would hope that ERP could lead to more effective capacity planning when it is fully operating. But perhaps the most important capacity issue to raise is that, when ERP systems are being implemented, there could be a noticeable reduction in effective capacity because of the significant resources needed to ensure successful implementation.

Six Sigma

The Six Sigma approach was first popularised by Motorola, the electronics and communications systems company. When it set its quality objective as 'total customer satisfaction' in the 1980s, it started to explore what the slogan would mean to its operations processes. It decided that true customer satisfaction would only be achieved when its products were delivered when promised, with no defects, with no early-life failures and when the product did not fail excessively in service. To achieve this, Motorola initially focused on removing manufacturing defects. However, it soon

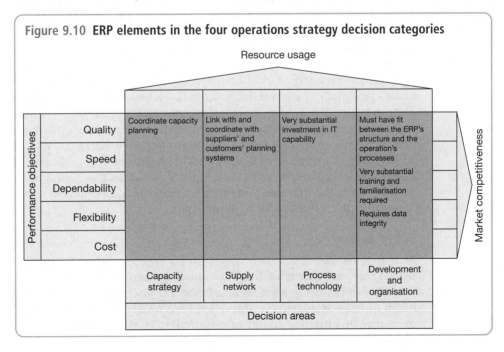

Figure 9.10 **ERP elements in the four operations strategy decision categories**

came to realise that many problems were caused by latent defects, hidden within the design of its products. These may not show initially but eventually could cause failure in the field. The only way to eliminate these defects was to make sure that design specifications were tight (i.e. narrow tolerances) and its processes very capable.

What is Six Sigma?

Motorola's Six Sigma quality concept was so named because it required that the natural variation of processes (± 3 standard deviations) should be half their specification range. In other words, the specification range of any part of a product or service should be ± 6 the standard deviation of the process. The Greek letter sigma (σ) is often used to indicate the standard deviation of a process, hence the Six Sigma label. How has the definition of Six Sigma widened to well beyond this rather narrow statistical perspective? General Electric (GE), which is probably the best known of the early adopters of Six Sigma, defined it as, *'a disciplined methodology of defining, measuring, analysing, improving, and controlling the quality in every one of the company's products, processes, and transactions – with the ultimate goal of virtually eliminating all defects'*. So, now Six Sigma should be seen as a broad improvement concept rather than a simple examination of process variation, even though this is still an important part of process control, learning and improvement.

The elements of Six Sigma

Although the scope of Six Sigma is disputed, among the elements frequently associated with Six Sigma are the following.

Customer driven objectives

Six Sigma is sometimes defined as *'the process of comparing process outputs against customer requirements'*. In taking on this definition, Six Sigma is conforming to what almost all of the new approaches to operations do, namely starting by emphasising the importance of understanding customers and customer requirements. The idea of comparing what processes can do against what customers want can be seen as an operational level articulation of the definition of operations strategy used in this book – reconciling market requirements against operations resource capabilities. Although the Six Sigma approach is inevitably narrower, it uses a number of measures to assess the performance of operations processes. In particular, it expresses performance in terms of defects per million opportunities (DPMO). This is exactly what it says, the number of defects which the process will produce if there were one million opportunities to do so. This is then related to the 'Sigma measurement' of a process and is the number of standard deviations of the process variability that will fit within the customer specification limits.

Use of evidence

Although Six Sigma is not the first of the new approaches to operations to use statistical methods (some of the TQM gurus promoted statistical process control for example) it has done a lot to emphasise the use of quantitative evidence. In fact much of the considerable training required by Six Sigma consultants is devoted to mastering quantitative analytical techniques. However, the statistical methods used in Six Sigma do not always reflect conventional academic statistical knowledge as such. Six Sigma emphasises observational methods of collecting data and the use of experimentation to examine hypothesis. Techniques include graphical methods, analysis of variance, and two-level factorial experiment design. Underlying the use of these techniques is an emphasis on the scientific method, responding only to hard evidence, and using statistical software to facilitate analysis.

Structured improvement cycle

The structured improvement cycle used in Six Sigma is called DMAIC (pronounced de-make) cycle (see Figure 9.11). The DMAIC cycle starts with defining the problem or problems, partly to understand the scope of what needs to be done and partly to define exactly the requirements of the process improvement. Often at this stage a formal goal or target for the improvement is set. After definition comes the measurement stage. This is an important point in the cycle, and the Six Sigma approach generally, which emphasises the importance of working with hard evidence rather than opinion. This stage involves validating the problem to make sure that it really is a problem worth solving, using data to refine the problem and measuring exactly what is happening. Once these measurements have been established, they can be analysed. The analysis stage is sometimes seen as an opportunity to develop hypotheses as to what the root causes of the problem really are. Such hypotheses are validated (or not) by the analysis and the main root causes of the problem identified. Once the causes of the problem are identified, work can begin on improving the process. Ideas are developed to remove the root causes of problems, solutions are tested and those solutions that seem to work are implemented, formalised and results measured. The improved process needs then to be continually monitored and controlled to check that the improved level of performance is being sustained. After this point the cycle starts again and defines the problems which are preventing further improvement. Remember though, it is the last point about both cycles that is the most important – the cycle starts again. It is only by accepting that in a continuous improvement philosophy these cycles quite literally never stop and that improvement becomes part of every person's job.

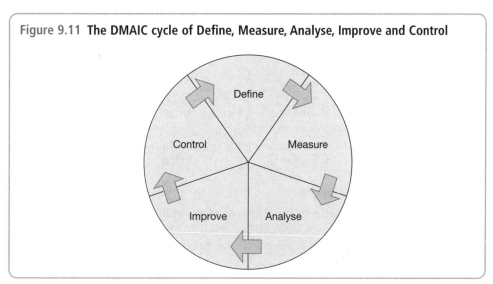

Figure 9.11 **The DMAIC cycle of Define, Measure, Analyse, Improve and Control**

Structured training and organisation of improvement

The Six Sigma approach holds that improvement initiatives can only be successful if significant resources and training are devoted to their management. It recommends a specially trained cadre of practitioners, many of whom should be dedicated full-time to improving processes as internal consultants. The terms that have become associated with this group of experts (and denote their level of expertise) are: Master Black Belt, Black Belt and Green Belt. Master Black Belts are experts in the use of Six Sigma tools and techniques as well as how such techniques can be used and implemented. Primarily Master Black Belts are seen as teachers who can not only guide improvement projects, but also coach and mentor Black Belts and Green Belts who are closer to the day-to-day improvement activity. They are expected to have the quantitative analytical skills to help with Six Sigma techniques and also the organisational and interpersonal skills to teach and mentor. Given their responsibilities, Master Black Belts are expected to be employed full time on their improvement activities. Black Belts can take a direct hand in organising improvement teams. Like Master Black Belts, Black Belts are expected to develop their quantitative analytical skills and also act as coaches for Green Belts. Black Belts are dedicated full time to improvement, and although opinions vary on how many Black Belts should be employed in an operation, some organisations recommend one Black Belt for every hundred employees. Green Belts work within improvement teams, possibly as team leaders. They have significant amounts of training, although less than Black Belts. Green Belts are not full-time positions; they have normal day-to-day process responsibilities but are expected to spend at least 20 per cent of their time on improvement projects.

Process capability and control

Not surprisingly, given its origins, process capability and control is important within the Six Sigma approach. Processes change over time, as does their performance. Some aspect of process performance (usually an important one) is measured periodically (either as a single measurement or as a small sample of measurements). These are then plotted on a simple time-scale. This has a number of advantages. The first is to check that the performance of the process is, in itself, acceptable (capable). They can also be used to check if process performance is changing over time, and to check on the extent of the variation in process performance.

Process design

Latterly Six Sigma proponents also include process design into the collection of elements that define the Six Sigma approach. This is somewhat surprising because process design (or rather, redesign) is implicit in the DMAIC cycle. Presumably, by formally including this element, practitioners are emphasising the need to improve whole processes rather than individual elements of a process.

Process improvement

Some of the ideas of continuous improvement are also now formally included in Six Sigma, but it does not confine itself to continuous improvement only. In fact Six Sigma projects may often be relatively wide in scope and aim to achieve relatively large improvements.

Criticisms of Six Sigma

One common criticism of Six Sigma is that it does not offer anything that was not available before. Its emphasis on improvement cycles comes from TQM, its emphasis on reducing variability comes from Statistical Process Control, its use of experimentation and data analysis is simply good quantitative analysis. The only contribution that Six Sigma has made, argue its critics, is using the rather gimmicky martial arts analogy of Black Belt, etc. to indicate a level of expertise in Six Sigma methods. All Six Sigma has done is package pre-existing elements together in order for consultants to be able to sell it to gullible chief executives. In fact it's difficult to deny some of these points. Maybe the real issue is whether it is really a criticism. If bringing these elements together really does form an effective problem solving approach, why is this a problem? Six Sigma is also accused of being too hierarchical in the way it structures it various levels of involvement in the improvement activity (as well as the dubious use of martial arts derived names such as Black Belt). It is also expensive. Devoting such large amounts of training and time to improvement is a significant investment, especially for small companies. Nevertheless, Six Sigma proponents argue that the improvement activity is generally neglected in most operations and if it is to be taken seriously, it deserves the significant investment implied by the Six Sigma approach. Furthermore, they argue, if operated well, Six Sigma improvement projects run by experienced practitioners can save far more than their cost.

There are also technical criticisms of Six Sigma. Most notably that in purely statistical terms the normal distribution which is used extensively in Six Sigma analysis does not actually represent most process behaviour. Other technical criticisms (that are not really the subject of this book) imply that aiming for the very low levels of defects per million opportunities, as recommended by Six Sigma proponents, is far too onerous.

Lessons from Six Sigma

If one were cynical one would argue that the real lesson from Six Sigma is that with a scientific sounding title and a set of commonsense analytical tools, consultants can sell anything. But whether one accepts that or not, one cannot deny the success of how Six Sigma has been sold. So maybe a more charitable view is that there is a genuine hunger for, and appreciation of, evidence-based improvement tools. Certainly, one can argue that before Six Sigma there was too little emphasis on evidence-based and statistical analysis. Softer and more cultural and behaviour-based approaches are useful, but they must be balanced with more rigorous quantitative perspectives.

Where does Six Sigma fit into operations strategy?

Figure 9.12 again categorises some of the elements of Six Sigma in the four operations strategy decision areas. In fact it shows that Six Sigma is very much biased towards infrastructural decision making. One could argue that Six Sigma's emphasis on process control is a function of how process technology is managed, but it is very much towards the infrastructural end of process technology strategy. All the other elements of Six Sigma are firmly in the development and organisation category. In other words, Six Sigma is more about how the systems, procedures, organisational structure and routines of the business are shaped rather than how its physical presence is configured.

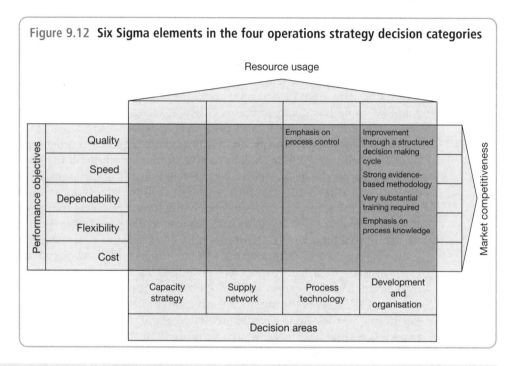

Figure 9.12 **Six Sigma elements in the four operations strategy decision categories**

The figure shows a matrix with "Resource usage" at the top, "Performance objectives" (Quality, Speed, Dependability, Flexibility, Cost) down the left side, "Market competitiveness" on the right, and "Decision areas" (Capacity strategy, Supply network, Process technology, Development and organisation) along the bottom. In the cells under Process technology: "Emphasis on process control". Under Development and organisation: "Improvement through a structured decision making cycle", "Strong evidence-based methodology", "Very substantial training required", "Emphasis on process knowledge".

> **Example** **Six Sigma at Xchanging**[16]

> *'I think Six Sigma is powerful because of its definition; it is the process of comparing process out-puts against customer requirements. Processes operating at less than 3.4 defects per million oppor-tunities means that you must strive to get closer to perfection and it is the customer that defines the goal. Measuring defects per opportunity means that you can actually compare the process of, say, a human resources process with a billing and collection process.'*

Paul Ruggier, head of Process at Xchanging, is a powerful advocate of Six Sigma, and credits the success of the company, at least partly, to the approach.

Xchanging, created in 1998, is one of a new breed of companies, operating as an out-sourcing business for 'back office' functions for a range of companies, such as Lloyds of London, the insurance centre. Xchanging's business proposition is for the client company to transfer the running of the whole or part of its back office to Xchanging, either for a fixed price or one determined by cost savings achieved. The challenge Xchanging faces is to run that back office in a more effective and efficient manner than the client company had man-aged in the past. So, the more effective Xchanging is at running the processes, the greater its profit. To achieve these efficiencies, Xchanging offers larger scale, a higher level of process expertise, focus and investment in technology. But above all, it offers, a Six Sigma approach. Paul Ruggier says:

> *'Everything we do can be broken down into a process. It may be more straightforward in a manu-facturing business, frankly they've been using a lot of Six Sigma tools and techniques for decades. But the concept of process improvement is relatively new in many Service companies. Yet, the con-cept is powerful. Through the implementation of this approach we have achieved 30 per cent pro-ductivity improvements in six months.'*

The company also adopts the Six Sigma terminology for its improvement practitioners – Master Black Belts, Black Belts and Green Belts. Attaining the status of Black Belt is very much sought after as well as fulfilling, says Rebecca Whittaker, a Master Black Belt at Xchanging:

'At the end of a project it is about having a process which is redesigned to such an extent, that is simplified and consolidated and people come back and say, "It's so much better than it used to be". It makes their lives better and it makes the business results better and those are the things that make being a Black Belt worthwhile.'

Rebecca was recruited by Xchanging along with a number of other Master Black Belts as part of a strategic decision to kick start Six Sigma in the company. It is seen as a particularly responsible position by the company and Master Black Belts are expected to be well versed in the Six Sigma techniques and be able to provide the training and know how to develop other staff within the company. In Rebecca's case she has been working as a Six Sigma facilitator for five years, initially as a Green Belt then as a Black Belt.

Typically, a person identified as having the right analytical and interpersonal skills will be taken off their job for at least a year, for training and immersed in the concepts of improvement and then sent to work with line staff as project manager/facilitator. His or her role as Black Belt will be to guide the line staff to make improvements in the way they do the job. One of the new Black Belts at Xchanging, Sarah Frost, is keen to stress the responsibility she owes to the people who will have to work in the improvement process:

'Being a Black Belt is about being a project manager. It is about working with the staff and combining our skills in facilitation and our knowledge of the Six Sigma process with their knowledge of the business. You always have to remember that you will go onto another project but they (process staff) will have to live with the new process. It is about building solutions that they can believe in.'

Some common threads

Before adopting any of the 'approaches to operations' that we have covered in this chapter it is worth considering the extent to which one should be influenced by the experiences of other organisations, especially when packaged as 'best practice'. It may be that operations that rely on others to define what is 'best practice', are always limiting themselves to currently accepted methods of operating or currently accepted limits to performance. 'Best practice' is not 'best' in the sense that it cannot be bettered, it is only 'best' in the sense that it is the best one can currently find. Accepting this may prevent operations from ever making the radical breakthrough or improvement that takes the concept of 'best' to a new and fundamentally improved level. Furthermore, because one operation has a set of successful practices in the way it manages its operations does not mean that adopting those same practices in another context will prove equally successful. It is possible that subtle differences in the resources within a process (such as staff skills or technical capabilities) or the strategic context of an operation (for example, the relative priorities of performance objectives) will be sufficiently different to make the adoption of seemingly successful practices inappropriate.

But, even if one accepts 'best practice' as distilled into the new approaches that we have reviewed, there are some important points to consider.

Senior managers sometimes use these new approaches without fully understanding them.

In this chapter we have chosen to very briefly explain five of the approaches sometimes referred to as 'operations strategies'. One could easily have extended this list of five to include several others such as Total Preventive Maintenance (TPM), Lean Sigma (a combination of lean and Six Sigma), and so on. But these five in our view constitute a representative sample of the most commonly used approaches. Nor do we have the space to describe them fully. Each of the approaches is the subject of several books that describe them in great detail. There is no shortage of advice from consultants and academics as to how they should be used. Yet, it is not difficult to find examples of where senior management have embarked on a programme of using one or more of these approaches without fully understanding them. And if senior management do not understand these approaches, how can the rest of the organisation take them seriously? The details of Six Sigma or lean, for example, are not simply technical matters. They are fundamental to how appropriate the approach could be in different contexts. Not every approach fits every set of circumstances. So understanding in detail what each approach means must be the first step in deciding whether it is appropriate.

All these approaches are different.

There are clearly some common elements between some of these approaches that we have described. The most obvious element being the idea of a customer-centric perspective. Furthermore, as these approaches develop over time, they may acquire elements from elsewhere. Look how Six Sigma has developed beyond its process control roots to encompass many other elements. Yet, there are also differences between them and these differences also need to be understood. For example, one important difference relates to whether the approaches emphasise a gradual, continuous approach to change, or whether they recommend a more radical 'breakthrough' change. Another difference concerns the aim of the approach. What is the balance between whether the approach emphasises *what* changes should be made or *how* changes should be made? Some approaches have a firm view of what is the best way to organise the operation's processes and resources. Other approaches hold no particular view on what an operation should do but rather concentrate on how the management of an operation should decide what to do. Put in operations strategy terms this distinction is similar to that between the content and process of operations strategy. Figure 9.13 places each of the five approaches on these two dimensions.

Just as different authors have differing views as to the exact nature of some of these approaches, one could position them on the two dimensions shown in Figure 9.13 in slightly different ways. Nevertheless there are some important differences between the approaches which should be recognised. First, they differ in the extent that they prescribe appropriate operations practice. ERP, for example, is very clear in what it is recommending. Namely, that all systems and databases should be integrated. It may also have something to say about how this should be achieved but the focus of ERP is what should happen rather than how it should happen. To a slightly lesser extent both BPR and lean are the same. They have a definite list of things that operations resources should or should not be – processes should be end-to-end, non-value added work should be eliminated, inventory should be reduced, technology should be flexible, and so on. Contrast this with both Six Sigma and TQM that focus to a far greater extent on how operations should be improved. Six Sigma

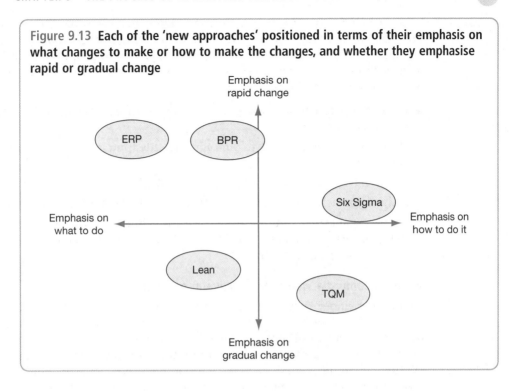

Figure 9.13 Each of the 'new approaches' positioned in terms of their emphasis on what changes to make or how to make the changes, and whether they emphasise rapid or gradual change

in particular has relatively little to say about what is good or bad in the way operations resources are organised (with the possible exception of it emphasising the negative effects of process variation). Its concern is largely the way improvements should be made: using evidence, using quantitative analysis, using the DMAIC cycle, and so on. They also differ in terms of whether they emphasise gradual or rapid change. BPR is explicit in its radical nature while ERP, in what it is recommending, implicitly assumes a fairly dramatic change. By contrast TQM and lean both incorporate ideas of continuous improvement. Six Sigma is relatively neutral on this issue and can be used for small or very large changes.

These approaches are not strategies but they are strategic decisions

So, are any of these approaches that we have described in this chapter operations strategies? Remember that our definition of operations strategy is the reconciliation of market requirements and operations resource capabilities. Implicit in this definition, and indeed in everything we have discussed in this book, is the idea that an individual enterprise's market requirements and their operations resource capabilities are to some extent unique to that enterprise. Even companies competing in ostensibly the same market for the same customers will generally have to position themselves slightly differently. Certainly, given that there is an infinite number of ways that they can organise their resources, they are likely to have different operations resource capabilities. The essence of an operations strategy is that it is individual and specific to one organisation at one point in time. By contrast, the approaches we have described in this chapter are generic in nature. That is after all why they are attractive: they offer generic advice that is broadly applicable across a range of businesses. That is also why they are not strategies. And that is why senior managers who adopt them as operations strategies are deluding themselves.

Nevertheless, none of them is incompatible with a sensible operations strategy. They can all be considered as part of a strategy, either in terms of its content or its process. In fact, the choice of which, if any, approach to adopt is an important strategic decision. Before adopting any of the approaches at least some of the following issues should be considered.

- Does the approach have the potential to add value in terms of the requirements of our customers?
- Have similar organisations to ours adopted this approach and what is their experience of using it?
- Do we have the resources (expertise, capacity, budget) to adopt the approach?
- Is this approach compatible with other strategic decisions that we have made?
- Are we capable of communicating the ideas behind the approach and carrying out the necessary training and development to ensure that all staff understand how it fits into the company's strategy?

Avoid becoming a victim of improvement 'fashion'

Finally, remember that operations improvement has, to some extent, become a fashion industry with new ideas and concepts continually being introduced as offering a novel way to improve business performance. There is nothing intrinsically wrong with this. Fashion stimulates and refreshes through introducing novel ideas. Without it, things would stagnate. The problem lies not with new improvement ideas, but rather with some managers' becoming a victim of the process, where some new idea will entirely displace whatever went before. Most new ideas have something to say, but jumping from one fad to another, will not only generate a backlash against any new idea, but also destroy the ability to accumulate the experience that comes from experimenting with each one. Avoiding becoming an improvement fashion victim is not easy. It requires that those directing the strategy process take responsibility for a number of issues.

(a) They must take responsibility for improvement as an ongoing activity, rather than becoming champions for only one a specific improvement initiative.

(b) They must take responsibility for understanding the underlying ideas behind each new concept. Improvement is not 'following a recipe' or 'painting by numbers'. Unless one understands *why* improvement ideas are supposed to work, it is difficult to understand *how* they can be made to work properly.

(c) They must take responsibility for understanding the antecedents to a 'new' improvement idea, because it helps to understand it better and to judge how appropriate it may be for one's own operation.

(d) They must be prepared to adapt new idea so that they make sense within the context of their own operation. 'One size' rarely fits all.

(e) They must take responsibility for the (often significant) education and learning effort that will be needed if new ideas are to be intelligently exploited.

(f) Above all they must avoid the over-exaggeration and hype that many new ideas attract. Although it is sometimes tempting to exploit the motivational 'pull' of new ideas through slogans, posters and exhortations, carefully thought out plans will always be superior in the long run, and will help avoid the inevitable backlash that follows 'over-selling' a single approach.

SUMMARY ANSWERS TO KEY QUESTIONS

How does Total Quality Management fit into operations strategy?

Total Quality Management (TQM) is a philosophy of how to approach the organis-ation of quality improvement that stresses the 'total' of TQM. It puts quality and improvement generally at the heart of everything that is done by an operation. It provides a checklist of how to organise operations improvement. It has also been developed into a more prescriptive form as in the European Foundation for Quality Management (EFQM) Excellence Model.

How do Lean Operations fit into operations strategy?

The lean approach aims to meet demand instantaneously, with perfect quality and no waste'. It can be seen as having four elements; customer-based demand triggers, syn-chronised flow, enhanced improvement behaviour, and waste elimination. However, the lean concept implies some sacrifice of capacity utilisation. It occurs because, when stoppages occur in the traditional system, buffers allow each stage to continue working and thus achieve high capacity utilisation. There is far less buffering in lean processes.

How does Business Process Reengineering fit into operations strategy?

Business Process Reengineering (BPR) is the fundamental rethinking and radical redesign of business processes to achieve dramatic improvements in critical, con-temporary measures of performance, such as cost, quality, service and speed. The approach strives for dramatic improvements in performance by radically rethinking and redesigning the process using 'end-to-end' processes and by exploiting the power of IT to integrate processes.

How does Enterprise Resource Planning fit into operations strategy?

Enterprise Resource Planning (ERP) is an enterprise-wide business solution that inte-grates the planning, resource allocation and control activities of all parts of the busi-ness, the better to make informed planning and control decisions. However the practical implementation of this idea has proved to be very complex and expensive. If a businesses current processes do not fit with the structure of whatever ERP pack-age is purchased, they can either change their processes to fit the ERP package, or modify the software within the ERP package to fit their processes. Both of these options involve costs and risks.

How does Six Sigma fit into operations strategy?

Six Sigma is a disciplined methodology of defining, measuring, analysing, improving, and controlling the quality in every one of the company's products, processes, and transactions – with the ultimate goal of virtually eliminating all defects. Although it started as a statistical process control-based concept, it is now a broad improvement concept rather than a simple examination of process variation. It stresses the use of (preferably quantitative) evidence in decision making, systematic problem solving and the use of improvement specialists called Black Belts, Green Belts, etc.

What place do these new approaches have in operations strategy?

These approaches are not strategies in themselves (operations strategy specific to one organization at one point in time), they are generic in nature, but they are strategic decisions. But none of them is incompatible with operations strategy, they can all be considered as part of a strategy. It is also important to understand fully any approach before it is adopted because all the approaches are different. Some emphasise gradual change, others more radical change. Some hold a view of the best way to organise resources, others concentrate on how to decide what to do. So the focus of ERP is what should happen rather than how it should happen. BPR and lean are similar. But both Six Sigma and TQM focus more on how operations should be improved. BPR is explicit in its radical and ERP implies dramatic change. TQM and lean, on the other hand, both incorporate ideas of continuous improvement, whereas Six Sigma can be used for small or very large changes.

Further reading

Bicheno, J. (2004) *The New Lean Toolbox: Towards Fast, Flexible Flow*. Buckingham, UK: Picsie Books.

George, M.L., Rowlands, D. and Kastle, B. (2003) *What Is Lean Six Sigma?* McGraw-Hill.

Liker, J. (2003) *The Toyota Way: 14 Management Principles from the World's Greatest Manufacturer*. McGraw-Hill Education.

Pande, P.S., Neuman, R.P. and Cavanagh, R. (2002) *Six Sigma Way Team Field Book: An Implementation Guide for Project Improvement Teams*. McGraw-Hill.

Spear, S. and Bowen, H.K. (1999) 'Decoding the DNA of the Toyota production system', *Harvard Business Review*, September–October.

Vollmann, T., Berry, W., Whybark, D.C. and Jacobs, F.R. (2004) *Manufacturing Planning and Control Systems for Supply Chain Management: The Definitive Guide for Professionals*. McGraw-Hill Higher Education.

Wallace, T.F. and Krezmar, M.K. (2001) *ERP: Making It Happen*. John Wiley & Sons.

Womack, J.P. and Jones, D.T. (1996) *Lean Thinking: Banish Waste and Create Wealth in Your Corporation*. New York: Simon & Schuster.

Notes on the chapter

1 Feigenbaum, A.V. (1986) *Total Quality Control*. New York: McGraw Hill.
2 Deming, W.E. (1986) *Out of Crisis*. Cambridge and Boston, MA: MIT Center for Advanced Engineering Study.
3 Matsushito, K. (1985) 'Why the West Will Lose', *Industrial Participation*, Spring.
4 *The Economist* (2000) 'Was It All Worth It?', 24 April.
5 Deming, W.E. (1986) op. cit.
6 Kamata, S. (1983) *Japan in the Passing Lane: An Insider's Account of Life in a Japanese Auto Factory*. London: Allen and Unwin.
7 Schultz, K., McCain, J. and Thomas, L.J. (2003) 'Overcoming the dark side of worker flexibility', *Journal of Operations Management*, Vol. 21, pp. 81–92.
8 Spear, S. and Bowen, H.K. (1999) 'Decoding the DNA of the Toyota production system', *Harvard Business Review*, September–October.
9 Based on Karlsson, C. (1996) 'Radically new production systems', *International Journal of Operations and Production Management*, 16(11).
10 Davenport, T. (1995) 'Reengineering: the fad that forgot people', *Fast Company*, November.
11 Hammer, M. and Champy, J. (1993) *Reengineering the Corporation: A Manifesto for Business Revolution*. New York: Harper Business.
12 Johansson, H.J. (1993) *Business Process Reengineering: Break Point Strategies for Market Dominance*. New York: John Wiley & Sons.
13 Hammer, M. and Champy, J. (1993) op. cit.
14 For example, Davenport, T. (1995) op. cit.
15 Teach, E. (2004) 'Watch how you think', *CFO Magazine*, January.
16 Source: Discussion with staff at Xchanging.

The process of operations strategy – implementation

Introduction

No matter how sophisticated the intellectual and analytical underpinnings of a strategy, it remains only an aspiration until it has been implemented. So implementation is an important part of operations strategy even if it does come at the end of the operations strategy process. Yet, it is not always straightforward to make general points about the implementation process because it is very context dependent. That is, the way one implements any strategy will very much depend on the specific nature of the changes implied by that strategy and the organisational and environmental conditions that apply during its implementation. That is why, in this chapter, the emphasis is on how implementation is shaped by its context (see Figure 10.1).

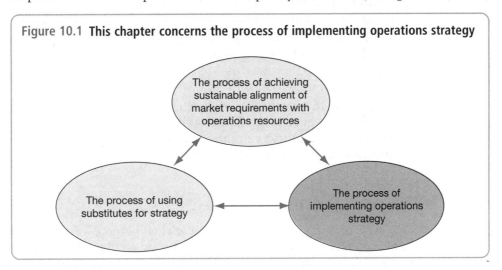

Figure 10.1 **This chapter concerns the process of implementing operations strategy**

The process of achieving sustainable alignment of market requirements with operations resources

The process of using substitutes for strategy

The process of implementing operations strategy

Successful operations depend not only on the nature and attributes of the resources contained within the firm but also on how those resources are organised, supported and developed.

KEY QUESTIONS

- *How does strategic context affect implementation?*
- *How does organisational context affect implementation?*
- *How does methodology affect implementation?*
- *How can project management affect implementation?*
- *How can participation affect implementation?*

What is implementation?

Implementation, in the context of operations strategy, means the organising of all the activities involved in making the strategy work as intended. And, while we wish to avoid simple prescriptions, it is important to reflect on the broad issues that implementation involves. The structure that we shall use to do this is known as the five Ps.[1] It identifies some of the key elements that characterise the strategy formulation process generally, but it also provides a useful structure for examining implementation. The five Ps are as follows.

1 *Purpose*. As with any management endeavour, the more clarity that exists around the ultimate goal, the more likely it is that the goal will be achieved. In our terms, a shared understanding of the relative changes in market position and operations resource capabilities, as well as the motivation, boundaries and context for developing the operations strategy is crucial.

2 *Point of entry*. Any analysis, formulation and implementation process is potentially politically sensitive and the support that the process has from within the hierarchy of the organisation is central to implementation success.

3 *Process*. The formulation process of operations strategy must be explicit. It is important that the managers who are engaged in putting operations strategies together actively think about the methodology that is being used.

4 *Project management*. Devising and implementing operations strategy is itself a project and needs to be managed as such. The basic disciplines of project management, such as stakeholder management, resource and time planning, controls, communication mechanisms, reviews, and so on, should be in place.

5 *Participation*. Intimately linked with the above points, the selection of staff to participate in the implementation process is also critical. So, for instance, the use of line managers and staff can provide 'real world' experience and the inclusion of cross-functional managers can help to integrate the finished strategy.

Purpose – the strategic context

One way of thinking about the underlying purpose of an operations strategy implementation is to use the 'line of fit', or alignment, concept introduced in Chapter 8. To recap, the idea is that operations strategy can be diagrammatically illustrated by its position relative to its operations resource capabilities, the requirements of its markets, and the degree of 'fit' or alignment between them. Chapter 8 focused on achieving sustainable alignment between operations resource capabilities and market requirements. It also stressed the difficulty of achieving alignment because of uncertain markets and operations resource capabilities. In Figure 10.2 moving along the market requirements dimension indicates a change in intended market performance. Moving along the operations resource capabilities dimension indicates changes in operations capabilities.

Using this model gives us a starting point for understanding the purpose of the operations degree of change involved in the strategy implementation. It is important to be clear regarding how much change is intended. So, if, on Figure 10.2, point A is the current operations strategy and point B is the intended operations strategy, it is necessary to develop an understanding of current and intended market requirements and operations resource capabilities. Certainly, without such an understanding, it is exceedingly difficult to expect the whole organisation to comprehend why, how, and how much, things are going to change when the new strategy is implemented. Yet providing guidance to those who will be carrying out the implementation, is not a straightforward task. We are again confronted with the tensions between seeing strategy as a plan that provides a 'grand design' for the operation on one hand, and seeing strategy as an emergent process that takes full account of the experiences that are derived from the day-to-day running of the operation and the day-to-day implementation of the new strategy. This means that any statement that articulates an intended change must be specific enough to provide useful guidance and yet broad enough to allow for adaptation of the implementation plan within an overall strategic direction.

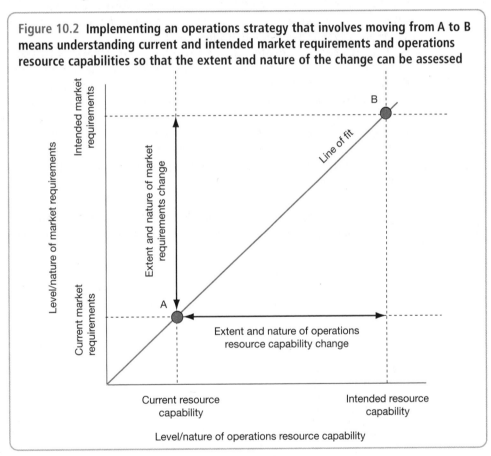

Figure 10.2 Implementing an operations strategy that involves moving from A to B means understanding current and intended market requirements and operations resource capabilities so that the extent and nature of the change can be assessed

But there is a problem. During the implementation from A to B in Figure 10.2 the balance between market requirements and operations resource capabilities may not always be maintained. Sometimes the market may expect something that the operation cannot (temporarily) deliver. Sometimes operations may have capabilities that cannot be exploited in the market. At a strategic level, there are risks deriving from a failure to achieve fit between operations resources and market requirements. And how to understand, and cope with, these risks during implementation should be part of any implementation plan.

Implementation risk – market and operations performance becoming out of balance

Particularly during implementation, when changes in both market positioning and operations resources are likely, the possibility of deviating from the 'line of fit' in Figure 10.2 is very real. This may be because some part of the implementation is not going to plan, for example, delays in the implementation of a new website means that customers do not receive the level of service they were promised. Or, it may be an inevitable and expected part of the implementation plan, for example, a firm may plan to install and de-bug a new IT system before it starts to use its potential to make promises to its market. Either way the deviation from alignment between market requirements and operations resources is exposing the firm to risk, and while there is no widely accepted definition for operations-related risk, our working definition of operations-related risk is: *operations risk is the potential for unwanted negative consequences from an operations-related event.*

Many risks can be related to the uncertainty associated with both the development of an operational resource-base and shifting market requirements. Any operations strategy implementation, therefore, must accommodate these risks. Figure 10.3 illustrates this idea. Moving above the diagonal implies that market performance (that is, the requirements and/or the expectations of the market) are in advance of the operation's capability to satisfy it. This is called external operations-related risk. The area below the diagonal implies that a firm has levels of competence or potential performance which are not being exploited in the marketplace. This is called internal operations-related risk.

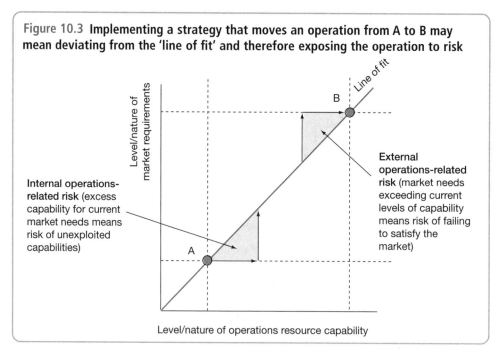

Figure 10.3 **Implementing a strategy that moves an operation from A to B may mean deviating from the 'line of fit' and therefore exposing the operation to risk**

Pure and speculative risk

A useful distinction is that between pure risks, involving events that will produce the possibility only of loss (or negative outcomes), and speculative risks that emerge from competitive scenarios and hold the potential for loss or gain (positive outcomes). A pure risk might be the risk that, while implementing a new blood testing strategy for HIV, a technician at a medical laboratory is involved in an accident that leads to possible infection. A speculative risk might be the risk associated with developing a new computer-based diagnostics and information infrastructure to enable the laboratory to offer a range of profitable new services. The risk here is that the technology may not work (or not work on time or in budget) or that the market will not want to pay for the new services. This is illustrated in Figure 10.4. The pure risk type of 'accident' involves a reduction in effective operations resource capability of the type represented by the movement between A and C. Speculative risk of the type represented by the new information infrastructure is represented by the possible outcomes B, D and E. Movement from A to B is positive in the sense that it represents a fulfilment of the intended outcome. Negative consequences are represented by point D where market requirements have increased as intended but operations capabilities have failed to match them, and E where operations capabilities have been increased but have not been fully exploited in the market.

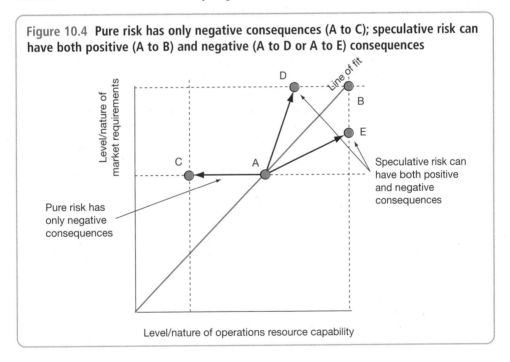

Figure 10.4 **Pure risk has only negative consequences (A to C); speculative risk can have both positive (A to B) and negative (A to D or A to E) consequences**

Controlling risk

Operations strategy practitioners are understandably interested in how an operation can avoid failure in the first place, or if it does happen, how they can survive any adverse conditions that might follow. In other words, how they can control risk. A simple structure for describing generic mechanisms for controlling risk uses three approaches.

- Prevention strategies – where an operation seeks to completely prevent (or reduce the frequency of) an event occurring.
- Mitigating strategies – where an operation seeks to isolate an event from any possible negative consequences.
- Recovery strategies – where an operation analyses and accepts the consequences from an event but undertakes to minimise or alleviate or compensate for them.

Prevention strategies

It is almost always better to avoid negative consequences than have to recover from them. The classic approach is to audit plans to try and identify causes of risk. For instance, by emphasising its use of 'fair trading' principles, the high street retailer The Body Shop was able to develop its 'ethical' brand identity as a powerful advantage, but it also became a potential source of vulnerability. When a journalist accused one of the firm's suppliers of using animal product testing, the rest of the media eagerly took up the story. To prevent this kind of accusation from resurfacing, the firm introduced a detailed auditing method to prevent any suspicion of unethical behaviour in their entire supply chain.

Mitigation strategies

Not all events can be avoided, but an operation can try to separate an event from its negative consequences. This is called mitigation. For example, look at the way that an operation deals with exposure to currency fluctuations. After the collapse of communism in the early 1990s, a multinational consumer goods firm began to invest in the former Soviet Union. Their Russian subsidiary sourced nearly all products from its parent's factories in Germany. Conscious of the potential volatility of the rouble, the firm needed to minimise its exposure to a devaluation of the currency. Any such devaluation would leave the firm's cost structure at a serious disadvantage and without any real option but to increase their prices. Financial tools were available to mitigate currency exposure. Most of these allowed the operation to reduce the risk of currency fluctuations but involved an 'up front' cost. Alternatively, the company could restructure its operations strategy in order to mitigate its currency risk, developing its own production facilities within Russia. This may reduce, or even eliminate, the currency risk, although it would probably introduce other risks. A further option was to form supply partnerships with other Russian companies. Again, this would not eliminate risks but could shift them to ones that the company feels more able to control.

Recovery strategies

Recovery strategies can involve a wide range of activities. They include the (micro) recovery steps necessary to minimise an individual customer's dissatisfaction. This might include apologising, refunding monies, reworking a product or service, or providing compensation. At the same time, operations have to be prepared for the (macro) major crises that might necessitate a complete product recall or abandonment of service. The question that an operations strategy needs to consider is, 'At what point do we reach the limit of avoidance and mitigation strategies before we start to rely on recovery strategies?'

Example **Planning for recovery**[2]

It was a product recall that attracted more than usual negative media coverage. Cadbury's the confectionary manufacturer recalled seven product lines accounting for more than a million chocolate bars. This was the result of potential salmonella contamination caused by a leaking pipe in a production factory. Initially a decision was taken not to recall any products, but this was reversed later. According to Chris Woodcock, managing director of Razor, a risk assessment firm:

'... this is a classic case of a business needing to consider all the reputational and brand-protection aspects of a possible food safety, technical problem before deciding whether or not to recall. The logical, technical facts are often not enough on their own to influence a decision on recall or no-recall. It is also vital to assess emotional and brand associations.'

Particularly where a brand is trusted to the extent of Cadbury's, recovery planning is vital. In this case the scientific justification for a recall was considered when it was first discovered that the pipe leaking had caused the low levels of salmonella.

'There was possibly still a good case for reconsidering the longer-term brand damage should the no-recall decision subsequently escape into the public domain. It was the apparent lack of transparency that attracted most criticism in media and expert commentary.'

But the Cadbury incident is far from being an isolated case. The number of product recalls is increasing as firms try to protect their reputations from the harm caused by faulty goods, according to Reynolds Porter Chamberlain a London law firm.

'Corporate reputations have become more fragile as consumers increasingly use the internet and other media to share and publicise information about faulty products. The Sony laptop battery debacle, which saw nearly 10 million battery packs recalled, is a perfect example. The growth of sites such as YouTube meant millions of consumers saw videos of a computer spontaneously catching fire due to the fault. The legal costs and compensation paid out can be colossal, so the need to recall quickly is vital, and so is insurance cover. With consumers becoming ever more litigious, companies are playing it safe and recalling even where the risk of a liability is slight. They know the courts and the press will punish them if they are seen as dragging their feet.'

Point of entry – the organisational context

We can think about the organisational context of implementation in two ways. First, it is important to recognise that different organisational structures have different attributes when it comes to implementing operations strategies. While it is not strictly within the scope of this text to examine the complexities of organisational design, it is necessary to understand how some of these characteristics affect implementation. Second, it is worthwhile examining the organisational position and role of whoever is charged with implementing the operation's strategy. Here we assume that there is some type of organisational team, function, or unit that has been allocated the responsibility for implementation, the key question being, 'How in practical terms do they relate to the rest of the operation's organisation?'

Organisational design

Organisational designs have been changing in response to the dual, and often conflicting, pressures of serving turbulent markets, whose requirements are continually changing, while at the same time preserving, and even extending, the essential capabilities that enable them to differentiate themselves from competitors. The organisation's structure is therefore not just the context of the implementation process, it also represents the corporate memory of how strategy has shifted and accommodated to these pressures over time. And, while there are many different ways of defining 'organisation structure', we see it as the way in which tasks and responsibilities are divided into distinct groupings, and how the responsibility and coordination relationships between the groupings are defined. This includes the informal relationships which build up between groups as well as their more formal relationships.

Perspectives on organisations[3]

How we illustrate organisations says much about our underlying assumptions of what an 'organisation' is and how it is supposed to work. For example, the illustration of an organisation as a conventional 'organogram' implies that organisations are neat and controllable with unambiguous lines of accountability. Even a little experience in any organisation demonstrates that rarely, if ever, is this the case. Nor does it take much more experience to question whether such a mechanistic view is even appropriate, or desirable. In fact, seeing an organisation as though it was unambiguously machine-like is just one of several metaphors commonly used to understand the realities of organisational life. One well-known analysis by Gareth Morgan proposes a number of 'images' or 'metaphors' which can be used to understand organisations.

Organisations are machines

The resources within organisations can be seen as 'components' in a mechanism whose purpose is clearly understood. Relations within the organisation are clearly defined and orderly, processes and procedures that should occur usually do occur, and the flow of information through the organisation is predictable. Such mechanical metaphors are popular because they appear to impose clarity on what is usually seen as deviant, messy behaviour within the organisation. Indeed, where it is important to impose clarity (as in much operations strategy analysis) such a metaphor can be useful. It is, however, a particularly limiting way of thinking about organisations. Flexibility and creativity are not emphasised, nor is independence of thought or action.

Organisations are organisms

Organisations are also living entities. Their behaviour is dictated by the behaviour of the individual humans within them. Individuals, and therefore the organisation, adapt to circumstances just as different species adapt to the environmental conditions in which they need to survive. The organism image helps us to understand how organisations interact with their environment, work through their life cycle and relate to other 'species' of organisation. This is a particularly useful way of looking at organisations if parts of the environment (such as the needs of the market) change radically. The survival of the organisation depends on its ability to exhibit sufficient flexibility to respond to its environment. However, the natural environments in which real organisms live are reasonably well understood, and are independent of the views of the organism itself. The social and political environment in which organisations exist is partly a function both of how they act and how they choose to see the environment. Organisations, even in the same industry, may see the opportunities and threats in very different ways.

Organisations are brains

Organisations process information and make decisions. No machine, or perhaps even organism, comes close to the degrees of sophistication of which a human brain is capable. Organisations, like brains, make decisions. They balance conflicting criteria, weigh up risks and decide when an outcome is acceptable. They are also capable of learning, changing their model of the world in the light of experience. This emphasis on decision making, accumulating experience and learning from that experience is important in understanding organisations. Brains, like organisations, are capable of developing and of organising themselves. However, organisations are clearly not unitary entities like brains. They consist of conflicting groups where power and control are key issues.

Organisations are cultures

An organisation's culture is usually taken to mean its shared values, ideology, pattern of thinking and day-to-day ritual. Different organisations will have different cultures stemming from their circumstances and their history. Because an organisation's internal structure and view of itself are influenced by its culture, we can think of an organisation as an expression of its culture. A major strength of seeing organisations as cultures is that it draws attention to their shared 'enactment of reality'. Within this the symbolism present in processes and procedures is seen to be important. Looking for the symbols and shared realities within an organisation allows us to see beyond whatever that organisation may formally say about itself. Unfortunately 'culture' has, in many organisations, come to be seen as something that can be changed at whim. Although managers can influence the evolution of culture, they cannot control it as if it were an air conditioning unit.

Organisations are political systems

Organisations, like communities, are governed. The system of government is rarely democratic, but nor is it usually a dictatorship. Within the mechanisms of government in an organisation are usually ways of understanding alternative philosophies, ways of seeking consensus (or at least reconciliation) and sometimes ways of legitimising opposition. Individuals and groups seek to pursue their aims through the detailed politics of the organisation. They form alliances, accommodate power relationships and manage conflict. Formal structures of authority may not always reflect the reality of influence and power. Such a view is useful in helping organisations to legitimise politics as an inevitable aspect of organisational life. However, seeing organisations exclusively as political systems can lead to cynicism or the pursuit of organisational power for its own sake.

Forms of organisation structure

Most organisation designs attempt to divide an organisation into discrete parts which are given some degree of authority to make decisions within their part of the organisation. All but the very smallest of organisations needs to delegate decision making in this way if for no other reason than that it prevents decision making over-load. More positively, it allows specialisation in so much as decisions can be taken by the people who are the most familiar with the relevant part of the organisation. The main issue is what dimension of specialisation should be used when grouping parts of the organisation together. There are three basic approaches to this:

- Group resources together according to their *functional purpose* – so, for example, sales, marketing, operations, research and development, finance, etc.

- Group resources together by the *characteristics of the resources themselves* – this may be done, for example, by clustering similar technologies together (extrusion tech-nology, rolling, casting, etc.). Alternatively, it may be done by clustering similar skills together (audit, mergers and acquisitions, tax, etc.). It may also be done according to the resources required for particular products or services (chilled food, frozen food, canned food, etc.).

- Group resources together by the *markets* which the resources are intended to serve – again this may be done in various ways. Markets may be defined by location, with distinct geographical boundaries (North America, South America, Europe and Middle East, South East Asia, etc.). Alternatively, markets may be defined by the type of customer (small firms, large national firms, large multinational firms, etc.).

Within a single organisation, resources can be grouped in several different ways. Moreover, the lines of responsibility and direct communication linking the resource clusters can also be configured in different ways. There is an infinite number of poss-ible organisational structures. However, some pure types of organisation have emerged that are useful in illustrating different approaches to organisational design, even if, in their pure form, they are rarely found.

The U-form organisation

The unitary form, or U-form, organisation clusters its resources primarily according to their functional purpose. Figure 10.5 (a) shows a typical U-form organisation with a pyramid management structure, each level reporting to the managerial level above. Such functionally based structures can prize narrow process efficiency above both customer service and the ability to adapt to changing market circumstances. The classic disease of such bureaucratic structures is that efficiency becomes an end in itself, while the broader set of organisational goals count for little when compared to narrow cost objectives. Worse, functions may become primarily concerned with their own survival, power and security. Even so, if the tendency to excessive bureau-cratisation is avoided, the U-form has one clear advantage – it keeps together intan-gible expertise within the function. This can promote a climate in which technical knowledge is created and shared amongst a community of functional experts. The problem then with the U-form organisation is not so much the development of capabilities but with the flexibility of their deployment.

The M-form organisation

This form of organisational structure emerged because the functionally based structure of the U-form was cumbersome when companies became large, often with complex, markets. It groups together either the resources needed for each product or service group, or alternatively, those needed to serve a particular geographical market, in separate divisions. Within each division, resources may be organised using the conventional functional U-form. The separate functions such as operations will be distributed throughout the different divisions (see Figure 10.5 (b)). This can reduce economies of scale and the operating efficiency of the structure. However, it does allow each individual division to focus on the specific needs of its markets, enabling it to tailor the nature and extent of its services to what each market requires.

Matrix forms

Matrix structures are a hybrid, usually combining the M-form with the U-form. In effect, the organisation has simultaneously two different structures (see Figure 10.5 (c)). In a matrix structure each resource cluster has at least two lines of authority, for example both to the division and to the functional groups. So an operations manager may be directly responsible to his or her division head, while at the same time having a (sometimes weaker) reporting responsibility to the head of the operations function for the whole company. Sometimes reporting relationships may be even more complex. For example, a team of accountants in a large accountancy firm could be responsible to the head of their technical specialism (for example, audit or taxation), the industry sector specialism (e.g. construction, financial services, etc.) and their regional market (United States, Europe, Far East, etc.). While a matrix organisation ensures the representation of all interests within the company, its drawbacks are its complexity, its cost and the potential it creates for considerable role ambiguity.

The N-form organisation

The 'N' in N-form stands for 'network'. In N-form organisations, resources are clustered into groups as in other organisational forms, but with more delegation of responsibility for the strategic management of those resources. N-forms have relatively little hierarchical reporting and control. Each cluster of resources is linked to the others to form a network, with the relative strength of the relationships between clusters changing over time, depending on circumstances (see Figure 10.5 (d)). Senior management set broad goals and attempt to develop a unifying culture but do not 'command and control' to the same extent as in other organization forms. They may, however, act to encourage any developments they see as beneficial to the organisation as a whole. N-forms have been described as organisations:

> 'where information about the whole is stored in each part of the organization. This means that strategy, guiding principles of behaviour, and access to detailed information are widely shared in the organization. It implies a 'firm as a brain' model of action rather than a 'brain of a firm' model – the entire firm is supposed to think and act directly on thinking'.[4]

Figure 10.5 (a) U-form organisations give prominence to functional groupings of resources; (b) the M form separates the organisation's resources into separate divisions; (c) matrix form structures the organisation's resources so that they have two (or more) levels of responsibility; (d) N form organisations form loose networks internally between groups of resources and externally with other organisations

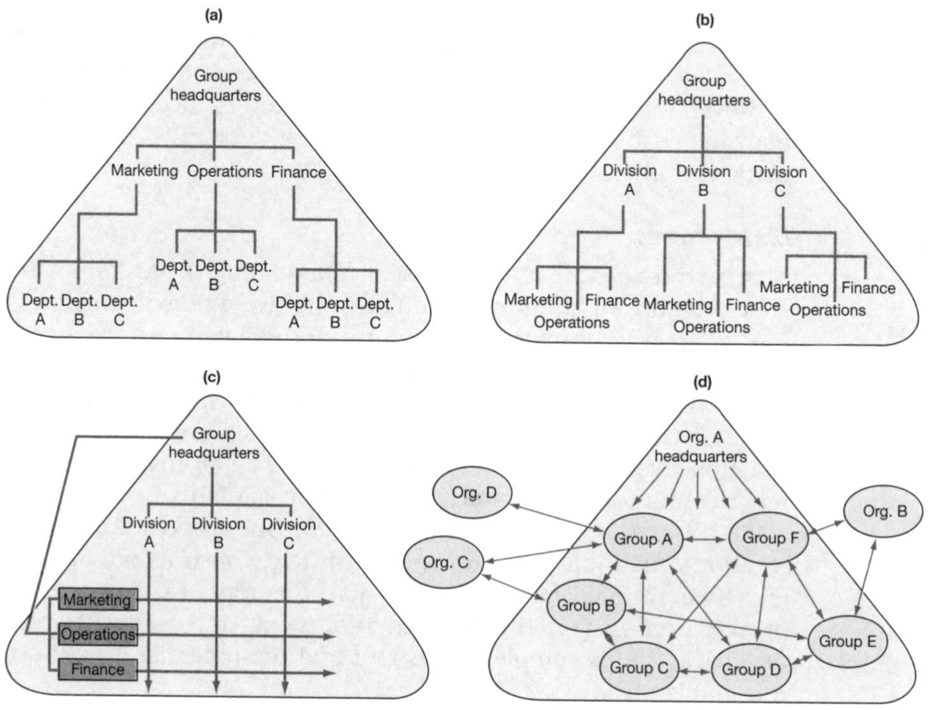

Organisational structure and implementation

The way in which any business organises its resources will have an effect on its ability to develop those resources, but the link between organisational design and its effectiveness at implementing strategy is less clear than most operations strategy decisions. Designing an organisation to achieve specific objectives will never guarantee that those objectives are achieved. Rather the task of organisational design is to create the setting which encourages the desired performance. Managing implementation in a single coherent functional authority poses very different challenges to implementation in a loose and fluid network-based organisation.

Table 10.1 summarises some of the implications of the various organisational forms for the operations function. The *degree of specialisation* within operations is usually high in U-form organisations. Specialist departments devoted to each area of quality, planning and control, process design, purchasing and so on, can flourish because of the economies of scale and scope within the function. Operations departments may have to become more generalist in M-form, matrix structures, and especially N-form organisations. Similarly, the *degree of centralisation* is, by definition, high in the U-form structure and reduces as operations resources are dispersed in M-, matrix and N-forms. However, as resources become less centralised, control becomes both more difficult and less appropriate, so the *degree of discretion* which operations managers have to make decisions independently must increase. Also, along with more decentralisation and more independence comes an increasing *complexity of communications* as organisation structure moves from simple U-forms to less straightforward N-forms. When the communication is between operations and other functions, U-form organisations tend to rely on the relatively formal channels implied by its hierarchical nature, likewise the M-form. However, matrix organisations, with their several 'dotted line' relationships, need substantial informal as well as formal relationships to make them work. N-form organisations are, again by definition, relationship based, and these sometimes fluid and flexible relationships necessarily build more informal than formal lines of communication.

So, how does organisation structure affect implementation? In fact it's not a straightforward question to answer. Different organisational structures have (as we have seen) different strengths. This means that each is better at some aspects of implementation than the others. Because U-form organisations have the capability to hold a high degree of technical specialisation, they are particularly adept at implementations where the risk of technical failure is high. If nothing else, this kind of organisation should be better at judging the degree of technical risk incurred. Similarly, because of the relatively high degree of centralisation of the operations function, U-form organisations should have an advantage in coordinating an implementation with many different elements and/or workstreams. However, if an implementation calls for a significant degree of learning and flexibility, the more flexible organisation forms such as matrix and N-form structure will be superior. This type of organisation has the degree of delegated authority to respond quickly to events and the relationship both with other functional areas and with the external environment, to adapt in a responsive manner. So, to some extent, there is a trade-off between complexity and uncertainty. The more formal U-form and M-form structures having the potential to cope with complexity. The more flexible matrix and N-form structures being more adept at coping with uncertainty. Remember though, we are only commenting on the *potential* of these structures to cope with different types of implementation. The reality will depend on how well the organisations are managed.

Table 10.1 The operations function in different organisational forms

Organisational form	Degree of 'technical specialisation'	Degree of centralisation	Degree of delegated authority	Relationship with other functions	Relationship with external environment
U-form	High	High	Low	Formal	Formal/limited
M-form	↑	↑	↑	↑	↑
Matrix form	↕	↕	↕	↕	↕
N-form	Low	Low	High	Informal	Informal/many points of contact

The role of 'central operations' in implementation

A particularly important organisational relationship that can have a profound impact on strategy implementation is that between those in the operations function who have responsibility for formulating strategy and those who run the day-to-day operations tasks. Of course, these two sets of people may be one and the same. Particularly in small organisations there is simply not enough 'organisational slack' to resource a separate 'operations strategy formulation' function. However, in larger organisations it is now common to have a function or department devoted to the broader aspects of formulating the way in which operations should be managed and resources allocated. We shall call this group of people 'central operations'. This distinction between central operations and day-to-day operations managers is often termed 'staff' and 'line' roles.

'Staff' and 'line' in operations

People occupying classic 'staff' positions have a monitoring, planning and shaping role. They are the ones who are charged with building up the company's operations capability. They may look forward to the way markets are likely to be moving, judge the best way to develop each part of the operation, and keep an eye on competitor behaviour. All of which are tasks which need close liaison with marketing planners, product and service development and finance. They are also tasks which need some organisational 'space' to be performed effectively. They are certainly not tasks which coexist readily with the hectic and immediate concerns of running an operation. These people constitute what could be termed 'central operations'. People occupying 'line' roles are those who run the day-to-day operations. Theirs is partly a reactive role, one which involves finding ways round unexpected problems: reallocating labour, adjusting processes, solving quality problems, and so on. They need to look ahead only enough to make sure that resources are available to meet targets. Theirs is the necessary routine. Knowing where the operation is heading, keeping it on budget and pulling it back on course when the unexpected occurs: no less valuable a task than the developer's but very different.

While these descriptions are clearly stereotypes, they do represent two types of operations task. The issue, for organisational design, is whether it is wise to separate them organisationally. It may cause more problems than it solves. Although it allows each to concentrate on their different jobs, it also can keep apart the two sets of people who have most to gain by working together. Here is the paradox: the development function does need freedom from the immediate pressures of day-to-day management but it is crucial that it understands the exact nature of these pressures. What makes the operation distinctive? Where do the problems occur? What improvements would make most difference to the performance of the operation? Questions only answered by living with the operation, not cloistered away from it. Similarly, the day-to-day operations manager has to interpret the workings of the operation, collect data, explain constraints, and educate developers. Without the trust and cooperation of each, neither set of managers can be effective.

Four types of central operations function

Here we are particularly concerned with how headquarters *operations* staff can act to create value for their company and its individual operations. Central operations could be involved in any of the four headquarters parenting responsibilities.

Particularly though, they tend to become involved in the provision of central functional services, in its broadest sense. This includes the provision of central resources which could provide technical advice, information systems capabilities, laboratory testing services, improvement teams, quality procedures, environmental services, and so on. It also could be taken to mean the general coordination of all operations activity in the different parts of the company. This may include the compilation of performance statistics, the encouragement of inter-operations learning, and the development of broad operations strategies.

Within this, how central operations exercises its responsibilities very much depends on the view it has of operations strategy and development. For example, we can use the dimensions which define the perspectives on operations strategy described in Chapter 1.

- *Top-down or bottom-up?* If central operations has a predominantly top-down view of the world, it is likely to take a programmatic approach to its activities, emphasising the implementation of overall company strategy. Conversely, if it takes a bottom-up view, it is more likely to favour an emergent model of operations development where individual business operations together contribute to the overall building of operations expertise.

- *Market requirements or operations resource focus?* If central operations takes a market requirements view of operations development, it is likely to focus on the explicit performance achieved by each business operation and how far that performance serves to satisfy the operation's customers. An operations resource focus, on the other hand, emphasises the way in which each business operation develops its competences and successfully deploys them in its marketplaces.

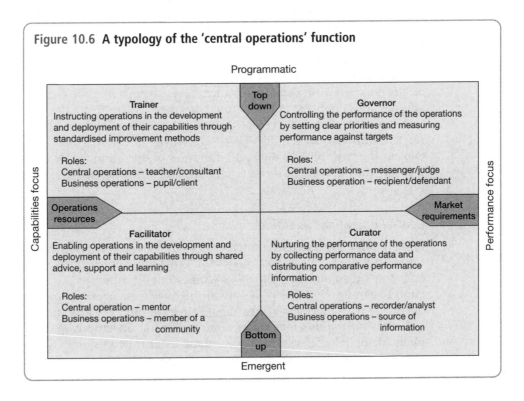

Figure 10.6 **A typology of the 'central operations' function**

We can use these two dimensions to define a typology of the central operations function as shown in Figure 10.6. It classifies central operations into four pure types called governors, curators, trainers and facilitators, a typology based on Merali and McGee's work.[5] Although, in practice, the central operations function of most businesses is a combination of these pure types, usually one type predominates.

Central operations as governor

Here we use the term 'governor' to describe the role of central operations first in its imperial sense. The ancient Roman Empire ruled its provinces by appointing governors whose job it was to impose the will of the Emperor and Senate on its possessions. They acted as the agent of a central authority, interpreting the Imperial will and arbitrating over any disputes within the framework of central rule. The word governor, however, is also used in mechanics to denote the mechanism which prevents an engine running out of control and damaging itself. Central operations of this type interpret strategy in terms of market performance, set clear goals for each business operation, judge their performance and, if performance is not to target, want to know the reason why. They are likely to have a set of predetermined responses to 'fix' operations that do not perform up to requirements and tend to expect results to improve in the short term.

Central operations as curator

Central operations can be concerned primarily with performance against market requirements without being top-down. They may take a more emergent view by acting as the repository of performance data and ideas regarding operations practice for the company as a whole. We use the term 'curator' to capture this idea. Curators collect information and examples so that all can be educated by examining them. Central operations, therefore, will be concerned with collecting performance information, examples of best practice, and so on. They will also be concerned with disseminating this information so that operations managers in different parts of the business can benchmark themselves against their colleagues and, where appropriate, adopt best practice from elsewhere. The term curator can also be taken to mean more than a collector. It can also imply someone who nurtures and cares for the exhibits. So central operations acting as curators may also analyse and explain the performance data and examples of operations practice they collect. In this way they educate business operations and encourage debate around operations practice.

Central operations as trainer

Moving from the market requirements to the operations resources emphasis shifts the focus more to the development of internal capabilities. If the mindset of central operations is top-down their role becomes one of a 'trainer'. Trainers go to some effort to develop clear objectives, usually derived from overall company strategy, and devise effective methods of instructing their 'pupils'. Because the specific needs of individual operations may differ, 'trainer' central operations may devise improvement methodologies which can, to some extent, be customised to each business operation's specific needs. However, their approach is likely to be common with a relatively coherent and centralised view of operations development. Even if individual business operations do initiate contact with central operations, they do so in the role of clients seeking advice on central policy from 'consultants' who bring a standardised approach. These internal consultants can, however, accumulate considerable experience and knowledge.

Central operations as facilitator

In some ways this final type of central operations is the most difficult to operate effectively. Central operations are again concerned with the development of operations capabilities but do so by acting as facilitators of change rather than instructors. Their role is to advise, support and generally aid the development and deployment of capabilities through a process of mentoring business operations. They share responsibility with the business operations in forming a community of operations practice. The development of the relationships between central operations and business operations is crucial in encouraging shared learning. The value placed on these relationships themselves becomes the prime, though somewhat diffused, mechanism for control of the improvement process. Implicit in this type of central operations is the acceptance of a relatively long-term approach to operations development.

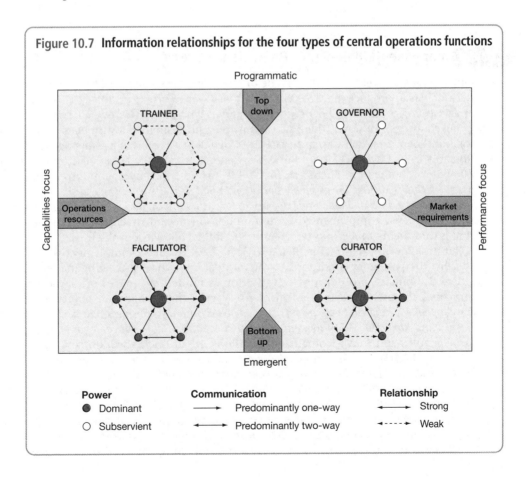

Figure 10.7 Information relationships for the four types of central operations functions

Central operations and information networks

The different types of central operations will play different roles within the information network which connects business operations to central operations and to each other. Figure 10.7 illustrates the likely nature of these information networks. In both the governor and trainer types, central operations is the dominant power player. Their vision of what the individual business operations should be doing dominates the rest of the network. When the emphasis is on individual business operations performance, as in the governor type, there is relatively little, if any, communication between the businesses. Because operations resource competences are more diffuse than hard performance measures, the trainer type will have to accommodate the needs and views of business operations to some extent and also rely on individual business operations having some, albeit weak, sharing of operations practice. Central operations which adopt a more emergent approach implicitly accept a two-way relationship between themselves and the business operations; only in this way can central operations be aware of emergent practice. The curator type, by publishing comparative performance data, is, to some extent, encouraging some communication between the individual business operations. The facilitator type of central operations, however, is entirely dependent on regular, strong and two-way communication between themselves and the community of business operations which they guide.

Example **Implementing Renault's Romanian strategy[6]**

One of Louis Schweitrer's ambitions before he retired as Chairman of the French carmaker Renault was to produce the '$5,000 car'. His goal was to produce a low-cost vehicle targeted at developing countries (80 per cent of consumers who have never owned a car live in developing countries). However, there also seems to be surprisingly buoyant demand in the West for utilitarian cars. Schweitrer succeeded when Renault started producing the Logan in Romania in its Dacia operation. But when Renault bought the Dacia plant in Pitesti, about 100 miles south-west of Bucharest, in 1999 it was described by one industry commentator as, '*one of the scruffiest car assembly operations I had seen in years. Dark, dismal and more like hell's kitchen than a manufacturing operation, it was hardly conducive to producing quality products*'. Now, having implemented a €500 million turnround strategy, it is turning out a car that is thoroughly modern in terms of fit and finish, but without the frills.

But in achieving its strategy, Renault/Dacia have needed to implement it in a manner that fits the particular conditions of the product and where it is being made. In a region where the public perception of privatisation is tainted by images of cowboy capitalists enriching themselves, François Fourmont, Dacia general manager, points out that '*you have to make it clear that you are very serious about running a business that benefits both shareholders and Romania. When Renault comes to a country, it does not come for only a few years.*' Yet, Renault had to make some harsh decisions. It cut Dacia's workforce from more than 27,000 to 12,500. '*We had no choice*', said Fourmont, '*our first responsibility is to make money, because that is the only way we can survive as a business*', he explains. '*Once we have that basis, we can start to think about other factors. And many of the fired workers were retrained and subsequently found jobs with the suppliers that had moved their production to the area.*'

In Romania, given the turbulence of the move from a centrally planned economy towards a market economy, it was also particularly important to work closely with state and local governments, especially over social issues. The company has had to address environmental concerns and develop a network of local suppliers that can produce to an international standard of quality. Many of the firms, including multinationals like Valeo, are now based on-site. Renault also put continuous training at the heart of Dacia's business, although at first it was a challenge. But, argues Fourmont, *'the more efficient and better trained the workforce is, the more likely they are to withstand competition from abroad, allowing the company to reward staff better for their good performance and quality product'*. One worker, who had been with Dacia for more than a decade, remembered what life was like before Renault took over:

> *'It was hard work, with a lot of effort and very little satisfaction. People were suspicious [of the changes] at first, especially when the job cuts came. But then they saw the company was serious and they began to trust Renault.'*

The design of the car was critical to its low cost. Renault designed a car that was modern but without costly design elements and superfluous technology. Production costs for the Logan were estimated at $1,089 per car, less than half the $2,468 estimate for an equivalent Western auto. 'The Logan is the McDonald's of cars', says Kenneth Melville, who headed the Logan design team. *'The concept was simple: Reliable engineering without a lot of electronics, cheap to build and easy to maintain and repair.'* To keep costs low, Renault adapted the platform used for its other small cars and then slashed the number of components by more than 50 per cent. The dashboard is one continuous injection-moulded part, vs. up to 30 pieces for a top-of-the-line Renault. The rear-view mirrors are symmetrical, so they can be used on both the left and right side of the car. Renault also opted for a flat windshield: curves result in more defects and higher costs.

Sourcing from local suppliers was another critical factor, as was encouraging Renault's existing suppliers to set up shop on a new supplier park within the Dacia factory complex. This was not easy because many suppliers were sceptical about the whole project. But they were won over; now 65 per cent of parts bought in from suppliers are produced locally, with 26 of Renault's existing suppliers agreeing to set up nearby, seven of them inside the supplier park.

Partly as a result of the Logan's low-cost objectives and simple design, assembly at the Romanian plant was implemented almost entirely without robots. This overcame some of the problems from using state-of-the-art technologies in a region where support services are relatively underdeveloped, and it lets Renault capitalise on the country's low labour costs. Now, Renault is ramping up production of the Logan from Russia to Morocco. *'The investment in manufacturing is relatively low, so you can have factories that don't have to produce huge volumes to finance themselves'*, says Christoph Stürmer, senior analyst at researcher Global Insight in Frankfurt. Renault has already expanded its output in Romania and is creating the world's largest logistical project that will ship Logan cars in bits so that they can be assembled in Russia, Morocco, India, Iran and Colombia.

Process – the methodological context

By methodology we simply mean the methods and the approach that are taken to formulate a strategy. As we said in Chapter 8, there are many 'stage models' (a model that sets down the stages involved in formulating a strategy) that are recommended by both consultants and academics. The two academic models that we described in Chapter 8 were the Hill Methodology and the Platts–Gregory Procedure. We will not repeat these models or the general advice that we covered in Chapter 8. Nevertheless, it is worth making two further points.

The first may seem obvious but is worth stating. It is important to have some kind of methodology or stage model in place. While accepting that, in practice, many important strategic ideas 'emerge' rather than are formulated in a deliberative manner (see our discussion in Chapter 1) and accepting the validity of the 'bottom-up' approach, there are still important advantages in having some kind of model in place.

- It provides a discipline for strategic thinking. Remembering the criteria that we applied to the operations strategy matrix in Chapter 1 – comprehensiveness, coherence, correspondence, and criticality – a model provides an opportunity to incorporate these simple criteria if only as a checklist.

- It brings to the fore the whole concept of methodology. There may be a tendency in some senior management teams to concentrate on the (sometimes technical) content of strategic decisions rather than the process of how they are made. A stage model makes the process explicit. Put simply, it forces managers to think about how and why they are making decisions as well as what decisions they are making.

- It makes communication easier. Especially in very large organisations, disseminating an overall strategic vision and how the firm wants to move forward is a significant challenge. There is a trade-off involved here. On one hand, one could attempt to communicate a sophisticated message regarding the strategy that is being pursued and how it should be implemented, but this is difficult to get over throughout a large company without the risk of misinterpretation. On the other hand, one can simplify the message which makes it easier to communicate, but may be over-simplified given the complexities and realities of the operations in which the strategy is being implemented. Even the simplest of stage models helps to communicate relatively complex messages and so, to some extent, overcomes this trade-off.

The second point to make about methodology concerns the relationship between operations management and operations strategy. As one reaches the implementation stage of operations strategy the nature of the task becomes ever closer to operations management. Changes in strategy are, after all, manifested eventually as changes in the way operations processes operate on a day-to-day basis. Also, many of the techniques useful in the implementation stage are the conventional improvement techniques and approaches (such as those treated in Chapter 9) that are the subject matter of operations management. The implication of this is that effective operations strategy implementation is dependent upon the organisation having a sound understanding of operations management principles and practice. One cannot hope to overlay an operations strategy (no matter how good) over the top of an intrinsically chaotic set of operations processes. In other words, getting operations strategy right also depends on getting operations management right.

Implementation costs

It is worth emphasising that any implementation methodology will need to account for the costs of implementation. These costs include both the direct and/or investment costs of providing whatever additional resources the strategy requires, and also what could be termed the adjustment cost of making any changes. By adjustment costs we mean the losses that could be incurred before the new strategy is functioning as intended.

Calculating the true costs of implementing any strategy is notoriously difficult. This is particularly true because more often than not, 'Murphy's Law' seems to prevail. This law is usually stated as, 'if anything can go wrong, it will'. This means that most implementations will incur 'adjustment costs' before the strategy works as expected. This effect has been identified empirically in a range of operations, especially when new types of process technology are involved. Specifically discussing technology-related implementation (although the ideas apply to almost any implementation), Bruce Chew of the Massachusetts Institute of Technology argues that adjustment costs stem from unforeseen mismatches between the new technology's capabilities and needs and the existing operation. New technology rarely behaves as planned and as changes are made, their impact ripples throughout the organisation. Figure 10.8 is an example of what Chew calls a Murphy Curve.[7] It shows a typical pattern of performance reduction (in this case, quality) as a new process technology is introduced. It is recognised that implementation may take some time, therefore allowances are made for the length and cost of a 'ramp-up' period. However, as the operation prepares for the implementation, the distraction causes performance actually to deteriorate. Even after the start of the implementation this downward trend continues and it is only weeks, indeed maybe months later that the old performance level is reached. The area of the dip indicates the magnitude of the adjustment costs, and therefore the level of vulnerability faced by the operation.

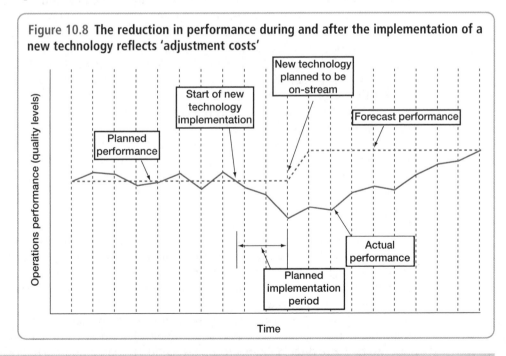

Figure 10.8 The reduction in performance during and after the implementation of a new technology reflects 'adjustment costs'

Project management – the delivery context

An implementation is a project. And it shares some of the same characteristics as all other projects, where a project is '... *a set of activities with a defined start point and a defined end state, which pursues a defined goal and uses a defined set of resources'.* Therefore, all implementations will need to be 'project managed'. In fact, large-scale implementations may need to be managed as 'programmes'. The distinction between 'projects' and 'programmes' is that a programme has no defined end point. Rather it is an ongoing process of change. Individual projects, may be individual sub-sections of an overall programme, such as an integrated skills development programme. Programme management will overlay and integrates the individual projects. Generally, it is a more difficult task in the sense that it requires resource coordination, particularly when multiple projects share common resources, as emphasised in the following quotation:

> *'Managing projects is, it is said, like juggling three balls – cost, quality, and time. Programme management . . . is like organizing a troupe of jugglers all juggling three balls and swapping balls from time to time.'*[8]

Implementation project difficulty

Some implementations are more difficult than others because of their scale, uncertainty, and complexity. This is illustrated in Figure 10.9. Large-scale implementations involving many different types of resources with durations of many years will be more difficult to manage, both because the resources will need a high level of management effort, and because implementation objectives must be maintained over a long time period. Uncertainty also affects implementation. Very novel implementations are likely to be especially uncertain with ever-changing objectives, leading to planning difficulty. When uncertainty is high, the whole implementation process needs to be sufficiently flexible to cope with the consequences of change. Similarly, implementation projects with high levels of complexity, such as multi-organisational projects, often require considerable control effort. Their many separate activities, resources and groups of people involved, increases the scope for things to go wrong. Furthermore, as the number of separate activities in a project increases, the ways in which they can impact on each other increases exponentially. This increases the effort involved in monitoring each activity. It also increases the chances of overlooking some aspect of the implementation which may be deviating from the plan. Most significantly, it increases the 'knock-on' effect of any problem.

Stakeholders

All implementation projects have stakeholders who must be included in its planning and executions. By stakeholders we mean the individuals and groups who have an interest in the project process or outcome. Individual stakeholders are likely to have different views on a project's objectives that may conflict with other stakeholders. At the very least, different stakeholders are likely to stress different aspects of a project. So, as well as any ethical imperative to include as many stakeholders as possible in an implementation, it also can prevent problems later in the implementation. There may also be more direct benefits from a stakeholder-based approach. Powerful stakeholders may shape the implementation at an early stage, making it more likely that they will support the project.

Figure 10.9 Implementation project difficulty is determined by scale, complexity, and uncertainty

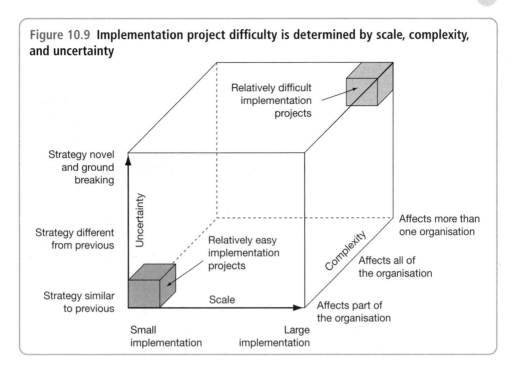

The power–interest grid

Managing stakeholders can be a subtle and delicate task, requiring significant social and, sometimes, political skills. It is based on three activities, identifying, prioritising, and understanding the stakeholder group. One approach to discriminating between different stakeholders, and more important, how they should be managed, is to distinguish between their power to influence the project and their interest in doing so. Stakeholders who have the power to exercise a major influence over the project should never be ignored. At the very least, the nature of their interest, and their motivation, should be well understood. But not all stakeholders who have the power to exercise influence over a project will be interested in doing so, and not everyone who is interested in the project has the power to influence it. The power–interest grid, shown in Figure 10.10, classifies stakeholders simply in terms of these two dimensions. Although there will be gradations between them, the two dimensions are useful in providing an indication of how stakeholders can be managed in terms of four categories.

Stakeholders' positions on the grid gives an indication of how they might be managed. High power, interested groups must be fully engaged, with the greatest efforts made to satisfy them. High power, less interested groups require enough effort to keep them satisfied, but not so much that they become bored or irritated with the message. Low power, interested groups need to be kept adequately informed, with checks to ensure that no major issues are arising. These groups may be very helpful with the detail of the project. Low power, less interested groups need monitoring, but without excessive communication. Some key questions that can help to understand high priority stakeholders include the following.

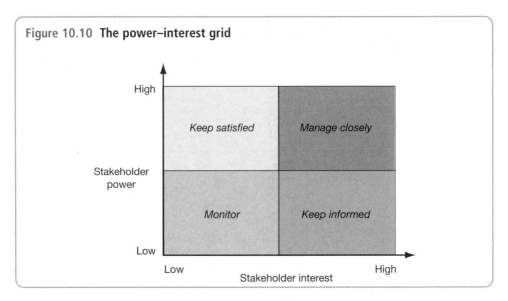

Figure 10.10 **The power–interest grid**

- What financial or emotional interest do they have in the outcome of the implementation? Is it positive or negative?
- What motivates them most of all?
- What information do they need?
- What is the best way of communicating with them?
- What is their current opinion of the implementation project?
- Who influences their opinions? Do some of these influencers therefore become important stakeholders in their own right?
- If they are not likely to be positive, what will win them around to support the implementation?
- If you don't think you will be able to win them around, how will you manage their opposition?

Implementation project planning

All implementations need some degree of planning. The planning process fulfils four distinct purposes. It determines the cost and duration of the implementation, it determines the level of resources that will be needed, it helps to allocate work and to monitor progress, and it helps to assess the impact of any changes to the implementation. It is a vital step, but it could be repeated several times during the implementation's life as circumstances change. This is not a sign of implementation failure or mismanagement. In uncertain implementations, in particular, it is a normal occurrence. The process of implementation project planning involves five steps shown in Figure 10.11.

Identify activities

Some implementations are too complex to be planned and controlled effectively unless they are first broken down into manageable portions. This is achieved by structuring the implementation into a 'family tree'; that specifies the major tasks or

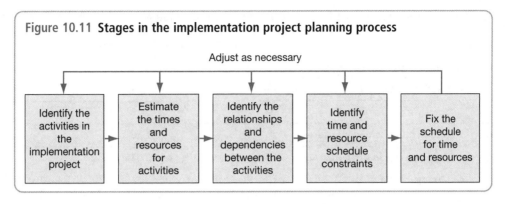

Figure 10.11 **Stages in the implementation project planning process**

sub-implementations. These in turn are divided up into smaller tasks, called work packages, with its own objectives. The output from this is called the work breakdown structure (WBS) and shows 'how the jigsaw fits together'. It also provides a framework for building up information for reporting purposes. For example, Figure 10.12 shows the work breakdown structure for an implementation to design a new information interface (a website screen) for a new sales knowledge management system that is being installed in an insurance company.

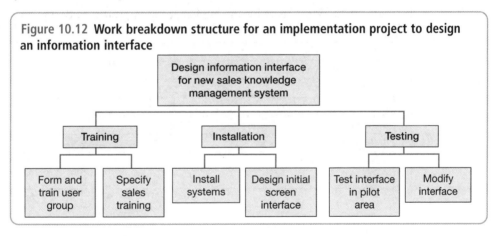

Figure 10.12 **Work breakdown structure for an implementation project to design an information interface**

Estimate times and resources

The next stage in planning is to identify the time and resource requirements of the work packages. Without this it is impossible to define what should be happening at any time during the execution of the implementation. Estimates may never be perfect but they can be made with some idea of how accurate they might be. Table 10.2 includes time (in days) and resource (in terms of the number of IT developers needed) estimates for the sales system interface design implementation.

Identify the relationships and dependencies between the activities

All the activities in the implementation will have some relationship with one another. In the case of the sales system interface design activities a and b can be started without any of the other activities being completed. Activity c cannot begin until activity a has been completed, nor can activity d. Activity e can only start when both activities b and d have been completed, and activity f can only start when

Table 10.2 **Time, resource and relationships for the sales system interface design implementation**

Code	Activity	Immediate predecessor(s)	Duration (days)	Resources (developers)
a	Form and train user group	none	10	3
b	Install systems	none	17	5
c	Specify sales training	a	5	2
d	Design initial screen interface	a	5	3
e	Test interface in pilot area	b, d	25	2
f	Modify interface	c, e	15	3

activities c and e have been completed. There are several techniques that help to handle time, resource and relationships complexity (for example, critical path analysis) which are outside the strategic scope of this book. The simplest of these techniques is the Gantt chart (or bar chart). Figure 10.13 shows a Gantt chart for the activities that form the sales system interface implementation. The bars indicate the start, duration, and finish time for each activity.

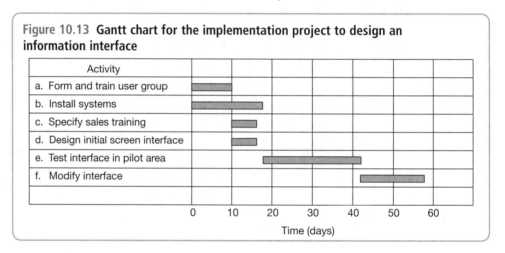

Figure 10.13 **Gantt chart for the implementation project to design an information interface**

Identify time and resource schedule constraints

Once estimates have been made of the time and effort involved in each activity, and their dependencies identified, it is possible to compare implementation requirements with the available resources. The finite nature of critical resources – such as staff with special skills – means that they should be taken into account in the planning process. This often has the effect of highlighting the need for more detailed re-planning.

Fix the schedule

Implementation planners should ideally have a number of alternatives to choose from. The one which best fits implementation objectives can then be chosen or developed. However, it is not always possible to examine several alternative schedules, especially in very large or very uncertain implementations, as the computation could be prohibitive. However, modern computer-based project management software is making the search for the best schedule more feasible.

Incorporate learning into project management

Techniques such as Gantt charts are necessary to plan and control implementation projects so as to meet cost and time goals. Yet, while conventional implementation project management remains a necessary condition for effective implementation, it may not by itself be sufficient to achieve strategically successful implementation. A more 'thoughtful' model of implementation project planning is needed to cope with the challenges involved in most implementations. Implementation project management needs to consider the potential for failure and recognise that not only will failures happen but that they can be viewed as an opportunity for learning. One very clear manifestation of a company's commitment to learning can be seen in the role of pilot or trial operations. The idea of running a complete 'experiment' of a new strategy is a very powerful one. However, sometimes potential delays combine with cost pressures to turn a pilot into a 'first-off' without giving any time to reflect upon the lessons learnt. The problems that arise should not only be solved, they should also be seen as an opportunity that allows knowledge to be gained which can improve the strategy and the process of implementation. The positive role of failure has to be recognised. In the context of implementation (especially if the overall resource change is significant), adopting a strategy of 'intelligent failure' is critical. Failure can occur without necessarily triggering organisational blame and recrimination.

Resource and process 'distance'

The degree of learning, and the degree of difficulty in the implementation process will depend on the degree of novelty of any new resources and the changes required in the operation's processes. The less that the new resources are understood (influenced perhaps by the degree of innovation) the greater their 'distance' from the current resource base of the operation. Similarly, the extent to which an implementation requires an operation to modify its existing processes, the greater the 'process distance'. The greater the resource and process distance, the more difficult any implementation is likely to be. This is because such distance makes it difficult to adopt a systematic approach to analysing change and learning from mistakes. Those implementations which involve relatively little process or resource 'distance' provide an ideal opportunity for organisational learning. As in any classic scientific experiment, the more variables that are held constant, the more confidence you have in determining cause and effect. Conversely, in an implementation where the resource and process 'distance' means that nearly everything is 'up for grabs', it becomes difficult to know what has worked and what has not. More importantly, it becomes difficult to know *why* something has or has not worked (see Figure 10.14).

Participation – the operational context

It is 60 years since Coch and French[9] argued that a key mechanism for overcoming resistance to change was to include the people to whom the change would happen

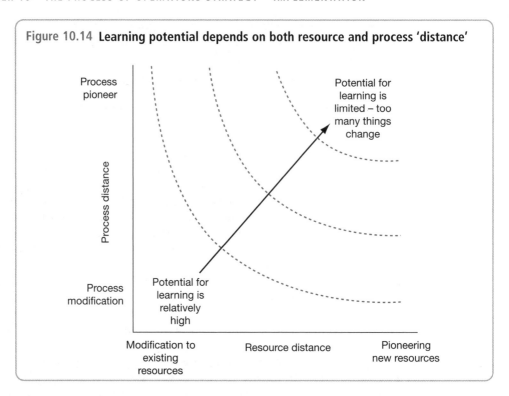

Figure 10.14 **Learning potential depends on both resource and process 'distance'**

Example Empty shelves mean 'a failure to implement'[10]

Lawrence Christensen, Sainsbury's new logistics boss, was blunt in his assessment of the UK based supermarket's radical supply chain implementation. *'Our rivals watched in utter disbelief'*, he said. *'Competitors looked on in amazement as Sainsbury poured millions into implementing new IT systems and replaced 21 depots with a handful of giant automated "fulfilment factories"'*.

Sainsbury had first devised a strategy for a new faster and more efficient supply chain strategy in 2000 when its former chief executive signed a £1.8 billion seven-year contract with Accenture, a business services firm, to modernise its IT and take on 800 of its staff. The problem turned out to be how the strategic objectives were put into practice. It was a huge project, with highly automated facilities and totally reconfigured IT systems. Eventually the cost reached £3 billion over four years, with new technology installed across all the company's distribution network. Yet, during this time the company slipped into third place in the UK grocery market that it once led, behind Tesco and Asda. *'In hindsight, the heavy reliance on automation was a big mistake, especially for fast moving goods'*, said Laurence Christensen. *'When a conventional facility goes wrong, you have lots of options. You have flexibility to deal with issues. When an automated "fulfilment factory" goes wrong, frankly, you're buggered.'* Most damning was the way that Sainsbury:

> *'... pressed on with the implementation of the automated facilities before proving that the concept worked at the first major site, Hams Hall in Birmingham. I'd have at least proved that one of them worked before building the other three. Basically, the whole company was committed to doing too much, too fast, trying to implement a seven-year strategy in a three-year timescale.'*

One industry analyst claimed that Sainsbury's just tried to do too much at the same time, reconfiguring its logistics, reducing the number of distribution sites, increasing the scale of the remaining operations, implementing a totally new over-complex IT system, outsourcing its day-to-day running, installing radical and largely untried automation, and so on. And by 2004, Justin King, Sainsbury's Chief Executive, admitted the scale of the problem:

'Our supply chain systems and automated depots are not fully operational. And the IT systems that were built to back up that have not delivered. The IT cost is a greater proportion of sales than they were three years ago. The system was developed to account for stock but the system can't see the stock on the shelves. The problems happen most often when we revamp a range. The system could not allocate the range because it could not see that we had taken old stock off the shelves. Every store is now going to manually update the stock levels on its shelves.'

Plans were immediately set in place to reorganise store backrooms, and local forecasting teams were established at every regional distribution centre to serve as a local point of contact for stores. A business transformation review suggested implementing a six-pronged strategy covering: people, industrial relations, processes, operations, automated equipment, and product wastage. Shortly after the supermarket announced that it would:

● get rid of 750 head office jobs and replace them with 3,000 in-store staff;

● write off £260 million in costs associated with flawed IT and supply chain systems;

● stop using its automated supply chain system, closing some newly automated depots, and revert back to manual processes for stock-level management;

● renegotiate its business transformation contract with lead contractor Accenture.

in the process, and allow them to influence what changes would take place. After all, by including people in the decision process, they are more likely to 'buy in' to the change. Also, involving users in the design of the processes affected by implementation allows designers to access their detailed knowledge and experience. This is especially important because some elements of strategy may be developed, at least partially, by external contractors and consultants. Although they may understand the details of the strategy, they often lack sufficient practical understanding of the organisational context of its implementation.

Professor Dorothy Leonard of Harvard Business School argues that the often used term 'user involvement' is insufficiently precise because it covers a multitude of different approaches to interaction, each with its own advantages and disadvantages. She proposes a model of four different modes of user involvement, each of which offers a progressively greater degree of descriptive and prescriptive value. (She was referring to implementation involving new process technology, but her ideas have wider applicability.)

1 *Delivery mode.* When users (and managers for that matter) have very little knowledge of any new resources needed for the strategy, it is relatively easy for external vendors or internal developers to treat the implementation project like a product to be finished and then delivered to the client. This 'over the wall' mode of development requires almost no interaction with users and, where interaction exists, the feedback may have little impact beyond possibly improving the next generation of technology. The critical strategic question is whether such a one-way flow of information is sufficient to help develop underlying operational resources and capabilities.

2 *Consultancy mode.* The next mode, requiring slightly more user interaction, is closer to a classic consultancy implementation project. Designers/vendors recog-

nise that there are established patterns of work (routines etc.) in the processes that they are helping to change and invest time asking questions of experienced users. Again, although this accesses more of the firm's operational resources, it does not necessarily contribute to their development because the flow of information remains largely one way.

3 *Co-development mode.* This mode is much closer to a form of partnership. This approach can be very effective when levels of uncertainty are high (either the developers' uncertainty about the existing system or users' uncertainty about any new resources). This is because there is relatively little pre-existing knowledge to be captured and exploited.

4 *Apprenticeship mode.* Users wanting a greater degree of independence from developers often seek a mode of implementation whereby lead users are almost 'apprenticed' to the developer. This radically changes the nature of the implementation process, moving it much closer to what we described in an earlier section as 'learning'. Such an approach is normally more time and money intensive but from a capability-building perspective it is very attractive.

Dorothy Leonard suggests three useful dimensions for thinking about different types of users:

● *Form of expertise.* Certain users might be the best operatives in the organisation but this does not guarantee that they are capable of articulating what it is they do. Equally, they may well lack the critical skills to question a system development process.

● *Representativeness.* Earlier we discussed the value of adopting a pilot approach to implementation. Doing so poses a problem common in all scientific experiments. Namely, 'is it representative of a broader sample or did something atypical occur during the experiment?' This is an issue that needs to be considered when selecting user participants for any implementation project. Are their skills and experience representative of the rest of the organisation?

● *Willingness.* A basic question perhaps, but some studies[11] have shown that levels of user satisfaction amongst implementation participants are related to the level of involvement they originally wanted in the process, compared with the involvement they actually had. Anyone who is forced to spend more time than they believe reasonable on an implementation project may resent it, regardless of the outcome.

Increasing the level of user involvement is, of course, not unambiguously positive. Truly radical solutions do not always emerge from discussions limited to current experience. Such a limited range of experience can also lead to the development of processes that address today's rather than tomorrow's difficulties. Despite such concerns, the benefits of increased user involvement in overcoming process 'distance' are usually regarded as significant.

Prerequisites for effective involvement

Although there is no simple formula that will ensure everyone's' commitment to making strategic implementation a success, there are some key elements of basic human resource practice than can facilitate successful involvement. Here we group these elements in a structure known as the 'CEO Principle'. This means simply that, for people to be involved effectively in an implementation they must:

● have the confidence that involvement will be a positive experience;

● have the education which will allow them to contribute intelligently; and

● be allowed the opportunity to participate in the implementation process.

Confidence that involvement will be a positive experience

One of the most important elements affecting people's confidence in their ability to contribute is an organisational culture that makes it clear that its people are an important strategic resource that can directly affect its success. If, through its actions and its communications, an organisation makes it clear that everyone's individual efforts can have an impact on what happens in the organisation, most people will feel that their contributions are worthwhile. Just as importantly, the opposite is also true. If people feel that they cannot influence what happens, why should they bother participating? The same argument applies to how people regard their security within the organisation. By security we mean both the obvious issues such as job security or salary security and more subtle types of security, such as security that their reputation will not suffer by making suggestions which are not supported by others in the organisation. Unless one has a future in the organisation, why become fully involved?

A factor that can negatively affect confidence is confusion over what a strategy is trying to achieve. An unambiguous and shared vision of the overall purpose of the implementation is clearly a help in moving everyone towards the same goal. Charismatic leadership can sometimes achieve this, but even where this exists effective communication is equally important. Remember though that for people to have the confidence to participate, communication should be a two-way street. That is, individuals should feel that they can, without any threat to their own security, communicate their views honestly upwards in the organisation. Certainly, the ability to communicate upwards can be enhanced by support from colleagues and team members as well as through more formal statements of individual empowerment.

Education in the necessary skills

Experience at a job is not always sufficient to ensure effective participation. Experience must be structured and contextualised through education, training and development. Education allows individuals to generalise their experience so that it can be used in different contexts. It also provides a shared language and body of knowledge that helps in the generation of innovative ideas, as we discussed earlier. But education in the basics of (in this case) operations management and operations strategy must also be complemented by education about what the strategy implementation is trying to achieve. The general term for this is 'policy deployment'. This is the way in which high-level strategic objectives are translated into more specific objectives and measurements appropriate for each individual group within the organisation. Of course, this presupposes two things. First, that a clearly articulated and coherent implementation plan exists, and second, that there is an appropriate process in place to 'cascade' and communicate the purpose of the strategy and its implementation down the organisation.

For education to thrive there must be learning. For learning to be an important element in an organisation's culture, both individuals and the organisation in general must learn how to learn. Amongst other things this means never wasting an opportunity to learn. And many of the best opportunities to learn come from the mistakes that one makes. It may be something of a cliché, but mistakes really are one of the most valuable sources of learning. They provide an opportunity to discuss and debate exactly why things went wrong and what can be done about it in the future. Of course, this will not happen if an organisation routinely punishes its employees for every mistake they make. And many organisations do claim that they punish mistakes only when there has been a clear dereliction of duty or when individuals refuse to learn from their mistakes. Yet, relatively few organisations have managed to build a culture which genuinely exploits the full potential of being able to learn from mistakes. Those that have come close to it (including the much quoted example of Toyota, see Chapter 9) have, over the years, developed a culture of continuous improvement based on a problem solving methodology that emphasises the importance of learning.

Opportunity to participate in the implementation process

Individuals may be supremely confident and soundly educated, yet unless they are provided with the opportunity to participate, their contribution will remain untapped. Those organisations who see implementation simply as a set of tasks, devised by senior management and communicated 'down the line' which people simple have to carry out, are not providing the opportunity for individuals to participate. The most obvious way to provide opportunities for participation is to expect employees to participate in planning the implementation itself. But organisational space must be provided to allow this. It cannot simply be expected that employees will participate in implementation planning in addition to an already excessive load. Some organisations programme formal workshops or team meetings to provide opportunities for participation. Some also include implementation planning as part of their appraisal process. Whatever mechanisms are used, the overall intention is to foster a feeling of ownership of the implementation process. This may be facilitated by devolving decision making downwards in the organisation, perhaps using self-managed teams. However, especially in large organisations, this may work against other attempts to coordinate activities across the organisation as well as conflicting with any attempt to promote a single and unambiguous vision for the organisation. Such devolved decision making however may be appropriate where the implementation climate has high level of uncertainty, individual staff member's technical expertise is important, and the organisation is relatively small.

SUMMARY ANSWERS TO KEY QUESTIONS

How does strategic context affect implementation?

During implementation the balance between market requirements and operations resource capabilities may not always be maintained. The market may expect something that the operation cannot (temporarily) deliver, or operations may have capabilities that cannot be exploited in the market. This results in risks deriving from a failure to achieve fit between operations resources and market requirements. Understanding, and coping with, these risks should be part of any implementation plan. Here a distinction should be made between pure risks (that will produce the possibility only of loss) and speculative risks (that hold the potential for loss or gain). Both are important in shaping implementation plans.

How does organisational context affect implementation?

Different organisational structures have different attributes when it comes to implementing operations strategies. Some structures are better at some aspects of implementation than others. U-form organisations have a high degree of technical specialisation and are appropriate where the risk of technical failure is high. U-form organisations, because of the high degree of centralisation of the operations function, can coordinate implementations with many different elements. But, if an implementation calls for a significant degree of learning and flexibility, matrix and N-form structure will be superior. So, there is some trade-off between complexity and uncertainty. More formal U-form and M-form structures can cope with complexity, more flexible matrix and N-form structures can cope with uncertainty.

How does methodology affect implementation?

Methodology means the methods and the approach that are taken to formulate a strategy. The first may seem obvious but is worth stating. It is important to have some kind of methodology or stage model in place. It provides a discipline for strategic thinking, it brings to the fore the whole concept of methodology, and it makes communication easier, especially in very large organisations. An explicit methodology also emphasises that effective operations strategy implementation is dependent upon the organisation having a sound understanding of operations management principles and practice.

How can project management affect implementation?

An implementation is a project, sharing the same characteristics as all other projects, so all implementations will need to be 'project managed'. However, large-scale implementations will be more difficult to manage, as are very novel implementations. But most implementation projects will have various stakeholders, the management of which requires social and political skills. One approach is to distinguish between stakeholders' power to influence the project and their interest in doing so. All implementation projects also need planning so as to determine the cost and duration of the implementation, the level of resources that will be needed, the allocation of work and the monitoring of progress. However, implementation project planning needs to consider the potential for failure and recognise that not only will failures happen but that they can be viewed as an opportunity for learning.

How can participation affect implementation?

A key aspect of overcoming resistance to the changes implied by any implementation is to include the people to whom the change would happen in the process, and allow them to influence what changes would take place. Doing so improves the likelihood of them 'buying in' to the change. Also, involving users in the design allows those managing the implementation to access their detailed knowledge and experience. This is especially important because some elements of strategy may be developed, at least partially, by external contractors and consultants. Although there is no simple formula to ensure commitment to an implementation, there are some basic human resource practices than can facilitate successful involvement. For people to be involved effectively in an implementation they must, have the confidence that involvement will be a positive experience, have the education which will allow them to contribute intelligently, and be allowed the opportunity to participate in the implementation process.

Further reading

Bettley A., Mayle, D. and Tantoush, T. (eds) (2005) *Operations Management: A Strategic Approach*. London: Sage.

Grant, R. (2004) *Contemporary Strategy Analysis*, 5th edn. Oxford: Blackwell Publishing.

Hayes, R.H., Pisano, G.P., Upton, D.M. and Wheelwright, S.C. (2004) *Operations, Strategy, and Technology: Pursuing the Competitive Edge*. John Wiley & Sons.

Macmillan, H. and Tampoe, M. (2000) *Strategic Management: Process, Content and Implementation*. Oxford University Press.

McCalman, J. and, Paton, R.A. (2000) *Change Management: A Guide to Effective Implementation*, 2nd edn. London: Sage.

Pearce, J.A. (2006) *Formulation, Implementation and Control of Competitive Strategy*, McGraw-Hill.

Notes on the chapter

1 Platt, K.W., Mill, J.F., Neeley, A.D., Gregory, M.J. and Richards, A.H. (1996) 'Evaluating the manufacturing strategy process', *International Journal of Production Economics*, Vols. 46–7.

2 Sources: Moynihan, T. (2007) 'Product recalls up 20% as firms act quickly to shore up reputations', *The Guardian*, 19 February; Woodcock, C. (2007) Comment on Cadbury's recall, on http://www.continuitycentral.com.

3 Morgan describes these and other metaphors in Morgan, G. (1986) *Images of Organization*. London: Sage.

4 Sölvell, O. and Zander, I. (1995) 'Organization of the dynamic multi-national enterprise', *International Studies of Management and Organization*, Vol. 24, pp. 17–38.

5 Merali, Y. and McGee, J. (1998) 'Information competences and knowledge creation at the corporate centre', in Hamel, G., Prahalad, C.K., Thomas, H. and O'Neal, D. (1998) *Strategic Flexibility*. New York: John Wiley & Sons. Here we use somewhat different terminology.

6 Sources: Lewis, A. (2005) 'Renault's Romanian route: Renault's Dacia plant gears up to build a quality, $5,000 car for Eastern Europe', *Automotive Industries*, February; Richardson, B. (2006) 'Renault tunes up Romania's top carmaker', BBC News website.

7 Chew, W.B., Leonard-Barton, D. and Bohnm, R.E. (1991) 'Beating Murphy's Law', *Sloan Management Review*, Spring.

8 Newton, R. (2005) *Project Manager*. Harlow, UK: Financial Times Prentice Hall.

9 Coch, L. and French, J.P.R., Jr. (1948) 'Overcoming resistance to change', *Human Relations*, No. 1, pp. 512–32.

10 Sources: Watson, E. (2005) 'Automation left Sainsbury "buggered" when it failed', *Food Manufacture*, 4 November; Knights, M. (2004) 'Sainsbury's dumps inefficient systems: but IT experts say IT isn't purely to blame for poor performance in recent months', *Computing*, 21 October; Computing Staff (2004) 'Sainsbury's admits IT systems are flawed and goes back to manual systems', *IT WEEK, Computing*, 19 October; The Economist (2004) 'The trouble with IT: Britain's oldest supermarket tries to turn itself around', 21 October.

11 Doll, W.J. and Torkzaden, G. (1989) 'A discrepancy model of end-user computing involvement', *Management Science*, 35(10), pp. 1151–71.

CASE STUDIES

1 BUNGE LIMITED

Jonathan West

'We are at a very special moment in the history of Bunge. We have reached one plateau. Now, we need to go to the next round of change. We constantly need intellectual jolts to the company.'

(Alberto Weisser, CEO of Bunge Limited)

In July 2002, Bunge, a global agribusiness and food company, announced that it would purchase Cereol, a global oilseed processor, based in France. The acquisition would transform Bunge, making it the world's leading oilseed-processing company, and give it a more balanced geographic footprint, as well as access to new products, but would substantially increase the complexity of the company's product lines, locations and personnel.

Less than a year before, on 2 August 2001, Alberto Weisser, Bunge's CEO, rang the opening bell on the New York Stock Exchange, as Bunge successfully went public after more than 180 years as a private company. The company had primary operations in North and South America and worldwide distribution capabilities. Bunge was the largest processor of soybeans in the Americas and among the world's leading exporters of soybean products. It was the largest fertiliser producer and supplier to farmers in Latin America. It was also a leader in vegetable oil and wheat-based food products for food manufacturers, food service companies[1] and consumers. Bunge's net sales in 2001 were $11.5 billion (see Exhibits 1 and 2 for Bunge's financials).

Bunge had undergone a dramatic transformation over the past decade. The company was established in Europe in the early nineteenth century. As recently as the early 1990s, it had faced financial problems and many expected it to exit the industry. Under new leadership, including Weisser as CFO, the company had returned to its roots in agribusiness and food, making a number of strategic acquisitions, divesting non-core businesses and restoring financial stability. Weisser, a Brazilian, was appointed Bunge's CEO in January 2000.

The acquisition of Cereol, for approximately $1.5 billion including debt, would be Bunge's largest to date. In early September 2002, Weisser prepared to meet with his Executive Committee to discuss how to manage the integration of Cereol. How would this affect Bunge's business and organisational model? Weisser cherished Bunge's decentralised management structure with decision making devolved to the regional units. He believed decentralisation reduced bureaucracy and allowed local managers to act fast and seize business opportunities. However, the potential always existed for decentralisation to result in decisions that benefited Bunge's regional companies, which were separate profit centers, rather than the company as a whole.

Source: Professor Jonathan West prepared this case. HBS cases are developed solely as the basis for class discussion. Cases are not intended to serve as endorsements, sources of primary data, or illustrations of effective or ineffective management. Copyright © 2001 President and Fellows of Harvard College. Reproduced with permission.

To create synergies between all Bunge's pieces, soon to include Cereol, coordination had to be optimised. Would Bunge's decentralised structure be scalable in an industry in which integration was, increasingly, the name of the game?

To reach Bunge's 35-person headquarters, Weisser walked through the company's recently created global agribusiness marketing centre. Bunge's traders were sourcing raw and processed oilseeds and grains from the company's operations in the United States, Brazil, and Argentina. They marketed these products worldwide: soy-protein meal to poultry feeders in Asia; edible vegetable oil to food manufacturers in the Middle East; and corn and wheat to millers in the Mediterranean. Ocean vessels were chartered to carry the products across the globe. This trade was supported by Bunge's vast network of physical assets: grain elevators, processing plants, trucks, barges, railcars and sales offices. In 2001, Bunge had originated, processed and marketed more than 70 million tons of grains, oilseeds and fertilisers, a three-fold increase since 1997.

Agribusiness

In terms of production, the most important oilseed was soybeans and the most important grains were wheat and corn. Between them, they accounted for more than 65 per cent of US crop area planted in 2001. Although these grains and oilseeds were grown throughout the world, a number of countries could not produce enough to supply their population's needs, either due to a shortage of agricultural land or unsuitable climatic conditions, and needed to import grains. Gigantic quantities of these products traversed the world. In 2001, for example, more than 160 million tons of soybeans were consumed worldwide (see Exhibit 5). The United States, Brazil, and Argentina accounted for more than 80 per cent of world soybean and corn exports and more than 50 per cent of world wheat exports. Because of differences in growing seasons, northern and southern hemisphere nations supplied the world market at different times of the year.

In the past decade, growth in agricultural production had moved toward South America largely because of cost advantages and the larger tracts of arable land available there (see Exhibit 3 for relative production costs and Exhibit 4 for soybean production in South America). In the next 20 years, more than 60 per cent of the growth in global grain exports was expected to come from South America. In Brazil, a huge expansion of cultivation was occurring in the interior of the country – the largest undeveloped area for farming in the world. Indeed, by 1999–2001, Brazil and Argentina's soybean and product exports had grown from less than 10 per cent in the 1960s to nearly 50 per cent.[2]

In the longer term eastern Europe, Russia and the Ukraine were expected to resume their historic role as grain exporters.[3] This would require major investments in transport, storage, and processing infrastructure in these countries. The main driver of growth in demand for food and feed was income and population growth in developing countries.[4]

Wheat was the world's principal food grain and corn was the world's most important animal feed grain. Soybeans were processed or 'crushed' to produce two main products, vegetable oil and protein meal.[5] Most soybean oil was refined for human food products such as cooking oil, margarine and shortening. Soybean meal was the dominant protein meal supplement for animal feed,[6] particularly for poultry and hogs, accounting for 65 per cent of world consumption. Unlike wheat flour, soybean meal and oil were economically transportable over large distances and the US, Brazil and Argentina were all major exporters of soybean products (see Exhibit 5).

Lags in the adjustment of agricultural supply and commodity processing capacity to changes in demand made agribusiness highly cyclical. Until 2000, the industry continued the downcycle that had begun with the Asian crisis in 1997. Overcapacity in oilseed processing, after a rapid expansion between 1997 and 1999, put pressure on crush margins, which averaged under $10 per ton in 1999 compared to a long term average of $18 per ton (see Exhibit 6). Crush margins picked up since 1999 because of growth and discipline in capacity management. The downcycle forced a number of smaller players out of the market and in 2000, large processors closed several soybean-processing plants to reduce overcapacity. Margins were also improved by the EU ban on meat and bone meal and improvements in Asian economies.

Biotechnology had already had a significant impact on agribusiness, and was projected to grow in importance in coming years. Since their commercial introduction in 1996, genetically modified (GM) seeds with 'input traits',[7] had been rapidly adopted by farmers in the United States and Argentina. In Brazil, although the government had prohibited the commercial planting of GM crops, it was estimated that 20–40 per cent of soybeans in the south were GM.[8] The introduction of GM crops into the food chain, particularly in grains and oilseeds for human consumption, had precipitated a consumer backlash in Europe. In the US, some food manufacturers had banned GM ingredients, while Japan and Korea announced plans to begin labeling unprocessed GM corn and soybeans. In the future, Agbiotech companies planned to introduce higher value-added GM crops, with nutritional and medicinal benefits for consumers, 'output traits'. In 2001, in response to multiple food crises, the EU proposed legislation requiring that all foods and feeds be traceable back to their origin. To capture the value created through output traits, modified grains had to be kept separate from commodity grains, or 'Identity Preserved' (IP).[9] The existing agribusiness system was very efficient at storing, transporting and processing large quantities of homogeneous commodities. It was not designed to manage a multiplicity of IP grains.

The value chain

The growing, handling, processing and marketing systems for grains and oilseeds were similar, and storage and transport were usually common (see Exhibit 7). Farmers generally sold their production to the closest elevator in order to minimise transportation costs. Elevators were facilities that served as consolidation and storage points. Production was then transported by truck, rail or barge to terminal elevators where larger quantities were consolidated for export or sale to processors serving the domestic and export markets. Grain was diverted from the distribution stream by competitive bidding from livestock producers, feed companies and corn and soybean processors. Grain was exported for processing at destination or processed domestically and the products exported. The chain could involve a single integrated grain company or multiple companies with several changes in ownership and with prices established many times at different locations. Grain was increasingly exported in higher value forms such as refined vegetable proteins, fructose and meats. This trend had reduced the role of grain exports in the US marketing system.

Economics

Grains, oilseeds, and their basic products were traded widely with clearly defined quality standards and transparent pricing. Customers bought mainly on price, although service and relationships could be important additional differentiators. Margins were slim and volatile (see Exhibit 8 for cost and margin structures). For higher value-added processed food products, innovation and brands were more important.

There were significant economies of scale in processing agricultural commodities. The main limitation on the size of processing plants[10] was not engineering but rather sourcing sufficient quantities of inputs year-round and having a readily accessible market for products. The largest plants were located in ports where they could draw on a large grain catchment area and export worldwide.

Risk management was fundamental in agribusiness. Uncertainties over supply and demand, related to factors such as weather, farmer's planting decisions, economic growth, trade policy and consumer tastes in different areas of the world, led to volatile prices for agricultural commodities. Price risks could be largely hedged through liquid futures markets such as the Chicago Board of Trade. These futures markets also acted as global price discovery mechanisms.

Bunge: 180 years in agribusiness

In 1818, a German merchant, Johann Peter Bunge, founded Bunge & Co. in Amsterdam, Holland, to merchandise grains and imports from the Dutch colonies. In 1859, the company moved to Antwerp where Bunge & Co. became one of the world's leading commodity traders.

The company moved its base to Argentina in 1884, to trade the country's rapidly expanding grain exports.[11] Bunge grew in tandem with Argentina's agribusiness, investing initially in commodity processing and food manufacturing and later expanding into many other businesses to become Argentina's largest private company. In the 1970s, during a period of political turmoil in Argentina, Bunge moved its head-quarters from Buenos Aires to Sao Paulo, Brazil. The 1970s saw the 'Brazilian miracle', a time of rapid growth and Bunge became one of the country's largest employers.

By the 1980s, Bunge was a diversified conglomerate with subsidiaries spanning the manufacture of textiles, paint, chemicals, cement, banking, insurance and real estate. Although a number of the group's companies were listed on local stock markets, the group remained private with shares held by descendants of the founders. The group's senior management continued to be drawn from the share-holders with family members running different regions independently.

Turnaround

Bunge's companies in South America had grown and worked in a protected environment and were not prepared for the international competition that came with the opening of the Brazilian and Argentine economies in the early 1990s. A fundamental review of the group's strategy concluded that Bunge must refocus on its consumer foods and agribusiness operations, divest non-core assets, and introduce professional management. Weisser, who joined as chief financial officer (CFO) in 1993, recollected:

'In South America Bunge diversified too far. It was very successful and money was rein-vested in the same countries. The group had a very inefficient holding structure.[12] We found that there was money in the wrong companies and debt in the wrong places. The US operations were on a sound footing and there were other pockets of a disciplined, decentralised, entrepreneurial company, but in Argentina and Brazil controls were weak. The structure was over heavy. The shareholders decided to make the company professional. We introduced discipline and began restructuring.'

Between 1992 and 1998, Bunge sold many non-core businesses, including Bunge Paints, the largest paint manufacturer in South America. In 1997, further focusing its strategy, Bunge returned to its roots in agribusiness, largely exiting the consumer foods business.[13] In the same year, Bunge took a critical step towards implementing its new strategy, acquiring Ceval Alimentos, Brazil's largest soybean processor. *'The move was smart'*, noted Ben Pearcy, Strategic Planning Director, *'because Brazil is the fastest growing region in the world in agriculture. We became the leader in oilseed processing in Brazil and gained a strong position in Argentina. If we hadn't done that acquisition, we wouldn't be positioned as we are today. It was a smart move but also fortuitous.'*[14]

In 1999, Bunge moved its headquarters from Sao Paulo to New York as part of its preparations for the IPO. Going public on 2 August 2001, Bunge sold 17.6 million new shares, just more than 20 per cent of total stock outstanding, at $16 per share. Weisser explained the rationale for the IPO:

'Firstly, the company needs to grow. There are many opportunities and our competitors have deep pockets. Shares are a good currency and public companies have better access to capital markets. Secondly, we need to provide liquidity for our shareholders.'

See Exhibit 9 for Bunge's stock price chart.

Strategy

Weisser's goal was for Bunge to become the best integrated agribusiness and food company in the world. He was convinced that in addition to its strong market positions, the company could differentiate itself by its business model and its organisation and culture. He explained the company's business model:

'We need to be integrated in the whole chain. We have really focused on integration and the most defining factor for integration is logistics. At Bunge, logistics doesn't just mean transportation – we mean getting the right product to the right customer, in the right quantity, at the right time and the right price.'

Weisser believed that superior logistics would give Bunge a cost advantage over companies that competed in only one part of the value chain. It would also enable Bunge to offer customers better service, for example traceability. He saw three dimensions to logistics: transport; having the right industrial footprint and locationally advantaged production assets; and *'extremely good management in the capture and analysis of information'*.[15]

Operations

Agribusiness

Bunge's agribusiness division consisted of grain origination, oilseed processing and international marketing.

Grain origination

Worldwide soybean demand was growing at an annual rate of 4.5 per cent and it was expected that population growth and rising incomes in the developing world would sustain this trend.[16] Bunge was strategically growing its grain origination network in Brazil and handled nearly one third of Brazil's soybeans.[17] It was the leading soybean originator and one of the largest consumers of logistics services in the country.[18] Furthermore, since there were fewer sources of crop financing than in the US, Bunge was directly involved in providing financial services to farmers in Brazil.[19] Bunge also had a strong origination position in Argentina. In the United States, Bunge was the leading handler of soybeans, corn and wheat in the southern Mississippi region. Bunge was more export-oriented than most of its competitors and, so, operated a number of strategically located port facilities in the United States, Brazil and Argentina. In 2001, Bunge used more than 50 per cent of the oilseeds and grains it originated in its own processing operations, the rest being sold to third parties

Oilseed processing

Bunge was the largest oilseed processor in the Americas and the third largest in the United States in 2001 (see Exhibit 10 for the evolution of Bunge's oilseed processing segment and Exhibit 11 for global market shares). Virtually all soybeans used were supplied by Bunge's own grain origination. Following the acquisition of an Argentine agribusiness firm in 2002, Bunge became the largest soybean processor and the second largest exporter of agricultural products in Argentina.[20]

Bunge was the largest soybean processor in Brazil. In Brazil, most of Bunge's crushing plants were located in Brazil's south and centre-west near soy growing centres or ports and most had attached edible oil refineries. Bunge exported nearly 80 per cent of its Brazilian soybean meal, and 65 per cent of its soybean oil production. Bunge planned to build two new crushing facilities in Brazil's north-east and centre-west regions in the world's fastest growing agricultural area.[21]

In the United States, Bunge's seven crushing plants were located either in the primary poultry producing areas, soybean producing areas, or on the primary river tributaries for export.

International marketing

Despite its history as an international grain trader with a global network of offices, by the 1990s Bunge had retreated to become primarily an originator and processor of oilseeds and grains. Bunge sold the majority of its products delivered 'free on board' (FOB) ship in ports in the United States, Brazil and Argentina (as the world's principal exporters these countries were often collectively termed 'the origins'). These were bought by traders, many of whom were Bunge's direct competitors, who aggregated end-customer demand, chartered ships, and provided services such as financing, storage and distribution at destination. Significant margins were being earned in international trade in which Bunge did not share and the lack of end-customer contact meant that while Bunge had a good understanding of grain origination dynamics it had only a second-hand perspective on destination trends. This limited the effectiveness of its hedging and risk management activities.

Changes in the international grain trade made a local marketing presence even more important:

> 'The nature of the export market has changed dramatically from large centralised buyers based in the Former Soviet Union or China, to broader, more diversified and discerning private buyers. Export contracts have changed: instead of their being comprised of a few large purchases of crops with standardised specifications, they have become much smaller, and have more differentiated quality and service requirements.'[22]

Bunge Global Markets (BGM)

By the late 1990s, in the wake of industry consolidation, Bunge saw an opportunity to reestablish itself in the international marketing arena. In 1998, it established BGM to build an international marketing capability. BGM had four main activities: marketing physical products, freight, risk management and trade finance. 'The value of BGM is in taking our origin capacity, linking with customers, and managing the risks in between: commodity, credit, interest rate, foreign exchange, freight and political', a BGM manager explained.

Archie Gwathmey, Managing Director for BGM, spoke of BGM's evolution:

> 'We developed first the global customer bases – in oil, soybeans, corn and wheat and saw that our costs were going up faster than our revenues. While we were trying to perform these functions we were also trying to measure and look at [BGM] as a stand-alone company. We understood that the key to having a viable business model was to layer additional services and capabilities so we started and developed a trade structured finance business where we were able to leverage trade flows in areas where we had high local working capital costs. We also tried to develop our economic analysis and build a system to read global markets better. We spent a lot of time promoting the team concept among our various players (other Bunge companies at the origins). We indicated where and how we see the market evolving, for example, and the only way we're going to be effective at this, from a pricing standpoint as well as from presenting to our global customer base, is if we do this together.'

BGM had grown rapidly. In 2001 alone, Bunge's international marketing volumes doubled while gross profit quadrupled, and operating income grew more than six times. Soy products accounted for 70 per cent of BGM's sales in 2001, although many customers required a mix of grains and oilseed products. Based in White Plains, New York, by 2002, BGM had opened more than 20 offices including Geneva, Singapore, Shanghai, Jakarta, Hamburg, Rome, Istanbul and Miami (see Exhibit 12). BGM was managing more than 100 chartered ocean going vessels and leased warehouse space at several destination points. In Italy and Portugal it had also leased crushing plants, supplying raw materials and marketing the resulting oil and meal. In Turkey it was constructing a port and in India, it lead the growth of Bunge's domestic processing business, expanding a crush plant and refinery.

BGM was organised along two axes – distribution businesses and product lines. Product lines covered global functions such as trade-structured finance, ocean freight, and certain risk management activities. Distribution businesses, organised regionally at the main destinations, were focused on serving customers in their local markets. While distribution businesses made their own decisions, they did so in the context of a global plan provided by BGM's product lines so, *'you don't have 15 people going to a particular market to buy soybeans because all the buying is channelled together and all the planning and logistics is similarly channelled'*, said Gwathmey.

BGM took inputs from destination marketing offices as they assessed world demand and import needs. Similarly, Bunge's origin offices conveyed their expectations of exportable surplus given current market circumstances and price structure. This information was synthesised at BGM, giving all Bunge companies a view of supply and demand in the world and insights into where surpluses and shortages were developing. This would help them manage their capacity and price risk, for example, selling capacity forward to lock in margins or increasing grain purchases in the interior. Gwathmey explained, *'The key position [for Bunge] is how we're going to play the cards in terms of managing our global capacity – where are we going to crush more, crush less – how we're going to manage our global risk in terms of having the right offsets between our risks in different categories.'*

Fertiliser

Bunge's fertiliser division benefited from agricultural growth in Brazil since land in the *cerrados* (savannas) required regular applications of phosphate fertilisers. Brazil, the fourth largest fertiliser market in the world,[23] grew by more than 70 per cent between 1991 and 1998 (see Exhibit 13). Bunge was the only integrated fertiliser producer in Brazil, participating in all stages of the business from mining of raw materials to selling of mixed fertilisers. Fertiliser was a cyclical business – demand was closely linked to agricultural acreage, fertiliser intensity, and credit avaialble to farmers. In 1996, Bunge had planned to sell its small fertiliser business. However, after studying the industry further, *'we saw we had a fantastic opportunity to grow the business and create value'*, Weisser explained. *'We saw some synergies but underestimated them.'* Through a series of eight acquisitions Bunge expanded its product lines, improved its access to raw materials and became Latin America's leading fertiliser producer in 2002. See Exhibit 14 for growth of Bunge's fertiliser division.

More than 75 per cent of Bunge's sales were direct to 60,000 farmers in Brazil, but Brazilian farmers typically did not have the financial resources to buy the required fertilisers without the help of financing from agribusiness companies. *'So, instead of giving [farmers] money who then buy fertiliser with some of the money, you give them fertiliser and you know what the money is being spent on and the farmer pays you [back] in soybeans. So you internalise and reduce the credit risk'*, Pearcy said. In 2001, more than 10 per cent of Bunge's fertiliser sales, up to 5 per cent in 2000, were made in conjunction with crop financing. This was expected to increase to 20 per cent over time. Bunge also wanted to see if its integrated fertiliser model would work with its grain origination to manage credit risk in other areas such as Argentina. In the future, Bunge intended to deepen its relationship with farmers by providing additional services such as selling seeds, chemicals, other financial services and technical advice. It was also considering managing similar risks for other companies such as agrochemical firms in return for a fee.

Bunge's scale in fertiliser gave it significant cost advantages in acquiring raw materials, financing, processing and logistics, in an industry characterised by low brand equity and little product differentiation. Weisser explained:

'We bring the grain to the port but we are able to negotiate to get a better rate to trans-port fertilisers back to the hinterlands [of Brazil]. It's not a huge thing, but it adds a couple of cents per ton when you negotiate the back-haul. Or, if you start chartering 50–100 ships, once you have the knowledge about freight, you can also do the importing for other Brazilian fertiliser companies to bring in the potassium so integration starts to have all kinds of benefits.'[24]

Bunge was the single biggest buyer of road freight in Brazil because of the large quantities it moved using trucks. Its bulk fertiliser blending facilities were being located close to soybean elevators to integrate fertiliser sales with grain origination and the two divisions established shared delivery and transshipment points. Speaking of the importance of links between the two divisions, Weisser said, *'the focus on the farmer, the logistics advantage, with the backhaul, financing, credit risk – [it is all about] efficiency, efficiency and efficiency – whatever you can do to reduce costs'*.

Food products

Through its food products operations in the United States and Brazil, including oils and shortenings, consumer products, wheat and corn milling, bakery products and soy ingredients, Bunge served the food service, food manufacturing and retail gro-cery markets. The food products business allowed Bunge to counterbalance some of the cyclicality in its fertiliser and agribusiness divisions. Bunge was refocusing its efforts in the food products business, having concentrated on its agribusiness and fertiliser operations in the recent past. Globally, Bunge used 20 per cent of its edible oil production in its food products division.

In developed markets, the retail and consumer food market had changed rapidly in recent years. Agribusiness companies were beginning to enter categories such as branded edible oil, in which returns were tied more to risk management and raw material access, for instance. Bunge, too, had to consider how far down the value chain it wanted to participate and to what extent. Bunge aimed to selectively par-ticipate in food products markets in which it could realise synergies with its agribusi-ness in procurement and risk management.

Soy ingredients

The soy ingredients market was growing at a rate of 11 per cent per year and offered favorable profit margins (see Exhibit 15 for diversity of soy products). However, Bunge was still a relatively small competitor, with sales under $100 million in 2001 (see Exhibit 16). Bunge manufactured soy-based food ingredients such as isolated soy proteins (ISP) and lecithin.[25] It was one of only three major global producers of ISP.[26] There were substantial technological barriers to producing ISP and Bunge had developed proprietary production technology in this area. Bunge's major soy ingre-dient production facility was in Brazil, a low-cost production area, and Bunge had recently invested in a new plant dedicated to the production of ISP, doubling its pro-duction capacity. The facility was among the world's most sophisticated and was designed to meet the strict requirements of pharmaceutical industry customers. Bunge planned on developing a new line of soy-based ingredients to meet nutraceu-tical food demands.[27]

Acquisition of Cereol

Cereol was the number four soy processor in the United States and the leading oilseed processor in Canada. Its US assets, located in the eastern cornbelt, were very complementary to Bunge's and would make Bunge a strong number two to ADM. Cereol also operated oilseed processing plants in western Europe. These primarily pocessed soybeans imported from the Americas. Western Europe was the largest market for protein meals in the world and Cereol's assets would allow Bunge to participate in the region's demand for domestically crushed meal.

In eastern Europe, Cereol had established a leading position in the oilseed processing industry with the privatisations of the early 1990s. Gwathmey was enthusiastic, *'We look at eastern Europe as a platform for growth in many areas – even areas outside of the ones we're buying. Grain production will expand, protein production will expand and there will be significant opportunities for us to leverage our capabilities and our strengths in the market there.'*

Cereol was integrated downstream in many of its European markets. It was the world's leading producer of bottled branded vegetable oil, marketing a billion bottles annually.

Cereol had a strong soy ingredients business and was a global leader in soy concentrates and lecithins. These products complemented Bunge's existing soy ingredients portfolio. Cereol had production assets in the United States and western Europe, a large sales force, and was widely respected by food industry customers for its innovation and long tradition.

Weisser noted that the increased sale of the combined company was important because,

> *'[I]n agribusiness, it is so important to be efficient. It is highly competitive – few businesses are as transparent as commodities and the acquisition is very imortant to address scale and efficiency, and enables us to reduce logistics expenses. [The acquisition] fits like a glove on your hand. It adds to scale, efficiency and growth, and we're gaining it at an attractive price.'*[28]

See Exhibit 17 for Bunge's position in oilseed processing.

Organisation and culture

A decentralised management structure

Weisser had inherited a decentralised structure from the days when Bunge was privately run. He strongly believed this could be a source of competitive advantage for the company. His professional experience had shown him what could happen at a centralised organisation:

> *'[I] saw hundreds of smart initiatives that were not implemented – not even articulated. The ideas would not even reach a decision point so people start getting disenchanted and soon don't even talk about their ideas. Also, with a large headquarters and centralisation, there can be a lot of politics, fiefdoms, much time wasted deciding who is right or wrong between the regions and the headquarters.'*

At the same time, Weisser recognised that Bunge's decentralised structure had caused problems in the past when its companies had become highly diversified in the absence of an aligned mission. Weisser saw that 'to be competitive on a global basis, you have to have an aligned mission. Especially since our business is global, you cannot have regions going in different directions. It might have been fine in the past but in the current environment where the business is so global, you have to be aligned.' Nevertheless, Weisser wanted Bunge to maintain the decentralised management structure:

> *'The beauty of being decentralised is that every region is very different. We have local management that knows the people. So, if our focus is to be very efficient and farmer- and customer-focused, these local people have to know how things work. In Argentina, for example, they are all Argentines, in Brazil, Brazilians and so on. They can react to the needs of the market with greater speed because we recognise opportunities faster. We are seen as a local player, and not an ugly multinational. Also, we are able to hire very good local talent, people who are bright and intelligent and take initiative, and who find the space to move. They don't like being in organisations that are stiff and rigid, where you just follow routines.'*

There were only 35 people in Bunge's headquarters in White Plains, NY. *'In other companies you have a large head office, an aristocracy, slower decision-making'*, explained Flavio Sa Carvalho, Bunge's chief personnel officer. *'There is nothing of that here. It is a tremendous competitive advantage.'* In the past, the company did not have managers for its three divisions; the heads of Bunge's regional operating companies reported directly to the CEO (see Exhibit 18). In 2001, Bunge had appointed a managing director of its food products division with responsibility for coordinating strategy, and in 2002, a managing director for its newly created soy ingredients division.

Bunge's ten-person Executive Committee, composed of the heads of Bunge's companies and key corporate officers, met four times a year. In the past two years, Weisser had encouraged this Committee to develop from being focused primarily on reporting performance towards becoming the global leadership team of Bunge. The Committee was increasingly involved in setting global strategy. In addition it was becoming an important forum for negotiation and discussion when decision-making cut across regional boundaries.

Challenges of decentralisation

Bill Wells, Bunge's CFO, saw a challenge posed by Bunge's structure: *'How do you run an integrated company in a decentralised manner? How do you obtain synergies across P&L lines and how do you correctly identify those functions that need to be centralised and which functions truly need to be decentralised?'*

In preparation for Bunge's IPO, its financial functions had become more centralised. Consequently, Bunge's companies could no longer take advantage of good local borrowing opportunities because the company as a whole needed to have a proportion of its debt funded at the holding company level to maintain its investment grade rating. Corporate functions such as treasury, financial control and planning, capital expenditure controls and strategic planning were centrally located. There was also a small human resources group. All other functions, such as business–customer contact, were devolved to country-based units that were still separate profit centres. Wells stated, *'The bias [at Bunge] is that if something should not be centralised then it definitely would not be. And if there is any doubt, then it should be decentralised.'*

Wells felt that Bunge's decentralised model was more scaleable than a centralised structure in which, *'if you keep building a larger and larger command infrastructure, you end up with the Pentagon. With a relatively small centre, you do not have to grow as fast and you can add outside functions and get a networking type effect – that's what we're striving for.'*

Weisser elaborated on the challenges of having a decentralised structure:

> *'The job of the centre is made more difficult because with profit and loss responsibility decentralised it is much more difficult to give instructions or directions. We have to convince – it is a more cumbersome way of getting alignment. If you are centralised, you give an order and it is implemented. So, the problem is much more complicated at our company.*
>
> *'The alignment takes a little more time, there is friction, and there is some inefficiency. Especially with the global initiatives, you need a lot of energy to get them implemented, and sometimes they don't get perfectly implemented. For example, because we have freight negotiations within the same country with different businesses, we sometimes don't optimise freight. But on the other hand, if our regional companies are responsible for their P&L, we want to give them the leeway to negotiate. I'm prepared to accept a certain level of inefficiency to maintain the entrepreneurial spirit. The limit of integration is the point at which bureaucracy takes over and kills this spirit.'*

To promote global coordination, Weisser had established a number of collaborative initiatives. These were in areas such as logistics, training and development, productivity, and innovation. Each initiative was championed by a member of the Executive Committee rather than being driven from headquarters. Team members were drawn from within the various companies and they participated in the initiatives alongside their other responsibilities.

Information technology (IT) was a particularly challenging area. Many in Bunge perceived an opportunity to better coordinate and leverage information across the company. Bunge did not have a global information system, other than e-mail. *'Information is all in little pockets'*, a manager explained. *'There could be tremendous power if we aggregated it.'* Bunge had an IT council that acted as a clearinghouse for broad company-wide issues, coordinating IT between companies. While there were incremental margins that could be captured, *'like money to be saved by buying equipment in bulk'*, there was the issue, Wells said, of, *'giving people liberty to make their own specifications and adapting things to their local business is also important. How do we try to fit those things together?'* Some had suggested that Bunge should appoint a Chief Information Officer and invest in a global IT infrastructure. This would be a major change from Bunge's existing model.

Challenges at BGM

Because BGM interfaced with all of Bunge's companies in the origins, yet was a stand-alone profit centre, its challenge was particularly acute. Gwathmey explained, *'Everyone is optimised for their local business. And the challenge for Bunge is to ensure that we're focused on building the business rather than just a segment of the chain.'*

Pearcy explained:

> *'Our challenge is that value bounces around in the value chain over time, depending on what is going on in global markets. It may be that in a certain stage in time, there is profitability in the demand side, other times profitability at the origin. Ultimately you have to make trade-offs: there are decisions that can cost certain parts of the business some-*

thing but can benefit another part, and at the moment there are separate profit centres. We have to behave in a very flexible integrated fashion and yet at the same time, Bunge has a culture that's very focused on the bottom line. Each of the countries is also focused on their own bottom line. This creates strong potential for friction and tension between them.'[29]

For example, tensions could arise around a commodity's transfer price. A Bunge manager explained with an example:

'A production unit would negotiate the price of their material on an FOB basis. The way they would negotiate would be to tell BGM – your competitor is paying X and we have a broker calling up and telling us he will pay one or two dollars more if we offer it. So, for you at BGM to buy it from us, you have to pay at least this price. But you would only know there really was someone if you allowed it to happen. That is, you would only find out the truth if you broke Bunge's entire reason for creating BGM. The transfer price issue in the origins was a big issue even a year ago. Basically, we, at BGM, ended up paying too much.'

Operational decisions in the origins could also affect BGM. Gwathmey explained how some structural inefficiency in Bunge's Brazilian ports resulted in delays in loading vessels:

'[We] have vessels whose charter costs are $10,000 a day. If we can execute those freight programs in two days rather than five or six, then that money stays at Bunge. But till we started to measure and look at that, the economic cost was not obvious because in Brazil, it wasn't a cost that the local profit centre bore.'[30]

The company worked to address such issues by deepening personal relationships between BGM and Bunge's regional units. *'We're visiting customers together, making sure that the people in charge of production at [the] origin and the person in charge of marketing have the same goals – they know with who, and where and how we're going to do business'*, said a BGM manager. As a result, friction had dissipated but some felt that it was inherent in a decentralized structure with separate profit centres.

Culture

Weisser was convinced that the company's management style, its values, collaborative initiatives and people were a source of differentiation. He believed that, *'you can only be decentralised, entrepreneurial, informal and practical and efficient if at the same time you can have a shared mission, strategy, incentives, teamwork and values'*. Values such as integrity, openness and trust, teamwork, an entrepreneurial spirit, farmer and customer focus, were to be promoted within Bunge since, *'you cannot have a decentralised organisation with an entrepreneurial spirit and at the same time be efficient if you don't have these strong values'*.[31]

Bunge's efforts in the last few years to regain global alignment of its mission and strategy among its various companies had resulted in a change of culture. Many people were recruited from other companies. *'Bunge is more entrepreneurial. There is a desire within Bunge to create a new industry model that doesn't replicate the models that are already out there, but draws on the elements of the different companies people came from'*, noted Pearcy. Wells observed, *'Over the last few years, there is a feeling of really being a winning team because we've had success after success, and that builds on itself and people start to be motivated by that. People like to be part of something successful.'*

Because of the company's small centre, it was not always clear exactly how things were done at Bunge. One outcome of this, Pearcy felt was that, *'people at Bunge are better at dealing with ambiguity and uncertainty, and looking for a creative solution'*. Unlike its large North American competitors, Bunge was seen as multicultural with some, such as Pearcy, seeing a distinct South American flavour, particularly a Brazilian one:

'Meetings can switch to Portuguese easily. People are very friendly, informal, pragmatic, deal with change fast, and are entrepreneurial. That is the positive side of business in Brazil. Bunge should always feel a special relationship with Brazil. Even after Cereol, such a big part of our business is in Brazil – you've got to understand how Brazil works – have to have a feel for what Brazil is like, the language, the culture, the geography.'

Industry evolution

Bunge's competitors included other integrated agribusiness companies, trading companies, farm cooperatives, and regional players.[32] Competitors were often both important customers and suppliers to each other in the liquid agricultural commodity markets. However, over the past decade, the industry had undergone considerable consolidation, with many firms exiting (see Exhibit 19).

In recent years, trading-focused companies such as Continental and Andre, historically a major force, faced financial problems and were either acquired, exited the industry, or played a sharply reduced role. As information became more available it was harder for them to take advantage of inefficiencies in global markets. In addition, without origination and processing assets they found it hard to source commodities efficiently. Similarly, farmer-owned cooperatives, long an important force in agribusiness, did not operate globally, and now played a diminished role.

ADM and Cargill, both integrated agribusiness companies, were Bunge's primary competitors (see Exhibit 20 for key metrics on these companies). They were each larger and more diversified than Bunge. Both operated in oilseed processing, and also wet corn processing,[33] wheat milling, and other products and services, including grain trading, transport and financial services (see Exhibit 21 and Exhibit 22 for ADM's and Cargill's financials).

ADM, based in Decatur, Illinois, was highly centralised and US-focused with nearly 70 per cent of revenues coming from North America. It was dedicated to being the lowest cost provider in each segment in which it operated, and was seen as more market-share and production oriented than customer driven. It visualised itself as a large food input and fuel *'factory, in which raw commodities entered at one end and exited as value-added products.'* ADM led the growth of the US soybean processing industry in the 1970s, wet-corn processing in the 1980s, and the production of lysine (a feed additive) and other bio-products in the 1990s. Recently, ADM had aggressively increased its international grain marketing activity, opening overseas offices and taking a majority ownership stake in AC Toepfer International, a grain-trading company. Toepfer had more than 40 sales offices worldwide and traded 40 million tons of grains annually.

Cargill, formed in Minnesota in 1865 and based in Minneapolis, was the largest private company in the world with sales of $50 billion in 2002. Cargill's activities included trading and processing commodities such as oilseeds, corn, wheat, fertiliser, beef, sugar, coffee, fruit juice, cocoa, salt and rubber. Cargill was active throughout the agribusiness chain, from supplying inputs to farmers to selling processed foods to consumers, although its strength was in commodity processing. Cargill had aggressively leveraged its capabilities in commodity trading, logistics, and processing into non-food businesses including steel mini-mills and metal trading. Cargill's financial services business had grown to make a major contribution to the company's results. Its activities included trading financial assets, risk management services and trade and structured finance.

In the last two years, Cargill initiated a fundamental review of its business. Its new strategy was to become *'a premier provider of customer solutions in food and agriculture'*. Cargill hoped to develop its value-added operations, increase innovation and enhance its customer focus. Cargill traditionally employed a highly structured, centralised organisation. In an effort to increase returns and become more entrepreneurial, Cargill had recently reorganised, attempting to push profit responsibility down to nearly 100 business units and reducing overhead.

Bunge also faced an emerging competitor group with strong regional positions, particularly in Asia. These companies invested throughout Southeast Asia and in mainland China. They were active in the poultry industry (China was the world's largest meat consumer, producing nearly 40 per cent of the world's total), feed milling, and commodity processing, including soybeans, wheat, and especially palm oil. A number of international companies, such as ADM, had entered joint ventures with these groups to penetrate the Chinese market.[34] *'They are very strong'*, Gwathmey explained. *'They are both strategic and opportunistic. They understand government and politics, and have the right timing.'* These groups were important customers for Bunge's grain and oilseed exports, while at the same time, by building domestic processing capacity, they competed with products imported from North and South America.

Integrating Cereol

With the addition of Cereol, Bunge would be exporting into the European market as well as producing locally, since Cereol had processing assets in Europe. Consequently, *'the complexity of our organisation will be much greater'*, observed Weisser. *'We will have to find a good solution to the issues that have to be dealt with globally and the issues that have to be dealt with locally. It will be more complicated to define these, especially when it relates to Europe, which is the largest consuming market in the world of meal and oil.'* A BGM manager elaborated:

> *'Today we're shipping soybean meal [and] marketing in Europe. Cereol is also a crusher in Europe. Very often, we need to make decisions at the destination in the local market, such as how to satisfy the local demand base with both local crush and the import of soybean meal. The mix is what determines profitability. So, we have to coordinate distribution opportunities on imports with local crush to optimise the value chain. But there are times when we want to position the company to optimise profitability, and not run destination capacity and ship more from origin.'*
>
> *'It will be very much a coordination issue and to what extent we can have common incentives. The decisions are largely commercial, such as: How do we position capacity and ourselves in the marketplace from a risk perspective? That's defining for success in our business. There is a fine line in a high volume business: a dollar per ton is meaning-*

ful to the bottom line. Marginal differences in profitability can have a huge impact. We're now going to be the largest oilseed processor, and there is not a lot of differentiation in our business – a ton of meal produced in Brazil means a ton can't be produced in Europe or the United States. These things are very fungible and there is only so much demand in the world. When one is big, and if one happens to be decentralised, the decentralised structure may not allow for optimisation.'

Conclusion

In recent years, Bunge had focused its corporate strategy, making a series of acquisitions to grow its agribusiness and fertiliser divisions. It had shifted from being a confederation of small regional companies to become a global giant. Now, with the acquisition of Cereol, Bunge had to reconsider how it was going to balance integration with its decentralised business model. Gwathmey articulated the problem:

'The biggest issue is people and how we manage the system. It's a management structure issue. As we mature and move into new regions, we have natural conflict in terms of optimising for the whole. Going forward, the value creation challenge for Bunge is how well we play the global cards, how we optimise logistics from the standpoint of making sure that the decisions we make will work for the whole rather than for one particular country business.'

BGM provided analysis, guidance and *'there was a certain moral authority of product lines'* but, ultimately, decisions on how much to buy, when to sell, and to whom to sell, resided with separate profit centres. Should BGM assume greater control over such decisions? Was BGM's model of building consensus to achieve results incompatible with Bunge's larger scale and integrated business model? Or, did the benefits of decentralisation outweigh such concerns? Weisser wanted Bunge to be the world's best integrated agribusiness company. Would the acquisition of Cereol require a change in Bunge's organisational model?

Notes on the case

1 The food service industry consisted of prepared meal providers including restaurants, hotels and institutions.
2 Schnepf, R.D., Dohlman, E. and Bolling, C. *Agriculture in Brazil and Argentina: Developments and Prospects for Major Field Crops.* Market and Trade Economics Division, Economic Research Service, USDA, WRS-01-3.
3 In 2000, Ukrainian grain output was expected to be half its peak Soviet levels.
4 Pinstrup-Andersen, *et al.* (1999) 'World food prospects: critical issues for the early twenty first century', *International Food Policy Research Institute*, October.
5 Soybeans were approximately 80 per cent meal and 20 per cent oil by volume. Because of its relatively higher value, oil accounted for between 30 per cent and 50 per cent of the total soybean product value.
6 Usually mixed with corn, soybean meal had the best conversion rate from vegetable protein to animal protein.
7 Input traits were genetic traits that reduced a farmer's need for herbicide, pesticide and fertiliser inputs.
8 Schnepf, R.D., Dohlman. E. and Bolling. C. Op. cit., p. vii.
9 Agbiotech companies aimed to build IP systems in partnership with the major agribusiness

companies. In 1998, Cargill and Monsanto agreed to each invest $50 million annually in a joint venture to develop, source, process and market agricultural products with output traits.

10 The average capacity of soybean processing plants in the United States had increased from approximately 1,000 tons per day in the 1970s to more than 3,000 tons per day in the 1990s. The world's largest plant, located at a port in Argentina, processed 12,000 tons per day.

11 Argentine wheat cultivation grew from 500,000 hectares in the early 1870s to 8 million hectares in 1913.

12 Bunge had more than 100 holdings and companies in Brazil alone.

13 It sold Molinos Rio de La Plata, Argentina's largest consumer foods company, Gramoven, a leading consumer foods company in Venezuela, and Bunge Defiance, a milling and baking business in Australia.

14 Case writer interview with Ben Pearcy, 30 August 2002.

15 Case writer interview with Alberto Weisser, 30 August 2002.

16 Bunge Annual Report (2001), p. 21.

17 Ibid.

18 In Brazil, about 80 per cent of soybeans were trucked to market for distances upwards of 800 miles. Long stretches of highways in the interior were dirt.

19 Crop financing loans were typically secured by the farmer's crop and a mortgage. The loans carried market interest and were repaid in soybeans or other grains.

20 Based on volumes; in March 2002, Bunge acquired La Plata Cereal, an Argentine agribusiness company.

21 Bunge Annual Report (2001) p. 22.

22 Nelson, David and Bianco, David (1999) 'Presentation to the World Food and Agribusiness Congress', *Credit Suisse First Boston*, 30 June.

23 After China, the United States and India.

24 Case writer interview with Alberto Weisser, 30 August 2002.

25 Soy ingredients were traditionally used as functional ingredients in food manufacturing. Soy proteins were widely used in the processed meat and baking industries for their binding, emulsification and flavour-enhancing capabilities. Lecithins were used as an emulsifier in chocolate, margarine, sweet biscuits and beverages.

26 The others were DuPont's Protein Technologies and ADM, both located in the United States.

27 Soy-based food ingredients were at the forefront of the growing nutraceutical foods – foods intended to produce specific health benefits – market. This was fuelled by consumer concern over diet, an ageing population, and increasing healthcare costs.

28 Case writer interview with Alberto Weisser, 30 August 2002.

29 Case writer interview with Ben Pearcy, 30 August 2002.

30 Case writer interview with Archie Gwathmey, 30 August 2002.

31 Case writer interview with Alberto Weisser, 30 August 2002.

32 This review does not include Bunge's many industry-specific competitors in fertilisers, consumer foods and food service.

33 Corn would be 'wet-milled' to produce high-value food ingredients such as sweeteners, or industrial products such as ethanol or starch. By 2000, corn wet-milling accounted for 18 per cent of US corn consumption, up from 8 per cent in 1970.

34 ADM had a one-third interest in a joint venture with Wilmar that had recently constructed 10 new crushing plants in China and was the leading oilseed processor in the country. These plants processed a mix of local and imported soybeans.

Exhibit 1 Bunge Limited financial summary ($ million – financial year ending 31 December)

	1997	1998	1999	2000	2001	First Half 2001	First Half 2002
Net sales	7,484	9,103	8,075	9,667	11,484	5,161	5,787
Gross Profit	458	670	612	683	963	366	504
SG&A	338	374	332	388	436	–	–
Income from Operations	120	296	280	295	527	172	265
Non-operating income (expense)[a]		(120)	(296)	(234)	(263)	(205)	(115)
Net Income	83	92	(5)	3	134	29	72
ASSETS							
– Trade Receivables	510	516	511	873	881		
– Inventories	1,200	1,194	1,172	1,311	1,368		
Total Current Assets	3,571	3,262	2,441	3,427	3,284		
– PPE	1,587	1,584	1,268	1,859	1,669		
Total assets	6,092	5,814	4,611	5,854	5,443		
LIABILITIES & EQUITY							
– Trade Payables	912	886	748	839	775		
– Short Term Debt	605	1,203	708	1,268	803		
Total Current Liabilities	2,487	2,714	2,146	2,746	2,346		
– Long-Term Debt	1,257	935	793	1,003	830		
– Equity	1,453	1,495	1,197	1,139	1,376		
Total liabilities and equity	6,092	5,814	4,611	5,854	5,443		

Source: the company.
[a]Interest and foreign exchange.

Exhibit 2 Bunge business segment selected financial data ($ million)

Agribusiness	1998	1999	2000	2001
Net external sales	5,894	5,517	6,327	8,412
Income from operations	162	92	91	311
Total assets	3,115	2,595	2,938	2,745

Fertilisers	1998	1999	2000	2001
Net external sales	625	605	1,466	1,316
Income from operations	47	106	153	187
Total assets	810	694	1,731	1,654

Food Products	1998	1999	2000	2001
Net external sales	2,584	1,953	1,874	1,756
Income from operations	83	92	52	48
Total assets	1,558	1,068	956	886

Source: the company.

Exhibit 3 **Comparison of total cost of production and transport of soybeans to export market in northern Europe between Sapezal, Mato Grosso, Brazil and Jefferson, Iowa, USA**

	Cost per acre		Cost per bushel	
	Iowa	Mato Grosso	Iowa	Mato Grosso
Seed	$21.00	$11.00	$.42	$.20
Fertiliser & lime	25.00	70.00	.50	1.27
Herbicides & insecticides	30.00	36.00	.60	.65
Labour	14.00	5.00	.28	.09
Machinery	34.00	29.00	.68	.53
Other	15.00	16.00	.30	.29
Total non-land costs	$139.00	$167.00	$2.78	$3.03
Transportation costs to northern Europe				
– from Jefferson, Iowa*	42.50		.85	
– from Sapezal, Mata Grosso**		83.05		1.51
Land cost	$140.00	$23.00	$2.80	$.42
Total cost	$321.50	$273.05	$6.43	$4.96
Yield per acre	50	55		

Source: Duffy, Mike and Smith, Darnell, Iowa State University, November 2000.
*Rail (200 miles) – barge (1,450 miles) from Jefferson, Iowa to New Orleans and ocean vessel to northern Europe.
**Truck (580 miles) – barge (600 miles) from Sapezal, Mato Grosso to Itacoatiara and ocean vessel to northern Europe.

Exhibit 4 **Global soybean production: South America as the new growth area**

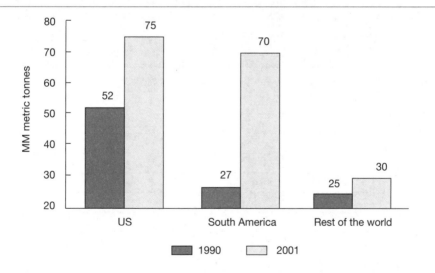

Exhibit 5 World soybean crush evolution (million metric tonnes crushed)

	Brazil	USA	Argentina	EU	China	India	Other	World
1995	21.3	38.3	9.1	15.1	7.8	3.1	17.7	112.4
1996	20.4	37.9	10.4	14.2	7.3	3.7	18.0	111.9
1997	18.9	40.4	10.5	15.1	9.0	3.5	19.5	116.8
1998	21.9	43.6	15.9	16.4	10.4	4.5	19.1	131.7
1999	21.5	43.7	17.1	15.8	12.1	4.4	20.8	135.3
2000	21.1	42.8	17.0	14.9	17.0	4.6	21.8	139.3
2001–2005E	24.7	47.9	20.2	16.4	21.9	5.5	24.9	161.5
2006–2010E	29.6	52.3	24.4	17.3	24.5	7.2	27.6	182.9

Source: compiled from OilWorld.

Exhibit 6 Soybean crushing margins (Chicago Board of Trade US $/ton and US $/bushel)

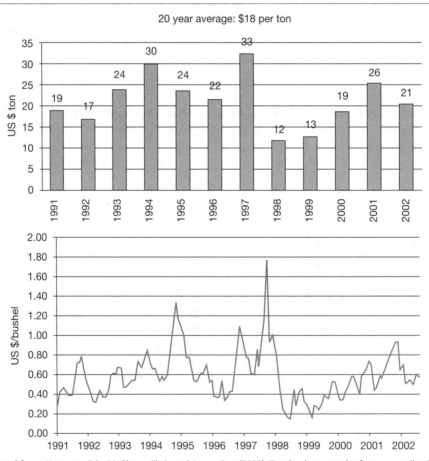

20 year average: $18 per ton

Source: adapted from: Katzman, Eric, McGlone, Chris and Jones, Pen (2002) 'Food – down on the farm … agribusiness', *Deutsche Bank*, August, p. 32.

Note: one metric tonne = 36.74 bushels of soybeans.

Exhibit 7 **Soybean value chain from farm to retail**

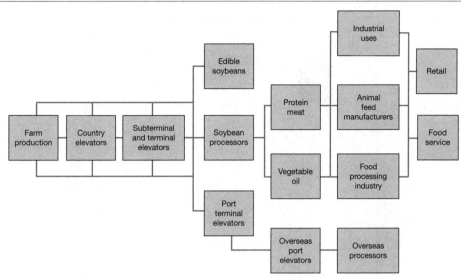

Source: the casewriter.

Note: elevators = silos.

Exhibit 8 **Illustrative agribusiness economics ($ per metric tonne)**

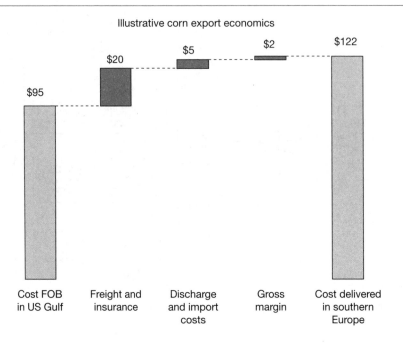

Illustrative corn export economics

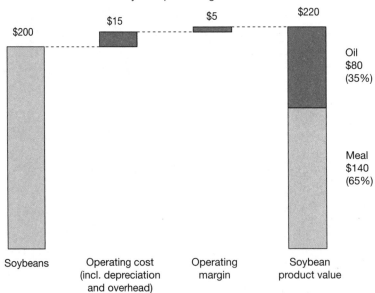

Illustrative soybean-processing economics

Source: the casewriter.

Exhibit 9 **Bunge's stock price vs. S&P**

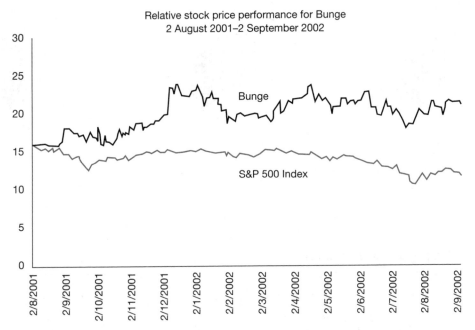

Relative stock price performance for Bunge
2 August 2001–2 September 2002

Source: Datastream.

Exhibit 10 **Evolution of Bunge's oilseed processing (million tons of capacity)**

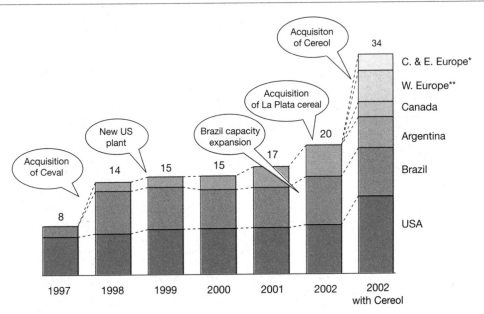

Source: the company
*Germany, Austria, Poland, Hungary, Ukraine, Romania.
**France, Spain, Italy.

Exhibit 11 Soybean crushing market shares, 2001

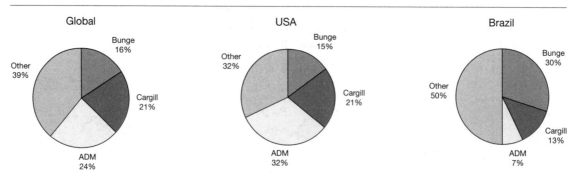

Source: company data (prior to acquisition of Cereol).

Exhibit 12 Bunge global markets offices

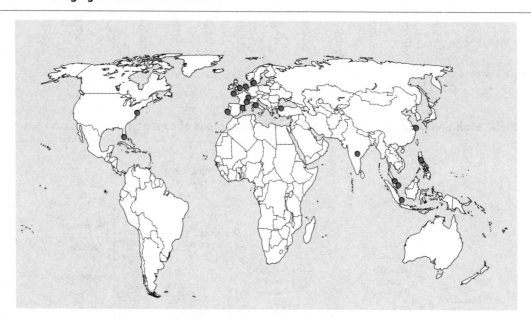

Source: the company.

Exhibit 13 **Brazilian fertiliser growth, indexed to 1991**

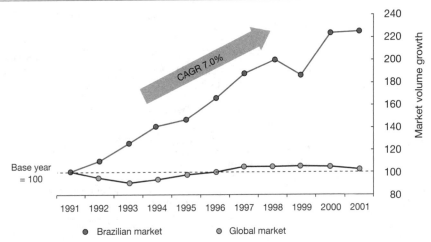

Source: compiled from data provided by the Brazilian Fertilizer Association.

Exhibit 14 **Evolution of Bunge's retail fertiliser business (million tons of NPK)**

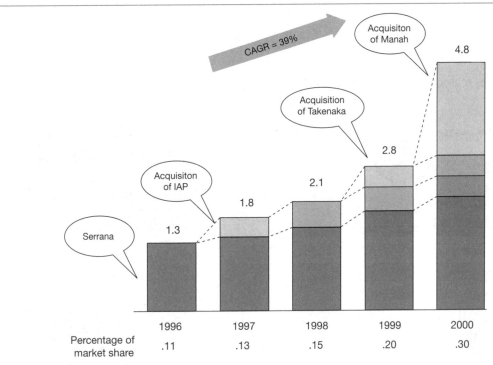

Source: the company.

Exhibit 15 **The soybean product tree**

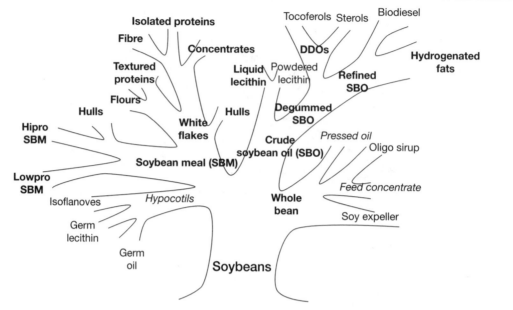

Source: the company.

Note: products in bold were by Bunge.

Exhibit 16 **Soy ingredients market share, 2001**

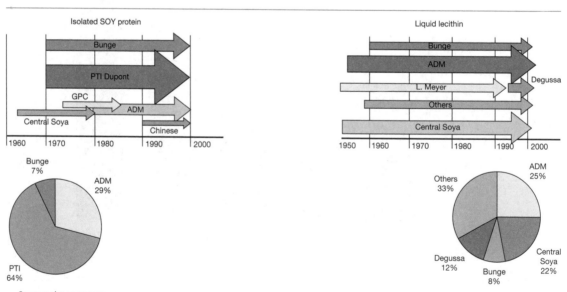

Source: the company.

Note: Central Soya is Cereol's US-based company.

Exhibit 17 Bunge's position in oilseed processing

Region	Bunge today	Bunge/Cereol
South America	No. 1	No. 1
USA	No. 3	No. 2
Canada	Not active	No. 1
Eastern Europe	Not active	No. 1
Western Europe	Small toll crush	No. 3
Asia	India	India
Globally	No. 3	No. 1

Source: the company.

Exhibit 18 Bunge Limited organisation

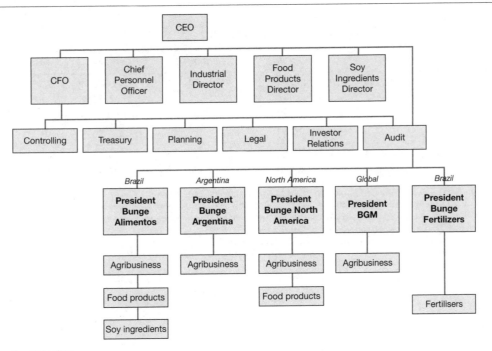

Source: the casewriter.

Note: positions in bold are members of Bunge's Management Executive Committee.

Exhibit 19 Evolution of the competitive field in grains and oilseeds

	1995	2001
Origination	ABC, Ceval, Continental Grain, Dreyfus, Farmland, Andre, Glencore, ConAgra	ABC, Dreyfus, ConAgra
Processing	ABC, Ceval, Dreyfus, Cereol	ABC, Dreyfus, Cereol
Marketing and distribution	ABC, Dreyfus, Andre, Continental Grain, Glencore, Nidera, Tradigrain, Toepfer, Premjee	ABC, Dreyfus, Nidera
ABC = ADM, Bunge, Cargill		

Source: the company.

Exhibit 20 Key metrics for Bunge and its competitors, 2001

US$ million	ADM	Cargill	Bunge	Cereol[c]	Bunge/Cereol
Net sales	20,051	49,204	11,484	4,587	16,071
EBITDA	1,492	2,407[b]	694	229[d]	923
Net income	383	358	134	63	197
Total assets	14,340	26,803	5,443	2,431	7,874
CapEx	300[a]	893[b]	230	80	310
Oilseed capacity (mmt)	30	30	21	13	34
Employees	22,834	90,000	17,360	5,751	23,111

Source: Cereol Annual Report; Bunge Annual Report; ADM Annual Report; Cargill web site,
http://www.cargill.com/finance/highlights.htm accessed 13 September 2002; and analyst reports as noted.
[a]Estimate. Nelson, David and Park, Nancy (2001) 'Archer Daniels Midland', *Credit Suisse First Boston*, 30 October, p. 16.
[b]Morley, Kevin (2002) 'Cargill', *Credit Suisse First Boston*, 22 March, p. 5.
[c]Cereol figures reported in euros and converted to US$ at 1.1289 euros/US$.
[d]Estimate. Digard, François (2001) 'Cereol-Refining Business', *ING Barings*, 9 August 2001, p. 16.

Exhibit 21 **ADM financials ($ millions), fiscal year ends 30 June**

	1991	1992	1993	1994	1995	1996	1997	1998	1999	2000
Sales	8,468	9,231	9,811	11,374	12,672	13,314	13,853	16,108	14,283	12,876
– Oilseeds	4,149	4,708	4,906	5,687	7,643	8,125	8,860	10,152	8,494	7,219
– Corn	2,540	2,677	2,747	2,957	2,477	2,561	2,171	2,154	1,855	1,950
– Wheat	847	923	1,275	1,479	1,384	1,644	1,631	1,491	1,378	1,358
– Other	932	923	883	1,251	1,168	984	1,191	2,312	2,556	2,350
Op. income	617	748	738	766	1,213	914	802	760	531	490
Net income	467	504	505	484	796	697	554	403	265	301
Capital exp.	468	480	394	514	559	801	780	703	671	428
Acquisitions	345	21	200	258	55	29	430	371	136	30
Current assets	2,532	3,213	3,922	3,911	3,713	4,384	4,284	5,452	5,790	6,162
Net P, P&E	2,695	3,060	3,215	3,538	3,762	4,114	4,709	5,323	5,567	5,277
LT debt	980	1,562	2,039	2,021	2,070	2,003	2,345	2,847	3,192	3,277
Equity	3,922	4,492	4,883	5,045	5,854	6,114	6,050	6,505	6,241	6,110
ROE	11.9%	11.2%	10.3%	9.6%	13.6%	11.4%	9.2%	6.8%	4.5%	4.9%

Source: ADM Annual Reports.

ADM – new reporting structure	1999	2000	2001
Net sales and other operating income	18,510	18,612	20,051
Oilseeds and corn	10,727	10,109	10,464
Agricultural services	3,574	4,640	5,644
Other	4,209	3,863	3,943
Op. income	531	490	701
Net income	265	301	383
Capital exp.	671	428	300
Acquisitions	136	30	100
Current assets	5,790	6,162	6,150
Net P, P&E	5,567	5,277	4,920
LT debt	3,192	3,277	3,351
Equity	6,241	6,110	6,332
ROE	4.5%	4.9%	6.05%

Source: ADM Annual Reports.

Exhibit 22 **Cargill, Inc. financial highlights 1995–2001 ($ million), fiscal year ends 30 June**

	1995	1996	1997	1998	1999	2000	2001	2002
Sales	50,907	55,979	55,695	51,418	45,697	47,602	49,204	50,826
Net earnings	671	902	814	468	597	480	358	827
Current assets	13,951	14,991	16,500	19,930	16,356	15,355	17,473	18,779
Property and other assets	5,359	6,022	6,921	7,139	8,221	8,813	9,330	10,708
Total assets	19,310	21,013	23,421	27,069	24,577	24,168	26,803	29,487
Current liabilities	11,258	11,908	12,800	15,507	12,272	11,377	13,464	14,346
Net worth	5,174	5,942	6,592	6,836	7,165	7,461	7,524	8,143

Source: adapted from data at Cargill website, http://www.cargill.com/finance/highlights.htm accessed 9 September 2002.

IKEA'S GLOBAL SOURCING CHALLENGE: INDIAN RUGS AND CHILD LABOUR

Christopher A. Bartlett, Vincent Dessain and Anders Sjöman

In May 1995, Marianne Barner faced a tough decision. After just two years with IKEA, the world's largest furniture retailer, and just two months into her new job as business area manager for carpets, she was faced with a decision of cutting off one of the company's major suppliers of Indian rugs. While such a move would disrupt supply and affect sales, she found the reasons to do so quite compelling. A German TV station had just broadcast an investigative report naming the supplier as one that used child labour in the production of rugs made for IKEA. What frustrated Barner was that, like all other IKEA suppliers, this large, well-regarded company had recently signed an addendum to its supply contract explicitly forbidding the use of child labour on pain of termination.

Even more difficult than this short-term decision was the long-term action Barner knew IKEA must take on this issue. On one hand, she was being urged to sign up to an industry-wide response to growing concerns about the use of child labour in the Indian carpet industry. A recently formed partnership of manufacturers, importers, retailers, and Indian NGOs was proposing to issue and monitor the use of 'Rugmark', a label to be put on carpets certifying that they were made without child labour. Simultaneously, Barner had been having conversations with people at the Swedish Save the Children organisation who were urging IKEA to ensure that its response to the situation was 'in the best interest of the child' – whatever that might imply. Finally, there were some who wondered if IKEA should not just leave this hornet's nest. Indian rugs accounted for a tiny part of IKEA's turnover, and to these observers, the time, cost and reputation risk posed by continuing this product line seemed not to be worth the profit potential.

The birth and maturing of a global company[1]

To understand IKEA's operations, one had to understand the philosophy and beliefs of its seventy-year old founder, Ingvar Kamprad. Despite stepping down as CEO in 1986, almost a decade later, Kamprad retained the title of honorary chairman and was still very involved in the company's activities. Yet, perhaps even more powerful than his ongoing presence were his strongly held values and beliefs that long ago had been deeply embedded in IKEA's culture.

Source: Professor Christopher A. Bartlett, Executive Director of the HBS Europe Research Center, Vincent Dessain and Research Associate Anders Sjöman prepared this case. Some supplier names and company information has been disguised for confidentiality. HBS cases are developed solely as the basis for class discussion. Cases are not intended to serve as endorsements, sources of primary data, or illustrations of effective or ineffective management. Copyright © 2006 President and Fellows of Harvard College. Reproduced with permission.

Kamprad was 17 years old when he started the mail-order company he called IKEA, a name that combined his initials with those of his family farm, Elmtaryd, and parish, Agunnaryd, located in the forests of southern Sweden. Working out of the family kitchen, he sold goods such as fountain pens, cigarette lighters and binders which he purchased from low-priced sources and then advertised in a newsletter to local shopkeepers. When Kamprad matched his competitors by adding furniture to his newsletter in 1948, the immediate success of the new line led him to give up the small items.

In 1951, to reduce product returns, he opened a display store in nearby Älmhult village to allow customers to inspect products before buying. It was an immediate success, with customers travelling seven hours from the capital Stockholm by train to visit. Based on the store's success, IKEA stopped accepting mail orders. Later Kamprad reflected,

> 'The basis of the modern IKEA concept was created [at this time] and in principle it still applies. First and foremost, we use a catalogue to tempt people to visit an exhibition, which today is our store. [. . .] Then, catalogue in hand, customers can see simple interiors for themselves, touch the furniture they want to buy and then write out an order [. . .]'[2]

As Kamprad developed and refined his furniture retailing business model he became increasingly frustrated with the way a tightly-knit cartel of furniture manufacturers controlled the Swedish industry to keep prices high. He began to view the situation not just as a business opportunity but also as an unacceptable social problem that he wanted to correct. Foreshadowing a vision for IKEA that would later be articulated as 'creating a better life for the many people', he wrote:

> 'A disproportionately large part of all resources is used to satisfy a small part of the population. [. . .] IKEA's aim is to change this situation. We shall offer a wide range of home furnishing items of good design and function at prices so low that the majority of people can afford to buy them. [. . .] We have great ambitions.'[3]

The small newsletter soon expanded into a full catalogue. The 1953 issue introduced what would become another key IKEA feature: self-assembled furniture. Instead of buying complete pieces of furniture, customers bought them in flat packages and put them together themselves at home. Soon, the 'knock-down' concept was fully systemised, saving transport and storage costs. In typical fashion, Kamprad turned the savings into still lower prices for his customers, gaining an even larger following among young post-war householders looking for well designed but inexpensive furniture. Between 1953 and 1955, the company's sales doubled from SEK 3 million to SEK 6 million.[4]

Managing suppliers: developing sourcing principles

As its sales took off in the late 1950s, IKEA's radical new concepts began to encounter stiff opposition from Sweden's large furniture retailers. So threatened were they that when IKEA began exhibiting at trade fairs, they colluded to stop the company from taking orders at the fairs, and eventually even from showing its prices. The cartel also pressured manufacturers not to sell to IKEA, and the few that continued to do so often made their deliveries at night in unmarked vans.

Unable to meet demand with such constrained local supply, Kamprad was forced to look abroad for new sources. In 1961, he contracted with several furniture factories in Poland, a country still in the Communist eastern bloc. To assure quality output and reliable delivery, IKEA brought its know-how, taught its processes, and even provided machinery to the new suppliers, revitalising Poland's furniture industry as it did so. Poland soon became IKEA's largest source and, to Kamprad's delight, at much lower costs – once again allowing him to reduce his prices.

Following its success in Poland, IKEA adopted a general procurement principle that it should not own its means of production but should seek to develop close ties by supporting its suppliers in a long-term relationship.[5] Beyond supply contracts and technology transfer, the relationship led IKEA to make loans to its suppliers at reasonable rates, repayable through future shipments. 'Our objective is to develop long-term business partners', explained a senior purchasing manager. 'We commit to doing all we can to keep them competitive – as long as they remain equally committed to us. We are in this for the long run.'

Although the relationship between IKEA and its suppliers was often described as one of mutual dependency, suppliers also knew that they had to remain competitive to keep their contract. From the outset they understood that if a more cost-effective alternative appeared, IKEA would try to help them respond, but if they could not do so, it would move production.

In its constant quest to lower prices, the company developed an unusual way of identifying new sources. As a veteran IKEA manager explained: 'We do not buy products from our suppliers. We buy unused production capacity.' It was a philosophy that often led its purchasing managers to seek out seasonal manufacturers with spare off-season capacity. There were many classic examples of how IKEA matched products to supplier capabilities: they had sail makers make seat cushions, window factories produce table frames, and ski manufacturers build chairs in their off-season. 'We've always worried more about finding the right management at our suppliers than finding hi-tech facilities. We will always help good management to develop their capacity.'

Growing retail: expanding abroad

Building on the success of his first store, Kamprad self-financed a store in Stockholm in 1965. Recognising a growing use of autombiles in Sweden, he bucked the practice of having a downtown showroom and opted for a suburban location with ample parking space. When customers drove home with their furniture in flat packed boxes, they assumed two of the costliest parts of traditional furniture retailing – home delivery and assembly.

In 1963, even before the Stockholm store had opened, IKEA had expanded into Oslo, Norway. A decade later, Switzerland became its first non-Scandinavian market, and in 1974 IKEA entered Germany which soon became its largest market (see Exhibit 1 for IKEA's worldwide expansion). At each new store the same simple Scandinavian-design products were backed up with a catalogue and off-beat advertising, presenting the company as 'those impossible Swedes with strange ideas'. And reflecting the company's conservative values, each new entry was financed by previous successes.[6]

During this expansion, the IKEA concept evolved and became increasingly formalised. (Exhibit 2 summarises important events in IKEA's corporate history.) It still built large, suburban stores with knock-down furniture in flat packages which the customers brought home to assemble themselves. But as the concept was refined, the company required that each store followed a pre-determined design, set up to maximise customers' exposure to the product range. The concept mandated for instance that the living room interiors should follow immediately after the entrance. IKEA also serviced customers with features such as a play room for children, a low-priced restaurant, and a 'Sweden Shop' for groceries that had made IKEA Sweden's leading food exporter. At the same time, the range gradually expanded beyond furniture to include a full line of home furnishing products such as textiles, kitchen utensils, flooring, rugs and carpets, lamps and plants.

The emerging culture and values[7]

As Kamprad's evolving business philosophy was formalised into the IKEA vision statement, *'to create a better everyday life for the many people'*, it became the foundation of the company's strategy of selling affordable, good quality furniture to mass market consumers around the world. The cultural norms and values that developed to support the strategy's implementation was also, in many ways, an extension of Kamprad's personal beliefs and style. *'The true IKEA spirit'*, he remarked, *'is founded on our enthusiasm, our constant will to renew, on our cost-consciousness, on our willingness to assume responsibility and to help, on our humbleness before the task, and on the simplicity of our behaviour.'* As well as a summary of his aspiration for the company's behavioural norms, it was also a good statement of Kamprad's own personal management style.

Over the years a very distinct organisation culture and management style emerged in IKEA reflecting these values. For example, the company operated very informally as evidenced by the open-plan office landscape, where even the CEO did not have a separate office, and the familiar and personal way all employees addressed each other. But that informality often masked an intensity that derived from the organisation's high self-imposed standards. As one senior executive explained, *'Because there is no security available behind status or closed doors, this environment actually puts pressure on people to perform.'*

The IKEA management process also stressed simplicity and attention to detail. *'Complicated rules paralyse!'*, said Kamprad. The company organised 'anti-bureaucrat week' every year, requiring all managers to spend time working in a store to re-establish contact with the front line and the consumer. The work pace was such that executives joked that IKEA believed in 'management by running around'.

Cost consciousness was another strong part of the management culture. *'Waste of resources'*, said Kamprad, *'is a mortal sin at IKEA. Expensive solutions are often signs of mediocrity, and an idea without a price tag is never acceptable.'* Although cost consciousness extended into all aspects of the operation, travel and entertainment expenses were particularly sensitive. *'We do not set any price on time'*, remarked an executive, recalling that he had once phoned Kamprad to get approval to fly first class. He explained that economy class was full, and that he had an urgent appointment to keep. *'There is no first class in IKEA'*, Kamprad had replied. *'Perhaps you should go by car.'* The executive completed the 350-mile trip by taxi.

The search for creative solutions was also highly prized with IKEA. Kamprad had written, *'Only while sleeping one makes no mistakes. The fear of making mistakes is the root of bureaucracy and the enemy of all evolution.'* Though planning for the future was encouraged, over analysis was not. *'Exaggerated planning can be fatal,'* Kamprad advised his executives. *'Let simplicity and common sense characterise your planning.'*

In 1976, Kamprad felt the need to commit to paper the values that had developed in IKEA during the previous decades. His thesis, *Testament of a Furniture Dealer*, became an important means for spreading the IKEA philosophy particularly during its period of rapid international expansion. (Extracts of the *Testament* are given in Exhibit 3.) Specially trained 'IKEA ambassadors' were assigned to key positions in all units to spread the company's philosophy and values by educating their subordinates and by acting as role models.

In 1986, when Kamprad stepped down, Anders Moberg, a company veteran who had once been Kamprad's personal assistant, took over as President and CEO. But Kamprad remained intimately involved as chairman, and his influence extended well beyond the ongoing daily operations: he was the self-appointed guardian of IKEA's deeply embedded culture and values.

Waking up to environmental and social issues

By the mid-1990s, IKEA was the world's largest specialised furniture retailer. Sales for the IKEA Group for the financial year ending August 1994 totalled SEK 35 billion (about $4.5 billion). In the previous year, more than 116 million people had visited one of the 98 IKEA stores in 17 countries, most of them drawn there by the company's product catalogue which was printed yearly in 72 million copies in 34 languages. The privately held company did not report profit levels, but one estimate put its net margin at 8.4 per cent in 1994, yielding a net profit of SEK 2.9 billion (about $375 million).[8]

After decades of seeking new sources, in the mid-1990s IKEA worked with almost 2,300 suppliers in 70 countries, sourcing a range of around 11,200 products. Its relationship with its suppliers was dominated by commercial issues, and its 24 trading service offices in 19 countries primarily monitored production, tested new product ideas, negotiated prices, and checked quality. (See Exhibit 4 for selected IKEA figures in 1994.) That relationship began to change during the 1980s, however, when environmental problems emerged with some of its products. And it was even more severely challenged in the mid-1990s when accusations of IKEA suppliers using child labour surfaced.

The environmental wake-up: formaldehyde

In the early 1980s, Danish authorities passed regulations to define limits for formaldehyde emissions permissible in building products. The chemical compound was used as binding glue in materials such as plywood and particleboard, and often seeped out as gas. At concentrations above 0.1 mg/kg in air, it could cause watery eyes, headaches, a burning sensation in the throat and difficulty breathing.[9] With IKEA's profile as a leading local furniture retailer using particleboard in many of its products, it became a prime target for regulators wanting to publicise the new standards. So when tests showed that some IKEA products emitted more formaldehyde than was allowed by legislation, the case was widely publicised and the company was fined. More significantly – and the real lesson for IKEA – was that due to the publicity, its sales dropped 20 per cent in Denmark.

In response to this situation, the company quickly established stringent requirements regarding formaldehyde emissions, but soon found that suppliers were failing to meet its standards. The problem was that most of its suppliers bought from sub-suppliers, who in turn bought the binding materials from glue manufacturers.

Eventually, IKEA decided it would have to work directly with the glue producing chemical companies, and with the collaboration of companies such as ICI and BASF, soon found ways to reduce the formaldehyde off-gassing in its products.[10]

A decade later, however, the formaldehyde problem returned. In 1992, an investigative team from a large German newspaper and TV company found that IKEA's best-selling bookcase series, Billy, had emissions higher than German legislation allowed. This time however, the source of the problem was not the glue but the lacquer on the bookshelves. In the wake of headlines describing 'deadly poisoned bookshelves', IKEA immediately stopped both the production and sales of Billy bookcases worldwide and corrected the problem before resuming distribution. Not counting the cost of lost sales and production or the damage to goodwill, the Billy incident was estimated to have cost IKEA $6 to $7 million.[11]

These events prompted IKEA to address broader environmental concerns more directly. Since wood was the principal material in about half of all IKEA products, forestry became a natural starting point. Following discussions with both Greenpeace and WWF (formerly World Wildlife Fund, now World Wide Fund for Nature), and using standards set by the Forest Stewardship Council, IKEA established a forestry policy stating that IKEA would not accept any timber, veneer, plywood or layer-glued wood from intact natural forests or from forests with a high conservation value. This meant that IKEA had to be willing to take on the task of tracing all wood used in IKEA products back to its source.[12] To monitor compliance, the company appointed forest managers to carry out random checks of wood suppliers and run projects on responsible forestry around the world.

In addition to forestry, IKEA identified four other areas where environmental criteria were to be applied to its business operations: adapting the product range; working with suppliers; transport and distribution; and ensuring environmentally conscious stores. For instance, in 1992, the company began using chlorine-free recycled paper in its catalogues; it redesigned the best-selling OGLA chair – originally manufactured from beech – so it could be made using waste material from yogurt cup production; and it redefined its packaging principles to eliminate any use of PVC. The company also maintained its partnership with WWF resulting in numerous projects on global conservation, and funded a Global Forest Watch programme to map intact natural forests worldwide. In addition, it engaged in an ongoing dialogue with Greenpeace on forestry.[13]

The social wake-up: child labour

In 1994, as IKEA was still working to resolve the formaldehyde problems, a Swedish television documentary showed children in Pakistan working at weaving looms. Among the several Swedish companies mentioned in the film as importers of carpets from Pakistan, IKEA was the only high-profile name on the list. As IKEA's newly appointed business area manager for carpets, Marianne Barner recalled the shockwaves that the TV programme sent through the company:

'The use of child labour was not a high-profile public issue at the time. In fact, the UN Convention on the Rights of the Child had only been published in December, 1989. So, media attention like this TV programme had an important role to play in raising awareness on a topic not well known and understood – including at IKEA ... We were caught completely unaware. It was not something we had been paying attention to. For example,

I had spent a couple of months in India learning about trading, but got no exposure to child labour. Our buyers met suppliers in their city offices and rarely got out to where production took place . . . Our immediate response to the programme was to apologise for our ignorance and acknowledge that we were not in full control of this problem. But we also committed to do something about it.'

As part of its response, IKEA sent a legal team to Geneva to seek input and advice from the International Labour Organization (ILO) on how to deal with the problem. They learned that Convention 138, adopted by the ILO in 1973 and ratified by 120 countries, committed ratifying countries to working for the abolition of labour by children under 15 or the age of compulsory schooling in that country. India, Pakistan and Nepal were not signatories to the convention.[14] Following these discussions with the ILO, IKEA added a clause to all supply contracts – a 'black-and-white' clause as Barner put it – stating simply that if the supplier employed children under legal working age, the contract would be cancelled.

To take the load off field trading managers and to provide some independence to the monitoring process, the company appointed a third party agent to monitor child labour practices at its suppliers in India and Pakistan. Because this type of external monitoring was very unusual, IKEA had some difficulty locating a reputable and competent company to perform the task. Finally, it appointed a well-known Scandinavian company with extensive experience in providing external monitoring of companies' quality assurance programmes, and gave it the mandate not only to investigate complaints but also to undertake random audits of child labour practices at suppliers' factories.

Early lessons: a deeply embedded problem

With India being the biggest purchasing source for carpets and rugs, Barner contacted Swedish Save the Children, UNICEF and the ILO to expand her understanding and to get advice about the issue of child labour, especially in South Asia. She soon found that hard data was often elusive. While estimates of child labour in India varied from the government's 1991 census figure of 11.3 million children under 15 working[15] to Human Rights Watch's estimate of between 60 and 115 million child labourers,[16] it was clear that a very large number of Indian children as young as five years old worked in agriculture, mining, quarrying and manufacturing, as well as acting as household servants, street vendors or beggars. Of this total, an estimated 200,000 were employed in the carpet industry, working on looms in large factories, small subcontractors, and in homes where whole families worked on looms to earn extra income.[17]

Children could be bonded – essentially placed in servitude – in order to pay off debts incurred by their parents, typically in the range of 1,000 to 10,000 rupees ($30 to $300). But due to the astronomical interest rates and the very low wages offered to children, it could take years to pay off such loans. Indeed, some indentured child labourers eventually passed on the debt to their own children. The Indian government stated that it was committed to the abolition of bonded labour which had been illegal since the Children (Pledging of Labour) Act passed under British rule in 1933. The practice continued to be widespread, however, and to reinforce the earlier law, the government passed the Bonded Labour System (Abolition) Act in 1976.[18]

But the government took a less absolute stand on unbonded child labour which it characterised as *'a socio-economic phenomenon arising out of poverty and the lack of development'*. The Child Labour (Prohibition and Regulation) Act of 1986 prohibited the use of child labour (applying to those under 14) in certain defined 'hazardous industries', and regulated children's hours and working conditions in others. But the government felt that the majority of child labour involved *'children working alongside and under the supervision of their parents'* in agriculture, cottage industries and service roles. Indeed, the law specifically permitted children to work in craft industries *'in order not to outlaw the passage of specialised handicraft skills from generation to generation'*.[19] Critics charged that even with these laws on the books, exploitative child labour – including bonded labour – was widespread because laws were poorly enforced and prosecution rarely severe.[20]

Action required: new issues, new options

In the autumn of 1994, after managing the initial response to the crisis, Barner and her direct manager travelled to India, Nepal and Pakistan to learn more. Barner recalled the trip:

'We felt the need to educate ourselves, so we met with our suppliers. But we also met with unions, politicians, activists, NGOs, UN organisations and carpet export organisations. We even went out on unannounced carpet-factory raids with local NGOs; we saw child labour and we were thrown out of some places.'

On the trip, Barner also learned of the formation of the Rugmark Foundation, a recently initiated industry response to the child labour problem in the Indian carpet industry. Triggered by a consumer awareness programme started by human rights organisations, consumer activists and trade unions in Germany in the early 1990s, the Indo-German Export Promotion Council had joined up with key Indian carpet manufacturers and exporters and some Indian NGOs to develop a label certifying that the hand-knotted carpets to which it was attached was made without the use of child labour. To implement this idea, the Rugmark Foundation was organised to supervise the use of the label. It expected to begin exporting rugs carrying a unique identifying number in early 1995. As a major purchaser of Indian rugs, IKEA was invited to sign up to Rugmark as a way of dealing with the ongoing potential for child labour problems on products sourced from India.

On her return to Sweden, Barner again met frequently with Swedish Save the Children's expert on child labour. *'The people there had a very forward looking view on the issue, and taught us a lot'*, said Barner. *'Above all, they emphasised the need to ensure you always do what is in the best interests of the child.'* This was the principle set at the heart of the UN Convention on the Rights of the Child (1989), a document with which Barner was now quite familiar (see Exhibit 5 for Article 32 from the UN Conventions on the Right of the Child).

The more Barner learned the more complex the situation became. As a business area manager with full P&L responsibility for carpets, she knew she had to protect not only her business, but also the IKEA brand and image. Yet, she viewed her responsibility as broader than this: she felt the company should do something that would make a difference in the lives of the children she had seen. It was a view that was not universally held within IKEA where many were concerned that a very proactive stand could put the business at a significant cost disadvantage to its competitors.

A new crisis

Then, in the spring of 1995, a year after IKEA began to address this issue, a well-known German documentary maker notified the company that a film he had made was about to be broadcast on German television showing children working at looms at Rangan Exports, one of IKEA's major suppliers. While refusing to let the company preview the video, the film maker produced still shots taken directly from the video. The producer then invited IKEA to send someone to take part in a live discussion during the airing of the programme. Said Barner, *'Compared to the Swedish programme which documented the use of child labour in Pakistan as a serious report about an important issue, without targeting any single company, it was immediately clear that this German-produced programme planned to take a confrontational and aggressive approach aimed directly at IKEA and one of its suppliers.'*

For Barner, the first question was whether to recommend that IKEA participate in the programme, or decline the invitation. Beyond the immediate public relations issue, she also had to decide how to deal with Rangan Exports' apparent violation of the contractual commitment it had made not to use child labour. And finally, this crisis raised the issue of whether the overall approach IKEA had been taking to the issue of child labour was appropriate. Should the company continue to try to deal with the issue through its own relationships with its suppliers? Should it step back and allow Rugmark to monitor the use of child labour on its behalf? Or should it recognise that the problem was too deeply embedded in the culture of these countries for it to have any real impact, and simply withdraw?

Notes on the case study

1 This section draws on company histories detailed in Torekull, Bertil (1998) *Leading by Design – The IKEA Story*. New York: Harper Business, and on the IKEA web site, available at http://www.ikea.com/ms/en_GB/about_ikea/splash.html, accessed 5 October 2005.

2 Ingvar Kamprad, as quoted in Torekull, B. (1998), ibid., p. 25.

3 Quoted in Bartlett, Christopher A. and Nanda, Ashish (1990) 'Ingvar Kamprad and IKEA', *HBS*, No. 390–132 (Boston: Harvard Business School Publishing).

4 Ibid.

5 This policy was modified after a number of eastern European suppliers broke their contracts with IKEA after the fall of the Berlin wall opened new markets for them. IKEA's subsequent supply chain problems and the loss of substantial investments led management to develop an internal production company, Swedwood, to ensure delivery stability. However, it was decided that only a limited amount of IKEA's purchases (perhaps 10 per cent) should be sourced from Swedwood.

6 By 2005, company lore had it that IKEA had only taken one bank loan in its corporate history – which it had paid back as soon as the cash flow allowed.

7 This section draws on Bartlett, C.A. and Nanda, A. (1990), op. cit.

8 Estimation in Pettersson, Bo (2004) 'Hans släpper aldrig taget', *Veckans Affärer*, 1 March, pp. 30–48.

9 Description of formaldehyde based on 'Formaldehyde' entry on public encyclopaedia Wikipedia, available at http://en.wikipedia.org/wiki/Formaldehyde, accessed 5 October, 2005.

10 Based on case study by The Natural Step, 'Organizational Case Summary: IKEA', available at http://www.naturalstep.org/learn/docs/cs/case_ikea.pdf, accessed 5 October 2005.

11 Ibid.

12 *IKEA – Social and Environmental Responsibility Report 2004*, p. 33, available at http://www.ikea-group.ikea.com/corporate/PDF/IKEA_SaER.pdf, accessed 5 October 2005.

13 Ibid., pp. 19–20.

14 Ratification statistics available on ILO web site, page entitled 'Convention No. C138 was ratified by 142 countries', available at http://www.ilo.org/ilolex/cgi-lex/ratifce.pl?C138, accessed 4 December 2005.

15 Indian government policy statements, 'Child Labor and India', available at http://www.indianembassy.org/policy/Child_Labor/childlabor_2000.htm, accessed 1 October 2005.

16 Human Rights Watch figures, available at http://www.hrw.org/reports/1996/India3.htm, accessed 1 October 2005.

17 US State Department (2000) *Country Reports in Human Rights*, February, available at http://www.state.gov/g/drl/rls/hrrpt/2000/, accessed 1 October 2005.

18 Indian government policy statements, op. cit.

19 Ibid.

20 Human Rights Watch data, op. cit.

Exhibit 1 IKEA stores, fiscal year ending August 1994

a. Historical store growth

	1954	1964	1974	1984	1994
Number of stores	0	2	9	52	114

b. Country's first store

Year	First store (with city) Country	City
1958	Sweden	Älmhult
1963	Norway	Oslo
1969	Denmark	Copenhagen
1973	Switzerland	Zürich
1974	Germany	Munich
1975	Australia	Artamon
1976	Canada	Vancouver
1977	Austria	Vienna
1978	Netherlands	Rotterdam
1978	Singapore	Singapore
1980	Spain	Gran Canaria
1981	Iceland	Reykjavik
1981	France	Paris
1983	Saudi Arabia	Jeddah
1984	Belgium	Brussels
1984	Kuwait	Kuwait City
1985	United States	Philadelphia
1987	United Kingdom	Manchester
1988	Hong Kong	Hong Kong
1989	Italy	Milan
1990	Hungary	Budapest
1991	Poland	Platan
1991	Czech Republic	Prague
1991	United Arab Emirates	Dubai
1992	Slovakia	Bratislava
1994	Taiwan	Taipei

Source: IKEA web site, http://franchisor.ikea.com/txtfacts.html, accessed 15 October 2004.

Exhibit 2 IKEA history: selected events

Year	Event
1943	IKEA is founded. Ingvar Kamprad constructs the company name from his initials (**I**ngvar **K**amprad), his home farm (**E**lmtaryd), and its parish (**A**gunnaryd)
1945	The first IKEA ad appears in press, advertising mail order products
1948	Furniture is introduced into the IKEA product range. Products are still only advertised through ads.
1951	The first IKEA catalogue is distributed
1955	IKEA starts to design its own furniture
1956	Self-assembly furniture in flat packs is introduced
1958	The first IKEA store opens in Älmhult, Sweden
1961	Contract with Polish sources, IKEA's first non-Scandinavian suppliers. First delivery is 20,000 chairs
1963	The first IKEA store outside Sweden opens in Norway
1965	IKEA opens in Stockholm, introducing the self-serve concept to furniture retailing
1965	IKEA stores add a section called the 'The Cook Shop', offering quality utensils at low prices
1973	The first IKEA store outside Scandinavia opens in Spreitenbach, Switzerland
1974	A plastic chair developed at a supplier that usually makes buckets
1978	The BILLY bookcase is introduced to the range, becoming an instant top seller
1980	One of IKEA's best-sellers, the KLIPPAN sofa with removable, washable covers, is introduced
1980	Introduction of LACK coffee table, made from a strong, light material by an interior door factory
1985	The first IKEA Group store opens in the USA
1985	MOMENT sofa with frame built by a supermarket trolley factory is introduced. Wins a design prize
1991	IKEA establishes its own industrial group, Swedwood

Source: adapted from *IKEA Facts and Figures,* 2003 and 2004 editions, and IKEA internal documents.

Exhibit 3 *'A Furniture Dealer's Testament'* – a summarised overview

In 1976, Ingvar Kamprad listed nine aspects of IKEA that he believed formed the basis of the IKEA culture together with the vision statement, *'To create a better everyday life for the many people'*. These aspects are given to all new employees a pamphlet entitled, *A Furniture Dealer's Testament*. The following table summarises the major points.

Cornerstone	Summarised description
1. The Product Range – Our Identity	IKEA sells well-designed, functional home furnishing products at prices so low that as many people as possible can afford them.
2. The IKEA Spirit – A Strong and Living Reality	IKEA is about enthusiasm, renewal, thrift, responsibility, humbleness toward the task and simplicity.
3. Profit Gives Us Resources	IKEA will achieve profit (which Kamprad describes as a 'wonderful word') through the lowest prices, good quality, economical development of products, improved purchasing processes and cost savings.
4. Reaching Good Results with Small Means	'Waste is a deadly sin.'
5. Simplicity is a Virtue	Complex regulations and exaggerated planning paralyse. IKEA people stay simple in style and habits as well as in their organisational approach.
6. Doing it a Different Way	IKEA is run from a small village in the woods. IKEA asks shirt factories to make seat cushions and window factories to make table frames. IKEA discounts its umbrellas when it rains. IKEA does things differently.
7. Concentration – Important to Our Success	'We can never do everything everywhere, all at the same time.' At IKEA, you choose the most important thing to do and finish that before starting a new project.
8. Taking Responsibility – A Privilege	'The fear of making mistakes is the root of bureaucracy.' Everyone has the right to make mistakes; in fact, everyone has obligation to make mistakes.
9. Most Things Still Remain to be Done. A Glorious Future!	IKEA is only at the beginning of what it might become. 200 stores is nothing. 'We are still a small company at heart.'

Source: adapted by case writers from: IKEA's, *A Furniture Dealer's Testament;* Torekull, Bertil (1998) *Leading by Design: The IKEA Story.* New York: Harper Business, p. 112; and own interviews.

Exhibit 4 IKEA in figures 1993/94 (fiscal year ending 31 August 1994)

a. Sales

Country/region	SEK billion	Percentage
Germany	10.4	29.70
Sweden	3.9	11.20
Austria, France, Italy, Switzerland	7.7	21.90
Belgium, Netherlands, United Kingdom, Norway	7.3	20.80
North America (USA and Canada)	4.9	13.90
Czech Republic, Hungary, Poland, Slovakia	0.5	1.50
Australia	0.4	1.00
	35.0	

b. Purchasing

Country/region	Percentage
Nordic countries	33.4
East and central Europe	14.3
Rest of Europe	29.6
Rest of the world	22.7

Source: IKEA Facts and Figures 1994.

Exhibit 5 The UN Convention on the Rights of the Child: Article 32

1. States Parties recognize the right of the child to be protected from economic exploitation and from performing any work that is likely to be hazardous or to interfere with the child's education, or to be harmful to the child's health or physical, mental, spiritual, moral, or social development.

2. States Parties shall take legislative, administrative, social, and educational measures to ensure the implementation of the present article. To this end, and having regard to the relevant provisions of other international instruments, States Parties shall in particular:

   (a) Provide for a minimum age for admission to employment.

   (b) Provide for appropriate regulation of hours and conditions of employment.

   (c) Provide for appropriate or other sanctions to ensure the effective enforcement of the present article.

Source: excerpt from 'Conventions on the Right of the Child', from the web site of the Office of the United Nations High Commissioner for Human Rights, available at http://www.unhchr.ch/html/menu3/b/k2crc.htm, accessed October 2005.

3 FROM RUSSIA WITH LOVE[1]

Peter William Stonebraker and Sergey Nicholaievich Polbitsyn

Part I – to America in trust

The low midday sun reflected across the frozen lake speckled with windblown snow that had covered Ekaterinburg the night before. To Nicholai Antonovich, Senior Vice-President for Manufacturing of Urals Machine Consortium (UMC), the whole of Siberia felt full of light and exuded a special warmth that only could be understood by one who had lived there many years. In two hours, the sun would set and darkness would quickly veil this land; then the only warmth would be in the brightly frosted windows and the hearts inside. 'Nature can be so deceptive', murmured Nicholai. 'But, then what to say about people?' He reflected on his recent visit to America and his growing friendship with Bill Stone, Director of Operations of American Mining Equipment Company (AME). However, other new forces were now apparent in the development of the Joint Agreement between their two companies.

Though it had taken several days since his return from Chicago to readjust to Russian time, it would take many months to fully digest the events of the one-week visit. This trip had been extremely important for UMC, as well as for Ekaterinburg. The recent economic turmoil in Russia had caused tremendous disruption and loss, in addition to personal privation. Managers of large and small enterprises that had been profitable and stable only a few short years ago now had to find a new niche and new buyers. Russian businesses could no longer sell to Uzbekistan or Poland. The Uzbeks could not pay and the Poles preferred to buy higher quality German goods. It would be hard to find the right decision.

Before the collapse of the Soviet Union, almost 20 years ago, there were no problems like this. Life was a comfortable mix of winter evenings with family and close friends, stable and full employment, summer vacations at southern resorts, and full faith in the premise that capitalism would ultimately be defeated. The main management task was to produce the required goods at the required time, which necessitated networking, as well as technical knowledge and decision making. Those skills were no longer required; now problems were mostly financial, caused by the rouble's decline. Barter and unpaid wages were widespread. Management and labour needed to work together as stockholders of former state-owned firms, on the verge of economic ruin.

Source: This case was written by Professor Peter William Stonebraker, Professor of Operations Management at Northeastern Illinois University, and Sergey Nicholaievich Polbitsyn, former Associate Dean of the Economics Faculty of Urals State Pedagogic University in Ekaterinburg (Svaerdlovsk), Russia, as a basis for classroom discussion with support from USIS and other organisations. It is part of the CIBER Case Collection, sponsored by the Indiana University Center for International Business Education and Research and distributed by the European Case Clearing House (ECCH) at Babson. Copyright © 2004 by Peter William Stonebraker and Sergey Nicholaievich Polbitsyn. Reproduced with permission.

The accounting books still showed a prosperous company. Orders were received, components and parts were produced and assembled goods were shipped to customers, and taxes were paid. But where was the cash? More than 50 per cent of the customers could not pay. *Neplatzhy*, it was called, the refusal or inability to pay bills. But the company must pay its bills, particularly to workers, because under privatisation, they were now shareholders of the company. Unpaid workers would not rebel, they could do worse. They could sell their shares to some *biznezman*. And there were many *biznezmen* in Ekaterinburg now, with government contacts and the ability to manipulate stock and acquire control of solid Russian businesses. But, if labour did sell their stock, they could lose everything. Thus, in many firms, a cautious, informal accord had developed between labour and management. With bitterness, Nicholai reflected over the irony that capitalist practices, initially proposed by Karl Marx but developed in the West, had brought much corruption to Siberia. He resolved not to let it happen at UMC. But the old guard bureaucracy did not understand that times were changing. For these reasons, his visit to Chicago, his friendship with Bill Stone, and the success of the Joint Agreement were very important.

He loved the expression that he learned from Bill. 'These are challenging times', they joked, but, as Nicholai reflected, the words had a different meaning in Chicago than in Ekaterinburg. Nicholai Antonovich clearly understood that UMC had to be rebuilt from the foundation up; everything must change. The first priority would be the corporate structure. He had to protect and train the workers, but at the same time eliminate management jobs and make the company truly profitable. Automation and information systems were top priorities, particularly in management of costly inventories, as were quality and investment in new equipment. It all had to be done, and with little money. He hoped that the Joint Agreement to exchange technology and work jointly in several global markets would provide the necessary currency and support, as well as the incentive for management to change. He had gone to America full of confidence that his company, with its long history and renowned name, could easily establish a mutually profitable joint operation with the American company.

Those had been the expectations. Next Monday, Nicholai Antonovich would present the results of his visit to the Board of General Directors. He took a clean sheet of paper and wrote the title: *Results of the Visit of the Representative of the Urals Machine Consortium to the American Mining Equipment Company*. He put down his pen on the desk, leaned back in his chair, and tried to build the chain of his impressions of his visit to Chicago.

This third visit to America was an important opportunity for Nicholai Antonovich to enhance the detail of his vision of the future for Russian manufacturing operations. He knew that the Russian craftsmen had technical skills to produce the best equipment in the world; their professional loyalty and dedication were also excellent, and their pay (roughly $80 per month) made UMC highly competitive in building labour-intensive products such as custom mining equipment. However, Nicholai also understood that they must learn something far more important. 'For 70 years we make work under communist economic model, and there's no our fault', Nicholai had told Bill. 'But trouble is we do no know work in market economy.'

Nicholai liked to compare Siberia and America. America was where the British king sent its prisoners. Then for years, people from Europe and other places moved to America, searching for opportunity. Siberia had the same destiny. The czars, then commissars, shipped prisoners to Siberia. Then people from Russia and other eastern

European countries moved to Siberia, looking for land and opportunity. Siberia proved rich in resources, such as oil, minerals and timber, and had become a land of opportunity and a melting pot. As he had told Bill, the biggest difference between Siberia and America was that Americans 'bought their freedom, and dearly, with blood', while Siberia would stay as part of Russia forever.

Nicholai Antonovich had taken to Chicago the accounting information, blueprints of floor plans, and copies of the *Urals Machine Consortium: 200 Glorious Years of Management by the People*, issued in 2002 on the company's 200th anniversary. He had tried to anticipate any question, and development. His fear was that the visit would be reduced to a tourist trip or perhaps the Americans would be suspicious that he just wanted to immigrate. But the stakes were too high to permit that.

He arrived in Chicago's O'Hare Airport at two in the afternoon after an exhausting journey. In Moscow he transferred from Domodedovo national airport, crossed the city by metro to Sheremetyevo international airport, and then took a twelve-hour flight to Chicago. He had flown economy class, thinking that business class would appear to his hosts to be a luxury.

The customs officer checked his passport and papers and surprised Nicholai by quickly returning them with an open smile. 'I wish good luck in business', he said in his emigrant Russian dialect. He was met by Bill Stone and the new interpreter, Masha, who had been hired to assist with the 'Russian Project'. Masha had come to Chicago from St Petersburg some 10 years earlier and thought that in 10 years she had become 110 per cent American. The huge limo ('longer than the drive track of our shovels', thought Nicholai) awaited them. Inside, Nicholai wanted to express greetings to Bill from many friends in Russia and ask about his visit agenda and other businesses matters, but Masha continued to chirrup about how lucky Nicholai was to be able to see America, and how it was too bad that he had had few opportunities to visit another country. In his broken English, Nicholai finally interjected that he had made two prior trips to America and been in China and Vietnam in the late sixties, although under another name. Bill, who had served there at the same time, quickly understood his friend's smirk and interrupted Masha, asking her to let their guest relax.

Bill handed Nicholai a packet that contained his agenda, some biographical information about senior executives, and some details about the company, all translated into Russian. Bill also gave Nicholai a very special, Russian-printed invitation to visit their house over the weekend. Masha grimaced as they lapsed into talk of events and friends in Ekaterinburg, Bill speaking in his broken Russian and Nicholai practising his newly learned English. They had learned from past visits that the greatest understanding occurred when they forced themselves to speak in the other person's language.

From the airport, the limo drove toward downtown. 'Why do we go this way?', Nicholai asked Bill. 'Your plant is north of Chicago, is it not?'

Masha jumped in, with pride in her voice, 'Oh, in America, top managers stay downtown; I reserved a suite for you on the seventieth floor with a full lake view.'

'This is something I could not even imagine', Nicholai said to himself.

'The welcome dinner is scheduled this evening at seven', continued Masha. 'It won't be late, and in the morning you can rest from your trip.'

'I have never before eaten dinner at five o'clock in the morning', Nicholai responded tersely, looking at his watch, which he had not yet changed to local time.

At 6:00, he was awakened from an all-too-brief nap by a telephone message that

Masha would pick him up in 30 minutes to take him to the welcome dinner. During the car ride Masha asked about his suite and how he liked the lake front view, and chirped breezily about various Chicago skyscrapers.

Nicholai felt that the dinner was really nice and relaxing. Bill introduced Nicholai to John Halbersen, an open Scandinavian and President of AME. Halbersen thanked Nicholai for coming to Chicago, then commented, with Masha translating, 'We understand you have come here with a strong wish to advance the Joint Agreement. We will work with you toward this goal; however, you must understand that we are business people. We do promise to be honest and truthful with you.'

'I really appreciate your openness', Bill heard Masha translate Nicholai's response. 'But, I want to suggest that if we try to make decisions as businessmen, there is a 90 per cent probability that the decisions will be wrong. We need to first establish our friendship and trust, and then discuss our joint strategy and the Joint Agreement, not at the plant level, but far above.'

In two hours, the dinner was over; they had agreed to meet the next morning and begin the detailed discussions. Bill gently chided Nicholai for the directness of his comments to the President, but Nicholai was too tired to understand.

The next morning, Masha took Nicholai to meet the Marketing Group. Though the translation process was slow, they asked many questions. Nicholai sometimes felt that he did not understand the meaning of the questions, and sometimes saw that his answers caused amazement. The Marketing Group members were not impressed with the history of his company or the extensive business ties in Europe and Central and South Asia. On several occasions, it appeared to Nicholai that the questions were hidden in excess and indirect verbiage, confusing to understand.

It was a relief when Bill and several of the senior people from the Marketing Group joined him for lunch. He found the American lunch to be more functional, and less formal and time-consuming than the Russian *obyed*. He started to ask questions of his hosts; he was interested in basics. What are the main tasks of the Marketing Group, how do they communicate with other departments, and what reports are made to senior executives? He also asked them how they survey markets and how they decide which markets to enter. Many Americans had never met a 'real' Russian, and certainly not a senior manager of one of their global competitors. The give and take was dynamic, often punctuated by misunderstandings and disagreements over language. But, as the afternoon wore on, the language skills of Bill and Nicholai were supplemented by translation, and clarity and understanding gradually emerged. That 'small lesson', as Bill called the lunch meeting, lasted all afternoon.

Similar meetings with accountants and production managers were scheduled for the next day. AME accountants were conservative and did not accept most of his information, which was based on Soviet bookkeeping. 'We do not see how you can make profits; we do not see how you can calculate costs', they said. And, Nicholai had to acknowledge, that was true. 'My dear friends', he finally responded, 'imagine situation in which you are selling a labour-intensive and customized product in distant markets requiring extensive transportation. Government agreements mandate that you to sell at 80 per cent of competitor's price to assure that you hold market share. ['Oh good', Nicholai said to himself. 'I now use business words that I learned yesterday. I wonder how that will translate.'] Labour costs are 5 per cent of the competition labour costs, and more than 50 per cent of transactions are based on barter, not open markets. Under those circumstances, how do you use accounting methods to calculate costs and profits of firm?'

After lunch ('I positively like sandwiches for lunch'), Nicholai met with the production team, Bill's area. Bill started with a short plant tour, where Nicholai, with permission, videotaped the extensive automation and material handling equipment. He then showed how functional managers in scheduling, inventory, purchasing, production planning and quality control retrieved information from the computer system and viewed the entire supply chain as an integrated decision. It was a very exact process, each data record was interdependent with other items of information; costs were reduced because there was no surplus or slack, and materials were sourced and controlled globally.

'Bill', Nicholai asked, 'tell me what happen if you get virus in net or if error data entered?'

Bill, along with his management, grinned understandingly. 'If we get a virus', Bill said, 'it would shut us down. Even if there is one error, possibly a model number of a customer order, then, it would be helpful to have Russian managers with your intuitive skills and long tenure to solve the problem. You see, Nicholai, though we have virus shields and daily backup tapes to protect us, reconstructing transactions is difficult and time-consuming. If we have to go manual, we lose control.'

After the plant tour, Nicholai met with the plant management team in a round table discussion. That meeting proved Bill's words. The management team could not understand how Russian managers could schedule work without computerised data bases, could control quality using mostly judgemental evaluation by worker and could anticipate and resolve problems intuitively. In his turn, Nicholai was amazed that American managers could trust their computer displays, without instinctively feeling the pulse of the plant. Nicholai was given example formats of forecasting, scheduling, inventory, quality control and human resource management computer printouts. During the meeting, several managers checked the PDAs to reschedule their afternoon activities, causing Nicholai to openly comment that few Russian mangers would need a PDA to remember their schedules for them. The discussions went late and were interrupted only when they had to leave for a scheduled meeting with John Halbersen.

In Halbersen's office, Nicholai discussed the final and most substantial part of his visit, the briefing of the Joint Agreement, scheduled for the following Monday afternoon. Masha spoke at length to Halbersen about the main issues that were discussed during the last four days. Halbersen did not ask Nicholai any questions, by paced the office. After a minute or so of silence, he finally said that for Monday's meeting, they would invite several more people.

'It will not be easy to adopt any decisions, and I want more input about the Joint Agreement from our staff', he said, with Masha dutifully translating. Nicholai was stunned; he had thought the Joint Agreement was fully accepted and that only a few details remained. He wanted to ask further questions of John Halbersen, but Bill's frown said: 'No.'

That evening, Nicholai joined Bill at his hone in the Chicago suburbs for dinner and the promised weekend. Eva Maria had prepared *kurnik* (Russian chicken) and *blinski* (potato pancakes). Toasts of white wine were exchanged and greetings and gifts were given from Nicholai's wife, Galena Ivanova. Katja, Bill's daughter, wore her broach of Urals gems and played a Tchaikovsky piano concerto; son Eric demonstrated a computer game. Bill translated awkwardly, yet the warmth of the evening and smiles of all said far more. Later that evening, the two friends sat in the cozy TV room in Bill's basement. While sipping Jack Daniels ('It really is not quite like Russian Vodka', thought Nicholai.), they discussed Nicholai's visit. Both were pleased to meet again, and both wished the Joint Agreement to succeed. At the same time, Bill was visibly bothered.

'You know, Nicholai, when I came back from Russia, I was excited about the Joint Agreement. However, some of our senior managers are not as enthusiastic. The Director of Finance, for example, can invest money in a plant in South America, in inventory, in new production technology, or in buying back some stock. Those options all give us rapid and easily calculated return, with little risk. In your case, we have no assurance that we can get back the capital, to say nothing about interest.'

'Wait!!! Wait!!! Whose ideas are those, Bill Louisovich? Yours or someone else? Where did this all come from? And why interpreter reports results of visit directly to President? Do you remember words of accountant, that Russian balance sheet not work in a country with market economy? Maybe she is right, but I know it works very well in my country. We find useful business information in balance sheets, and managers and employees, because of long experience, make right decision to grow productivity. Russian labour is among least expensive, most loyal and stable, and highest skilled in world. My English is no very good, but interpreter never said that, I would have heard.'

Bill recognised the seriousness of Nicholai's tone and that he had used the patronymic form of address (Louisovich – son of Louis), an expression of respect for the family. 'Kolya' (a nickname for Nicholai). 'Kolya, cool down. I understand that you are upset, but you must understand, the Joint Agreement will require long-term investments and we need to present it to the Board of Directors and to the stock-holders. It is easy for you because you only need to convince your twelve-person Board of General Directors, but we must explain our plans to thousands.'

'Not true, that is old Russia', interjected Nicholai. We just informally speak with each shareholder, often labourers or retirees. This is much difficult process than open stockholder meetings.'

'Okay, you got me there', Bill acknowledged. 'You know, Masha was recommended by Wes Sykes, our VP of Finance', stated Bill thoughtfully. 'Are you sure you are right about the mistranslations?'

Nicholai discussed with Bill each of the situations with the Present, the Marketing Group and the Accounting Section. Finally, Bill commented: 'Okay, I know an MBA student, Grisha, from the Russian Far East; I think that she knows enough about American business to help us on this.'

Nicholai spent all of Saturday and Sunday with Grisha as Bill looked on and offered occasional advice. As Nicholai explained the problems, together they prepared a detailed SWOT analysis of the Joint Agreement, and a comparable analysis of AME business both with and without the Joint Agreement. Grisha helped Nicholai to adapt to the American presentation style. They simplified arcane Russian accounting assumptions and emphasised the importance of the strong political and social support for the Joint Agreement.

Late Monday afternoon, Nicholai heaved a sigh of relief as he concluded the formal presentation. He could see that the AME managers, some 55 in total, were impressed, and Grisha's translation was understood by all. As he concluded the formal remarks, Nicholai spontaneously summarised his own vision of the problems that his company faced and opportunities for the future cooperation with AME. 'We Russians must rid ourselves of Iron Curtain in our minds', Nicholai noted. Then he added: 'I now see that Americans also have Iron Curtain. The question is: will we gradually develop a working relationship to destroy both curtains, better understanding each other and working for the long term joint benefit?'

President Halbersen was visibly moved. He joined the group in spontaneous applause, then stood to shake Nicholai's hand. 'Now I see the situation more clearly', he said. 'I see more opportunities than before. Your visit is of extreme importance to us. I am going to ask the Board to consider an initial 10–15 person staff exchange visit for several weeks, followed by a pilot integration project, and long-term technology training, exchanges and business integration. I am sure we can find a segment of business where our mutual interests are aligned.'

Before leaving Chicago, Nicholai spent a day with Grisha and Bill. They visited the Mercantile Exchange and Water Tower. Even in the cold winter, tourists were sightseeing, enjoying the 'warmth' of Chicago. And the whole day, they talked about Russia, about the changes in the country, in the economy, and in people's minds. They visited Marshal Fields to buy a sweater for Galena Ivanovna. The clerk showed them a beautiful discontinued item on sale, and then explained that she got a bonus for selling discontinued items. Nicholai was overwhelmed by such marketplace incentives.

The blast of the factory whistle caused Nicholai to bolt. He placed several reports and folders, and the *Results of the Visit . . .* pages, in his satchel. He would have to do his own analysis of how to sell the Board of General Directors and then how to communicate with the stockholders on the visit and on the necessity of the changes that it would bring. What models could he use? ('On, American management again.') Or should he communicate just his impressions and feelings? 'How do you explain the importance of capitalism to people who have known only socialism and planning', he mused, 'and who see little direct and immediate benefit (either personal or corporate) to change?'

Part II – from Russia with love

Bill Stone sank heavily into his stuffed chair and gazed absently out the corner window to the grey Chicago winterscape. It had been a tough day; implementation of the new supply chain software had gone smoothly, but there were problems with the team-building training. And, he was still recovering from the trip to Ekaterinburg. The eleven-hour time difference, the extreme Siberian cold, and the never-ending social schedule had taken their toll. Yet, the Joint Agreement between the American Mining Equipment Company (AME) and the Urals Machine Consortium (UMC) now seemed workable. Nicholai's report to the UMC Board of General Directors had been approved. Both companies were major international manufacturers of mining equipment, such as steam shovels and ore trucks. As AME's recently appointed Director of Operations, it was Bill's job to make the Joint Agreement work.

Bill routinely thumbed through his inbox and mail, and then turned to his laptop, where an icon in the corner announced the receipt of a new e-mail:

Dear Bill

Hope return travel to Chicago was good and not tired, and you have now time to discuss our meetings and situation with Joint Agreement. We so pleasured your visit us and thanks for all assistants. Much we have done since you leave. Heavy shovel assembly committee meet and discuss plans for revised schedule and Director was discussed with Region Planning Committee needs for more planning in manufacturing and safety of stamping machines. We thank to you for wonderful friendship; Galena Ivanovna sends best greetings to Eva Maria.

Most sincerely
Nicholai Antonovich

Bill's thoughts wandered through the cold evening mist to Ekaterinburg, almost half a world away, in the Ural Mountains, gateway to Siberian resources. In Soviet times, Ekaterinburg was called Sverdlovsk; now it was the third largest city in the Russian Federation. For many years during the cold war, Ekaterinburg, was a closed city due to military and defence industries there. Foreigners could not enter and residents could not leave without authorisation. In the 1960s, Gary Powers, the American U-2 spy pilot, had been shot down near there. Even today, many plants are known only by numbers or codes assigned to conceal their identity and the nature of the production.

Nicholai Antonovich and Galena Ivanovna (Russian middle names often reflectd the father's name or patronymic – son of Anton, daughter of Ivan) had been wonderful hosts during the seven-day visit. There were performances of the opera and symphony, both among the best in Russia, and visits to family homes. Bill was given the position of honour on the sofa at the cramped family dinner table and entertained with violin recitals by children and slide presentations of vacation camping trips to the Black Sea. Nicholai had toasted the great opening of Russia to the West since Peter the Great and a lasting reduction of Russian xenophobia.

But the days had been all business. Breakfasts of strong powdered coffee, rolls, cheese, and sausage were hosted by the Director General of UMC, Vladimir Vasiliovich Fyodorov, and attended by Deputy directors and staff members. Conversations started with polite enquiries about family and accommodations, but quickly focused toward specific topics of the Joint Agreement, such as product mix or the schedule of technology transfers. *Obyed*, or dinner, in the middle of the day, was more formal; silver chafing dishes and four or five courses, starting with soup and rich dark water bread, then salad, an entree with vegetables and potatoes, and desert, followed by liqueur. Chocolate and local beer were ubiquitous and coffee was served from an ornate procelain samovar.

Mornings and afternoons involved plant tours and meetings with staff and committee groups, government officials, and private bankers. At one such meeting, the Governor of Sverdlovsk *oblast* (roughly equivalent of a US state) gave Bill strong assurances that the Joint Agreement would be supported by both regional and national governments. Bill's attempt to speak Russian had helped and his language, though often ungrammatical, was understood and appreciated by all; however, business discussions moved laboriously through Irena and Natasha, who took turns translating. Words and meanings were repeated and clarified; often a one-word translation for a term was not available. Thus, terms were described, but there was no way to effectively communicate specific concepts, such as material requirements planning or supply chain integration, for which there was no corresponding notion in Russian. Though the Joint Agreement had been signed, as Bill looked deeper into the details, he saw some inconsistencies and felt there might be further misunderstandings. John Halbersen, AME's President, would certainly want him to address these issues next Thursday at the Monthly Planning Update Conference.

The Joint Agreement was clear: AMC and UMC had agreed to a ten-year programme of joint development consisting of several phases. The first phase would involve visits and exchanges of mid-level managers and staff focused toward training and the general integration of planning processes. This would lead to a second phase involving standardisation of information reporting and decision-making processes in specific areas, including inventory, quality measurement and production design. The third phase, manufacture of specific parts and components at disparate facilities for shipment to customers and on-site assembly anywhere in the world, was the ultimate goal of the Joint Agreement.

This market segmentation and cooperation offered competitive advantages to both companies, particularly over Asian competitors. Specialisation and focus would reduce costs and improve efficiencies. Additionally, integrated scheduling of their complementary, roughly two-year order-lead-time products would stabilise schedules at each company. However, Bill had seen little indication of strategic planning or use of long-, mid- and short-range business forecasting by his Russian counterparts; he was also concerned that Joint Agreement deliveries might be slowed if UMC's non-agreement business received a higher priority.

His Russian colleagues had confirmed, and reconfirmed, their commitment to the Joint Agreement; they apologised for the turbulence of the government regulatory environment, the financial environment, and their consequent inability to plan and forecast accurately. In fact, they had described examples of vacillating taxation, environmental, and safety policies. Two years previously, for example, a 100 per cent tax increase, based on product value, had been levied on all facilities that generated even low levels of sulphur emissions. As exports, products within the Joint Agreement were exempted, but other UMC production was not. It took six months of lobbying and numerous defaults and bankruptcies to convince the government to change the tax. One day, a letter was received from the Central Economic Commission, stating that the tax had been cancelled and the Minister for Environmental Affairs had been fired.

Conversations with Derwin Karsten, the Shop Manager at Factory 14 and UMC employee for 60 years, had also given Bill a much deeper appreciation of the strength of character of Russian labour. Derwin described his employment by the firm at age ten and the movement of the plant from Leningrad (now St Petersburg) in 1941, just before the Nazi army blockaded the city. He depicted, often with a sneer, his many experiences with the Soviet central planning system. He described rail cars, with bills of lading showing full loads of production, that, in fact, were shipped empty, and commissioners who minimised production plans so they could easily make their personal quotas.

Yet, when asked about the future of Russian manufacturing, Derwin smiled broadly with a toothless grin: 'Now that ... the future, it be good. But, we have many work to do, so we get rapidly started. Problem is . . . worker know how to work, but manager only understand how work under . . . strict plan.' Derwin grinned, 'But, Russian worker with help of friends and comrades do anything. Russian worker know how to team and work for social good of all.'

There were other problems. Orders were produced when management knew that there were no buyers, and other orders were cancelled due to lack of parts or the purchaser's inability to pay. The rouble had inflated by 50 per cent in the past year, and by 600 per cent in the prior year. Bill again reviewed several translations of the long-range forecasts provided by UMC. Valerie Borisovich Larionov, Chief of Economic Planning, had used the quarterly and annual historical data, with the simple moving average and seasonal forecasting methods. Mechanically, the forecasting projections were correctly calculated, but the high error rates bothered Bill. Of course, forecasting with small unit values was always difficult, but, with that much error, why bother to forecast? Without a good forecast, strategic planning was tough and there was little indication that the forecasting was more than a mathematical exercise. He remained concerned with what appeared to be a general disregard for integrated planning, forecasting, and scheduling, starting at the long term, then disaggregating to execution.

The plant tours were extremely interesting. Ivan Alexandrovich Okhrimyenko, Chief Deputy Engineer, explained production flows and equipment needs. Most of the equipment was older; a few lathes were American, dating from the Lend-Lease Programme in the 1930s. Plant equipment, however, was clean and well maintained. Some European, computer-controlled equipment supplemented the general-purpose equipment, and workers proudly demonstrated skills with either technology; however, several expressed the need for state-of-the-art computer-assisted-manufacturing equipment. In fact, Bill saw little indication of system automation during his entire visit. Bar codes were not used and data capture, when done, was manual. Such activities as scheduling, inventory mangaement, and forecasting were done manually by a part-time university economics professor. Some materials, particularly case hardened steel, were held in excess of expected needs, while other materials, usually rubber and plastic parts, were expedited on a weekly basis. Shortages in numerous commodities had resulted in the development of a secondary dealer-to-dealer market.

Replacement and spare parts had been designed and manufactured locally. Bill visited the facilities of a subcontractor that provided aluminum castings for various motor and gear parts. The facility, about eight kilometres from the UMC plant, consisted of a roughly 40,000 square foot metal building. Ten to fifty-gallon cauldrons were used to melt the minerals in a semi-enclosed coal furnace. Test chemicals assured the correct composition for alloys, and molten metal was then scooped in hand-held dippers and poured into formed depressions in a 'sand box' on the floor. As the metal cooled, a wooden or metal 'cap' was used to mould the upper side of the part. Finished parts were then lathed, ground or milled to tolerance, and the scrap recycled. During that visit, Nicholai had noted with pride that several weeks previously, because the phone system was out, a manager had taken the tramway, then walked to the plant to deliver an urgent message for expedited parts delivery. The plant had worked for three days straight, and the job had been delivered on time.

Quality control was the workers' responsibility, but parts were designed to tolerate high variances, which made quality control less of a problem. Engines required run-in times of 20 hours or more, and as Ivan Alexandrovich explained: 'if it will run for 20 hours, it's good for life'. Bill had also attended several training sessions in statistical process control given by the university professor, but he heard employees complain that the equipment would not hold desired settings.

The production process was labour intensive. In fact, it was very costly to fire workers, Nicholai Antonovich explained, because the company would have to contribute six months' salary to the workers' unemployment compensation. Thus, many cash-strapped companies, including UMC, had resorted to under-paying workers, skipping monthly cheques or paying in bartered goods or food. Even so, UMC was supportive of its labour force, which averaged 22 years with the company. Though many executives openly expressed a need for improved technology and training, most clearly affirmed that technology improvements would not cause workforce reductions.

Safety appeared to be a more immediate problem. Bill noted the presence of high noise levels and lack of hearing protection in the engine testing room and near several of the stamping operations. Also, most equipment did not have hand or foot safety guards. For example, Bill watched as a woman placed metal plates in a stamping machine, and with a foot trigger, released the stamp. As the machine recovered, she pulled the stamped part out with her fingers. He asked Ivan Alexandrovich what protected the the woman's fingers; Ivan's response was to tap his finger against the side of his head and say: 'This'. With the exception of some computer skills, the labour force demonstrated high levels of discipline and training. Since UMC was a former state-owned business, the average monthly pay of $80 was higher than most businesses in the area. Nevertheless, to live comfortably all adult family members must work. The UMC cafeteria provided free employee meals, and the company offered a relatively generous retirement plan. However, with inflation, the stipend was of little value.

The distribution centre through which UMC received parts and shipped their partially assembled equipment was on the trans-Siberian rail line, connected to the plant by a spur. Storage sheds contained unmarked cartons on pallets that were moved by handcarts and a sporadically functioning forklift. Gantry cranes lifted heavier assemblies on rail cars that were picked up by the daily Trans-Siberian Express. Bill marvelled at the lack of markings or records, but was told that the distribution manager and crew know location, product, and number of every shipment that went through the facility. Historical records were retained in shoebox-like files. The distribution manager proudly stated that, in 25 years, he had never lost a shipment.

The managers he had met impressed him. Several, who might be described as 'angry young men', were in their late thirties, and had been employed by the company for some 15 or more years. Bill quickly realised that, although Russian families focused on female-associated values (matronymic), that few women had management jobs. Some men, like Ivan Alexandrovich, had travelled to western Europe to visit companies and had developed an initial understanding of market-driven economies and supply chain management processes. These new managers clearly had found a common language with senior labourers and rejected the established bureaucratic directors in their firms.

On Sunday, Bill was invited to visit Nicholai's *dacha* (a country cottage or home – often a Russian's only real property because many lived in state-owned apartments in the city), which was, by train, some thirty kilometres from Ekaterinburg. They stepped off the train in a snowstorm and walked along a rutted dirt and gravel road that diminished to a logging path covered by two feet of snow, passing through a seemingly endless pristine white birch forest. Twenty minutes later, they entered the unlocked log cabin, lit the wood stove, and warmed some tea and *bitochki* (potato or meat cakes), provided by Galena Ivanovna. Fruit juice-sized glasses of vodka warmed their hearts long before the heat from the wood stove permitted them to take off their mittens. On the train ride back to the city, Nicholai commented: 'friendships develop more rapidly in cold country air, not in heated city flats'.

Even in his short visit, Bill had started to feel appreciation for the mystique of Russia, the vast untapped mineral and human resources, the power of life-long friendships, and the tremendous strength of stoic life styles and work ethics. As

Vladimir Vasilovich had stated at the first breakfast meeting, 'To do business in Russia, particularly in Sverdlovsk *oblast*, you must become friends first'.

Bill glanced at his watch and tossed the reports back in the file folder. He would suggest to the Monthly Planning Update a multi-stage process to develop the Joint Agreement with UMC. But how should he define the specific steps? What could be the impact of 'translation misunderstandings' and 'cultural differences'? Should he start with a more technical evaluation, or would a general SWOT (strength, weaknesses, opportunities, threats) analysis be appropriate? For both firms, cost management was critical, but then so was quality. AME had invested more than $30 million in their own software and training to integrate with suppliers and customers; how much would it cost to build a corresponding system in Ekaterinburg?

But, for now, Bill had a briefing to give next Thursday. He tossed the folders in his briefcase and headed for the door. Eva Maria would have a good supper ready and he wanted to sleep on this one a bit.

Note on the case study

1 The authors would like to express their appreciation for support in this project from the US Information Service, the Soros Foundation, Northeastern Illinois University, Urals State Pedagogic University and Urals State Vocational Pedagogical University. Additionally, the comments and suggestions from the CIBER reviewer notably enhanced this case, for which the authors are grateful.

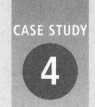

MCDONALD'S CORPORATION

David Upton

Whether in Moscow or Massachusetts, the same experience would greet a customer in any of the 12,611 McDonald's quick-service restaurants worldwide. McDonald's had distinguished itself in the quick-service industry through its remarkable consistency across all units. To competitors and customers alike, the Golden Arches – the corporate emblem that adorned every restaurant – symbolised pleasant, fast service and tasty, inexpensive food.

In the United States alone, McDonald's served over 20 million customers every day.[1] Although such a number testified to the restaurant chain's success, it also suggested a troubling question for management. With McDonald's already serving so many customers, how could it possibly attract more business? External pressures reinforced the dilemma. Demographic trends were reshaping American eating habits while competitors were attacking the quick-service giant from all sides. From chains specialising in speed and service, to those offering wider variety and those that featured deeply discounted menus, McDonald's faced competitors poised to challenge the industry leader on all fronts. McDonald's had built its success on a legendary operating system that amazed competitors and the financial community by generating an average annual return on equity of 25.2 per cent from 1965 through 1991, and an average annual earnings growth of 24.1 per cent. However, sales per unit had slowed between 1990 and 1991, causing management to wonder whether the company's operating system, so vital in guaranteeing uniform quality and service at every McDonald's outlet, was suited to the new circumstances the company faced.

Top managers faced a vexing challenge: To what extent should McDonald's change its operations strategy to accommodate the growing need for flexibility and variety in products. Was it merely tweaking, or a dramatic change, that would support the company's volume growth objectives?

The Speedee Service System

Dick and Mac McDonald opened their first drive-in restaurant in 1941, relying on carhops – waiters who went from car to car – to take orders from patrons parked in the restaurant's large lot. In 1948, the brothers abandoned their popular format and introduced self-service windows, 15-cent hamburgers, french fries and milk shakes. They standardised their preparation methods (in what they termed the 'Speedee

Source: Professor David Upton and Doctoral Candidate, Joshua Margolis, prepared the original version of this case, 'McDonald's Corporation', HBS Case No. 693-028. This version was prepared by Professor Roy Shapiro. HBS cases are developed solely as the basis for class discussion. Cases are not intended to serve as endorsements, sources of primary data or illustrations of effective or ineffective management. Copyright © 2002 President and Fellows of Harvard College. Reproduced with permission.

Service System') with exact product specifications and customised equipment. Every hamburger, for example, was prepared with ketchup, mustard, onions and two pickles; the ketchup was applied through a pump dispenser that required just one squirt for the required amount. Ray Kroc, who held the national marketing rights to the multimixers used in the restaurants to make milk shakes, met the McDonald brothers in 1954. He was so impressed by their restaurant and its potential that he became a national franchise agent for the brothers, and founded the McDonald's chain. Like the McDonald brothers' first restaurant in San Bernardino, California, the McDonald's chain featured a limited menu, low prices and fast service. From the moment in 1955 when he opened his first McDonald's, in Des Plaines, Illinois, Kroc made the operating system his passion and his company's anchor. Whereas many competitors could prepare products that were similar to McDonald's, most focused on recruiting franchisees, which they promptly ignored, and on identifying the lowest-cost suppliers. Kroc, on the other hand, sought (1) to make sure McDonald's products were of consistently high quality, (2) to establish a unique operating system, and (3) to build a special set of relationships between the McDonald's corporation, its suppliers, and its franchisees (see Exhibit 1).

Getting it right – again and again

McDonald's designed its operating system to ensure consistency and uniformity across all outlets. Operating procedures guaranteed customers the same quality of food and service visit after visit, store after store. Every hamburger, for example, was dressed in exactly the same way: mustard first, then ketchup, onions, and two pickles. One competitor marvelled at McDonald's record of consistency: 'I've been to McDonald's in Tokyo, Vienna, and Australia, and I get a great sense of having the same product from each one of their locations. Most people haven't been able to bring the discipline needed in fast food to get that type of consistency.'

McDonald's operating system concentrated on four areas: improving the product; developing outstanding supplier relationships; improving equipment; and training and monitoring franchisees. In its quest for improvement, McDonald's revolutionised the entire supply chain, introducing innovations in the way farmers grew potatoes and ranchers raised beef, altering processing methods for both potatoes and meat, and inventing efficient cooking equipment tailored to the restaurant's needs. Most revolutionary, perhaps, was McDonald's attention to detail. Never before had a restaurant cared about its suppliers' product beyond the price, let alone the suppliers' methods of operation.

McDonald's was able to spend as much time and effort as it did in perfecting its operating system because it restricted its menu to 10 items. Most restaurants in the 1960s and 1970s offered a variety of menu items, which made specialisation and uniform standards rare and nearly impossible. Fred Turner, one of Kroc's original managers and later senior chairman of McDonald's, stressed the critical importance of menu size in attributing success of the company's operating system: 'It wasn't because we were smarter. The fact that we were selling just 10 items, had a facility that was small, and used a limited number of suppliers created an ideal environment for really digging in on everything.'

Turner developed the first operations manual in 1957, which, by 1991, reached 750 detailed pages. It described how operators should make milk shakes, grill hamburgers and fry potatoes. It delineated exact cooking times, proper temperature settings, and precise portions for all food items – even prescribing the quarter ounce of onions to be placed on every hamburger and the 32 slices to be obtained from every pound of cheese. French fries were to be $\frac{9}{32}$ of an inch, and to ensure quality and taste, no products were to be held more than 10 minutes in the transfer bin.

McDonald's patrolled suppliers and franchisees scrupulously. The meat in McDonald's hamburgers, for example, had particular specifications: 83 per cent lean chuck (shoulder) from grass-fed cattle and 17 per cent choice plates (lower rib cage) from grain-fed cattle. Fillers were unacceptable. Whereas other restaurants merely accepted what suppliers provided and complained only when meat was visually inferior, McDonald's routinely analysed its meat in laboratories.

In 1991, McDonald's spent $26.9 million on its field service operation to evaluate and assist each of its restaurants. Each of the company's 332 field service consultants visited over 20 restaurants in the United States several times every year, reviewing the restaurants' performance on more than 500 items ranging from rest-room cleanliness to food quality and customer service. Turner was the first corporate employee to visit and evaluate each restaurant, and, as early as 1957, he summarised his evaluations by assigning a letter grade to a restaurant's performance in three categories: quality, service and cleanliness (QSC). For more than 30 years, therefore, McDonald's had prided itself on QSC and a fourth letter – V for value.[2]

McDonald's meticulous attention to detail and careful analysis of quality and procedures did not come from an unbending need for regimentation. Instead, McDonald's sought to study every component of its operation to learn what worked and what failed, to determine how best to offer consistently good service and food. Whereas other chains ignored both franchisees and suppliers, McDonald's sought to elicit commitment from them – commitment that required not only adherence but experimentation. Turner explained: *'We were continuously looking for a better way to do things, and then a revised better way to do things, and then a revised, revised better way.'*

Suppliers

A simple handshake secured every arrangement between McDonald's and a supplier, and it symbolised the way McDonald's revolutionised the entire relationship. Jim Williams, head of Golden State Foods, which supplied McDonald's with meat, contrasted the traditional supplier/restaurant relationship with the changes McDonald's introduced:

> *'Deals and kickbacks were a way of life. How long you let a guy stretch out his payments was more the determining factor of whether you got the business than the quality of the product you were selling. Kroc brought a supplier loyalty that the restaurant business had never seen. If you adhered to McDonald's specifications, and were basically competitive on price, you could depend on their order.'*

When McDonald's first approached the established food processing giants, such as Kraft, Heinz and Swift, the restaurant chain received a cold response. The established suppliers refused to accept McDonald's concepts and specifications and continued to concentrate solely on the retail market. Only small, fledgling suppliers were willing to gamble on McDonald's, and in turn, McDonald's created a whole new set of major institutional vendors. Each McDonald's restaurant ordered 1,800 pounds of hamburger meat per week and 3,000 pounds of potatoes. By meeting McDonald's strict standards and price requests, suppliers were guaranteed future volumes from a burgeoning restaurant chain. A supplier described the novel relationship that developed:

> 'Other chains would walk away from you for half a cent. McDonald's was more concerned with getting quality. They didn't chisel on price and were always concerned with suppliers making a fair profit. A lot of people look on a supplier as someone to walk on. But McDonald's always treated me with respect even when they became much bigger and didn't have to. That's the big difference, because if McDonald's said "Jump", an awful lot of people would be asking "How high?"'

Suppliers grew alongside McDonald's and were thus carefully attuned to the company's needs. As one supplier commented, 'You've got to be deaf, dumb, and ignorant to lose McDonald's business once you have it'.

Franchisees

McDonald's referred to its 3,500 US franchisees as its partners for good reason. By 1992, McDonald's generated 39 per cent of its revenues from franchise restaurants. When Ray Kroc first sold franchises, he made sure that his 'partners' would make money before the company did, and he insisted that corporate revenue come not from initial franchise fees but from success of the restaurants themselves. That philosophy continued to be at the centre of McDonald's franchise and operating practices.

Franchise owners did indeed see themselves as partners, developing such products as the Filet-O-fish sandwich and the Egg McMuffin in the 1960s and the McDLT in the 1980s. Franchisees also formed powerful regional cooperatives for both advertising and purchasing. Their regional advertising budgets enabled them to 'customise' local promotions while also supporting national programmes, and the buying cooperatives gave franchisees a channel for challenging suppliers to be innovative, even when those suppliers were meeting corporate requirements.

Together with corporate management and suppliers, franchisees infused McDonald's with an entrepreneurial spirit. All three partners balanced one another, just as the entrepreneurial inventiveness within each balanced their collective emphasis on disciplined standards of quality.

Cooking up products

Nothing exemplified the success of McDonald's operating system like the development of its food. From french fries to Chicken McNuggets, McDonald's had distinguished its menu offerings by drawing both on the rigorous operating system, with its focus on uniformity, and on the orchestra formed by corporate management, suppliers and franchisees.

In pursuit of the perfect fries

When McDonald's first began operating, french fried potatoes accounted for approximately 5 per cent of the entire US potato crop. By 1985, french fries accounted for more than 25 per cent of the US market. McDonald's had made french fries standard fare for an American meal, but more important for McDonald's, french fries became the restaurant chain's most distinctive item. Ray Kroc was well aware of the importance of the chain's fries:

> 'A competitor could buy the same kind of hamburger we did, and we wouldn't have anything extra to show. But the french fries gave us an identity and exclusiveness because you couldn't buy french fries anywhere to compete with ours. You could tell the results of tender loving care.'

McDonald's did indeed apply tender loving care in preparing its french fries. At first the company simply monitored the way french fries were cooked in its restaurants, trying to determine the exact temperature and settings that yielded the best french fries. They discovered, however, that temperature settings on the fryers had little connection to the temperature of the oil in the vat once cold potatoes were dropped in. By putting temperature sensors in the vat and on potato slices, McDonald's charted temperature readings during the cooking process. When a batch of cold, wet potatoes were thrown into a vat of melted shortening, the shortening's temperature dropped radically. Each batch of fries fell to a different temperature, but, McDonald's researchers discovered, the fries were always perfectly cooked when the oil temperature rose three degrees above the low temperature point. This discovery enabled the company to design a fryer that produced perfect french fried potatoes every order.

The initial research team eventually learned that potatoes also need to be cured for three weeks to produce perfect french fries: in that period of time the sugars within potatoes convert into starches. To prevent excessive browning and permit uniform crispness through the fry, McDonald's only accepted potatoes with a 21 per cent starch content. Members of the company's field operations staff visited produce suppliers with hydrometers, a floating instrument that measured the starch content of potatoes when immersed in a bucket of water.

As the number of McDonald's outlets grew to over four hundred in the early 1960s, the company's potato consumption surpassed six million pounds a year. That gave McDonald's and its suppliers sufficient purchasing power to influence growers of Idaho Russet potatoes to adhere to planting practices that yielded potatoes with high starch content. McDonald's also began looking for potato processors willing to invest in storage facilities with sophisticated temperature controls.

In the early 1960s, Jack Simplot, a major potato grower who supplied 20 per cent of McDonald's potatoes, approached McDonald's with an idea for improving the chain's french fries. He agreed to spend $400,000 to put Idaho Russets in cold storage during the summer, when they typically were not available. During the summer months, McDonald's relied on California white potatoes, less suited to production of crisp french fries. Although his gamble failed, and all of the stored potatoes rotted, Simplot returned with another, bolder suggestion in 1965. He recommended that McDonald's consider converting from fresh to frozen potatoes. Reluctant though the company was to tamper with its renowned french fries, Ray Kroc recognised the distribution problems involved in supplying fresh potatoes to his growing chain. Simplot pitched his idea to Kroc on the basis not of price but of qualiy, as he later explained:

> 'They were having a hell of a time maintaining potato quality in their stores. The sugar content of the potatoes was constantly going up and down, and they would get fries with

every colour of the rainbow. I told him that frozen fries would allow him to better control the quality and consistency of McDonald's potato supply.'

McDonald's studied the freezing process carefully learning that the traditional process robbed structure and flavour from french fries. Ice crystals would form in the potato during freezing, rupturing the starch granules. McDonald's developed a process to dry french fries with air, run them through a quick frying cycle, then freeze them. This reduced the moisture in the frozen fry while preserving its crispness. Simplot volunteered to build the initial production line that implemented this process, and by 1992, his company supplied McDonald's with 1.8 billion pounds of french fries – close to 50 per cent of the chain's domestic potato business. Only a small, local supplier when he first approached McDonald's, Simplot's organisation grew to a $650 million frozen potato processing giant.

McDonald's even improved the way restaurant crews filled orders for french fries. Operators had complained that employee productivity suffered because the metal tongs traditionally used to fill french-fry bags proved clumsy. In response, a McDonald's engineer, Ralph Weimer, designed a V-shaped aluminum scoop with a funnel at the end that enabled operators to fill a french-fry bag in one motion and, in addition, align the fries in the same vertical direction within the bag.

Fast break from competitors: breakfast and the McMuffin

In June 1976, McDonald's franchisees introduced the chain's most significant new product: not just a new menu item but a new meal – breakfast. Most operators were sufficiently busy keeping their restaurants open between 11:00 a.m. and midnight, but a Pittsburgh franchisee looked at these hours as a limitation that offered an opportunity: *'We were paying rent, utilities, and insurance 24 hours a day, but we were only open for business for half that time. We had all those morning hours before 11:00 a.m. to do some business.'*

This franchisee began opening his restaurant at 7:00 a.m., serving coffee, doughnuts, sweet rolls, pancakes, and sausage. Without detracting from McDonald's existing menu, he generated entirely new business.

Other franchisees would agree to extend morning hours only if they happened upon a breakfast item that promised enormous sales growth. Herb Peterson, a franchise operator in Santa Barbara, California believed that to launch a new meal, McDonald's required a unique product that could be eaten like all other McDonald's foods – with the fingers. He turned to a classic egg dish – Eggs Benedict – for inspiration.

In 1971, he developed a sandwich and a special utensil that could, in classic McDonald's style, guarantee foolproof production of the sandwich. A cluster of six Teflon-coated rings could be used on a grill to give eggs the rounded shape of an English muffin while giving them the look and taste of poached eggs. When a slice of cheese and bacon were added, McDonald's had developed the cornerstone product of its breakfast menu: the Egg McMuffin.

McDonald's rolled out a complete breakfast menu in 1976, featuring the Egg McMuffin, hotcakes, scrambled eggs, sausage, and Canadian-style bacon. McDonald's had again distinguished itself from competitors, none of whom responded until the mid-1980s, by which time McDonald's held a virtual monopoly on breakfast, which accounted for 15 per cent of average restaurant sales.

McDonald's once again turned to suppliers for support in developing the Egg McMuffin; some were responsive while others lost a revolutionary opportunity. Pork processors, for example, worked with McDonald's to build equipment that could cut round slices of bacon instead of strips.

Chicken comes to the golden arches

In the late 1970s, McDonald's official chef, Rene Arend, tried to develop an onion product – deep-fried chunks of onion – but the variation in onion supplies made it difficult to control quality. Instead, CEO Fred Turner suggested that Arend substitute bite-sized chunks of deep-fried chicken.

McDonald's immediately turned to two suppliers to help develop the product in record time. Gorton, the original supplier of fish for McDonald's Filet-O-Fish sandwich, was selected to solve the breading and battering challenge as it had done previously with fish. McDonald's handed the most difficult challenge to Keystone, one of McDonald's meat suppliers: find an efficient way to cut chicken into bite-sized, boneless chunks. Arend, meanwhile, developed four sauces to accompany the nuggets. The collaborative effort between McDonald's and its suppliers produced breakthroughs that made the new product, Chicken McNuggets, not only possible but unique: a modified hamburger-patty machine that cut boneless chicken into nuggets, for example, and a special batter that gave the nuggets the taste and appearance of being freshly battered.

By March 1980, just five months after beginning work on McNuggets, McDonald's was testing them in a Knoxville restaurant. Within three years of introducing Chicken McNuggets throughout its chain, McDonald's was deriving 7.5 per cent of domestic sales from its newest product. The giant of the hamburger business had suddenly become the second-largest chicken retailer in the food-service industry, positioned behind Kentucky Fried Chicken. Keystone's efforts on behalf of McDonald's again provided proof of the success bred by loyalty: by 1992, Keystone had 65 per cent of McDonald's chicken business, transforming the meat supplier into a major chicken producer as well.

Competitors and growth

McDonald's had built the most successful quick-service franchise in the world, maintaining phenomenal growth for over 35 years. Distinguishing itself from other chains by adhering tenaciously to an operating system focused on uniformity, it worked with its franchisees and suppliers as partners to improve the operating system and introduce new products. But as management reviewed McDonald's performance in recent years, many wondered if the company's traditional strategy still suited the dramatic changes it now seemed to face.

McDonald's share of the US quick-service market had dropped from 18.7 per cent in 1985 to 16.6 per cent in 1991, even though the company gained sales from a bigger quick-service 'pie'. Despite this, between 1988 and 1990, sales per US outlet dropped an average of 3.7 per cent in real dollars. After years of double-digit income growth, McDonald's 1991 net US income grew just 7.2 per cent to $860 million. It was estimated that by 1995, profit from overseas outlets would surpass profit from US outlets. Overseas business, in fact, showed the greatest growth in recent years, with operating income rising from $290 million in 1987 to $678 million in 1991.

Although international expansion clearly offered McDonald's its most fertile frontier, McDonald's had to concentrate on US operations. There were 2,500 franchisees in the United States, over 8,814 restaurants (1,416 company-operated), and 25 per cent of company revenues came from franchise fees based on a percentage of sales. US business accounted for 60 per cent of profits, and it simply had to be bolstered.

Moreover, McDonald's had to consider demographic trends. Hamburger consumption had dropped from 19 per cent of all restaurant orders in 1982 to 17 per cent of all orders in 1990 (hamburger consumption at McDonald's had nevertheless increased over the same time period). Increasingly, though, consumers were becoming more conscious of nutrition and dietary options without compromising taste. The change in dietary preference was, however, certainly not universal, and there was a strong constituency of customers who continued to enjoy McDonald's traditional fare.

The quick-service industry had grown at an average annual rate of 8.7 per cent in the 1980s but was projected only to keep pace with inflation during the 1990s. Perhaps most confusing in its implications, the number of meals eaten off the premises of quick-service restaurants had increased from 23 per cent per cent in 1982 to 62 per cent in 1990. McDonald's responded with double drive-through windows to keep pace with changing consumer preference, as well as new venues for its restaurants, such as schools, sporting arenas, museums, airports, and hospitals. It also developed new smaller restaurants, less expensive than its traditional designs, which could service customers profitably in 'seam' areas between existing McDonald's restaurants.

New competition

The once simple quick-service market had been complicated by the entry of specialist competitors who had emulated McDonald's strategy to capture their own segment of the market. Michael Quinlan, chairman of McDonald's, acknowledged just how fierce the competition had become. *'Our competition is much tougher, no question about it. And not just in numbers but in quality.'* McDonald's most menacing competition no longer came from Burger King, Wendy's, or Kentucky Fried Chicken – the traditional rivals.

Chili's and Olive Garden catered to customers searching for full-service and greater variety. Both were family-style restaurants where patrons sat down to be served. Menus offered a wide variety of foods, yet prices remained competitive with those at McDonald's (see Exhibit 2 for McDonald's menu). Casual dining restaurants were likely to grow in the 1990s as their most frequent patrons – people between the ages of 40 and 60 – increased in number by about 20 million.

Two hamburger chains, Sonic and Rally's, offered drive-through service only and specialised in delivering burgers fast. For four years Sonic sales per restaurant grew an average of 11.3 per cent per annum, and in 1991 alone, sales per unit increased 13 per cent. There were 1,150 Sonic units and 327 Rally's.[3] Taco Bell featured Mexican food and a menu with 26 items under one dollar. Along with Kentucky Fried Chicken and Pizza Hut, Taco Bell was owned by PepsiCo and had seen the greatest increase in sales of any quick-service chain in the late 1980s. By learning from McDonald's, Taco Bell shifted food preparation to outside suppliers, reduced kitchen space in its outlets, and used a cost-based strategy to compete – prices were always kept low. Between 1988 and 1991, Taco Bell served 60 per cent more customers and sales rocketed 63 per cent.

Early responses from McDonald's

McDonald's drew on its traditional strengths to respond to competitors' challenges and customers' new habits. Careful product development, closely gauged to customer tastes, again formed the focus of attention as McDonald's turned to suppliers and franchisees for assistance. To address concerns about nutrition, McDonald's had introduced salads, chicken and muffins. In conjunction with Keystone and Auburn University, it developed the first ever 91 per cent fat-free burger, McLean Deluxe. Keystone also convinced McDonald's to experiment with chicken fajitas, which proved an instant success in initial tests. The chicken arrived precooked and seasoned, so it only required heating and did not slow operations. The fajitas sold well in market tests and were soon scheduled for national introduction.

Just as McDonald's had spent five years perfecting its breakfast menu for national rollout, the company spent seven years developing a pizza suitable for its restaurants. Meticulous product development included design of advanced technology, as it had when McDonald's engineers introduced a special french-fry scoop and a grill that prepared hamburgers in half the time by cooking them on both sides simultaneously. Now McDonald's engineers had invented a pizza oven that could cook McDonald's pizza in under five minutes. In addition, McDonald's was developing new staging equipment – high-tech temperature and moisture controlled cabinets – that would allow parts of a product to be prepared ahead of time without detracting from food quality. Toasted buns, for example, could be stored in these containers without becoming dried out.

In early 1991, McDonald's returned to a value menu, cutting prices an average 20 per cent. Cheeseburgers sold for only 69 cents, and McDonald's Happy Meals™ – complete children's meals (sandwich, fries, drink and toy in a colourful box) – for just $1.99. As a result, sales of hamburgers increased by 30 per cent and customer counts rose. Revenues and profits, however, increased less dramatically.

These initial moves suggested a fundamental tension between McDonald's expanded efforts to provide greater value, on the one hand, and enhanced variety, on the other. As Fred Turner noted, *'We're a penny-profit business'*, and with a value menu, volume was critical. That made the chain's hallmark of speed more vital than ever, yet a wider variety of menu offerings posed the risk of slowing each unit's service. Variety and value had to be carefully balanced. Management's challenge was to sustain McDonald's painstaking attention to products and service in achieving that balance.

Flexibility and growth

McDonald's had achieved success by focusing on a simple formula: limited menu, low prices, and fast service. The golden arches symbolised a uniform product – primarily burgers, fries and shakes – delivered in a consistent manner. Whereas uniformity and consistency had formed McDonald's focal point for 35 years, the company's new advertising slogan seemed to suggest a subtle yet significant shift: 'What You Want Is What You Get at McDonald's Today'. Catering to customers had always been the company's focal point, but to meet changing and divergent customer needs, McDonald's was exploring many different options, and management thought a basic question had to be answered. Would the chain's new concern with flexibility in meeting customers' changing needs require a fundamental change in McDonald's bedrock strategy? Or was this just a new, albeit incredibly complicated, situation once again adaptable to the company's traditional approach?

Early responses to new customer desires and intensifying competition represented just a piece of the company's maelstrom of creative activity. Further efforts were in progress as well. For example, McDonald's had developed a number of new building prototypes, from drive-through-only models to compete with Rally's and Sonic, to small cafes suitable for small towns. Menu diversification offered the greatest area of experimentation. A wide range of items was being tested, including lasagne, carrot sticks, corn on the cob, fruit cups, and oven-baked chicken. McDonald's was also looking for new ways to address nutritional concerns revolving around calcium deficiency and sodium and fat reduction.

McDonald's changes to date had not threatened its traditional operating system, but increased variation throughout the chain – whether in menu offerings, building plans, or eating experience – would pose formidable challenges to McDonald's in maintaining its remarkable quality control and speed of service. The operating system had been constructed to ensure uniformity, quality, and speed at all McDonald's restaurants. If the chain intended to offer a wider variety of foods, such as spaghetti and meatballs or baked chicken, it could disrupt an operating system built around a limited menu.

McDonald's traditional rival, Burger King, afforded an example of the dangers contained in variety. Burger King flame-broil – *if* the flame-broiled Burger King burgers were cooked correctly. But flame-broiled hamburgers were inconsistent in quality and Burger King was not able to implement an operating system that could sustain consistency across all units.

Increasing variety posed another potential dilemma for McDonald's. As the chain responded to pricing challenges from competitors like Taco Bell, higher volume became imperative. To generate higher volume at each restaurant, speed became even more important, and speed could not be risked on a cornucopia of new products. Although the new menu items McDonald's had thus far tested, such as chicken fajitas, had not clogged operations and were well-received by franchisees, McDonald's had to guarantee similar smoothness with some of the more exotic products under consideration, whether chicken, spaghetti or corn on the cob.

The sheer number of additional products could also detract from the speed of service. McDonald's perfected its operating procedures and equipment in part to accommodate its workforce, whose annual turnover rate was greater than 100 per cent (nevertheless, the lowest in the industry). While McDonald's commitment to training continued to set the industry standard, no McDonald's outlet could afford to engage in complicated preparation processes for new products that might work at cross-purposes with speed of service.

If those challenges did not prove sufficiently daunting to the quick-service giant, it also had to consider restaurant image if it hoped to expand its business through enhanced variety. McDonald's had built its image as the place for hamburgers and quick service – not for other food and not for casual dining. If people sought Mexican food, they would go to Taco Bell. If people wanted pizza, they would go to Pizza Hut. If they wanted to sit down to a leisurely, reasonably priced meal, Olive Garden, Chili's, Perkin's, TGI Friday's, and Friendly's all came to mind before McDonald's. Not only did McDonald's have to extend its own image, it also had to confront the established reputations of competitors.

These challenges appeared especially troubling because dinner presented perhaps the final frontier of potential growth. Only 20 per cent of McDonald's sales came from dinner, and to entice customers to visit the golden arches for dinner required a new menu – as it had for breakfast – and even a different ambiance. To defend against competitors, McDonald's could not introduce dinner items one by one. Competitors could tout their specialties and thus respond easily. McDonald's, therefore, had to present an entire dinner menu at once, and the earliest possible date for such a rollout appeared to be the spring of 1993.

Dinner differed in other ways too. Lunch and breakfast customers were most concerned with speed and convenience, but dinner was more of an event, and customers expected full meals and more complete service. Tablecloths and table service, for example, did not seem out of the question. With 62 per cent of 1990 quick-service sales coming from off-premises eating, compared to just 23 per cent in 1982, the trends for lunch and breakfast seemed to be headed in the opposite direction.

While these competitive pressures mounted, a new challenge had been growing: protecting the environment. While many companies had seen the outbreak of environmentalism in the late 1980s as a threat – McDonald's saw an opportunity: the chance of knitting a responsible environmental policy into its evolving operations strategy.

Management considered all of these challenges and knew McDonald's would like to maintain the same core menu, operating systems, and decor. The chain nonetheless would have to allow greater latitude across units and provide a broader variety of products and experiences for the customer. But would there still be such a thing as a standard McDonald's?

Notes on the case

1 With 250 million people living in the United States, McDonald's was serving roughly 8 per cent of the US population daily.
2 Franchisees could not be graded on value because it violated antitrust regulations, which prohibited rigid pricing and required independent business owners be given the latitude to set prices on their own.
3 Therrien (1991) 'The Upstarts Teaching McDonald's A Thing or Two' *Business Week*, 21 October, p. 122.

Exhibit 1 McDonald's original menu

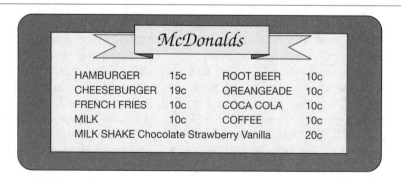

Exhibit 2 McDonald's menu, 1992

APPROVED NATIONAL MENU ITEMS – Listed on Menu Boards – (Effective 6/1/92)

Regular Menu Items

1. Hamburger	19. Medium Fries
2. Cheeseburger	20. Large Fries
3. Quarter Pounder with Cheese	21. Lowfat Milk Shakes
4. Big Mac	22. 1% Milk
5. McLean Deluxe (and cheese option) (8, 12, 16 oz.)	23. Drink – Child Size (12 oz.)
6. McChicken Sandwich	24. Drink – Small (16 oz.)
7. McNuggets – 6 Piece	25. Drink – Medium (21.9 oz.)
8. McNuggets – 9 Piece	26. Drink – Large (32 oz.)
9. McNuggets – 20 Piece	27. Orange Juice
10. Happy Meal – Hamburger	28. Coffee (8, 12, 16 oz.)
11. Happy Meal – Cheeseburger	29. Decaffeinated Coffee Fresh Bewed
12. Happy Meal – 4 pc. McNuggets	30. Hot Tea
13. Filet	31. Iced Tea (12, 16, 21.9, 32 oz.)
14. Chunky Chicken Salad	32. Apple Pie
15. Chef Salad	33. Chocolate Chip Cookie
16. Garden Salad	34. McDonaldland Cookies
17. Side Salad	35. Sundaes
18. Small Fries	36. Cones

Breakfast Menu Items

1. Egg McMuffin
2. Sausage McMuffin w/Egg
3. Big Breakfast
4. Hotcakes and Sausage
5. Sausage Biscuit
6. Sausage/Egg Biscuit
7. Bacon/Egg/Cheese Biscuit
8. Breakfast Burrito
9. Hash Browns
10. Apple Bran Muffin (fat free)
11. Cereal (Wheaties & Cheerios)

APPROVED NATIONAL 'VALUE MENU COMBOS' – Listed on Menu Board – (Effective 6/1/92)

Regular Menu   *Breakfast*

1. Big Mac, Lg. Fry, Med. Drink	1. Egg McMuffin, any size drink
2. 2 Cheeseburgers, Lg. Fry, Med. Drink	2. Bacon Egg & Cheese Biscuit, any size drink
3. Quarter Pounder w/Cheese, Lg. Fry, Med. Drink	3. Sausage McMuffin w/Egg, any size drink
[a]4. McChicken, Lg. Fry, Medium Drink	[a]4. Sausage Biscuit w/Egg, any size drink

[a]The #4 position can be used as a flexible option with provided options being McLean Deluxe, 2 Chicken Fajitas, Filet-O-Fish, or Hotcakes during Breakfast.
Source: company document.

5 KUHN FLOWERS

Thomas G. Disantis

Bill Cutting and Harry Graham, co-executives of Kuhn Flowers, drove along the St John's River after visiting the Kuhn Flowers store in the Ortega neighbourhood of Jacksonville, Florida. Although their offices were located at the company's headquarters in the Beach Boulevard store, Cutting and Graham enjoyed visiting Kuhn Flowers' other locations to talk with employees and see that the stores were running smoothly. Kuhn Flowers had a family company feel to it; a legacy of the founder, Robert Kuhn. Many of the company's employees, for example, had been working for Kuhn Flowers for five years or more and were intensely dedicated to the company.

Since taking over the company in 2001, Cutting and Graham had continued the company's success (see Exhibits 1 and 2 for recent financial information) including maintaining its position as the largest retail florist in the Jacksonville area for the past 30 years. In comparison, its closest competitors among other retail florists in the area were only about a quarter of its size.

Despite this success, Cutting and Graham were concerned about the changes that the floral industry had experienced during recent years. One such change was the increasing competition among channels, especially between retail florists like Kuhn Flowers and mass-market retailers such as supermarkets, Wal-Mart, and club stores. Developments in the industry's supply chain had also made it easier for larger companies to import flowers directly from growers at lower cost without diminishing the quality of the flowers.

As Cutting and Graham turned onto Beach Boulevard, they discussed how these and other changes would affect Kuhn Flowers and how the company might have to change to address them.

Company history[1]

Kuhn Flowers was founded by Robert Kuhn in Jacksonville, Florida, in 1947 after he returned from serving in the navy during World War II. While developing the company in its early stages, Kuhn focused on a number of attributes that still define Kuhn Flowers to this day. First, instead of relying on business from walk-in customers, Kuhn actively pursued the telephone order and delivery business. This not only provided customers with a way to order flowers without the hassle of driving to the store, but it also provided Kuhn with the ability to market to two customers at the same time: the purchaser and the recipient. Kuhn continuously expanded the delivery area served by Kuhn Flowers, which became a key element in the company's

Source: This case was prepared by Thomas G. Disantis (MBA 2004), under the supervision of Professors Paul W. Farris and Ervin R. Shames. It was written as a basis for class discussion rather than to illustrate effective or ineffective handling of an administrative situation. Copyright © 2004 by the University of Virginia Darden School Foundation, Charlottesville, VA. All rights reserved.

growth. Second, Kuhn established the company's pledge to provide exceptional service to its customers, including a 100 per cent guarantee of customer satisfaction with the flowers they received. Finally, Kuhn realised the importance of being known as a quality provider of flowers and used advertising and promotions to increase awareness about his company. Through his efforts, Kuhn Flowers became the largest and most successful retail florist in north-east Florida by the 1970s. When Kuhn decided to retire in 1984, he sold his business to Exotic Gardens, a floral company in South Florida.

Bill Cutting and Harry Graham became involved with Kuhn Flowers during this time. Cutting joined the company in 1958 and eventually became Kuhn's right-hand man. He worked with Kuhn until 1974 when he left to take a position with Floral Transworld Delivery, better known as FTD. When Kuhn retired in 1984, Cutting returned to Kuhn Flowers, and at Kuhn's suggestion Exotic Gardens hired him to run the Jacksonville operation. Graham, meanwhile, had been involved with the Kuhn Flowers business since the 1970s as the company's banker. Cutting and Graham met when Cutting returned to the company in 1984, and the two had been friends ever since.

After Kuhn's retirement, Cutting continued his legacy of careful development and expansion. It was during this time, for example, that the company expanded to the four stores operated by Kuhn Flowers. Cutting explained his reasoning for expanding to other locations:

'As the city grew, it became harder to deliver to our customers because of both the increase in the number of customers and the increase in traffic congestion. We added locations to address these challenges. It's important to note that we expanded only if the opportunity was right, and we were able to expand or acquire the business at a price that was fair and did not put undue burden on ourselves. We also made sure that the stores weren't pulling customers away from each other.'

In 1999, Exotic Gardens sold Kuhn Flowers to Gerald Stevens, a newly established company that was in the midst of creating a nationwide, vertically integrated flower operation by rolling up local flower shops and other floral businesses. The effort ultimately failed, and Gerald Stevens declared bankruptcy in 2001. As a part of the roll up, Kuhn Flowers was caught in the middle of Gerald Stevens' rise and fall. Cutting recalled:

'The people who ran Gerald Stevens didn't have a background in the flower business, and they didn't understand our business here at Kuhn Flowers. They tried to make a lot of changes that I had to fight against because they would have destroyed the company that we had created. I was helped by the fact that we were making a lot of money for them and that I have been involved with the flower business for many years, but it was still a difficult time.'

After Gerald Stevens failed, Cutting and Graham together proposed to buy Kuhn Flowers from the bankrupt company. Graham remembered:

'Within a year of Gerald Stevens coming in, it was apparent they were in trouble, and we started talking about buying the business. Bill and my sons were also working for Kuhn Flowers at the time. When they declared Chapter 11, we engaged an attorney and Bill told management that we were interested in purchasing. I looked at it as a good investment with a good operating partner.'

In November of 2001, Cutting and Graham closed the deal and have managed the company since then.

Changes in the flower industry

As a retail florist, Kuhn Flowers had been impacted by the continuing changes within the floral industry as a whole. One change that had dramatically affected the floral industry was the increase in imported cut flowers (see Exhibit 3). The use of refrigerated shipping containers for air shipments along with genetic advancements that have increased the strength and duration of the flower's life after harvest have broadened the industry's geographic scope. As Cutting declared: '*A flower that is in the ground in Columbia on Friday can be in one of our arrangements by Monday*'. Imported flowers have relative cost advantages over domestically grown flowers, and imported flowers now make up a majority of the cut flowers purchased in the United States.[2]

These developments have also provided large floral operations, including retail florists, supermarkets, and club stores, with the ability to bypass floral wholesalers and purchase their flowers directly from the grower. While this did not eliminate the need for the wholesaler in the supply chain, it gave large flower sellers the chance to realise significant cost savings and to exert influence with their suppliers.

Another development in the floral industry was the increasing competition among retail channels. Two major groups of retail channels in particular have been at the forefront of this competition: (1) Traditional retail florists (i.e. stores that sell flowers, arrangements, and other such goods and also provide services for weddings, funerals, and other occasions); and (2) mass-market retailers such as supermarkets and discount retail stores (i.e. stores that sell a broad range of household products that also have a floral department within the store).

Retail florists used to be among the few retail channels available to the floral customer aside from buying direct from a nursery. That changed in the 1970s as supermarkets introduced floral items in their stores beginning first with popular potted plants but later including cut flowers and bouquets.[3] Other mass-market retailers, such as discount retail stores, also began to introduce floral products on their sales floor. The primary reason for the rise of mass-market retailers as a channel for the floral industry was the convenience that they offered the customer with their floral purchases.[4] Initially this did not provide a threat to the traditional retail florist because supermarkets and other mass-market retailers had a reputation for poor quality.[5] But it was not long before mass-market retailers improved the quality of their flower offerings while they provided customers with a convenient place to shop for their floral purchases.[6]

This increasing competition from the mass-market retail channel has had an impact on the traditional retail florist. While the industry as whole has been steadily growing over the past 10 years, the share of the industry represented by retail florists has decreased (see Exhibit 4). Several factors are involved with this decrease in share. One contributing factor has been the decline in the number of florists (see Exhibit 5). A mitigating factor, however, has been the increasing average amount per customer transaction at retail florists (see Exhibit 6). As a result of these trends in the marketplace, the role of retail florists has changed from the provider of everyday flower purchases to the provider of flowers for special occasions. Bruce Wright, editor of the trade magazine *Flowers&*, explained:

'What is happening to retail florists today is similar to the experience of the local bakery. 20 or 30 years ago, you went to the local baker for your everyday purchases such as a loaf of bread. Now, you go to the local supermarket for most of your everyday purchases because of the convenience and you go the local bakery only for special occasions.'

Two other recent changes in the retail channel have affected the flower industry. First, online direct florists, such as ProFlowers and KaBloom, were new but important developments in the flower industry. In this channel, retailers either grew the flowers themselves or had close ties to growers and were able to provide rapid turnaround in their deliveries to customers. Second, 'order gatherers' such as 1-800-FLOWERS had been a developing trend in the industry. Order gatherers performed the same task as FTD.[7] The difference was, however, that the order gatherers did not receive any incoming orders; instead, they pocketed the 20 per cent originating charge. This was a threat to retail florists because they could not afford to fulfil too many orders with an immediate 20 per cent discount.

The dynamics in the retail channel aspect of the flower industry were continuing to change. Giant Foods, for example, allowed customers to order flower arrangements online to be available for pickup at their retail locations. Wal-Mart also hinted that it would include flower delivery as part of a variety of new services that it would offer.[8] This possibility became a reality in the spring of 2004 when Wal-Mart promoted a new online floral delivery service through Post & Petal Flowers (see Exhibit 7).

Kuhn Flowers[9]

Customers who walked into the company's Beach Boulevard store may have considered it a flower shop, but to the employees, the store was actually the hub of the company's operations. In fact, sales space for walk-in customers accounted for only one-third of the building; the rest was dedicated to the coolers that maintained the inventory, a large area for employees to assemble flower arrangements, a fully staffed call centre to receive telephone orders, and the company's headquarters (see Exhibit 8).

Kuhn Flowers' operational model was one aspect of the business that distinguished the company from its competition of traditional retail florists and mass-market floral retailers. One feature of this operational model was the company's focus on receiving, fulfilling and delivering flower orders from local customers over the telephone. While traditional florists and mass-market retailers generally relied on walk-in business to generate orders, 85 per cent of Kuhn Flowers' local sales (i.e. those not involving a wire service) originated from local telephone orders.

A second feature of the operational model was the company's focus on selling arrangements that had been pre-made and were awaiting sale and shipment in the company coolers. Instead of beginning an arrangement after the customer placed an order like many traditional florists, Kuhn Flowers predominantly sold arrangements that had been made before the order was placed. These arrangements were available from the Kuhn Flowers' catalogue, which was updated every two years, and during certain holiday periods (see Exhibit 9). While customised orders could be created for customers who wished them, 90 per cent of the arrangements sold were arrangements found in the catalogue.

A critical component of this operational model was the ability to accurately predict demand for each particular arrangement. The forecasts were created by the executive team at the Beach Boulevard headquarters with help and input from operational managers at the other retail locations. Harry Graham explained:

'Demand is forecasted based on historical information and a best guess of the expected increase. We forecast demand for each store and send them product to meet the forecast. It is then up to the manager at each store to adjust and revise the estimates during the day to meet the needs of the customers.'[10]

As a result, each of the three other Kuhn Flower retail stores acted as the spokes to the Beach Boulevard hub in this system, and their inventory was stocked and supplied by the Beach Boulevard location using the demand projections. Each store also delivered arrangements to customers, increasing the quality of service provided to customers.[11] Because of the effectiveness of this system, Kuhn Flowers was able to offer a two-hour turnaround to its customers.[12]

Cutting and Graham's focus on sales and operational metrics not only supported smooth operations, but both also believed that the numbers must be paid attention to if Kuhn Flowers was to remain in touch with its customers. As Cutting explained:

'It's vital to remain attuned to your customers and paying attention to the numbers allows us to do this. For example, if we look at the sales data and see that the price per order has increased significantly, we know that we have a problem attracting the everyday customer. This isn't sustainable. So we'll run a promotion to drive traffic and get that number back to a more reasonable level.'

The typical order for a Kuhn Flowers arrangement was handled in the following way. Before an order was placed for a particular arrangement, the raw cut flowers were delivered either from the wholesaler or directly from the grower and were put into inventory coolers. Throughout the day, flower arrangers created a specific number of each arrangement that was determined by the forecasted projection of demand for that arrangement. The efficiency of this process was enhanced by the use of a predeveloped 'recipe' for each arrangement. This recipe told the arranger how many of each type of flower that should be placed in the arrangement and how the arrangement should be put together. Once the arrangements were completed, they were put into a cooler to await delivery.

A customer wanting to purchase an arrangement called Kuhn Flowers' main number. If the customer had ordered before, the sales operator could tell who the customer was and had learned the customer's sales history through the company's customer database. Once the order was placed, it was checked for accuracy and sent to the delivery area. The deliverer reviewed the order and picked the arrangement from the cooler to be delivered along with other orders to be delivered at that time. The arrangement was then delivered.

A second aspect of the business that differentiated Kuhn Flowers from its competition was the marketing strategy that the company followed. Influencing this strategy was how Kuhn Flowers approached the customer. According to Cutting:

'Customers care about two things when they purchase a flower arrangement. They want flowers that are going to last for a long time, and they want to have a lot of flowers in the arrangement. Therefore, that is what we focus on: selling only the freshest flowers and providing value with the customer's purchase. If a customer is unhappy in any way with their purchase or with the flowers that have been delivered to them, Kuhn will replace the item with no questions asked. We think that it is important that customers are 100 per cent satisfied with the quality of the flowers they are receiving.'

In addition to quality, Kuhn Flowers focused on providing the customer with a high level of service, and this was reflected at all levels and in all departments in the company. Deliverers, for example, would bring up the morning paper from the bottom of the driveway along with the delivery, and they have even been known to help a customer take out the trash. Also, the employees working at the stores would carry the purchase to the customer's car or re-open the store if a customer arrived after the store had closed.

Another key aspect of the Kuhn Flowers marketing strategy was that it was focused on satisfying the needs of the customer who was interested in the everyday purchase of flowers. Cutting said:

'The reason supermarkets and other mass-market retailers have done well in the flower market is because traditional retail florists have chased customers away. Florists have made shopping at their stores inconvenient because they've focused on the big occasion purchase rather than the everyday purchase. Convenience for the customer is just as important as the product that you are selling them.'

This convenience was provided both over the phone and in the store. The ordering process over the phone had been designed to be efficient and easy for the customer. Sales calls were targeted to be no longer than four minutes in length and even shorter during the busy periods. At the store, customers would find arrangements and stems that were out on the sales floor instead of behind or inside coolers. As a result, 39 per cent of Kuhn Flowers' sales came from everyday purchases (see Exhibit 10). *'We provide a level of quality and service that cannot be matched by mass-market retailers while providing customers with a convenient place to buy their flowers'*, Cutting said.

While about 70 per cent of their sales came from individual customers, Kuhn Flowers served corporate customers as well. These included real estate and law offices that used flowers and flower arrangements typically as a method for expressing gratitude to new or important clients. Although corporate customers were an important part of the Kuhn Flowers business, they presented important risks as well. Harry Graham explained:

'Having too much of your business with one customer presents two risks. First, you become dependent on that customer for the success of your business, and second, you have your focus taken away from all of your other customers. This explains why we do not service weddings. They involve a lot of work and they can take our attention away from our main business. They also are variable; they do not provide a steady stream of business.'[13]

Although Kuhn Flowers focused its business on quality and service, the company did not let this influence the way that products were priced. As Cutting explained:

'We want to keep our flowers affordable to all customers, and we price for the customer and not for the occasion. This means that we don't raise our prices really high just because it's Valentine's Day. Customers have come to expect value for what they receive from Kuhn Flowers and that is why we price for the customer.'

Pricing was also used to compete against both groups of retail channels. Individual stems, for example, were priced competitively with mass-market retailers while arrangements were priced to compete with other retail florists.

Advertising and promotion were also important components of the Kuhn Flowers marketing mix. *'Since we're the largest florist in this market, we have to maintain awareness of our brand among the current residents as well as make new residents aware that we exist. With the level of growth and transition among the Jacksonville population, it's important to continue to attract new customers'*, said Graham. Kuhn Flowers spent up to $500,000 per year for television, radio, and print placements, coupons, and other promotional items such as brochures and mailings. The year-round advertising and promotion provided a consistent message with the goal of maintaining their brand image as a stable company that was a part of the community.

Going forward

Bill Cutting and Harry Graham continued to discuss how they would manage the business as they entered the Beach Boulevard store. Walking to their offices, they passed rows and rows of employees assembling flower arrangements. They wondered if the success that Kuhn Flowers had enjoyed in the past would be influenced by the continuing changes in the floral industry and whether they would have to make changes to their business in order to maintain its current position. Cutting and Graham knew that Kuhn Flowers was a successful business; they just wanted to make sure that it stayed that way.

Notes on the case

1 The subject matter of this section is primarily drawn from company documents and interviews with Harry Graham and Bill Cutting.

2 US Department of Agriculture (2002) *Floriculture and Nursery Crops: Yearbook 2003*, June.

3 Pyle, Kathleen (2001) 'Chain Reaction', *Flowers&*, August.

4 'Floral Trend Tracker', *Society of American Florists*, Spring 2003.

5 Pyle, K. op. cit.

6 Major, Meg (2004) 'Full Bloom', *Progressive Grocer*, 1 July.

7 Although FTD provided numerous support services to member florists, its primary role was the routing and settling of orders between FTD-affiliated florists in different cities. If an order was requested in a florist in City A to be delivered to City B, FTD routed the order to the FTD florist in City B for a fee. The original florist in City A received 20 per cent of the order value, and the florist in City B received the other 80 per cent for fulfilling the order.

8 Useem, Jerry (2003) 'One Nation under Wal-Mart', *Fortune*, 3 March.

9 The subject matter of this section is primarily drawn from company documents and interviews with Harry Graham and Bill Cutting.

10 A factor which helped in the success of this system was that up to 90 per cent of the customers who called in to Kuhn Flowers to place an order were unsure what arrangement to purchase. The sales operator was responsible for helping the customer to determine which arrangement was best to purchase given the customer's needs and the arrangements that were available.

11 On a typical day, 13 lorries were used to cover 35 different routes. Each lorry averaged about 30 orders a day. Kuhn Flowers charged $8.95 for delivery service. Labour and vehicle costs typically averaged $7.00 per delivery.

12 Approximately 20 per cent of customers asked for same-day delivery depending on the time of the year.

13 The largest corporate customer provides 125 orders per month and accounts for approximately $200,000 in sales per year.

Exhibit 1 Kuhn Flowers: income statement for quarter ending 31 March 2004, and years ending 31 December 2003 and 31 December 2002

	31/3/2004	*31/12/2003*	*31/12/2002*
Revenue from local sales			
Fresh flowers	$ 1,305,630	$ 4,315,025	$ 4,453,786
Greenhouse	$ 194,338	$ 717,106	$ 1,037,183
Other local sales	$ 159,373	$ 989,693	$ 610,108
Total revenue from local sales	$ 1,659,341	$ 6,021,824	$ 6,101,077
Revenue from other sales			
Incoming sales	$ 190,644	$ 710,888	$ 616,631
Delivery charges	$ 250,010	$ 910,282	$ 852,631
Wire comissions	$ 67,367	$ 285,443	$ 344,632
Other income	$ 102,780	$ 395,852	$ 394,899
Total revenue from other sales	$ 610,801	$ 2,302,465	$ 2,208,793
Gross sales	$ 2,270,142	$ 8,324,289	$ 8,309,869
Less: discounts and allowances	$ (37,085)	$ (167,154)	$ (159,180)
Net sales	$ 2,233,057	$ 8,157,135	$ 8,150,689
Cost of goods sold			
Materials	$ 755,554	$ 2,593,321	$ 2,678,267
Labour	$ 322,686	$ 1,144,425	$ 1,309,236
Other	$ 68,809	$ 252,113	$ 208,319
Total cost of goods sold	$ 1,147,049	$ 3,989,859	$ 4,195,822
Gross margin	$ 1,086,008	$ 4,167,276	$ 3,954,867
Sales, general, & administrative	$ 880,338	$ 3,384,327	$ 3,508,537
Earnings before tax	$ 205,670	$ 782,949	$ 446,330

Exhibit 2 **Kuhn Flowers: balance sheet for quarter ending 31 March 2004 and years ending 31 December 2003, 31 December 2002 and 31 December 2001**

ASSETS	31/3/2004	31/12/2003	31/12/2002	31/12/2001
Current assets				
Cash & cash equivalents	$ 141,803	$ 374,607	$ 521,435	$ 416,344
Accounts receivable	$ 340,792	$ 549,756	$ 563,332	$ 617,738
Prepaid expenses	$ 13,168	$ 24,951	$ 17,000	$ 14,270
Inventory	$ 98,422	$ 98,422	$ 135,484	$ 135,676
Total current assets	**$ 594,185**	**$ 1,047,737**	**$ 1,237,251**	**$ 1,184,028**
Non-current assets				
Fixtures & furniture	$ 127,741	$ 127,741	$ 127,740	$ 115,445
Computer equipment	$ 119,414	$ 119,414	$ 115,326	$ 140,295
Vehicles	$ –	$ –	$ –	$ 50,395
Leasehold improvement	$ 157,570	$ 157,570	$ 145,116	$ 130,613
Goodwill	$ 1,614,018	$ 1,614,018	$ 1,614,017	$ 1,614,017
Other non-current assets	$ 17,117	$ 18,891	$ 45,753	$ 51,385
Accumulated depreciation	$ (218,363)	$ (195,945)	$ (101,049)	$ (18,509)
Total non-current assets	**$ 1,817,496**	**$ 1,841,688**	**$ 1,946,903**	**$ 2,083,641**
TOTAL ASSETS	**$ 2,411,682**	**$ 2,889,425**	**$ 3,184,154**	**$ 3,267,669**
LIABILITIES				
Current liabilities				
Accounts payable	$ 349,650	$ 529,522	$ 486,213	$ 603,194
Short-term borrowing	$ 75,434	$ 475,434	$ –	$ –
Accruals	$ 162,609	$ 205,678	$ 222,004	$ 136,399
Sales tax payablee	$ 17,911	$ 30,125	$ 30,522	$ 30,928
Deferred revenue	$ 16,096	$ 6,863	$ 5,514	$ 3,227
Total current liabilites	**$ 621,700**	**$ 1,247,623**	**$ 744,253**	**$ 773,748**
Non-current liabilities	**$ –**	**$ –**	**$ 1,153,333**	**$ 1,473,333**
TOTAL LIABILITIES	**$ 621,700**	**$ 1,247,623**	**$ 1,897,586**	**$ 2,247,081**
PARTNERS CAPITAL	**$ 1,789,981**	**$ 1,641,802**	**$ 1,277,883**	**$ 1,020,588**
TOTAL LIABILITIES & PARTNERS CAPITAL	**$ 2,411,682**	**$ 2,889,425**	**$ 3,175,469**	**$ 3,267,669**

Exhibit 3 Imports of cut flowers (1992–2002) ($000)

Source country	1992	1993	1994	1995	1996	1997	1998	1999	2000	2001	2002
Canada	$ 4,133	$ 4,584	$ 5,772	$ 7,455	$ 10,012	$ 14,871	$ 15,554	$ 15,477	$ 17,809	$ 17,959	$ 17,053
Mexico	$ 11,898	$ 13,930	$ 15,368	$ 23,191	$ 19,522	$ 23,649	$ 25,186	$ 27,224	$ 29,621	$ 29,415	$ 27,495
Other Central America	$ 15,395	$ 16,687	$ 21,679	$ 22,360	$ 23,892	$ 25,983	$ 26,540	$ 25,025	$ 24,961	$ 18,082	$ 18,415
Total North America	**$ 31,426**	**$ 35,201**	**$ 42,819**	**$ 53,006**	**$ 53,425**	**$ 64,503**	**$ 67,281**	**$ 67,726**	**$ 72,391**	**$ 65,456**	**$ 62,963**
Domican Republic	$ 1,639	$ 1,872	$ 1,510	$ 1,172	$ 1,480	$ 1,390	$ 1,198	$ 1,244	$ 1,133	$ 1,530	$ 1,820
Other Carribean	$ 998	$ 515	$ 539	$ 659	$ 575	$ 414	$ 169	$ 81	$ 152	$ 219	$ 215
Total Caribbean	**$ 2,637**	**$ 2,387**	**$ 2,049**	**$ 1,832**	**$ 2,055**	**$ 1,805**	**$ 1,367**	**$ 1,325**	**$ 1,286**	**$ 1,749**	**$ 2,035**
Columbia	$ 231,397	$ 251,837	$ 270,219	$ 321,273	$ 366,395	$ 359,620	$ 360,626	$ 343,684	$ 347,242	$ 302,450	$ 289,554
Ecuador	$ 15,244	$ 19,575	$ 26,080	$ 50,498	$ 68,210	$ 83,497	$ 90,119	$ 92,299	$ 89,249	$ 99,722	$ 87,252
Peru	$ 2,316	$ 1,082	$ 538	$ 582	$ 1,295	$ 1,617	$ 1,019	$ 1,598	$ 2,478	$ 2,334	$ 1,700
Other South America	$ 1,453	$ 1,386	$ 2,494	$ 1,737	$ 1,739	$ 2,318	$ 3,576	$ 3,904	$ 3,633	$ 3,832	$ 3,765
Total South America	**$ 250,410**	**$ 273,880**	**$ 299,330**	**$ 374,090**	**$ 437,638**	**$ 447,051**	**$ 455,339**	**$ 441,486**	**$ 442,602**	**$ 408,338**	**$ 382,270**
Netherlands	$ 51,080	$ 53,460	$ 57,116	$ 61,162	$ 59,005	$ 61,774	$ 69,200	$ 61,645	$ 71,639	$ 67,070	$ 71,256
France	$ 2,253	$ 2,047	$ 2,025	$ 2,370	$ 2,079	$ 1,980	$ 1,966	$ 1,656	$ 1,413	$ 833	$ 754
Italy	$ 1,332	$ 1,128	$ 823	$ 1,058	$ 788	$ 825	$ 1,431	$ 1,241	$ 1,127	$ 988	$ 1,127
Other EU	$ 807	$ 845	$ 1,136	$ 839	$ 868	$ 954	$ 1,332	$ 847	$ 1,018	$ 761	$ 959
Total European Union	**$ 55,472**	**$ 57,480**	**$ 61,100**	**$ 65,428**	**$ 62,740**	**$ 65,533**	**$ 73,929**	**$ 65,389**	**$ 75,196**	**$ 69,653**	**$ 74,095**
Israel	$ 1,610	$ 1,828	$ 2,094	$ 3,029	$ 3,350	$ 3,832	$ 4,468	$ 4,345	$ 5,821	$ 6,888	$ 7,332
Thailand	$ 4,378	$ 4,275	$ 4,323	$ 4,606	$ 4,189	$ 3,766	$ 2,921	$ 2,599	$ 3,008	$ 2,714	$ 2,841
China	$ 217	$ 523	$ 777	$ 302	$ 685	$ 377	$ 683	$ 1,698	$ 1,421	$ 1,360	$ 1,015
India	$ 885	$ 978	$ 1,871	$ 3,749	$ 2,927	$ 1,140	$ 848	$ 652	$ 672	$ 799	$ 731
Other Asia	$ 604	$ 481	$ 469	$ 417	$ 242	$ 432	$ 376	$ 267	$ 1,119	$ 1,336	$ 868
Total Asia	**$ 7,694**	**$ 8,085**	**$ 9,534**	**$ 12,103**	**$ 11,393**	**$ 9,547**	**$ 9,296**	**$ 9,561**	**$ 12,041**	**$ 13,099**	**$ 12,786**
Australia	$ 2,898	$ 2,614	$ 2,808	$ 2,405	$ 2,295	$ 2,372	$ 2,356	$ 2,498	$ 2,518	$ 2,235	$ 1,571
New Zealand	$ 616	$ 805	$ 1,002	$ 1,181	$ 1,339	$ 1,668	$ 2,078	$ 2,261	$ 2,420	$ 3,165	$ 3,253
Other Oceana	$ 4	$ –	$ 2	$ –	$ –	$ 3	$ 6	$ 20	$ 26	$ –	$ –
Total Oceana	**$ 3,518**	**$ 3,419**	**$ 3,811**	**$ 3,586**	**$ 3,634**	**$ 4,043**	**$ 4,440**	**$ 4,779**	**$ 4,963**	**$ 5,400**	**$ 4,823**
South Africa	$ 533	$ 841	$ 445	$ 607	$ 736	$ 1,269	$ 1,545	$ 1,134	$ 1,020	$ 1,058	$ 868
Other Africa	$ 556	$ 677	$ 818	$ 717	$ 851	$ 1,250	$ 1,162	$ 900	$ 842	$ 627	$ 1,544
Total Africa	**$ 1,089**	**$ 1,518**	**$ 1,263**	**$ 1,323**	**$ 1,587**	**$ 2,520**	**$ 2,707**	**$ 2,034**	**$ 1,862**	**$ 1,685**	**$ 2,412**
Rest of the world[1]	**$ 119**	**$ 212**	**$ 197**	**$ 156**	**$ 78**	**$ 44**	**$ 4**	**$ 66**	**$ 120**	**$ 89**	**$ 81**
Total imports of cut flowers	$ 352,366	$ 382,182	$ 420,104	$ 511,524	$ 572,550	$ 595,045	$ 614,362	$ 592,366	$ 610,461	$ 565,468	$ 541,466
Cut flowers produced in the US[2]	$ 425,950	$ 384,811	$ 404,384	$ 383,316	$ 365,198	$ 422,816	$ 367,042	$ 389,898	$ 390,244	$ 378,428	$ 373,899
Total US consumption of cut flowers	$ 778,316	$ 766,992	$ 824,488	$ 894,840	$ 937,748	$ 1,017,862	$ 981,404	$ 982,264	$ 1,000,705	$ 943,896	$ 915,364
% from imports	45.27%	49.83%	50.95%	57.16%	61.06%	58.46%	62.60%	60.31%	61.00%	59.91%	59.15%

Notes:
1. Includes other Europe, New independent states, and central Asia.
2. Net of exports.
Source: US Department of Agriculture, Economic Research Service.

Exhibit 4 **Retail florists' share of floral sales (1993–2003) ($ in billions)**

	Total industry sales	*Retail florist sales*	*% of total sales*
1993	$ 12.60	$ 6.50	51.59
1994	$ 13.30	$ 6.60	49.62
1995	$ 14.00	$ 6.70	47.86
1996	$ 15.00	$ 7.10	47.33
1997	$ 15.70	$ 7.30	46.50
1998	$ 16.40	$ 7.70	46.95
1999	$ 17.10	$ 7.90	46.20
2000	$ 18.00	$ 8.10	45.00
2001	$ 18.10	$ 8.80	48.62
2002	$ 18.20	$ 9.10	50.00
2003	$ 19.10	$ 8.50	44.50

Sources: US Department of Commerce, Bureau of Economic Analysis, Personal Consumption Expenditures US Department of Commerce, Census Bureau. Courtesy: Society of American Florists.
Note. The remainder of total industry sales consists of flower sales at garden centres, department stores, discount chain stores, home improvement stores, hardware stores, supermarkets, drug stores, etc.

Exhibit 5 **Retail florists with payroll (1997–2001)**

1997	26,200
1998	25,617
1999	24,798
2000	24,197
2001	23,870

Source: Society of American Florists.

Exhibit 6 **Spending per customer transaction (1993–2003)**

	Retail florists		Non-retail florists	
	Arrangements	Unarranged flowers	Arrangements	Unarranged flowers
1993	$ 31.26	$ 15.15	$ 27.48	$ 6.38
1994	$ 33.31	$ 17.17	$ 28.16	$ 6.81
1995	$ 34.48	$ 17.21	$ 29.32	$ 6.51
1996	$ 37.15	$ 17.98	$ 31.36	$ 6.86
1997	$ 38.63	$ 17.22	$ 31.78	$ 7.34
1998	$ 40.12	$ 18.68	$ 32.93	$ 7.40
1999	$ 39.69	$ 18.28	$ 32.68	$ 7.70
2000	$ 42.86	$ 25.17	$ 34.42	$ 8.46
2001	$ 45.41	$ 23.36	$ 35.71	$ 8.45
2002	$ 43.09	$ 22.93	$ 34.18	$ 8.39
2003	$ 44.73	$ 24.25	$ 31.71	$ 8.43

Source: American Floral Endowment Consumer Tracking Study. Courtesy: Society of American Florists.

Exhibit 7 Wal-Mart advertisement

Exhibit 8 **Kuhn Flowers, Beach Boulevard location**

Main sales floor with assembly area in the back

Recently made arrangements in assembly area

Exhibit 8 (continued)

Finished arrangements in inventory awaiting shipment

Cut stems on the sales floor

Exhibit 9 Sample page from Kuhn Flowers' arrangement catalogue

Exhibit 10 Kuhn Flowers: sales by customer purchase occasion

Holidays	26.0%
Funerals	20.0%
Birthdays	10.0%
Anniversaries	5.0%
Everyday purchases	39.0%

6 INDITEX: ZARA AND BEYOND

Michael Lewis

In 1963 Amancio Ortega Gaona started Confecciones GOA to manufacture women's pyjamas and lingerie products for garment wholesalers. In 1975, after one customer cancelled a large order, the firm opened a retail outlet in La Coruña. The Zara store was popular and during the next 10 years others opened in all major Spanish cities. The Inditex corporate structure was created in 1985 and in December 1988, the first overseas Zara store opened in Porto, Portugal, followed shortly by New York in 1989 and Paris in 1990. Today, Inditex, has eight different business formats, 63,000 employees and more than 3,000 stores in 64 countries. It is undoubtedly a major player in the global fashion industry. During the first half of 2006, its turnover grew by 23 per cent to €3,746 million and its net profit grew by 20 per cent to €295 million (consolidated turnover for 2005 was €6,741 million and profit €803 million). Equally significant, however, given very challenging conditions in many of its key markets, store sales increased by 5 per cent, compared to 0.5 per cent for key rival H&M – perhaps helping to explain how the firm exceeded analyst estimates for the seventh consecutive quarter. Zara remains the largest Inditex division: in 2006 its 990 stores in 63 countries accounted for 65 per cent of total Inditex sales.

Zara

In 1975, the first Zara store was simply intended to be an outlet for cancelled orders but a more fundamental lesson was also learnt, the benefits of having 'five fingers touching the factory and five touching the customer'. Ten years later this principle transformed the evolution of the company. Over a 12-month period from 1985–1986, the firm's entire manufacturing capacity was switched to producing exclusively for the rapidly growing Zara chain and a sophisticated logistics system was created. Today, Zara is able to offer cutting edge fashion at affordable prices because its operating model exerts control over almost the entire garment supply chain (retailing, design, purchasing and logistics).

Retailing

At the heart of the operating model is the store. Zara locates its stores in expensive prime retail locations, selected after extensive market research, but much of the selling space is left empty in order to create a pleasant, spacious and uncluttered shopping environment. The layout of the stores, the furniture, and even the window displays are all designed at La Coruña, and a 'flying team' from headquarters is usually dispatched to a new site to set up the store. Location, traffic and layout are crucial for Zara because it spends relatively little on advertising. A typical Zara store has women's, men's and children's sections, with a manager in charge of each. Women's wear accounted for almost 60 per cent of sales, with the rest equally divided between men's wear and children's wear. The store manager is usually also the head of the women's section. Zara places a great deal of emphasis on training its sales force and strongly emphasises internal promotion. Store employee remuneration is based on a combination of salary and bonus derived from overall store sales. Although store managers are responsible for the 'profit and loss' of their respective stores, La Coruña controls prices, transfer costs, and even a certain amount of merchandising and product ordering. In practice, the critical performance measures for the store managers relate to the precision of their sales forecasts (communicated through the ordering process) and sales growth. A simple yet key measure followed by senior managers was the rate of improvement of daily sales from year-to-year – for example, sales on the third Wednesday of June 2007 compared to the third Wednesday of June 2006.

To its customers, Zara offers fashionably exclusive (yet low cost) product. Individual stores hold very low levels of inventory – typically only a few pieces of each item – and this can mean that a store's entire stock is on display. Indeed, it is not unusual to find empty racks by the end of a day's trading. This creates an additional incentive for customers to buy on the spot (because if a customer chooses to wait, the item might be sold out and may never be made again) and allows Zara to both carry less overall inventory and have less unsold items that have to be discounted in end-of–season sales than its competitors. In an industry where discounting means that the average product fetches only 60 per cent to 70 per cent of its full price, Zara manages to collect 85 per cent. This approach means that stores are completely reliant on regular and rapid replenishment of newly designed products. Stores must place their orders at predesignated times – if a store misses its ordering deadline, it has to wait – and receive shipments twice per week. Zara also minimise the risk of oversupply by keeping production volumes low at the beginning of the season and reacting quickly to orders and new trends during the season. The industry average 'pre-season inventory commitment' – the level of production and procurement in the supply chain in, say, late July for the fall/winter season – ranges from 45 per cent to 60 per cent of anticipated sales. At Zara it is only 15 per cent to 20 per cent. The 'in-season commitments' at Zara are 40 per cent to 50 per cent whereas the industry average ranges from almost nothing to a maximum of 20 per cent.

Design

Zara designs all its products. It has almost 300 staff in its headquarters 'commercial team' – comprising 200 designers plus market specialists and buyers. Together they produce designs for approximately 40,000 items per year from which about 10,000 are selected for production. Unlike their industry peers, these teams work both on next season's designs and, simultaneously and continuously, also update the current season's designs. Women's, men's and children's designers sit in different halls in a modern building attached to the Inditex headquarters. In each of these big open spaces designers occupy one side, market specialists the middle, and buyers (procurement and production planners) the other side. There are several big round tables in the central area of each hall for impromptu meetings and comfortable chairs and racks of the latest fashion magazines and catalogues fill the walls. There is an air of informality and openness. The firm tries hard to encourage a collegial and dynamic atmosphere (e.g. it is a young team and there are deliberately no design 'prima donnas') and inspiration is sought from myriad global sources (e.g. trade fairs, discotheques, catwalks, magazines). Extensive feedback from the store network also forms an integral part of the design process.

Designers produce sketches by hand and discuss them with colleagues. The sketches are then redrawn using CAD where further changes and adjustments, for better matching of weaves, textures, colours etc., are made. Before moving further through the process, it is necessary to determine whether the design can be produced and sold at a profit. The next step is to make a sample, often completed in the sample making shop in one corner of each hall.

Market specialists have responsibility for dealing with specific stores. As experienced employees, who have often been store managers themselves, they emphasise establishing personal relationships with the managers of 'their' stores. They are in constant contact, especially by phone, discussing sales, orders, new lines and other matters. Equally, stores rely heavily on these discussions with market specialists before finalising orders. Augmenting their extensive phone conversations, store managers are supplied with a specially designed hand-held digital device to facilitate the rapid and accurate exchange of market data. Final decisions concerning what products to make, when, and in what volumes are normally made collectively by the relevant groups of designers, market specialists, and buyers and after the decision is taken the buyers (also very experienced staff) take charge of the total order fulfilment process: planning procurement and production requirements, monitored warehouse inventories, allocated production to various factories and third-party suppliers and kept track of shortages and oversupplies.

Production

Zara manufactures a significant proportion of its products – mainly the most fashionable – in its own network of Spanish factories (most of which are located in and around the La Coruña complex). These factories generally work a single shift and are managed as independent profit centres. The rest of its products are procured from outside suppliers, in 2005 63 per cent of these were located in Europe and neighbouring countries, and most of the rest (33%) in Asia. With its relatively large and stable base of orders, Zara is a preferred customer for almost all its suppliers. The make or buy decisions are usually made by the procurement and production planners. The key criteria for making this decision are required levels of speed and expertise, cost-effectiveness, and availability of sufficient capacity. If the buyers cannot obtain desired prices, delivery terms, and quality from Zara factories, they are free to look outside. For its in-house production, Zara obtain 40 per cent of its fabric supply from another Inditex-owned subsidiary, Comditel (Zara accounts for almost 90 per cent of its total sales). Over half of these fabrics are purchased undyed to allow faster response to mid-season colour changes. To facilitate quick changes in printing and dyeing, Zara also work closely with Fibracolor (a dyestuff producer part owned by Inditex). The rest of the fabrics come from a range of other suppliers, none account for more than 4 per cent of Zara's total production in order to minimise any dependency on single suppliers and encourage maximum responsiveness from them.

After in-house CAD controlled piece cutting, Zara uses subcontractors for all sewing operations. The subcontractors themselves often collect the bagged cut pieces, together with the appropriate components (like buttons and zippers) in small trucks. There are some 500 sewing subcontractors in very close proximity to La

Coruña (in the Galicia region) and most work exclusively for Zara. Zara closely monitors their operations to ensure quality, compliance with labour laws, and above all else adherence to the production schedule. Subcontractors then bring back the sewn items to the same factory, where each piece is inspected during ironing (by machine and by hand). Finished products are then placed in plastic bags with proper labels and then sent to the distribution centre. A system of aerial monorails connects ten of the factories in La Coruña to the distribution centre. Completed products procured from outside suppliers are also sent directly to the distribution centre. Zara uses a sampling methodology to control the incoming quality.

Logistics

Speed is clearly an over-riding concern for Zara logistics: as one senior manager put it: 'For us, distance is not measured in kilometres, but in time'. The integrated logistics system is able to fulfil orders (i.e. from receipt of order at the distribution centre to arrival of goods at the store) within 24 hours for Europe, 48 hours for America and a maximum of 72 hours for Asia. Compared to similar companies in the industry, shipments are almost flawless – 98.9 per cent accurate with less than 0.5 per cent shrinkage. Although Inditex support their eight different formats with seven logistics centres in Spain (with another planned for Madrid), Zara's major distribution centres are in La Coruña and Zaragoza. The La Coruña centre is a five-storey, 50,000 m^2 facility that employs some of the most sophisticated and up-to-date automated systems: many developed by Zara/Inditex staff with the support of a Danish supplier. With a workforce of 1,200, the distribution centre normally operates four days per week with the precise number of shifts depending on the volume of products that have to be distributed. Orders for each store are packed into separate boxes and racks (for hanging items) and are typically ready for shipment eight hours after they have been received. Interestingly, although the original distribution centre was only operating at around 50 per cent of its full capacity, the nature of the operating system and its ambitious growth plans, saw Inditex open a new €100 million logistics centre in Zaragoza in 2002. Zara also has other smaller warehouses (e.g. Brazil, Argentina and Mexico) in order to cope with distance and different seasons in the southern hemisphere. Contractors, such as Keunhe and Nagel, using vehicles bearing Zara's name, pick up the merchandise at La Coruña and deliver it directly to Zara's stores in Europe. The vehicles run to published schedules (like a bus timetable). For example, an order for a store in the Netherlands catches the truck leaving La Coruña at 6 a.m. on Thursday. It is also easy to schedule a pick up at a specific destination for transport back to La Coruña (for example a shipment from China to be picked up at the port of Rotterdam). Products shipped by air are flown from either the airport in La Coruña or the larger airport in Santiago.

The future for Inditex?

In parallel with its overseas expansion, Inditex has successfully managed its risk profile by diversifying its retail offerings – a strategy only recently emulated by great rival H&M –- by acquiring and developing a number of new formats (2005 data for store numbers): *Skhuaban* (Kiddy's Class in Spain and Portugal) specialise in children's fashion (149 stores); *Pull and Bear* offer causal style to young people (427 stores); *Massimo Dutti* offers higher quality designs (369 stores); *Bershka* aims to be more fashionable (368 stores); *Stradivarius* focuses on young women (263 stores); *Oysho* provides lingerie and underwear product (154 stores). The most recently developed chain, *Zara Home*, is Inditex's first non-garment format and is focused on the home furnishings market (110 stores). Inditex, as the corporate parent, is responsible for some central administration (HR and legal services, etc.) together with services, like logistics technology, that are shared across the eight chains, but each of the eight brands operates with a great deal of commercial autonomy. What binds these formats together is a shared commitment to 'fashion at affordable prices' and the adoption of similar models for the fast control of the total supply chain.

DELTA SYNTHETIC FIBRES (DSF)

Nigel Slack

'When you are a small player in this business you really do need to develop your own approach to doing business. We are not in the same game as BASF or DuPont. Our key objectives have always been based on three things – niche markets, focused production and innovative products.'

(Paul Mayer – CEO, Delta Synthetic Fibres)

By the standards of the synthetic fibre industry, DSF was a very small, but international and technically successful company. For over eight years the company had been heavily dependent on one range of products based on the polymer 'Britlene', which it had developed itself in the late 1990s. By 2004, Britlene products accounted for 97 per cent of total revenue (the other 3 per cent came from the sale of licences). In fact, since it was founded in the 1970s, the company had always limited itself to a single product range at one time. The original product range 'Teklon' had been replaced by 'Deklon', which had in turn been replaced by 'Britlene'. None of these product changes had required substantial changes to the company's processes.

'I guess that, until now, we have been lucky in only having one product range to concentrate on. This means that the early parts of our manufacturing process have to cope with relatively little variety. There are different grades and variants of the basic Britlene polymer but only five or six main varieties, with around 10 or 12 "specials", which we make for specific customers. The real variety comes later on in the process, in the extrusion stage and especially in the finishing and packing stages. We have 35 extrusion "patterns" which, together with 17 "finishes" and 10 to 12 pack types, means that we have potentially around seven thousand ways of producing each polymer grade. Of course, as usual, 20 per cent of possible end product codes account for 80 per cent of our output. However, I feel it is important that we should try and control this variety. Not only does it add complexity to the process, it will become an even greater problem if we do not tackle it before we start producing Britlon as well as Britlene.'

(Paul Mayer, CEO)

The Britlene range was used mainly as a 'blend fibre' in heavy-duty clothing, although smaller quantities were used to produce industrial goods such as tyre cord, flexible industrial drives and insulating sleeves. Its main properties were very high wear resistance, together with high thermal and electrical insulation. Sales of Britlene products, especially in the United States had started to fall off in 2004 as competitor products eroded DSF's traditional markets. These products rarely matched the technical specification of the Britlene products but were significantly less expensive.

From Britlene to Britlon

In 2004 the company had developed a new product range built around a new polymer to be known as Britlon. Britlon polymers had all the properties of Britlene but were superior in their strength, heat resistant qualities and electrical insulation. It was hoped that these additional properties would open up new clothing uses (for example, as a substitute for mineral wool) as well as allowing entry into the far larger markets associated with thermal and electrical insulation. By late 2004, after some delays, the major technical and engineering problems associated with bulk production of the Britlon range seemed to have been solved.

> 'Britlon has come later than we hoped. Partly this is because it is a genuine advance in product formulation and we had some difficult technical problems to overcome. I have to admit though that partly the delay was due to not starting Britlon development early enough. Our Marketing colleagues have been telling us for some time that an enhanced product range could have a significant impact on the market around this time. Yet now, because of construction lead-times, we are in the position of not being able to introduce the Britlon range into the market until early 1999.'

(Paul Mayer, CEO)

The basic production method for both the Britlene and Britlon ranges was similar to that of most synthetic fibres. An oil-based organic chemical is polymerised (a process of joining several molecules into a long chain) in conditions of intense pressure and heat, often by the addition of a suitable catalyst. This polymerisation takes place in large autoclaves (like an industrial pressure cooker). The polymer is then extruded (forced through a nozzle like the rose of a garden watering can), rapidly cooled and then finished in a variety of ways, for example, spun on to cones or collected in bales. After this, a variety of different conversion processes were used to add value before the product was shipped to the customer.

The later stages of the production processes were relatively flexible. With some 'change-over' losses in productivity, the equipment could be used to process most types of fibre with little modification. However, the early stages in the process, particularly the polymerisation stage, were usually designed for one range of polymer and might need substantial modification before a different polymer range could be made. For this reason a new Britlon line or a Britlene line converted to produce the Britlon range, could only produce Britlon products, just as a Britlene line could only produce Britlene products.

Current facilities

Currently the Britlene range was produced at the company's three factories: Teesside in the UK, Hamburg in Germany and Chicago in the USA. The largest site was Teesside with three lines. There was one line at each of the other two sites. All five production lines had a nominal design capacity of 5.5 million kg per year of Britlene. However, after allowing for change-over losses, maintenance and holidays, expected output was around 5 million kg per year. Each plant operated on a 24 hours per day, seven days per week basis.

The cost of raw materials was more or less the same at each location, but labour costs, general employment costs, local taxation and energy costs did vary. The

Hamburg plant had the highest production costs followed by the Chicago plant, with the Teesside plant having the lowest cost per kg produced (at full utilisation). However, the cost differences between the plants were less than the differences in the input costs. Partly this was because of higher productivity at both the Hamburg and Chicago plants, and partly because all three Teesside lines were relatively old and prone to breakdown.

DSF's markets

The largest single market for the Britlene range was still the UK, although the percentage of sales to UK customers had declined from over 60 per cent in 1998 to around 41 per cent in 2004. The potential for volume growth was greatest in the Far East markets, especially South East Asia, and least in the UK. Earnings growth potential however was likely to be greatest in continental Europe and the USA. In terms of market sector sales, both industrial and domestic clothing were growing only slowly for DSF, while the company's sales into general industrial markets had grown from practically nothing in 1990 to around 13 per cent of sales in 2004 and were likely to grow further in the next five years especially in the USA. Thermal and electrical insulation markets, after fast growth in the early 2000s, had grown only slowly over the last two years.

'We are trading in two quite different types of market. Clothing, both industrial and domestic, is relatively predictable, and we are established suppliers with a relatively large share of a very small market. The industrial and insulation markets however are far larger in themselves and we have only a tiny share. In the clothing markets we are competing, usually on price, against very similar products. In the other markets we are competing against a whole range of different materials, usually on product performance and supply flexibility.'

(Tim Williams, Vice-President Marketing)

Exhibit 1 shows market volumes for 2004.

Tim Williams also saw the new Britlon product range changing the sales profile of the company.

'Britlon products will be based on a technically superior material which is also likely to be marginally less expensive to produce. We should be able to, at least, maintain our share of the clothing market and possibly stop the margin erosion we have suffered in this sector over the last few years. But the real benefits are going to show in the Insulation and, to only a slightly less extent, in the Industrial markets. The improved strength and insulation properties of the Britlon range should let us capture a greater share of a larger and more profitable market. Also, because we will have two product ranges, we can differentiate between different market needs in different parts of the world. The future will be one where we will have far more choice as to how we position ourselves in our markets. But it will also be one where we will face increased level of market uncertainty.'

Exhibit 2 shows the aggregated volume and price forecasts for both products for 2005 through to 2010.

Creating a Britlon capability

The production process needed to manufacture the Britlon range was very similar to that used for the Britlene range, however a totally new type of polymerisation unit would be needed prior to the extrusion stage. Also the technologies for polymerisation were mutually exclusive. Britlon and Britlene products could not be produced on the same line. Early in the development of Britlon, DSF had approached Alpen GmbH, an international chemical plant construction company, for help on a large-scale plant design of the new unit. Together they produced and tested an acceptable design for the new line and had explored different construction methods. Essentially there were two ways of acquiring Britlon capacity. DSF could convert the old Britlene-based lines, or it could construct entirely new lines.

For a conversion a new polymer unit would need to be constructed alongside the old line (without interfering with production). When complete it would be connected to the extrusion unit which would itself require only minor conversion. Alpen were quoting a lead-time of two years for both the construction of a new Britlon line or to convert an old Britlene plant to Britlon production.

> 'The long lead-times which are being quoted for constructing this type of process are partly a result of a high level of demand for Alpen's services because of their reputation for providing sound technical solutions in process design. Also, I guess they are a bit cautious because of the technical novelty of the Britlon process.'
>
> (Liam Flaherty, Vice-President Operations)

Although the lead-time for building a new line was the same as for a conversion, the capital cost of the latter was lower. Exhibit 3 shows the capital estimates for both conversion and new lines. Economies of scale were such that, whether converted or built new, the capacity of Britlon plants would be around 5 million kg per year.

Focus or flexibility?

Liam Flaherty, the Vice-President of Operations, based at Teesside, was keen to take advantage of the opportunities provided by the introduction of the Britlon range. In particular, he wanted to avoid concentrating exclusively on the problems posed in the short-term by the introduction of new Britlon capacity.

> 'I know that getting the capacity expansion strategy right must be a priority. It is a major investment programme for the company and we must keep tight control of how the new capacity is installed. However, we are also laying down the structure of the company's operations for the long-term. In effect we are moving, for the first time, into being a "two product range" company. This presents us with a whole range of issues which either we have not faced before or we have avoided confronting.'
>
> (Liam Flaherty, Vice-President Operations)

Liam had already identified what he regarded as some of the key questions in a report to Paul Mayer. These were as follows.

- Should every site produce both product ranges, or should we try and develop 'Centres of Expertise' for the two product ranges?
- Even if all three sites do produce both product ranges, should each site specialise in one part of each product range?

- How can we make sure that all sites understand their contribution to the company's overall operations capability? In other words, should strategic operations decisions still be made at the centre or should we allow each site some degree of autonomy in developing their own strategies for their markets or their product ranges?

- In the longer term should we give different sites different roles in developing our overall operations capability? For example, Chicago has shown particular enthusiasm (and enjoyed some success) in improving both productivity and flexibility on its line. It has done this mainly through a series of incremental technology improvements to the process. Because of this, should it be given responsibility for process improvement, even though traditionally this responsibility has been seen as belonging to the central technical resource at Teesside?

- Following from this last point, what should be the role of our central technology resource? In the past it has been good at understanding the practicalities of implementing modifications to our existing technology in a 'top-down' way. However, it has been less good at motivating and training factory level operations people in the three sites to take responsibility on themselves for improvement.

- How can we link our technology/operations capabilities with sales and marketing? So far we have prospered through pushing our new technologies out into the market, but this is unlikely to be successful in the future. Although Britlon's enhanced performance will give a major boost to sales, increasingly it will be small product modifications which will win us extra business. I'm sure there will be some big technology breakthroughs in the future. But we can't wait for these to come through every few years. The future is more likely to be one of fast development and response to specific customer needs in a wider variety of markets.

The capacity working group

In the autumn of 2004 Paul Mayer set up the capacity working group to consider the introduction of the new product range and all its implications. However, he did place some limits on what the company would do.

'Liam is right, we have to consider the underlying issues and assumptions behind the reconfiguration of our operations, but for the time being we need to confine ourselves to existing sites. In the short-term the creation of an entirely new site would increase the complexities of multi-site operation to an unacceptable level. Conversely, the complete closure of one of the three existing sites is, I consider, a waste of the manpower and physical resources that we have invested in that location. I believe expansion could take place at one, two or all of the existing sites. In the future however all things are possible. For example, it may make sense to develop a new site in Asia both to service the growing Eastern markets and to take advantage of lower costs.'

(Paul Mayer, CEO)

Exhibit 1 **Current market volumes by product and region, 2004 (millions of kg)**

Market sectors	UK	Continental Europe	USA	Far East
Clothing – industrial	8.04	3.74	1.69	1.84
Clothing – domestic	1.22	0.09	N.A.	N.A.
Clothing – general	0.52	1.02	1.10	0.73
Thermal insulation	0.41	0.39	1.01	N.A.
Electrical insulation	0.18	0.64	1.10	0.98
Total	10.37	5.88	4.90	3.55

Exhibit 2 **Forecasts Britlene and Britlon ranges**

	Potential sales	
	Britlene (all products) millions of kg p.a.	Britlon (all products) millions of kg p.a.
2004 (actual)	24.7	
2005	22	
2006	20	
2007	17	3 (assuming availability)
2008	13	16
2009	11	27
2010	10	29
	Average price forecast (p. per kg)	
	Britlene (across all products)	Britlon (across all products)
2005	98	–
2006	98	–
2007	95	125
2008	90	120
2009	85	120
2010	85	120

Exhibit 3 Estimated Britlon capital costs

The table below gives estimated costs and stage payments required by Alpen for Britlon polymer line and extrusion unit construction.

Type of order	Cost (£ million)	Timing	
Whole *new* 'Britlon' line including polymer and extrusion units	4.8	Begin Onstream	6 months from order 2 years from order
Conversion of 'Britlene' line to 'Britlon' line	3.0	Begin Onstream	6 months from order 2 years from order

The cost of a new plant is payable in three six-monthly instalments – £1,000,000 being due one year after ordering; £1,000,000 due six months later and the balance on completion.

The cost of a conversion is payable in three six-monthly instalments of £1,000,000; one year and 18 months from the order and on completion.

THE GREENVILLE OPERATION

Nigel Slack

In Greenville, South Carolina, is the largest piece of technology within the Carlsen group, described by the company as *'the most advanced machine of its type in the world, which will enable us to achieve new standards of manufacturing excellence for products requiring absolute cleanliness and precision in production'* and *'a quantum leap in harnessing economies of scale, new technology and new forms of organisation to provide **the** plant of the 21st century'*.

The Greenville plant was joining Carlsen's, two existing US plants in North Carolina, 100 km from the new plant. Both the old plants offered precision custom coating and laminating services to a wide range of customers, amongst the most important being, Phanchem for whom it made dry photoresist imaging films, a critical step in the printed wiring board manufacturing process. Yet, although the Greenville plant was seen as being right for the 21st century, its origins lay back in 1998.

'The Big One'

Nineteen ninety-eight was a traumatic year for Carlsen's photoresist imaging business. Prior to that, it had been the clear market leader based on high quality, competitive costs and excellent working relationships with its customers. So when Grade Graphics, the company's major competitor, introduced a new coating technology, enabling it to produce product at levels of cleanliness significantly better than Carlsen, the shock was severe.

> We paid millions in customer rejections and the coating machine was down for eight months. Imagine it; we just didn't make any of this product line for eight months! it was a very painful experience. Up to then we had acted as though we would always be the best. It was this competitive failure which woke us up.
>
> (Will Small, Vice-President and General Manager, Carlsen Custom)

By modifying its own coating technology, the company overcame the worst of its problems and by mid-1999 had recovered most of its market share. Yet, the experience had convinced Carlsen that it should be considering more radical manufacturing methods. A team, led by Will Small, was formed to create a concept for a coating machine that would push the boundaries of process technology further than anything considered previously, with a large capacity, faster speed, state-of-the-art automation and ultra clean conditions. This could result in lower costs and very high quality levels.

Source: Revised October 2006. Some data have been changed for reasons of commercial confidentiality. This case is for the purposes of class discussion, and is not intended to illustrate either good or bad management practice.

'We called this machine "The Big One". It was a kind of design exercise I guess, but with a very serious intent. it was a "mind-expanding" experience yet with a clear business goal'.
(Greg Russell, Engineering Manager, Greenville)

However, shortly after the creation of the 'The Big One' concept, market forecasts were revised downwards and the project was abandoned. However, all who had participated in the 'The Big One' team were convinced of the value of the process.

'During the time of incubation which followed the exercise many of the ideas that we had put into "The Big One" were changed and modified as new technology became available and as our ideas developed. But "The Big One" had planted the seed so the effort that we put in, although aborted at the time, did lead us to be able to be more effective when we got to the point of doing it in reality.'
(Greg Russell)

'The Big One' resurrected

By 2000, forecasts of demand once again indicated a need for extra coating capacity and work started on examining how this extra capacity might be provided. It was thought that a new low-cost operation could secure a very large part of Phanchem's future business – perhaps even an exclusive agreement to supply 100 per cent of their needs.

After consideration three options were presented to Carlsen's board.

A. Expand an existing site by building a new machine within existing site boundaries. This would provide around 120 to 130 million square feet (MSF) per year of additional capacity and require somewhat less than $15 million in capital expenditure.

B. Build a new facility alongside the existing plant. This new facility could accommodate additional capacity of around 150 MSF per year but, unlike option A, would also allow for future expansion. Initially this would require around $18 million capital.

C. Set up a totally new site with a much larger increment of capacity (probably around 250 MSF per year). This option could also incorporate much of the 'The Big One', ultra clean technology which had been explored previously. This option would be much more expensive, almost certainly in excess of $28 million.

Will Small and his team initially favoured option B but in discussion with Carlsen Group senior management, opinion shifted towards the more radical option C.

'It may have been the highest risk option but it held considerable potential and it fitted with the Carlsen Group philosophy of getting into high-tech specialised areas of business. So we went for it.'
(Will Small)

The option of a very large, ultra clean, state-of-the-art facility also had a further advantage – it could change the economics of the photoresist imaging industry. Worldwide demand and capacity did not immediately justify investing in such a large increase in capacity. In fact, there was probably some overcapacity in the industry. But a 'The Big One' type operation would provide a level of quality at such low costs that, if there was overcapacity in the industry, it would not be Carlsen's capacity which would by lying idle.

Designing the new plant

Detailed decisions were needed in four interrelated areas.

- Capacity – what type of factory should be built, how big should it be, and where should it be built?
- Technology – what type of coating technology should be installed?
- Organisation – what type of work organisation would be appropriate for the new plant?
- Supply relationships – what should be the relationship with Phanchem?

Capacity

The team considered two options for the coating machine capacity. The first was to install two coating lines, each with around 150 MSF per year. This was a reasonably ambitious option given that the largest machine existing at that time had a capacity of around 100 MSF per year. However, this paled beside the second option which was to install a single prototype machine with a capacity of over 250 MSF per year. Although risky and requiring more technological development, it would be more effective in its use of capital and, potentially, would allow very efficient use of labour. The risk was that effective capacity might be reduced because of lower yields from such a big and untried machine, especially if there were changeover losses.

The location of the new plant would also have to be decided. It should be within two to three hours' drive of the division's headquarters, and also had to be a non-attainment area for ozone under US Environmental Protection Agency (EPA) rules. It would need good communications, be near an interstate highway and preferably close to an interstate intersection. Furthermore, it should be reasonably close to an airport and be in an area that would attract professionals because of the 'quality of life' available.

> 'We contacted the government representatives of both North Carolina and South Carolina. Interestingly those in South Carolina were much more receptive. The North Carolina guys did not seem to be as excited at the prospect of the new plant.'
>
> (Greg Russell)

The site at Greenville was selected partly because of the cooperation from the South Carolina authorities and partly because of the intrinsic attractiveness of the area. In retrospect, it was felt that perhaps not all the effort expended on choosing a site was justified.

> 'One of the things we learnt from the whole process of finding a site was that we ought to not necessarily go for the best site possible. Rather look until you've found something which meets your needs and then stop'.
>
> (Will Small)

Technology

Two decisions regarding the design of the process technology faced the team. First, what type of drying technology to incorporate within the line? And second, what kind of feed system should be installed to deliver the coating material to the coating heads? The decision over the drying technology was a choice between traditional and radical options. A traditional approach involved drying using relatively low energy levels applied to the material over a long web path. The more radical solution was to subject the material to higher energy levels over a shorter web path. A major advantage of high energy drying was that, if it worked, it would give significantly lower capital costs, and potentially slightly lower processing costs. However, there were risks in choosing high energy systems because quality levels were sometimes difficult to control.

A similar decision faced the team over the technical design of the feed system which transported the coating material to the coating heads after mixing. Sophisticated, computer controlled feed systems involving complex piping arrangements between the mixing and coating areas were available on the market. Although expensive, these seemed to offer convenient linking with process control technology, less physical handling of the material, and greater flexibility. On the other hand, a simple piped system was both considerably less expensive and more robust.

Focus or flexibility?

It became clear that there was one issue which was underlying all the team's discussions – how flexible should the process be? Should the team assume that they were designing a plant which would be dedicated exclusively to the manufacture of photoresist imaging film for the foreseeable future, and ruthlessly cut out any technological options that would enable them to manufacture other products, or should they design a more general purpose plant which was suitable for photoresist imaging film, but could be adapted to coat other products? It proved a difficult decision.

- The advantages of the more flexible option were obvious, *'At least it would mean that there was no chance of me being stuck with a plant and no market for it to serve in a couple of year's time.'* (Harry Barton, Plant Manager)
- But the advantages of a totally dedicated plant were less obvious, although there was a general agreement that both costs and quality could be superior in a focused plant.

The team decided on a mixture of the adventurous and the conservative, deciding to go for a single large machine, but using robust, conventional drying and feed line technologies. They also decided to focus on a relatively non-flexible single dedicated large machine.

'You can't imagine the agonies we went through when we decided not to make this a flexible machine. Many of us were not comfortable with saying, "This is going to be a photoresist machine exclusively, and if the market goes away we're in real trouble". We had a lot of debate about that. Eventually we more or less reached a consensus for focus but it was certainly one of the toughest decisions we ever made.'

(Harry Barton)

The capital cost savings of a focused facility and operating costs savings of up to 25 per cent were powerful arguments, as was the philosophy of total process dedication.

'The key word for us was focus. We wanted to be quite clear about what was needed to satisfy our customer in making this single type of product. As well as providing significant cost savings to us it made it a lot easier to identify the root causes of any problems because we would not have to worry about how it might affect other products. It's all very clear. When the line

was down we would not be generating revenue! It would also force us to understand our own performance. At our other plants, if a line goes down, the people can be shifted to other responsibilities. We don't have other responsibilities here – we're either making it or we're not.'

(Greg Russell)

Work organisation

In the same way that many of the technical ideas which found their way into the Greenville plant had their origins some years earlier, so the pattern of work organisation and the concept of self-managed team work had been discussed for some time. The Greenville project provided the opportunity to use them. However, before committing themselves, the team members drew up a list of 15 reasons why they *should* adopt the self-managed work team approach and 15 reasons why they *should not* do so. These are set out in the table below.

Reasons why we should do it	Reasons why we should not do it
It will allow us to change rapidly	We are currently successful
Enriches jobs for all employees	We are inexperienced in using/implementing such a concept
Increases employee 'ownership'	Starting a new operation. We have plenty going on as it is
Greater technical requirements demand it	Culture of people we recruit or transfer might not adapt to it
More fulfilling for all employees involved	We do not have the support of Middle Management
If it leads to high quality, it will lead to lower cost	It is a big piece of our business to risk
Therefore, we think this method will increase our profitability	Increased training costs/employee costs. We might have to pay more to get more
Involves all employees in a joint venture to achieve customer satisfaction	Risks, personnel policies, legalities, etc.
If our objective is to stay number one, we must change our people/management philosophy to stay abreast, etc.	Immediate impact on other Carlsen plants
May be the last opportunity to do this for 10 years	We may not have enough time to do it right
Competition may try it before us	Unmet expectations by more high calibre employees
It will attract a higher-calibre employee (flexible, thinking)	Uncertain consequences of failure. Would we be better off for having tried and failed or better off not to try?
People are the way you think they are	Are we willing to reward for success
Our value statement – *'Let's walk like we talk regarding the worth and dignity of people, quality, customers, etc.'*	Takes away some (or all) management control
The people we recruit will want change	Human beings resist change

Recruiting the work teams

The team members were in favour of going ahead with the team approach and early in 2003 they started the recruitment process. Over 1,500 applicants for the positions of production technician were interviewed. Two hundred passed this initial screening, from which 100 were selected for team interviews that involved four people from marketing, technical and manufacturing. The team interviews whittled the 100 down to 28, with whom the company started pre-employment classes. This consisted of four, four-hour sessions per week over nine weeks. Both morning and evening sessions were conducted in order to accommodate people who were working a second- or third-shift job. The pre-employment classes were also intended to test the candidates' willingness to stretch themselves and their desire to join the company. Out of the 24 who completed the training programme, 19 who excelled in team exercises and interactive skills were selected to join the firm. All 19 accepted.

Starting up

The plant started producing in June 2003, with a capacity at start-up of 325 MSF per year, working on a seven day basis. Notwithstanding some initial teething troubles it was, from the start, a technical and commercial success. In October 2000 a contract was signed with Phanchem to supply 100 per cent of Phanchem's needs for the next 10 years. Phanchem's decision was based on the combination of manufacturing and business focus which the Greenville team has achieved, a point stressed by Harry Barton:

'Co-locating all necessary departments on-site was seen as particularly important. All the technical functions and the marketing and business functions are now on site. Our other plants are 60 km from their marketing and support functions. Yet those 60 km are really significant. In terms of the mind-set, it might as well be 600 km.'

Will Small was also convinced that Greenville's team-based approach was the foundation of the plant's success:

'Our associates are now well used to the idea that nothing ever stays the same, that we have to adapt, change, and improve no matter how successful we are. They understand business objectives and customer needs as well as any manager. It was certainly the only time in my career when I saw a work team take over a machine which still had some problems to iron out and yet immediately took responsibility for it themselves.'

Developing the supply relationship

At the time of the start-up, product produced in Greenville was shipped to Phanchem's facility in Massachusetts, over 1,000 km away. This distance caused a number of problems including some damage in transit and delays in delivery. However, the relationship between Carlsen and Phanchem remained sound; helped by the two companies' co-operation during the Greenville start-up.

'We had worked closely with them during the design and construction of the new Greenville facility. More to the point, they saw that they would certainly achieve cost savings from the plant, with the promise of more savings to come as the plant moved down the learning curve.'

(Harry Barton)

With the 100 per cent supply agreement, Carlsen and Phanchem increasingly adopted a partnership philosophy towards the business. In particular the idea of a physically closer relationship between Carlsen and Phanchem was explored.

> *'During the negotiations with Phanchem for our 100 per cent contract there had been some talk about co-location but I don't think anyone took it particularly seriously. Nevertheless there was general agreement that it would be a good thing to do. After all, our success as Phanchem's sole supplier of coated photoresist was tied in to their success as a player in the global market, what was good for Phanchem was good for Carlsen.'*

(Will Small).

Several options were discussed within and between the two companies. Phanchem had, in effect, to choose between four options:

- Stay where they were in Massachusetts.
- Locate in the same part of the country but not too close to Carlsen.
- Locate on the adjacent site across the road from the Greenville plant.
- Co-locate within an extension built to the Carlsen plant at Greenville.

The state of the Carlsen–Phanchem relationship

The closeness of the relationship between the two companies was a result of their staff working together in solving the issues involved in starting the Greenville plant. Partly also it was born from adversity. Carlsen's engineers had hit problems with the line's winding mechanism. They found that the problems derived from 'bowed' paper cores. Moving to more rigid steel cores eliminated the problem. But, until rigid plastic cores could be sourced, Phanchem staff had to cope with the heavier loads. Carlsen engineers were impressed by their customer's willingness to help out by doing this while they worked on finding suitable lighter cores. A second problem concerned the auto-splicer. Carlsen's engineers were not convinced that the auto-splicer would work consistently on a long-term basis. Yet, Phanchem could not afford any interruption to supplies from Greenville if the auto-splicer failed. To prevent this happening, Carlsen's engineers rushed through a capital approval for $400,000 to install an accumulator that would ensure the continuity of supply to Phanchem.

> *'The splicing problem was potentially very serious. But we made a conscious effort to keep the customer fully informed. In fact, they were very helpful in doing anything they could to help us sort the problem. Partly because we worked together on that problem the relationship has grown stronger and stronger. They have become a real part of the partnership rather than someone waiting on the side lines expecting product to come to them. They agonised when we failed and they shared the sense of achievement when we succeeded.'*

(Harry Barton)

Evaluating the co-location options

Relatively early in the discussions between the two companies, the option of 'doing nothing' by staying in Massachusetts was discounted. The advantages of some kind of move, both in cost savings and in ease of communications, were significant. The option of Phanchem moving to a site 45 km from Greenville was considered but rejected because it had no advantages over locating even closer to the Greenville plant. Phanchem also strongly considered building and operating a facility across the road from the Greenville plant. But eventually the option of locating in a building attached to Carlsen's coating plant was the preferred option.

> 'There was a lot of resistance to having a customer on the same site as ourselves. At one stage we said we would never do it. No one in Carlsen had ever done it before and we couldn't imagine working so closely with a customer. The step from imagining our customer across the road to imagining them on the same site took some thinking about. It was a matter of getting used to the idea, taking one step at a time.'

(Will Small)

Yet, the more the options were discussed, the more it became obvious to both companies that the best plan was to have Carlsen build an extension to the Greenville plant and lease it to Phanchem. Co-location would have a significant impact on Phanchem's competitiveness by reducing their operating costs. This would enable them to gain market share by offering quality film at attractive prices, thus increasing volume for Carlsen. The managers at the Greenville plant also looked forward to an even closer operational relationship with the customer

The proposal

By August of 2002 the Greenville managers presented their proposal for extending the plant, but to their surprise the proposal was not well received by Carlsen's main board when it was presented at a capital budget meeting.

> 'We were beaten up severely at that meeting. Providing factory space seemed a long way from our core business. Although we understood that this company is not in the real estate business, we felt we had a good package and could put together a leasing deal which was profitable in its own right and enhance our ability to make profit in our main business of coating.'

(Will Small)

However, after several months of persuasion, the proposal was eventually approved by the end of 2005. Nevertheless, there was still concern over actually sharing a facility, and as a condition the board insisted that the door between the two companies areas should be capable of being locked from both sides.

The customer becomes a paying guest

The construction of the new extension proceeded smoothly with no significant deviations from the design or timeframe. Phanchem took occupancy in October 2006 and was slitting sellable product within one week of moving in. The construction and commissioning of the new facility was also a model of cooperation.

> 'We involved the customer from the very beginning. The few problems which our customer had in moving down here were really problems of shifting their operations rather than any interface problems with us. In fact we could help in the installation of their

equipment. Our maintenance people looked after some of their equipment for a while until they got settled in.'

(Harry Barton)

Now, all visitors to the plant are shown the door that had to be 'capable of being locked from both sides' and asked how many times they think it has been locked. The answer, of course, is 'never'.

9

TURNROUND AT THE PRESTON PLANT

Nigel Slack

'Before the crisis the quality department was just for looks, we certainly weren't used much for problem solving, the most we did was inspection. Data from the quality department was brought to the production meeting and they would all look at it, but no one was looking behind it.'

(Quality Manager, Preston Plant)

The Preston plant of Rendall Graphics was located in Preston, Vancouver, across the continent from their headquarters in Massachusetts. The plant had been bought from the Georgetown Corporation by Rendall in March 2000. Precision coated papers for ink-jet printers accounted for the majority of the plant's output, especially paper for specialist uses. The plant used coating machines that allowed precise coatings to be applied. After coating, the conversion department cut the coated rolls to the final size and packed the sheets in small cartons.

The curl problem

In late 1998 Hewlett-Packard (HP), the plant's main customer for ink-jet paper, informed the plant of some problems it had encountered with paper curling under conditions of low humidity. There had been no customer complaints to HP, but their own personnel had noticed the problem, and they wanted it fixed. Over the next seven or eight months a team at the plant tried to solve the problem. Finally, in October of 1999 the team made recommendations for a revised and considerably improved coating formulation. By January 2000 the process was producing acceptably. However, 1999 had not been a good year for the plant. Although sales were reasonably buoyant the plant was making a loss of around $2 million for the year. In October 99, Tom Branton, previously accountant for the business, was appointed as Managing Director.

Slipping out of control

In the spring of 2000, productivity, scrap and re-work levels continued to be poor. In response to this, the operations management team increased the speed of the line and made a number of changes to operating practice in order to raise productivity.

'Looking back, changes were made without any proper discipline, and there was no real concept of control. We were always meeting specification, yet we didn't fully understand how close we really were to not being able to make it. The culture here said, "If it's within specification then it's OK" and we were very diligent in making sure that the product which was shipped was in specification. However, Hewlett-Packard gets "process

charts" that enables them to see more or less exactly what is happening right inside your operation. We were also getting all the reports but none of them were being internalised, we were using them just to satisfy the customer. By contrast, HP have a statistically-based analytical mentality that says to itself, "You might be capable of making this product but we are thinking two or three product generations forward and asking ourselves, will you have the capability then, and do we want to invest in this relationship for the future?"'

(Tom Branton)

The spring of 2000 also saw two significant events. First, Hewlett-Packard asked the plant to bid for the contract to supply a new ink-jet platform, known as the Vector project, a contract that would secure healthy orders for several years. The second event was that the plant was acquired by Rendall.

'What did Rendall see when they bought us? They saw a small plant on the Pacific coast losing lots of money.'

(Finance Manager, Preston Plant)

Rendall was not impressed by what it found at the Preston plant, which was making a loss and had only just escaped from incurring a major customer's disapproval over the curl issue. If the plant did not get the Vector contract, its future looked bleak. Meanwhile, the chief concern continued to be productivity, but also, once again, there were occasional complaints about quality levels. However, HP's attitude caused some bewilderment to the operations management team.

'When HP asked questions about our process the operations guys would say, "Look we're making roll after roll of paper, it's within specification. What's the problem?"'

(Quality Manager, Preston Plant)

But it was not until summer that the full extent of HP's disquiet was made:

'I will never forget June of 2000. I was at a meeting with HP in Chicago. It was not even about quality. But during the meeting one of their engineers handed me a control chart, one that we supplied with every batch of product. He said "Here's your latest control chart. We think you're out of control and you don't know that you're out of control and we think that we are looking at this data more than you are." He was absolutely right, and I fully understood how serious the position was. We had our most important customer telling us we couldn't run our processes just at the time we were trying to persuade them to give us the Vector contract.'

(Tom Branton)

The crisis

Tom immediately set about the task of bringing the plant back under control. They first of all decided to go back to the conditions which prevailed in the January, when the curl team's recommendations had been implemented. This was the state before productivity pressures had caused the process to be adjusted. At the same time the team worked on ways of implementing unambiguous 'shutdown rules' that would allow operators to decide under what conditions a line should be halted if they were in doubt about the quality of the product they were making.

'At one point in May of 2000 we had to throw away 64 jumbo rolls of out-of-specification product. That's over $100,000 of product scrapped in one run. Basically that was because they had been afraid to shut the line down. Either that or they had tried to tweak the line while it was running to get rid of the defect. The shut-down guidelines in effect say, "We are not going to operate when we are not in a state of control". Until then our operators just couldn't win. If they failed to keep the machines running we would say, "You've got to keep productivity up". If they kept the machines running but had quality problems as a result, we criticised them for making garbage. Now you get into far more trouble for violating process procedures than you do for not meeting productivity targets.'

(Engineer, Preston Plant)

This new approach needed to be matched by changes in the way the communications were managed in the plant.

'We did two things that we had never done before. First, each production team started holding daily reviews of control chart data. Second, one day a month we took people away from production and debated the control chart data. Several people got nervous because we were not producing anything. But it was necessary. For the first time you got operators from the three shifts meeting together and talking about the control chart data and other quality issues. Just as significantly we invited HP up to attend these meetings. Remember these weren't staged meetings, it was the first time these guys had met together and there was plenty of heated discussion, all of which the Hewlett-Packard representatives witnessed.'

(Engineer, Preston Plant)

At last something positive was happening in the plant and morale on the shop floor was buoyant. By September 2000 the results of the plant's teams' efforts were starting to show results. Process were coming under control, quality levels were improving and, most importantly, personnel both on the shop floor and in the management team were beginning to get into the 'quality mode' of thinking. Paradoxically, in spite of stopping the line periodically, the efficiency of the plant was also improving.

Yet, the Preston team did not have time to enjoy its emerging success. In September of 2000 the plant learned that it would not get the Vector project because of the recent quality problems. Then Rendall decided to close the plant:

'We were losing millions, we had lost the Vector project, and it was really no surprise. I told the senior management team and said that we would announce it probably in April of 2001. The real irony was that we knew that we had actually already turned the corner.'

(Tom Branton)

Convincing the rest of the world

Notwithstanding the closure decision, and convinced that their overall performance could be substantially improved, the management team in Preston set about the task of convincing both HP and Rendall, that the plant could be viable. The team figured it would take three things. First, it was vital to continue to improve quality. Second, costs had to be brought down so as to lower the break-even volume of the plant substantially. Third, the plant had to create a portfolio of new product ideas which could establish a greater confidence in future sales.

First – quality

Progressing with their quality initiative involved establishing full statistical process control (SPC) and increasingly capable processes. (Exhibits 1 and 2 show how process variation reduced through this period and how process capability improved.) It also meant establishing quality consciousness and problem solving tools throughout the plant.

> 'We had people out there, professional engineers and operators, who saw themselves as concerned with the project rather than the processes that made it. But taking time out for quality meetings and discussing process performance and improvement, we got used to discussing the basic capabilities that we needed to improve.'
>
> (Quality Manager, Preston Plant)

Second – get costs down

Working on cost reduction was inevitably going to be painful. The first task was to get an understanding of what should be an appropriate level of operating costs.

> 'We went through a zero-based assessment to decide what an ideal plant would look like, and the minimum number of people needed to run it. By the way, in hindsight, cutting numbers had a greater impact on cost than the payroll saving figures seems to suggest. If you really understand your process, when you cut people it cuts complexity and makes things clearer to understand.'
>
> (Tom Branton)

Although most staff had not been informed of Rendall's closure decision, they were left in no doubt that the plant had its back to the wall.

> 'We were careful to be very transparent. We made sure that everyone knew whether they would be affected or not. I did lots of walking around explaining the company's position. There were tensions and some negative reactions from the people who had to leave. Yet most accepted the business logic of what we were doing.'
>
> (Tom Branton)

By December of 2000 there were 40 per cent fewer people in the plant than two months earlier. All departments were affected. Surprisingly the quality department shrank more than most, moving from 22 people down to nine.

> 'When the plant was considering down-sizing they asked me, "How can we run a lab with six technicians?" Remember that at this time we had 22 technicians. I said, "Easy. We get production to make good paper in the first place, and then we don't have to control all the garbage. That alone would save an immense amount of time. Also, having someone working with the suppliers so that we can guarantee to give production good material and take that problem out of the equation saves people as well."'
>
> (Quality Manager, Preston Plant)

Third – work on new products

Several new ideas were investigated; including some that were only possible because of the plant's enhanced capability. The most important of these became known as 'Greenwrap', a product, aimed particularly at the Japanese market. Short of landfill space, newsprint companies wanted their suppliers to ship newsprint in a wrap that could be repulped. Producing a protective wrap that was recyclable, an effective barrier against moisture, and could keep the newsprint free of welts and buckles was technically difficult. However, the plant's newly acquired capabilities allowed it to develop appropriate coatings at a cost that made the product attractive.

Out of the crisis

In spite of their trauma in the autumn, the plant's management team faced Christmas of 2000 with increasing satisfaction, if not optimism for the plant's future. In December it made an operational profit for the first time for over two years. By spring of 2001 even HP, at a corporate level, were starting to look more favourably on the Preston plant. It was becoming obvious to HP that the plant really had made a major change. More significantly, HP had asked the plant to start work on trials for a new product – 'heavyweight' paper.

April 2001 was a good month for the plant. It had chalked up three months of profitability (which was to be the start of routine double-digit return on sales). HP formally gave the heavyweight ink-jet paper contract to Preston, and were generally more up-beat about the future.

At the end of April, Rendall reversed its decision to close the plant.

The future

Both 2001 and 2002 were profitable years for the Preston plant. By the end of 2002 the plant had also captured the majority of Hewlett-Packard's Canadian business and was being asked to work on several other large projects.

'Hewlett-Packard now seems particularly keen to work with us. I'm sure that one reason is that we have been obliged to understand their way of doing business. It has helped us with our own suppliers also. We have already given considerable assistance to our main paper supplier with improving their own internal process control procedures. Recently we were in a meeting with people from all different parts of HP. There was all kinds of confidential information going around. But you could never tell that there was an outsider (us) in the room. They were having arguments amongst themselves about certain issues and no one could have been there without feeling that basically we were a part of that company. In the past they've always been very close with some information. Basically the change is all down to their new found trust in our capabilities.'

(Tom Branton)

Exhibit 1 **Typical process control charts (May 1998)**

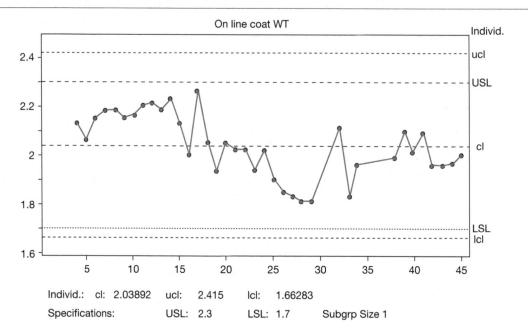

On line coat WT

Individ.: cl: 2.03892   ucl: 2.415   lcl: 1.66283
Specifications: USL: 2.3   LSL: 1.7   Subgrp Size 1

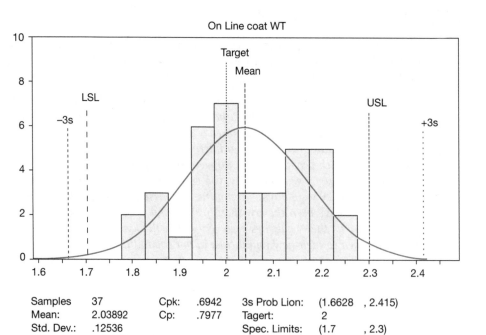

On Line coat WT

Samples	37	Cpk:	.6942	3s Prob Lion:	(1.6628	, 2.415)
Mean:	2.03892	Cp:	.7977	Tagert:	2	
Std. Dev.:	.12536			Spec. Limits:	(1.7	, 2.3)
Skewness:	−.19322			Est % outside:	(.343	, 1.864)

Exhibit 2 Typical process control charts (January 1999)

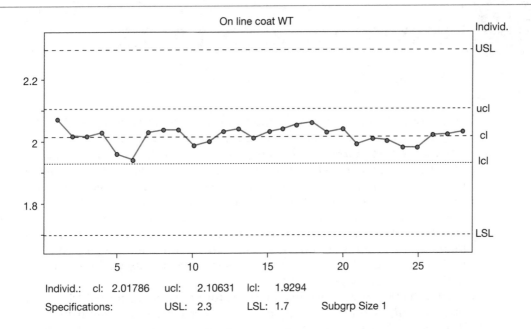

Individ.: cl: 2.01786   ucl: 2.10631   lcl: 1.9294
Specifications: USL: 2.3   LSL: 1.7   Subgrp Size 1

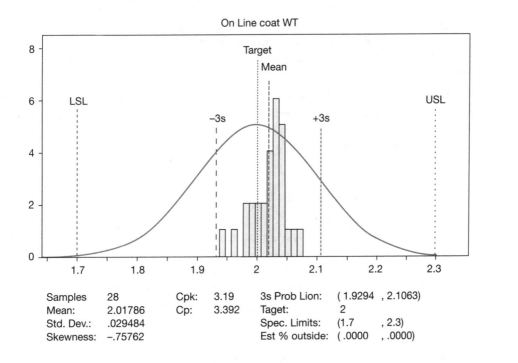

Samples	28	Cpk:	3.19	3s Prob Lion:	(1.9294 , 2.1063)
Mean:	2.01786	Cp:	3.392	Taget:	2
Std. Dev.:	.029484			Spec. Limits:	(1.7 , 2.3)
Skewness:	−.75762			Est % outside:	(.0000 , .0000)

DISNEYLAND RESORT PARIS

Nigel Slack

In August 2006, the company behind Disneyland Resort Paris reported a 13 per cent rise in revenues, saying that it was making encouraging progress with new rides aimed at getting more visitors. *'I am pleased with year-to-date revenues and especially with third quarter's, as well as with the success of the opening of Buzz Lightyear Laser Blast, the first step of our multi-year investment programme. These results reflect the group's strategy of increasing growth through innovative marketing and sales efforts as well as a multi-year investment programme. This performance is encouraging as we enter into the important summer months'*, said Chairman and Chief Executive Karl L. Holz. Revenue for the quarter ending 30 June rose to €286.6 million ($362 million) from €254 million a year earlier. The results helped to boost overall profits at Disney Company, and the company's stock price soared.

Yet, it hadn't always been like that. The fourteen-year history of Disneyland Paris had more ups and downs than any of its rollercoasters. The company had hauled itself back from what some commentators had claimed was the brink of bankruptcy in 2005. In fact, from 12 April 1992 when Euro Disney opened through to this more optimistic report, the resort had been subject simultaneously to both wildly optimistic forecasts and widespread criticism and ridicule. An essay on one critical internet site (called 'An Ugly American in Paris') summarised the whole venture in this way:

> *'When Disney decided to expand its hugely successful theme park operations to Europe, it brought American management styles, American cultural tastes, American labor practices, and American marketing pizzazz to Europe. Then, when the French stayed away in droves, it accused them of cultural snobbery.'*

The 'magic' of Disney

Since its founding in 1923, The Walt Disney Company had striven to remain faithful in its commitment to *'producing unparalleled entertainment experiences based on its rich legacy of quality creative content and exceptional storytelling'*. It did this through four major business divisions: Studio Entertainment, Parks and Resorts, Consumer Products, and Media Networks. Each segment consists of integrated businesses that worked together to *'maximise exposure and growth worldwide'*.

Source: This case was prepared by Nigel Slack of Warwick Business School, Warwick University, United Kingdom, using published sources of information. It does not reflect the views of the Walt Disney Company, who should not be held responsible for the accuracy or interpretation of the information or views contained in this case. It is not intended to illustrate either good or bad management practice. Copyright © 2006 Nigel Slack.

In the Parks and Resorts division, according to the company's description, customers could experience the *'magic of Disney's beloved characters'*. It was founded in 1952, when Walt Disney formed what is now known as 'Walt Disney Imagineering' to build Disneyland in Anaheim, California. By 2006, Walt Disney Parks and Resorts operated or licensed 11 theme parks at five Disney destinations around the world. They were, Disneyland Resort, California, Walt Disney World Resort, Florida, Tokyo Disney Resort, Disneyland Resort Paris, and their latest park, Hong Kong Disneyland. In addition, the division operated 35 resort hotels, two luxury cruise ships and a wide variety of other entertainment offerings. But in the history of the Walt Disney Company, perhaps none of its ventures had proved to be as challenging as its Paris Resort.

Service delivery at Disney resorts and parks

The core values of the Disney Company and, arguably, the reason for its success, originated in the views and personality of Walt Disney, the Company's founder. He had what some called an obsessive focus on creating images, products and experiences for customers that epitomised fun, imagination and service. Through the 'magic' of legendary fairytale and story characters, customers could escape the cares of the real world. Different areas of each Disney Park are themed, often around various 'lands' such as Frontierland, Fantasyland, Tomorrowland and Adventureland. Each land contains attractions and rides, most of which are designed to be acceptable to a wide range of ages. Very few rides are 'scary' when compared to many other entertainment parks. The architectural styles, decor, food, souvenirs, and cast costumes were all designed to reflect the theme of the 'land', as were the films and shows.

Although there were some regional differences, all the theme parks followed the same basic setup. Over the years, Disney had built up a reputation for imaginative rides. Its 'imagineers' had years of experience in using 'auto animatronics' to help recreate and reinforce the essence of the theme. The terminology used by the company reinforced its philosophy of consistent entertainment. Employees, even those working 'back stage', were called cast members. They did not wear uniforms but 'costumes', and rather than being given a job they were 'cast in a role'. All park visitors were called 'guests'.

Disney employees were generally relatively young, often of school or college age. Most were paid hourly on tasks that could be repetitive even though they usually involved constant contact with customers. Yet, employees were still expected to maintain a high level of courtesy and work performance. All cast members were expected to conform to strict dress and grooming standards. Applicants to become cast members were screened for qualities such as how well they responded to questions, how well they listened to their peers, how they smiled and used body language, and whether they had an 'appropriate attitude'.

All Disney parks had gained a reputation for their focus (some would say obsession) with delivering a high level of service and experience through attention to operations detail. To ensure that their strict service standards were met they had developed a number of specific operations policies.

- All parks employed effective queue management techniques such as providing information and entertainment for visitors.

- Visitors (guests) were seen as having a role within the park. They were not merely spectators or passengers on the rides, they were considered to be participants in a play. Their needs and desires were analysed and met through frequent interactions with staff (cast members). In this way they could be drawn into the illusion that they were actually part of the fantasy.

- Disney's stated goal was to exceed their customers' expectations every day.

- Service delivery was mapped and continuously refined in the light of customer feedback.

- The staff induction programme emphasised the company's quality assurance procedures and service standards. These were based on the four principles of safety, courtesy, show and efficiency.

- Parks were kept fanatically clean.

- The same Disney character never appears twice within sight – how could there be two Mickeys?

- Staff were taught that customer perceptions are both the key to customer delight, but also are extremely fragile. Negative perceptions can be established after only one negative experience.

- Disney University was the company's in-house development and learning facility with departments in each of the company's sites. The University trained Disney's employees in its strict service standards as well as providing the skills to operate new rides as they were developed.

- Staff recognition programmes attempted to identify outstanding service delivery performance as well as *energy, enthusiasm, commitment, and pride*.

- All parks contained phones connected to a central question hot-line for employees to find the answer to any question posed by customers.

Tokyo Disneyland

Tokyo Disneyland was owned and operated by the Oriental Land Company. Disney had designed the park and advised on how it should be run. In return, they received 10 per cent of all admissions revenues, and 5 per cent of food and souvenir revenues. The Tokyo project was considered a great success. Japanese customers revealed a significant appetite for American themes, American brands, and already had a good knowledge of Disney characters. Feedback from visitors at the Tokyo Park was extremely positive. Visitors commented on the cleanliness of the park, the efficiency of staff members, and the courtesy with which they were treated. Visitors also appreciated the Disney souvenirs (a wider range than in the American parks) because giving gifts is deeply embedded in the Japanese culture. Although the Tokyo park was almost identical to Disney's Californian park, there had been no complaints about the dilution of Japanese culture by so strong an American themed entertainment. The Japanese operators had added many new attractions since its opening. Many signs were written in English as were cast members' name badges. Similarly, many of the live shows and attractions were conducted in English and although almost all visitors to the park were Japanese, only one out of its thirty restaurants sold Japanese food.

The success of the Tokyo Park was explained by one American living in Japan:

'Young Japanese are very clean-cut. They respond well to Disney's clean-cut image, and I am sure they had no trouble filling positions. Also, young Japanese are generally comfortable wearing uniforms, obeying their bosses, and being part of a team. These are part of the Disney formula. Also, Tokyo is very crowded and Japanese here are used to crowds and waiting in line. They are very patient. And above all, Japanese are always very polite to strangers.'

Disneyland Tokyo had opened in 1982. Because Disney was wary of losing money on the Japanese venture it decided not to own the Tokyo site – a decision it came to regret. Disney also regretted allowing hotels owned by other companies to be built at its earlier US Disneyland parks, to the extent that Disney only owned about 25 per cent of hotels in the vicinity. It decided that it would take full control of Euro Disney and all its hotels.

Disneyland Paris

By 2006 Disneyland Paris consisted of three parks: the Disney village, Disneyland Paris itself and the Disney Studio Park. The village was comprised of stores and restaurants; Disneyland Paris was the main theme park; and Disney Studio Park has a more general moviemaking theme. Yet, the idea of a European park was not new. Because many of Walt Disney's most successful animations were taken from European literature, he had always wanted to build a park in Europe. In the event, his wish wasn't completed until 25 years after his death. But when the Walt Disney Company planned its European venture, its reputation was riding high and it was confident of success. At the time of the European park's opening, more than two million Europeans visited the US Disney parks, accounting for 5 per cent of the total visitors. The company's brand was strong and it had over half a century of translating the Disney brand into reality. The name 'Disney' had become synonymous with wholesome family entertainment that combined childhood innocence with high-tech 'imagineering'.

Alternative locations

Formal plans to build a European Disney Park were first considered as early as 1975. Initially, as well as France, Germany, Britain, Italy and Spain were all considered as possible locations, though Germany, Britain and Italy were soon discarded from the list of potential sites. The decision soon came to a straight contest between the Alicante area of Spain, which had a similar climate to Florida for a large part of the year and the Marne-la-Vallée area just outside Paris. Certainly, winning the contest to host the new park was important for all the potential host countries. The new park promised to generate more than 30,000 jobs.

It was the French location that eventually won out, partly because of the close proximity to the large population of the Paris conurbation and the city's attraction as a tourist centre. Also its central positioning within Western Europe was though to be crucial to if it was to attract sufficient visitors. Early concerns that the park would not have the same sunny, happy feel in a cooler climate than Florida were allayed by the spectacular success of Disneyland Tokyo in a location with a similar climate to Paris. The first letter of agreement was signed with the French government in December 1985, and started to draw up the financial contracts during the following spring. Robert Fitzpatrick, a key organiser of the 1984 Los Angeles Olympics, was appointed as the Euro Disney President, and construction started on the 2,000 hectare site in August 1988. But from the announcement that the park would be built in France, it was subject to a wave of criticism. One critic called the project a *'cultural Chernobyl'* because of how it might affect French cultural values. Another described it as *'a horror made of cardboard, plastic, and appalling colours; a construction of hardened chewing-gum and idiot folk lore taken straight out of comic books written for obese Americans'*. However, as some commentators noted, the cultural arguments and anti-Americanism of the French intellectual elite did not seem to reflect the behaviour of most French people, who *'eat at McDonalds, wear Gap clothing, and flock to American movies'*.

The major advantage of locating in Spain was the weather. However, the eventual decision to locate near Paris was thought to have been driven by a number of factors that weighed more heavily with Disney executives. These included the following:

- There was a site available just outside Paris which was both large enough and flat enough to accommodate the park.
- The proposed location put the park within a two-hour drive for 17 million people, a four-hour drive for 68 million people, a six-hour drive for 110 million people and a two-hour flight for a further 310 million or so.
- The site also had potentially good transport links. The Euro Tunnel that was to connect England with France was due to open in 1994. In addition, the French autoroutes network and the high-speed TGV network could both be extended to connect the site with the rest of Europe.
- Paris was already a highly attractive vacation destination and France generally attracted around 50,000,000 tourists each year.
- Europeans generally take significantly more holidays each year than Americans (five weeks of vacation as opposed to two or three weeks).
- Market research indicated that 85 per cent of people in France would welcome a Disney park in their country.
- Both national and local government in France were prepared to give significant financial incentives (as were the Spanish authorities) including an offer to invest in local infrastructure, reduce the rate of value added tax on goods sold in the park, provide subsidised loans, and value the land artificially low to help reduce taxes. Moreover, the French government were prepared to expropriate land from local farmers to smooth the planning and construction process.

The resort was to be 49 per cent owned by the Walt Disney Company and 51 per cent owned by a company called Euro Disney SCA which was quoted on the French stock exchange. Initially all shares were offered to European investors. The Walt Disney Company was to receive management fees and royalty fees based on the park's revenues as well as an incentive-based management fee calculated on the park's cash flow.

Designing Disney Land Resort Paris

Phase 1 of the Euro Disney Park was designed to have 29 rides and attractions as well as six hotels with over 5,000 rooms in total. In addition, the park had a championship golf course together with many restaurants, shops, live shows, and parades. Although the park was designed to fit in with Disney's traditional appearance and values, a number of changes were made to accommodate what was thought to be the preferences of European visitors. For example, market research indicated that Europeans would respond to a 'wild west' image of America. Therefore, both rides and hotel designs were made to emphasise this theme. Disney was also keen to diffuse criticism, especially from French left-wing intellectuals and politicians, that the design of the park would be too 'Americanised' and would become a vehicle for American 'cultural imperialism'. To counter charges of American imperialism, Disney gave the park a flavour that stressed the European heritage of many of the Disney characters, and increased the sense of beauty and fantasy. They were, after all, competing against Paris's exuberant architecture and sights. For example, Discoveryland featured storylines from Jules Verne, the French author. Snow White (and her dwarfs) was located in a Bavarian village. Cinderella was located in a French inn. Even Peter Pan was made to appear more 'English Edwardian' than in the original US designs.

Disney conceded to the pressure for French to be the language of the park with English taking second place. The American actor, Vincent Price's voice-over for the Phantom Manor, that was used initially, was replaced by a French actor. Only Price's maniacal laugh remained. In keeping with their desire to make this park more 'European', even the story behind the Disneyland Paris Phantom Manor (named The Haunted Mansion in the US versions), although open to interpretation, was changed to include bits of *The Phantom of the Opera* and *Great Expectations*. Main Street USA, built in the idealised style of America at the beginning of the twentieth century, contained ornate shopping arcades one of which (diplomatically!) contains an exhibition telling the history behind the presentation of the Statue of Liberty by France to the USA in a spirit of friendship.

Because of concerns about the popularity of American 'fast-food', Euro Disney introduced more variety into its restaurants and snack bars, featuring foods from around the world. In a bold publicity move, Disney invited a number of top Paris chefs to visit and taste the food. Some anxiety was also expressed concerning the different 'eating behaviour' between Americans and Europeans. Whereas Americans preferred to 'graze', eating snacks and fast meals throughout the day, Europeans generally preferred to sit down and eat at traditional meal times. This would have a very significant impact on peak demand levels on dining facilities. A further concern was that in Europe (especially French) visitors would be intolerant of long queues. To overcome this, extra diversions such as films and entertainments were planned for visitors as they waited in line for a ride.

Discoveryland was new for a Disney park, it was based on the concept of the future based on past European Visionaries. Fantasyland was also new in that it had it's own new 'European' attractions, along with a newly created castle especially for Euro Disney. Adventureland gained some extra new areas, again with a more authentic 'European' look than in previous parks.

Before the opening of the park, Euro Disney had to recruit and train between 12,000 and 14,000 permanent and around 5,000 temporary employees. All these new employees were required to undergo extensive training in order to prepare them to achieve Disney's high standard of customer service as well as understand operational routines and safety procedures. Originally, the company's objective was to hire 45 per cent of its employees from France, 30 per cent from other European countries, and 15 per cent from outside of Europe. However, this proved difficult and when the park opened around 70 per cent of employees were French. Most 'cast members' were paid around 15 per cent above the French minimum wage.

Espace Euro Disney (an information centre) was opened in December 1990 to show the public what Disney was constructing. The 'casting centre' was opened on 1 September 1991 to recruit the cast members needed to staff the park's attractions. But the hiring process did not go smoothly. In particular, Disney's grooming require-ments that insisted on a 'neat' dress code, a ban on facial hair, set standards for hair and fingernails, and an insistence on 'appropriate undergarments' proved contro-versial. Both the French press and trade unions strongly objected to the grooming requirements, claiming they were excessive and much stricter than was generally held to be reasonable in France. Nevertheless, the company refused to modify its grooming standards.

Accommodating staff also proved to be a problem, when the large influx of employees swamped the available housing in the area. Disney had to build its own apartments as well as rent rooms in local homes just to accommodate its employees. Notwithstanding all the difficulties, Disney did succeed in recruiting and training all its cast members before the opening.

The park opens

The park opened to employees, for testing during late March 1992, during which time the main sponsors and their families were invited to visit the new park. The formal press preview day was held on 11 April 1992, and the park finally opened to visitors on 12 April 1992. When opening the new resort, Roy Disney, nephew of Walt Disney, spoke of his *'emotional homecoming for the Disney family, which traced its roots to the French town of Isigny-sur-Mer'*. The opening was not helped by strikes on the commuter trains leading to the park, staff unrest, threatened security problems (a terrorist bomb had exploded the night before the opening) and protests in sur-rounding villages who demonstrated against the noise and disruption from the park. The opening day crowds, expected to be 500,000, failed to materialise, however, and at close of the first day only 50,000 people had passed through the gates.

Disney had expected the French to make up a larger proportion of visiting guests than they did in the early days. This may have been partly due to protests from French locals who feared that their culture would be damaged by Euro Disney. Also all Disney parks had traditionally been alcohol-free. To begin with Euro Disney was no different. However, this was extremely unpopular, particularly with French visi-tors who like to have a glass of wine or beer with their food. But whatever the cause, the low initial attendance was very disappointing for the Disney Company.

It was reported that, in the first nine weeks of operation, approximately 1,000 employees left Euro Disney, about one half of whom 'left voluntarily'. The reasons cited for leaving Disney's employment varied. Some blamed the hectic pace of work and the long hours that Disney expected. Others mentioned the 'chaotic' conditions in the first few weeks. Even Disney conceded that conditions had been tough immediately after the park opened. Some leavers blamed Disney's apparent difficulty in understanding 'how Europeans work'. *'We can't just be told what to do, we ask ques-tions and don't all think the same'*. Some visitors who had experience of the American parks commented that the standards of service were noticeably below what would be acceptable in America. There were reports that some cast members were failing to meet Disney's normal service standard:

'... even on opening weekend some clearly couldn't care less ... My overwhelming impression ... was that they were out of their depth. There is much more to being a cast member than endlessly saying "Bonjour". Apart from having a detailed knowledge of the site, Euro Disney staff have the anxiety of not knowing in what language they are going to be addressed [in] ... Many were struggling.'

It was also noticeable that different nationalities exhibited different types of behaviour when visiting the park. Some nationalities always used the waste bins while others were more likely to drop litter. Most noticeable were differences in queueing behaviour. Northern Europeans tend to be disciplined and content to wait for rides in an orderly manner. By contrast, some southern European visitors *'seem to have made an Olympic event out of getting to the ticket taker first'.*

The press in a number of countries debated whether Euro Disney really knew what it was trying to be. Is it an American theme park in Europe? Is it a theme park that exploits the European heritage of Disney characters? Had the park any connection at all with France, its host country? Is there a fundamental difference between Europeans and Americans in the type of entertainment that they appreciate? Is it even possible to devise a theme park that can please so many different nationalities and cultures? Others claimed that the nature of the European work force was such that they could never achieve the US standards of Disney service:

'The Disney style of service is one with which Americans have grown up. There are several styles of service (or lack of it) in Europe; unbridled enthusiasm is not a marked feature of them.'

Nevertheless, not all reactions were negative. European newspapers also quoted plenty of positive reaction from visitors, especially children. Euro Disney was so different from the existing European theme parks, with immediately recognisable characters and a wide variety of attractions. Families who could not afford to travel to the United States could now interact with Disney characters and *'sample the experience at far less cost'.*

The first phase of development (the theme park, hotel complex and golf course) had gone massively over budget. And attendance figures failed to improve much (by May the park was only attracting around 25,000 visitors a day instead of the predicted 60,000). Moreover it appeared that only three in every 10 visitors were native French. Seven weeks after the opening of the park, visitor attendance was reported at 1.5 million, a disappointment for the park which had expected 11 million visitors in its first year, and when Euro Disney announced its first quarter revenues of $489,000,000, it also said that it would make a loss in its first financial year. Again, the loss was blamed on disappointing attendance figures. Nevertheless, the company pointed out that Disney's other theme parks had made comparable losses in their first year of operation, and anyway, it was foolish to try to predict future attendance so early in the park's history. However, the Euro Disney company stock price started a slow downward spiral, rapidly losing almost a third of its value.

The next 15 years

By August 1992 estimates of annual attendance figures were being drastically cut from 11 million to just over 9 million. Euro Disney's misfortunes were further compounded in late 1992 when a European recession caused property prices to drop sharply, and interest payments on the large start-up loans taken out by Euro Disney forced the company to admit serious financial difficulties. Also the cheap dollar resulted in more people taking their holidays in Florida at Walt Disney World.

At the first anniversary of the park's opening, in April 1993, Sleeping Beauty's Castle was decorated as a giant birthday cake to celebrate the occasion, however, further problems were approaching. Criticised for having too few rides, the roller coaster Indiana Jones and the Temple of Peril was opened in July. This was the first Disney roller coaster that included a 360-degree loop, but just a few weeks after opening emergency brakes locked during a ride, causing injuries to some guests. The ride was temporarily shut down for investigations. Also in 1993 the proposed Euro Disney phase 2 was shelved due to financial problems. Which meant Disney MGM Studios Europe and 13,000 hotel rooms would not be built to the original 1995 deadline originally agreed upon by The Walt Disney Company. However, Discovery Mountain, one of the planned phase 2 attractions, did get approval.

By the start of 1994, rumours were circulating that the park was on the verge of bankruptcy. Emergency crisis talks were held between the banks and backers with things coming to a head during March when Disney offered the banks an ultimatum. It would provide sufficient capital for the park to continue to operate until the end of the month, but unless the banks agreed to restructure the park's $1 billion debt, the Walt Disney company would close the park, and walk away from the whole European venture, leaving the banks with a bankrupt theme park and a massive expanse of virtually worthless real estate. Disney then forced the bank's hand by calling the annual stockholder meeting for 15 March. Shortly before the stockholder meeting, Michael Eisner, Disney's CEO, announced that Disney was planning to pull the plug on the venture at the end of March 1994 unless the banks were prepared to restructure the loans. Faced with no alternative other than to announce that the park was about to close, just before the annual meeting the banks agreed to Disney's demands. This effectively wrote off virtually all of the next two years' worth of interest payments, and granted a three-year postponement of further loan repayments. In return, the Walt Disney Company wrote off $210 million in unpaid bills for services, and paid $540 million for a 49 per cent stake in the estimated value of the park, as well as restructuring its own loan arrangements for the $210 million worth of rides at the new park.

In May 1994, the connection between London and Marne-la-Vallée was completed, along with a TGV link, providing a connection between several major European cities. By August the park was starting to find its feet at last, and all of the park's hotels were fully booked during the peak holiday season. Also, in October, the park's name was officially changed from Euro Disney to 'Disneyland Paris', in order to, *'show that the resort now was named much more like it's counterparts in California and Tokyo'* and to link the park more closely with the romantic city of Paris. Some commentators noted that the name change would disassociate the resort in people's minds with controversy, debts and politics. The end of year figures for 1994 showed encouraging signs despite a 10 per cent fall in attendance caused by the bad publicity over the earlier financial problems. And by the end of March 1995 Disney executives were predicting that Disneyland Paris might break even by the end of 1995.

1995 saw the opening of the new roller coaster, not after all to be called 'Discovery Mountain' but 'Space Mountain de la Terre à la lune', because it was decided that the new name was more exciting. Unlike its counterparts in Tokyo, Florida and California, it was not housed in a big white dome, but in a very ornate Victorian futuristic style dome. Intensive marketing of Space Mountain on television channels all over Europe and the release of the popular movie *Pocahontas* contributed to an improvement in the resort's financial results. In fact, the Euro Disney resort complex did announce its first annual operating profit in November 1995, helped by the opening of Space Mountain in June.

In 1997 the five-year celebrations included, a new parade with Quasimodo and all the characters from the latest Disney blockbusting classic, *The Hunchback of Notre Dame*, the *'Year To Be Here'* marketing campaign, the resort's first Hallowe'en celebration and a new Christmas parade.

A new attraction was added in 1999, 'Honey I Shrunk The Audience', making the audience the size of a bug while being invited to Inventor of the Year Award Ceremony. This was the more modern replacement to the ageing 3D movie Captain EO. However, the planned Christmas and New Year celebrations were disrupted when a freak storm caused havoc, destroying the Mickey Mouse glass statue that had just been installed for the Lighting Ceremony and many other attractions. Also damaged were trees next to the castle, the top of which developed a pronounced lean, as did many street signs and lamp posts.

Disney's 'Fastpass' system was introduced in 2000. This was a new service that allowed guests to use their entry passes to gain a ticket at certain attractions and return at the time stated and gain direct entry to the attraction without queueing. Two new attractions are opened, 'Indians Jones et le temple du péril' and 'Tarzan le recontre' starring a cast of acrobats along with Tarzan, Jane and all their Jungle friends with music from the movie in different European languages.

In 2001 the 'ImagiNations Parade' was replaced by the 'Wonderful World of Disney Parade' which received some criticism for being 'less than spectacular' with only eight parade floats. Also Disney's 'California Adventure' was opened in California.

The Resort's tenth Anniversary saw the opening of the new Walt Disney Studios Park attraction. The Disney-MGM Studios at the Walt Disney World Resort, Florida, had already proved to be a major success and the original concept for the Paris studios had first been studied in 1992, shortly before the park opened. The concept, which was based on the world of cinema, seemed perfectly adaptable to the expectations of a European audience so development for the new park was started in 1997 when a small team of Disney Imagineers were asked to design it. In parallel to this, opinion leaders from the worlds of French and European cinema, culture and media were consulted about the project. R. Julienne, the famous French stunt designer, was among the first Europeans to work with Disney on the new Theme Park's concept. Also, in this year, Disneyland Paris was renamed Disneyland Resort Paris, the original park was also renamed Disneyland Park to accommodate the new Walt Disney Studios.

André Lacroix from Burger King was appointed as CEO of Disneyland Resort Paris in 2003, to *'take on the challenge of a failing Disney park in Europe and turn it around'*. Increasing investment, he refurbished whole sections of the park, increased the numbers of dancers to the ageing 'Wonderful World of Disney Parade' and introduced the Jungle Book Carnival in February to increase attendance during the slow months.

By 2004, attendance had increased but the company announced that it was still losing money. It again renegotiated its €2.4 billion debt to the Walt Disney Company and French financial institutions. Losses were attributed partly to the costs of opening Walt Disney Studios two years earlier, just as the world theme park business slumped in the wake of the American terrorist attacks. New hotels were opened (not owned by Disney) close to the park which meant increased competition for the park's own hotels.

The positive news of 2006 was well received. As one commentator put it:

> '[W]ould Disney, the stockholders, the banks, or even the French government make the same decision to go ahead if they could wind the clock back to 1987? Is this a story of a fundamentally flawed concept, or was it just mishandled?'

Questions

1. What markets are the Disney resorts and parks aiming for?
2. Was Disney's choice of the Paris site a mistake?
3. What aspects of its parks' design did Disney change when it constructed Euro Disney?
4. What did Disney *not* change when it constructed Euro Disney?
5. What were Disney's main mistakes from the conception of the Paris resort through to 2006?

Some events in overview of the history of Disneyland Resort Paris

1955	Disneyland, California opens
1971	Walt Disney World opens in Orlando, Florida
1982	Epcot Center opens in Orlando, Florida
1984	Tokyo Disney opens
1987	The announcement that the resort on Marne-la-Vallée had been chosen as the place to build the newest Magic Kingdom (called Euro Disney then). Construction starts with a plan to complete in five years
1989	Disney-MGM Studios Theme Park opens in Orlando
1992	The grand opening of Euro Disney resort with a cast of thousands there to meet the demand that did not materialise
1993	The second year of Euro Disney's operations. On the 12 April the castle was renamed from Le château de la belle au Bois dormant to the Le château du Gâteau
1994	Stand-off with French banks over taking away some of Euro Disney's debt that had accumulated because of lower than expected revenues and the project due to going over budget. On 14 March agreement is reached with the French banks and Euro Disney stays open. The company would pay fewer royalties to the Walt Disney Company and more money from the Walt Disney Company would be invested into the resort
1995	Opening of the new roller coaster proves a great success
1996	Planet Hollywood was opened within the resort
1997	The Park open for five years
1998	Disney's Animal Kingdom opened in Orlando
1999	Storm disrupts the Park's operations.
2000	Disney's 'Fastpass' introduced
2001	Disney's California Adventure opened in California
2002	The tenth Anniversary and Walt Disney Studio opened in Paris
2003	André Lacroix from Burger King is appointed as CEO of Disneyland Resort Paris
2004	The company announces that it is still losing money and again renegotiates its €2.4 billion debt to the Walt Disney Company and French financial institutions
2006	Rise in revenues reported

Index